Microprocessor Systems

Hardware, Software, And Applications

JAMES W. STEWART

DeVry Institute of Technology
Woodbridge, New Jersey

PRENTICE HALL, *Englewood Cliffs, New Jersey 07632*

Library of Congress Cataloging-in-Publication Data

Stewart, James W.
  Microprocessor systems : hardware, software, and applications / James W. Stewart.
  p. cm.
  Includes bibliographical references.
  ISBN 0-13-582396-X
  1. Microprocessors. I. Title.
QA76.5.S777 1990
004.16—dc20   89-38275
                                                 CIP

Editorial/production supervision: Merrill Peterson
Interior design: Joan Stone
Cover design: 20/20 Services Inc.
Manufacturing buyer: Dave Dickey

© 1990 by Prentice-Hall, Inc.
A Division of Simon & Schuster
Englewood Cliffs, New Jersey 07632

All rights reserved. No part of this book may be reproduced, in any form or by any means, without permission in writing from the publisher.

Printed in the United States of America
10 9 8 7 6 5 4 3 2 1

ISBN 0-13-582396-X

Prentice-Hall International (UK) Limited, *London*
Prentice-Hall of Australia Pty. Limited, *Sydney*
Prentice-Hall Canada Inc., *Toronto*
Prentice-Hall Hispanoamericana, S.A., *Mexico*
Prentice-Hall of India Private Limited, *New Delhi*
Prentice-Hall of Japan, Inc., *Tokyo*
Simon & Schuster Asia Pte. Ltd., *Singapore*
Editora Prentice-Hall do Brasil, Ltda., *Rio de Janeiro*

Contents

Preface ix

---- chapter 1 ----

Architecture of a Microcomputer 1

    1.1   Introduction, *1*
    1.2   The CPU, *4*
    1.3   Memory, *8*
    1.4   Input/Output (I/O), *15*
    1.5   Bus Structures, *17*
    1.6   Address Decoding, *21*
    1.7   Speed, *25*
    1.8   Summary, *27*
           Chapter Review, *27*

---- chapter 2 ----

The 8085 Microprocessor 29

    2.1   Introduction, *29*
    2.2   Hardware Overview, *30*
    2.3   CPU Timing, *34*

2.4 The 8085 Programming Model, *41*
2.5 8085 Instruction Set Overview, *43*
2.6 The 8155/8156 Support Chip, *52*
2.7 Summary, *59*
Chapter Review, *59*

---

chapter 3

Introduction to Assembly Languages   62

3.1 Introduction, *62*
3.2 Instruction Statements, *67*
3.3 Addressing Modes, *72*
3.4 Pseudo-Operations and Directives, *74*
3.5 Macro Assemblers, *79*
3.6 Conditional Assembly, *81*
3.7 Summary, *83*
Chapter Review, *83*

---

chapter 4

Programming and the 8085   85

4.1 Introduction, *85*
4.2 Subroutines, *88*
4.3 Making Passes, *92*
4.4 Some Smooth Moves, *94*
4.5 A Modicum of Math, *97*
4.6 A Little Logic, *102*
4.7 Jump Around the Loop, *108*
4.8 Control Structure, *113*
4.9 Rotates and Shifts, *115*
4.10 Binary Coded Decimal (BCD), *117*
4.11 Miscellaneous Stuff, *122*
4.12 Summary, *127*
Chapter Review, *127*

---

chapter 5

Interrupts and DMA   130

5.1 Introduction, *130*
5.2 Interrupts, *130*
5.3 Interrupt Constraints, *133*

- 5.4 The 8085 Interrupts, *137*
- 5.5 Direct Memory Access (DMA), *145*
- 5.6 The 8257 Programmable DMA Controller, *147*
- 5.7 Summary, *153*
  Chapter Review, *153*

---

chapter 6

Interfacing: Hardware and Software   155

- 6.1 Introduction, *155*
- 6.2 Mechanical Switches, *156*
- 6.3 Solid State Switches, *164*
- 6.4 Solenoids and Relays, *168*
- 6.5 Displays and Printers, *173*
- 6.6 Handshaking, *178*
- 6.7 Centronics Parallel Interface, *179*
- 6.8 IEEE-488 Bus (GPIB), *181*
- 6.9 RS-232C (EIA-232) Serial Interface, *184*
- 6.10 Some 8155 Applications, *187*
- 6.11 Some Interrupt-Driven Applications, *189*
- 6.12 Analog/Digital Interfacing, *193*
- 6.13 Summary, *197*
  Chapter Review, *197*

---

chapter 7

The Z80 Processor   199

- 7.1 Introduction, *199*
- 7.2 Hardware Overview, *200*
- 7.3 Programming Model, *207*
- 7.4 Instruction Set Overview, *210*
- 7.5 Moving and Searching, *216*
- 7.6 Arithmetic and Logic, *219*
- 7.7 Rotates and Shifts, *221*
- 7.8 Jumps and Looping, *222*
- 7.9 Input/Output, *223*
- 7.10 Calls and Returns, *225*
- 7.11 Bit Manipulation, *225*
- 7.12 Interrupts, *226*
- 7.13 Context Switching, *231*
- 7.14 Summary, *233*
  Chapter Review, *233*

___ chapter 8 ___

The 8051 Single-Chip Microcontroller   **235**

8.1 Introduction, *235*
8.2 8051 Hardware Overview, *236*
8.3 CPU Timing, *238*
8.4 Memory Organization, *238*
8.5 SFR Space: Special Function Registers, *241*
8.6 I/O Ports, *244*
8.7 Timer/Counters, *246*
8.8 Serial Port Interface, *249*
8.9 Interrupts, *252*
8.10 Instructions and Addressing, *255*
8.11 Instruction Groups, *260*
8.12 Single-Bit Boolean Processor, *262*
8.13 System Examples: External ROM, RAM, I/O, *264*
8.14 Summary, *267*
       Chapter Review, *268*

___ chapter 9 ___

Programming and the 8051   **270**

9.1 Introduction, *270*
9.2 Finite State Machines, *271*
9.3 Example Programs, *276*
9.4 Summary, *284*
       Chapter Review, *284*

___ chapter 10 ___

Peripheral Devices   **286**

10.1 Introduction, *286*
10.2 The 8255 Programmable Peripheral Interface, *287*
10.3 The 8279 Keyboard/Display Interface, *297*
10.4 The LTC1091 Data Acquisition Chip, *309*
10.5 The 8251A Programmable USART, *315*
10.6 Summary, *325*
       Chapter Review, *325*

chapter 11

The 8086 Microprocessor   **327**

11.1 Introduction, *327*
11.2 The 8086 Architecture, *328*
11.3 The Minimum Mode Interface, *336*
11.4 Interrupt Vectoring, *339*
11.5 Minimum Mode Timing, *340*
11.6 The Programming Model, *344*
11.7 8086 Assembly Language, *346*
11.8 Summary, *349*
       Chapter Review, *350*

chapter 12

System Design Techniques   **351**

12.1 Introduction: The System Design Cycle, *351*
12.2 Top-Down vs. Bottom-Up Design, *355*
12.3 System Requirements for the Project, *355*
12.4 System Specifications for the Project, *357*
12.5 Hardware Design, *360*
12.6 Software Design, *361*
12.7 Software Modularization for the Project, *363*
12.8 Pseudo-Code for the Project, *366*
12.9 Assembly Language for the Project, *374*
12.10 System Integration and Evaluation, *381*
12.11 Summary, *383*
        Chapter Review, *384*

appendices

A   Project Design   **385**

B   8085 Instruction Set Summary   **404**

C   Z80 Instruction Set Summary   **406**

D   8051 Instruction Set Summary   **408**

E   8086 Instruction Set Summary   **412**

| F | ASCII and EBCDIC Tables | 417 |

Answers to Selected Questions and Problems   422

Index   427

Preface

This text is targeted for a comprehensive course, or sequence of courses, in microprocessor hardware and software for engineering and technology students. It includes two common 8-bit CPUs (the 8085 and the Z80), a single-chip controller (the 8051), and an introduction to a 16-bit CPU (the 8086), together with their assembly languages. Also included are several commonly used peripheral devices and a treatment of hardware interfacing.

Although not a prerequisite, it would be helpful if the student has some familiarity with personal computers and has taken introductory courses in programming (such as BASIC) and digital devices. It is assumed that the student is familiar with binary and hexadecimal numbers. Each chapter includes an introduction, a summary, and questions for review. A separate instructor's manual is available.

It is the author's experience that learning about microprocessors and programming is not a spectator sport. To really grasp the subject, the student must get hands-on experience. To back up the belief, this text includes two features not found in many similar texts. First, software support: Specifically, a cross-assembler and simulator are available that will allow the student to write, assemble, run, and debug 8085 software directly on a personal computer under MS-DOS. Any text editor can be used to write the source code as long as it produces ASCII text files. Second, hardware support: The complete design of a single-board computer, including monitor program software, is included in Appendix A, thus giving the student the opportunity to build an inexpensive 8085-based trainer. The monitor program forms the basis of the chapter on software design methodology (Chap. 12).

The monitor software for the single-board computer, as well as the material in Chapter 12 and its associated appendix, was written by Professor G. Thomas Huetter. It is based on the notes of a very successful system design course that Dr. Huetter has developed and taught to senior level students at DeVry Technical Institute (Woodbridge, New Jersey).

An effort has been made to keep the text readable as well as accurate and thorough. Special terminology is introduced as needed and defined in context. In order to learn a subject such as microprocessors, it is necessary to focus on real hardware, as insight is often in the details. The 8085 is used as an introduction to microprocessors because of its simplicity and availability. However, the chapter on 8085 programming goes beyond a mere description of the instruction set. An emphasis is put on techniques. So, while this book focuses mainly on the Intel family of devices, the hardware issues and software ideas that are involved, once they are understood, can be "ported" to any other device.

A Note to Students: From time to time in history, some thought, some invention, some product of the human mind changes forever the way we all live. Consider the printing press or the concept of the scientific method. The ideas of people like Isaac Newton in the seventeenth century led to the start of modern science in the eighteenth century and to the explosion of technology and production in the nineteenth that we call the Industrial Revolution. The symbolic piece of that era's technology, literally its driving force, was the steam engine.

Today we are at the beginning of another technological revolution, one based on ideas in the fields of electronics, solid state physics, artificial intelligence, and information theory. And, like the Industrial Revolution, our age is both symbolized and driven by a piece of technology: the computer. The steam engine was able to put the equivalent of muscle into a machine; to this day we speak of the "horsepower" of an engine. The computer has the ability to put the equivalent of brain into a machine, so we begin to speak of the "intelligence" of our systems. There is much debate over whether computers can ever "think" in the way that people do. There is no argument, however, that computers can do things that until only recently required the services of thinking people.

Large, centralized steam engines could only be used in factories; the mechanization of everyday things such as washing clothes and cutting grass had to await the electric motor and the internal combustion engine. In the same way, only institutions could use large, centralized computers until the invention of the microprocessor in the early 1970s. Now cars, appliances, military weapons, even teddy bears may contain the power of computer technology.

Small, inexpensive computers, sophisticated software techniques, and high-speed data communications are combining to bring about profound changes in the quality of our lives. This book is an introduction to the engine of that change: the microprocessor. It is also an invitation for you to participate in shaping that change for the benefit of us all.

Here is a suggestion: When studying new material we may feel there is so much to learn that we can't see the forest for the trees. A useful technique is to read everything twice—once to see the forest and then again to see the trees. In other words, try to get the overall picture first. Formulate that picture into words and write it down in your notes. Then go back and see how the details fit in. If necessary, reformulate your overall view. It may take several iterations of the loop. Another suggestion: Microprocessor technology, as well as all electronics technology, is characterized by new developments. To keep abreast, try to spend some time every week in your school's library reading articles in the trade journals and professional publications. And don't be afraid to contact manufacturers to ask for their literature; they will be glad to send it to you. You've heard it before but it's still true: Education is a lifelong process, so get into the habit early.

A final note: Please feel free to mark this book up. Underline key sentences, highlight important words, make notes in the margins. A textbook is an educational tool, and as such it works best when "customized" by the user.

I wish to thank the following for their help on this project: Alice Barr of Prentice Hall, Dale Bandy of Silicon Systems, Robert Scott of Linear Technology, Jim Bull of Micro Link, Paul Papaioannou of DeVry Chicago, Warren Foxwell of DeVry Lombard, John Morgan of DeVry Texas, David Delker of Kansas State University, Arnold Gugarty of Wentworth Institute of Technology, and my former student Randy Echterling. Last, but far from least, I wish to thank my good friend and teacher Véronique Henriksen for her long time support and encouragement.

Jim Stewart
Piscataway, NJ

*This book is dedicated to those I teach,
and to all those who taught me.*

chapter 1

Architecture of a Microcomputer

OBJECTIVES

Upon completion of this chapter, you should be able to

1. Give a short history of computers
2. Understand and use the special terminology to describe microprocessors
3. Explain what a microprocessor is, what its main components are, and what they do
4. Describe the use and importance of bus structures
5. Explain what is involved in the concept of processor speed

1.1 INTRODUCTION

This chapter describes in general terms the various subsystems of a microcomputer and the ways they interrelate—that is, the architecture of the microcomputer. Terms are defined and general concepts stressed. A more detailed examination of the architecture is left to later chapters dealing with specific microprocessor devices. Many terms are introduced in this chapter so that the student can begin to "learn the language"; the short definitions given are not intended to be exhaustive.

1.1.1 Some History

The history of the computer is relatively short. In the nineteenth century, Charles Babbage designed a machine to perform calculations according to a stored set of instructions. He was assisted by Ada, the countess of Lovelace, who was the world's first programmer. Unfortunately, the limitations of nineteenth-century technology stymied Babbage's efforts to build a working model. In the twentieth century, the theory of mechanized computation was further developed by such people as John von Neumann and Alan Turing. An early digital computer built with relays was designed by Howard Aiken in 1944. The first electronic digital computer was built by John Atanasoff during the late 1930s. The ENIAC, the most famous early machine, was built at the University of Pennsylvania during World War II. Completed in 1946, it used a room full of vacuum tubes and could work for only a few hours at a time.

The commercial use of computers had to await the coming of the transistor in the early 1950s. Integrated circuit technology of the 1960s dramatically lowered the cost and size of circuitry and brought about the minicomputer. The minicomputer started the move of computers out of large institutions and into the hands of individual users in laboratories and factories, although the cost was still too high for the average person to afford.

In 1971, something revolutionary happened in the world of computers. The first general-purpose device to contain all the basic parts of a processor on a single chip, the microprocessor, was born. It was the Intel 4004, a 4-bit central processing unit developed at Intel by Ted Hoff, Federico Faggin, and Stan Mazor. In the following year the 8-bit 8008 was introduced. Interestingly, Intel developed the 8008 as a special device for Datapoint Corporation, a terminal manufacturer. Although the corporation had specified its design, Datapoint subsequently decided not to use the device because of speed and cost considerations. Intel then tried to sell the 8008 as a general-purpose device and discovered that a need (and thus a potential market) did indeed exist for an integrated circuit processor. The 8080, an improved version, soon followed and found immediate application in a wide range of products. An enormous success, the 8080 was the processor used in the first "home computer," which was sold as a mail-order kit for $350 by a company called MITS. An improved version of the 8080 appeared in the late 1970s as the 8085 and is discussed in detail in this text.

Other semiconductor manufacturers soon introduced their own devices. As is typical of a new technology, many different designs were marketed, but not all were successful. The successes included the MOS Technologies 6502 (used in the Apple II), the Motorola 6800, and the Zilog Z80. The power of a computer was now available with only a handful of chips costing relatively few dollars.

By the 1980s, microprocessors had grown in speed and capability. Single-chip computers were available. Word size had grown from 8-bit to 16-bit to 32-bit. Sophisticated software was available at relatively low cost. Now it was possible for the average person to buy for a few hundred dollars computing power that would have cost a few million dollars only 30 years earlier. But the real revolution was

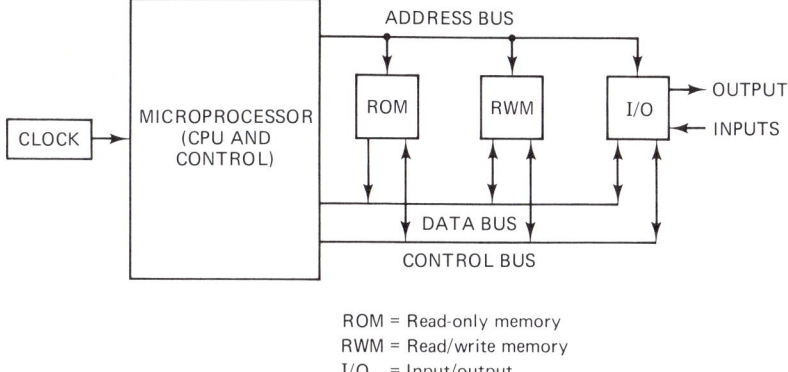

Figure 1.1 Block diagram of a microcomputer. (*Source:* Adapted from Kenneth Short, *Microprocessors and Programmed Logic*, © 1981, P. 12. Reprinted by permission of Prentice-Hall, Inc., Englewood Cliffs, N.J.)

the computerization of everything—from automobiles to zoological equipment—made possible by the microprocessor. Today, the combination of microprocessors with robotics, telecommunications, and artificial intelligence promises a future of exciting new applications. This book is an introduction to that future.

1.1.2 Parts of a Microcomputer

A *microcomputer* is a system made up of a microprocessor, memory, input/output, and an interconnecting bus structure (see Fig. 1.1). Each part of the system may be a separate device, or the whole system may be integrated into a single chip. The parts of a microcomputer are described in the following sections.

1.1.3 Bits, Bytes, Words, Addresses

The basic unit of information in a computer is the *bit,* which stands for binary digit. A bit can have only the values 0 or 1 (low or high). A group of 8 bits is called a *byte*. A group of 4 bits, half a byte, is sometimes called a *nibble*. The *word length* of a processor is the size of the group of bits it is designed to use as a single unit or word. Thus, when speaking of an 8-bit, or 16-bit, or 32-bit machine, we are referring to its word length.

    A microprocessor requires various *registers* to hold groups of bits, some as big as the word size and some bigger. Some of the registers are also *counters* and can be incremented or decremented (add 1 or subtract 1), as well as have entire groups of bits moved into or out of them. One of the registers, the program counter (PC) (or instruction counter; IC), is used to hold binary numbers representing the *addresses* of instructions stored in memory. The size of the program counter, which is usually bigger than the word length, determines the memory space. The *memory space* is how many memory locations the processor can get to (address) directly and is equal to 2^N, where N is the number of bits in the PC register.

> **EXAMPLE 1.1**
>
> The 8085 processor has an 8-bit word length and a 16-bit address length. How many words can it address?
>
> **SOLUTION** $2^{16} = 65,536$. The 8085 can directly address 64K bytes of memory, where 1K is equal to 1024 (not 1000). Memory sizes are given in multiples of 1K.

1.2 THE CPU

The microprocessor itself contains a *CPU* (central processing unit), together with various counters, registers, and logic circuits required for the CPU to do its job. The central processor is the main component of a microcomputer; it's where the action takes place.

1.2.1 Clock, Reset, Watchdog Timer

A CPU is a sequential state machine, and as such, it requires a *clock* to synchronize the internal transitions from state to state as it carries out its operations. The number of clock pulses required by the CPU to perform a basic operation is called a *machine cycle*. Also required is a *reset* input to put the CPU into a defined initial state when it is first powered up or to return the CPU to such a state from a severe error that locks up the processor.

Microprocessors built using NMOS semiconductor technology are dynamic devices. That is, they use the system clock input for internal refresh as well as timing and require a clock frequency higher than some specified minimum value to ensure proper operation. In contrast, the typical CMOS microprocessor is static and can be operated at an arbitrarily low clock rate. A CMOS microprocessor can be single-stepped by using a switch to generate clock pulses manually. The terms *static* and *dynamic* are explained further in Sec. 1.3.3.

Often a piece of equipment must operate with little or no human intervention. In such a case, if something happens to lock up the CPU, it is important that the system be able to recover by resetting the CPU itself. One technique is the so-called watchdog timer. A *watchdog timer* is a circuit that will wait a fixed amount of time for a signal from the CPU. If the signal arrives while the timer is waiting, it will restart the wait period. If the watchdog "times out" before it gets the signal, it will automatically reset the CPU. Such a circuit can be built with an integrated circuit such as the popular 555 timer.

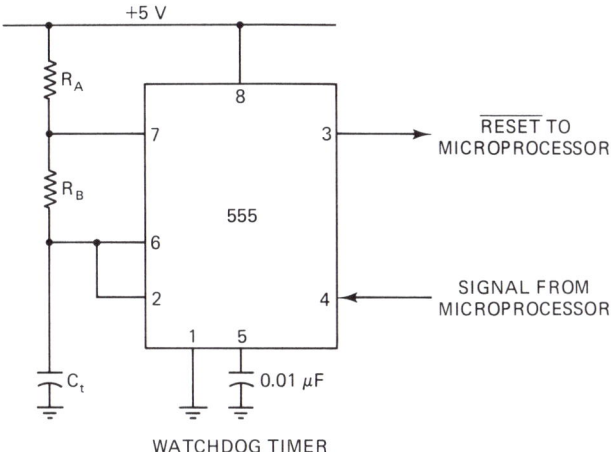

WATCHDOG TIMER

EXAMPLE 1.2

Use a 555 to design a watchdog timer. It should have a wait time of approximately 1 sec and produce a pulse of at least 0.1 sec.

SOLUTION We will use the 555 in astable mode and assume that it causes a reset when its output (pin 3) goes low. The 555 output will stay high until capacitor Ct charges up. A periodic output signal from the processor will pulse the transistor to discharge Ct. We will arbitrarily pick Ct to be 1 µF. The 555 output is low during its discharge time (T2) given by T2 = 0.693 · Rb · Ct, so

$$0.1 = 0.693 \cdot Rb \cdot 1 \times 10^{-6}$$
$$Rb = 0.1/(0.693 \cdot 1 \times 10^{-6})$$
$$Rb = 144,300$$

We will make Rb 150K, which is a standard value close to 144,300. The charging time for Ct is given by T1 = 0.693 · (Ra + Rb) · Ct, so

$$1 = 0.693 \cdot (Ra + 150,000) \cdot 1 \times 10^{-6}$$
$$Ra = 1/(0.693 \cdot 1 \times 10^{-6}) - 150,000$$
$$Ra = 1,293,001$$

We will make Ra 1.5 Meg, which is a standard value close to 1,293,001.

1.2.2 Instructions, IR, MAR

Instructions are the commands, encoded as binary numbers and held in memory, that tell the microprocessor what to do. The main job of the CPU is to fetch (read) instructions and then execute them—the *fetch-execute* cycle. The address of the next instruction is held in the program counter. When the microprocessor is reset, the PC will contain some initial address, usually all zeros. As each instruction is fetched, the contents of the PC will be automatically increased (by an amount equal to the length of the instruction) so as to point to the next instruction in sequence. Some instructions (e.g., JUMP) change the contents of the PC when they are executed. Other instructions reference the memory to load or store data. Such instructions put addresses onto the address bus through the *memory address register* (MAR), which is similar to, but distinct from, the program counter.

Processors using the standard Von Neumann architecture multiplex the PC and the MAR onto a common address bus and fetch both instructions and data over a common data bus. Processors using the so-called Harvard architecture have an address bus and a fetch bus for instructions and a separate address bus and read/write bus for data.

Once it is fetched, an instruction is held in the *instruction register* (IR) while the CPU decodes it. Some high-performance processors have an instruction *pipeline* (also called an instruction *queue*), which is a group of registers that allow a number of instructions to be *prefetched* and held while waiting to get into the IR. The prefetching is done while the CPU is executing the current instruction, and parts of the prefetched instructions may be executed simultaneously with the instruction in the IR in a technique called *overlap*. Getting an instruction from the pipeline is much faster than getting it from the memory, so the throughput of the CPU is increased by not having to wait for the next instruction. Similarly, some processors have an on-chip *cache* memory to hold frequently used data. Reading from cache is much faster than reading from external memory.

The general format of an instruction is an op-code followed by one or more operands. The *op-code* tells the CPU what operation to do; the *operands* specify on what piece of data the operation is performed. Instructions can be different lengths, usually multiples of a byte.

1.2.3 Control Unit and Microcode

The *control unit* is the part of the CPU that reads the instruction in the IR and enables the appropriate hardware in the processor to execute the instruction. Some processors decode instructions directly using hardware. More commonly, a microprocessor will implement the instruction in the IR by executing a series of more primitive instructions called *microinstructions* or *microcode*. The microcode is held in a *control memory,* which is usually embedded in the CPU chip. Some processors keep the control memory on a separate chip so that it can be changed to give the processor a different instruction set.

1.2.4 CPU Modes

In many of the newer 16-bit and 32-bit microprocessors, instruction execution depends on the CPU being in one of two modes: privileged (also called supervisory) or user. In *privileged* mode, all instructions may be executed. In *user* mode, certain instructions (e.g., HALT) will not be executed. The division into two modes allows the microprocessor to be used in systems where a piece of software known as the *operating system* runs in privileged mode and all other programs, typically called *applications,* run in user mode under the control and supervision of the operating system. Such a system prevents an application from "crashing" the computer (either by accident or design), as any attempt by a user to do something not allowed in its mode will cause a "trap," meaning the operating system will step in and take charge.

1.2.5 Accumulators, Scratchpads, Pointers

The typical CPU (but not all) contains one or more accumulators, equal in size to the word length. The *accumulator* is the main working register of the CPU. The result of an ALU operation (see Sec. 1.2.6) is left in the accumulator, where it may, in turn, become the operand of the next operation. Input and output usually flow through the accumulator.

A CPU also may have general-purpose word-length registers that can be used for temporary storage. These registers are sometimes called *scratchpads*. A CPU may also have one or more *pointer* registers (also called *index* registers) that are used to hold addresses. Special instructions can then get at memory locations by referring to the pointer instead of using the numeric address itself. Because the contents of a pointer can be incremented, decremented, or changed by the program, the pointer is a versatile feature. In some CPUs the scratchpad registers (sometimes in pairs) can be used as pointers.

1.2.6 The ALU

Some instructions move data around; other instructions perform calculations on the data. Calculations are done in a CPU by the *arithmetic and logic unit* (ALU). The ALU does adding and subtracting, as well as shifting, comparing, ANDing, and ORing.

1.2.7 Flags and Program Status

The CPU contains a special register, often called the *program status word* (PSW), that contains the *flag bits*. The flag bits are *set* or *cleared* (made 1 or 0), depending on results of CPU operations. Some instructions can "test" the flags, meaning that the execution of the instruction depends on whether a certain flag bit (or bits) is high or low. Some typical flags are sign, carry, zero, and overflow. Other flags, such as auxiliary carry and subtract, may also be present.

A flag bit usually refers to the state of the accumulator because most of the CPU work is done there. The *sign bit* is simply the *most significant bit* (MSB) of the accumulator after an ALU operation. When the content of the accumulator is being treated as a signed number, an MSB of 0 indicates positive and a 1 indicates negative. The *carry* flag can be thought of as an extra accumulator bit—for example, the ninth bit of an 8-bit accumulator. Any operation that causes a result exceeding the accumulator by 1 bit will set the carry; otherwise, the carry is clear.

Overflow occurs when the result of an arithmetic operation on signed numbers causes an erroneous carry into the sign bit. Because bits of the result are lost, overflow represents an error. The function of overflow should not be confused with that of the carry flag (see Chap. 4). The *zero* flag will be set by any operation that leaves all the bits in the accumulator equal to zero. The operation must be one using the ALU; just moving all zeros into the accumulator will not set the zero flag.

1.3 MEMORY

The set of instructions that tell the microcomputer what to do is called the *program*. The program, and perhaps tables of data, are stored in memory locations either on the microprocessor chip itself or in external memory chips. Memory devices are classified into two basic types: read-only memory (ROM) and read/write or random-access memory (RAM) (see Secs. 1.3.2 and 1.3.3). Some processors, such as the 8051, contain both RAM and ROM.

1.3.1 Storage: Program, Data, Page, Segment

The total memory space can be divided into *program storage* and *data storage*. Such a division is usually just semantic because most processors treat memory as one continuous space. However, some processors (e.g., the 8051) have physically separate program and data storage with separate addresses.

Another division of memory space is into *pages* and *segments*. Typical sizes are 256 bytes for a page and 64K bites for a segment. While often used simply as convenient descriptions, some processors actually handle memory in such fixed blocks. An example is the 8086, which uses segment addressing.

1.3.2 ROM, EPROM, Volatility

As the name implies, read-only memory (ROM) devices can only be read by the microcomputer. To write into a ROM device requires a ROM programmer, which is separate from the microcomputer. Some ROM devices can be written to only once, whereas others can be erased and reprogrammed. A chip called a UVEPROM (or just EPROM) is an *erasable-programmable read-only-memory* that is erased by exposing the chip to ultraviolet light in a special fixture.

ROM is usually nonvolatile, meaning that it does not lose its contents even when power is removed or it is disconnected from the system. Thus, ROM is often used to store the programs used by microcomputers. Programs so stored are referred to as *firmware*, which is derived from the terms *software* (the program) and *hardware* (the memory chip itself). In other words, firmware is software permanently embedded in hardware.

Another form of ROM is the *electrically alterable read-only memory* (EAROM). An EAROM is similar to an EPROM except that it can be programmed and erased under control of the microprocessor. Note that EPROMs and EAROMs can be erased and reprogrammed only a limited number of times before they fail.

1.3.3 RAM: Static, Dynamic, Battery Backup

The term *random access* was originally used to distinguish a memory device from one that was sequential access, such as magnetic tape. The term is now used to indicate that a memory device can be written to, as well as read, by a processor. The term *read/write* memory means the same as RAM.

Because a semiconductor RAM is essentially a large number of transistors on a chip, it is volatile. If power is removed, whatever was stored on the chip is lost. However, a RAM chip can be made nonvolatile by using *battery backup*. A battery is wired into the microprocessor system in such a way that during normal operation the RAM is powered by the system supply. But when power is lost, the RAM is automatically switched over to battery power, thus preserving its contents. The battery can be rechargeable, such as the nickel-cadmium battery, or it can be a primary cell type, such as the lithium. Some RAM chips are available with built-in batteries.

Another distinction is between static and dynamic RAM chips. *Static* memory devices store bits in bistable latch circuits (flip-flops) on the chip. In contrast, *dy-*

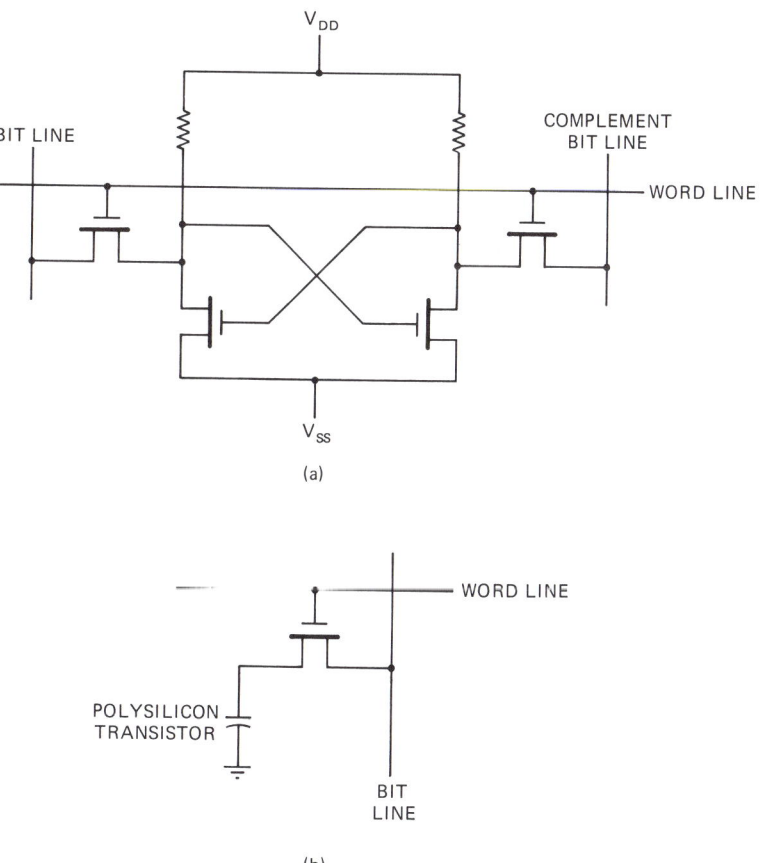

Figure 1.2 Comparison of (a) static and (b) dynamic RAM cells.

namic memory chips store bits in the form of stored charge on the gates of the integrated transistors. See Fig. 1.2. The charge is very small and tends to "bleed off," requiring that the bits be recharged periodically to maintain their data. The recharging occurs every few milliseconds when the processor accesses the memory chip during a special refresh cycle. Although the need for refresh cycles complicates the design of the memory subsystem, dynamic devices store more bits in less space and at lower cost than do static devices.

1.3.4 The Stack: Push, Pop, Call

Although RAM is used to hold programs and data, the CPU requires that a portion of RAM be set aside in the form of a *stack* for use by certain important operations. The stack gets its name from the stack of plates in a cafeteria. When a plate is taken off the top, another plate pops up to take its place. When new plates are added to the stack, the old plates are pushed down. The terms *push* and *pop* are carried over to memory stacks, which, in effect, work the same way. Stacks are described as being last-in, first-out, or *LIFO*, because the last thing pushed on will be the first thing popped off. See Fig. 1.3.

The stack is accessed sequentially by the CPU using a special address register called the *stack pointer* (SP), which points to the top of the stack. A push instruction will copy the contents of a register to the (hopefully) empty space at the top of the stack and the stack pointer will be advanced to point to the next location up the stack. A pop instruction will copy the top of the stack into a register and the SP will be adjusted to point to the next location down the stack. ("Up" and "down" are relative and depend on the processor.) The stack grows with every push and contracts with every pop. There must, eventually, be a pop for every push, or the stack will grow until it overflows—overwriting other parts of RAM and causing the system to crash. (The term *pull* is sometimes used for pop.)

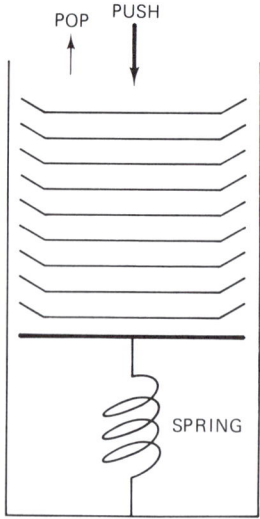

Figure 1.3 Pictorial version of LIFO.

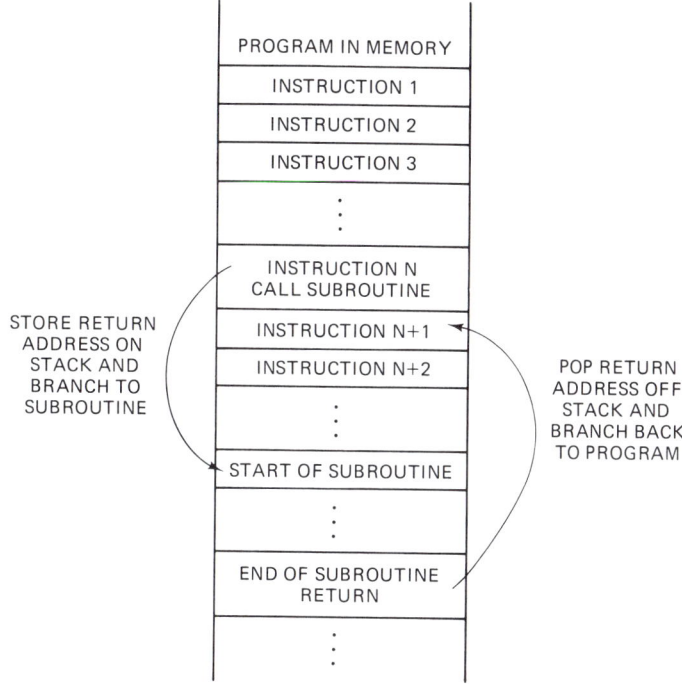

Figure 1.4 Call to a subroutine.

The most important use of the stack is in a call to a subroutine. Subroutines are considered in detail in Chapter 4. Briefly, a *subroutine* is a group of instructions written at one place in the program that can be executed from any other place. A *call* is an instruction that tells the CPU to go to the starting address of the subroutine and execute it. The last instruction in the subroutine is a *return*, which tells the CPU to go back to the main part of the program. The CPU knows the address of where it left the main program because a call instruction causes an automatic push of the return address onto the stack before branching to the subroutine. The return instruction causes an automatic pop of the return address off the stack and back into the program counter (assuming, of course, that the subroutine has not altered the stack). See Fig. 1.4.

1.3.5 Memory Speed and Devices

The speed of a memory chip is its *access time*, measured as the time between asking the chip for data and actually getting valid data from it. *Cycle time* refers to the time between successive accesses.

Access time can vary, depending on how the memory chip is asked. A typical ROM chip will have inputs called *chip select* (CS) and *output enable* (OE), as well as address and data lines. CS and OE are usually *active-low*, with CS being essentially an extra address pin and OE controlling output on the 3-state data pins. The

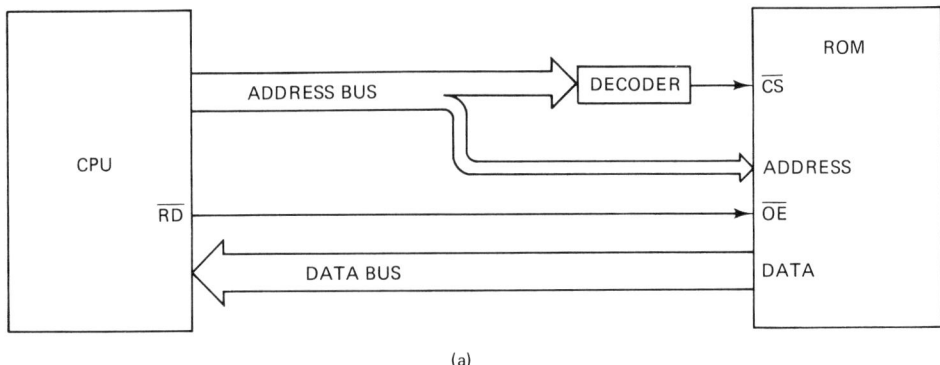

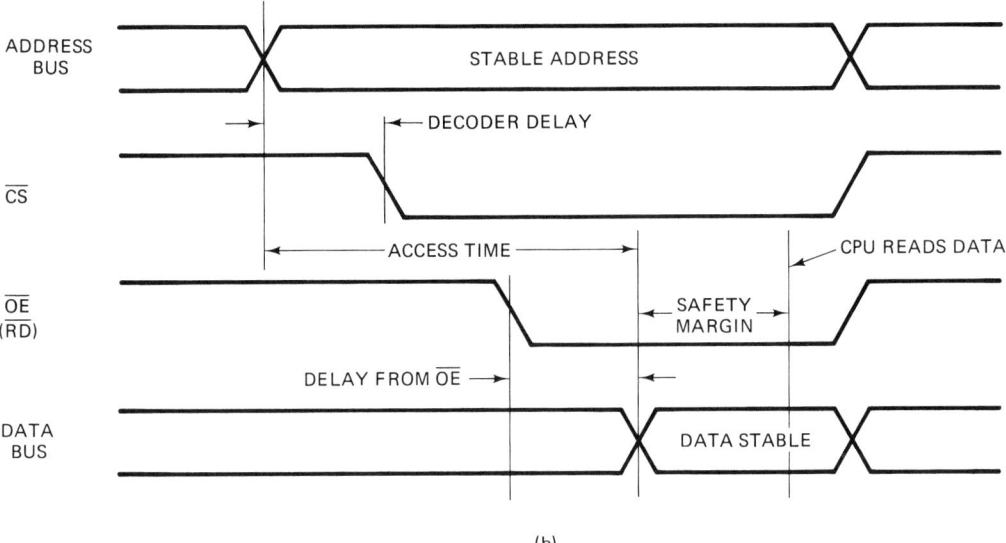

Figure 1.5 (a) Block and (b) timing diagrams of access time.

term *3-state* (or *three-state*) refers to the three possible output states: high (1), low (0), and floating (high impedance or disconnected). Such devices are used to share a common bus. (*Note:* The term *tristate* means 3-state, but it is a registered trademark of National Semiconductor Corporation.) The CS signal is usually derived by decoding the higher address bits, and OE is driven by the CPU read control line (RD). See Fig. 1.5. Note that the CPU also generates a write control signal (WR) for writing to RAM devices.

In some memory devices, such as the 2764 EPROM (see Fig. 1.6), the chip-select function is called *chip enable* (CE) and has an additional function of putting the chip into a low-power standby mode when not enabled, during which OE will be ignored. One way to access such a device is to give it a valid address, assert

2764A

Pin Names

A_0–A_{12}	Addresses
$\overline{CE}$	Chip Enable
$\overline{OE}$	Output Enable
O_0–O_7	Outputs
$\overline{PGM}$	Program
N.C.	No Connect
D.U.	Don't Use

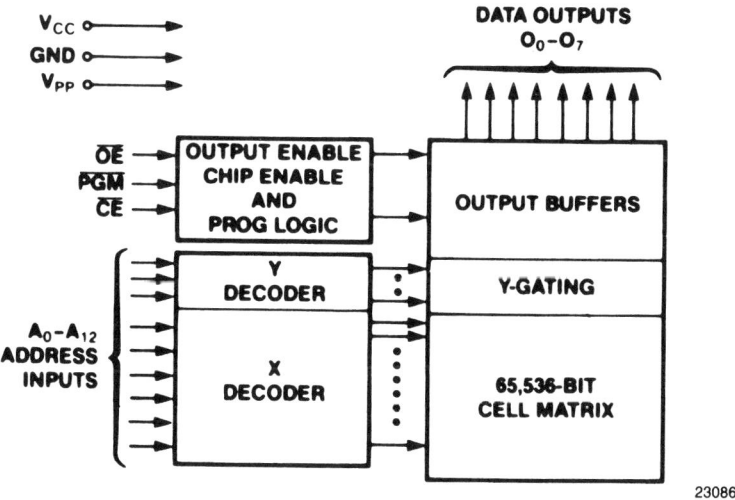

Figure 1.6 The 2764 EPROM. (*Source:* Reprinted by permission of Intel Corporation, Copyright © Intel Corporation 1988.)

CE, and then assert $\overline{OE}$ using RD. An alternative is to ground the CE pin so that the chip is always enabled. To access the device, just give it a valid address and then assert $\overline{OE}$. Access time will be quicker at the expense of higher power consumption in the memory chip, an example of the speed-power trade-off common in digital systems.

A typical RAM chip (see Fig. 1.7) does not have an $\overline{OE}$ pin, but it does have a read/write (R/W) control pin. Driving R/W to the read state causes the RAM to

#M039

HM6264ASP-12, HM6264ASP-15, HM6264ASP-20, HM6264ALSP-12, HM6264ALSP-15, HM6264ALSP-20

JANUARY, 1986

⊕ HITACHI

8192-word x 8-bit High Speed Static CMOS RAM

■ FEATURES

- High Density 300 mil 28 pin Package
- Low Power Standby   Standby: LP 0.01mW (typ.)
  Low Power Operation   P 0.1mW (typ.)
- Fast access Time   Operating: 15mW/MHz (typ.)
- Single +5V Supply   120ns/150ns/200ns (max.)
- Completely Static Memory . . . No clock or Timing Strobe Required
- Equal Access and Cycle Time
- Common Data Inputs and Outputs, Three State Outputs
- Directly TTL Compatible: All Inputs and Outputs

(DP-28N)

■ BLOCK DIAGRAM

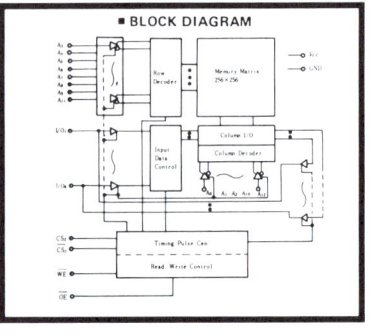

■ PIN ARRANGEMENT

NC	1	28	V_{CC}
A_{12}	2	27	$\overline{WE}$
A_7	3	26	CS_2
A_6	4	25	A_8
A_5	5	24	A_9
A_4	6	23	A_{11}
A_3	7	22	$\overline{OE}$
A_2	8	21	A_{10}
A_1	9	20	$\overline{CS_1}$
A_0	10	19	I/O_8
I/O_1	11	18	I/O_7
I/O_2	12	17	I/O_6
I/O_3	13	16	I/O_5
GND	14	15	I/O_4

(Top View)

■ ABSOLUTE MAXIMUM RATINGS

Item	Symbol	Rating	Unit
Terminal Voltage *	V_T	−0.5 ** to +7.0	V
Power Dissipation	P_T	1.0	W
Operating Temperature	T_{opr}	0 to +70	°C
Storage Temperature	T_{stg}	−55 to +125	°C
Storage Temperature (Under Bias)	T_{bias}	−10 to +85	°C

* With respect to GND.   ** Pulse width 50ns: 3.0 V

■ TRUTH TABLE

$\overline{WE}$	$\overline{CS_1}$	CS_2	$\overline{OE}$	Mode	I/O Pin	V_{CC} Current	Note
X	H	X	X	Not Selected	High Z	I_{SB}, I_{SB1}	
X	X	L	X	(Power Down)	High Z	I_{SB}, I_{SB1}	
H	L	H	H	Output Disabled	High Z	I_{CC}	
H	L	H	L	Read	Dout	I_{CC}	
L	L	H	H	Write	Din	I_{CC}	Write Cycle (1)
L	L	H	L	Write	Din	I_{CC}	Write Cycle (2)

X : H or L

Figure 1.7 Typical RAM chip. (*Source*: Courtesy of Hitachi America, Ltd. This manual may, wholly or partially, be subject to change without notice.)

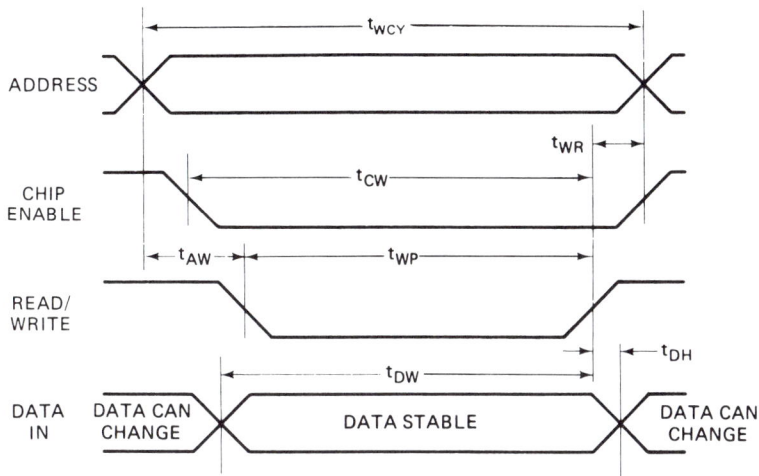

t_{WCY} = Cycle time
t_{CW} = Time chip select (chip enable) must be stable before another transition on R/W
t_{WR} = Time address must be stable before another R/W transition
t_{AW} = Address to read/write delay (address setup)
t_{WP} = Minimum read/write pulse width
t_{DW} = Minimum data setup time
t_{DH} = Data hold time after R/W change

Figure 1.8 Write timing diagram for RAM chip. (*Source:* Adapted from Kenneth Short, *Microprocessors and Programmed Logic,* © 1981, P. 47. Reprinted by permission of Prentice-Hall, Inc., Englewood Cliffs, N.J.)

put data on the bus, similar to OE in a ROM. RAM chips typically have faster access times than ROM chips, which allows the R/W pin to be driven by the CPU RD line. See Fig. 1.8.

1.4 INPUT/OUTPUT (I/O)

To do something useful, a microcomputer must be able to exchange information with the real world—that is, hardware other than the memory and the CPU. Usually, a computer must *interface* with keyboards, displays, LEDs, switches, disk drives, and other such *I/O devices*.

1.4.1 Ports and Memory Mapping

Microcomputers connect to I/O devices through *ports,* which are connections consisting of groups of parallel bit lines going into and out of the computer. A single-bit port is called a *serial* port. Ports often have addresses separate from memory addresses and special instructions to access them. Some systems use *memory-mapped I/O,* where the I/O devices are treated like memory locations, and all the instructions that access memory can then be used for input and output.

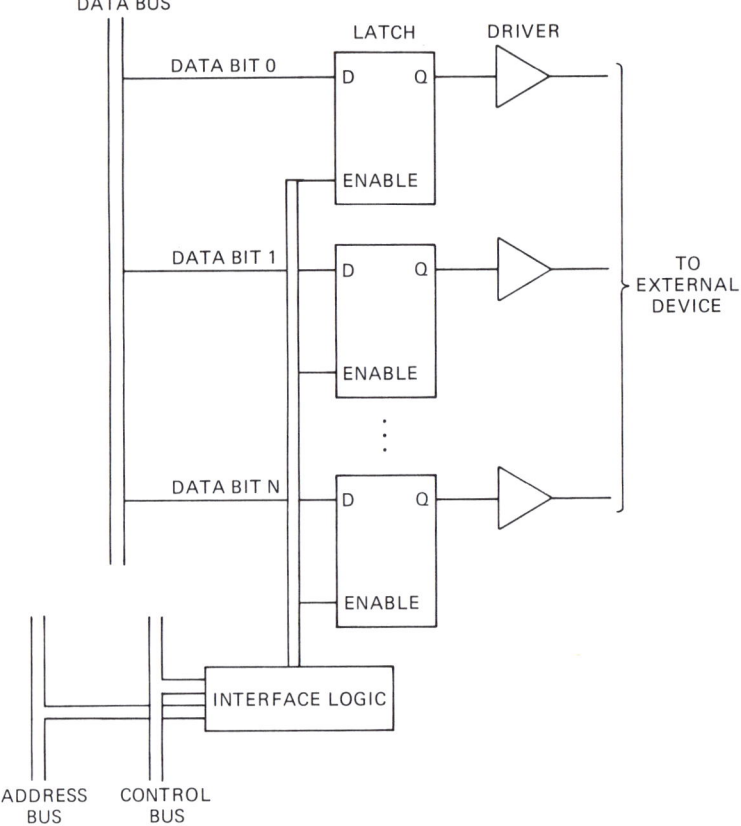

Figure 1.9 Simplified output port.

1.4.2 Latches, Drivers, Peripheral Devices

Often a separate chip containing *latches* and *drivers* is connected to the system bus to implement the I/O function of the microcomputer system. The data sent to a port address will go through the chip and into the real-world I/O device. See Fig. 1.9. Some I/O devices, described as *bus compatible,* contain hardware that allows them to be connected directly to the microprocessor bus. Such circuits are called peripheral devices and are discussed in detail in Chapter 10.

1.4.3 Interrupts

Related to the idea of I/O is the idea of an *interrupt.* Microprocessors are often used to monitor and control external processes such as machine tools and communications links. In such systems, often called real-time systems, events will happen that require immediate attention from the processor. By activating the appropriate pin on the CPU or peripheral chip, an external device can interrupt whatever the CPU is doing and cause it to branch to an interrupt service routine. The process is similar to a subroutine call. Interrupts are examined further in later chapters.

1.5 BUS STRUCTURES

Because the CPU, the memory, and the I/O ports may be on separate chips, a means must exist to interconnect them. That means is the microprocessor *bus structure*. The entire structure usually consists of three buses: the *address bus*, the *data bus*, and the *control bus*, each carrying the information implied by its name. The buses are parallel connections, typically wires or traces of copper on a printed circuit board, and each of the chip packages has pins to connect to buses.

1.5.1 Bus Width and Multiplexing

The width of a bus is usually a multiple of a byte but is no wider than what it is carrying. For example, a CPU with an 8-bit data word would use an 8-bit data bus but not a 16-bit data bus. Another CPU may have a 16-bit word and use a 16-bit bus, or, like the 8088, it might use an 8-bit bus, sending out the 16-bit word as 2 sequential bytes.

The number of bus lines is often limited by the number of pins that can be reasonably placed on a device package rather than the number of bits required. In such cases, the pins are time-shared or *multiplexed,* meaning that the same pins do double duty. The 8085 uses the same eight pins to carry the 8-bit data word as well as half the 16-bit address. External hardware must capture the bits in a latch to demultiplex and hold them for the complete machine cycle.

1.5.2 Unidirectional, Bidirectional, 3-State

Some buses carry bits in only one direction; they are *unidirectional*. For example, the address bus goes from the CPU out to the memory and peripheral devices. *Bidirectional* buses carry bits in both directions. The data bus, for example, must carry bits from the CPU to the memory during a write cycle and from the memory back to the CPU during a read cycle.

Because a typical system has multiple sources of data (ROM, RAM, I/O, CPU) but only one data bus, the devices not currently using the bus must let go of it. If more than one device tries to get on the same bus at the same time, the result is bus contention or collision, which is a system error.

The normal states for a digital device are high and low. A third state is for the device to become a virtual open circuit by going into a high-impedance or floating condition. When a device is not selected to use the data bus, it puts its data pins into the floating 3-state mode to effectively disconnect itself from the bus.

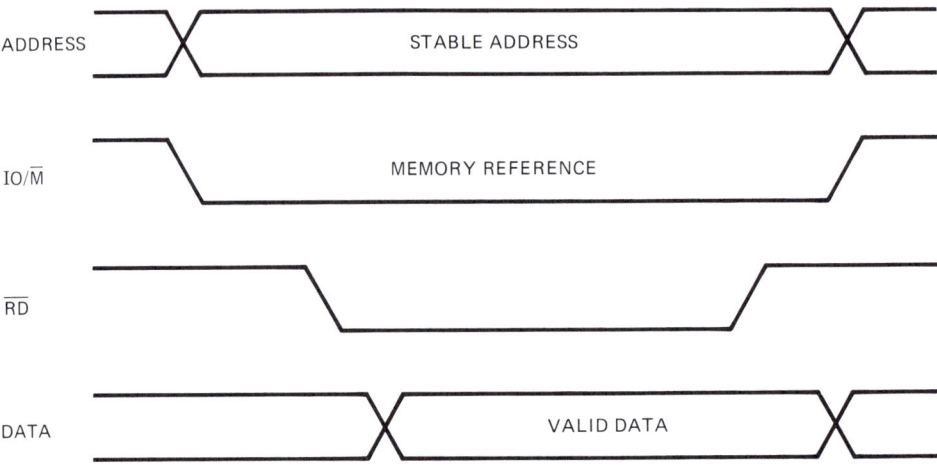

Figure 1.10 Typical memory read cycle.

1.5.3 Bus Operation

To illustrate the interaction of the three buses, we can go through a typical memory read cycle, as shown in Fig. 1.10. First the CPU puts out the address of the location in memory to be read, together with control signal IO/M (part of the control bus) that tells whether the read is from memory or from an I/O device having the same address. After allowing time for the address to become stable, the CPU will assert another control line ($\overline{RD}$) that tells the memory chip that the operation is a read (instead of a write) and do it now. While $\overline{RD}$ is active, the memory chip will put the data onto the data bus for the CPU to read. When $\overline{RD}$ becomes inactive, the memory chip data pins go back to the floating 3-state condition.

1.5.4 Wait States

A read operation requires a fixed number of clock pulses for the CPU to execute it. The time required, therefore, depends on the frequency of the clock. However, memory chips and other bus devices have a minimum access time required for them to put valid data on the bus after they are addressed. If the CPU read cycle time is shorter than the access time, data will be lost.

To allow slower devices to be used on the bus, the typical CPU has a special control input (e.g., the 8085 READY pin) that will stretch out the machine cycle by forcing the CPU to execute *wait states*. When addressed, the slow device must assert the wait control until it puts the data on the bus. Thus, wait states synchronize slow data devices to the bus.

1.5.5 Card Cages and Motherboards

The term *bus* as used so far refers to the chip level structure defined by the microprocessor architecture. The term can also be used to refer to a higher level structure implemented in the packaging of the system.

Typically, chips are soldered onto printed circuit cards, which, in turn, are pushed into enclosures known as *card cages*. The chips also can be soldered onto *daughterboards* that plug into a single large *motherboard*. Either way, a standardized scheme of interconnecting the small boards must be defined—in other words, a bus. An example of such a bus is the one used in IBM-compatible personal computers. Another is the STD bus, shown in Fig. 1.11. The term *backplane* also refers to interconnection schemes of boards plugged into connectors, especially in larger computers.

The main advantage of a board level bus is that devices from various manufacturers, using different chip level buses, can be "mixed and matched" in the same system as long as the signals at the edge of each card conform to the packaging bus standard. Systems designers sleep better at night knowing that if a sole-source chip from manufacturer X is no longer available, a similar device from vendor Y can be substituted using a different board but plugging into the same edge connector.

A sole-source device is one that is only available from a single manufacturer or vendor. In contrast, a device available from two or more manufacturers is described as having a *second source*. Many designers will not use sole-source items as key parts in a system for fear of having to redesign or scrap the system if the sole source stops making the part. Chip manufacturers with an original design will often set up second sources by licensing another company to produce the device in exchange for a payment on each chip sold (a royalty). If two manufacturers grant each other licenses for their proprietary designs, the arrangement is called cross-licensing.

1.5.6 Bus Problems

In addition to bus contention (see Sec. 1.5.2), some other problems that can be encountered on a bus are loading, transients, and cross-talk.

Loading problems occur because device outputs are limited in the amount of ac and dc power they can provide to drive the inputs of other devices. If an output tries to drive too many inputs, it will not be able to maintain the correct voltage levels to distinguish a binary 1 from a binary 0 and bits will be lost.

Devices called *buffers* are used to prevent loading problems. An output of a device such as a microprocessor can be connected to the input of a buffer and the output of the buffer can drive the inputs of many other devices. For bidirectional signals such as data lines, a two-way type of buffer, a transceiver, is required; for unidirectional signals such as address lines, a one-way buffer, a driver, is used. When several devices are sharing signal lines such as data lines, the buffers used would be 3-state devices.

STD BUS FUNCTIONAL SPECIFICATIONS

The STD Bus pin-out connectors are organized into four functional groups:
DUAL POWER BUSES - Pins 1-6 and 53-56
DATA BUS - Pins 7-14
ADDRESS BUS - Pins 15-30
CONTROL BUS - Pins 31-52
The descriptions of all pin-out functions are listed in (b). This chart lists the mnemonic function and signal flow direction for each pin of the STD Bus. Further physical definitions of the STD Bus are shown in (a). The STD Bus requires that each card have a 56-pin (dual 28) card edge connector and that the mother-board connectors be spaced at least 0.5 inches on center.

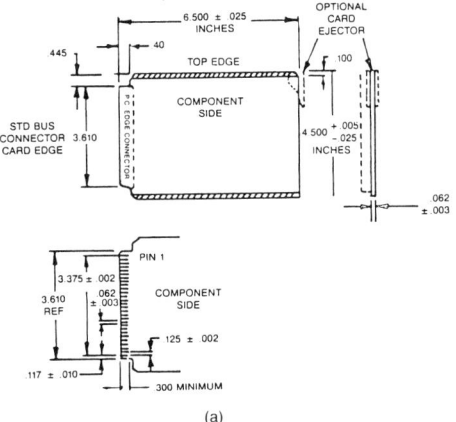

(a)

	PIN	COMPONENT SIDE SIGNAL NAME	SIGNAL FLOW	DESCRIPTION	PIN	CIRCUIT SIDE SIGNAL NAME	SIGNAL FLOW	DESCRIPTION
LOGIC POWER BUS	1	Vcc	In	Logic Power (+5 VDC)	2	Vcc	In	Logic Power (+5 VDC)
	3	GND	In	Logic Ground	4	GND	In	Logic Ground
	5	VBB #1/VBAT	In	Logic Bias #1/Bat Pwr	6	VBB #2/DCPD*	In	Logic Bias #2/Pwr Dwn
DATA BUS	7	D3/A19	In/Out	Data Bus/Address Ext	8	D7/A23	In/Out	Data Bus/Address Ext
	9	D2/A18	In/Out		10	D6/A22	In/Out	
	11	D1/A17	In/Out		12	D5/A21	In/Out	
	13	D0/A16	In/Out		14	D4/A20	In/Out	
ADDRESS BUS	15	A7	Out	Address Bus	16	A15	Out	Address Bus
	17	A6	Out		18	A14	Out	
	19	A5	Out		20	A13	Out	
	21	A4	Out		22	A12	Out	
	23	A3	Out		24	A11	Out	
	25	A2	Out		26	A10	Out	
	27	A1	Out		28	A9	Out	
	29	A0	Out		30	A8	Out	
CONTROL BUS	31	WR*	Out	Write to Memory or I/O	32	RD*	Out	Read Memory or I/O
	33	IORQ*	Out	I/O Address Select	34	MEMRQ*	Out	Memory Address Select
	35	IOEXP	In/Out	I/O Expansion	36	MEMEX	In/Out	Memory Expansion
	37	REFRESH*	Out	Refresh Timing	38	MCSYNC*	Out	CPU Machine Cycle Sync.
	39	STATUS 1*	Out	CPU Status	40	STATUS 0*	Out	CPU Status
	41	BUSAK*	Out	Bus Acknowledge	42	BUSRQ*	In	Bus Request
	43	INTAK*	Out	Interrupt Acknowledge	44	INTRQ*	In	Interrupt Request
	45	WAITRQ*	In	Wait Request	46	NMIRQ*	In	Nonmaskable Interrupt
	47	SYSRESET*	Out	System Reset	48	PBRESET*	In	Pushbutton Reset
	49	CLOCK*	Out	Clock from Processor	50	CNTRL*	In	AUX Timing
	51	PCO	Out	Priority Chain Out	52	PCI	In	Priority Chain In
AUXILIARY POWER BUS	53	AUX GND	In	AUX Ground	54	AUX GND	In	AUX Ground
	55	AUX +V	In	AUX Positive (+12 VDC)	56	AUX −V	In	AUX Negative (−12 VDC)

*Low-level active indicator

(b)

Figure 1.11 STD bus. (*Source:* Courtesy of Micro-Link Products.)

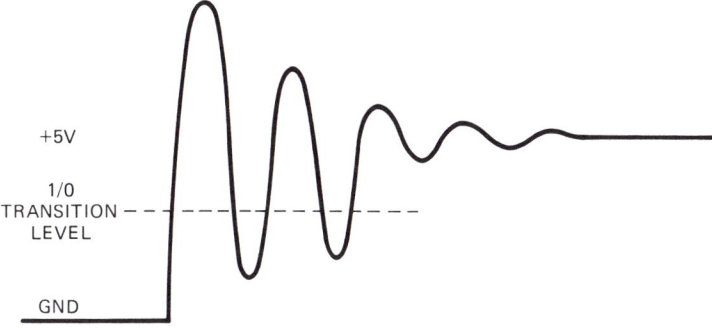

Figure 1.12 Ringing.

Transients occur because of the fast rise and fall times of the signals in a typical digital system. It can be shown mathematically using Fourier analysis that signals, such as square waves and pulses, that have fast rise times generate many high-frequency sinusoidal harmonics. At high frequencies, even the small amounts of capacitance and inductance associated with the bus connections can form tuned circuits and transmission lines that give rise to a reflection of energy and ringing, a rapid fluctuation in voltage (see Fig. 1.12).

Ringing causes a digital signal to alternate rapidly between high and low level at a time when it should have a steady state, thus causing an intermittent type of error when the signal is read. Ringing can be reduced by terminating the signal lines with resistors. A discussion of termination techniques is beyond the scope of this book.

Cross-talk occurs when a signal on one line is capacitively coupled to another line where it doesn't belong. Like ringing, cross-talk occurs most frequently when signals have fast rise and fall times. Cross-talk can be reduced by careful board and bus layout. Avoid running critical signal lines parallel to each other, or separate them with ground traces. Do not bundle signal wires together. Use ground planes on printed circuit boards.

1.6 ADDRESS DECODING

A typical microprocessor system will contain multiple memory and I/O devices. For example, there may be a ROM chip to hold the program, a RAM chip to hold the stack and data, a serial I/O chip for data communications, and a parallel I/O chip to interface to an LED display. To select the appropriate chip, the address bus, together with some of the control bus signals, must be *decoded*.

1.6.1 Distinctions: Memory or I/O, Read or Write

As discussed in Sec. 1.5, the typical microprocessor has a single data bus that all memory and I/O must share, so somehow memory and I/O chips must be turned on and off as needed. To do so, the typical memory or I/O chip will have a chip-select

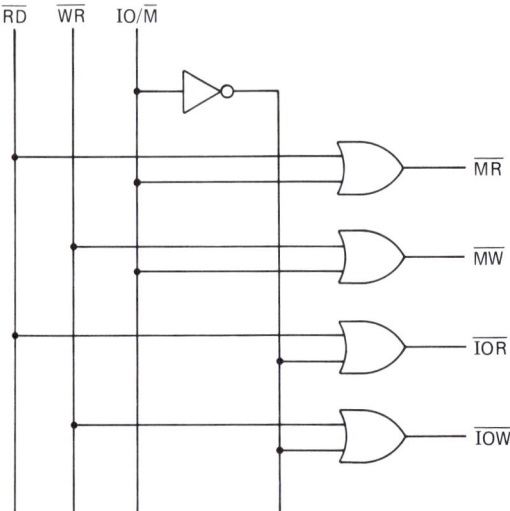

Figure 1.13 Combined $\overline{RD}$, $\overline{WR}$, and IO/$\overline{M}$ control signals.

(CS) pin. When CS is asserted (i.e., made active), the chip will drive the data bus; otherwise, the chip will let go of the bus by making its outputs float. A typical system will use gate circuits to combine address and control from the CPU into a chip-select signal.

For systems having separate memory and I/O space, it is necessary to determine whether a given address refers to a memory location or an I/O port. To allow this determination to be made, the CPU must supply a control signal. For example, the 8085 supplies the IO/$\overline{M}$ signal, which is high when the CPU is accessing (reading from or writing to) an I/O port and low when the CPU is accessing memory.

Once a memory or I/O chip has been selected, it must know whether it should read data off the bus or write data onto the bus. Again, the CPU must supply control signals. For example, the 8085 supplies the two signals $\overline{RD}$ and $\overline{WR}$ to indicate read and write, respectively. The terms *read* and *write* are from the point of view of the CPU: When the processor writes to a chip, the chip will read the data off the bus. The memory or I/O chip will usually accept the $\overline{RD}$ and $\overline{WR}$ signals directly. The $\overline{RD}$, $\overline{WR}$, and IO/$\overline{M}$ control signals may be combined, as shown in Fig. 1.13, to obtain separate pairs of signals: memory read and write ($\overline{MR}$ and $\overline{MW}$) and I/O read and write ($\overline{IOR}$ and $\overline{IOW}$). Note that even if a chip has been selected, its data output will remain in a high-impedance state until it is told to put the data on the bus by a $\overline{RD}$ signal. Likewise, a selected device will not read data off the bus until it receives a $\overline{WR}$ signal.

1.6.2 Linear Selection

For systems with a small number of ports and memory locations, a simple addressing scheme called *linear selection* may be used. With linear selection, the higher order address bus bits are connected directly to the chip selects and the lower order bits are connected to the chip address lines, as shown in Example 1.3. It is important to realize that of the bits used for chip selects, only one can be active at a time. A programmer must be careful to avoid selecting two or more devices when writing the code to address a given port or memory location.

EXAMPLE 1.3 Linear Selection

Draw a block diagram of a byte-oriented memory system using three 1K by 8-bit chips. Address bits A15, A14, and A13 should be used for linear selection. Show an addressing error.

SOLUTION   In Fig. 1.14 addresses 2000h to 23FFh are located in memory chip MEM1, addresses 4000h to 43FFh are in MEM2, and addresses 8000h to 83FFh are in MEM3. An address such as C001h would cause an error because it refers to locations in two different chips simultaneously; both would be placed on the data bus, causing a collision.

In Fig. 1.14 note that addresses 8401h, 8801h, and 8C01h are all equivalent to 8001h because address bus bits A11 and A10 are not used. Linear addressing uses a partial address, as described in Sec. 1.6.3. Also note that linear selection can cause nonsequential addresses. In Fig. 1.14 the next location above 23FFh is at address 4000h instead of 2400h; again, the reason is that A11 and A10 are not used. The three 1K blocks of memory are not contiguous in memory space.

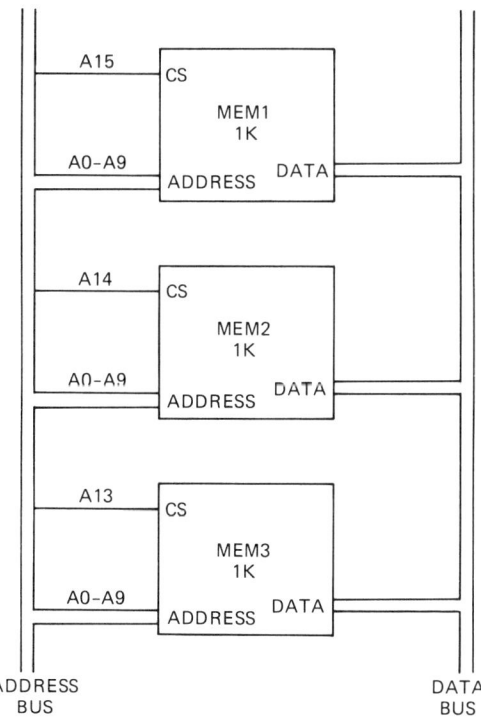

Figure 1.14 Linear selection.

Sec. 1.6   Address Decoding

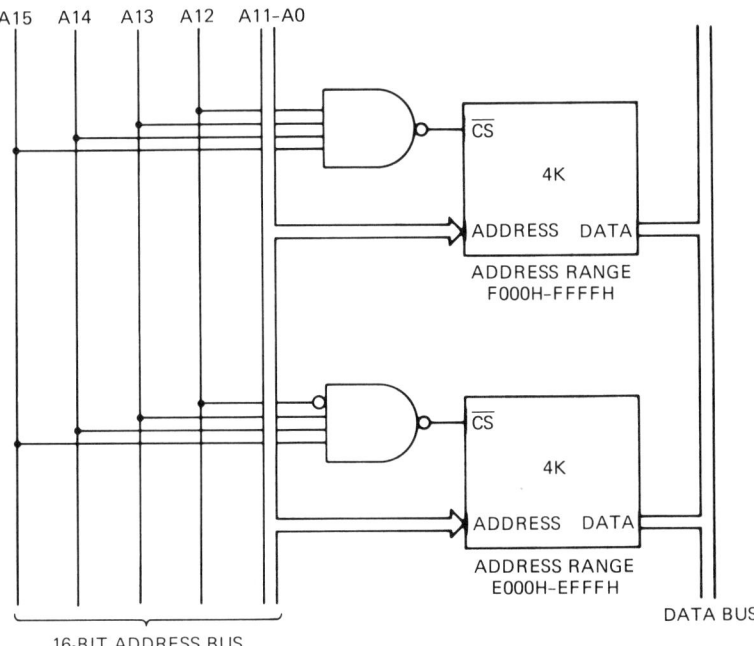

Figure 1.15 Full decoding.

1.6.3 Full and Partial Decoding

When a system has more memory than can be supported by linear selection, the higher order address bus bits must be decoded with gates to drive the appropriate chip select. If all the address bus bits are used, addresses are *fully decoded* and memory locations will have unique addresses. If some of the address bits are not used, then addresses are *partially decoded* and some locations will have multiple addresses (but a given address should not refer to multiple locations).

EXAMPLE 1.4 Full Decoding

Draw a block diagram of a byte-oriented memory using two 4K by 8-bit chips and full decoding. Addresses should be at the top end of memory space. What happens if an unimplemented location is addressed?

SOLUTION   See Fig. 1.15. If the CPU tries to read a nonexistent location in a fully decoded memory, nothing will drive the data bus when $\overline{RD}$ is asserted and the CPU will read either all 1s (high states) or a random number. If it tries to write to a nonexistent location, the data are simply lost.

1.7 SPEED

When comparing the speeds of two different microcomputer systems, it is tempting to look only at their CPU clock frequencies. For example, a 5-MHz processor should be "faster" than a 4-MHz CPU. But the speed we are really interested in is how fast the system does the application for which it was designed, not how fast the clock runs.

1.7.1 Throughput and Instructions

One aspect of speed is *throughput,* the number of instructions executed per second. The 4-MHz CPU may have a higher throughput than the 5-MHz if instructions in the 4-MHz unit require fewer machine cycles or if each machine cycle requires fewer clock pulses to complete.

Another factor is how well the CPU *instruction set* matches the program requirements. For example, if a program does a lot of numeric calculations (number crunching) but the CPU lacks specific MULTIPLY and DIVIDE instructions, then all the arithmetic will have to be done by repeated addition and subtraction. A CPU with the necessary instructions may do the calculations faster even though it has a slower clock. An alternative approach, known as a reduced instruction set computer (RISC), uses a small set of instructions that execute very rapidly. Conventional complex instruction set computers are sometimes referred to as CISCs.

1.7.2 Buses and Memory

The organization of the bus structure, at both the chip and package levels, has an effect on throughput. A 16-bit machine that uses an 8-bit bus will be slower than a 16-bit machine on a 16-bit bus, and may even be slower than an 8-bit machine on an 8-bit bus, depending on the architecture. The product of bus width and clock speed is sometimes called *bandwidth* and is a figure of merit when comparing speeds. Also, a fast CPU joined to a slow memory will have a lower throughput because it will be forced to execute wait states in any instruction that references memory.

1.7.3 Direct Memory Access (DMA)

As mentioned earlier, using the CPU to move data into or out of memory forms a bottleneck, as the CPU can move only one word at a time. DMA is a process by which a special controller chip takes over the bus and moves large blocks of data without involving the CPU. DMA is discussed further in Chapter 5.

1.7.4 Coprocessors, ASICs, DSPs

For systems used in applications requiring large amounts of specialized processing, throughput can often be greatly improved by using a special sort of peripheral called a *coprocessor*. As the name implies, a coprocessor chip is itself a microprocessor designed to do a specific job very fast. Whenever that job is called for in a program, the CPU gives it to the coprocessor, which does the job and gives the results back to the CPU. An example is the 8087 math coprocessor chip used with the 8086 CPU.

In some systems, speed can be increased by designing special hardware to perform specific functions instead of relying solely on software. Such hardware in the form of a custom-designed chip is called an *application specific integrated circuit* or ASIC. Typically, an OEM (original equipment manufacturer) will design the logic of an ASIC, but the actual chip fabrication will be done by a silicon foundry, an independent company that converts other companies' designs into integrated circuits. Often an ASIC is based on a core device, such as a microprocessor, which is made available (for a fee) by the semiconductor house that owns the design. In such cases, the microprocessor is said to be available as a ''cell'' for incorporation into ASIC designs.

In addition to increasing speed, ASICs can save money (and increase reliability) in production by reducing the chip count in a product. However, the initial cost of development may be too high for certain applications. To fill the space between general-purpose processors and ASICs, some chip manufacturers have come up with generic processors targeted at specific classes of application. Thus, a processor could be designed for use in automobiles and another with features for industrial control applications.

Digital signal processors (DSP chips) are another important class of devices designed to unburden the CPU. DSP chips use digital techniques to do functions, such as filtering, that were previously done by analog circuitry. However, DSPs can process signals (once they have been suitably digitized from their analog form) with an accuracy and sophistication often not possible with analog circuits.

1.7.5 Benchmarks

To really compare apples to apples in terms of speed, you want to compare how fast two different microprocessor systems will run a specific application. One way to do that is to write test programs called *benchmarks* that closely resemble the actual application. Each microcomputer will have the benchmark program written in its own instruction set, using its best features. The systems can then be run side by side and the times compared, giving a more valid measure of which is truly faster.

Standard benchmark programs have been developed for comparison purposes—for example, the Whetstone, which contains floating-point calculations, and the Dhrystone, which uses fixed point. However, the best benchmark is one that most closely matches your application. (A point of interest: Whetstone is the name of the benchmark developer, whereas Dhrystone appears to be a pun.)

1.8 SUMMARY

Microcomputers are systems consisting of four basic parts:

- The CPU, which does the actual processing
- The memory, which stores the program and the data
- The I/O, which allows access to the real world
- The bus structure, which connects the parts

The CPU was described as using the ALU as well as various registers and flags in order to fetch and execute the instructions. Regarding memory, we discussed RAM, ROM, and stack, as well as such terms as static, dynamic, and volatility. Under I/O we discussed ports and memory mapping. We also examined bus structures at both the chip and board levels, together with the use of wait states and the 3-state mode. The concept of speed in a microcomputer was discussed, together with the speed-related issues of interrupts and direct memory access.

CHAPTER REVIEW

Questions

1. Who was the first computer programmer?
2. Who designed the first stored program machine?
3. When and where was the first electronic computer built?
4. When was the first microprocessor released?
5. Name the four basic parts of a microcomputer.
6. What is the difference between a byte and a word?
7. What do the following initials stand for: CPU, ALU, PC, IR?
8. Why does a CPU require a clock?
9. Why does a CPU require a reset?
10. What is held in the program counter?
11. What is the purpose of an instruction queue?
12. What part of an instruction tells the CPU what to do?
13. Describe the importance of the accumulator.
14. What is a pointer register?
15. What does the ALU do?
16. What is the PSW?
17. How are flag bits used?
18. How does the carry flag differ from the overflow flag?
19. What is the sign bit?
20. How is the zero bit set?
21. Explain the difference between RAM and ROM.

22. What is firmware?
23. What does nonvolatile mean?
24. Explain the difference between static and dynamic RAM.
25. Give an example of an application where battery backup would be needed.
26. Explain the operation of a memory stack.
27. What does LIFO stand for?
28. What is stack overflow and what might cause it?
29. What is the difference between port-addressed I/O and memory-mapped I/O?
30. Describe a possible application for a serial port.
31. What is a peripheral device?
32. Name the three buses in the microprocessor bus structure.
33. Which bus is undirectional?
34. What is a multiplexed bus, and why is it used?
35. Explain what the 3-state mode is and why it is necessary.
36. Explain the use of wait states.
37. How does a board level bus differ from a chip level bus?
38. Explain one advantage of a board level bus.
39. Explain how a 4-MHz CPU can be faster than a 5-MHz CPU.
40. What is the advantage of using a coprocessor?
41. Explain the use of benchmark programs.
42. Why are interrupts necessary?

Problems

1. How many locations can a CPU address directly if it has a 24-line address bus?
2. Design a watchdog timer using a 555 that will wait 500 msec before generating a 200-msec active-low reset pulse.
3. Draw a block diagram of an 8K byte memory that uses 4K by 8-bit chips and linear selection with address bits A15 and A14. Are the two blocks of memory contiguous? Give an example of an address that would cause a collision.
4. Draw a block diagram of a byte-oriented memory using four 2K by 8-bit chips and full decoding. Addresses should start from 0000h and ascend. What happens if an unimplemented location is addressed?

chapter 2

The 8085 Microprocessor

OBJECTIVES

Upon completion of this chapter, you should be able to

1. Describe the function of each pin on the 8085
2. Draw the block diagram of an 8085
3. Read an 8085 timing diagram
4. Describe the 8085 programming model
5. Describe the basic functions of the 8085 instruction set
6. Draw the block diagram of an 8155

2.1 INTRODUCTION

In the late 1970s, Intel introduced the 8085 as an enhanced version of the then popular 8080 8-bit device. The 8085 took on many of the tasks that had required separate chips with the 8080 and could be used to implement a relatively minimal hardware system. More importantly, the 8085 was code compatible with the 8080 at the object code level. That meant that all the software developed for 8080-based systems could be used as is with new hardware designed around the 8085: The same ROM program could be used. It is a fact of life that the cost of developing software far exceeds the cost of developing hardware, so compatibility is an important consideration for both the manufacturers and users of microprocessors.

Although the 8085 is obsolescent when compared to newer devices such as the 8051, it is far from obsolete. Its simple structure makes it ideal as an introduction to microprocessors. Also, it is a good introduction to an important family of devices, as much of the philosophy of the 8085 can be seen in later Intel products, such as the 8086. In addition, the popular Z80 8-bit processor can be considered a hardware and software superset of the 8085. All but two 8085 machine code instructions (RIM and SIM) will execute on a Z80.

The 8085 was originally considered a general-purpose 8-bit microprocessor, but it is currently listed by Intel as an embedded controller. *Embedded controllers* are microprocessors used as the "brains" inside such noncomputer equipment as microwave ovens. "General purpose" now refers to 16-bit and 32-bit processors used in personal computers, development systems, and other such recognizably computer-type equipment. Several support chips have been developed (such as the 8155) that connect directly to the 8085 bus lines, allowing controller systems to be implemented with a low chip count.

2.2 HARDWARE OVERVIEW

2.2.1 Block Diagram

A functional block diagram of the 8085 is shown in Fig. 2.1. The CPU contains an 8-bit accumulator as well as six addressable 8-bit registers that can also be used as

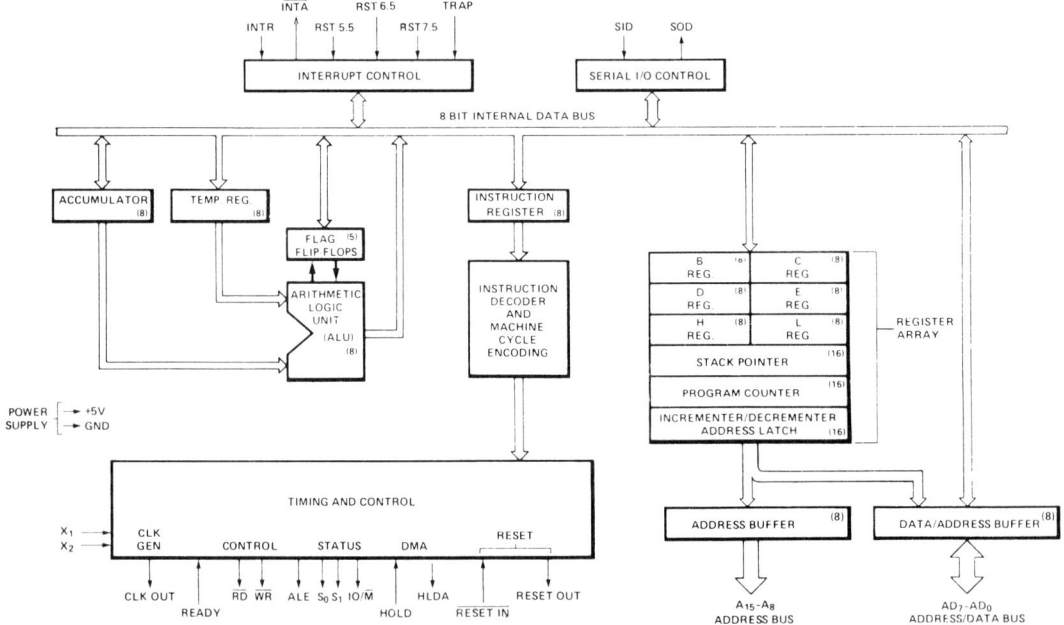

Figure 2.1 8085A CPU functional block diagram. (*Source:* Reprinted by permission of Intel Corporation, Copyright © Intel Corporation 1987.)

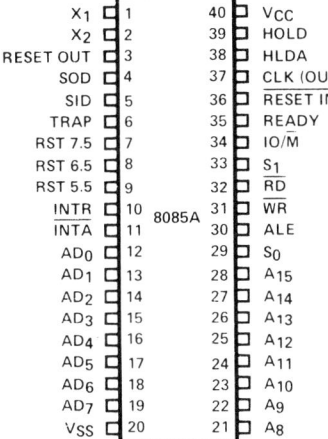

Figure 2.2 8085A pinout diagram. (*Source:* Reprinted by permission of Intel Corporation, Copyright © Intel Corporation 1987.)

three 16-bit registers. It has an 8-bit data width and a 16-bit memory address width and can address directly 64K bytes of memory. The 8085 also has an 8-bit port address width and can address 256 different ports (actually, 512 because an input port can have the same address as an output port but be physically distinct). It has a built-in clock oscillator and is available in a 6-MHz version. The device comes in a 40-pin DIP (dual inline pins) package, as shown in Fig. 2.2, and operates from a 5V supply. The function of each pin is described briefly in Table 2.1. Note the RST interrupt pins.

2.2.2 Bus Multiplexing and Loading

A significant aspect of the 8085 is its multiplexed bus. The 8-bit data bus shares the same pins as the lower half of the 16-bit address. To allow external devices to distinguish address bits from data bits, the 8085 outputs a pulse on its ALE (address latch enable) pin when address bits are on the bus lines.

Regarding bus loading and the need for buffering, the 8085 output pins will typically drive up to five LS TTL standard loads. The number of MOS devices that can be driven without buffering depends on the total capacitance being driven. An 8085 output pin can drive up to 150 pF without degradation and as much as 300 pF if the user is willing to derate the system timing and accept a lower reliability level.

2.2.3 Memory and I/O References

The memory space and the port space are separate in the 8085. Memory locations and I/O ports are similar in that the CPU can read from or write to them. Therefore, both memory locations and I/O ports have addresses. In the 8085, memory locations have 16-bit addresses and I/O ports have 8-bit addresses. The maximum number of memory locations is 2^{16}, or 65,536, and the maximum number of I/O ports is 2^8, or 256.

TABLE 2.1 8085A FUNCTIONAL PIN DEFINITION

Symbol	Function
A_8–A_{15} (Output, 3-state)	Address Bus: The most significant 8 bits of the memory address or the 8 bits of the I/O address, 3-stated during Hold and Halt modes and during RESET.
AD_{0-7} (Input/Output, 3-state)	Multiplexed Address/Data Bus: Lower 8 bits of the memory address or I/O address appear on the bus during the first clock cycle (T state) of a machine cycle. It then becomes the data bus during the second and third clock cycles.
ALE (Output)	Address Latch Enable: It occurs during the first clock state of a machine cycle and enables the address to get latched into the on-chip latch of peripherals. The falling edge of ALE is set to guarantee setup and hold times for the address information. The falling edge of ALE can also be used to strobe the status information. ALE is never 3-stated.
S_0, S_1, and $IO/\overline{M}$ (Output)	Machine cycle status:

$IO/\overline{M}$	S_1	S_0	Status
0	0	1	Memory write
0	1	0	Memory read
1	0	1	I/O write
1	1	0	I/O read
0	1	1	Op-code fetch
1	1	1	Interrupt Acknowledge
·	0	0	HALT
·	X	X	HOLD
·	X	X	RESET

· = 3-state (high impedance)
X = unspecified

$\overline{INTA}$ (Output)	INTERRUPT ACKNOWLEDGE: Is used instead of (and has the same timing as) $\overline{RD}$ during the instruction cycle after an INTR is accepted. It can be used to activate the 8259 Interrupt chip or some other interrupt port.
RST 5.5 RST 6.5 RST 7.5 (Inputs)	RESTART INTERRUPTS: These three inputs have the same timing as INTR except they cause an internal RESTART to be automatically inserted. The priority of these interrupts is ordered. These interrupts have a higher priority than INTR. In addition, they may be individually masked out using the SIM instruction.
TRAP (Input)	Trap interrupt is a nonmaskable RESTART interrupt. It is recognized at the same time as INTR or RST 5.5–7.5. It is unaffected by any mask or Interrupt Enable. It has the highest priority of any interrupt.
$\overline{\text{RESET IN}}$ (Input)	Sets the program counter to zero and resets the Interrupt Enable and HLDA flip-flops. The data and address buses and the control lines are 3-stated during RESET and because of the asynchronous nature of RESET, the processor's internal registers and flags may be altered by RESET with unpredictable results. $\overline{\text{RESET IN}}$ is a Schmitt-triggered input, allowing connection to an R-C network for power-on RESET delay. The CPU is held in the reset condition as long as $\overline{\text{RESET IN}}$ is applied.
V_{CC}	+5 volt supply.
V_{SS}	Ground reference.

TABLE 2.1 8085A FUNCTIONAL PIN DEFINITION (*continued*)

Symbol	Function
RESET OUT (Output)	Indicates CPU is being reset. Can be used as a system reset. The signal is synchronized to the processor clock and lasts an integral number of clock periods.
X_1, X_2 (Input)	X_1 and X_2 are connected to a crystal, LC, or RC network to drive the internal clock generator. X_1 can also be an external clock input from a logic gate. The input frequency is divided by 2 to give the processor's internal operating frequency.
CLK (Output)	Clock Output for use as a system clock. The period of CLK is twice the X_1, X_2 input period.
SID (Input)	Serial input data line. The data on this line are loaded into accumulator bit 7 whenever a RIM instruction is executed.
SOD (Output)	Serial output data line. The output SOD is set or reset as specified by the SIM instruction.
$\overline{RD}$ (Output, 3-state)	READ control: A low level on $\overline{RD}$ indicates the selected memory or I/O device is to be read and that the data bus is available for the data transfer, 3-stated during Hold and Halt modes, and during RESET.
$\overline{WR}$ (Output, 3-state)	WRITE control: A low level on $\overline{WR}$ indicates the data on the data bus is to be written into the selected memory or I/O location. Data are set up at the trailing edge of $\overline{WR}$, 3-stated during Hold and Halt modes, and during RESET.
READY (Input)	If READY is high during a read or write cycle, it indicates that the memory or peripheral is ready to send or receive data. If READY is low, the CPU will wait an integral number of clock cycles for READY to go high before completing the read or write cycle.
HOLD (Input)	HOLD indicates that another master is requesting the use of the address and data buses. The CPU, upon receiving the HOLD request, will relinquish the use of the bus as soon as the completion of the current bus transfer. Internal processing can continue. The processor can regain the bus only after the HOLD is removed. When the HOLD is acknowledged, the address, data, $\overline{RD}$, $\overline{WR}$, and IO/$\overline{M}$ lines are 3-stated.
HLDA (Output)	HOLD ACKNOWLEDGE: Indicates that the CPU has received the HOLD request and that it will relinquish the bus in the next clock cycle. HLDA goes low after the HOLD request is removed. The CPU takes the bus one-half clock cycle after HLDA goes low.
INTR (Input)	INTERRUPT REQUEST: Is used as a general-purpose interrupt. It is sampled only during the next to the last clock cycle of an instruction and during Hold and Halt states. If it is active, the program counter (PC) will be inhibited from incrementing and an $\overline{INTA}$ will be issued. During this cycle a RESTART or CALL instruction can be inserted to jump to the interrupt service routine. The INTR is enabled and disabled by software. It is disabled by Reset and immediately after an interrupt is accepted.

Source: Reprinted by permission of Intel Corporation, Copyright © Intel Corporation 1987.

When the CPU references (reads from or writes to) one of the devices connected to the bus, the device must know if the address on the bus is a memory address or a port address. To distinguish the two, the 8085 puts out the IO/$\overline{\text{M}}$ control signal along with the address. When IO/$\overline{\text{M}}$ is low, memory is being referenced; when it is high, an I/O port is referenced.

2.2.4 DMA and Other Features

The 8085 supports direct memory access (DMA). To request DMA, an external device asserts the HOLD line by pulling it high. The 8085 responds by suspending program execution, putting out a high level on the HLDA (hold acknowledgment) pin, and floating the address and data buses. HLDA will remain high as long as HOLD is held high. DMA in the 8085 is discussed in Chap. 5.

Other important features of the 8085 (also discussed in Chap. 5) include five prioritized interrupt input pins (four maskable and one nonmaskable), interrupt vectoring, a serial (i.e., 1-bit) input port, and a serial output port. The serial ports and interrupt mask have associated instructions SIM and RIM.

2.3 CPU TIMING

2.3.1 Reset

When power is first applied or after some event (such as a transient on the power supply) that disrupts the CPU, it is necessary to reset the 8085 to ensure proper operation. The reset-in pin is active-low, and must be held low for at least 10 msec. The 8085 supplies an active-high reset-out signal for the benefit of other chips (or peripheral devices) that must be reset in synchronization with the 8085. As a result of reset, certain actions will take place within the 8085, as summarized in Table 2.2.

Reset in can be accomplished manually with a momentary action normally open switch. Also, a circuit is commonly used to generate a reset when power is first turned on, such as the simple *power-on reset* circuit shown in Fig. 2.3. The circuit shown requires that the power supply (V_{CC}) rise from 0 to 5V rapidly, and may not work with a power supply having a *soft-start* feature, which goes from 0 to 5V slowly.

2.3.2 Clock Frequency

The 8085 contains an on-chip oscillator that requires a crystal to be connected between the pins designated X1 and X2. The clock frequency obtained will be half the crystal frequency, so a 3-MHz clock requires a 6-MHz crystal. The minimum clock frequency is 0.5 MHz, so the crystal must be at least 1 MHz.

Alternatively, the 8085 can be driven by an external clock signal. At frequencies below 6 MHz, the drive can be connected to X1, with X2 left floating. Above 6 MHz, both X1 and X2 must be driven by complementary waveshapes. Consult

TABLE 2.2 ACTIONS CAUSED BY RESET

Resets	Sets
Program counter	RST 5.5 mask
Instruction register	RST 6.5 mask
INTE FF	RST 7.5 mask
RST 7.5 FF	
Trap FF	
SOD FF	
Machine state FFs	
Machine cycle FFs	
Internally latched FFs for HOLD, INTR, and READY	

RESET IN does not explicitly change the contents of the 8085A registers (A, B, C, D, E, H, L) and the condition flags, but due to RESET IN occurring at a random time during instruction execution, the results are indeterminate. (Source: Reprinted by permission of Intel Corporation, Copyright © Intel Corporation 1987.)

the Intel documentation for details. Note that the 8085 provides a clock output on pin 37 (CLK) for use by other devices in the system that must be synchronized to the CPU.

2.3.3 Machine Cycles and T States

A *machine cycle* consists of a multiple number of T states, where the length of a T state is one period of the clock frequency. The CPU uses the machine cycles to fetch instructions and data from memory, to store data into memory, and to execute instructions. A typical machine cycle consists of three T states, except during an

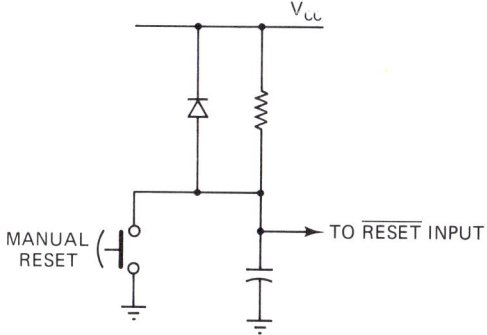

Figure 2.3 Power-on reset circuit. (*Source:* Reprinted by permission of Intel Corporation, Copyright © Intel Corporation 1987.)

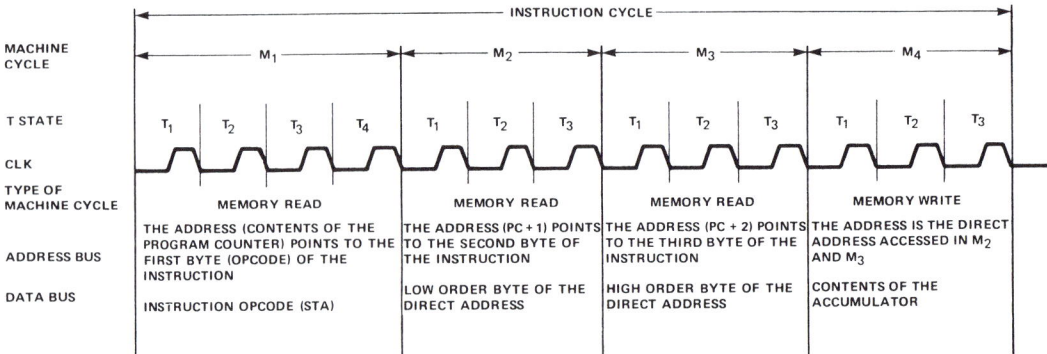

Figure 2.4 CPU timing for store accumulator direct (STA) instruction. (*Source:* Reprinted by permission of Intel Corporation, Copyright © Intel Corporation 1987.)

op-code fetch, which requires either four or six, depending on the type of instruction being fetched.

The timing for a store accumulator direct instruction is shown in simplified form in Fig. 2.4. The format of the instruction is STA abcdH, where STA is the mnemonic for store accumulator and abcdH represents a 2-byte address. STA abcdH will cause the CPU to store a copy of the contents of the accumulator into memory address abcdH. The instruction takes four machine cycles to execute.

During the M1 cycle, the first byte of the instruction (the op-code) is fetched: 32H, the machine code for STA. During the M2 cycle, the second byte of the instruction is fetched: cd, the low-order half of the 16-bit address abcdH. During the M3 cycle, the third byte of the instruction is fetched: ab, the high half of the address. (Because the CPU fetches from progressively higher memory locations, it is worth noting that 2-byte numbers are stored by the 8085 with the high-order byte in the higher address.) At this point, the CPU has read the entire instruction and is able to effect execution, so during M4 it writes the contents of the accumulator to memory location abcdH. Following M4 will be the M1 cycle of the next instruction.

The number of T states required for each instruction is given in the detailed instruction set in this chapter. Thus, the assembly language programmer can analyze and control the exact execution time of a program, something that is difficult to do in a high-level language.

The number of T states in a machine cycle can be increased by forcing the CPU to execute wait states (discussed in Sec. 1.5.4). The READY pin on the 8085 controls the generation of wait states. The timing for a memory (or I/O) read with and without wait states is shown in Fig. 2.5.

2.3.4 Clock Speed and Memory Access Time

It is possible to estimate the required speed of the memory device by examining the timing diagram in Fig. 2.6. The full address will be available to the memory device at the falling edge of ALE during T1 of the first machine cycle. The $\overline{RD}$ control signal goes active (low) during T2, and the CPU will read the data before $\overline{RD}$ goes

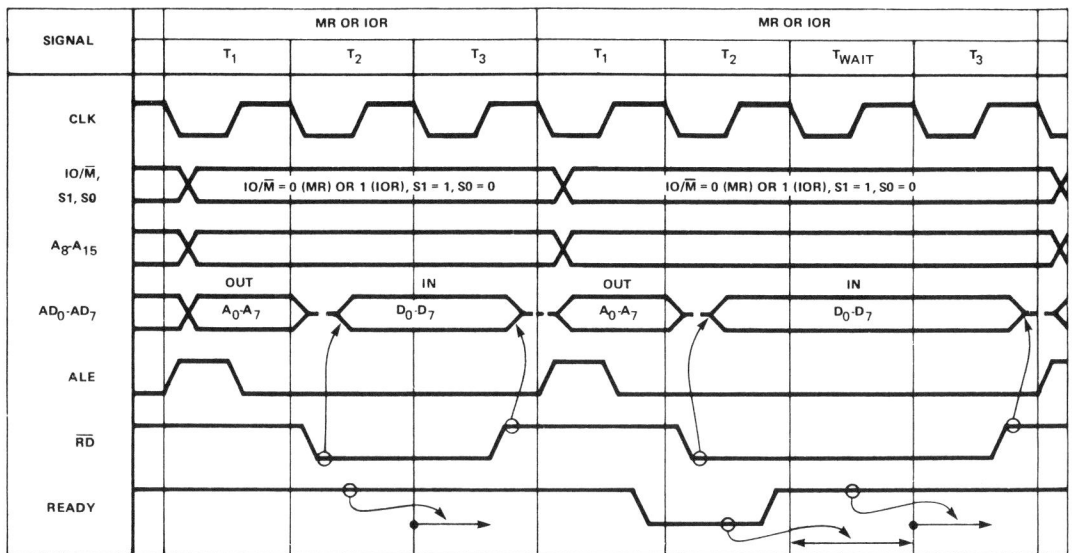

Figure 2.5 Memory read (or I/O read) machine cycles (with and without wait states). (*Source:* Reprinted by permission of Intel Corporation, Copyright © Intel Corporation 1987.)

high in T3. If we assume that the memory chip is accessed as soon as $\overline{RD}$ goes low, then the access time of the memory must be less than the length of the $\overline{RD}$ pulse, or a little more than one T state long.

Remember that one T state is equal to one clock period, which is the inverse of the clock frequency ($T = 1/f$). For example, an 8085 running at 3 MHz has a T state length of 333 nanoseconds (nsec), so it would require a memory device with

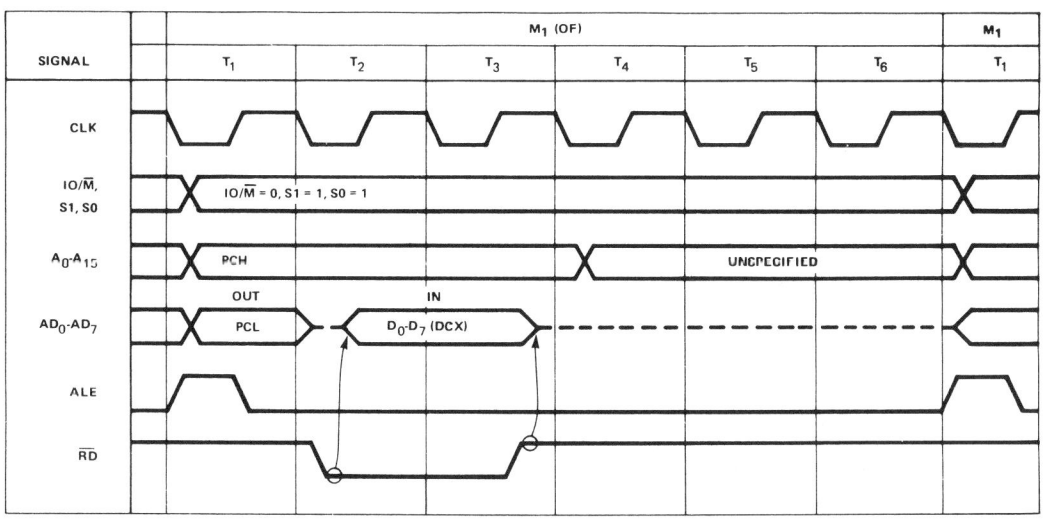

Figure 2.6 Op-code fetch machine cycle (of DCX instruction). (*Source:* Intel Corporation, Copyright © Intel Corporation 1987.)

Sec. 2.3   CPU Timing

MACHINE CYCLE		STATUS			CONTROL		
		IO/$\overline{M}$	S1	S0	$\overline{RD}$	$\overline{WR}$	$\overline{INTA}$
OPCODE FETCH	(OF)	0	1	1	0	1	1
MEMORY READ	(MR)	0	1	0	0	1	1
MEMORY WRITE	(MW)	0	0	1	1	0	1
I/O READ	(IOR)	1	1	0	0	1	1
I/O WRITE	(IOW)	1	0	1	1	0	1
INTR ACKNOWLEDGE	(INA)	1	1	1	1	1	0
BUS IDLE	(BI): DAD	0	1	0	1	1	1
	INA(RST/TRAP)	1	1	1	1	1	1
	HALT	TS	0	0	TS	TS	1

0 = Logic "0"   1 = Logic "1"   TS = High Impedance   X = Unspecified

(a)

Machine State	Status & Buses				Control		
	S1,S0	IO/$\overline{M}$	A_8-A_{15}	AD_0-AD_7	$\overline{RD},\overline{WR}$	$\overline{INTA}$	ALE
T_1	X	X	X	X	1	1	1†
T_2	X	X	X	X	X	X	0
T_{WAIT}	X	X	X	X	X	X	0
T_3	X	X	X	X	X	X	0
T_4	1	0*	X	TS	1	1	0
T_5	1	0*	X	TS	1	1	0
T_6	1	0*	X	TS	1	1	0
T_{RESET}	X	TS	TS	TS	TS	1	0
T_{HALT}	0	TS	TS	TS	TS	1	0
T_{HOLD}	X	TS	TS	TS	TS	1	0

0 = Logic "0"   1 = Logic "1"   TS = High Impedance   X = Unspecified

†ALE not generated during 2nd and 3rd machine cycles of DAD instruction.

*IO/$\overline{M}$ = 1 during T_4-T_6 states of RST and INA cycles.

(b)

Figure 2.7 (a) 8085A machine cycle chart. (b) 8085A machine state chart. (*Source:* Reprinted by permission of Intel Corporation, Copyright © Intel Corporation 1987.)

a maximum access time specification of about 400 nsec. The actual worst case speed given in the Intel data book for ALE-to-valid-data-during-read is 460 nsec, so our estimate is conservative. Consult the Intel documentation for a full description of timing.

2.3.5 Control Signals

There are seven different types of machine cycles, which can be distinguished by looking at the control signals (see Fig. 2.7a). The Intel literature refers to status and control signals, where the *status* signals are IO/$\overline{M}$, S1, and S0 and the *control* signals are $\overline{RD}$, $\overline{WR}$, and $\overline{INTA}$ (the last three are active-low). However, the term *status* commonly refers to registers in peripheral devices used for handshaking (see 8155 below). To avoid confusion, the signals discussed in section 2.6.3 are referred to as control signals.

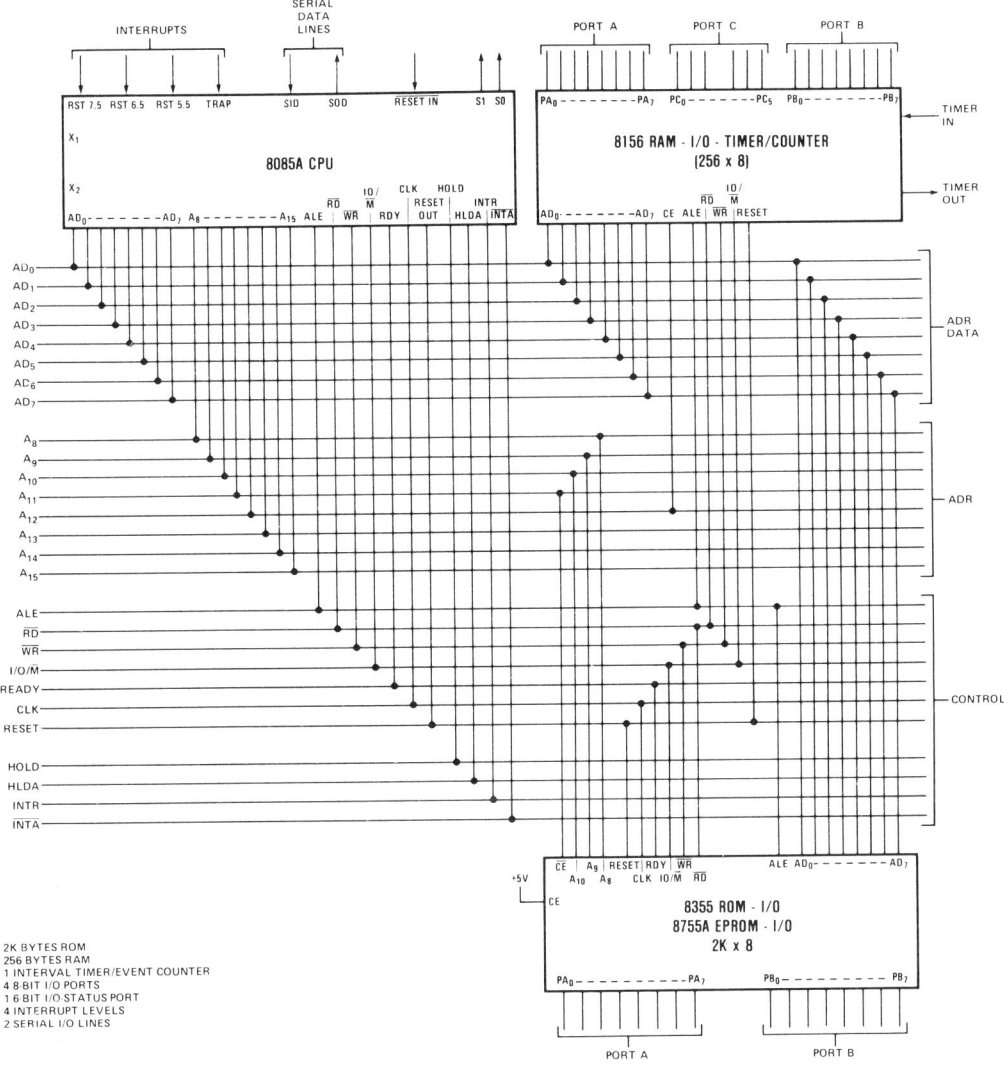

Figure 2.8 Special support chips for internal demultiplexing. (*Source:* Intel Corporation, Copyright © Intel Corporation 1987.)

The states of the control lines for each type of machine cycle are given in Fig. 2.7b. It is sometimes necessary during the design of a system to trouble-shoot hardware problems by looking at bus signals during specific parts of the instruction cycle. Using equipment such as a logic analyzer, it is possible to decode the control signals to trigger the test equipment at the critical parts of the cycle and capture the desired data.

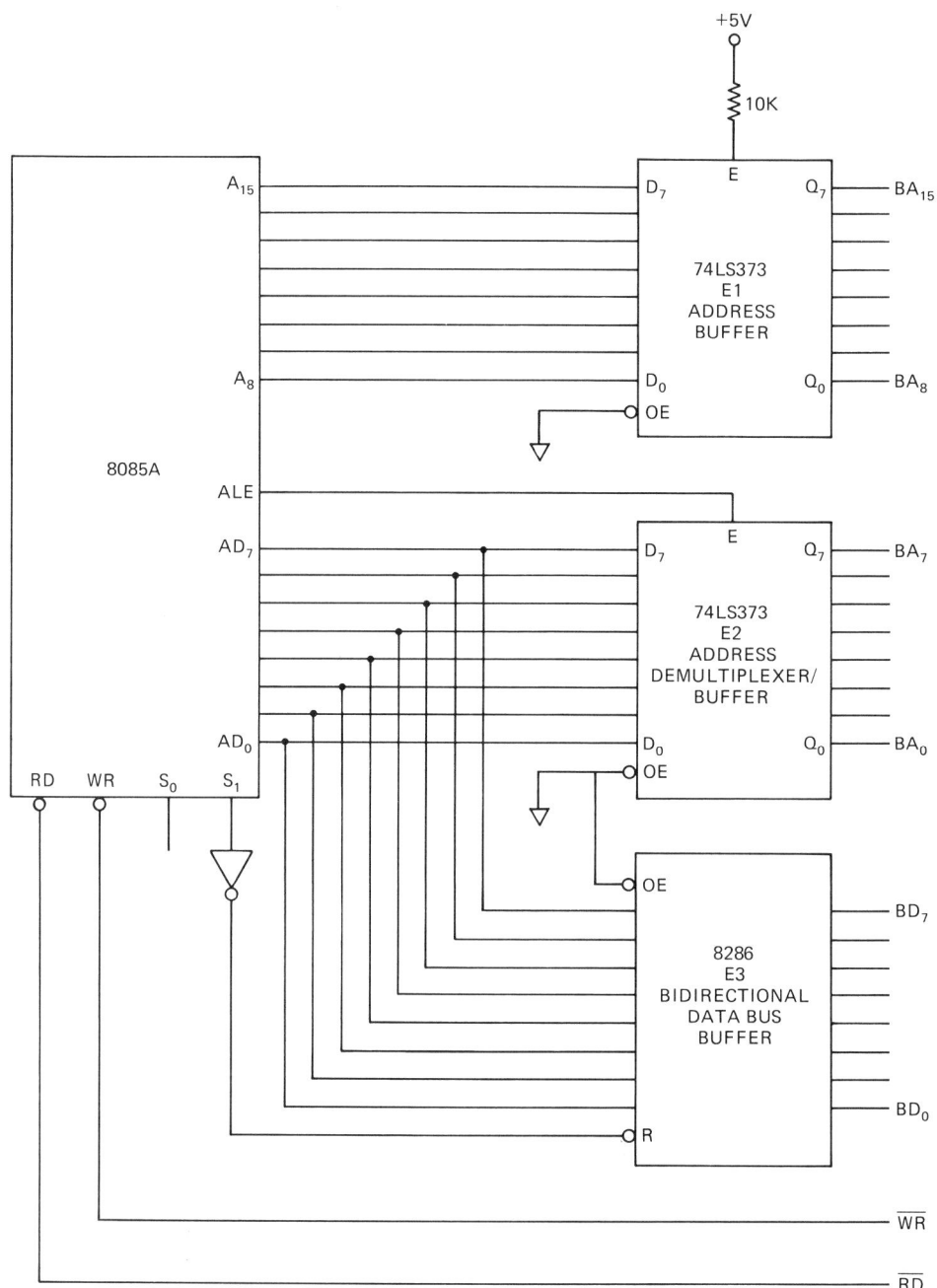

Figure 2.9 74LS373 octal latch for demultiplexing.

2.3.6 Address Demultiplexing

Refer to Fig. 2.6 and note that the 8085 puts the lower 8 bits of the 16-bit address on the AD0–AD7 lines during the T1 state, during which time the falling edge of ALE occurs. Data appear on the same lines at a later time in the machine cycle while ALE is low. Special support chips, such as those shown in Fig. 2.8, have been designed to interface directly to the 8085 and do the required demultiplexing internally. To interface general-purpose devices to the 8085, the address can be demultiplexed using a standard TTL device such as the 74LS373 octal latch, as shown in Fig. 2.9. As long as LE (latch enable) is high, the latch is *transparent*, meaning whatever appears on the input pins goes directly to the output pins. When LE goes low, the output pins of the octal latch will be "frozen" (latched) at their last state. Because ALE drives LE and AD0–AD7 drive the inputs, the output of the latch is always the lower 8 bits of the current address.

2.4 8085 PROGRAMMING MODEL

In this section we look at the flags and registers, which are the resources of the 8085 used by the assembly language programmer.

2.4.1 The Working Registers

As shown in Fig. 2.1, the 8085 contains an 8-bit accumulator (A in instructions), an 8-bit flag register, and six general-purpose 8-bit registers designated B, C, D, E, H, and L. Data can be moved between registers as well as between memory and registers. If a program is small enough to keep all its data in the registers, it will execute very quickly.

The registers can be paired as BC, DE, and HL to form 16-bit registers. Instructions that use register pairs BC and DE designate them with the first letter of the pair, such as B for BC and D for DE. The accumulator and flag register together are known as the *processor* (or program) *status word* (PSW). Instructions referring to the PSW use PSW as the designation. When used in instructions, the stack pointer is designated SP.

Although the 8085 will execute a few 16-bit operations, it is basically an 8-bit machine. The HL pair is used as a pointer register by a number of instructions that use indirect addressing, and in such instructions, the designation M is used to indicate that the 16-bit content of HL is the address of the byte being referenced (pointed to). Instructions that refer to register pair HL but do not use it as a pointer designate it as H.

The accumulator (A) is a special 8-bit register. It is used by the ALU to hold the results of arithmetic and logic operations and to exchange data with I/O ports. Also, it is the implied register for many instructions. In fact, most of the CPU action involves the accumulator.

2.4.2 The Flags

The flag register contains five flag bits, as shown in Fig. 2.10. The remaining three flag bits of the register are not defined and should not be used by the programmer. Various conditional instructions will test the flag values to control execution. The flags are as follows:

S   **Sign Flag:** The MSB of the accumulator (bit 7) is copied to the sign flag after an arithmetic or logic operation. If the contents of the accumulator are being used as a signed number, then a sign bit of 0 indicates a positive number and a 1 indicates a negative number.

Z   **Zero Flag:** Z is set to a 1 if an ALU operation on an 8-bit register results in the contents of the register going to zero. Note that moving zero into a register will not set Z because it doesn't involve the ALU.

AC   **Auxiliary Carry:** An 8-bit register can be used to hold two 4-bit BCD numbers. After an ALU operation, a carry may occur out of the lower BCD number into the higher (i.e., from bit 3 to bit 4). Such a carry will set AC to a 1. The DAA instruction (decimal adjust accumulator) will test AC, as it needs to restore the BCD numbers back to the correct format if such a carry occurs. (Logical ANDing will also set AC to 1.) The programmer is not usually required to test AC explicitly.

P   **Parity Flag:** After an ALU operation, an 8-bit register may contain an odd or even number of 1s. If the number of 1s is even, the P flag is set to a 1. If the number of 1s is odd, P is reset to 0. Note the distinction between an odd number and an odd number of 1s. The binary number 11100000 is even (224 in decimal) but contains an odd number of 1s (three).

CY   **Carry Flag:** The carry flag is set or reset according to the result of ALU operations on 8-bit registers, including rotates, as well as addition with 16-bit registers. The carry can be considered as the ninth bit of the accumulator. For example, the addition of two 8-bit numbers may produce a result too big to fit into the accumulator. The resulting carry out of the accumulator MSB will set the carry flag. The carry will also be set during subtraction if a "borrow" occurs (i.e., a bigger number is subtracted from a smaller number).

A flag is said to be *set* or *true* if its value is 1; it is *reset* or *clear* or *false* if its value is 0 (0 and 1 are the only two values a flag can have). The flags most often used in programming are CY and Z; the others are used only for certain specific functions.

D_7	D_6	D_5	D_4	D_3	D_2	D_1	D_0
S	Z		AC		P		CY

Figure 2.10 Five flag bits of the flag register. (*Source:* Reprinted by permission of Intel Corporation, Copyright © Intel Corporation 1987.)

2.4.3 The 16-Bit Registers

In addition to the register pairs discussed in Sec. 2.4.1, the 8085 contains the 16-bit program counter (PC) and stack pointer (SP) registers. They are accessible to the programmer but have specific uses.

The *program counter* always contains the address of the next instruction to be executed. After reset, PC will contain 0000. As instructions are fetched, the CPU automatically updates the program counter. Usually, the programmer does not have to deal explicitly with the contents of PC. The *stack pointer* contains the address of the top of the stack (as described in Sec. 1.3.4). The programmer must initialize SP to the beginning of the stack area in RAM before trying to use the stack. (Remember: Subroutines and interrupts use the stack.)

2.4.4 The Stack

As discussed in Chap. 1, the stack is an area set aside in RAM for temporary storage. The 8085 stack grows *downward* through memory, so SP is usually initialized to an address near the *high* end of RAM space. The 8085 stores 16-bit numbers on the stack, so registers are saved in pairs. For example, the instruction PUSH B stores the contents of both the B and C registers. The 8085 and similar processors *predecrement* SP. That is, SP is decremented by 1 *before* the first byte (B) is stored and then decremented again *before* the second byte (C) is stored. SP is left pointing to the second byte. Some other processors use *postdecrementing* (decrement after the move). Note that the content of the high half (B) will be stored in the stack at a higher memory address than the low half (C). The instruction POP B will remove 2 bytes from the stack and place them into registers B and C, with the content of the higher address placed in B. SP will be incremented by 2. As mentioned, the combination of the accumulator and the flag register is called the program status word (PSW), and the corresponding stack instructions are PUSH PSW and POP PSW. As usual, it is the responsibility of the programmer to ensure that the stack does not overflow, underflow, or otherwise get mangled.

2.4.5 The Interrupt Mask

The 8085 chip has interrupt pins labeled RST 5.5, RST 6.5, and RST 7.5, as well as one labeled TRAP (see Table 2.1). To control these interrupts, the 8085 contains an interrupt mask register that can be modified using the SIM (set interrupt mask) instruction. The 8085 interrupt system is described in detail in Chapter 5.

2.5 8085 INSTRUCTION SET OVERVIEW

Chapter 3 gives a detailed discussion of how to use the 8085 instruction set. Here we take a quick look at the instructions.

The 8085 instruction set can be divided into four groups: the data transfer group, the arithmetic and logical group, the branch control group, and the stack, I/O, and machine control group. Within a group, instructions will be 1, 2, or 3 bytes long, with the first byte always an op-code. The addressing modes used are direct, register, register indirect, and immediate, as described in Chap. 3. A detailed description of the instructions is given in Appendix B.

2.5.1 The Data Transfer Group

The *data transfer group* includes register to register move instructions, immediate 8-bit register move instructions, immediate 16-bit load instructions, and an assortment of 8- and 16-bit loads and stores using direct and indirect addressing. The instructions in the data transfer group are the following:

MOV r1,r2 [Move Register: where r1 and r2 are 8-bit registers] moves a *copy* of the content of r2 into r1 (r2 remains the same). 4 T states.

MOV r,M [Move from Memory: where r is an 8-bit register] moves a *copy* of the content of a memory location into register r. The content of register pair HL is used as the address of the location (i.e., HL is used as a pointer). Both HL and the memory location are unchanged. 7 T states.

MOV M,r [Move to Memory: where r is an 8-bit register] similar to MOV r,M except moves from the register to the memory location. Contents of the register and HL are unchanged. 7 T states.

MVI r,n8 [Move Immediate: where r is an 8-bit register and n8 is an 8-bit number] loads the number into the register. 7 T states.

MVI M,n8 [Move to Memory Immediate: where n8 is an 8-bit number] similar to MVI r,n8 except a memory location is used instead of a register (as explained for MOV M,r). 10 T states.

LXI rp,n16 [Load Extended Immediate: where rp is a register pair or the stack pointer (B, D, H, SP) and n16 is a 16-bit number] loads a number into a 16-bit register. 10 T states.

LDA adr [Load Accumulator Direct: where adr is a 16-bit address] loads the accumulator with a *copy* of the content of the memory location specified by the address. The contents of the memory location are not changed. 13 T states.

STA adr [Store Accumulator Direct: where adr is a 16-bit address] stores a *copy* of the content of the accumulator in the memory location specified by the address. The accumulator is not changed. 13 T states.

LHLD adr [Load HL Direct: where adr is a 16-bit address] loads the HL register pair with a *copy* of the contents of two successive memory locations starting at the address. L will be loaded from the byte at *address* and H will be loaded from the byte at *address+1*. The contents of memory are unchanged. 16 T states.

SHLD adr [Store HL Direct: where adr is a 16-bit address] stores a *copy* of the contents of the HL register pair into two successive memory locations starting at the address. L will be stored in *address* and H will be stored in *address + 1*. The contents of H and L are not changed. 16 T states.

LDAX rp [Load Accumulator Indirect: where rp is B or D, designating the BC or DE register pair] loads the accumulator with a *copy* of the content of a memory location. The address of the location is held in the register pair specified in the instruction. Both the content of memory and the contents of the register pair are unchanged (similar to MOV A,M). 7 T states.

STAX rp [Store Accumulator Indirect: where rp is B or D, designating the BC or DE register pair] stores a *copy* of the content of the accumulator in a memory location. The address of the location is held in the register pair specified in the instruction. Both the content of the accumulator and the contents of the register pair are unchanged (similar to MOV M,A). 7 T states.

XCHG [Exchange Contents of HL and DE] a quick way to swap pointers. No flags are affected. 4 T states.

Important note: These instructions have no effect on the flags.

2.5.2 The Arithmetic and Logic Group

The *arithmetic and logic group* contains instructions to add, subtract, increment, decrement, and rotate, as well as instructions to AND, OR, exclusive-OR, and compare. This group also contains some special instructions affecting the accumulator and the carry bit directly. Although most of the instructions in this group use 8-bit operands, addition can be performed with 16-bit operands. If a register is not explicitly given in an operand, it is generally the accumulator. It is important to remember that, with a few noted exceptions, instructions in this group can affect all the flags.

The instructions in the arithmetic and logic group are the following:

ADD r [Add Register: where r is an 8-bit register] adds the content of register r to the accumulator. Content of register r is unchanged (except for ADD A). All flags are affected. 4 T states.

ADD M [Add Memory] adds the content of a memory location to the accumulator. The 16-bit number in the HL register pair is used as the address of the location (i.e., HL is used as a pointer). All flags are affected. 7 T states.

ADC r [Add Register with Carry: where r is an 8-bit register] similar to ADD r except also adds the value of the carry bit (CY) to the accumulator. (For the purpose of this instruction, CY can be thought of as a hex number whose value can be either 00H or 01H.) The contents of register r are unchanged (except for ADC A). All flags are affected. 4 T states.

ADC M [Add Memory with Carry] similar to ADD M except also adds carry bit (as explained for ADC r). All flags are affected. 7 T states.

ADI n8 [Add Immediate: where n8 is an 8-bit number] adds the 8-bit number to the accumulator. All flags are affected. 7 T states.

ACI n8 [Add with Carry Immediate: where n8 is an 8-bit number] same as ADI n8 except adds carry bit (as explained for ADC r). All flags are affected. 7 T states.

DAD rp [Double Add: where rp is B, D, H, or SP] adds the contents of the specified register pair (or the stack pointer) to the contents of the HL register pair. Contents of the specified register pair are unchanged (except for DAD H). Only CY flag is affected. 10 T states.

SUB r [Subtract Register: where r is an 8-bit register] subtracts the content of register r from the accumulator. Content of r is unchanged (except for SUB A). All flags are affected. 4 T states.

SUB M [Subtract Memory] similar to SUB r except HL is used as a pointer (as described for ADD M). All flags affected. 7 T states.

SBB r [Subtract Register with Borrow: where r is an 8-bit register] similar to SUB r except also subtracts the value of the carry bit (CY) from the accumulator. (For the purpose of this instruction, CY can be thought of as a hex number whose value can be either 00H or 01H.) The content of register r is unchanged (except for SBB A). All flags are affected. 4 T states.

SBB M [Subtract Memory with Borrow] similar to SBB r except uses HL as a pointer (as described for ADD M). All flags affected. 7 T states.

SUI n8 [Subtract Immediate: where n8 is an 8-bit number] subtracts the 8-bit number from the accumulator. All flags are affected. 7 T states.

SBI n8 [Subtract with Borrow Immediate: where n8 is an 8-bit number] similar to SUI n8 except also subtracts carry bit (as explained for SBB r). All flags are affected. 7 T states.

INR r [Increment Register: where r is an 8-bit register] adds 1 to the 8-bit number in register r. All flags except CY are affected. 4 T states.

INR M [Increment Memory] adds 1 to the content of a memory location. The contents of the HL register pair are used as the address. All flags except CY are affected. 10 T states.

INX rp [Increment Extended: where rp is B, D, H, or SP] adds 1 to the 16-bit number in register pair rp. No flags are affected. 6 T states.

DCR r [Decrement Register: where r is an 8-bit register] subtracts 1 from the 8-bit number in register r. All flags except CY are affected. 4 T states.

DCR M [Decrement Memory] similar to DCR r except subtracts 1 from content of the memory location pointed to by HL. All flags except CY are affected. 10 T states.

DCX rp [Decrement Extended: where rp is B, D, H, or SP] subtracts 1 from the 16-bit number in register pair rp. No flags are affected. 6 T states.

RLC [Rotate Left] rotates contents of accumulator to the left by one bit position, copies MSB to CY. No other flags affected. 4 T states.

RRC [Rotate Right] rotates contents of accumulator to the right by one bit position, copies MSB to CY. No other flags affected. 4 T states.

RAL [Rotate Left through Carry] similar to RLC except CY is included to form a 9-bit rotation. No other flags affected. 4 T states.

RAR [Rotate Right through Carry] similar to RRC except CY is included to form a 9-bit rotation. No other flags affected. 4 T states.

ANA r [AND Register: where r is an 8-bit register] the content of register r is logically ANDed bit by bit with the content of the accumulator. The result is in the accumulator. All flags are affected; CY is cleared to 0 and AC is set to 1. (There seems to be no particular need to set AC; it's just an artifact of the way the instruction was implemented.) 4 T states.

ANA M [AND Memory] similar to ANA r except a memory location is used (as explained for ADD M). All flags are affected; CY is cleared to 0 and AC is set to 1. 7 T states.

ANI n8 [AND Immediate: where n8 is an 8-bit number] similar to ANA r except an 8-bit number is used instead of the contents of a register. All flags are affected; CY is cleared to 0 and AC is set to 1. 7 T states.

ORA r [OR Register: where r is an 8-bit register] the content of register r is logically ORed bit by bit with the content of the accumulator. The result is in the accumulator. All flags are affected; CY and AC are cleared to 0. 4 T states.

ORA M [OR Memory] similar to ORA r except a memory location is used (as explained for ADD M). All flags are affected; CY and AC are cleared to 0. 7 T states.

ORI n8 [OR Immediate: where n8 is an 8-bit number] similar to ORA r except a number is used (as explained for ANI n8). All flags are affected; CY and AC are cleared to 0. 7 T states.

XRA r [Exclusive-OR Register: where r is an 8-bit register] the content of register r is logically exclusive-ORed bit by bit with the content of the accumulator. The result is in the accumulator. All flags are affected; CY and AC are cleared to 0. (Note: XOR A will clear the accumulator.) 4 T states.

XRA M [Exclusive-OR Memory] the content of a memory location is logically exclusive-ORed bit by bit with the content of the accumulator. The result is in the accumulator. HL is used as a pointer (as explained for ADD M). All flags are affected; CY and AC are cleared to 0. 7 T states.

XRI n8 [Exclusive-OR Immediate: where n8 is an 8-bit number] the content of register r is logically exclusive-ORed bit by bit with an 8-bit number. The result is in the accumulator. All flags are affected; CY and AC are cleared to 0. 7 T states.

CMP r [Compare Register: where r is an 8-bit register] the content of register r is subtracted from the accumulator. However, the accumulator remains unchanged; only the flags are affected. 4 T states.

CMP M [Compare Memory] similar to CMP r except a memory location is used instead of a register. HL is used as a pointer (section 2.5). All flags are affected. 7 T states.

CPI n8 [Compare Immediate: where n8 is an 8-bit number] similar to CMP r except an 8-bit number is used instead of the content of a register. All flags are affected. 7 T states.

DAA [Decimal Adjust Accumulator] restores the accumulator to a BCD format following BCD addition (alas, it doesn't work for subtraction). All flags are affected. 4 T states.

CMA [Complement the Accumulator] the number in the accumulator is replaced with its one's complement. No flags are affected. 4 T states.

STC [Set Carry] CY is set to a 1. No other flags are affected. 4 T states.

CMC [Complement Carry] CY is changed to the opposite state. No other flags are affected. 4 T states.

2.5.3 The Branch Control Group

The *branch control group* contains the jump instructions together with the restarts, calls, and returns. The instructions in this group are used to change the flow of the program by changing the contents of the PC register. Normally, the CPU fetches instructions from sequential memory locations. By changing the contents of the PC, the instructions in this group cause the CPU to fetch instructions from other parts of memory, which makes possible the use of iteration (loops), subroutines, interrupts, and so on.

Jumps, calls, and returns can be unconditional or conditional. *Unconditional* instructions are executed as soon as they are encountered: JMP 2000H will cause execution to resume from location 2000H as soon as it is executed. The effect of a *conditional* instruction, however, depends on the state of a flag. Thus JZ 2000H will cause a jump to location 2000H only if the zero flag is true (Z = 1). If the zero flag is false (Z = 0), then the jump will not occur, and the instruction following JZ 2000H will be fetched.

Remember that the flags are affected by the results of other instructions in the program. The ability to change the flow of the program based on the results of the program is what gives a computer its power. Without that ability, a computer would be just an adding machine. With it, a computer can make decisions, enabling it to do anything that can be described as a sequence of if-then-else statements, that is, an *algorithm*.

Jumps can also be classified as absolute or relative. In an *absolute* jump, the complete address must be specified in the jump instruction. In a *relative* jump, an *offset*, usually 1 byte, is specified in the jump instruction. The offset is *added* to the current content of the program counter to cause a jump, so the exact address of the target of a relative jump depends on the address of the jump instruction itself. The 8085 only supports absolute jumps; other processors, though, such as the Z80, support both relative and absolute.

The instructions in this group do not affect the flags. The conditional jumps take ten T states if the condition is met (jump occurs) but only seven T states if the condition is not met (no jump). In the following, adr is a 16-bit address.

Jumps

JMP adr	[Jump] unconditional jump to address adr. 10 T states.
JNZ adr	[Jump Not Zero] jump if Z = 0 to address adr.
JZ adr	[Jump Zero] jump if Z = 1 to address adr.
JNC adr	[Jump Not Carry] jump if C = 0 to address adr.
JC adr	[Jump Carry] jump if C = 1 to address adr.
JPO adr	[Jump Parity Odd] jump if P = 0 to address adr.
JPE adr	[Jump Parity Even] jump if P = 1 to address adr.
JP adr	[Jump Plus] jump if S = 0 to address adr.
JM adr	[Jump Minus] jump if S = 1 to address adr.
PCHL	[Swap Contents of PC and HL Register Pairs] an unconditional jump using the contents of HL instead of a fixed address. 6 T states.

Calls and Restarts

Remember: When a call is executed, the current content of the program counter is automatically pushed onto the stack. Conditional calls require 18 T states if the condition is met (call occurs) but only 9 T states if the condition is not met (no call).

CALL adr	[Call] unconditional call to address adr. 18 T states.
CNZ adr	[Call Not Zero] call if Z = 0 to address adr.
CZ adr	[Call Not Zero] call if Z = 1 to address adr.
CNC adr	[Call Not Carry] call if C = 0 to address adr.
CC adr	[Call Carry] call if C = 1 to address adr.
CPO adr	[Call Parity Odd] call if P = 0 to address adr.
CPE adr	[Call Parity Even] call if P = 1 to address adr.
CP adr	[Call Plus] call if S = 0 to address adr.
CM adr	[Call Minus] call if S = 1 to address adr.
RST n	[Restart: where n is 0, 1, 2, 3, 4, 5, 6, or 7]. A call to one of the predefined addresses (see Chapter 5). 12 T states.

Returns

Remember: When a return is executed, an address is popped off the stack and into the program counter register PC. Conditional returns require 12 T states if the condition is met (return occurs) but only 6 T states if the condition is not met (no return).

RET	[Return] unconditional return. 10 T states.
RNZ	[Return Not Zero] return if Z = 0.

RZ   [Return Zero] return if Z = 1.
RNC   [Return Not Carry] return if C = 0.
RC   [Return Carry] return if C = 1.
RPO   [Return Parity Odd] return if P = 0.
RPE   [Return Parity Even] return if P = 1.
RP   [Return Plus] return if S = 0.
RM   [Return Minus] return if S = 1.

2.5.4 The Stack, I/O, and Machine Control Group

As the name states, the instructions in the *stack, I/O, and machine control group* include stack, input and output, interrupt enable/disable, and other instructions to control the state of the CPU during program execution. The instructions in this group are the following:

PUSH rp   [Push: where rp is B, D, H, or PSW] pushes a *copy* of the contents of the register pair designated onto the stack. The registers are not changed. Note that the stack pointer cannot be pushed: rp cannot be SP. No flags are affected. 12 T states.

POP rp   [Pop: where rp is B, D, H, or PSW] pops 2 bytes off the top of the stack into the register pair designated. As with PUSH, rp cannot be SP. No flags are affected. 10 T states.

SPHL   [Move HL to SP] *a copy* of the contents of the HL register pair is moved into SP. Allows the stack pointer to be initialized from HL. Compare to LXI SP,abcdH (LXI rp,n16). No flags are affected. 6 T states.

XTHL   [Exchange HL with the 2 bytes on top of the stack] no flags are affected. A quick way to swap pointers. 16 T states.

IN pn   [In: where pn is an 8-bit port address] inputs a byte from the addressed port into the accumulator. No flags are affected. 10 T states.

OUT pn   [Out: where pn is an 8-bit port address] sends a *copy* of the content of the accumulator out to the addressed port. No flags are affected. 10 T states.

DI   [Disable Interrupts] no flags are affected. 4 T states.

EI   [Enable Interrupts] takes effect after the subsequent instruction (see explanation in Chap. 5). No flags are affected. 4 T states.

NOP   [No Operation] just kills time. No flags are affected. 4 T states.

HLT   [Halt] causes the CPU to suspend its fetch-execute cycle until either a reset or an interrupt occurs. No flags are affected. 5 T states.

RIM   [Read Interrupt Mask] see Chap. 5. No flags are affected. 4 T states.

SIM   [Set Interrupt Mask] see Chap. 5. No flags are affected. 4 T states.

A complete description of the instruction set, including hex op-codes, is in Appendix B.

2.5.5 Some Examples

8085 programming is examined in detail in Chap. 4. Here we look at a few simple examples of using the instruction set.

EXAMPLE 2.1 Direct and Indirect Moves

Write 8085 instructions to get a byte from location 2000h and copy it to location 2001h.

SOLUTION

1. Using direct addressing:

```
            LDA   2000H
            STA   2001H
```

2. Using indirect addressing:

```
            LXI   H, 2000H
            MOV   A, M
            INX   H
            MOV   M, A
```

Solution 1 is self-explanatory. In solution 2, we first load the HL register pair with the address 2000h. We then use that address to get the memory byte into the accumulator. The address is incremented by 1 to 2001h and used to move the byte in the accumulator back to memory.

EXAMPLE 2.2 Immediate and Register Arithmetic

Get the number 5 into the accumulator, subtract 3, and store the result in register B.

SOLUTION

1. Using immediate subtraction:

```
            MVI   A, 5
            SUI   3
            MOV   B, A
```

2. Using register subtraction:

```
            MVI   A, 5
            MVI   B, 3
            SUB   B
            MOV   B, A
```

In both cases, note that the result of the subtraction is left in the accumulator and a copy moved to B.

EXAMPLE 2.3 A Simple Loop

Write 8085 instructions to increment the accumulator and send the result out to I/O port address 4 in a continuous loop.

SOLUTION

```
LOOP:   INR   A
        OUT   04
        JMP   LOOP
```

Note the use of the label LOOP. More is said about labels in subsequent chapters.

2.6 THE 8155/8156 SUPPORT CHIP

The 8155 is a support chip specifically designed to work with the 8085 and interfaces directly to the 8085 buses. It contains 256 bytes of static RAM, two 8-bit and one 6-bit programmable ports, and a 14-bit counter/timer. The 8156 is the same device but with an active-high chip enable; the 8155 chip enable is active-low. In the rest of this section we refer to the 8155, but the information applies to the 8156 as well. In Chap. 3 we write some example programs using the 8155.

The 8155 comes in a 40-pin DIP package, as shown in Fig. 2.11. The block diagram is shown in Fig. 2.12. Notice that the 8155 has an input pin for the ALE output of the 8085. The 8155 will automatically demultiplex address and data. The 8155 also has an input pin for the 8085 IO/$\overline{\text{M}}$ output signal, so the 8155 will automatically distinguish I/O references from memory references.

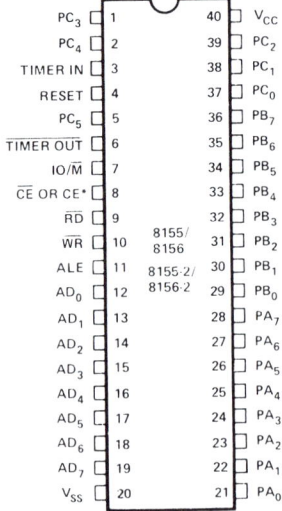

Figure 2.11 Pin configuration. (*Source:* Reprinted by permission of Intel Corporation, Copyright © Intel Corporation 1987.)

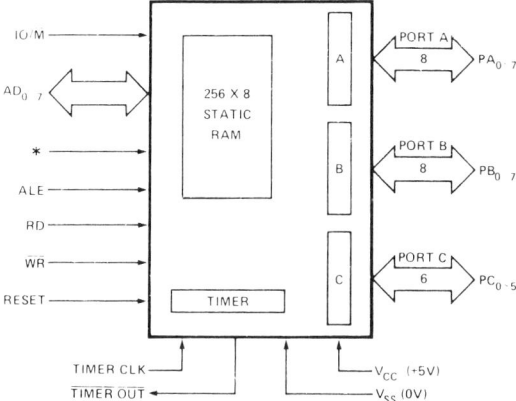

*: 8155/8155-2 = $\overline{CE}$, 8156/8156-2 = CE

Figure 2.12 Block diagram. (*Source:* Reprinted by permission of Intel Corporation, Copyright © Intel Corporation 1987.)

2.6.1 The 8155 Registers

As shown in Fig. 2.13, the 8155 contains seven registers at six different I/O port addresses. Two registers, command and status, share a single address and are referred to as the *command/status register* (CSR). When writing to CSR, the data go to the command register; when reading from CSR, the data come from the status register.

In Fig. 2.14, only the last 3 bits of the 8-bit port addresses are shown numer-

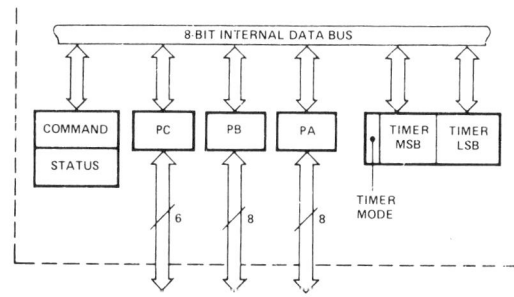

Figure 2.13 8155/8156 internal registers. (*Source:* Reprinted by permission of Intel Corporation, Copyright © Intel Corporation 1987.)

I/O ADDRESS†								SELECTION
A7	A6	A5	A4	A3	A2	A1	A0	
X	X	X	X	X	0	0	0	Interval Command/Status Register
X	X	X	X	X	0	0	1	General Purpose I/O Port A
X	X	X	X	X	0	1	0	General Purpose I/O Port B
X	X	X	X	X	0	1	1	Port C — General Purpose I/O or Control
X	X	X	X	X	1	0	0	Low-Order 8 bits of Timer Count
X	X	X	X	X	1	0	1	High 6 bits of Timer Count and 2 bits of Timer Mode

X: Don't Care.
†: I/O Address must be qualified by CE = 1 (8156) or $\overline{CE}$ = 0 (8155) and IO/$\overline{M}$ = 1 in order to select the appropriate register.

Figure 2.14 I/O port and time addressing scheme. (*Source:* Reprinted by permission of Intel Corporation, Copyright © Intel Corporation 1987.)

ically, whereas the other 5 bits are shown as Xs. Even though AD0–AD7 are connected to the 8155, it only decodes the lower three address lines for port references. The upper five address lines must be decoded with external logic and used to drive the 8155 chip select. Thus, the 8-bit addresses used in programs to reference the 8155 are system dependent.

2.6.2 The Command/Status Register

Before trying to use the resources of the 8155, the programmer must set them up by writing a special byte to the 8155 command register, which will retain the byte until it is overwritten with a new value (or until a reset). As shown in Fig. 2.15, each bit of the command register has its own function:

> Bits 0 and 1 control the direction of ports A and B.
> Bits 2 and 3 control the direction and mode of port C.
> Bits 4 and 5 are interrupt enables (allow optional use of port C bits as interrupt pins).
> Bits 6 and 7 control the counter/timer.

Table 2.3 details the function of each pin of port C in the four alternative port C modes: ALT 1, ALT 2, ALT 3, and ALT 4.

Each bit of the status register also has a specific meaning, as shown in Fig. 2.16. The two major uses of status are when ports A and/or B are being used in handshake mode and in checking the state of the timer/counter. Such uses are examined in later chapters.

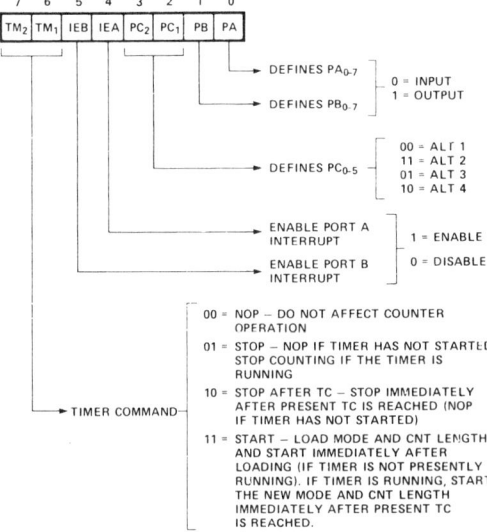

Figure 2.15 Command register bit assignment. (*Source:* Reprinted by permission of Intel Corporation, Copyright © Intel Corporation 1987.)

TABLE 2.3 PORT CONTROL ASSIGNMENTS

Pin	ALT 1	ALT 2	ALT 3	ALT 4
PC0	Input port	Output port	A INTR (port A interrupt)	A INTR (port A interrupt)
PC1	Input port	Output port	A BF (port A buffer full)	A BF (port A buffer full)
PC2	Input port	Output port	A $\overline{\text{STB}}$ (port A strobe)	A $\overline{\text{STB}}$ (port A strobe)
PC3	Input port	Output port	Output port	B INTR (port B interrupt)
PC4	Input port	Output port	Output port	B BF (port B buffer full)
PC5	Input port	Output port	Output port	B $\overline{\text{STB}}$ (port B strobe)

Source: Reprinted by permission of Intel Corporation, Copyright © Intel Corporation 1987.

2.6.3 Input, Output, Handshaking

After a reset, ports A, B, and C are automatically inputs. Writing to an input port has no effect. Using the CSR, ports A and B can be independently configured as either input or output but not input/output. They cannot be used as bidirectional ports. Two of the port C modes allow it to be used as either an input (ALT 1) or an output (ALT 2) 6-bit port. ALT 3 splits port C into 3 output bits and 3 handshake bits for port A, and ALT 4 splits port C into handshake bits for both ports A and B.

Handshaking is done using bits called *strobe* (STB) and *buffer full* (BF). A third bit is labeled *interrupt* (INTR). Note that INTR does not automatically generate a CPU interrupt. The port C pin designated INTR can, if desired, be connected to one of the 8085 interrupt pins or it can be left unconnected. The state of INTR can be read from the corresponding interrupt request bit in the status register.

The use of STB and BF depends on whether data are being written (output) or read (input). Assume the CPU wants to send data through port A of the 8155 to an external device using handshaking. Assume also that the CSR has been properly configured. The sequence of events (see Fig. 2.17) is as follows:

1. The CPU does an OUT to port A; INTR goes low.
2. The data appear on the port A lines and stabilize.

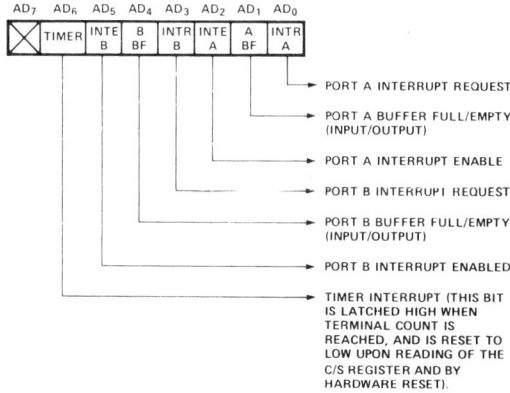

Figure 2.16 Status register bit assignment. (*Source:* Reprinted by permission of Intel Corporation, Copyright © Intel Corporation 1987.)

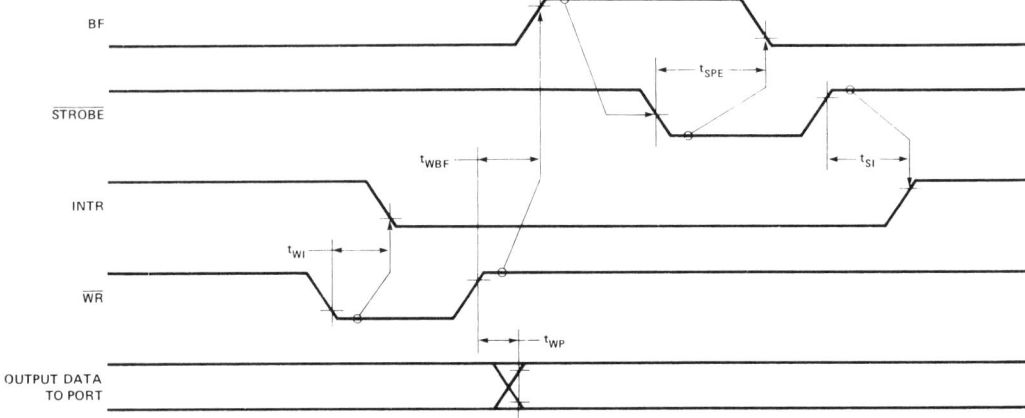

Figure 2.17 Strobed output mode. (*Source:* Reprinted by permission of Intel Corporation, Copyright © Intel Corporation 1987.)

3. BF goes high, telling the external device that data are available.
4. The external device reads the data.
5. The external device pulses STB low to tell the 8155 that the data were read.
6. BF goes low, indicating port A is free; INTR goes high.

Now let's assume that the external device wants to send data to the CPU through port B using handshaking. The sequence of events (see Fig. 2.18) is as follows:

1. The external device puts data on the port B lines.
2. The external device indicates data are available by pulsing STB low.

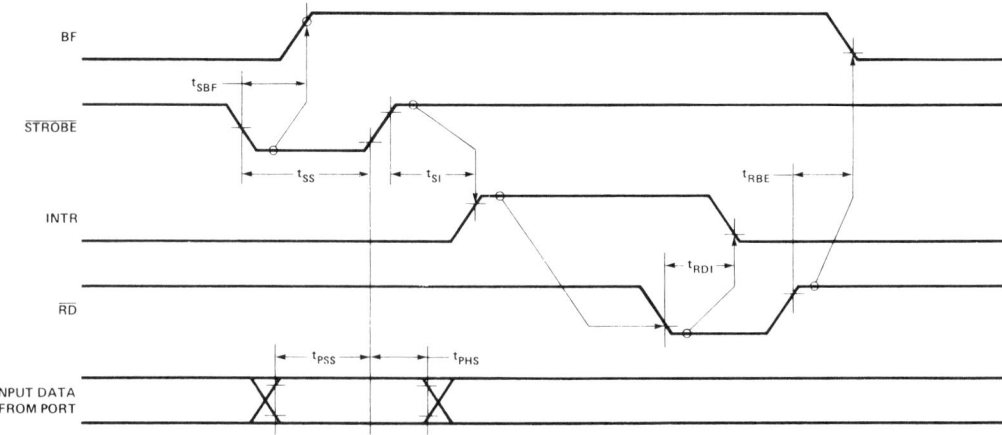

Figure 2.18 Strobed input mode. (*Source:* Reprinted by permission of Intel Corporation, Copyright © Intel Corporation 1987.)

3. BF goes high, telling the external device that the 8155 has the data; INTR goes high.
4. The CPU eventually reads the data from port B; INTR goes low.
5. BF goes low, telling the external device that the CPU has the data.

For both input and output, the state of BF can be read by the CPU from the status register of CSR. The I/O program can periodically check BF or can be interrupted by INTR (assuming it is connected to an 8085 interrupt pin) and use an interrupt service routine (see Chapter 5).

2.6.4 The Counter/Timer

The counter/timer is a 14-bit down counter with input and output pins labeled TIMER IN and TIMER OUT on the 8155 chip. Although called a counter/timer, it was not designed to be used as an *event counter* (e.g., to count how many widgets pass an electric eye). Rather, the 8155 timer was designed to take an input frequency and divide it down to a lower output frequency in one of four output waveforms:

1. Continuous square wave
2. Continuous negative-going pulse train
3. Single wide negative-going pulse (single square wave)
4. Single narrow negative-going pulse

Figure 2.19 shows the waveforms, together with their corresponding *mode bits*. The programmer must set up the timer by writing 2 bytes to the low and high halves of the 16-bit *timer length register*. As shown in Fig. 2.20, the two MSBs of the high byte are the mode bits.

Operation of the timer is controlled by bits 6 and 7 of the CSR command register. The preset count and the mode can be changed while the timer is running (changed "on the fly"), but a START command must be sent to CSR to force the timer to use the new values.

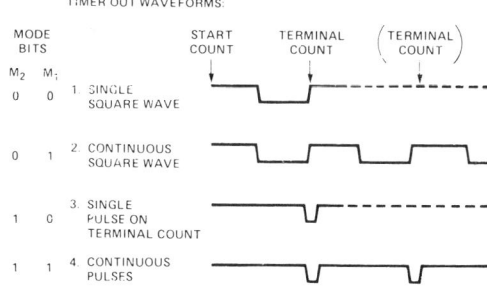

Figure 2.19 Timer modes. (*Source:* Reprinted by permission of Intel Corporation, Copyright © Intel Corporation 1987.)

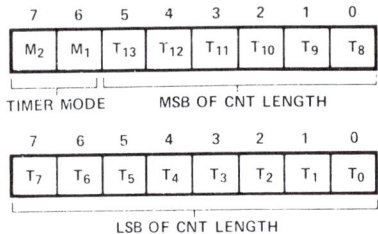

Figure 2.20 Timer format. There are four modes to choose from: M_2 and M_1 define the time mode, as shown in Fig. 2.19. (*Source:* Reprinted by permission of Intel Corporation, Copyright © Intel Corporation 1987.)

2.6.5 RAM

The 8155 contains 256 bytes of read/write memory (RAM). During a memory reference, the 8155 will decode the lower 8 bits of the 16-bit address on the AD0–AD7 lines. The upper 8 address bits (A8–A15) must be decoded with external logic and used to activate the 8155 chip-enable (CE) pin. Depending on the system, linear selection, partial decoding, or full decoding may be used.

2.6.6 Configuring the 8155

Configuring the 8155 means sending a control byte to the CSR. See Examples 2.4 and 2.5.

> **EXAMPLE 2.4 Configuring the 8155**
>
> Write 8085 instructions to configure the 8155 with all ports as output. Stop the timer and disable interrupts. Assume the CSR is at address 80h.
>
> SOLUTION We must load the appropriate 8-bit control word into the accumulator and output it to the CSR. Looking at Fig. 2.15, we see that, to stop the timer, the two most significant bits must be 01. The next 2 bits control the interrupts and must be 00 to disable them. The next 2 bits control port C. Looking at Table 2.3, we see that port C must be in ALT 2 to be all output. Referring back to Fig. 2.15, bits 3 and 2 must be 11 for ALT 2. The last 2 bits control the direction of ports A and B, and must be 11 for both to be output ports. Putting it all together, the control word is 01001111 in binary or 4F in hex.
>
> The required 8085 instructions are
>
> ```
> MVI   A, 4FH
> OUT   80H
> ```

> **EXAMPLE 2.5 Another 8155 Configuration**
>
> Write the 8085 instructions to configure the 8155 so that port A is input, port B is output, and port C is input. Interrupts are disabled. Also, we wish to divide down a 1000-Hz signal to get a 1-Hz square wave. Assume 8155 port addresses start at 80h (see Fig. 2.14).

SOLUTION   As in the previous example, we will use the information in Fig. 2.15 and Table 2.3 to put together the 8-bit control word. Since we will be using the counter/timer, the first 2 bits will be 11. The next 2 bits will be 00 to disable the interrupts. ALT 1 is used for port C input, so the next 2 bits are 00. To direct ports A and B, the last 2 bits are 10. The control word is 11000010 in binary or C2 in hex.

However, before we output the control word to the CSR, we must initialize the counter by outputting the 16-bit count length to the 8155 as 2 bytes, as shown in Fig. 2.20. To obtain 1 Hz from 1000 Hz, we must divide by 1000; therefore, the count length must be equal to 1000. Decimal 1000 is 3E8 in hex or 1111101000 in binary. Breaking the binary into 8-bit halves, we get 00000011 for the high half and 11101000 for the low half. Fig. 2.20 shows that bits 7 and 6 of the high byte select the timer mode. Referring to Fig. 2.19, we see that 01 is required for a square-wave output, so the high byte should be 01000011 or 43h. The low byte is E8h. The required instructions are

```
MVI   A,43H
OUT   85h
MVI   A,0E8H
OUT   84H
MVI   A,0C2H
OUT   80H
```

2.7 SUMMARY

In this chapter we have looked at the hardware of the 8085 8-bit microprocessor, including such features as a multiplexed address/data bus, serial ports, and vectored interrupt pins. We also looked at the programming model containing the A, B, C, D, E, H, and L registers, as well as the use of register pairs HL, BC, and DE and the program status word (PSW). This chapter also included a hardware description of the 8155 support chip, which contains three programmable ports, 256 bytes of RAM, and a 14-bit timer.

CHAPTER REVIEW

Questions

1. When was the 8085 introduced for commercial use?
2. What is an embedded controller?
3. Draw the block diagram for the 8085.
4. Describe the 8085 multiplexed bus.
5. How many LS TTL loads can an 8085 output pin typically drive?
6. What limits the number of MOS loads an output pin can drive?

7. What is the largest memory size the 8085 can address directly?
8. How many I/O ports can the 8085 address directly?
9. How does the 8085 distinguish memory from I/O references?
10. Which 8085 pin is used to initiate DMA?
11. What is a serial port?
12. What happens to the 8085 during reset?
13. Modify the circuit of Fig. 2.3 to allow the use of a soft-start power supply (if you have digital circuit experience).
14. A 4-MHz crystal would give what clock frequency?
15. What crystal frequency is required for a 1-μsec T state?
16. What is fetched during the M1 T state?
17. If a 2-byte number is stored in memory, which half is stored at the higher address?
18. When choosing memory devices, what determines the maximum acceptable access time?
19. By looking at the bus lines, how could you distinguish an op-code fetch from a memory read of data?
20. Describe the function of ALE.
21. Name all the registers and register pairs in the 8085.
22. What is the PSW?
23. To what does "M" refer?
24. Name and describe the 8085 flags.
25. Which flags are most commonly used by a programmer?
26. What happens to the content of SP after a PUSH?
27. Where in RAM is the stack normally located?
28. Compare and contrast MOV r1,r2 with MOV r,M.
29. Compare and contrast LDAX B with MOV A,M.
30. Compare and contrast LXI H,abcd with XTHL.
31. Compare and contrast LXI SP,abcd with SPHL.
32. Compare and contrast ADD B with ADC B.
33. Compare and contrast SUB D with SBI 05.
34. Which group of instructions never affects the flags?
35. Which arithmetic instruction(s) affect no flags?
36. Compare conditional and unconditional jumps.
37. Draw the block diagram for the 8155.
38. Describe the 8155 CSR.
39. Describe I/O using handshaking.
40. Describe the 8155 counter/timer.

Problems

1. Write the 8085 instructions to add without carry the content of the A and B registers and save the result in the C register.
2. Repeat Prob. 1 but add with carry.

3. Write the instructions to get address 1230h into the HL register pair and then use it as a memory pointer to load 2 consecutive bytes from memory into registers D and E.
4. Write the instructions needed to configure an 8155 to make all ports input, enable the interrupt pin for port A only, and stop the timer. Assume port addresses start at 10h.
5. Assuming the configuration of Prob. 4, write the instruction to input a byte from port B.
6. Modify the instructions of Prob. 4 so that the 8155 will generate a series of continuous pulses at a rate of 1000 Hz, assuming an input of 500,000 Hz.

chapter 3

Introduction to Assembly Languages

OBJECTIVES

Upon completion of this chapter, you should be able to

1. Understand and use the special terminology of assembly languages
2. Explain what an assembler is and why assembly language is useful
3. Describe the structure of an assembly language statement and the use of directives
4. Describe the various addressing modes
5. Explain a development system

3.1 INTRODUCTION

A computer requires a step-by-step list of instructions called a program that tells it exactly what to do. However, the only thing a computer can actually read and process is a binary number. A microprocessor (or any computer) is designed to recognize a group of binary numbers as its *native* or *primitive instruction set*. Such an instruction set makes up the *machine language* for a processor. Although pure numbers are fine for machines, people are more comfortable with words and names. As we will discuss, an assembly language is a machine language with words replacing the numbers.

3.1.1 Mnemonics

In the very early days, programs were actually entered into a computer as binary numbers using toggle switches on the machine's front panel, or the computer might read the numbers as holes punched into cards or paper tapes. Either way, such programming could not be called user-friendly. To write programs that could be read and understood by people, programmers used short words or letter combinations to represent the operation codes *(op-codes)*. For example, the word ADD might be written to stand for the binary number 11000110, which would be the machine code for the addition instruction. Such short words are called *mnemonics,* from a Greek word meaning "an aid to memory."

3.1.2 The Assembler: A Translator

At first, programmers had to translate the mnemonics back into binary numbers by hand and then enter them into the computer. It wasn't long, however, before computers were enabled to do the tedious job of translation. Using a device with an alphanumeric keyboard, such as a teletype, a person could enter programs written with mnemonics directly into the computer. Pressing a key on a teletype machine produces a binary code representing the character on the key. Thus, a mnemonic such as ADD would be represented by three binary numbers. A program written with words is said to be in *symbolic* form.

After the program was entered in symbolic form, a special translator program was run that would recognize the binary numbers making up the mnemonics and produce the binary op-codes. The translator program is called an *assembler,* and programs written in the mnemonic form are called *assembly language* (or *assembler language*) programs.

3.1.3 Assembly: A Low-Level Language

An assembly language has a one-to-one correspondence to the underlying machine language. The main difference is that the assembly language allows the numeric op-codes to be replaced by mnemonics and the numeric operands to be replaced by symbolic names. The manufacturer of the microprocessor also defines (and copyrights) the mnemonics for its products. Each microprocessor has its own unique assembly language, although some (e.g., the 8085 and the Z80) may, to a certain extent, be compatible at the machine code level. Assembly languages are classified as *low-level* languages, in contrast to *high-level* languages such as BASIC or PASCAL.

3.1.4 Why Use Assembly Language?

Programs written in a high-level language can be run on computers built with different microprocessors, whereas programs written in assembly language can be executed only on computers built with the microprocessor for which the assembler was designed. Also, high-level languages contain instructions that allow a programmer to do, in a few lines of code, operations that would take many lines of code in assembly language. So why use assembly? There are several reasons:

1. Assembly language gives the user full access to the power of the processor. Because high-level languages must run on any machine, they do not allow the programmer access to processor-specific features. A high-level language defines a *virtual machine*, which hides features of the real processor from the programmer.
2. Assembly language allows direct control of hardware features such as I/O ports, CPU registers, and memory. High-level languages usually do not allow such control. Much of what is called *systems programming* is done in assembly.
3. Assembly language allows a skilled programmer to write "tight code"—that is, a program written with the fewest machine code instructions and able to execute in the least amount of time. Programs written in a high-level language must still be translated down to machine code by a translator program called a *compiler*. However, even the best compilers are not as efficient as a skilled human programmer (at least not yet). For applications requiring very compact code, such as those using a single-chip controller with on-board ROM, assembly is often preferred.
4. Assembly language allows a programmer to fine-tune the timing of a program. Interrupt-driven real-time applications often require precise control over the execution times of critical parts of the program, which is often difficult to achieve in a high-level language.

3.1.5 Editors and Source Files

Before writing a line of code, a good programmer will have already designed the program using flowcharts, pseudo-code, or some other technique. (Program design is discussed in Chapter 12.) After designing the program, the programmer writes the actual assembly language code ("codes it up") using a program called an *editor*. An editor allows the programmer to enter a program from a keyboard while monitoring it on a CRT display; he or she can then make any additions, deletions, or corrections and save the program on a hard or floppy disk. The stored program can be retrieved by the editor for further changes.

Editors in common use with microprocessors use the ASCII code to represent the letters, numbers, figures, and punctuation marks on the keyboard. A *programmer's editor* uses the ASCII code exclusively. Some word processor types of editors mix special non-ASCII codes with the standard ASCII characters. Such word processor editors should not be used to write programs because microprocessor assemblers will only accept ASCII character codes. The file that the editor stores on disk is called a *source file*.

3.1.6 Object Files, List Files, Loaders, Linkers

The job of the assembler is to read the source file and create a new file containing a translation of the source file. The assembler does not alter the source file. The new file, often called an *object file*, created by the assembler contains the numeric codes required by the microprocessor. In addition, the assembler will generate a *list file*, which can be printed out. A list file contains each line of source code together with the machine code translation.

If the object file can be loaded into the microprocessor's memory and run "as is," then it is called an *absolute file* or a *binary file*. Often it is the case that the numeric addresses of memory references in a program depend on where in memory the program will be placed for execution. However, the numeric value of the beginning address may not be known at the time the program is written but will be determined when the program is actually loaded into memory. In such a case the object file must be created in a form called a *relocatable file*, and a program called a *loader* will adjust all program addresses to their absolute numeric value as it loads the program into memory. After a relocatable object file has had its address references adjusted and is ready for execution, it is called a *load module*.

Large programs must be broken down into smaller parts (or modules) so that a single programmer can work on manageable pieces of code or so that a team of programmers can work simultaneously. The result is a collection of relocatable object files that must be combined into one final program. The combining is done by a program called a *linker*, which makes sure all references to memory locations contain the correct addresses. Sometimes the linker and the loader are combined into one program. Also, collections of useful routines that can be used in many different programs are brought together into *libraries*, from which they can be linked into new programs as the need arises.

Because large programs often consist of many modules, changes made to one module may require other modules to be changed as well. A *configuration control* program can be used to keep track of all such changes automatically. In addition, it can reassemble and relink the modules into a new version of the program and it saves previous versions in an *archive*.

3.1.7 Development Systems

The computer used to write and assemble a program is part of a *development system* or a *work station*. A development system provides the hardware and software tools needed to write and debug programs. Sometimes the development system is used to write software for a different processor than the one contained in the development system itself. In such a case, a *cross-assembler* is required. A cross-assembler will run on the development system processor but will produce as its output machine code to run on a different processor. The microprocessor-based piece of equipment that will eventually run the program produced by the cross-assembler is called the *target system*. The 8085 assembler available with this book is a cross-assembler. It runs on an IBM personal computer or clone. The single-board computer described in Appendix A (or any similar board) can be used as a target system.

A development system usually has a piece of equipment for transferring or *downloading* the output of a cross-assembler into the memory of the target system. Such equipment may be capable of writing into the on-board memory of a single-chip computer as well as into an EPROM device. The equipment that programs the microprocessor memory may require an absolute load module or, alternatively, a *hex file*.

Many development systems include *emulation* as a powerful design tool. One version, called *in-circuit emulation,* allows the development system to take the place of the microprocessor in the target system. A cable plugs into the socket where the microprocessor would go and connects the development system to the target system. During program execution, special *debugger* software allows the programmer to examine and alter the contents of CPU registers, flags, and memory locations. Execution can be single-stepped, and modifications to the program can be made and tested instantly.

The VM85 8085 simulator program available with this book gives some of the flavor of emulation. A *simulator* is a program that models in software the behavior of hardware, allowing the user to find errors in a design before any hardware is built. However, because real hardware can sometimes behave in unexpected ways, the usefulness of a simulation is limited by how faithfully it represents the hardware.

3.1.8 Assembler Passes and Errors

The typical assembler is called a *two-pass* assembler, meaning that it reads the source file twice. Two passes are required because some information needed to complete the translation of the beginning of the program may not be found until the end of the program. Information is gathered during the first pass, and the actual translation is done during the second pass. Figures 3.1 and 3.2 show the steps involved in each pass.

A mistake in using the language properly is called a *syntax* error. An example of a syntax error is misspelling a mnemonic. The usual practice is for the assembler to report all errors in the listing file. The generation of a usable object file is voided by errors. *Semantic* errors, or errors in the design of the program, will not be caught by the assembler but must be found by testing.

3.1.10 The Programming Model

The term *programming model* refers to the way a programmer must view a computer. Whereas a hardware designer must be concerned with such details as bus loading and power supply voltages, the programmer is concerned with those features of the processor that relate to writing code. Besides the instruction set, the programming model includes such things as the sizes and names of all the registers, the memory map showing the address ranges of RAM and ROM, I/O port addresses, handshaking sequences, and details of any special processor features that may be used in a program.

Assembly language gives the programmer full access to all features of the processor, so it is essential that the programmer fully understand what the processor can and cannot do. The programming model is the image of the machine that the programmer must keep in mind while designing and writing the program.

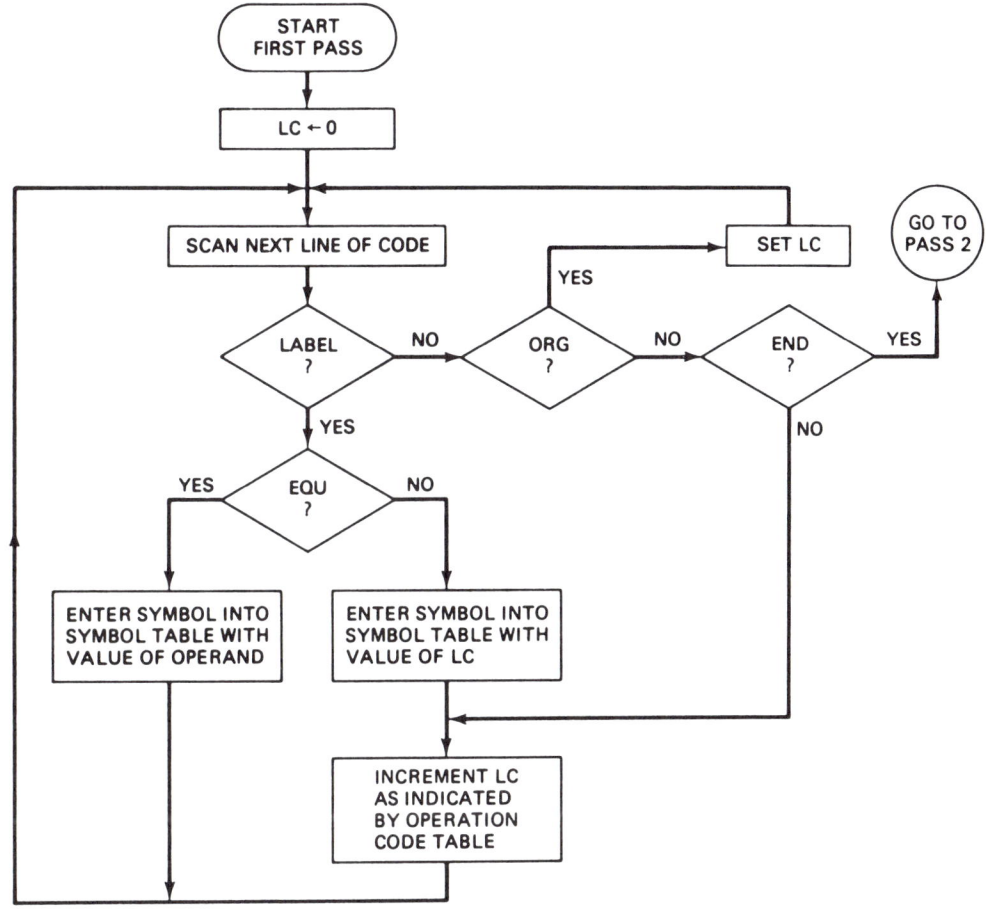

Figure 3.1 Simplified flowchart of the first pass of a two-pass assembler. (*Source:* Kenneth Short, *Microprocessors and Programmed Logic,* © 1981, p. 162. Reprinted by permission of Prentice-Hall, Inc., Englewood Cliffs, N.J.)

3.2 INSTRUCTION STATEMENTS

A typical *statement* in an assembly language consists of an optional *label,* followed by an operation mnemonic, followed by one or more operands. A comment may follow on the same line, separated from the statement by a semicolon. Comments are optional, but it is good programming practice to include enough comments to make the program as self-documented as possible for the benefit of whoever has to modify the program during its lifetime. Even programs you write yourself can seem unintelligible to you six months later if they are not well documented. Typically, much more time is spent on *maintenance* (i.e., modifying and debugging) than on writing programs in the first place.

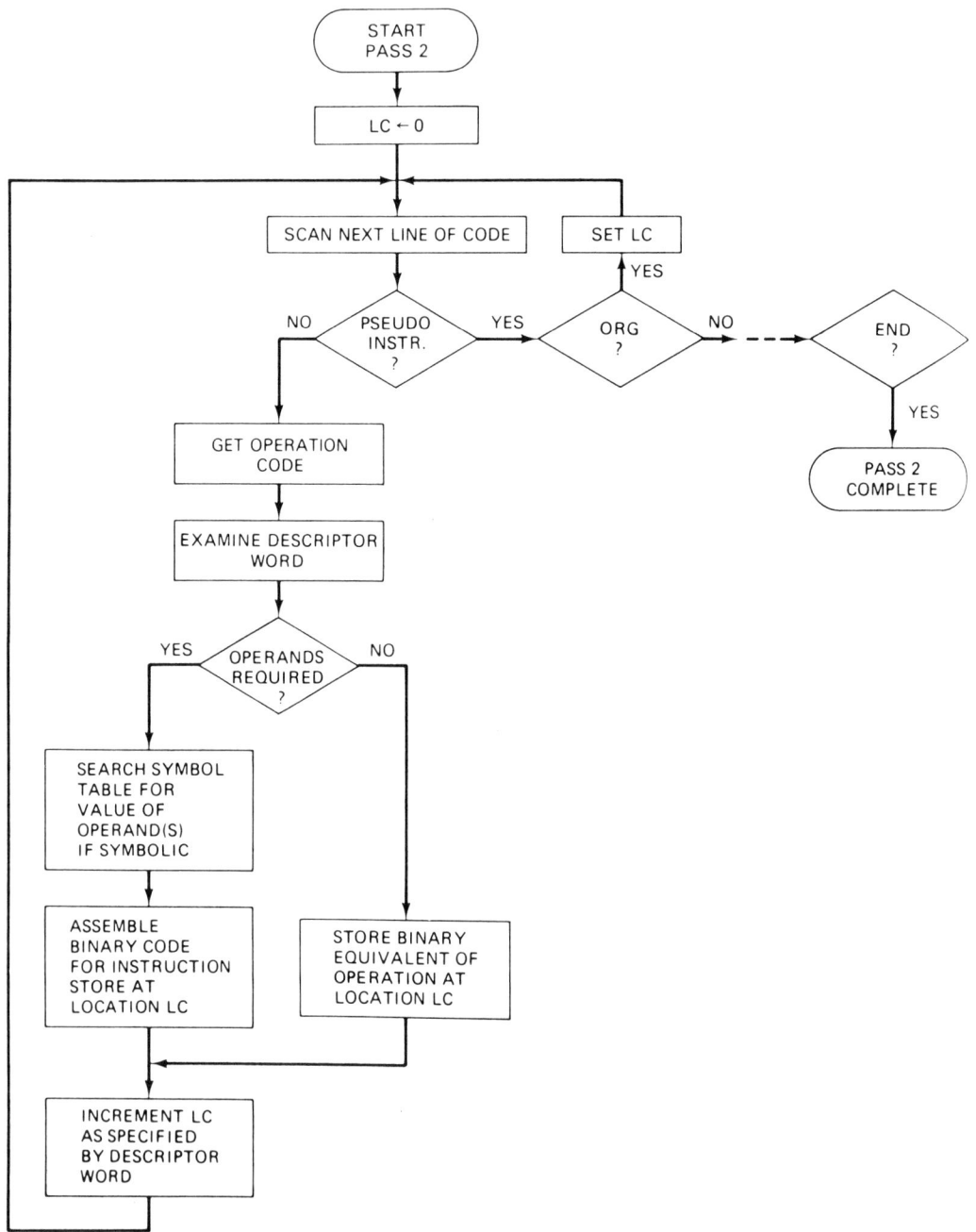

Figure 3.2 Simplified flowchart of the second pass of a two-pass assembler. (*Source:* Kenneth Short, *Microprocessors and Programmed Logic,* (© 1981, p. 163. Reprinted by permission of Prentice-Hall, Inc., Englewood Cliffs, N.J.)

EXAMPLE 3.1

Some example statements:

```
    ;     THIS IS A COMMENT
MAIN:   MVI A,45;   LOAD ACCUMULATOR
LP1:    INR A
        JMP LP1
```

MAIN: and LP1: are labels; MVI, INR, and JMP are mnemonic op-codes; A, 45, and LP1 are operands.

3.2.1 Labels and Names

Note that labels must begin with a letter and terminate with a colon. They can be used as operands in other statements because a label is actually a symbolic representation of a numeric memory address. The assembler will determine the numeric value of a label during pass 1 and store it in the assembler's *symbol table*. During pass 2, when the assembler encounters the label again, it will look up the value in the symbol table as it translates the symbolic assembly language into numeric machine language.

A *name* is similar to a label in that it is a symbolic representation of a numeric value. Names are associated with a value in an *equate statement*. An equate is not a part of the microprocessor's instruction set but is a feature of the assembler itself. Such features, called pseudo-operations (or assembler directives), are discussed in Sec. 3.4.

EXAMPLE 3.2 EQU

An example equate:

```
        FIVE   EQU   5
```

Unlike labels, names do not usually end with a colon. After they have been defined, names can be used as operands in instructions:

```
        MVI   A,FIVE
```

Both names and labels must begin with a letter and usually may not contain spaces, punctuation marks, or special characters such as # or @. The assembler user's manual will also specify the maximum number of characters that names and labels may contain, as well as the maximum number of names and labels that the symbol table will hold. Another limitation on names and labels is that they cannot be the same as any key words. *Key words* are typically the names of flags and registers, op-code mnemonics, and pseudo-operations.

3.2.2 Operands

Operands can be numeric or symbolic. Symbolic operands may be labels or names, or they may be fixed symbols defined by the assembly language itself, such as the designations of registers in the CPU. See Example 3.3

> **EXAMPLE 3.3 Operands**
>
> ```
>           MOV  A,B
>           MVI  A,FIVE
> ```
>
> The first instruction moves the content of the B register into the A register; the assembler will know what A and B refer to. The second instruction moves the value of the symbol FIVE into the A register. The assembler will recognize A, but will only know the value of FIVE if the name has been defined in an EQU statement.

3.2.3 Numbers and Radix

Most assemblers allow numbers to be represented in several bases, with decimal usually the normal or *default* base. The term *radix* is often used for the base of a number; a decimal number has a radix of ten (base 10). Other common bases are hexadecimal (base 16), octal (base 8), and binary (base 2).

The assembler determines the base of a number by looking for a letter at the end of the number. No letter indicates the default base, D indicates a decimal number, H indicates a hexadecimal number, O or Q indicates an octal number, and B indicates a binary number. Thus, the number 10 is ten, 10H is sixteen, 10Q is eight, and 10B is two.

Care must be used with hexadecimal (hex) numbers because of the letters A through F. To convince the assembler that something is a number, it must start with a digit in the range 0 to 9.

> **EXAMPLE 3.4 Writing Hex Numbers**
>
> The hex number F2H looks like a name to the assembler, and it will try to find the value in the symbol table. Therefore, F2H should be written as 0F2H to avoid an error.

Also, if you forget the H at the end of a hex number, the assembler may or may not see it as an error.

> **EXAMPLE 3.5 Writing Binary Numbers**
>
> Assuming the default base is decimal, the number 1A will be detected as an error, but the hex number 1B will be read as if it were a valid binary number.

3.2.4 Characters and Strings

In a computer, all symbols are ultimately represented by numbers, including all the numbers, letters, and punctuation marks on a keyboard. The numbers used to represent keyboard characters are *codes*. The code most commonly used with microcomputers is *ASCII* (American Standard Code for Information Interchange). Another common code is *EBCDIC* (Extended Binary Coded Decimal Interchange Code), used by IBM in its larger machines.

To represent a character code in assembly language, enclose the character between single quote marks (apostrophes). See Example 3.6.

EXAMPLE 3.6 Characters

An assembler will read 5 as the number 05H but will read '5' as 35H, which is the numeric value of the ASCII code for the character 5. In the same manner, 'A' will evaluate to 41H, which is the ASCII code for the letter A.

A *string* is a group of characters enclosed between single quotation marks such as 'this is a string'. Note that when counting characters in a string the spaces (blanks) must also be counted. See Example 3.7.

EXAMPLE 3.7 Strings

The string 'this is a string' contains 16 characters.

3.2.5 Expressions

It is often useful to let the assembler calculate the values for symbols using mathematical expressions. An *expression* is made up of arithmetic combinations of numbers and symbols such as 2+3*VAR, where VAR is a previously defined name. The normal operator precedence is usually observed, meaning multiplication and division are done before addition and subtraction. Terms inside parentheses will be done first.

EXAMPLE 3.8 Expressions

The expression 3*1+2 will evaluate to 5; 3*(1+2) will evaluate to 9.

Expressions can be used as operands in statements and in pseudo-operations. See Example 3.9.

EXAMPLE 3.9 Expressions as Operands

```
            MVI    A,3*FIVE-1
    TWO     EQU    2
    FIVE    EQU    3+TWO
            MVI    B,'A'+1
```

Note that TWO had to be defined before it could be used in an EQU statement, but FIVE was used in an instruction before it was defined. The reason is that EQU statements are evaluated during pass 1 in the order they appear, whereas operands in instructions are evaluated during pass 2. Note also that the last statement in the example will put the value 42H into the B register when it is executed.

3.3 ADDRESSING MODES

An important consideration in judging the power of a processor is the number of different ways instructions can access the memory, that is, the processor's *addressing modes*. In this section we examine several typical methods. The term *load* is used to mean that the processor is reading data from memory into a register; the term *store*, writing data into memory.

3.3.1 Register Addressing

In processors with multiple general-purpose registers, the fastest way to move data around is from register to register. *Register addressing* uses the predefined names of the registers in the instruction.

EXAMPLE 3.10

The 8085 instruction MOV A,B moves a copy of the contents of register B into register A. The operand names A and B are part of the assembly language.

3.3.2 Direct Addressing

In *direct addressing* the instruction contains the complete address of the memory location it is trying to reference. The address may be in numeric or symbolic form. Instructions using direct addressing are limited to the one memory location they specify, so loading from a hundred sequential locations would require a hundred different instructions.

EXAMPLE 3.11

The two 8085 instructions LDA LABL1 and LDA 1234H are equivalent if LABL1 appears in the program as the label of the location with address 1234H or has been defined as 1234H with an EQU.

3.3.3 Immediate Mode

Immediate mode is a method of putting a constant value into a register or memory location during program execution. It is a modification of addressing methods such as register or direct. For example, the 8088 instruction to load the number 12H into register AL is MOV AL,12H. In some assembly languages (e.g., 8085) the form of the mnemonic is changed to indicate immediate mode, so the equivalent move instruction would be written MVI A, 12H. Once the program is assembled, immediate operands have a fixed value; they *cannot* be changed by the program.

3.3.4 Indirect Addressing

Indirect addressing gets around the limitation of direct addressing by using a pointer to hold an address. The pointer may be a memory address or a register. Instructions can then refer to that pointer instead of the actual address. When the processor executes the instruction, it will use the number in the pointer as the address. Thus, the same instruction can be used to access many different locations simply by changing the pointer contents.

EXAMPLE 3.12

In the following Z80 instructions

```
LD   HL, 1000H
LD   A, (HL)
```

the HL register pair is being used as a pointer and is initialized to hold address 1000H. The instruction LD A,(HL) will move a copy of the contents of memory location 1000H into register A. Note the parentheses around HL. The same instruction without the parentheses would mean "move the contents of the HL register pair into the accumulator," which can't be done. Thus, notation such as parentheses is needed to show when a register is to be used as a pointer. The equivalent 8085 instructions are

```
LXI   H, 1000H
MOV   A, M
```

3.3.5 Paged Addressing

Paged addressing can be considered a variation on indirect addressing. Let's assume that the processor uses a 16-bit address, giving a maximum address space of 64K bytes (note that 1K is 1024). A 64K memory can be thought of as 256 *pages*, with each page consisting of 256 bytes. An 8-bit number is required to specify a page while another 8-bit number can specify a byte within a page.

In processors supporting paged addressing, an 8-bit *page register* is used to hold the page number. The contents of the page register can be altered by the program. An instruction can supply the 8-bit byte address either directly or indirectly, and the processor will concatenate the two 8-bit numbers into a 16-bit memory address when the instruction is executed.

3.3.6 Base, Index, Displacement

Base displacement is a variation on indirect addressing that is somewhat similar to paged addressing but much more powerful. A *base register* (under software control) is used to hold a full-length address. Instructions that use the base register may supply a *displacement* number that will be added to the contents of the base register at execution to form a memory address. The displacement may be an immediate operand or the contents of another register.

Some processors contain an *index register*, which can be used with the displacement register. The index register also is loaded with an address. Instructions can then reference both the base and index registers as well as supply a displacement. When such an instruction is executed, the memory location address will be the sum of the base, the index, and the displacement. To increase the power of indexed addressing, some instructions may cause the processor to increment (or decrement) the contents of the index register automatically when they are executed. The 8086 (see Chap. 11) uses base, index, and displacement.

3.3.7 Relative Addressing

Relative addressing is similar to base-displacement addressing with the program counter taking the place of the base register. An instruction using relative addressing will supply a signed 8-bit *offset*, which is added to the contents of the program counter. In a signed number, the MSB is the sign bit and the lower 7 bits are the magnitude, so the range of addresses is within 128 bytes either forward or backward from the location of the relative instruction itself.

The most common use of relative addressing is a JUMP RELATIVE instruction. Some assemblers will allow the programmer to use a generic JUMP instruction. If the target of the jump is within relative range, the assembler will produce the op-code for a relative jump; otherwise, it will produce the code for an absolute jump. Relative jump instructions are shorter and execute faster than absolute jumps. The Z80 and 8051 use relative jumps; the 8085 does not.

3.3.8 Implied Addressing

In *implied addressing*, the operands, which are usually registers, are fixed and are not explicitly specified in the instruction. An example is the 8085 instruction CMA, which complements the contents of the accumulator.

3.4 PSEUDO-OPERATIONS AND DIRECTIVES

Pseudo-operations—sometimes also called *assembler directives*—look like assembly language instruction statements, but actually they are instructions to the assembler itself. They do not take up memory space in the final program. Psuedo-operations allow the programmer to control certain operations during the assembly process.

The mnemonic op-codes in an assembly language are determined by the designers of microprocessors and are different from processor to processor. Pseudo-ops are more or less standard for all assemblers, although any given assembler may use a variation of a particular pseudo-op or not use it at all. There are many possible assembler directives. In this section we look at some of the more important ones. Note that some assemblers precede directives with a period, such as .ORG, to differentiate them from instructions.

3.4.1 ORG and END

ORG stands for "origin" and allows the programmer to determine the address of the first instruction in a program. If there is no ORG statement at the beginning of a program, the assembler will assume a default value, typically 0000. As each instruction is assembled, it will be assigned by the assembler to the next available address unless another ORG statement is encountered. Some assembly languages use LOC (for "location") in place of ORG.

EXAMPLE 3.13 Use of ORG

```
        ORG  1000H;
L1:     MOV  A,B;
        ORG  1500H;
L2:     JMP  L1;
```

The assembler will associate the label L1 with address 1000H, which is where it assumes the translated version of MOV A,B will eventually be loaded in memory. The label L2 will be associated with address 1500H. The assembler assumes nothing about all the empty locations between the two instructions shown.

The END statement tells the assembler where to stop assembling. There must be only one END directive, and it should be the last line in the program because the assembler will ignore everything after it. Omitting the END will cause an error in assembly.

3.4.2 EQU and SET

As discussed in Sec. 3.2.1, EQU allows the programmer to bind a value to a name. Some assembly languages use an equal sign (=) in place of EQU. However, once a name is defined with an EQU, it may not be redefined.

EXAMPLE 3.14 Use of EQU

```
VAR  EQU  2;   definition
MVI  A, VAR
VAR  EQU  3;   redefinition (error)
MVI  B, VAR
```

These lines of code would cause the assembler to report an error.

SET is similar to EQU, except that it allows a name to be redefined.

EXAMPLE 3.15 Use of SET

```
VAR  SET  2    temporary definition
MVI  A, VAR
VAR  SET  3    new definition
MVI  B, VAR
```

This code allows the name VAR to be used twice with different values.

3.4.3 Memory Allocation: DS, DB, DW

Memory locations can be defined and initialized to data values by the use of *define storage* (DS), *define byte* (DB), and *define word* (DW) statements.

DS allows the programmer to set aside a block of memory without putting anything into it. See Example 3.16.

EXAMPLE 3.16 Use of DS

```
          ORG 1000H ; anything after
STOR: DS 5          ; a semicolon is
          MOV A,B   ; a comment
```

This code will set aside 5 bytes of memory starting at address 1000H. Also, the address of the first byte is associated with the label STOR. The instruction MOV A,B will be stored at address 1005H.

DB allows the programmer to initialize 1 or more bytes of memory to specific values. See Example 3.17.

EXAMPLE 3.17 Use of DB

```
       ORG  1000H;
TWO    EQU  2;
L1:    DB   3+TWO;
       DB   '2';
MSG:   DB   'HELLO';
```

The EQU statement does not take up memory space in the program because it is a pseudo-op. Address 1000H, associated with the label L1, will contain the numeric value 05. Address 1001H will contain the character '2', which is numeric value 32H in ASCII. Locations 1002H through 1006H will contain the values 48H ('H'), 45H ('E'), 4CH ('L'), 4CH ('L'), 4FH ('O'). The label MSG will have the value 1002H, the address of the first character in the five-character string.

The DW directive is similar to DB except that a 2-byte word is initialized instead of a single byte. Usually DW does not allow character strings, but will allow expressions. See Example 3.18.

EXAMPLE 3.18 Use of DW

```
              ORG  2000H;
    ADR1:     DW   1234H;
    ADR2:     DW   ADR1+5;
```

Label ADR1 is equal to 2000H and ADR2 is equal to 2002H. The content of memory starting at location 2002H is 1239H.

Some processors (e.g., the 8085) store the high-order byte in the higher memory location, whereas other processors (e.g., the 8051) do the reverse. The result is that

```
              DW   1234H;
```

may or may not be equivalent to

```
              DB   12H;
              DB   34H;
```

depending on the processor for which the assembler was written.

It is important to note that when writing programs that will be executed from ROM, you cannot use DB or DW to initialize the RAM. You should use immediate mode instructions instead.

3.4.4 Code and Data Segments: CSEG, DSEG

Relocatable assemblers (i.e., those that produce relocatable object files) require directives concerning address references that are not required in absolute assemblers. Relocatable assemblers allow the programmer to partition the program memory space into two regions: a *code segment* and a *data segment*. Special directives such as CSEG and DSEG are used to tell the assembler what lines of the program belong in which segment.

EXAMPLE 3.19 CSEG and DSEG

```
              CSEG
              LXI  B, VAR1;
              DSEG
    VAR1:     DB   12;
    VAR2:     DB   34;
              CSEG
              JMP  NEXT;
```

In the final load module, the JMP instruction will follow the LXI instruction in memory since they are both in the code segment. Although it appears that JMP and LXI are separated by 2 bytes of defined data, they are actually sequential because the two DB statements are in the data segment, a completely different part of memory.

EXAMPLE 3.20 Addresses in Segments

```
CSEG
ORG   0100H;
DSEG
ORG   0100H;
```

It seems that the code and data segments have been assigned to the same place in memory. However, in a relocatable assembler, the ORG statements are relative to the beginning addresses of the segments, which, in turn, are determined by the loader program. The programmer can tell the loader at what addresses the segments will start. Thus, ORG 0100H in the data segment might translate to actual address 1823H in memory and ORG 0100 in the code segment might correspond to address 0400H in memory.

Another reason for separate code and data segments has to do with the physical memory. In the target system, such things as instructions and constants (ROMable code) can be placed in ROM, whereas changeable variables (data) must be kept in RAM. The use of CSEG and DSEG in the source program makes it easy to separate ROMable from non-ROMable code. As mentioned, do not use DB or DW to initialize RAM data in the DSEG if the code will be executed from ROM in the target system.

3.4.5 PUBLIC and EXTERNAL

When relocatable object files (or modules) are linked together to form a larger program, it is often the case that a label or variable name will be defined in one module but used in several others. Such *external references* can be resolved by the linker but require the use of directives to prevent the assembler from assuming that a name not found in the symbol table is an error. The exact mnemonics used depend on the assembler, but they are usually called *PUBLIC* and *EXTERNAL*. The term *GLOBAL* is the same as PUBLIC.

A public directive usually precedes a list of symbols, as in Example 3.21.

EXAMPLE 3.21

```
PUBLIC   VAR1, VAR2, LABL1
```

The values of the symbols must be defined in the same module that declares them public. The relocatable assembler will save the public symbols in a special section of the object file so that they can be referenced by name in other modules. Any given symbol can be declared public in only one module.

For a public symbol to be used in other modules, it must be declared as external in each module that wants to use it (except for the module that declared it as public). A symbol that has been declared as public in one module can be used in a second module with a different meaning as long as the second module defines it without declaring it as either public or external.

EXAMPLE 3.22

```
          EXTERNAL   VAR1, VAR2
```

3.5 MACRO ASSEMBLERS

Often, certain sequences of instructions are found to form a block of code that is repeated at many places in the same program. As a convenience, the programmer may wish to associate a symbolic name with the instruction sequence, and everywhere the sequence occurs it can be replaced with its name. A symbolic name that represents such a block of code is called a *macro,* and assemblers that support macros are called *macro assemblers*.

3.5.1 Macros and Subroutines

Macros should not be confused with subroutines. A subroutine is a processor function and involves such overhead as saving register contents, pushing and popping the return address, and branching to a different part of memory to find the subroutine instructions—all of which happen when the program is executed. In contrast, macros are a feature of the assembler. When the assembler finds a macro in the program it expands it, meaning that the assembler replaces the macro name with the block of code it represents.

From a programming point of view, it may seem that much of what a subroutine does can be done by a macro. However, note that the use of subroutines makes a program shorter but slower, whereas the use of macros makes it longer but faster. A useful technique is to combine macros and subroutines. A subroutine call can be embedded in a macro together with all the instructions needed to save and restore the environment—all the registers and flags that must be preserved from alteration by the subroutine. Such a technique can save the programmer a lot of tedious coding and also prevent errors.

EXAMPLE 3.23 A Simple Macro

Assume TOTAL is a macro name. The following

```
          MVI    A, VAR1;
          TOTAL
          MVI    A, VAR2;
```

would expand to be

```
         MVI   A, VAR1;
         PUSH  PSW      ; part of TOTAL
         CALL  SUM      ; part of TOTAL
         POP   PSW      ; part of TOTAL
         MVI   A, VAR2;
```

assuming that TOTAL had been defined to mean the three instructions shown.

3.5.2 Macro Definition

The exact form of a macro definition depends on the particular assembler being used, so what follows can be considered as generic. The assembly language user's manual will give the correct form.

A macro is defined by creating a *template* (also called a *prototype*) associated with the macro name. The *body* of the macro is the group of instructions in the template that will be substituted at every place where the macro name appears in the program. The beginning and end of the macro template are delimited by a pair of directives such as MACRO and ENDM.

An important part of a macro definition is the list of *formal parameters*. When the macro is *called* (or *invoked*) in the program, the call supplies actual parameters that will be substituted for the formal parameters when the macro is *expanded*. Look at Example 3.24.

EXAMPLE 3.24   Macro Parameters

```
         SUM    MACRO   $X, $Y, $Z
                MOV     A, $X
                ADD     $Y
                ADD     $Z
                MOV     $X, A
                ENDM
```

Note that the name of the macro, SUM, appears on the same line as the MACRO directive, which is, in turn, followed by the formal parameter list. Also note that the formal parameters use the $ character to mark them as special symbols (different assemblers may use other characters, such as # or %). Normally, a macro definition may not include another macro definition.

Now suppose that the macro in Example 3.24 is invoked in a program with the statement

```
         SUM   B, C, D;
```

It will be expanded by the assembler into

```
            MOV    A, B
            ADD    C
            ADD    D
            MOV    B, A
```

Note how the formal parameters of the template have been replaced by the actual parameters of the invocation. Different invocations can use different actual parameters.

3.5.3 Labels in Macros

If a label appears in the body of a macro, then repeated invocations would lead to the same label being used for different addresses, a redefinition error. To get around the problem, the macro definition will include a special string in labels such as #SYM. When the macro is invoked, #SYM will be replaced in the expansion by a four-digit hexadecimal number. The number will be incremented by 1 at every call, so that no two labels will be the same.

EXAMPLE 3.25 Labels in Macros

```
    DELAY    MACRO
             PUSH   A
             MVI    A, 100H
    L#SYM    DEC    A
             JNZ    L#SYM
             POP    A
             ENDM
```

The first time the macro DELAY is used, L#SYM will be replaced by L0001. In a second invocation it will be replaced by L0002, in a third by L0003, and so forth. Such special strings should not appear in the list of formal parameters.

3.6 CONDITIONAL ASSEMBLY

It is often the case that several different versions of a program are required. For example, several models of a microprocessor-based product may be sold with each model adding a few options onto a basic design. The software for each model would be basically the same, but some of the code would depend on the options. Instead of maintaining a separate program for each model, it is possible to maintain a single program with several *conditional* sections of code.

3.6.1 Conditional Directives

As the name implies, code designated for *conditional assembly* will be translated into machine code only if certain conditions are true when the program is assembled. Special directives, such as IF and ENDIF, are used to indicate the beginning and end of the conditional section of code. Conditional blocks may be *nested*, meaning that one conditional block may be completed inside another.

> **EXAMPLE 3.26   Conditional Assembly**
>
> A conditional block:
>
> ```
> IF    COND1
> MOV   A,B
> ENDIF
> ```
>
> The symbol COND1 will be evaluated at assembly. If it evaluates to true, then the line MOV A,B will become part of the program. If COND1 evaluates to false, then MOV A,B will be ignored. In this context false usually means a numeric value of zero and true any nonzero value.

3.6.2 Compound Conditions

The condition following the IF directive can be compounded from several symbols using both arithmetic expressions and logic operators. Use of an arithmetic expression is given in Example 3.27.

> **EXAMPLE 3.27**
>
> ```
> IF    2*VAR-10
> MVI   A,5
> ENDIF
> ```
>
> If 2*VAR-10 equals zero, then the instruction will be ignored.

Use of logic operators is shown in Example 3.28.

> **EXAMPLE 3.28**
>
> ```
> IF    (M1 AND M2) OR (Q3 GT 5)
> MVI   A,5
> ENDIF
> ```
>
> For the condition to be true, both the variables M1 *and* M2 must be true at the same time *or* the variable Q3 must be greater than 5.

Common relational operators are the following:

EQ	equal	Example:	IF (X EQ 5)	is true if X = 5.
GT	greater than	Example:	IF (X GT 5)	is true if X = 6 or more.
LT	less than	Example:	IF (X LT 5)	is true if X = 4 or less.
NOT	logic inversion	Example:	IF NOT (X GT 5)	is true if X = 5 or less.

3.7 SUMMARY

In this chapter we have looked at what an assembler is and what it does. We described source files, list files, and object files, as well as editors, linkers, loaders, and libraries. We examined the format of an instruction, together with various addressing modes, and assembler directives. Finally, we explained the use of macros and conditional assembly.

CHAPTER REVIEW

Questions

1. What is a mnemonic?
2. What does an assembler do?
3. How does an assembly language differ from a high-level language?
4. How is a source file prepared?
5. What is an object file?
6. What does a loader do?
7. What does a linker do?
8. What does "relocatable" mean?
9. What is meant by an assembler pass?
10. What is the reason for having two passes?
11. What is the difference between syntax errors and semantic errors?
12. What is in a programming model?
13. Why should comments be included in a program?
14. What is the difference between a label and a name?
15. What is a radix?
16. What are some typical number bases used in assemblers?
17. What is the difference between a character and a string?
18. Write a typical expression using numbers and symbols.
19. Explain register addressing.
20. Compare direct and indirect addressing.
21. Explain immediate mode.
22. Explain base-displacement addressing.
23. Describe an application that would make use of base, index, and displacement.
24. What is an assembler directive, and how does it differ from an instruction?

25. What does ORG do?
26. What is the difference between EQU and SET?
27. Explain what each of the following do: DS, DB, DW.
28. Explain the use of CSEG and DSEG.
29. Explain the use of PUBLIC and EXTERNAL.
30. What is a macro, and why is it used?
31. Compare macros to subroutines.
32. Explain the use of formal parameters.
33. How are labels handled in macros?
34. What is conditional assembly, and why use it?
35. What does "nesting" mean?

Problems

1. Write an 8085 program that starts at location FE00h and adds the content of register B to the accumulator and halts. Show use of the END statement.
2. Write a short 8085 program using the EQU and SET directives.
3. Write a short program starting at 0000h using DS, DB, and DW directives. Calculate the numeric addresses of all the instructions.
4. Write a macro template to subtract one register from another. The registers will be specified in the macro invocation.
5. Use IF and ENDIF so that INR A will be included in a program only if SW1 is true and either X1 or X2 is false.

chapter 4

Programming and the 8085

OBJECTIVES

Upon completion of this chapter, you should be able to

1. Read 8085 assembly language programs and explain what they do
2. Write short programs using the 8085 instruction set
3. Write programs using subroutines
4. Explain the use of pointers, flags, and masking

4.1 INTRODUCTION

This chapter examines the use of the 8085 instruction set. However, it is also a tutorial on assembly language techniques in general. Although expressed in 8085 code, the techniques can be used with any processor simply by recoding them in the assembly language of that processor. In other words, the ideas in this chapter can be "ported" to any microprocessor.

Sometimes students come to a course on microprocessors with the preconceived idea that assembly language is difficult, despite the fact of having mastered another language such as BASIC. There are two reasons for that feeling. First, assembly language is unfamiliar. However, the skills acquired by programming in BASIC can be applied to assembly because they consist mainly of thinking through the task at hand in a logical and sequential way. Familiar techniques, such as looping, are also used in assembly language. The second reason assembly language may, at first, seem difficult is that high-level languages such as BASIC hide many of the processing details. The advantage is portability, as a program written in BASIC should run on any machine that has a BASIC interpreter. The disadvantage is that the full power of the processor is not directly available to the BASIC programmer.

Assembly language gives the programmer full access to the resources of the computer. If it can't be done in assembly, it can't be done. Assembly is not the language of choice for many applications. High-level languages, especially structured languages such as C and PASCAL, often save much time and effort in writing and debugging large programs. However, when using microprocessors as embedded controllers in ROM-based equipment, or when writing driver routines to interface to I/O devices, or when trying to optimize a certain critical routine in a large program, assembly language is often the best option. And the best way to learn assembly language is by doing it. It's like learning to ride a bicycle. At first, the movements seem unnatural and the ride is a little shaky. After a while, though, it seems quite natural and the ride is swift and sure. All it takes is practice.

4.1.1 Getting Started

Often the most difficult problem a novice programmer has is where to begin. Systems design techniques are discussed at length in Chapter 12, but in general, we must do something like these five steps:

1. Clarify what it is you want to do by writing out a concise description of the program's task.
2. Try to identify those aspects of the task that are critical or in some way limiting, such as speed, I/O, memory size, and the like. Certain hardware/software trade-offs may have to be made in the system design at this point.
3. Break the task down into a logical sequence of subtasks, for example, by using a flowchart. Note what things must be done at the beginning (initialization) and at the end of the task.
4. Start writing the code for the subtasks. See if the assembly language has instructions to do what you want directly. If not, can it be done indirectly? For example, the 8085 does not have a 16-bit register pair to register pair MOV instruction, but you can get the same effect with a PUSH and a POP.
5. Test each subtask code module to see if it works. Then integrate the modules into the final program and test. Remember that testing cannot prove that a program is bug-free; it only proves that the bugs you tested for aren't there. There may be bugs your test just doesn't find.

Once you have gotten started, bear in mind that nobody, not even an experienced programmer, can sit down and write a perfect program in one pass. Just as one must troubleshoot and fine-tune a hardware design, so one must do with a software design. In the same way that you gain hardware skills through experience, you will gain software skills by recognizing patterns and structure while writing and debugging code. The process of designing and writing software is by its nature iterative, the so-called software development cycle. However, proper planning can reduce substantially the number of iterations required.

4.1.2 Flowcharts, Design Languages, Walk-Throughs

When designing a program it is useful to have a way of outlining what the program does before writing the code. In other words, we design the algorithm before we write the program.

The word *algorithm* comes from the name of the Muslim mathematician al-Khwarizmi. His book, *al-jebr w'al-mugabala*, was translated into Latin in 1145 under the title *Algebra*. An algorithm is the "game plan" of how to solve some problem or accomplish some task. It is actually an abstraction, as the same algorithm can be expressed in different computer languages. A *program* is the actual implementation of an algorithm.

Two ways of designing algorithms are flowcharts and design languages. *Flowcharts* are a graphical way of outlining a program using a set of standard symbol shapes. Several different shapes have been defined, but we will keep it simple by using only three: ovals, rectangles, and diamonds. In addition, small circles will be used for connection points. Ovals (often boxes with rounded sides) indicate the beginning and end of a routine, rectangles indicate a block of code that does a specific task, and diamonds indicate decision points. See the flowchart in Fig. 4.1.

Although flowcharts are well suited for outlining the large-scale structure of a program, they tend to get so large as to be unreadable when applied at the code

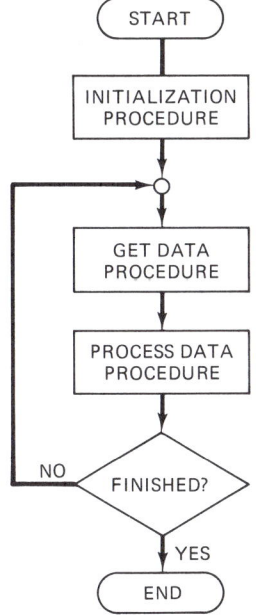

Figure 4.1 Typical flowchart.

level in a big program. Also, there is no easy way to execute a flowchart to demonstrate its correctness.

An alternative is to use a structured *design language*. Some such languages exist only on paper and are called pseudo-code. Others, such as PASCAL, have been implemented as real languages; a program initially designed in that language can be executed to see how it works before it is translated into assembly language. More is said about design language in Chapter 12. Later in this chapter we look at assembly language versions of structured code.

A *walk-through* is a technique where the programmer explains the program to other programmers, usually team members on the same project, who try to find the flaws in the design. It is usually done at the flowchart or design language level in order to catch design errors before much time is spent in detailed programming.

4.2 SUBROUTINES

We discussed the basic idea of a subroutine in Chap. 2. In this section we look at why subroutines are useful. Throughout this chapter we will write example programs in the form of a subroutine, just for the practice. Some examples simply show the use of the instructions and do not necessarily "do something." Other examples will be more interesting. Also, the calling routines (usually called MAIN in this section) are often written as program fragments rather than complete programs. If you want to try running them on a trainer, you can always add a HALT instruction (HLT) at the end. You may find it useful to refer to the instruction descriptions given in Chapter 12 as you read the code.

4.2.1 The Enemy: Complexity

In the early days of programming, people tended to write programs in which every part was connected to every other part by large numbers of GOTO types of statements (jumps). The technique came to be called "spaghetti code" because of the way a program looked when drawn as a flowchart. If a programmer tried to change any part of the program, it would often cause strange and unexpected things to happen—so-called side effects—in other parts of the program. (In the C language, the term "side-effect" has a somewhat different meaning.)

Getting such a program to work became a long and tedious cycle of finding and fixing bugs and then finding and fixing the bugs caused by the previous fixes. With larger projects, such as operating systems, people found that for every 100 bugs they fixed, they would generate 101 new ones. In other words, the test-fix-test cycle would not converge for programs over a certain size. A complexity barrier had been reached. (As a historical note, the term *bug* comes to us from that fateful day when an early computer built with relays stopped working for no apparent reason. The problem was traced to an insect that had gotten itself caught between a pair of relay contacts. Once the computer was "debugged," it worked fine!)

4.2.2 A Friend: Subroutines

Many tools and techniques have been developed for dealing with complexity, some of which are examined in Chapter 12. Arguably the most important of those tools is *modularization:* breaking the program down into small, self-contained sections *(modules)* that do a limited, well-defined function. In assembly language we can implement modules in the form of subroutines. Some of the advantages of using subroutines are the following:

- It allows a complex program to be broken down into smaller, simpler modules that are easier to understand and debug.
- Programs can be shorter because the code for a subroutine appears once, but can be used many times in the program.
- The work of writing a large program can be divided among many programmers, all working simultaneously.
- It allows debugging to be confined to the faulty module without side effects spreading throughout the program. That is, the module is encapsulated.
- Modules can be kept in a library for reuse in other programs, thus saving future software costs.

Subroutines may be *nested,* meaning that a subroutine may call another subroutine, which, in turn, may call another subroutine, and so forth. The level of nesting refers to the order of calls. If MAIN calls SUB1, which then calls SUB2, SUB1 would be at the first level and SUB2 would be at the second level of nesting. Subroutines that can call themselves are *recursive*. Subroutines that can be placed anywhere in memory and executed without having to alter any instructions are *position independent*. *Multitasking* systems can run several programs simultaneously. A subroutine that can be called by two or more programs simultaneously is *reentrant*.

If instructions are stored in RAM, then a program can modify its own code as it executes by overwriting parts of the instructions. Such a program is called *self-modifying*. With very few exceptions, writing self-modifying code is a very bad idea because it is so difficult to debug.

Although usually not significant, using subroutines does slow down execution due to the overhead of pushing, branching, popping, and returning. When absolutely necessary, it is possible to gain speed at the expense of increased memory size by rewriting a program with the subroutines expanded (much like macros) into in-line code, eliminating the overhead associated with calling and returning.

4.2.3 Do It with Style

For the sake of clarity, subroutines (as well as variables, pointers, etc.) should be given names that give some clue as to what they do. For example, a subroutine to take square roots should be called something like SQRT rather than SUB27.

Also in the name of clarity we must consider *style*. Unless there is some important reason to do otherwise, it is better to write code that is straightforward and clear rather than clever but obscure. The reason is that the most time, effort, and money are spent on maintaining software after it is first written. A tried and true piece of code may be a cliché, but everyone knows what it does. Sometimes, in order to get the maximum speed out of a critical routine, it is necessary to be as clever as possible. In such a case, clear and detailed documentation is essential. There are cases where large amounts of very clever, but undocumented, software had to be discarded because the original programmer had left the company. It was actually cheaper to rewrite it than to fix it.

Formal documentation is discussed in Chapter 12. At a less formal level, documentation should include the generous use of comments in an assembly language program. Try to make the source file as *self-documenting* as possible. At a minimum, the comments should tell what the subroutine does, what it expects as input, what it gives as output, and what registers and memory locations it changes. Remember, comments don't cost anything; they don't take up memory space or reduce speed because the assembler ignores them.

4.2.4 Save the Environment

When a subroutine is called (by the calling routine, naturally), it should do its work and return without causing unwanted changes in the flags, register contents, or any other important resource. In other words, it should not cause accidental changes in the program's environment. To help prevent such side effects, the first thing a subroutine should do is PUSH onto the stack all the registers it intends to use. Just before it returns, the subroutine should POP them off the stack. Remember that a stack is LIFO (last-in, first-out), so registers must be POPed off in the reverse order they were PUSHed on.

EXAMPLE 4.1

The subroutine in this example would be called by the instruction CALL SUBR, and the contents of A, B, C, D, E, and the flags would be the same after the call is complete (subroutine returns) as they were before the call was executed. Note the use of comments.

```
          SUBR:     PUSH PSW    ; save Acc and Flags
                    PUSH B      ; save BC reg pair
                    PUSH D      ; save DE reg pair

                       <rest of subroutine>

                    POP D       ; restore DE
                    POP B       ; restore BC
                    POP PSW     ; restore Acc and Flags
                    RET         ; from SUB
```

In addition to the reasons already given, you should get into the habit of using comments because they are invaluable when, six months later, you have to make a change to your own program and can't remember for the life of you what the thing does.

Sometimes a subroutine must change a register or memory location as part of what it does. For example, a subroutine may take the square root of a number and return the result in the accumulator (see the discussion on parameter passing in Sec. 4.3). Obviously, the content of the accumulator will be different after the call. In such cases the programmer should include comments in the subroutine explicitly stating what gets changed.

Although we do not want hidden side effects, we often do want to hide detail in a subroutine. For example, a programmer may not care how a library subroutine for taking square roots actually works as long as what it does is completely documented. The programmer calling the routine just wants to pass it a number and get back the root without anything weird happening. The *interface* to the subroutine is through the explicitly passed parameters.

4.2.5 The Stack Pointer

The stack pointer (SP) must be initialized before any subroutines are called, any PUSH or POP instructions are executed, or any interrupts are allowed to occur.

EXAMPLE 4.2

The program here contains the instruction LXI SP,1000H as the first line of MAIN. In subsequent examples, if we do not explicitly load SP, just assume that it was done in some prior (and not shown) part of the program. Although SP can also be loaded from the HL register pair with the instruction SPHL, the occasions for doing so are few.

```
MAIN:    LXI     SP, 1000H   ; INITIALIZE STACK
         MVI     B,35H       ; PUT HEX 35 INTO REG B
         MVI     C,23H       ; PUT HEX 23 INTO REG C
         CALL    SWAPBC      ; CALL SUBROUTINE
         HLT                 ; HALT

                               *
                               *
                               *

SWAPBC:  PUSH    PSW         ; SAVE ACC AND FLAGS
         MOV     A,C         ; SAVE CONTENTS OF C
         MOV     C,B         ; PUT CONTENTS OF B IN C
         MOV     B,A         ; PUT CONTENTS OF C IN B
         POP     PSW         ; RESTORE ACC AND FLAGS
         RET                 ; RETURN FROM SWAPBC
```

4.3 MAKING PASSES

As mentioned in Sec. 4.2.4, sometimes subroutines must change the value of some variable or parameter. A key issue is how to pass that variable to the subroutine and then pass the results back to the calling routine—in other words, *parameter passing*.

4.3.1 Global Variables

One approach is to not pass anything and instead use *global variables* in a *common data area*. For example, a memory location could be used to hold the value of some important quantity. All calling routines and all subroutines would "know" the name and address of the variable in memory. Any subroutine that used that quantity would simply read it from memory, use it, and possibly overwrite the old value with a new one. Although eliminating the problem of passing, global variables increase the probability of side effects occurring in the subroutine that are hidden from the main or calling routine.

4.3.2 Passing in Registers

If only a few simple variables are needed, they can be passed in the *registers*. For example, a program may want to find the square root of an 8-bit number stored in a memory location. It could fetch the number from memory into the accumulator. It could then call the square root subroutine, passing the number in the accumulator. The subroutine would take the square root and pass the result back to the calling routine in the accumulator. Meanwhile, the original number is still in memory untouched, as both the main routine and the subroutine worked on a copy of the variable. Such a method is often called *pass by value*.

4.3.3 Passing Pointers

Sometimes a subroutine must work on variables that cannot be passed in registers. For example, a quantity may be a record consisting of a name, address, and telephone number all stored as ASCII characters in a predefined format. In such cases it is often convenient to pass the address of the beginning of the variable. Also, certain I/O devices, like disk drives, typically move blocks of data in and out of fixed buffer areas in memory. The calling routine can pass to the subroutine a pointer to the beginning of the buffer. In the 8085, the HL register pair is often used to hold such a pointer. Passing the address of a parameter is often called *pass by reference*.

If a subroutine needs several parameters residing in noncontiguous memory locations, then passing a single pointer is not enough. A pointer to each parameter will be needed. The solution is to use a *table* of pointers. The table is stored as consecutive memory locations, so only a single pointer to the first entry in the table need be passed to the subroutine. Each entry is the address of a parameter and can be used by the subroutine to fetch the parameter itself. See Fig. 4.2.

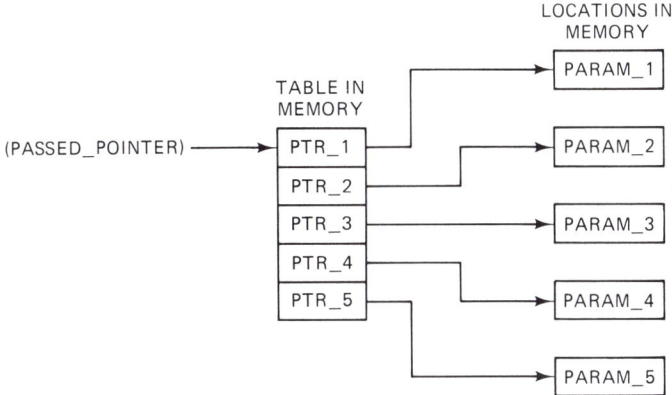

Figure 4.2 Pointer table.

4.3.4 Passing in the Stack

It is possible to pass variables in the *stack*. One technique is as follows. Before calling the subroutine, the calling routine will push the variables it wants to pass to the subroutine onto the stack. If the number of things pushed is itself a variable, then the last thing the calling routine must push is the *count* of variables pushed. The subroutine is then called.

Because calling the subroutine causes the return address to be automatically pushed onto the stack, the first thing the subroutine must do is pop the return address off the stack and put it aside for safekeeping. Then the subroutine pops off the stack the count of variables that are being passed (assuming it was pushed on). Next the subroutine pops off the stack all the variables that were pushed on by the calling routine and saves them in a scratchpad area of memory. Then the subroutine must save the environment, as discussed in sec. 4.2.4.

After it completes its job, the subroutine can pass values back to the calling routine (assuming the calling routine expects them) by pushing them onto the stack. Finally, the subroutine must push the return address back onto the stack so that it will be there when the subroutine executes a return instruction.

A useful trick to implement this scheme is to use the two-instruction sequence POP H followed by XTHL. The POP instruction gets the return address into the HL register pair and moves SP to point at the first parameter (pair of bytes) on the stack. The XTHL instruction then swaps HL with the top of stack, thus removing the first parameter off the stack and replacing it with the return address. The procedure can be repeated until all the parameters have been removed from the stack.

An alternate technique works as follows. The calling routine pushes parameters onto the stack, creating a *stack frame,* and then calls the subroutine. The subroutine copies the content of the stack pointer to a register pair to be used as a pointer, for example, HL. The parameters can then be picked off the stack as needed, using, for example, MOV A,M.

Note that the subroutine does not remove parameters from the stack but only copies them into registers with MOVs. After the subroutine returns, the calling routine must POP off the stack the parameters it had PUSHed on before the call. If the calling routine expects to get a result passed back on the stack from the subroutine, then it must make a space for it by pushing a *dummy parameter* onto the stack before the call. The subroutine can then replace the dummy value with the actual result before returning.

Obviously, care must be taken to preserve the integrity of the stack when using it to pass parameters, as N pushes matched by N − 1 pops eventually spells *crash*.

4.3.5 Passing the Flag Bits

Often individual flag bits are used to pass status information from a subroutine back to the calling routine. A common practice is to use the carry bit (CY) to indicate an error condition. For example, if the subroutine executes normally, it will return with CY false (reset). If the subroutine could not complete its function because of some problem (e.g., attempted division by zero), it will return with CY true (set).

The carry can be set with the STC instruction. The 8085 does not have a corresponding clear-carry instruction, but CY can be reset several ways. If we know that CY is 1, we can complement it with CMC. We can use the arithmetic instruction SUI 0 or ADI 0 or even SUB A. We can use the logic instruction ANA A or OR A. Note that whereas STC and CMC affect only CY, the other instructions affect other flags and SUB A changes the accumulator. Arithmetic and logic instructions are discussed in sec. 4.5.

If there are several possible errors, the subroutine may return a code number in the accumulator to identify the specific error. Remember, this doesn't happen automatically; the programmer must write the appropriate code to implement such a scheme.

4.4 SOME SMOOTH MOVES

In this section we look at a few simple examples using instructions from the data transfer group as well as the IN and OUT instructions. Because a typical program spends 90 percent of its time doing moves, most processors have short, quick move instructions. The 8085 MOV r1,r2 instructions are 1 byte long.

4.4.1 Simple Register Moves

When trying to figure out what a piece of code does, it is a useful exercise to "play computer," meaning that as you read the instructions you also carry them out using pencil and paper. Just draw some boxes and label them with the names of the registers. Draw some additional boxes to represent memory locations. As you "execute" the instructions, write the appropriate values into the boxes, erasing any previous values. Try it in Example 4.3.

EXAMPLE 4.3

The program in Example 4.2 will swap the contents of registers B and C. The calling routine (MAIN) uses a 16-bit immediate move (immediate load) to initialize the stack pointer. It then uses 8-bit immediate moves to put two numbers into the B and C registers and calls SWAPBC to do the swap. After SWAPBC returns, the last instruction in MAIN is a halt. The processor would stop further execution until either an external reset or an interrupt occurred.

SWAPBC pushes PSW because it needs the accumulator as a working register. Remember that the call automatically pushed the return address on the stack, so pushing PSW displaces the return address stack position (actually, it's the stack pointer that's changed, but one usually thinks of things being "pushed down" the stack). Therefore, SWAPBC must pop PSW before it returns because the return address must be on top of the stack when RET is executed. SWAPBC uses register to register MOV instructions to do its work.

Note how the semicolons are aligned for the comments. A little extra care to make the program more readable is worth the effort.

4.4.2 Memory Moves and Pointers

Bytes can be moved back and forth between memory locations and registers, either directly or by means of pointers. Moving from memory to a register is called a *load;* moving from a register to memory is called a *store*. The term *directly* means the address is given in the instruction. The 8085 has the LDA and STA instructions to load and store the accumulator directly. Note that a direct address cannot be changed during execution because it is part of the instruction.

EXAMPLE 4.4

The short program here will load into the accumulator the content of memory location 0100h and then store it in location 0101h. The leading zeros are not required but they emphasize the 2-byte size of an address. Note that the last line is a *busy loop*. It is similar to a HALT instruction, but you can't get past it with an interrupt as you can from a HALT.

```
              LDA   0100H    ; MOVE BYTE INTO ACC
              STA   0101H    ; MOVE BYTE TO MEMORY
       HERE:  JMP   HERE     ; BUSY LOOP
```

Loading and storing may be done *indirectly,* meaning the address will not be part of the instruction but will be held in a pointer. Indirect addressing is much more useful than direct addressing because the address can be changed by the program during execution by changing the content of the pointer. The 8085 uses the HL register pair for most indirect moves, but BC and DE can be used for indirect loads and stores involving the accumulator. Also, the 8085 uses HL as a pointer for arithmetic and logic operations involving memory locations. Instructions that use HL as a pointer have the letter M (for memory) as an operand, such as MOV B,M. When using BC or DE, the accumulator can be loaded with the instructions LDAX B (uses BC) or LDAX D (uses DE). The corresponding store instructions are STAX B and STAX D.

There are several ways to get an address into HL. We can load H and L individually, either directly or from memory. We can use the LXI H,adr immediate load instruction, which puts the address adr into HL. HL can be loaded from memory using LHLD adr, which fetches the 16-bit number stored as 2 consecutive bytes at addresses adr and adr + 1 and loads it into HL. (The higher address byte goes into H and the lower address byte goes into L.) The complementary instruction is SHLD adr, which stores the contents of HL in memory. We can also swap the contents of HL and DE using XCHG, where DE may have been loaded using LXI D. The 8085 also has a special 1-byte instruction, XTHL, which swaps the top of the stack (i.e., the content of the 2 consecutive bytes in memory addressed by SP) with the contents of HL without affecting the stack pointer.

Once we have an address in HL, we can increment it to successively higher addresses using INX H and decrement it to successively lower addresses using DCX H. Likewise, the other register pairs can be incremented using INX B and INX D and decremented using DCX B and DCX D.

EXAMPLE 4.5

The program below reads in three characters from an input device and stores the first at memory location 1000h, the second at 1500h, and the third at 1200h. Equate statements are used to give names to the addresses and the port. Note the

```
        ;                       EQUATES
        PORT1   EQU     0F0H    ; INPUT DEVICE
        PNTR1   EQU     1000H   ; MEMORY POINTER 1
        PNTR2   EQU     1500H   ; MEMORY POINTER 2
        STACK   EQU     0F00H   ; TOP OF STACK


        ;                       MAIN PROGRAM

        MAIN:   LXI     SP,STACK    ; INITIALIZE STACK POINTER
                LXI     H,PNTR1     ; INITIALIZE HL
                LXI     B,PNTR2     ; INITIALIZE BC
                LXI     D,1200H     ; INITIALIZE DE
                CALL    CHAR        ; GET 1ST CHARACTER
                MOV     M,A         ; SAVE CHAR IN MEMORY
                CALL    CHAR        ; GET 2ND CHARACTER
                STAX    B           ; SAVE CHAR IN MEMORY
                CALL    CHAR        ; GET 3RD CHARACTER
                XCHG                ; EXCHANGE HL AND DE
                MOV     M,A         ; SAVE CHAR IN MEMORY

                            *
                            *
                            *

        CHAR:   IN      PORT1       ; INPUT CHAR FROM PORT
                RET                 ; RETURN
```

use of the leading zero for port address 0F0h. The assembler requires numbers to start with a digit. Strings starting with a letter, such as F0, would be interpreted as a name. Remember that equates are assembler directives (pseudo-operations) and do not translate into executable code. Note the use of separate comment lines, as well as comments at the end of instructions. Also note the use of blank lines. Blank lines are ignored by most assemblers and can be inserted for clarity.

Note the similarity of action of MOV M,A and STAX B. Also note the use of XCHG to swap the pointers in HL and DE so that the second time MOV M,A occurs, the character in the accumulator will be stored in location 1200h. Many assembly languages indicate indirect moves by the use of parentheses. Thus, MOV A, (HL) would be the equivalent of MOV A,M and MOV A, (BC) would be the equivalent of LDAX B.

4.5 A MODICUM OF MATH

In this section we look at a few example programs using the arithmetic instructions together with some conditional instructions. Remember, arithmetic (and logic) instructions *affect* the flags, whereas conditional instructions *test* the flags.

4.5.1 Simple Addition and Subtraction

EXAMPLE 4.6

```
        SUB   A           ;   INITIALIZE
        MVI   A,0FH       ;   PUT 0F IN ACC
        MVI   B,0F0H      ;   PUT F0 IN REG B
        ADD   B           ;   ADD B TO A
        ADI   01          ;   ADD ONE TO ACC
        SUI   00          ;   RESET CY
                  *
                  *
                  *
```

It is possible that before the program in Example 4.6 is executed, we have no idea as to the status of the flags or what is in the accumulator. The first instruction, however, subtracts the accumulator from itself. At that point we know the accumulator contains 00, as whatever was there before, A − A = 0. We also now know that the carry flag (CY) is 0 (reset) and the zero flag (Z) is 1 (set).

Next the program puts the number 0Fh in A and the number F0h in B. The content of B is then added to the content of A, leaving the number FFh in the accumulator, which is the largest number it can hold because FF hex = 11111111 binary. At this point both the carry and zero flags are low (reset). Then 01 is added immediately to the accumulator, causing its content to become 00 while also generating a carry, so both CY and Z are set. Finally, 0 is subtracted from the accumulator, which has no effect on the accumulator content but which does affect the flags. In particular, the Z flag stays set, but CY gets reset because the subtraction did not generate a carry.

It may seem that we could save a byte by replacing the 2-byte ADI 01 instruction with the 1-byte INR A inasmuch as they both add 1 to the accumulator. However, ADI affects the carry flag and INR does not. That may not seem important in this example, but in applications using conditional instructions that test the carry flag (e.g., JC), the distinction becomes crucial.

4.5.2 Including the Carry Bit

In Chapter 2 we said that the carry flag (CY) is like the "ninth bit" of the 8-bit accumulator. When the sum of adding two numbers is larger than 255 (FFh), or when a larger number is subtracted from a smaller one, the carry flag is set to 1. Otherwise, an arithmetic operation will reset CY to 0. Carry is essential for multiple-precision arithmetic, such as multiple-byte addition or subtraction. For addition, the *carry out* of one operation must be the *carry in* of the next. For subtraction, CY acts as a "borrow."

As an example, the instruction ADC M adds the number pointed to by the HL register pair to the accumulator. It also adds to the accumulator the value that was in CY just before the instruction was executed (consider CY as being 01h or 00h for the purpose of addition). After execution, CY may have a different value.

EXAMPLE 4.7

Just prior to execution of ADC M, assume that the accumulator contains 02 and the byte to be added (the one pointed to by HL) contains 03 and that the carry flag is set (CY = 1). After execution, the accumulator will contain 06 and carry will be reset (CY = 0). On the other hand, if CY had been 0 prior to execution, then the accumulator would have contained 05 after execution and CY would have stayed 0.

Now let's include the carry bit in a subtraction.

EXAMPLE 4.8

Assume that the accumulator contains 7. If the instruction SBI 2 (subtract with borrow immediate) is executed while CY is reset, the result will be 5 in the accumulator and CY will stay reset. If the same instruction is executed while CY is set, the result will be 4 in the accumulator; CY being set causes 1 to be "borrowed" from the accumulator before the 2 is subtracted. Again, CY will be reset at the end of the instruction because the number in the accumulator was bigger than what was being subtracted. If SBI 9 had been executed, CY would have been set because subtracting 9 from 7 requires a borrow. As to what will be in the accumulator, refer to Sec. 4.5.4.

4.5.3 Multiple-Byte Addition

EXAMPLE 4.9

```
        MAIN:      LXI    B,ADRN3   ; POINT TO LSB OF RESULT
                   LXI    D,ADRN1   ; POINT TO LSB OF NUMBR1
                   LXI    H,ADRN2   ; POINT TO LSB OF NUMBR2
                   SUB    A         ; CLEAR CARRY
                   CALL   ADDEM     ; ADD FIRST PAIR OF BYTES
                   CALL   ADDEM     ; ADD SECOND PAIR OF BYTES
                   CALL   ADDEM     ; ADD THIRD PAIR OF BYTES
                   CALL   ADDEM     ; ADD FOURTH PAIR OF BYTES
                                *
                                *
                                *
        ; SUBROUTINE ADDEM   ADD WITH CARRY TWO BYTES
        ; REQUIRES POINTERS IN BC, DE, HL
        ; POINTERS ARE INCREMENTED, SUM IS SAVED

        ADDEM:     LDAX   D         ; GET BYTE OF NUMBER 1
                   ADC    M         ; ADD BYTE OF NUMBER 2
                   STAX   B         ; SAVE RESULT
                   INX    B         ; INCREMENT
                   INX    D         ;    THE
                   INX    H         ; POINTERS
                   RET              ; RETURN FROM ADDEM
```

Consider the program in Example 4.9, which adds two 4-byte numbers together to get a 4-byte sum. When a byte from one number is added to the corresponding byte from the other number, it is possible that a carry is generated that must be included in the addition of the next pair of bytes. For that reason, the subroutine uses ADC M to add-with-carry. Also, ADDEM does not push the PSW because the state of CY has to be carried from one call to the next. Note that MAIN must clear CY before calling ADDEM for the first time. Also note that the INX instructions in ADDEM do not affect CY, or any other flags.

The program also demonstrates a typical use of pointers. The two numbers to be added are held in memory locations. Four consecutive bytes are used for each number, with the least significant byte held in the lowest address. The result will also be held in 4 consecutive bytes, also with the LSB in the lowest address. Three pointers are used: BC, DE, and HL. The BC register pair holds the address of the first (lowest) byte of the resultant sum, the DE register pair holds the address of the first byte of the first 4-byte number, and the HL register pair holds the address of the first byte of the second 4-byte number.

The calling routine (MAIN) *initializes* the pointers and the subroutine *increments* them. The subroutine also saves the result. The exact division of labor between calling routine and subroutine depends on the application, how general or specific you want the subroutine to be, and how much detail you want to hide in the subroutine.

4.5.4 Subtraction and Two's Complement

When the 8085 carries out a subtraction instruction such as SUB C, it actually does a mathematical trick. Instead of *subtracting* the number from the accumulator, it *adds* the two's complement of the number to the accumulator. The *two's complement* of a binary number is formed by first changing all the 1s to 0s and the 0s to 1s, which forms the *one's complement*. The next step is to add 1 to the one's complement. The result is the two's complement.

> **EXAMPLE 4.10**
>
> If a register holds 00111001, the one's complement is 11000110 and the two's complement is 11000111.

When a smaller number is subtracted from a bigger number, the result left in the accumulator will be the difference and the carry flag will be reset. However, if a bigger number is subtracted from a smaller number, the carry flag will be set and the number in the accumulator will be the two's complement of the difference (see Fig. 4.3). Thus, if a subtraction sets CY but we just want to know the magnitude of the difference, we will have to take the two's complement of the accumulator to get it. To take the two's complement of the accumulator, first form the one's complement with the CMA instruction and then add 1.

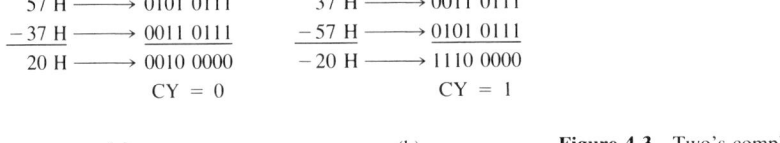

```
  57 H ⟶ 0101 0111          37 H ⟶ 0011 0111
 -37 H ⟶ 0011 0111         -57 H ⟶ 0101 0111
  20 H ⟶ 0010 0000         -20 H ⟶ 1110 0000
          CY = 0                    CY = 1

         (a)                        (b)
```

Figure 4.3 Two's complement.

4.5.5 16-Bit Operations

Other than INX and DCX, the only 16-bit arithmetic operation the 8085 supports is addition. The DAD instruction will add the content of a 16-bit register pair to the content of the HL pair and the result is left in HL. Only the carry flag is affected by DAD. As we saw earlier, INX and DCX affect no flags, so they can be used to advance pointers without affecting CY or Z.

An important use for DAD is to implement a base-displacement type of addressing. For example, suppose we have a table of 256 consecutive bytes stored in memory. To get the address of a particular byte in the table, we would have to add the 8-bit number of the byte (the displacement) to the 16-bit address of the first byte in the table (the base).

EXAMPLE 4.11

```
LXI   H,TABLE    ; ADDRESS OF TABLE
MVI   B,0        ; UPPER 8-BITS = 0
MVI   C,DSPL     ; DISPLACEMENT
DAD   B          ; BYTE ADDRESS
MOV   A,M        ; GET THE BYTE

      < REST OF PROGRAM >
```

The 8085 has no 16-bit register to register move instructions as such, but we can get the same effect using PUSH and POP instructions. For example, to do the equivalent of MOV HL,BC (an instruction that doesn't exist) we would use the instruction PUSH B followed by POP H.

4.5.6 Signed Numbers

The most significant bit (MSB) of the accumulator, bit 7, can be interpreted as a *sign bit*. The sign bit is the S flag. If the sign bit is 0, the number is positive; if the sign bit is 1, the number is negative. Only 7 bits are left for the magnitude. The number 01111111 is +127. The number 00000000 is zero. However, negative numbers contain the two's complement of the magnitude in the lower 7 bits. The signed number 11111111 represents −1, and 10000000 is −128.

When performing arithmetic operations on signed numbers, the programmer must be careful to watch the interactions of the S and CY flags. For example, if +1 and +1 (00000001 and 00000001) are added, the result is 00000010, or +2. The sign bit is correct and CY is reset. On the other hand, it is possible that two

TABLE 4.1 RESULTS OF ARITHMETIC ON SIGNED NUMBERS IN THE RANGE +127 TO −128

Operation	S	CY	Meaning
Add two positive numbers	0	0	Result OK
(S = 0 is positive)	0	1	Can't happen
(S = 1 is negative)	1	0	Overflow
	1	1	Can't happen
Add two negative numbers	0	0	Can't happen
	0	1	Overflow
	1	0	Can't happen
	1	1	Result OK
Add positive and negative numbers (subtraction)	0	0	Can't happen
	0	1	Result OK and is positive
	1	0	Result OK and is negative
	1	1	Can't happen

positive numbers, such as +127 and +1 (01111111 and 00000001) are added. The result is 10000000. Although CY is reset, the sign bit of the result is negative, so something is wrong. The explanation is that the magnitude of the result was bigger than 7 bits and an overflow occurred into the sign bit.

Likewise, if two negative numbers are added, such as −1 and −1 (11111111 and 11111111), the result will be 11111110. Note that even though CY is set, no overflow has occurred as the result is −2 in two's complement. On the other hand, adding −128 and −1 (10000000 and 11111111) will give 01111111. Now the sign bit indicates positive and CY is true. Taken together, they indicate an overflow. See Table 4.1.

When comparing signed numbers remember that compare instructions do not "look at" the S flag; they just compare one 8-bit binary number to another. Because the sign bit is actually the MSB of the accumulator, negative numbers (MSB = 1) will always look greater than positive numbers (MSB = 0) when compared.

4.6 A LITTLE LOGIC

In this section we look at the logic operations compare, AND, OR, and XOR (exclusive-OR) together with the concept of masking.

4.6.1 Using Compare

There are four key points to remember about *compare:*

1. Compare is a "dummy subtraction": the flags are affected as if a subtraction had occurred, but *no register contents change*.
2. Comparisons in the 8085 are made with respect to the accumulator: the "dummy subtraction" is from the accumulator.
3. If the numbers being compared are *equal*, Z is set; if they are *not equal*, Z is reset. In other words, Z acts like an *equal* flag.
4. If the number in the accumulator is *greater than* or *equal to* the compared number, CY is reset; if the number in the accumulator is *less than* the compared number, CY is set. Note that if *both* CY and Z are low, the number in the accumulator is *greater than*.

The 8085 has instructions to compare the accumulator with the content of a register, a memory location, or an immediate number.

> **EXAMPLE 4.12**
>
> The use of compare is shown in the program here, which uses a subroutine to find the bigger of two numbers. The program MAIN loads two numbers into registers B and C and calls BIGR, which returns the bigger number in the accumulator. Note that B and C remain unchanged. BIGR first moves the content of

B to the accumulator and then compares the accumulator to the content of C using CMP C.

```
MAIN:       LXI     H,PNTR      ; LOAD POINTER
            MOV     B,M         ; GET FIRST NUMBER
            INX     H           ; INCREMENT POINTER
            MOV     C,M         ; GET SECOND NUMBER
            CALL    BIGR        ; GET BIGGER NUMBER IN A

                     *
                     *
                     *

BIGR:       MOV     A,B         ; GET FIRST NUMBER
            CMP     C           ; COMPARE TO SECOND NUMBER
            RNC                 ; RETURN IF FIRST BIGGER
            MOV     A,C         ; GET SECOND NUMBER
            RET                 ; SECOND IS BIGGER
```

Remember that compare is a "dummy subtraction"; it doesn't change the accumulator, but it does affect the flags as if a subtraction had occurred (in this case A − C). During subtraction, the carry flag acts like a "borrow" flag. If *no* carry is generated (CY stays 0), then the content of the accumulator must be *equal to* or *greater than* the content of the register. If a carry *is* generated, then the number in the accumulator is *smaller than* the number in the register, causing a "borrow." Thus, if the CMP instruction does *not* generate a carry, then the number in the accumulator is the bigger number (or the numbers are equal).

The next instruction in BIGR is a return-no-carry (RNC), which will cause BIGR to return to MAIN (with a copy of the content of B still in the accumulator) if carry is false (CY = 0). If a carry *was* generated, then RNC will *not* cause a return. Carry being true tells us that the number in C must be bigger, so the next instruction is MOV A,C followed by an unconditional return (RET).

4.6.2 ANDing and Masking

The basic AND function is summarized in the truth table in Table 4.2, where the 2 bits being ANDed are b1 and b2 and the result is r. (Truth tables are sometimes written with T replacing 1 and F replacing 0.) Note that if b1 is 0, then r will also

TABLE 4.2 TRUTH TABLE FOR EXAMPLE AND FUNCTIONS

| \multicolumn{3}{c}{$r = b1 \cdot b2$} |
b1	b2	r
0	0	0
0	1	0
1	0	0
1	1	1

be 0 regardless of whether b2 is 0 or 1. On the other hand, if b1 is 1, then the value of r will be equal to the value of b2. That idea is central to the technique of masking (discussed below). A dot is customarily used to indicate AND, so the operation can be written as the equation $r = b1 \cdot b2$.

The 8085 has instructions to AND the accumulator with the content of a register, a memory location, or an immediate number. The operation is done on a bit-by-bit basis. Each bit in the accumulator is ANDed with the corresponding bit in the other number, and the result is left in the accumulator.

EXAMPLE 4.13

If the accumulator held 11010101 and register B held 11110000, then the instruction ANA B would leave 11010000 in the accumulator (the content of B would be unchanged).

An important use of the AND operation is *masking*. A specific bit or group of bits can be selectively examined by "masking off" the unwanted bits. We do that by ANDing the target byte with an appropriately chosen *mask* byte.

EXAMPLE 4.14

Suppose a byte is in the accumulator and all we want to know is whether the first and last bits (bit 7 and bit 0) are both low. The other 6 bits are don't cares. The mask would be the binary number 10000001, which is hexadecimal 81. We could use the immediate AND instruction ANI 81H to leave only the first and last bits of the accumulator untouched while causing the middle 6 bits to contain 0s (refer to Table 4.2). Because logic instructions affect the flags, we could use a conditional instruction that tests the zero flag, such as JZ, to determine if the 2 bits being tested are both low. If they are, then all the bits in the accumulator will be 0s and the Z flag will be set. If either bit 7 or bit 0 is high, then Z will be reset.

4.6.3 Masking and Compare

In Example 4.14 we tested the results of masking by looking at the zero flag. That works when we just want to know if a single bit is high or low. It also works if we want to see if several bits are all low at the same time. However, if we want to test a group of bits to see if it matches a certain pattern (other than all 0s), we will have to use a compare instruction after masking and then test the flags.

EXAMPLE 4.15

The program here could be used in a computerized lock. A person wishing to open the lock would insert a magnetically encoded card into a reader. The card reader would extract an 8-bit code off the card, which would then be read from an input port and compared to the correct combination. If the code is correct, the lock is opened. If the wrong code is entered, an alarm would sound.

```
                    *
                    *
                    *
    MASK   EQU   0FH       ; MASK = 00001111
    KEY    EQU   09        ; COMBINATION = 1001

           IN    LOCK      ; READ KEY CARD
           ANI   MASK      ; GET LOWER 4 BITS
           CPI   KEY       ; COMPARE TO COMBINATION
           JNZ   L1        ; JUMP IF NO MATCH
           MVI   A,02      ; IT MATCHED, OPEN
           JMP   L2        ; GO DO IT
    L1:    MVI   A,01      ; NO MATCH, ALARM
    L2:    OUT   DRVRS     ; OPEN OR ALARM
                    *
                    *
                    *
```

The program reads a byte from the input port labeled LOCK. The actual code is in the lower 4 bits and the correct combination is 1001. The output port DRVRS is connected to relay drivers: Bit 0 will open the lock when high and bit 1 will turn on an alarm when high.

4.6.4 ORing

The basic OR function is summarized in the truth table in Table 4.3, where the 2 bits being ORed are b1 and b2 and the result is r. Note that if b1 is 1, then r will be 1 regardless of whether b2 is 0 or 1. On the other hand, if b1 is 0, then the value of r will be equal to the value of b2. Compare Tables 4.3 and 4.2. A plus sign is customarily used to indicate OR, so the operation can be written as the equation r = b1 + b2.

The 8085 has instructions to OR the accumulator with the content of a register, a memory location, or an immediate number. The operation is done on a bit-by-bit basis. Each bit in the accumulator is ORed with the corresponding bit in the other number, and the result is left in the accumulator.

TABLE 4.3 TRUTH TABLE FOR EXAMPLE OR FUNCTION

\multicolumn{3}{c}{r = b1 + b2}
b1	b2	r
0	0	0
0	1	1
1	0	1
1	1	1

EXAMPLE 4.16

If the accumulator held 11010101 and register B held 11110000, then the instruction ORA B would leave 11110101 in the accumulator (the content of B would be unchanged).

4.6.5 XORing and Complementing

The basic XOR function is summarized in the truth table in Table 4.4, where the 2 bits being ORed are b1 and b2 and the result is r. Note that if b1 is 1, then r will be the opposite of b2. On the other hand, if b1 is 0, then the value of r will be equal to the value of b2. Another way to view it is that r will be false (0) when b1 and b2 are equal but r will be true (1) when b1 and b2 are different. Think of it as "one or the other but not both." Compare Tables 4.3 and 4.4. A plus sign inside a circle is customarily used to indicate XOR, so the operation can be written as the equation $r = b1 \oplus b2$.

The 8085 has instructions to XOR the accumulator with the content of a register, a memory location, or an immediate number. The operation is done on a bit-by-bit basis. Each bit in the accumulator is XORed with the corresponding bit in the other number, and the result is left in the accumulator.

EXAMPLE 4.17

If the accumulator held 11010101 and register B held 11110000, then the instruction XRA B would leave 00100101 in the accumulator (the content of B would be unchanged).

In the example, the upper 4 bits of the number in the accumulator were *complemented* (changed to the opposite state). Complementing, also called *inverting*, is an important use of XOR; any bit or group of bits can be complemented by XORing with the appropriate pattern (remember, 1 XOR 1 is 0 and 1 XOR 0 is 1). If

TABLE 4.4 TRUTH TABLE FOR EXAMPLE XOR FUNCTION

$r = b1 \oplus b2$		
b1	b2	r
0	0	0
0	1	1
1	0	1
1	1	0

an 8-bit number is XORed with itself, the result is all zeros, so the instruction XRA A is often used to clear the accumulator (it also clears the CY, Z, and AC flags).

To complement the entire accumulator, you could XOR it with 11111111 (FFh) using the instruction XRI OFFH, but the 8085 has a separate instruction just for that purpose: CMA. If the accumulator held 11001100 before executing CMA, it would hold 00110011 afterward. Complementing is equivalent to the logic operation NOT. That is, NOT 1 = 0 and NOT 0 = 1. The NOT operation is often shown as a bar above a variable, so NOT a = ā.

4.6.6 Bit Manipulation

Microprocessors are commonly used in control applications, such as machine control, robotics, industrial control, process control, HVAC (heating, ventilating, and air-conditioning), and SCADA (supervisory control and data acquisition). In such applications, a microprocessor must determine the state of the thing being controlled and then decide what, if any, action to take. For example, a microprocessor may periodically read the room temperature and then turn on either the heater or the air-conditioner.

Many of the inputs and outputs in a control application require only a single bit, as they can only be either on or off. Switches, thermostats, LEDs, relays, buzzers, solenoids, and motors are examples. All these inputs and outputs have to be connected to the I/O ports, typically using special driver or isolator circuits (see Chapter 6). Because a typical I/O port is 8 bits wide, it is very useful to be able to turn individual bits on and off independent of the adjacent bits. We can do that with ANDing and ORing.

ORing with a 1 always sets a bit: 1 OR x = 1. On the other hand, ORing a bit with 0 does not change it: 0 OR x = x. In order to force individual bits in the accumulator to 1 without changing other bits, OR it with a number that has 1s in the bit positions you want to force high and 0s in the other bit positions.

ANDing with a 0 always resets a bit: 0 AND x = 0. On the other hand, ANDing a bit with 1 does not change it: 1 AND x = x. In order to force individual bits in the accumulator to 0 without changing other bits, AND it with a number that has 0s in the bit positions you want to force low and 1s in the other bit positions.

EXAMPLE 4.18

Consider a microprocessor-based controller for traffic signal lights. Figure 4.4a shows a diagram of a string of such lights all connected to a common cable that is coming from an I/O port on the controller through an appropriate driver. When a byte is sent out the port, all the signal lights will read it. The upper 6 bits of the byte are used to form an address, and the lower 2 bits are used for a signal command, as shown in Fig. 4.4b. Each signal light contains circuitry to decode the byte and recognize its own address and the command. The fragment of code

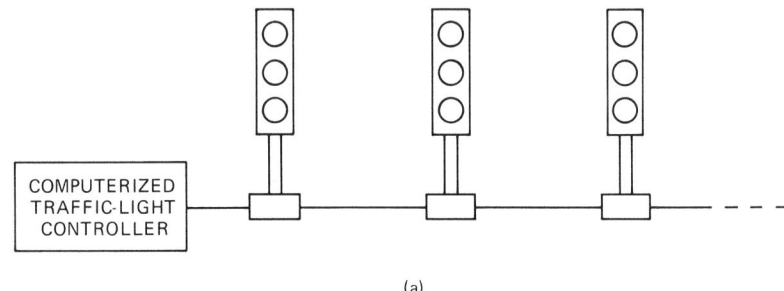

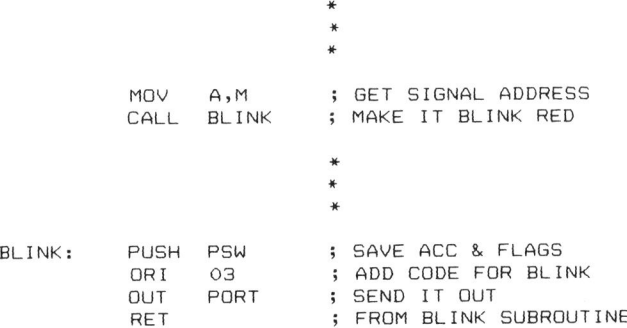

Figure 4.4 Microprocessor-based controller for traffic signal lights.

shown in the program here will get the address of a particular light from memory and then put the light into blink mode.

```
              *
              *
              *
       MOV    A,M          ; GET SIGNAL ADDRESS
       CALL   BLINK        ; MAKE IT BLINK RED
              *
              *
              *
BLINK: PUSH   PSW          ; SAVE ACC & FLAGS
       ORI    03           ; ADD CODE FOR BLINK
       OUT    PORT         ; SEND IT OUT
       RET                 ; FROM BLINK SUBROUTINE
```

4.7 JUMP AROUND THE LOOP

One of the most common programming techniques is *looping* to repeat, or *iterate*, execution of a section of the program. Iteration can be done simply by writing the same code *in line* as many times as needed, as shown in the following program.

```
            MOV   A,M
            OUT   PORT
            INX   H
            MOV   A,M
            OUT   PORT
            INX   H
            MOV   A,M
            OUT   PORT
            INX   H
                 *
                 *
                 *
```

Although it runs fast, in-line iteration can take up a lot of memory if it is repeated many times. Looping allows a block of code to be written once and executed many times by branching back to the beginning of it. The branching may be unconditional or conditional. Various conditions can be used to terminate the loop, such as reaching a preset *loop count* or encountering a special value in the accumulator, such as an *end-of-line* (EOL) character or an *end-of-file* (EOF) character. The specific characters used for EOF and EOL depend on the application.

4.7.1 Continuous Loops

The simplest loop is one that does not terminate. Such a loop is often used for programs that must run continuously, such as control programs.

EXAMPLE 4.19

The program here shows a continuous loop using an unconditional branch instruction (JUMP).

```
        LOOP:    NOP              ; BEGINNING OF PROGRAM
                 < REST OF PROGRAM >
                 JMP   LOOP       ; KEEP DOING IT
```

4.7.2 Loop Counting

A common type of loop is implemented by loading a count into a register and then decrementing the register each time the block of instructions inside the loop is executed. When the count gets to zero, the program *falls through* (exits) the loop.

EXAMPLE 4.20

The program in this example moves a block of 128 bytes from one part of memory to another. Note the use of pointers.

```
            MVI    C,128        ; INITIALIZE LOOP COUNTER
            LXI    H, 1000H     ; START OF 'FROM' AREA
            LXI    D, 2000H     ; START OF 'TO' AREA
    LOOP:   MOV    A,M          ; GET A BYTE
            STAX   D            ; PUT A BYTE
            INX    H            ; INCREMENT 'FROM' POINTER
            INX    D            ; INCREMENT 'TO' POINTER
            DCR    C            ; DECREMENT LOOP COUNT
            JNZ    LOOP         ; JUMP IF NOT DONE
            NOP                 ; EXIT LOOP HERE
                                 *
                                 *
                                 *
```

A word of caution: If the loop count number is not fixed but is read in, for example, from a port, then the loop counting procedure used in the program in Example 4.20 will not work. The problem is that, as written, the procedure *first* executes the code and *then* decrements the count. Because the count is a variable, it may have zero as a value. But if we decrement 00h we get FFh, so the JNZ instruction that tests the loop count will jump and we will iterate the loop an additional 255 times before we get back to zero and terminate! The problem can be fixed by checking the loop count for zero *before* using it.

EXAMPLE 4.21

The program here adds 1 to the loop count before entering the loop and then decrements and tests inside the loop *before* executing the code.

```
            LXI    H, 1000H     ; START OF 'FROM' AREA
            LXI    D, 2000H     ; START OF 'TO' AREA
            IN     PORT         ; GET LOOP COUNT
            INR    A            ; ADD 1 TO COUNT
            MOV    C,A          ; SET UP COUNT REG
    LOOP:   DCR    C            ; DECREMENT LOOP COUNT
            JZ     DONE         ; JUMP IF FINISHED
            MOV    A,M          ; GET  BYTE
            STAX   D            ; PUT  BYTE
            INX    H            ; INCREMENT 'FROM' POINTER
            INX    D            ; INCREMENT 'TO' POINTER
            JMP    LOOP         ; GO TEST FOR DONE
    DONE:   NOP                 ; EXIT LOOP HERE
                                 *
                                 *
                                 *
```

4.7.3 Conditional Loops

Instead of using a loop counter, it is often necessary to loop until a certain condition is met. For example, many programs use a single subroutine to send messages to a display such as a CRT. The messages, of course, may be different lengths, so we can't use a fixed loop count. However, if we end each message with a special character we can loop until that character is encountered.

EXAMPLE 4.22

This program uses '$' as an EOL character.

```
                        *
                        *
                        *
              LXI  H,MSGE_1   ; ADDRESS OF MESSAGE 1
              CALL DSPLY      ; DISPLAY MESSAGE
                        *
                        *
                        *
    DSPLY:    PUSH PSW        ; SAVE ACC & FLAGS
    DLOOP:    MOV  A,M        ; GET A CHAR
              CPI  '$'        ; END OF MESSAGE?
              JZ   DONE       ; YES, SO RETURN
              OUT  DISP       ; NO, SO DISPLAY CHAR
              INX  H          ; POINT TO NEXT CHAR
              JMP  DLOOP      ; GO GET CHAR

    DONE:     POP PSW         ; RESTORE ACC & FLAGS
              RET             ; FROM DSPLY
                        *
                        *
                        *
    MSGE_1    DB     'THIS IS MESSAGE 1 $'
    MSGE_2    DB     'SECOND MESSAGE $'
                        *
                        *
                        *
```

4.7.4 Timing Loops

The measurement and/or generation of time intervals, either exact or approximate, is a common requirement in many applications. Oftentimes the function is done by a peripheral chip designed for the purpose. However, simple timing jobs can be done in software using loops. For example, a printer controller may want to wait 1 sec after sending a carriage-return line-feed sequence (CR-LF) in order to allow the printhead to physically move back before printing more characters. After sending CR-LF, the controller program could call a subroutine that just kills time by executing a loop for 1 sec.

Each instruction in a loop takes a certain amount of time to execute. Those times are added to get the time for one complete loop. That time is then multiplied by the number of times the loop is executed to give the total time. Chapter 2 gives the number of T states for each 8085 instruction. Multiply the time for one T state by the number of T states to get the execution time for an instruction. Remember that the time for one T state is $1/f$, where f is the CPU clock frequency.

EXAMPLE 4.23

How long does it take for this loop to execute? Assume a 1-Mhz clock. (*Note:* The MVI is not part of the loop.)

```
            MVI   C, 3
LOOP:  NOP
       DCR   C
       JNZ   LOOP
```

SOLUTION The length of one T state is 1/1 MHz = 1 μsec. Looking up the number of T states for each instruction and multiplying by the number of times it is executed (iterations), we find

Instruction	T States	Iterations	Subtotals
NOP	4	3	12
DCR C	4	3	12
JNZ (jumps)	10	2	20
JNZ (no jump)	7	1	7
Total			51 T states

Loop time = 51 T states × 1 μsec/T state = 51 μsec.

Consider the subroutine DELAY in the following program. DELAY uses a loop within a loop. Each time the MVI C,NUM2 instruction is executed, the inner loop will execute repeatedly until C contains 00. The process will be repeated for each iteration of the outer loop. The total number of times that the inner loop executes is equal to the product of NUM1 and NUM2. For example, if NUM1 is 3 and NUM2 is 4 the inner loop will execute 12 times. Thus, the time DELAY takes to execute has three levels of control: a coarse adjustment using B, a fine adjustment using C, and a very fine adjustment (a tweak) by adding or subtracting NOPs from the inner loop.

```
DELAY:   PUSH   PSW         ; SAVE ACC & FLAGS
         MVI    B,NUM1      ; INITIALIZE OLOOP COUNTER
OLOOP:   MVI    C,NUM2      ; INITIALIZE ILOOP COUNTER

ILOOP:   DCR    C           ; DEC INNER LOOP COUNT
         NOP                ; KILL TIME
         NOP                ; KILL TIME
         NOP                ; KILL TIME
         JNZ    ILOOP       ; INNER LOOP JUMP

         DCR    B           ; DEC OUTER LOOP COUNT
         JNZ    OLOOP       ; OUTER LOOP JUMP

         POP    PSW         ; RESTORE ACC & FLAGS
         RET                ; FROM DELAY
```

Sometimes different manufacturers will make similar CPU chips that execute the same instruction set but with different numbers of clock pulses. An example pair is the Intel 8088 and the faster NEC V20. Unless the program is changed accordingly, timing loops will take less time when executing on the faster processor. Also, many 16-bit and 32-bit microprocessors use sophisticated architectures that can overlap the execution of instructions. In such processors, timing analysis is more complicated and may have to be done empirically (i.e., you measure it while the software runs).

4.8 CONTROL STRUCTURE

As mentioned earlier, programs are often designed at an abstract level using a structured design language to describe the algorithms involved—either a real language such as PASCAL or a pseudo-language. The flow of program execution can then be described by a small number of high-level control structures.

Control structures usually involve testing conditions that have a *Boolean* value—that is, they are either true or false. In high-level languages, such control structures exist as instructions in the language. In assembly language, they are constructs that must be implemented using the instructions available. We have already seen control structures at work but didn't know them by name.

4.8.1 IF-THEN-ELSE

The structure IF ⟨*condition*⟩ THEN ⟨*routine1*⟩ ELSE ⟨*routine2*⟩ will execute the code in routine 1 only if the condition is true. Otherwise, it executes the code in routine 2. The code designated routine 1 could be a subroutine, a block of code, or just a single line and likewise for routine 2. If there is no routine 2, it is an IF-THEN statement; that is, the ELSE part is optional. In assembly, the condition is the state of a flag bit that is tested with a conditional branch or a conditional call.

> **EXAMPLE 4.24**
>
> An IF-THEN-ELSE can be found in the subroutine BIGR in the program in Example 4.12. It can be read as IF B is bigger than C THEN return with B ELSE return with C.

4.8.2 FOR-DO

FOR ⟨*counter*⟩ = ⟨*first value*⟩ TO ⟨*last value*⟩ DO ⟨*routine*⟩ is the format of a FOR-DO loop. The counter is usually a register that initially contains the number *first value*. Each time the code in routine is executed, the counter is either incremented by 1 (if counting up) or decremented by 1 (if counting down). When counter equals *last value*, the looping stops and the code following the loop is executed.

Although it is possible to terminate a FOR-DO loop prematurely (before counter reaches last value) by branching out, it defeats the idea of using a structured approach. Premature termination is sometimes justified in order to branch to an error-handling routine in case of a severe error encountered while executing routine.

EXAMPLE 4.25

A FOR-DO loop is found in the program in Example 4.20, where register C is the counter with first value equal to 128 and last value equal to 0. The code from MOV A,M to INX D is the routine. Note that the instructions DCR C and JNZ LOOP are part of the loop structure.

4.8.3 WHILE-DO

The format of a WHILE-DO loop is WHILE ⟨condition⟩ DO *routine*. While the condition is true, the routine is executed. If the condition is false, the loop is terminated. Note that the condition is tested *before* each iteration of the loop. If the condition is false to begin with, the WHILE-DO loop will not execute at all.

EXAMPLE 4.26

A WHILE-DO loop is found in the program in Example 4.21, where the condition is that register C not contain 0. In other words, the statement "C does not contain 0" must be true for the loop to execute each iteration.

4.8.4 REPEAT-UNTIL

The structure REPEAT ⟨routine⟩ UNTIL ⟨condition⟩ is similar to the WHILE-DO loop except that the condition is checked *after* each iteration of routine. Loop execution is terminated when the condition is true. Note that, in contrast to a WHILE-DO loop, a REPEAT-UNTIL loop always executes at least once.

EXAMPLE 4.27

A REPEAT-UNTIL is shown below.

```
        LOOP:   IN   PORT1      ; GET FIRST BYTE
                MOV  B,A        ; SAVE IT
                IN   PORT2      ; GET SECOND BYTE
                ADD  B          ; ADD BOTH BYTES
                OUT  PORT3      ; SEND RESULT
                CPI  EOF        ; FINISHED?
                JNZ  LOOP       ; NO, PLAY IT AGAIN SAM
```

4.8.5 CASE-OF

A CASE statement is a generalized IF-THEN structure.

EXAMPLE 4.28

The action in the program here is that if variable equals value 1, then routine 1 is executed, if variable equals value 2, then routine 2 is executed, and so forth. If variable equals none of the listed values, then the default routine is executed.

(Not all versions of a CASE statement include an ELSE.) Note that only one of the routines will be executed for each execution of the CASE structure. It is left as an exercise for the reader to write an assembly language CASE structure, but first read Sec. 4.11.3, on jump tables.

```
CASE <variable> OF
  value1 : routine1
  value2 : routine2
  value3 : routine3
         *
         *
         *
  valueN : routineN
  ELSE   : default-routine
ENDCASE
```

4.9 ROTATES AND SHIFTS

It is useful for a processor to be able to move the contents of a register 1 or more bits to the left or right. If the bit shifted *out* one end of the register is also shifted *in* the other end, then the operation is a *rotate*. The 8085 does not have any pure shifts, but it does have two kinds of rotates, both of which affect CY. One kind rotates the 8-bit accumulator and the other includes CY for a 9-bit rotation. See Fig. 4.5.

RLC

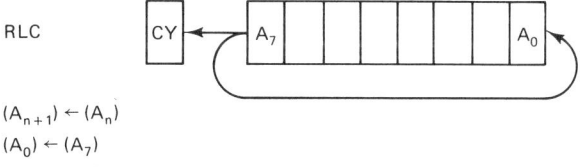

$(A_{n+1}) \leftarrow (A_n)$
$(A_0) \leftarrow (A_7)$
$(CY) \leftarrow (A_7)$

Figure 4.5 8085 rotates.

4.9.1 RLC and RRC

RLC is the instruction for *rotate accumulator left*, and RRC means *rotate accumulator right*. (Yes, you're right; they ought to be RAL and RAR, but they're not!) Both instructions will move a copy of the rotated bit into the carry flag (CY).

EXAMPLE 4.29

Assume the accumulator contains 00001111 and CY is 0. If RRC is executed, the accumulator will then contain 10000111 and CY will be 1. If the next instruction is RLC, then the accumulator will go back to 00001111 but CY will still be 1, as the 1 that is rotated out of the MSB and back into the LSB is also copied to CY. If another RLC is executed, then the accumulator will contain 00011110 and CY will be 0. Note how a rotate causes each bit in the accumulator to be "bumped over" to the adjacent bit position while the bit that gets "pushed out" the end just "wraps around" to fill in the empty position at the other end. A copy of the "pushed-out" bit is placed in CY.

4.9.2 RAL and RAR

RAL is the instruction for *rotate accumulator left through carry*, and RAR means *rotate accumulator right through carry*. RAL and RAR are similar to RLC and RRC but include the carry bit for a 9-bit rotation.

EXAMPLE 4.30

Assume the accumulator contains 11111111 and CY is 0. If RAR is executed, the accumulator will then contain 01111111 and CY will be 1. If the next instruction is RAL, then the accumulator will contain 11111111 again and CY will be back to 0.

4.9.3 Why Rotate?

A common use for rotates is to test a specific accumulator bit. For example, the program here reads a byte from a port. If bit 2 of that byte is high, then we want to call the subroutine; otherwise, we go back and read the port again. Instead of masking and testing, we will rotate the bit into CY and use a jump-no-carry.

```
LOOP:     IN    PORT1    ; GET BYTE
          RRC            ; GET BIT2
          RRC            ; INTO
          RRC            ; CY BIT
          JNC   LOOP     ; JUMP IF BIT2 LO

          CALL  SUB      ; CALL SUB IF BIT2 HI

                *
                *
                *
```

In the 8085, rotates can be used to simulate shift instructions. RAR and RAL can be used to act like shifts if we make sure that CY contains the right value before rotating. For logic shifts, CY should be reset to 0 (using, for example, SUI 0) before each rotate so that as bits are shifted out one end, zeros are shifted in the other end. For arithmetic shifts, CY should be reset to 0 before rotating left, but CY should be made equal to the MSB before rotating right. An arithmetic shift right propagates the sign bit, meaning that as bits get shifted out the LSB (into the proverbial bit bucket), all the higher order bits are moved to the right one position but the MSB retains its value.

EXAMPLE 4.31

If 10000111 was shifted right arithmetically, it would become 11000011.

A common use of shifts is multiplying or dividing a binary number by powers of 2. Each shift to the left multiplies by 2, and each shift to the right divides by 2.

> **EXAMPLE 4.32**
>
> If N = 00000100, then N = 4.
>
> Shift N left 1 bit (to 00001000) and N = 8.
> Shift N right 1 bit (to 00000010) and N = 2.

Another use for rotates is to swap the upper and lower 4-bit halves (nibbles) of the accumulator.

> **EXAMPLE 4.33**
>
> Assume the accumulator contains 00001111. After executing the four instructions RRC, RRC, RRC, and RRC, the accumulator will contain 11110000. (Note that four RLCs would do the same thing.)

4.10 BINARY CODED DECIMAL (BCD)

Because they are built with on/off circuits, computers naturally work with binary numbers, and because they are built with 10 fingers, most people naturally work with decimal numbers. In order to get a processor to deal with decimal numbers, the numbers must be encoded as groups of bits, as in *binary coded decimal* (BCD). BCD consists of a group of 4 bits with the binary weighting, left to right, of 8 4 2 1. Many I/O devices, such as thumbwheel switches and digital displays, use data in the form of BCD numbers.

> **EXAMPLE 4.34**
>
> Decimal 5 has the BCD code 0101; 9 has the code 1001.

Because 4 bits can be arranged 16 different ways (0000 to 1111) and there are only 10 decimal digits (0 to 9), some 4-bit combinations are not legal BCD codes: They are 1010, 1011, 1100, 1101, 1110, and 1111. The ALU in a typical processor cannot tell the difference between a BCD number and any other 4-bit binary number, so arithmetic operations on BCD numbers are liable to give results that are not legal in BCD. For BCD addition, the 8085 has the DAA instruction to "fix up" the results. Unfortunately, the 8085 DAA does not work for subtraction, so the "fix-up" must be done by the programmer, as we will see in an example.

4.10.1 Packed and Unpacked BCD

Inasmuch as a BCD number requires only 4 bits and there are 8 bits in a byte, we can store two BCD numbers per byte as *packed* BCD.

> **EXAMPLE 4.35**
>
> The 8-bit number 10010110 (96h) contains the packed BCD digits 9 and 6. Note that in a packed BCD number, the digit encoded in the upper 4 bits is worth 10 times as much as the digit encoded in the lower 4 bits.

If a byte contains a single BCD number in the lower 4 bits (the upper 4 bits are typically 0000), it is *unpacked* BCD. BCD numbers can be held in registers or memory locations in either packed or unpacked form. Packed is more convenient for multibyte arithmetic. The routine in the following program assumes that registers B and C contain unpacked BCD numbers with the more significant digit in B. The upper 4 bits of each are zeros. The program combines them into packed BCD in the accumulator.

```
            MOV   A,B      ; GET HIGH BCD
            RLC            ; SHIFT
            RLC            ; LOWER 4 BITS
            RLC            ; INTO
            RLC            ; UPPER 4 BITS
            ORA   C        ; PACK LOW BCD
                           *
                           *
                           *
```

4.10.2 Converting BCD to Binary

If a microprocessor reads a value from an input device, it is often a BCD number. If the value is to be used in a calculation, it may first have to be converted to a binary number. The subroutine in the following program (BCD2BN) inputs a two-digit packed BCD number from a port and converts it to binary. The result is returned in the accumulator.

```
BCD2BN:     PUSH  B        ; SAVE THE
            PUSH  D        ; REGISTERS
            IN    PORT     ; READ PACKED BCD
            MOV   B,A      ; SAVE PACKED BCD
            ANI   0FH      ; MASK OFF UPPER HALF
            MOV   D,A      ; SAVE THE UNITS
            MOV   A,B      ; RETRIEVE PACKED BCD
            ANI   0F0H     ; MASK OFF LOWER HALF
            CPI   0        ; IS MSD A ZERO?
            JZ    OVER     ; SKIP OVER IF YES

            RRC            ; MSD NOT ZERO, SO
            RRC            ; SHIFT IT DOWN TO
            RRC            ; LOWER 4 BITS FOR
            RRC            ; USE AS A COUNTER
            MOV   E,A      ; REG E IS LOOP COUNTER
```

```
                MVI     C,10        ; TEN INTO C FOR ADDING
                SUB     A           ; CLEAR THE ACCUMULATOR
        LOOP:   ADD     C           ; ADD TEN TO ACC
                DCR     E           ; ONE LESS 10 TO ADD
                JNZ     LOOP        ; JUMP IF NOT DONE
        OVER:   ADD     D           ; ADD THE UNITS
                POP     D           ; RESTORE THE
                POP     B           ; REGISTERS
                RET                 ; FROM BCD2BN
```

The two-digit packed BCD number represents a value in the range from 00 to 99. The upper 4 bits represent the *tens* digit, and the lower 4 bits represent the *units* digit. The subroutine simply unpacks the BCD and stores the number of tens in register E and the number of units in register D. Register E is used as a loop counter to add 10 to the accumulator the correct number of times. The units are then added to the sum of tens, so the number in the accumulator is the binary equivalent of the BCD quantity.

A couple of points should be noted. First, the subroutine has to check to see if the tens digit of the BCD number is zero. Without such a check, if the tens digit were zero, we would add 10 to the accumulator 256 times (as discussed in Sec. 4.7, on looping). Second, we used the instruction MVI C,10 to put 10 into register C. Remember that most assemblers assume a number is decimal unless indicated otherwise. The instruction could have been written MVI C,0AH, but 10 seems more natural than 0AH in this application.

4.10.3 Converting Binary to BCD

Some output devices, such as numeric displays, are designed to use BCD numbers. A binary number in the range from 00 to 99 can be converted to BCD for outputting to such a device. The subroutine in the following program (BN2BCD) converts the binary number in the accumulator to packed BCD and sends it out a port. The BCD is also returned in the accumulator.

```
        BN2BCD: PUSH    D           ; SAVE THE REGS
                LXI     D,0         ; PUT 00 IN D AND E
        LOOP1:  SUI     10          ; SUBTRACT A TEN
                JC      UNITS       ; JUMP IF NO MORE TENS
                INR     D           ; INCREMENT TENS DIGIT
                JMP     LOOP1       ; GET ANOTHER TEN
        UNITS:  ADI     10          ; CANCEL LAST TEN SUBTRACT
                MOV     E,A         ; WHAT'S LEFT IS UNITS
        OVER:   MOV     A,D         ; GET TENS DIGIT
                RLC                 ; AND MOVE IT
                RLC                 ; TO THE UPPER
                RLC                 ; FOUR BITS OF
                RLC                 ; PACKED BCD
                ADD     E           ; THE ONES DIGIT
                OUT     PORT        ; SEND BCD
                POP     D           ; RESTORE REGS
                RET                 ; FROM BN2BCD
```

Basically, the subroutine just counts the number of tens in the binary number by repeated subtraction. After all the tens have been removed, what's left is the number of units (ones).

4.10.4 BCD Addition

The following is a program to add two 8-digit BCD numbers X and Y. Each number is stored in memory as packed BCD in four consecutive locations. Except for the DAA instruction, the program is very similar to the one in Example 4.9.

```
MAIN:       LXI   H,XVALS     ; LOAD X POINTER IN HL
            LXI   D,YVALS     ; LOAD Y POINTER IN DE
            MVI   C,4         ; LOAD LOOP COUNT
            XRA   A           ; CLEAR CY
            PUSH  PSW         ; DUMMY PUSH
LOOP:       POP   PSW         ; RESTORE CY FOR SUBR
            CALL  ADDBCD      ; DO IT
            PUSH  PSW         ; SAVE CY FOR SUBR
            DCR   C           ; DECREMENT COUNT
            JNZ   LOOP        ; JUMP IF NOT DONE

            POP   PSW         ; EVERY PUSH NEEDS A POP
            HLT               ; WAIT HERE
                *
                *
                *
ADDBCD:     LDAX  D           ; GET BCD PAIR X
            MOV   B,M         ; GET BCD PAIR Y
            ADC   B           ; ADD THEM
            DAA               ; DECIMAL ADJUST ACC
            MOV   M,A         ; STORE SUM IN Y
            INX   H           ; ADVANCE X POINTER
            INX   D           ; ADVANCE Y POINTER
            RET               ; OUT OF HERE
```

The DAA instruction uses both the AC and the CY flags. If the *lower* 4 bits of the accumulator are 1001 (9) or less, DAA leaves them alone and AC is reset. If they are greater than 1001 (i.e., 1010 through 1111), DAA will subtract 1010 (10) from them and set AC, which becomes a carry-in to the upper 4 bits. For example, if the lower 4 bits are 1100, DAA will make them 0010 and set AC to a 1. Next, DAA will add AC to the *upper* 4 bits and then check to see if they exceed 1001. If they do, DAA subtracts 1010 from the upper 4 bits and sets CY. Note that subtracting 1010 and setting CY is the same as adding 0110.

At first glance, the calling routine MAIN has to do simultaneously two mutually exclusive things with the flags. It must use Z to continue looping with JNZ, but at the same time, it must preserve the value of CY between subroutine calls, as ADDBCD uses an add-with-carry (ADC B) for its multibyte addition. However, although the DCR C instruction in MAIN affects Z, it does *not* affect CY. If DCR did affect CY (as it might in some other processor), a solution would be to PUSH the PSW to save CY while you use Z and then POP it back to use CY. You would use a dummy PUSH before entering the loop as well as a compensating POP after leaving the loop.

4.10.5 BCD Subtraction

The problem here is that the 8085 DAA does not work for subtraction. One solution is to add the complement. As binary subtraction can be done by adding the two's complement, decimal subtraction can be done by adding the *ten's complement*. The ten's complement is formed by adding 1 to the *nine's complement*, which, in turn, is formed by subtracting each digit in the number from 9.

> **EXAMPLE 4.36 Subtraction Using Ten's Complement**
>
> The nine's complement of 28 is 71: 28 and 71 add up to 99. The ten's complement of 28 is then 71 + 1, or 72.
> To *subtract* 28 from 59, we would *add* 72 to 59, which gives (after using DAA) 131. Because the maximum decimal number the accumulator can hold is 99, 131 is actually 31 in the accumulator with CY set. The carry flag set indicates a *positive* result. Consider subtracting 28 from 20, which should give −8. We will *add* 72 (two's complement of 28) to 20 to get 92. Note that the addition causes CY to be reset, indicating a *negative* result; therefore the number in the accumulator, 92, is the *ten's complement* of the answer. To get the magnitude of the difference, just form the ten's complement of 92: (99 − 92) + 1 = 08.

The following is a program using addition of the ten's complement to subtract two packed BCD numbers.

```
SUBBCD:     PUSH  PSW       ; SAVE
            PUSH  B         ; ALL
            PUSH  D         ; REGISTERS
            PUSH  H         ; AND FLAGS

            LXI   H,VALS    ; SET UP POINTER
            MOV   B,M       ; GET BCD PAIR X
            INX   H         ; ADVANCE POINTER
            MOV   C,M       ; GET BCD PAIR Y
            MVI   A,99H     ; MAKE 9S
            SUB   B         ; COMPLEMENT OF X
            INR   A         ; MAKE 10S COMPLEMENT
            ADD   C         ; Y-X BY ADDING COMPLEMENT
            DAA             ; FIX UP RESULT
            MOV   M,A       ; SAVE RESULT

            POP   H         ; RESTORE
            POP   D         ; THE
            POP   B         ; REGISTERS
            POP   PSW       ; AND FLAGS
            RET             ; RETURN TO CALLER
```

4.11 MISCELLANEOUS STUFF

Here we look at a few common assembly language tasks and techniques.

4.11.1 ASCII Conversion

The ASCII character code (see Appendix F) is a 7-bit code used to represent upper- and lowercase letters and the digits, as well as punctuation marks and some special nonprinting symbols. A common task in programming is to convert hex numbers to ASCII characters for display. Equally common is the task of taking ASCII character input, for example, from a keypad, and converting it to hex numbers.

To convert a single hex digit in the range 0 to 9 to the equivalent ASCII character, just add 30h. For example 35h is the ASCII code for the character '5'. To convert a hex digit in the range A to F to the equivalent ASCII character, just add 37h. For example, 42h is the ASCII code for the character 'B'. Note the use of single quote marks to distinguish a character from a numeric value: 5 is a hex number, but '5' is an ASCII character. The subroutine HEX2ASC in the following program converts hex to ASCII.

```
HEX2ASC:    CPI   10         ; BIGGER THAN 9 ?
            JNC   LETRS      ; JUMP IF YES
            ADI   30H        ; NO, ADJUST FOR 0-9
            RET              ; BACK TO MAIN

LETRS:      ADI   37H        ; ADJUST FOR A-F
            RET              ; BACK TO MAIN
```

To convert an ASCII character in the range '0' to '9' to the equivalent hex number, just subtract 30h from the ASCII code. To convert an ASCII character in the range 'A' to 'F' to the equivalent hex number, just subtract 37h from the ASCII code. The subroutine ASC2HEX in the following program converts ASCII to hex.

```
ASC2HEX:    CPI   'A'        ; BIGGER THAN '9' ?
            JNC   LETR       ; JUMP IF YES
            SBI   30H        ; NO, ADJUST FOR '0'-'9'
            RET              ; BACK TO MAIN

LETR:       SUB   37H        ; ADJUST FOR 'A'-'F'
            RET              ; BACK TO MAIN
```

4.11.2 Look-Up Tables and Conversions

There are two software approaches for converting one thing to another. One approach is to take the thing to be converted as input to an algorithm and *calculate* the result. The other approach requires that all possible results be known and kept in memory. If the locations are consecutive, they form a simple *look-up* table. If the locations are dispersed through a certain block of memory, they form a *hash table*.

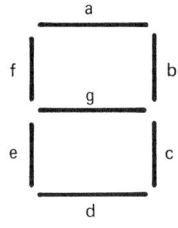

· dp (DECIMAL POINT)

ACCUMULATOR BIT:	7	6	5	4	3	2	1	0
DISPLAY SEGMENT:	dp	g	f	e	d	c	b	a

WHEN BIT = 1, SEGMENT IS ACTIVATED

Figure 4.6 Look-up table.   **Figure 4.7** Mapping of segments to accumulator bits.

In both look-up and hash tables, the thing to be converted is used to derive an address that points to the corresponding table entry. The result is then simply read from memory. Typically, using tables is faster than calculating a result, but it takes up more memory. Addresses in a look-up table are usually arrived at in some straightforward way, whereas those in hash tables usually require a short algorithm.

A typical use of a look-up table is the conversion of the hex numbers 0 through 9 to the codes necessary to drive a seven-segment display. Figure 4.6 shows the layout of a display with the segments designated a through g. To display a digit, the appropriate segments are turned on. For example, to display digit 4 requires segments b, c, f, and g to be activated. Using driver circuits attached to an output port, segments can be *mapped* to accumulator bits so that an OUT instruction will activate the display. Figure 4.7 shows such a mapping.

EXAMPLE 4.37

When the subroutine of the program below is called, it takes the content of the accumulator as a hex number and returns with the corresponding seven-segment code in the accumulator. The hex number in A is copied to register C while zero is put into register B. Thus, the register pair BC holds a number in the range 0000h to 0009h. The address of the beginning of the table is loaded into HL. The contents of BC are then added to HL to form the address of the desired byte in the table. The address is then used to move the byte to the accumulator.

```
HEX2SEG:  MOV   C,A         ; USE VALUE IN A
          MVI   B,0         ; AS DISPLACEMENT
          LXI   H,TABLE     ; BASE IS TABLE ADDRESS
          DAD   B           ; ADD DISPLACEMENT
          MOV   A,M         ; GET CODE FROM TABLE
          RET               ; RETURN IT IN ACC

TABLE:    DB    3FH         ; 0
          DB    06H         ; 1
          DB    5BH         ; 2
          DB    4FH         ; 3
          DB    66H         ; 4
          DB    6DH         ; 5
          DB    7DH         ; 6
          DB    07H         ; 7
          DB    7FH         ; 8
          DB    67H         ; 9
```

Sec. 4.11   Miscellaneous Stuff

In Example 4.37, the subroutine assumes the content of the accumulator is in the range 00 through 09 and doesn't check for an out-of-bounds value. It is left as an exercise for the reader to rewrite the routine so that it can handle an invalid input.

4.11.3 Jump Tables and Computed Calls

With a simple conditional jump, such as JZ, the program will go one of two ways: either execute the jump or fall through to the next instruction. But sometimes we want more than two choices. Depending on the result of an input instruction or a calculation, we may want to jump to one of N different addresses. A *jump table*, also called a *computed goto*, will let us do just that.

The 8085 PCHL instruction is designed to implement jump tables. The action of PCHL is to swap the content of the program counter (PC) with the content of the HL register pair. Because PC points to the next instruction to be executed, the effect of PCHL is to cause an immediate jump to the address that was in HL *before* PCHL was executed. HL can be filled by reading from a look-up table. For example, suppose that HL is pointing to an entry in a table of addresses. Example 4.38 shows a sequence of instructions that will get the address from the table and jump to it.

EXAMPLE 4.38

```
          MOV   E,M     ; GET LOWER HALF OF ADDRESS
          INX   H       ; INCREMENT TABLE POINTER
          MOV   D,M     ; GET UPPER HALF OF ADDRESS
          XCHG          ; EXCHANGE HL AND DE
          PCHL          ; JUMP TO ADDRESS
```

Consider an example that is a modification of the jump table idea. Suppose there are four possible places to go, each separated by 64 bytes of memory space. The four 16-bit addresses could be of the form XXXXXXXXBB000000, where the Xs represent the 8 upper bits and the Bs represent the two MSBs of the lower 8 bits. The high-order half of the address could be loaded immediately into H while the low-order half could be read in from a port. See the following program.

```
          UPPER   EQU   8100H       ; HIGH HALF OF ADDRESS
          PORT1   EQU   0F4H        ; INPUT PORT ADDRESS

                  ORG   1000H       ; START ADDRESS OF MAIN

          MAIN:   LXI   H,UPPER     ; SET UP H FOR PCHL
                  IN    PORT1       ; GET LOWER HALF-ADDRESS
                  MOV   L,A         ; SET UP L FOR PCHL
                  PCHL              ; JUMP

                  ORG   8100H       ; ADDRESS OF FIRST BLOCK
                  < FIRST BLOCK OF CODE >

                  ORG   8140H       ; ADDRESS OF SECOND BLOCK
                  < SECOND BLOCK OF CODE >
```

```
            ORG   8180H       ; ADDRESS OF THIRD BLOCK
              < THIRD BLOCK OF CODE >

            ORG   81C0H       ; ADDRESS OF FOURTH BLOCK
              < FOURTH BLOCK OF CODE >
```

Another modification of the jump table idea is a technique we might refer to as a *computed call*. Instead of jumping to an address, we will use PCHL to effectively call a subroutine. Unlike a real call, which automatically pushes the return address onto the stack, we must save it with a PUSH instruction. The RET will pop the saved address off the stack. See the following program.

```
   UPPER     EQU   8100H       ; HIGH HALF OF ADDRESS
   PORT1     EQU   0F4H        ; INPUT PORT ADDRESS

             ORG   1000H       ; START ADDRESS OF MAIN

   MAIN:     LXI   H,UPPER     ; SET UP H FOR PCHL
             LXI   D,THERE     ; SET UP RETURN ADDRESS

   LOOP:     IN    PORT1       ; GET LOWER HALF-ADDRESS
             MOV   L,A         ; SET UP L FOR PCHL
             PUSH  D           ; SAVE RETURN ADDRESS
             PCHL              ; CALL
   THERE:    JMP   LOOP        ; DO IT AGAIN

             ORG   8100H       ; ADDRESS OF SUBROUTINE 1
               < FIRST BLOCK OF CODE >
             RET               ; BACK TO THERE

             ORG   8140H       ; ADDRESS OF SECOND BLOCK
               < SECOND BLOCK OF CODE >
             RET               ; BACK TO THERE

             ORG   8180H       ; ADDRESS OF THIRD BLOCK
               < THIRD BLOCK OF CODE >
             RET               ; BACK TO THERE

             ORG   81C0H       ; ADDRESS OF FOURTH BLOCK
               < FOURTH BLOCK OF CODE >
             RET               ; BACK TO THERE
```

4.11.4 Multiplication and Division

Sophisticated processors have multiply and divide instructions. Also, they may use a math coprocessor to do it in hardware. On the 8085 we must do multiplication and division with a subroutine. An easy way to multiply is to use repeated addition. For example, to multiply 9 times 3, we can simply add 9 to the accumulator three times. Likewise, we can do division by repeated subtraction. For example, to divide 81 by 4 we can just keep subtracting 4 from 81 until CY gets set. CY set means we subtracted one too many 4s, so we should add back a 4 and stop. At this point you should be familiar enough with the 8085 assembly language to write such programs for yourself, so such examples are left to the reader.

The problem with multiplying by repeated addition is that the time required to execute gets longer as the numbers being multiplied get bigger. *Booth's algorithm* is a way to multiply that requires a fixed time to execute and is quicker than repeated addition for all but the smallest numbers. It is based on a *shift-and-add* technique.

EXAMPLE 4.39 Shift and Add

```
         111    Multiplicand
     X   101    Multiplier
         111
         000
         111
      100011    product     (7 × 5 = 35)
```

This problem shows us what we would do if we had to multiply the two 3-bit numbers 111 and 101. Note that we multiply digit by digit. When the multiplier digit is a 1, we copy the multiplicand down. When the multiplier digit is a 0, we copy down all 0s. In either case, we shift over one digit before we go to the next multiplier bit.

EXAMPLE 4.40 Booth's Algorithm

The program here uses Booth's algorithm to multiply two 8-bit numbers. Because the product could be up to 16 bits long, we will use register pairs. Note the use of a rotate instruction to test each multiplier bit for a high value as well as the conditional addition. Also note how the 16-bit number in DE is rotated by first rotating E through CY followed by rotating D through CY. Whatever was rotated *out* of the MSB of E will then be rotated *into* the LSB of D.

```
MULT:   IN    01          ; GET 8-BIT
        MOV   E,A         ; MULTIPLICAND
        IN    02          ; GET 8-BIT
        MOV   B,A         ; MULTIPLIER
        LXI   H,0         ; CLEAR HL
        MVI   D,0         ; CLEAR D OF DE PAIR
        MVI   C,8         ; 8-BIT MULTIPLY COUNT
LOOP:   MOV   A,B         ; RETRIEVE MULTIPLIER
        RRC               ; ROTATE RIGHT BIT TO CY
        MOV   B,A         ; SAVE ROTATED MULTIPLIER
        JNC   OVER        ; SKIP ADD IF BIT IS 0

        DAD   D           ; ADD IF BIT IS 1

OVER:   MOV   A,E         ; ROTATE THE 16-BIT
        RAL               ; MULTIPLICAND 1 BIT
        MOV   E,A         ; TO THE LEFT
        MOV   A,D         ; AND SAVE IT
        RAL               ; FOR NEXT TIME
        MOV   D,A         ; THROUGH THE LOOP
        DCR   C           ; DONE IT 8 TIMES?
        JNZ   LOOP        ; JUMP IF NO

        HLT               ; HALT IF YES
```

4.11.5 Multiple Stacks

Certain algorithms, such as the one used for evaluating an expression like Y = 2 + X * (1 + 3), are easier to implement as a sequence of pushes and pops on two separate stacks: one for the operators and another for the numbers. Also, it is sometimes convenient to have a separate stack area in memory for the sole purpose of passing parameters to subroutines.

The 8085 has only one stack pointer register, so we will have to save the contents of SP and jam a different value into it when we wish to use the other stack. When we want to use the first stack, we will have to restore the original stack pointer into SP. Note, however, that there is no PUSH SP instruction. If there were, it would lead to ambiguity because the 8085 decrements SP before it pushes. We can get SP into HL and then save it in memory by executing the instruction sequence

```
LXI   H,0        ; CLEAR HL TO ZEROS
DAD   SP         ; EFFECTIVELY MOVE SP TO HL
SHLD  SPTMP      ; SAVE SP AT ADDRESS SPTMP
```

We can then use LXI to put a new value in SP. To restore the original stack pointer we would use the instruction sequence

```
LHLD  SPTMP      ; GET OLD SP INTO HL
SPHL             ; COPY HL TO SP
```

4.12 SUMMARY

In this chapter we have seen how subroutines are used to overcome complexity through modularization. The importance of good documentation was emphasized. The use of pointers was demonstrated, as was the use of flags, including CY in multibyte arithmetic. The use of DAA in BCD arithmetic was shown, and signed numbers were examined. Logic operations in masking and bit manipulation was discussed. The technique of looping was demonstrated together with the concept of control structure. Rotates and shifts were examined. Finally, various techniques, such as look-up tables, were demonstrated.

CHAPTER REVIEW

Questions

1. Give an advantage and a disadvantage of programming at the assembly language level.
2. What is the first step when starting a program?
3. What is the purpose of modularization?

4. Why is documentation important?
5. What is the "environment"?
6. How can parameters be passed? Compare the methods of doing so.
7. What are the flags, and what do they represent? How are they used?
8. Explain what a pointer is and how it is used.
9. Compare and contrast direct and indirect moves.
10. How can HL be loaded with a 16-bit number?
11. Describe the 8085 16-bit arithmetic operations and the flags they affect.
12. Describe two's complement and how it it used.
13. Describe signed numbers. What is "overflow"?
14. Explain "masking."
15. Explain how individual bits in a register can be made 1 or 0 without affecting other bits.
16. Explain what a conditional loop is.
17. Compare and contrast a WHILE-DO loop with a REPEAT-UNTIL loop.
18. Compare and contrast a rotate with a shift.
19. Describe a use for a rotate and a use for a shift.
20. Compare BCD to binary.
21. Explain what packed and unpacked BCD are.
22. What is the function of DAA?
23. Explain what a look-up table and a jump table are.
24. Explain how Booth's algorithm works.

Programming Problems

When writing programs for the following problems, use subroutines where appropriate. If it helps, draw a flowchart.

1. Draw flowcharts for programs to implement IF-THEN-ELSE, FOR-DO, WHILE-DO, REPEAT-UNTIL, and CASE.
2. Write a subroutine that reads upper- and lowercase ASCII characters from port 1 and sends them out port 2 as uppercase only.
3. Write a program to pass two 8-bit numbers in the stack to a subroutine that adds them to get a 16-bit result that is passed back to the calling routine in the stack. The calling routine should put the result in HL before ending.
4. Write a program that passes two pointers to the subroutine in register pairs DE and HL. The subroutine should use the pointers to get 2 bytes from memory, which it then adds. The result is passed back in the accumulator.
5. Write a program to subtract one 4-byte number stored in memory from another with the result stored in memory. Assume the smaller number is subtracted from the bigger.
6. Write a program that adds two signed numbers and checks for overflow. If overflow occurs, set the accumulator to all zeros.
7. Write a program that uses a pointer to search through memory, starting at address 0200h, looking for the bit pattern 11000011. When found, the program should stop with the address in HL.

8. Write a program that will read a byte from port 1. It should then force bit 7 and bit 6 high and bit 1 and bit 0 low; the rest of the bits remain unchanged. Output the modified byte to port 2.
9. Assuming an 8085 with a 2-MHz clock, how much time does the program in Example 4.22 take?
10. Write a program that reads a byte from a port and then uses a rotate instruction in a loop to count the number of bits in the byte that are 1s.
11. Write a program to do division by repeated subtraction.
12. Write a program to implement a CASE statement.
13. Write a program to add three unpacked BCD numbers and get the answer as packed BCD. Assume the sum will not be bigger than 99.
14. Write a subroutine that, when passed an ASCII character for a hex number ('0'–'9', 'A'–'F'), will output the corresponding seven-segment code to port 1.

chapter 5

Interrupts and DMA

OBJECTIVES

Upon completion of this chapter, you should be able to

1. Explain what an interrupt is and how it works
2. Explain the interrupt structure of the 8085
3. Explain what DMA is
4. Explain how the 8257 chip works

5.1 INTRODUCTION

In this chapter we discuss interrupts and direct memory access.

5.2 INTERRUPTS

5.2.1 Servicing External Devices

The timing of events in external devices usually has no relationship to the timing of the CPU; in other words, real-world events are usually asynchronous to the processor. In order to monitor and control external devices, a microcomputer must have a method of responding to I/O requests and other external events in a timely manner.

5.2.2 Polling and Buffering

One way a processor deals with I/O devices is to ask them periodically (usually through I/O ports) if they need service; that is, to poll them. Often, a polled device will exchange blocks of information with the processor. The device will hold such blocks in its own memory, the buffer. The main drawback to polling is the amount of time the CPU spends checking the I/O device. Of course, if that is all the CPU has to do in life—in other words, if it is a dedicated controller—this is no problem.

> **EXAMPLE 5.1   A Polling Loop**
>
> ```
> LOOP:   IN    DEV1
>         CPI   READY
>         CZ    READ1
>         IN    DEV2
>         CPI   READY
>         CZ    READ2
>         JMP   LOOP
> ```
>
> This loop continuously polls two input devices (DEV1 and DEV2) to see if they are ready to be read. If a device is ready, the appropriate subroutine is called to read the device.

If the I/O device buffer either fills up or empties out while it is waiting for service, data may be lost or the device may stop working. Consider a printer. The processor initially will load the print buffer with text. But if the buffer runs out before the printer is polled again, printing will stop. Another example is digital communications equipment. If data keep coming in, the receiver buffer can overflow while waiting for the next poll. Also, real time applications, which require service from the processor as soon as the need occurs, cannot wait for a poll. Clearly, something better is called for. That something is an interrupt.

5.2.3 Basic Interrupt Action

I/O devices often require immediate service while the processor is in the middle of doing something else. The interrupt is a software-controlled hardware feature that, in an orderly manner, forces the processor to suspend what it is currently doing in order to service the I/O device. When it is finished with I/O, the processor will resume where it left off, much the same as a subroutine. Interrupts that can be blocked by software are called *maskable;* those that cannot be blocked are called *nonmaskable*. Interrupts that occur while masked are said to be *pending*.

An I/O device will request service by activating an interrupt pin on the CPU. If the CPU has enabled its interrupts in software, it will initiate its response, often with an acknowledgment signal to the I/O device. This request-acknowledge sequence is an example of handshaking.

The rest of the response is similar to a subroutine call. The CPU will push the return address onto the stack and branch to a predefined part of memory, where it expects to find the *interrupt service routine* which will handle the interrupting device. The last instruction in the routine will be a RETURN, which will pop the return address off the stack and into the PC register. The CPU will then resume program execution from the point where it was interrupted.

5.2.4 Multiple Interrupt Sources

It is possible to have many I/O devices sharing a single interrupt input. They may be wire-ORed, as shown in Fig. 5.1. When an interrupt occurs, the processor must first determine which device was the cause, as different devices need different services. One way is for the interrupt service routine to poll all the devices to find out which one called, perhaps by having the service routine read status lines from all the devices. But polling can be time-consuming. A faster way is for each interrupting device to point (like a vector arrow) to the place in memory where its service routine is stored. The CPU can then go there directly.

5.2.5 Vectored Interrupts

A *vectored interrupt* scheme can be implemented in several ways. A method in the 8080 was to have the interrupting device put a special type of call instruction onto the bus for the CPU to read in place of an instruction from memory. A simpler scheme, used in the 8085, is to have several interrupt pins on the CPU, each associated with a fixed address in memory. Separate I/O devices can then use separate pins to request an interrupt. Another approach, used in the Z80, is for the CPU to obtain the vector address from the interrupting device. A variation on the idea of vectoring is to have the interrupt cause the CPU to go to a location in memory that holds the *address* of the service routine instead of the routine itself. A *vector table* of such addresses can exist and be changed during execution of the main program to select different service routines.

5.2.6 Interrupt Priority

In a vectored interrupt system, a problem can arise if two devices request an interrupt at exactly the same time. Which gets serviced first? What is needed is a means of establishing priority.

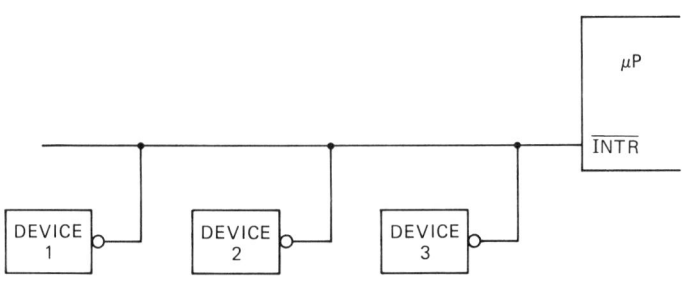

Figure 5.1 Wire-ORed I/O devices.

Polling establishes priority by the order in which the devices are polled; the highest priority is the first one on the list. Using separate interrupt pins allows a hardware solution; the pins are ranked in priority. Another scheme is to have a single interrupt pin but connect the interrupt sources to it in a "daisy chain." Each device must relay its request through a higher priority device, which, in turn, may pass it or block it. The highest priority device is the one closest to the CPU, and the device at the end of the chain has the lowest priority.

5.2.7 Interrupts and the HALT State

When a processor executes a HALT instruction, it will stop fetching instructions. However, the processor can still be interrupted. When it returns from the interrupt service routine, the processor will fetch the next instruction *after* the one last executed. The effect is that an interrupt can knock the processor out of a HALT state. It will resume execution with the instruction following the HALT.

5.2.8 Implementation, Levels, Reentrant Code

Although interrupt-driven systems can be very effective, they can also be tricky to implement. They must be well thought out, especially if interrupt service routines are, themselves, subject to being interrupted in a multilevel system. In a multilevel system it is possible that an interrupt service routine will be interrupted by a request to run the same service routine. In order for the routine to execute properly, it must be written in a form called reentrant.

Reentrant code does not alter itself or its environment. When a reentrant routine is entered, it saves the contents of all the registers and memory locations it expects to use so that they can be restored to their original values upon leaving. A common technique is to use the stack for storage, creating a stack frame for each invocation of the routine (see Chap. 4).

In critical real-time applications a thorough analysis of execution times must be done in terms of the timing requirements of the interrupt source. In addition, there is a latency time between requesting an interrupt and the start of the service routine.

5.3 INTERRUPT CONSTRAINTS

Microcontrollers, by definition, are constantly monitoring the state of some external machine or process. However, compared to the instruction execution time of a microprocessor, events in the real world (the external equipment being controlled) often occur very infrequently. Having the processor sit in a polling loop waiting for something to happen "out there" would be a waste of time. Therefore, devices such as the 8085, Z80, and 8051 have interrupt schemes allowing for multiple sources, vectoring, and priority. Interrupts are crucial to embedded controller performance and require the examination of three limiting factors: latency, density, and time limit.

5.3.1 Latency

Latency is the time elapsed from when an interrupt is asserted to when the interrupt service routine begins execution. It includes other factors besides the time required to save the return address and branch. In the case of a single interrupt source, there are only two situations:

1. Interrupts are enabled and the processor is executing an instruction in the main program. The instruction must complete before the interrupt is recognized, so the worst case latency will be increased by the time it takes to execute the longest instruction.
2. The main program is in a critical region where interrupts are disabled. At the end of the critical region the interrupts are reenabled. The worst case latency is then extended by the time it takes to execute the code in the longest critical region.

If there are multiple, prioritized interrupts, the situation is more complicated. In the following discussion we assume that interrupts are disabled when an interrupt service routine starts and are reenabled when it ends; interrupt service routines are not interrupted.

EXAMPLE 5.2   A Simple Latency Calculation

In Fig. 5.2 we want to know the latency for interrupt INT3, which occurs at time t1. The processor cannot respond, however, because it is already executing the service routine for lower priority interrupt INT4, which occurred prior to t1. But before INT4 completes, the higher priority interrupt INT2 occurs, so when INT4 does complete, INT2 starts and INT3 continues to wait. Only when INT2 completes can INT3 finally begin.

The total latency for INT3 includes the time it takes to execute the service routines for INT4 and INT2. In general, the worst case latency time for an inter-

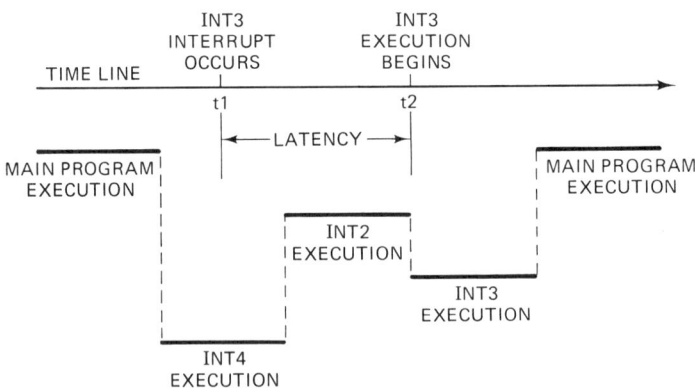

Figure 5.2

rupt must include the time to execute the single longest lower priority service routine as well as the time to execute all the higher priority service routines (plus whatever time it takes to get out of the main routine, as discussed above).

Note that the shorter time a high priority interrupt takes to complete the better. Also, the less frequently a high priority interrupt occurs the better, as we shall see in section 5.3.3.

5.3.2 Interrupt Density

The basic idea of interrupt density is the percentage of time the processor spends servicing interrupts.

EXAMPLE 5.3 Interrupt Density Calculation

If an interrupt occurs once every 10 sec and the service routine takes 2 sec to execute, then the percentage is

$$\text{Density} = (2/10) \times 100\% = 20\%$$

As the percentage approaches 100, the processor gets closer to being *interrupt bound*. When that happens, nothing gets done in the main routine because all processor time is used to service interrupts. The idea can be extended to multiple interrupt sources; see Example 5.4.

EXAMPLE 5.4 Detecting Interrupt-Bound Condition for Three Interrupt Sources

Suppose INT1 occurs at a frequency of F1 interrupts per second and takes T1 sec to execute its service routine. Likewise, INT2 has a frequency of F2 and takes T2 sec and INT3 occurs at the rate F3 and takes T3 sec. To guarantee that all interrupts have a chance to get serviced, the following inequality should be true:

$$(F1 \times T1 + F2 \times T2 + F3 \times T3) \times 100\% < 100\%$$

The inequality can be extended to any number of interrupt sources.

5.3.3 Interrupt Time Limit

Time and tide wait for no one, nor will most other real-time processes. When an interrupt occurs, the event that caused it may be able to wait only a short time for service before it's too late. For example, imagine a computerized remote probe sent to the surface of a planet. At some point in the descent, the altimeter generates an interrupt to fire the retrorocket. If the processor does not initiate the service routine quickly, the probe becomes scrap metal.

For any interrupt, if the latency time exceeds the maximum allowable waiting time, the system fails (perhaps catastrophically). We have discussed latency already, but now we must combine it with the idea of frequency.

EXAMPLE 5.5 Total Latency Time

We will modify Example 5.2, as shown in Fig. 5.3. Interrupt INT3 still has to wait for INT4 to finish, and again INT2 occurs before INT4 finishes and forces INT3 to wait more. But now the higher priority INT1 occurs before INT2 finishes and while that's executing, INT2 occurs again. INT3 must wait for INT4, INT1, and two occurences of INT2. Worst case, the total latency time (TLT) for INT3 would be

$$TLT3 = N1 \times T1 + N2 \times T2 + T4$$

where N1 is the number of times INT1 can occur and N2 is the number of times INT2 can occur before returning to the main program. As before, Ti is the time for the INTi service routine to execute.

To see if INT3 really has a chance, we will use TLT3 as follows. Let the period of time between INT3 interrupts be P3, where $P3 = 1/F3$, and F3 is the interrupts per second rate of INT3. Then, for INT3 to have a chance of getting service, the following must be true: TLT3 < P3. Also, if TMAX3 is as long as INT3 can wait before disaster, then TLT3 < TMAX3 must also be true. The calculation of TLT can be extended to as many interrupts as required, and the inequalities can be generalized to

$$TLTi < Pi \text{ and } TLTi < TMAXi$$

Note that if Tn is the longest of the interrupt service routines of lower priority than INT1, then TLT1 = Tn. In other words, the highest priority interrupt has the best chance of getting service quickly. INT2 has the second-best chance (TLT2 = N1 × T1 + Tn), and so on.

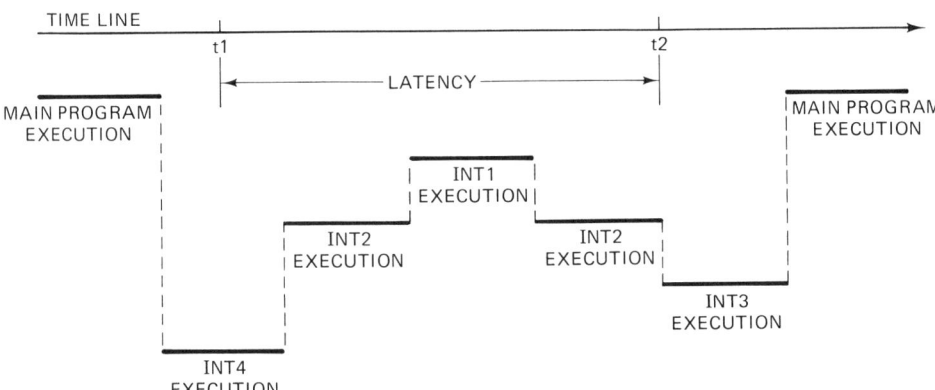

Figure 5.3

> **EXAMPLE 5.6 Interrupt Time Limit Calculation**
>
> Referring to Fig. 5.3, suppose INT3 occurs once per second, and it must be serviced within 400 msec. Assume that we have calculated the execution times of the other interrupts to be T1 = 25 msec, T2 = 50 msec, and T4 = 100 msec. Also assume that, by observing their frequency of occurrence, we know that N1 = 4 and N2 = 2. We calculate as follows:
>
> TLT3 = 4 × 25 msec + 2 × 50 msec + 100 msec = 300 msec
>
> F3 = 1/sec, so P3 = 1/F3 = 1000 msec; 300 msec < 1000 msec, so TLT3 < P3 is true; and 300 msec < 400 msec, so TLT3 < TMAX3 is also true. We conclude that INT3 will receive service in time.

For a more detailed mathematical analysis of interrupt timing, see Chapter 3 of *Design with Microcontrollers* by Peatman (McGraw-Hill).

5.4 THE 8085 INTERRUPTS

The basic interrupt operation has been described. The 8085 supports two different kinds of vectored interrupts. One requires the interrupting device to supply (indirectly) the vector. The other kind, the hardware restarts, uses special pins on the 8085 and is automatically vectored. Except for one (TRAP), the interrupts must be enabled in software by executing an EI (enable interrupts) instruction. The hardware restarts may also be individually masked on or off with software.

5.4.1 INTR and $\overline{\text{INTA}}$

The use of INTR (interrupt request) and $\overline{\text{INTA}}$ (interrupt acknowledge) is a carry-over from the 8080 processor. Assuming interrupts have been enabled in software, a device can initiate an interrupt by pulling INTR high. At the end of each machine cycle, the 8085 will check INTR. If INTR is high, the CPU will not fetch the next instruction from memory, but will expect the interrupting device to supply it instead. The CPU so indicates by asserting $\overline{\text{INTA}}$ in place of $\overline{\text{RD}}$. When the interrupting device sees $\overline{\text{INTA}}$ go low, it must place the first byte of an instruction onto the data bus. A multiple-byte instruction would require multiple $\overline{\text{INTA}}$ pulses. After reading that one instruction from the interrupting device, the CPU will resume reading from memory using $\overline{\text{RD}}$.

With a few exceptions (e.g., EI and DI) almost any instruction could, in principle, be used with $\overline{\text{INTA}}$. However, the 8085 instruction set contains a group of eight 1-byte instructions especially for the purpose called the *restarts:* RST 0 through RST 7. When a restart instruction is executed, it is the same as a subroutine call to one of eight fixed locations in the first page (i.e., the first 256 bytes) of memory. Table 5.1 lists the software restarts and their vector addresses.

TABLE 5.1 SOFTWARE RESTARTS AND THEIR VECTOR ADDRESSES

Instruction	Op-code	Vector address
RST 0	C7	0000H
RST 1	CF	0008H
RST 2	D7	0010H
RST 3	DF	0018H
RST 4	E7	0020H
RST 5	EF	0028H
RST 6	F7	0030H
RST 7	FF	0038H

EXAMPLE 5.7 Hardware Implementation of RST 2

Figure 5.4 shows a circuit to implement an RST 2 using a 74LS244 octal tristate buffer. The buffer has two output enable pins, $\overline{E1}$ and $\overline{E2}$, both active-low. The enable pins are tied together and connected to $\overline{INTA}$. The eight buffer inputs are connected to form the binary number 11010111, and the outputs are connected to the 8085 data bus. As long as $\overline{E1}$ and $\overline{E2}$ are held high, the buffer outputs will be in a high-impedance state. When INTR is asserted, the 8085 will pull $\overline{INTA}$ low, and the 8-bit number for RST 2 will be placed onto the bus, where it will be fetched and executed by the CPU.

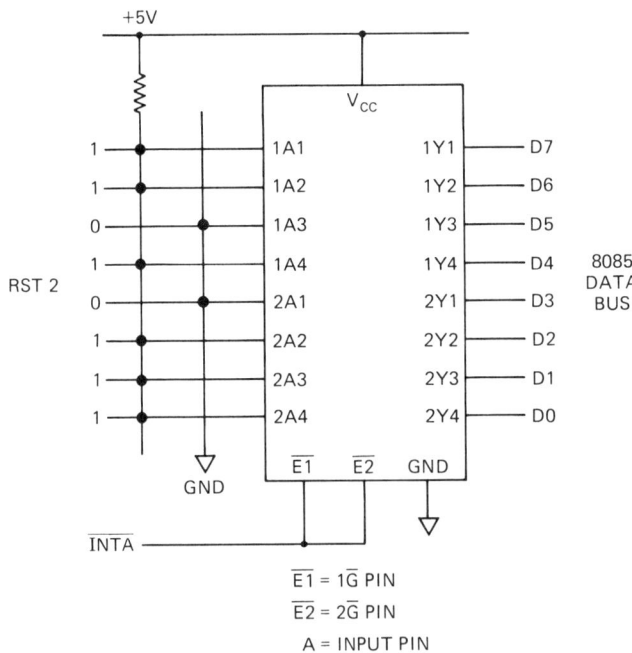

Figure 5.4 Circuit for hardware implementation of RST 2.

Remember that when an interrupt is executed, the contents of the program counter are pushed onto the stack as a return address. Next, the vector address (0010H for RST 2) is put into the PC to cause a jump to that location. After the jump, the CPU will start its fetch-execute cycle at that address, so the programmer must make sure that an appropriate instruction is there. Because there are only 8 bytes between the restart vector addresses (e.g., from 0010H to 0018H), it is common practice for the first instruction of the interrupt service routine to be a jump to another part of memory where the rest of the routine will be stored.

The last instruction in the interrupt routine is a return (RET), which will pop the return address off the stack and into the PC to allow the processor to continue from where it left off before the interrupt occurred.

5.4.2 Reenabling Interrupts

When an interrupt occurs, further interrupts are disabled until an EI instruction is executed. It is common to use EI immediately before returning. In order to allow RET to execute before interrupts are reenabled, EI has the property that it waits for the instruction *following* it to execute before EI takes effect.

Although it is possible to enable interrupts early in the interrupt service routine, it is usually not done because the interrupt itself could then be interrupted, and that interrupt, in turn, interrupted, and so on. The effect would be that interrupts could pile up before the first had a chance to finish, and there's a good possibility something nasty could happen, like stack overflow.

The effect of not executing EI until the end of the interrupt routine is to allow one interrupt to be serviced before responding to another. The TRAP interrupt, explained in Sec. 5.4.4, is an exception that can occur regardless of EI.

5.4.3 Hardware Restarts

The circuit described in the previous section assumes a single interrupt source requiring a single vector. If there are several sources, each requiring a different restart, then additional logic is required. If two or more interrupts occur at the same time, the logic must *arbitrate* the priority by deciding which one to put into effect. The logic must then put the correct restart instruction on the bus when $\overline{\text{INTA}}$ is asserted. (The 8259 programmable interrupt controller chip can be used with INTR, but a discussion of it is beyond the scope of this book.) If four or less interrupt sources are required, it is easier to use the *hardware restarts* built into the 8085 chip.

The hardware restart pins on the 8085 are labeled RST 5.5, RST 6.5, RST 7.5, and TRAP. As with INTR, the CPU will look for an interrupt request on the restart pins at the end of each instruction cycle. Like INTR, RST 5.5 and RST 6.5 must be held high until the interrupt occurs or they will be ignored. RST 7.5, however, is activated by a rising edge, that is, a low to high transition. Once the rising edge has occurred, it will be latched in so that the CPU will see it even if the pin is low when the CPU looks. Table 5.2 lists the vector addresses for hardware restarts; notice their locations with respect to the software restarts. The priority of

TABLE 5.2 INTERRUPT PRIORITY, RESTART ADDRESS, AND SENSITIVITY

Name	Priority	Address branched to (1) when interrupt occurs	Type trigger
TRAP	1	24H	Rising edge *and* high level until sampled
RST 7.5	2	3CH	Rising edge latched
RST 6.5	3	34H	High level until sampled
RST 5.5	4	2CH	High level until sampled
INTR	5	See note 2	High level until sampled

1. The processor pushes the PC on the stack before branching to the indicated address.
2. The address branched to depends on the instruction provided to the CPU when the interrupt is acknowledged.

Source: Reprinted by permission of Intel Corporation, Copyright © Intel Corporation 1987.

the interrupt sources also is given in Table 5.2. Note that TRAP has the highest priority and INTR has the lowest.

5.4.4 TRAP

The TRAP interrupt is a special case. It is nonmaskable, meaning that it cannot be disabled in software. In order to prevent false multiple interrupts, TRAP requires both a rising edge and a high level to be activated. If TRAP is activated, it must go low and then high again and be held in order to reactivate it.

A common use for TRAP is to allow the processor to fail gracefully during some catastrophic event. For example, an external circuit could be used to detect a drop in power supply voltage. The circuit would then activate TRAP to execute a routine to save all register contents in nonvolatile memory before total power failure. When power is restored, another routine could restore the register contents and continue on with the program. In a world where Murphy's law is usually in effect, the wise systems designer will consider all possibilities.

As with any other interrupt, when a TRAP interrupt occurs further interrupts are disabled. The effect is the same as executing DI, so an EI is required to reenable them. For any other interrupt source there would be no problem; the interrupt service routine simply would include an EI. However, a TRAP interrupt can occur even if the main program had executed a DI. If the TRAP service routine always included an EI, it might enable interrupts when the main program doesn't want them: a classic side effect type of software bug.

To get around the problem, the TRAP service routine should execute a RIM instruction, as described in section 5.4.7. The value of the interrupt enable flag obtained through RIM will be what it was *before* the interrupt occurred. If it was high, the TRAP service routine should do an EI before returning. If it was low, skip the EI.

5.4.5 Interrupt Masks

Except for TRAP, the hardware restarts can be enabled and disabled using the EI and DI instructions. While they are enabled, RST 5.5, RST 6.5, and RST 7.5 can also be controlled by *mask* bits, one for each restart. When a mask bit is set to 1, the corresponding restart is prevented from causing an interrupt (it is *masked off*). If an interrupt pin is activated while it is masked, it will be *pending*. When a mask bit is cleared to 0, the corresponding interrupt can occur if it is still pending. The relationship among EI, DI, interrupts, and masks is shown logically in Fig. 5.5. The mask bits can be set and cleared by the SIM (set interrupt mask) instruction and read by the RIM (read interrupt mask) instruction.

5.4.6 SIM

The SIM instruction has three functions:

1. Set or clear the interrupt masks for RST 5.5, RST 6.5, and RST 7.5
2. Reset the RST 7.5 input latch
3. Load the SOD (serial output data) latch

As shown in Fig. 5.6, SIM uses specific bits in the accumulator for each function, so the accumulator must be loaded with the correct bit pattern before SIM is executed:

- Bits 7 and 6 are used for serial data. If bit 6 is a 1, then the contents of bit 7 will be written to the SOD pin when SIM is executed. If bit 6 is a 0, then bit 7 becomes a "don't care," and will have no effect on SOD when SIM is executed. The advantage of bit 6 is that it allows the programmer to change masks without affecting SOD. (A hardware reset will reset SOD.)
- Bit 5 has no function; it may be left 1 or 0.
- Bit 4 can be used to clear (reset) the RST 7.5 interrupt latch. The latch will be cleared automatically if the 8085 is allowed to execute the RST 7.5 interrupt. However, if RST 7.5 is masked off, the programmer may wish to reset the latch explicitly by executing SIM with bit 4 set to 1. (The RST 7.5 latch is also cleared by a hardware reset.)
- Bit 3 is the *mask set enable* (MSE). If bit 3 is a 1, then bit 2, bit 1, and bit 0 will control the masks. If bit 3 is a 0, then bit 2, bit 1, and bit 0 are don't cares. The advantage of bit 3 is that it allows the programmer to use SOD without affecting the masks.
- Bit 2 is the RST 7.5 mask. When bit 2 is 0, the RST 7.5 interrupt is enabled. When bit 2 is a 1, the interrupt is masked off (disabled).
- Bit 1 is the RST 6.5 mask and works the same as bit 2.
- Bit 0 is the RST 5.5 mask and works the same as bit 2 and bit 1.

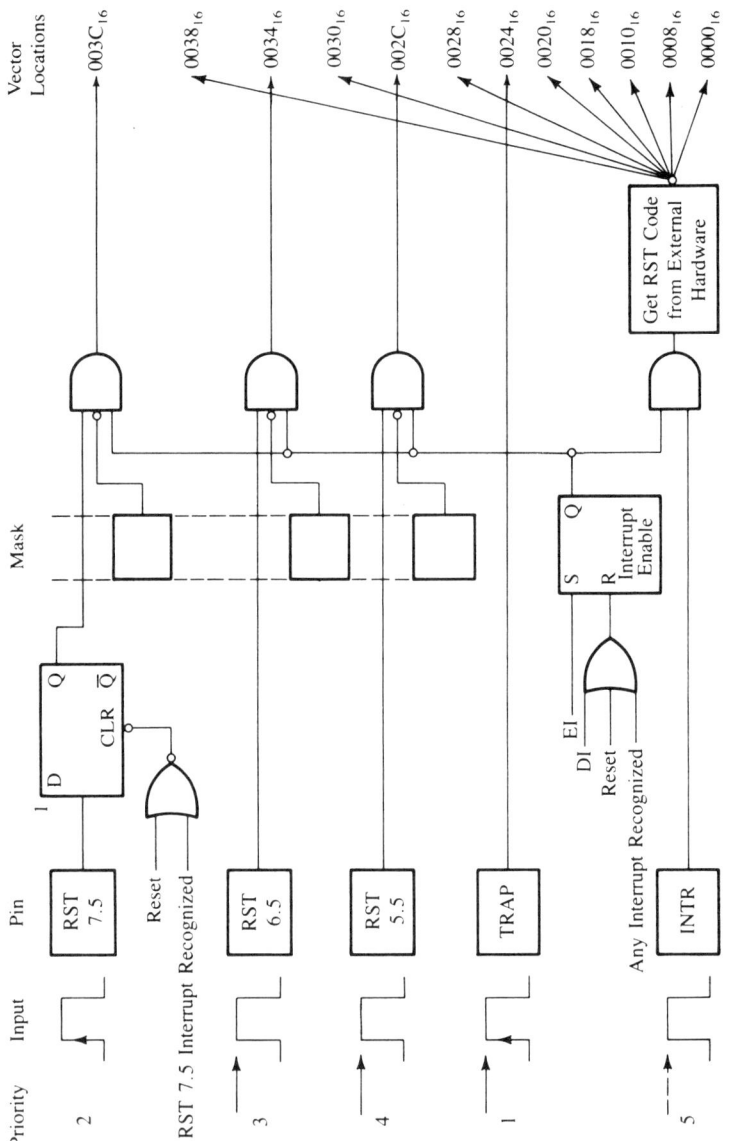

Figure 5.5 The 8085 interrupts and vector locations. (*Source*: Reprinted by permission of Intel Corporation, Copyright © Intel Corporation 1979.)

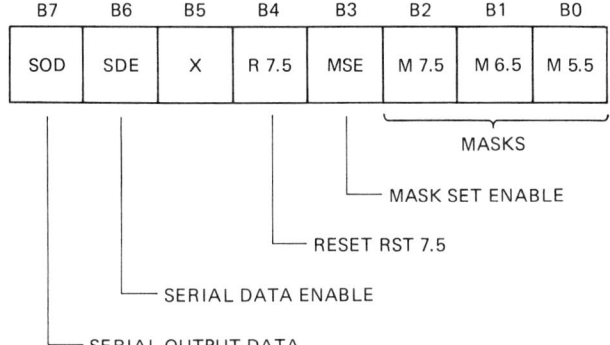

Figure 5.6 Accumulator before SIM.

A hardware reset will set the interrupt masks to 1, disabling RST 5.5, RST 6.5, and RST 7.5. Remember, TRAP cannot be masked.

5.4.7 RIM

When RIM is executed, bits will be loaded into the accumulator to give information about four things:

1. The status of the RST 5.5, RST 6.5, and RST 7.5 interrupt mask bits (0 = enabled and 1 = disabled, presumably the result of a prior SIM instruction or a reset).
2. The current status of the interrupt enable flag (1 = enabled). The flag will be set to 1 when EI is executed. It will be reset to 0 if DI is executed, if an interrupt occurs, or as the result of a hardware reset. (Note: Immediately following a TRAP interrupt, RIM will give the status of the interrupt enable flag prior to the TRAP. The TRAP service routine should include a RIM so that subsequent RIMs will yield the *current* status.)
3. Which hardware interrupts are pending.
4. Serial input data from the SID pin.

As shown in Fig. 5.7, following a RIM instruction the accumulator bits will be as follows.

- Bit 7 will be the value that was on the SID pin just prior to RIM.
- Bit 6 indicates if the RST 7.5 interrupt is pending (1 = pending). (RST 7.5 is edge-triggered; it stays pending unless recognized or reset.)
- Bit 5 indicates if the RST 6.5 interrupt is pending (1 = pending). (RST 6.5 is level-triggered; it must stay high to remain pending.)
- Bit 4 indicates if the RST 5.5 interrupt is pending (1 = pending). (RST 5.5 is level-triggered; it must stay high to remain pending.)
- Bit 3 is the interrupt enable (IE) flag (1 = enabled).

Sec. 5.4 The 8085 Interrupts

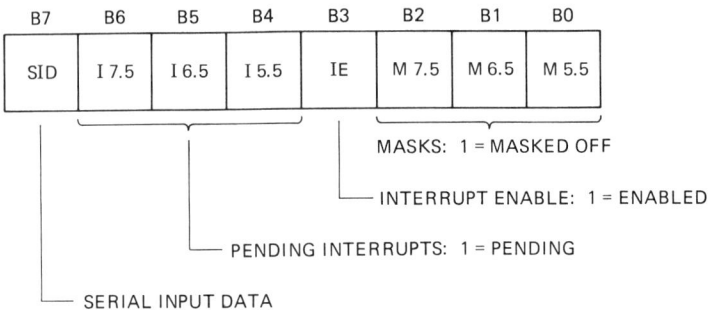

Figure 5.7 Accumulator after RIM.

- Bit 2 is the RST 7.5 mask bit (0 = enabled).
- Bit 1 is the RST 6.5 mask bit (0 = enabled).
- Bit 0 is the RST 5.5 mask bit (0 = enabled).

5.4.8 A Programming Example

In Chap. 6 we examine applications using the 8085 hardware restarts to generate interrupts. Here, in Example 5.8, we use the restart pins to implement a simple polling system.

EXAMPLE 5.8 Using a Restart for a Polling Loop

As shown in Fig. 5.8, we connect status lines from three devices to the RST 5.5, RST 6.5, and RST 7.5 pins on the 8085. However, they will not be used to generate interrupts. As external oscillator will drive the TRAP pin to generate periodically an interrupt and the TRAP service routine will check the status of the devices to see which need service.

In the program fragment shown here, note the use of RIM in the TRAP service routine. Also note the use of SIM to reset the RST 7.5 interrupt in the SR75 routine. Remember that RST 7.5 is latched, and because we are not allowing it to cause an interrupt, we must reset it in software.

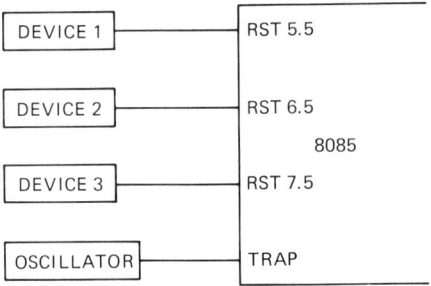

Figure 5.8 Restart for a polling loop.

144   Interrupts and DMA   Chap. 5

```
                ORG     0024H         ; RST 7.5 VECTOR ADDRESS

                RIM                   ; GET PENDING STATUS
                RLC                   ; IGNORE SID
                RLC                   ; GET I7.5
                CC      SR75          ; CALL SERV. ROUT. IF HI
                RLC                   ; GET I6.5
                CC      SR65          ; CALL SERV. ROUT. IF HI
                RLC                   ; GET I5.5
                CC      SR55          ; CALL SERV. ROUT. IF HI
                RET                   ; TO MAIN

                ORG     START         ; START OF MAIN PROG
        MAIN:   DI                    ; NO INTERRUPTS BUT TRAP
                MVI     A,1FH         ; R7.5=1 MSE=1 MASKS=1
                SIM                   ; INITIALIZE MASKS
                < REST OF MAIN PROGRAM >

        SR75:   NOP                   ;
                        < BODY OF SR75 >
                MVI     A,10H         ; RESET I7.5
                SIM                   ; DO IT
                RET                   ; TO TRAP ROUTINE
        SR65:   NOP                   ;
                        < BODY OF SR65 >
                RET                   ; TO TRAP ROUTINE
        SR55:   NOP                   ;
                        < BODY OF SR55 >
                RET                   ; TO TRAP ROUTINE
```

The frequency of the oscillator determines how often the devices are polled. However, the frequency cannot be set arbitrarily. Because TRAP cannot be blocked, we must make sure that there is enough time between interrupts to execute all three device routines (SR55, SR65, SR75), as well as the TRAP routine itself.

5.5 DIRECT MEMORY ACCESS (DMA)

The basic architecture of the traditional computer, as first delineated by John von Neumann, consists of a single CPU and a single memory with a single data channel (bus) interconnecting them. The problem with such a design is that all data must flow, one word at a time, through that data channel. Moving large blocks of data into and out of memory via the CPU is slow and prevents the CPU from doing other work while data are being moved. One way around the "Von Neumann bottleneck" is to use multiple-CPU parallel architecture, a discussion of which is beyond the scope of this book. Another way is direct memory access (DMA).

5.5.1 DMA Basic Description

DMA is a method of bypassing the CPU. A special DMA controller chip is used to take temporary control of the bus structure away from the CPU and move data rapidly into or out of memory. Of course, the CPU must be designed to support DMA and have the appropriate control signals (handshaking) to allow it.

DMA is typically used to transfer quickly large blocks of data between memory and an I/O device such as a disk drive or the frame buffer in a video system. We will examine two ways of doing DMA: burst and cycle stealing. In section 5.6 we will look at a specific DMA device.

5.5.2 DMA Controllers

A DMA controller is an interface between the I/O device and the bus structure. The CPU can control its mode of operation by accessing a special status and control register in the controller that the processor sees as a port address. Usually, a DMA controller will have multiple channels, meaning several I/O devices can share it on a priority basis. For each channel, the controller would have the following:

- A *DMA Address Register* to hold the address of the first memory location to access
- A *Count Register,* which holds the number of words to transfer
- *Request* and *Acknowledge* handshaking lines for the I/O device

The controller also has hardware to control the bus structure in order to read and write data.

In operation, an I/O device would request DMA transfer from the controller. The controller would then assert the DMA request line on the CPU. The CPU hardware (not under software control) will let go of the address and data lines by *floating* them (they are tristate outputs) and acknowledge the controller, which, in turn, will take control of the bus and acknowledge the I/O device. The controller will then proceed to move data between the I/O device and memory until the number in the count register is reached. The controller will then release the bus back to the CPU, which continues from where it left off.

5.5.3 Burst Mode

In *burst mode,* the controller transfers large blocks of data between the I/O device and memory. During burst mode transfers, the CPU must suspend any processing that uses the bus address and data lines. The rate of transfer is limited only by the access time of memory chips and the speed of the DMA controller. Burst mode DMA may not be appropriate if the processor is running a time-critical program.

5.5.4 Cycle Stealing and Transparent DMA

In *cycle stealing,* the transfer of individual data words is done in between the execution of program instructions. The DMA controller "steals" a few machine cycles every now and then. The effect is to make the DMA concurrent with CPU processing.

Even with cycle stealing, the CPU will be blocked if it tries to execute a read or write during DMA. A variation on cycle stealing that overcomes that problem is *transparent* DMA. In transparent DMA, special logic in the controller will detect when the CPU is executing instructions that do not require the address and data buses. DMA transfer can then be done without suspending the CPU, thus maintaining throughput and not disturbing any critical process timing.

5.6 THE 8257 PROGRAMMABLE DMA CONTROLLER

The 8257 is a four-channel DMA controller designed to be compatible with the 8085 and other 8-bit microprocessors. It can transfer blocks of 1 to 16,384 bytes. It comes in a 40-pin DIP and requires a single +5V supply. Figure 5.9 shows the block diagram and pin configuration.

The following discussion is simply an overview of the 8257. For a complete description, the reader should refer to the Intel literature.

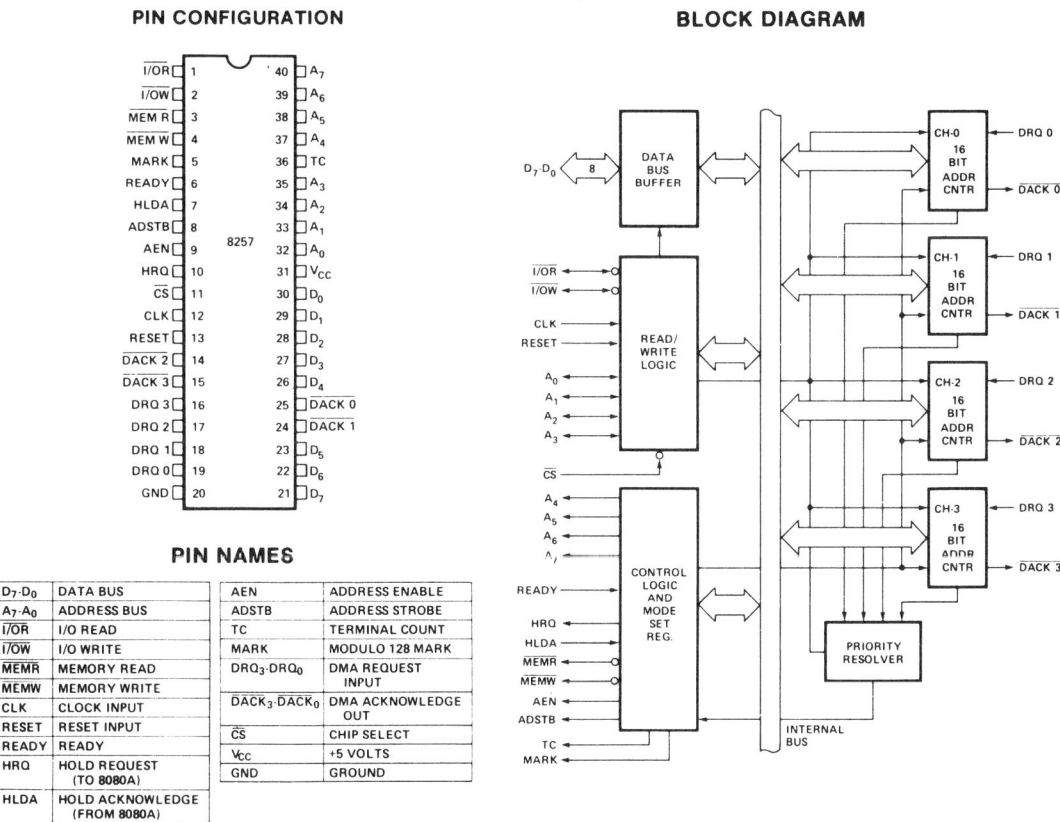

Figure 5.9 Block diagram of the 8257 DMA controller. (*Source:* Reprinted by permission of Intel Corporation, Copyright © Intel Corporation 1980.)

5.6.1 The Channels

The 8257 has four identical channels (CH0–CH3) to communicate with up to four external devices. Each channel has an associated pair of signals: DRQ (DMA request) and $\overline{\text{DACK}}$ (DMA acknowledge). The external devices would share the address and data bus with the microprocessor through tristate transceivers. Because the processor normally has control of the bus, the external device transceivers would normally be in the high-impedance state. An external device can use the bus only when the 8257 takes control.

Each channel has an associated pair of 16-bit registers: one to hold the DMA start address and the other to hold the byte count. Both must be initialized in software by the processor before a channel is enabled.

5.6.2 Operation

Available DMA services are read, write, and verify. To request service, a device will assert its DRQ line. If the request is granted, the 8257 will respond as follows:

1. The 8257 will assert its HRQ (hold request) line. HRQ is connected to the processor's DMA request line, such as the 8085 HOLD pin.
2. The processor lets go of the bus by putting its drivers into the high-impedance state and pulls the 8257 HOLDA pin high. The 8085 has a HOLDA output that would be used for the purpose.
3. The 8257 puts out the first address and pulses $\overline{\text{DACK}}$ to strobe the data on the bus, one pulse for each byte.
4. Step 3 is repeated for sequential addresses while the byte count is decremented.
5. When the byte count gets to zero, the 8257 TC (terminal count) pin goes high and DMA for that channel usually ends. Note that DRQ can be used to do the DMA in several bursts until TC says it is complete.

5.6.3 8257 Modes

The 8257 has two modes: master and slave. In the *master* mode it controls the bus and does DMA. In the *slave* mode, it is a peripheral chip with a chip-select ($\overline{\text{CS}}$) pin and internal registers addressed as I/O ports. $\overline{\text{CS}}$ can be tied to an address line because in master mode, $\overline{\text{CS}}$ is disabled. The 8257 is initialized in slave mode prior to doing DMA.

5.6.4 The Terminal Count Register

The start address is the address of the first memory location to be accessed. The byte count is held in the *terminal count register* (TCR). The lower 14 bits of the TCR specify the number of DMA cycles to be executed when the channel is enabled. Note that for N cycles, the number loaded into TCR should be N − 1. During

TABLE 5.3 TCR AND DMA ACTION

Bit 15	Bit 14	DMA action
0	0	Verify
0	1	Write
1	0	Read
1	1	Illegal

the Nth cycle, the 8257 TC pin will go high. TC high tells the external device that service on the block of bytes has been completed. The upper 2 bits of TCR specify the DMA action for the channel; as shown in Table 5.3.

Note that *write* means from external device to memory, whereas *read* means from memory to external device. During *verify,* no data are read or written, but the 8257 generates $\overline{DACK}$ pulses for each data byte as if transfer were taking place. The external device can use the pulses as timing for its own purposes.

5.6.5 The Mode Set Register

As shown in Fig. 5.10, the 8-bit mode set register is divided into two 4-bit halves. The lower 4 bits are enables. Setting one of them to a 1 enables the corresponding DMA channel. A 0 disables the channel. The upper 4 bits are used to select options for 8257 operation. We will not discuss AUTOLOAD and EXTENDED WRITE; they are normally reset to 0. The other two work as follows:

TC STOP: If the TC STOP bit is set, then the active DMA channel will be disabled (i.e., the channel enable bit will go to 0) when TC goes high. The enable bit for that channel will have to be set back to 1 by software to reenable it. If the TC STOP bit is low, then it is up to the external device to see the TC line go true and take the appropriate action.

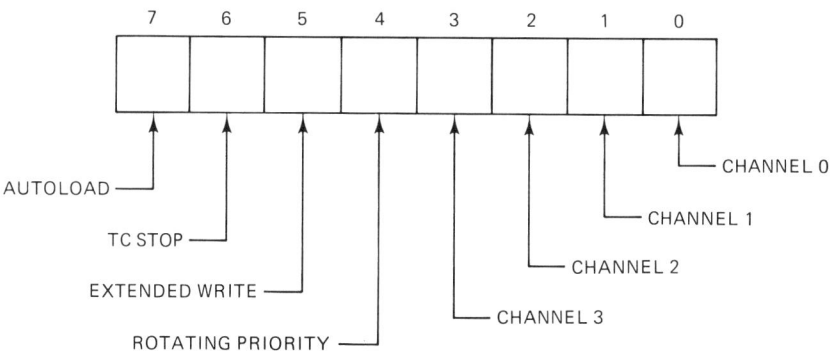

Figure 5.10 Mode set register.

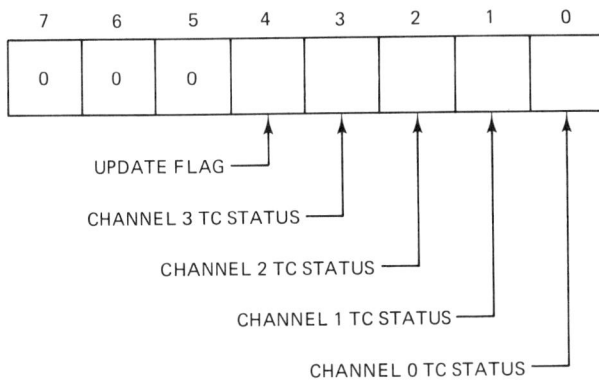

Figure 5.11 Status register.

ROTATING PRIORITY: If this bit is a 0, then the DMA channels have a fixed priority with CH0 being highest and CH3 lowest. If the bit is a 1, then the priority rotates. After a channel is serviced, its priority drops to last and the next channel becomes highest.

5.6.6 The Status Register

Figure 5.11 shows the 8-bit status register that can be read by the processor. The lower 4 bits tell when a channel has reached its terminal count. A bit value of 1 means the channel has completed its DMA action; a 0 means it has not. In nonautoload mode, a channel will have to be reenabled for more DMA after its TC STATUS bit goes high. The upper 3 bits are always 0 and have no significance. The UPDATE FLAG bit is used in autoload mode. Refer to Intel literature for details.

5.6.7 8257 Port Addresses

In slave mode, the 8257 registers are usually mapped to I/O ports. The upper 4 bits of the port address (A7–A4) can be decoded for $\overline{CS}$, and the lower 4 bits (A3–A0)

TABLE 5.4 A3–A0 BITS OF REGISTER ADDRESSES

Register	A3	A2	A1	A0
CH0 DMA address	0	0	0	0
CH0 terminal count	0	0	0	1
CH1 DMA address	0	0	1	0
CH1 terminal count	0	0	1	1
CH2 DMA address	0	1	0	0
CH2 terminal count	0	1	0	1
CH3 DMA address	0	1	1	0
CH3 terminal count	0	1	1	0
Mode set/status	1	0	0	0

will be used by the 8257 to select a register. Table 5.4 shows the A3–A0 bits of the register addresses.

Note that there is only one address for each register. Because the 8257 uses an 8-bit data bus, the 16-bit registers must be written to *twice*. The first byte written to a 16-bit register is the low byte; the second is the high byte. Also note that the mode set and status registers have the same address. Reading from that address gives STATUS; writing to it addresses MODE SET.

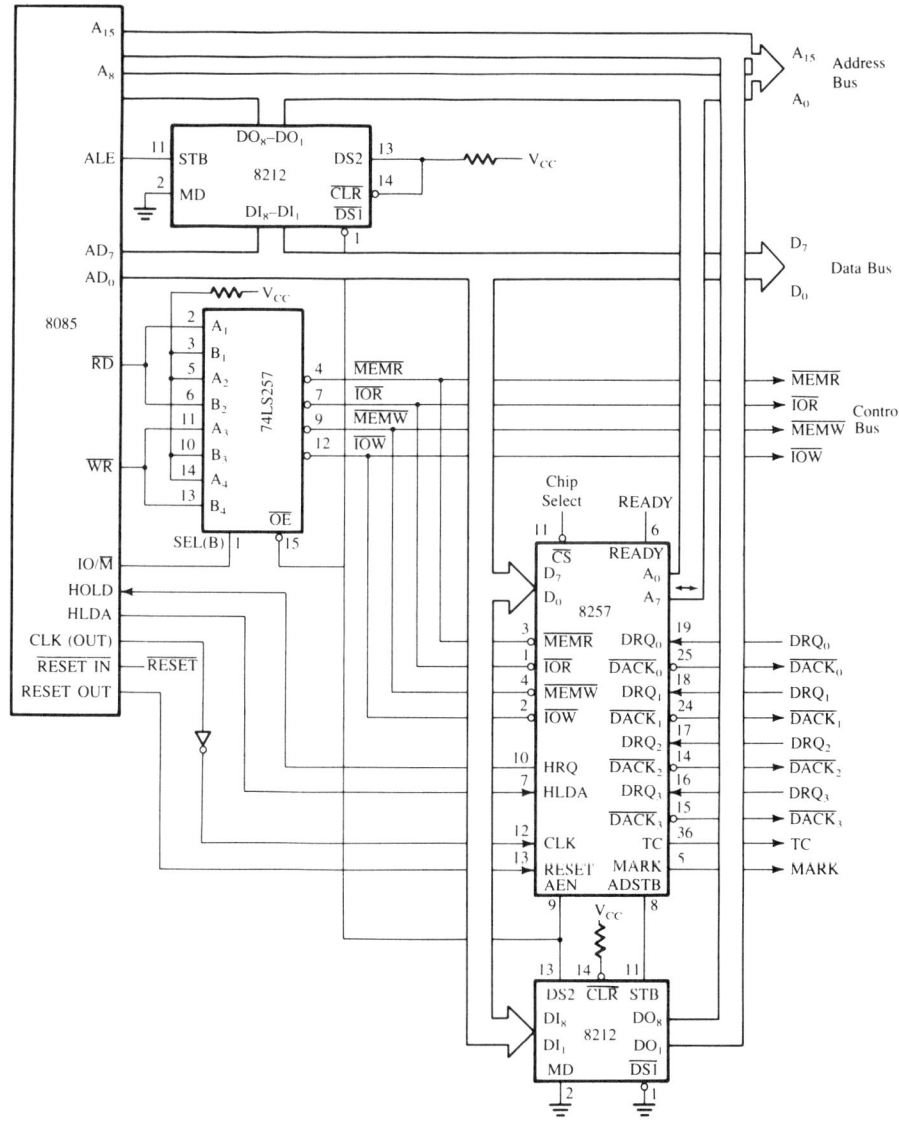

Figure 5.12 Schematic of interfacing 8257 DMA controller. (*Source:* Reprinted by permission of Intel Corporation, Copyright © Intel Corporation 1981.)

5.6.8 A Typical Circuit

Figure 5.12 shows an 8257 interfaced to an 8085. Several observations can be made regarding the circuit:

1. The 8257 does not have an ALE pin; it cannot demultiplex the data from the address on the lower 8 bits of the 8085 bus. The circuit uses an 8212 latch to do the demultiplexing.
2. The 8257 requires separate read and write signals for accessing I/O and memory. The circuit uses a 74LS257 multiplexer with a tristate output to generate $\overline{\text{MEMR}}$ and $\overline{\text{MEMW}}$ together with $\overline{\text{IOR}}$ and $\overline{\text{IOW}}$.
3. The decoding for the 8257 chip select is not shown. We can assume an appropriate value for the upper 4 bits of the port addresses.
4. HRQ from the 8257 goes to HOLD on the 8085. HOLDA from the 8085 goes back to HOLDA on the 8257. AEN from the 8257 goes to $\overline{\text{OE}}$ on the 74LS257. HRQ will force the 8085 to let go of the address and data buses, and AEN will force the 74LS257 to let go of the control bus. AEN also floats the 8212 used to demultiplex the data.
5. The circuit uses a second 8212 latch, enabled by AEN. The latch is used to hold the high-order 8 bits of the memory address during DMA. The 8257 sends the high-order bits to the 8212 over the data bus and uses ADSTB to strobe it into the latch.

5.6.9 A Programming Example

EXAMPLE 5.9 Using the 8257

The following is a program using the 8257. The program sets up the CH0 channel for an external device to write 4100 (1004h) bytes into memory starting at address 1000h. We will assign port addresses to the 8257 starting at F0H. Use of equates allows the program parameters to be changed easily.

Note that the channels are initialized before they are enabled. We assume that the system has been previously reset, so the 8257 channels are initially disabled.

```
;                       EQUATES
VERIFY    EQU    00H        ; UPPER 2 BITS = 00
WRITE     EQU    40H        ; UPPER 2 BITS = 01
READ      EQU    80H        ; UPPER 2 BITS = 10
PORTS     EQU    0F0H       ; 8257 PORTS
CH0ADR    EQU    PORTS+00   ; CH0 DMA ADDRESS
CH0TCT    EQU    PORTS+01   ; CH0 TERMINAL COUNT
MODSET    EQU    PORTS+08   ; MODE SET
STHI      EQU    10H        ; HI BYTE OF START ADDRESS
STLO      EQU    00H        ; LO BYTE OF START ADDRESS
CNTHI     EQU    10H        ; HI BYTE OF COUNT
CNTLO     EQU    04H        ; LO BYTE OF COUNT
```

```
;                    INITIALIZATION
         MVI    A,STLO      ; NOTE
         OUT    CHOADR      ; PORT
         MVI    A,STHI      ; ADDRESSES
         OUT    CHOADR      ; USED
         MVI    A,CNTLO     ; TWICE
         OUT    CHOTCT      ; FOR
         MVI    A,CNTHI     ; 16-BIT VALUES
         ORI    WRITE       ; ADD DMA ACTION BITS
         OUT    CHOTCT      ;
         MVI    A,41H       ; TC_STOP=TRUE CHO=ENABLE
         OUT    MODSET      ;
;        START MAIN PROGRAM
         < REST OF PROGRAM >
```

5.7 SUMMARY

In this chapter we considered the idea of an interrupt, both in general and in the specific case of the 8085 microprocessor. We described polled and vectored interrupts and examined the 8085 hardware restarts, together with the associated SIM and RIM instructions. The constraints on interrupts were analyzed in terms of latency, interrupt density, and time limits. Also, we examined direct memory access (DMA) and defined the terms *burst* mode, *cycle stealing,* and *transparency*. After a general description of DMA, we used the 8257 DMA controller as an example device.

CHAPTER REVIEW

Questions

1. Explain polling.
2. Explain in general what an interrupt is.
3. Explain vectoring.
4. Explain the interrupt structure of the 8085.
5. Explain what RIM and SIM do.
6. Compare and contrast maskable and nonmaskable interrupts.
7. Explain the interaction between interrupts and the HALT state.
8. Explain latency with an example.
9. Explain the time limit problem in interrupt-driven systems.
10. What does interrupt density refer to?
11. Explain in general what DMA is.
12. What are the basic functions of a DMA controller?
13. Compare cycle stealing and transparent DMA.
14. Describe the 8257 chip.

Problems

1. Following Example 5.2, assume a system has three prioritized interrupts: INT1, INT2, and INT3. INT1 has the highest priority and INT3 the lowest. INT1 takes 500 μsec and INT3 takes 300 μsec. Calculate the worst case latency time for INT2, assuming no multiple occurrences of INT3.
2. Calculate interrupt density as a percentage for an interrupt that occurs five times a second and takes 20 msec to execute.
3. A system is planned to have four interrupts with the following specifications:

Interrupt	Time to execute (μsec)	Frequency of occurrence (times/sec)
INT1	500	100
INT2	800	200
INT3	400	50
INT4	100	10

    Calculate whether or not the system will be interrupt bound.
4. Assume a four-interrupt system with the same time to execute numbers as given in Prob. 3. Calculate the total latency time for INT3 (TLT3) if INT1 can happen twice and INT2 can happen three times before INT3 gets its chance.
5. Repeat the problem in Example 5.6 with the following changes: T4 = 50 msec, N1 = 3, and INT3 occurs twice per second.
6. Draw the schematic for a hardware implementation of RST 3.
7. Write an 8085 program to use the 8257. Assume an external device uses channel 1 to write 256 bytes into memory starting at location 2000h.

chapter 6

Interfacing: Hardware and Software

OBJECTIVES

Upon completion of this chapter, you should be able to

1. Analyze a typical hardware/software interface
2. Write code to interface to various electromechanical devices
3. Write code to interface to various printers and displays
4. Explain interfaces such as Centronics, IEEE-488, RS-232C, and A/D
5. Write a simple interrupt I/O program

6.1 INTRODUCTION

When you stop to think about it, getting a microprocessor to do something for you in the real world is an amazing thing. First you have an idea of what you want done. Then you translate that idea into a program that is stored in the processor's memory. When the program executes, your idea acts itself out using the various I/O devices connected to the processor. It can get feedback through input sensors and change the flow of execution accordingly while it drives output devices to carry out its task. If we didn't know how it was done, we might be tempted to call it magic.

The place where information and control flow back and forth between the program and the real world is the interface. The exact meaning of the term *interface* depends on the context in which it is used, but usually it means more than just an I/O port. An interface can also include special hardware, such as an A/D converter, as well as special software, such as a subroutine to use the A/D (a driver routine). Also, information may have to be structured in a certain way to pass through the interface, as, for example, with a communications protocol such as RS-232. In this chapter we examine some typical interfacing issues, both hardware and software.

6.2 MECHANICAL SWITCHES

Mechanical switches are common input devices. They are discussed here in terms of hardware and software considerations.

6.2.1 Description and Nomenclature

A common mechanical switch construction is one or more pairs of contacts that can be *open* (not touching) or *closed* (touching). One contact of each pair is mounted on a movable piece called the *pole*. The pole can be in one of two positions, depending on whether or not the switch is *activated* (pressed). If a pole can close a contact pair in only one of the two positions, it is said to be *single throw*. If it can close a pair in both positions, it is called *double throw*. Also, *normally open* (N.O.) contacts close when a switch is activated, and *normally closed* (N.C.) contacts open when a switch is activated. Switches are drawn in their normal, deactivated (finger off the button) state.

Typical switch designations are SPST, for single-pole-single-throw, SPDT, for single-pole-double-throw, and DPDT, for double-pole-double-throw. When the number of poles exceeds two, a digit is used such as 4PDT for four-pole-double-throw. There are various mechanical means of actuation, such as push button, toggle, foot switch, and the like. A switch that is designed for use on machinery where some moving part of the machine will activate it is called a *limit switch*. Figure 6.1 shows the schematic symbols for several switches.

Mechanical switches also can be characterized as either *momentary* or *latched*. Many (but certainly not all) momentary switches are of the push-button type (see Fig. 6.2). A momentary switch stays activated only as long as you press it, whereas a latched switch (e.g., a toggle switch) will stay in the last position it was placed.

When choosing a switch, it must be "sized" for the application—that is, the contacts must be able to pass the required current and be able to interrupt the voltage

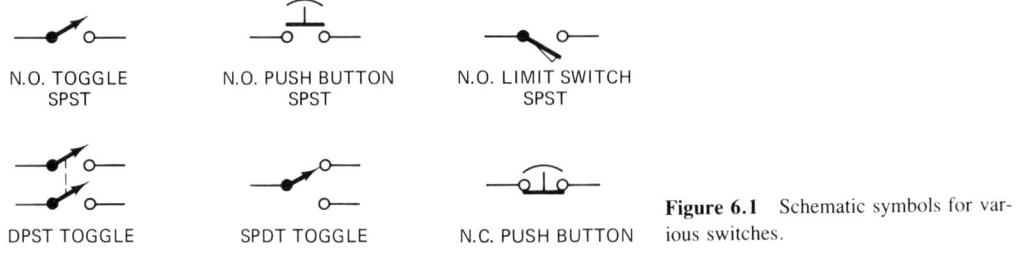

Figure 6.1 Schematic symbols for various switches.

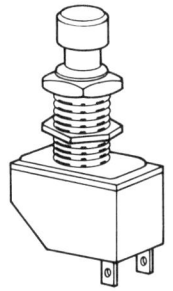

PUSHBUTTON SWITCH   **Figure 6.2** Push-button switch.

levels present on opening without excessive arcing. An undersized switch will have a short life expectancy.

EXAMPLE 6.1 A Dry Circuit

When a switch is used as an input to a microprocessor, it is usually a *dry circuit* application, meaning that the voltage and current levels are so low (microvolts and microamps) that they are not significant. Switch life can then be on the order of 10^4 to 10^6 activations, depending on mechanical quality.

A *rotary switch* (see Fig. 6.3) differs from those just described in that the rotating pole can have more than two throws. You could, for example, have a 4P10T rotary switch, but it would be called a four-pole-ten-position switch instead of a ten-throw switch. Rotaries are commonly used for selector switch types of applications. The contacts on rotary switches may be *break-before-make,* meaning that as the switch is rotated, the contact on the pole will leave one stationary contact completely (break) before it touches the next contact (make). Or else they can be *make-before-break,* meaning that as the switch is rotated, the contact on the pole will, for a brief time, short out two adjacent stationary contacts before coming to rest at the next position.

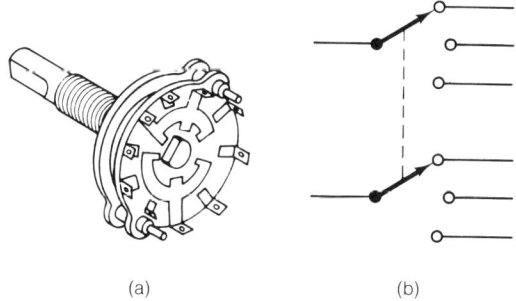

(a)   (b)

Figure 6.3 Two-pole-three-position rotary switch. Adapted from Patrick O'Conner, *Digital and Microprocessor Technology* © 1983, p. 145. Reprinted by permission of Prentice-Hall, Inc., Englewood Cliffs, N.J.

6.2.2 Contact Bounce and Debouncing

The moving parts of a switch have mass and springiness. What they don't have is a lot of resistance to their motion, or damping. Any springy mechanical system with low damping is going to exhibit oscillatory, or "bouncy," behavior. When a N.O. switch is activated, the contacts will come together and bounce off each other several times before finally coming to rest in a closed position (see Fig. 6.4). Such behavior is called *contact bounce* or *switch bounce*. Contacts bounce over a period of milliseconds (5–25 msec), whereas microprocessors can execute an entire subroutine in a period of microseconds. A common example is a keyboard on a CRT terminal. Each key is actually a switch. If you press the letter E, you want a single E to appear on the screen. A bouncy switch can make the processor think the key was pressed several times, and several Es will appear. Obviously, mechanical switches must be *debounced*.

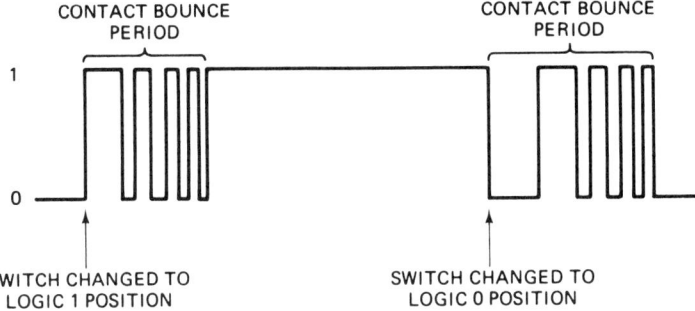

Figure 6.4 Multiple signal transitions caused by contact bounce of a mechanical switch. (*Source:* Kenneth Short, *Microprocessors and Programmed Logic*, © 1981, p. 332. Reprinted by permission of Prentice-Hall, Inc., Englewood Cliffs, N.J.)

EXAMPLE 6.2 Hardware Debouncing

Debouncing may be done in hardware, as shown in Fig. 6.5. Note the use of *pull-up* resistors to provide logic level voltages to the switch circuit.

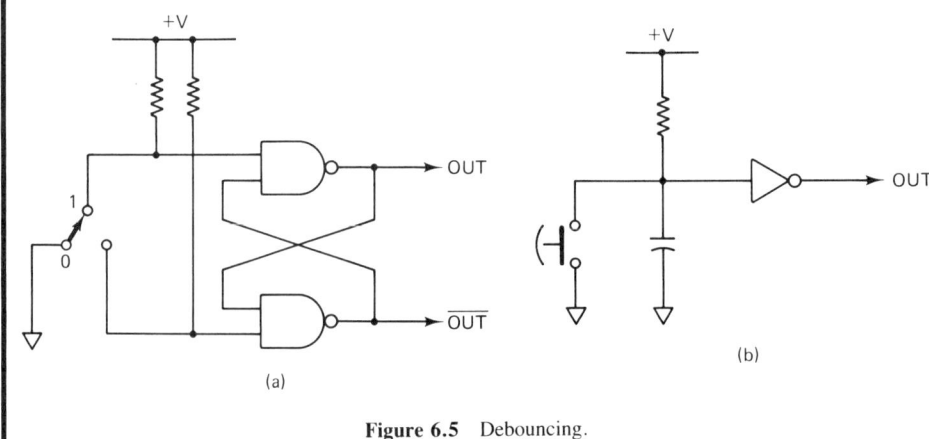

Figure 6.5 Debouncing.

Debouncing can also be done in software. Although a hardware solution may be practical for one or two switches, cost considerations often require a software solution for keypads and other applications using large numbers of switches. Note that, through use, switches tend to loose some of their springiness. The result is that the time it takes for bouncing to stop may *increase* as a switch gets older, and the debounce code that worked fine when the keypad was new may not work a year later unless you allowed for the change. Consult the switch manufacturer for data on worst case bounce time.

EXAMPLE 6.3 Software Debouncing

The program here shows the subroutine PCNT, which counts the number of times a momentary push button is pressed. When PCNT is called, it waits in LOOP1 for the switch to be pressed. When a contact closure is detected, PCNT updates the count (stored at memory location COUNT) and calls the DELAY subroutine to kill time waiting for the switch to stop bouncing. After returning from DELAY, PCNT then waits in LOOP2 for you to take your finger off the switch before it returns to the calling routine. Note that LOOP2 is just as necessary as the debounce delay to prevent multiple counts from a single switch press.

```
PCNT:      PUSH PSW           ; SAVE ACC & FLAGS

LOOP1:     IN   SWITCH        ; READ SWITCH
           CPI  OPEN          ; IS IT OPEN?
           JZ   LOOP1         ; IF YES, LOOK AGAIN

           LDA  COUNT         ; SWITCH CLOSED, SO
           INR  A             ; GET COUNT, ADD 1
           STA  COUNT         ; AND SAVE COUNT
           CALL DELAY         ; WAIT TIL BOUNCING STOPS

LOOP2:     IN   SWITCH        ; READ SWITCH AGAIN
           CPI  OPEN          ; STILL PRESSED?
           JNZ  LOOP2         ; IF YES, LOOK AGAIN

           CALL DELAY         ; CAN BOUNCE ON OPENING

           POP  PSW           ; RESTORE ACC & FLAGS
           RET                ; RETURN TO MAIN
```

6.2.3 Switch Arrays and Encoders

If a system uses only a few switches, their status can be read directly through an I/O port. When many switches are used in an array, such as a 16-switch hex keypad or a 64-switch typewriter style keyboard, other methods are used to read them. One method is to use a hardware *encoder*. Some switches, such as the *thumbwheel* switch shown in Fig. 6.6, come with built-in encoders. More commonly a circuit is required.

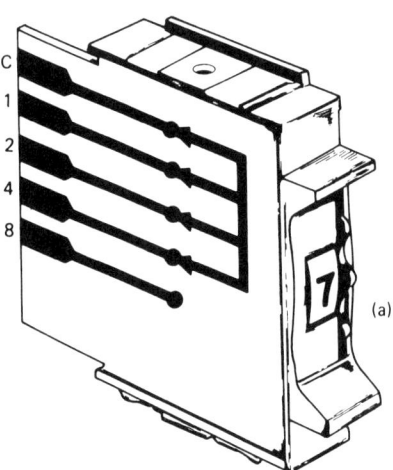

Figure 6.6 Thumbwheel switch. (a) Pictorial. (b) Truth table indicating which terminals are connected to common for each dial position. (*Source:* Adapted from Kenneth Short, *Microprocessors and Programmed Logic,* © 1981, p. 335. Reprinted by permission of Prentice-Hall, Inc., Englewood Cliffs, N.J.)

EXAMPLE 6.4 Encoding

In Fig. 6.7, 16 switches are shown connected to an encoder circuit. When any switch is pressed, the encoder will generate a 4-bit number corresponding to that particular switch. As soon as the 4-bit number becomes stable, a data-available (DAV) status bit will go true. When the switch is released, DAV goes false. Note that the encoder also debounces the switches, so DAV will go true only once for each key press.

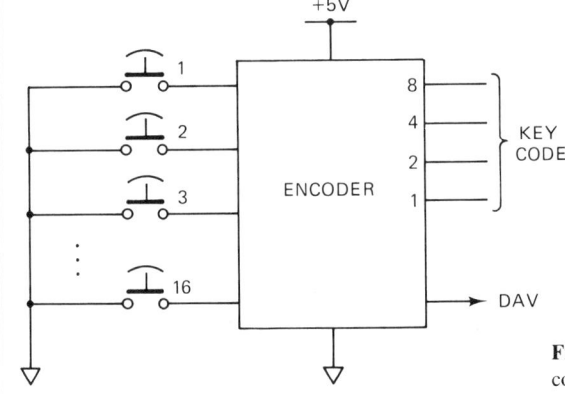

Figure 6.7 Switches connected to an encoder.

A problem occurs if more than one switch is pressed simultaneously. One solution is to have the encoder either ignore multiple key presses or output another status bit to indicate an error condition. A more useful approach is to have the encoder implement *rollover*. Rollover depends on the fact that even when two or more keys are pressed "simultaneously," in fact one switch will close before the other. In *two-key rollover,* the first contact closure is accepted and all subsequent closures are ignored until the first key is released. In *N-key rollover,* a second key press will be accepted before the first key is released. Although more complicated to implement, N-key rollover is preferred in applications such as terminal keyboards where rapid typing can easily cause multiple key presses.

6.2.4 Switch Matrix and Keyboards

For large numbers of switches, the direct connection shown in Fig. 6.7 is not practical because of the large number of connections required, one for each switch. The number of connections can be reduced by wiring the switches into rows and columns in an X-Y *matrix,* as shown in Fig. 6.8. The switches in a matrix are read by a *scanning process.*

In the typical matrix, the columns are connected to the logic 1 level by pull-up resistors. The rows are also held high but are driven low, one at a time, in a repeating cycle. Each time a row is driven low, the columns are read sequentially

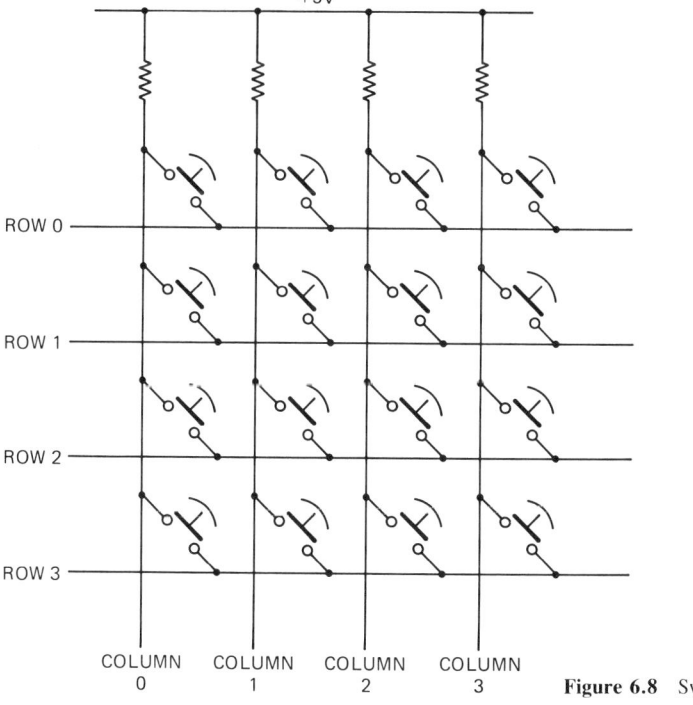

Figure 6.8 Switch X=Y matrix.

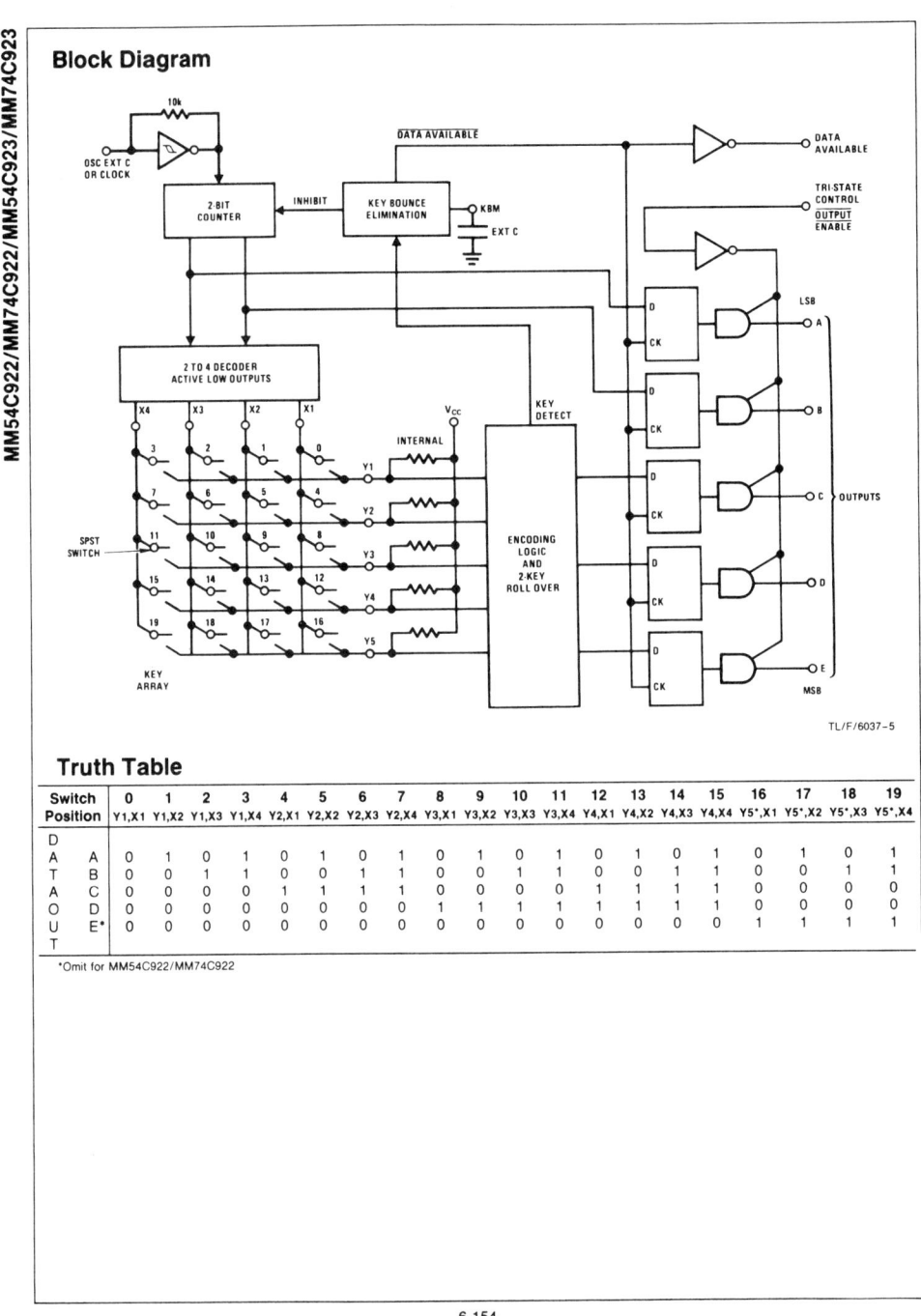

Figure 6.9 Integrated circuit 20-key keyboard scanner MM74C923. (*Source:* Reprinted with permission of National Semiconductor Corporation.)

to see which, if any, are low. Because the switches are N.O., if no key is pressed all the columns will remain high. If a key is pressed, a column will go low when the row that intersects that column at the closed switch is driven low. By knowing which row and column are low simultaneously, you can figure out which key was

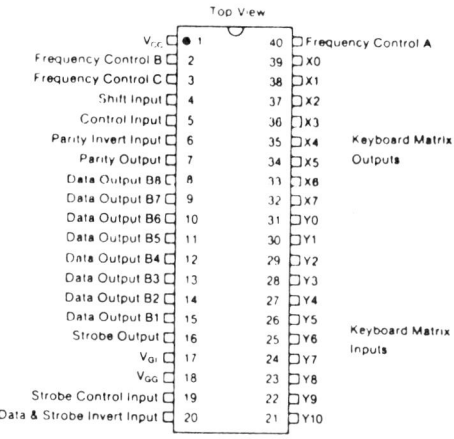

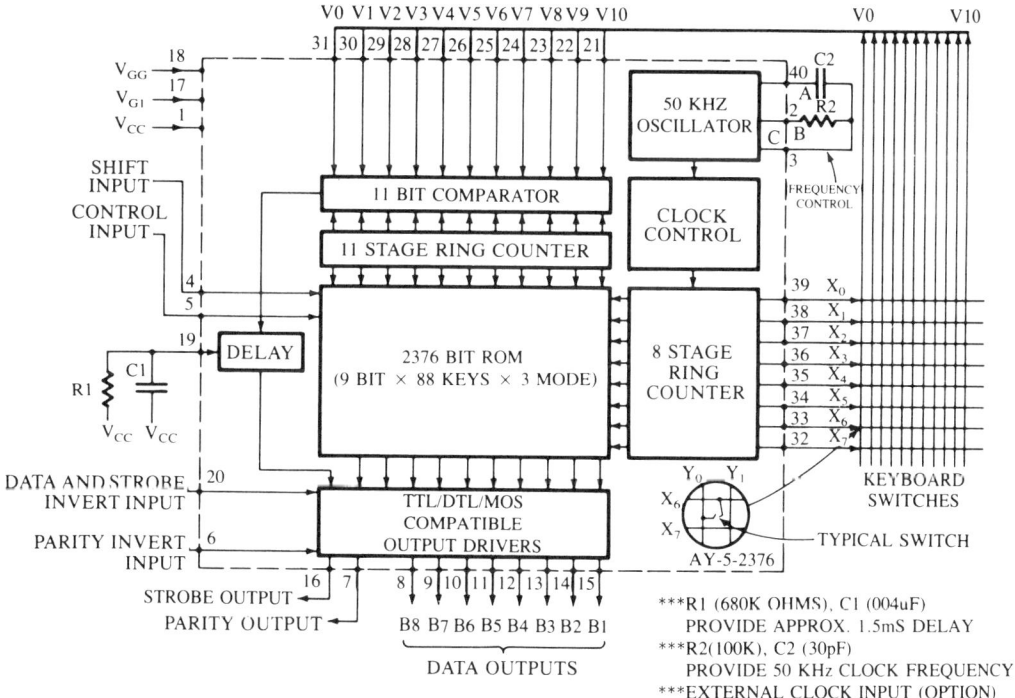

Figure 6.10 Pinout and block diagram of the AY-5-2376 keyboard encoder. (*Source:* Courtesy of General Instrument Corporation and Microchip Technology Incorporated.)

pressed. Note that the roles of the rows and columns can be reversed. Also note that the switches must be scanned rapidly compared to the speed of a key press, but that is not usually a problem.

A matrix can be scanned in software using I/O ports to drive the rows and read the columns. (Such software is developed in Chap. 12, on system design.) It can also be done in hardware with a chip designed for the purpose, such as the MM74C923 shown in Fig. 6.9. Some encoders just match a sequential binary number to each switch. When an encoder is built into a keyboard to form a separate device (a fully encoded keyboard), it is usually desirable that the encoder output a standard code for each labeled key. Thus, pressing the A key on a fully encoded ASCII keyboard will yield the hex number 41 at the output of the encoder together with a data-available signal. The encoder hardware may contain a combination of logic and ROM to generate the appropriate codes to match the keys. See Fig. 6.10.

A keyboard is not the only application for a switch matrix. Switch matrixes are often used to trace movement, such as pressure switches buried in a floor or fine wires embedded in a writing pad to follow the movement of a stylus.

6.3 SOLID STATE SWITCHES

If a microprocessor needs to read signals from an external transducer, such as a photo pickup, the voltage levels supplied by the device may not be compatible with the logic levels required at the I/O port. One solution is to use a transistor as a solid state N.O. switch.

EXAMPLE 6.5 A Transistor Switch

Refer to Fig. 6.11. When sufficient voltage is applied to the base (or gate, if using a FET device), the transistor turns on and acts like a switch closed to ground. When the voltage is removed from the base, the transistor turns off and acts like an open switch.

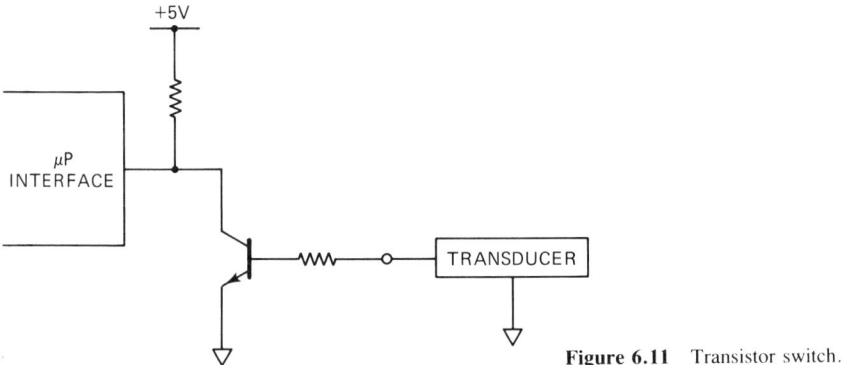

Figure 6.11 Transistor switch.

Transistors are much faster than mechanical switches and can last almost indefinitely when used properly. There are, however, two problems to consider: switching and isolation.

6.3.1 Switching and Hysteresis

The *switching* problem comes about because for some range of base voltage the transistor can act like a linear amplifier. The result is that if the signal from the transducer changes from the on level to the off level slowly, the transistor may rapidly turn on and off many times as it passes through its linear region. The effect is similar to contact bounce. The solution is to introduce some *hysteresis*.

Hysteresis in a switch means that the voltage needed to turn it on initially is higher than the voltage needed to keep it on. Likewise, the voltage at which the switch turns off is lower than the initial turn-on voltage. An IC device known as a Schmitt trigger gate is commonly used to introduce hysteresis, as shown in Fig. 6.12. The loop inside the gate symbol indicates hysteresis.

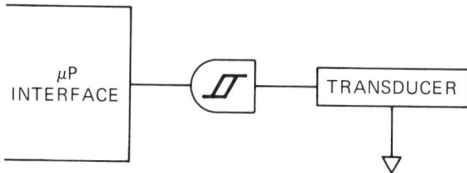

Figure 6.12 Switching problem solved by hysteresis.

6.3.2 Isolation

Isolation is required as a result of this variation of Murphy's law: *If a direct path exists between the outside world and the microprocessor, a destructively high voltage eventually will be applied to it*. The solution is to have a gap in the path through which signals only can be transmitted.

> **EXAMPLE 6.6 An Optoisolator**
>
> An optoisolator (Fig. 6.13) uses an LED and a phototransistor to transmit signals by light while allowing for separate grounds between voltages in the outside world and those inside the microprocessor-based equipment. Optoisolator IC chips can withstand hundreds (even thousands) of volts of difference between
>
>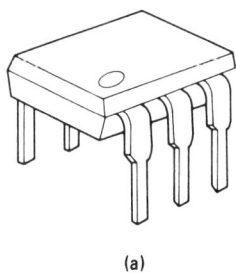
>
> (a)

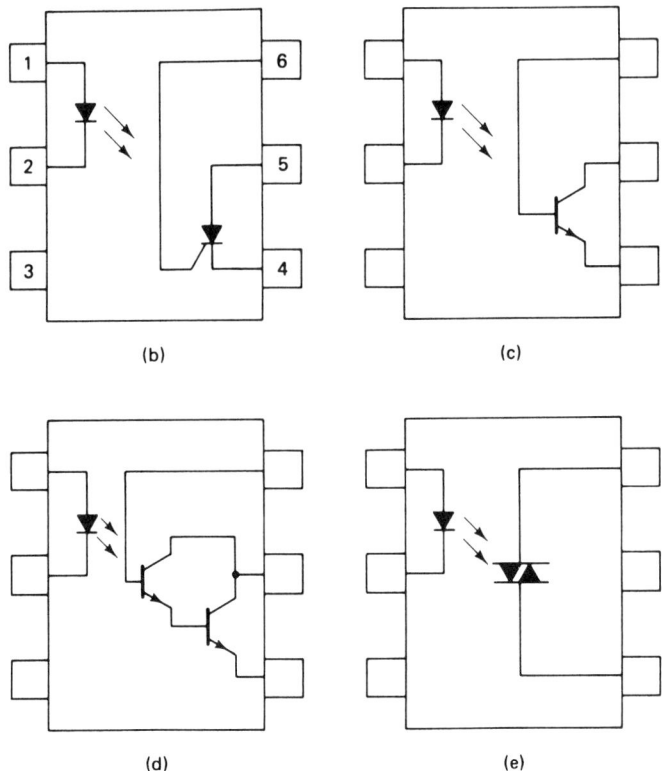

Figure 6.13 Optocoupler configurations. (a) Case 730A-01. (b) Photo SCR output. (c) Phototransistor output. (d) Photo Darlington output. (e) Phototriac output. Some commercially available types: (b) MOC3002. (c) 4N26. (d) MOC119. (e) MOC633A. (*Source:* Gayakwad/Sokoloff, *Analog and Digital Control Systems,* © 1988, p. 48. Reprinted by permission of Prentice-Hall, Inc., Englewood Cliffs, N.J.)

input and output ground levels (common mode voltage) and are available with built-in Schmitt triggering.

Note that isolation is as important for outputs as it is for inputs.

6.3.3 Shaft Encoders

A *shaft encoder* is a device that converts the position or rotation of a shaft into a digital signal. There are two basic types: *incremental* and *absolute*. Both types use a disk attached to the shaft. On the disk are concentric strips, and each strip is divided in a binary pattern that can be read by a pickup. The position resolution is determined by the number of divisions (pulses) per rotation.

EXAMPLE 6.7 Incremental Shaft Encoder

As shown in Fig. 6.14, a typical incremental encoder has three strips (tracks). One track, the index, produces one pulse per revolution. The other two tracks (A and B) produce many pulses per revolution. The two pulse trains are in quadrature, meaning they are 90 degrees apart. Counting the index pulses per minute (tachometry) gives rpm. Counting pulses on the other tracks with respect to the

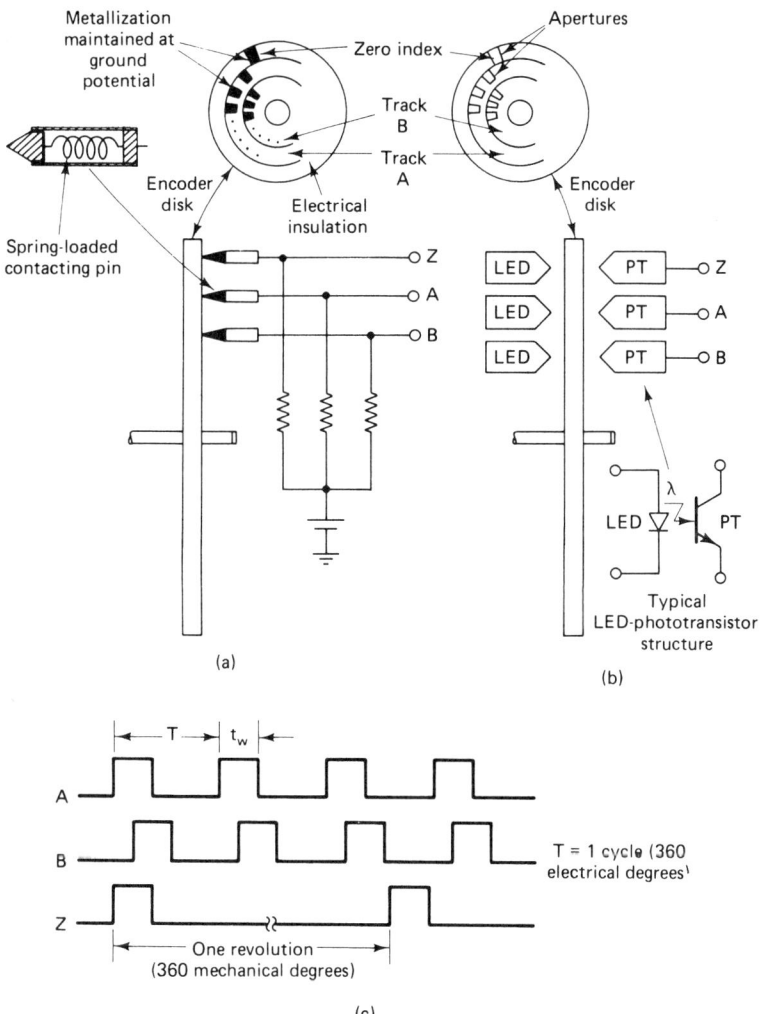

Figure 6.14 Incremental shaft position encoders. (a) Contacting type. (b) Optical type. (c) Encoder output waveforms. (*Source:* Gayakwad/Sokoloff, *Analog and Digital Control Systems,* © 1988, p. 84. Reprinted by permission of Prentice-Hall, Inc., Englewood Cliffs, N.J.)

index pulse gives the position of the shaft. Sensing the time sequence of the pulses on the two tracks (A-before-B or B-before-A) gives the direction of rotation. Because of their long life, incremental shaft encoders are often used instead of rotary switches in microprocessor-based equipment.

Figure 6.15 shows an absolute encoder. Note that for any angular position, the pickups would provide a unique binary number. The more tracks the better the resolution. Absolute encoders are typically more expensive than incremental encoders but have a built-in "memory" of their position. Absolute encoders often use a Grey code instead of simple binary encoding, so that between any two adjacent positions only one bit can change, thus reducing possible errors in reading.

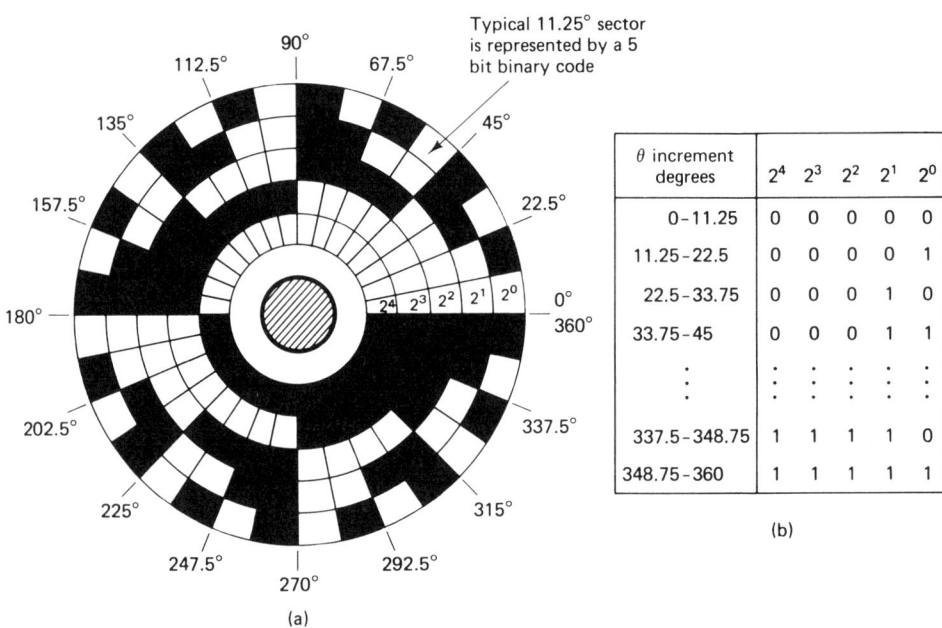

Figure 6.15 Absolute shaft position encoder. (a) Encoding disk (5-bit). (b) Angular code assignment truth table. (*Source:* Gayakwad/Sokoloff, *Analog and Digital Control Systems,* © 1988, p. 86. Reprinted by permission of Prentice-Hall, Inc., Englewood Cliffs, N.J.)

6.4 SOLENOIDS AND RELAYS

A *solenoid* is a coil of wire used to produce a magnetic field to move a steel actuator of some sort. When the actuator is used to close a pair of contacts, the device is called a *relay* (Fig. 6.16). Relays and solenoids are common in many kinds of equipment. An impact printer, for example, uses solenoids to drive the printhead and advance the paper. Relays are often used to turn large loads, such as ac motors, on and off.

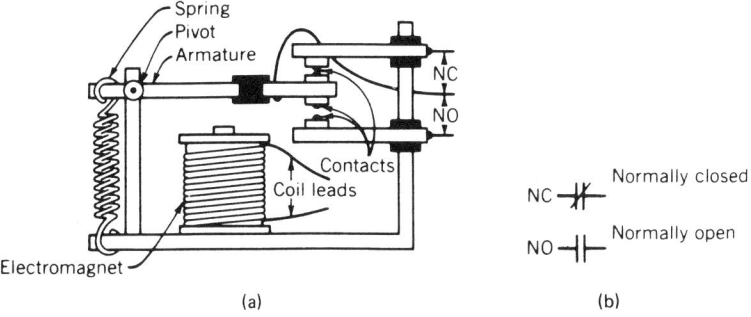

Figure 6.16 Electromagnetic Relay. (a) Simplified sketch. (b) Symbols showing normal relay contact state. (*Source: Industrial Electronics and Controls* by Martin Newman. Copyright © 1986 John Wiley & Sons. Reprinted by permission of John Wiley & Sons, Inc.)

6.4.1 Solenoid Drivers

Two things to know about solenoids: They can be electrically "noisy" and they often require a lot of current. The current requirements mean that most relays and solenoids require a transistor driver. The noise occurs as a short-duration voltage transient, or *spike,* when the current in the coil is abruptly turned off. The spike is due to the collapsing magnetic field inducing a voltage back into the coil, and its amplitude can be many times greater than the supply voltage. Protective circuitry is required to prevent spikes from damaging ("zapping") the transistor driver.

EXAMPLE 6.8 A DC Solenoid Driver

Figure 6.17 shows a typical solenoid driver for a dc coil, such as a control relay. The diode placed across the coil is the transient protection, as the spike voltage polarity will be opposite the applied voltage. The transistors are shown in a Darlington pair, which has a total current gain that is the product of the individual transistor gains. The gain of a Darlington is typically 2000 or more, so a 1-amp coil could be driven by 0.5 mA of current into the base. Darlingtons are available as integrated circuits.

Note that Fig. 6.17 also shows optical isolation. Not only does that provide protection from accidental voltages coming in "backwards" from the output, it also allows the coil to be driven from a separate power supply. Having the microprocessor and digital circuits share a power supply with relays and solenoids is asking for noise problems.

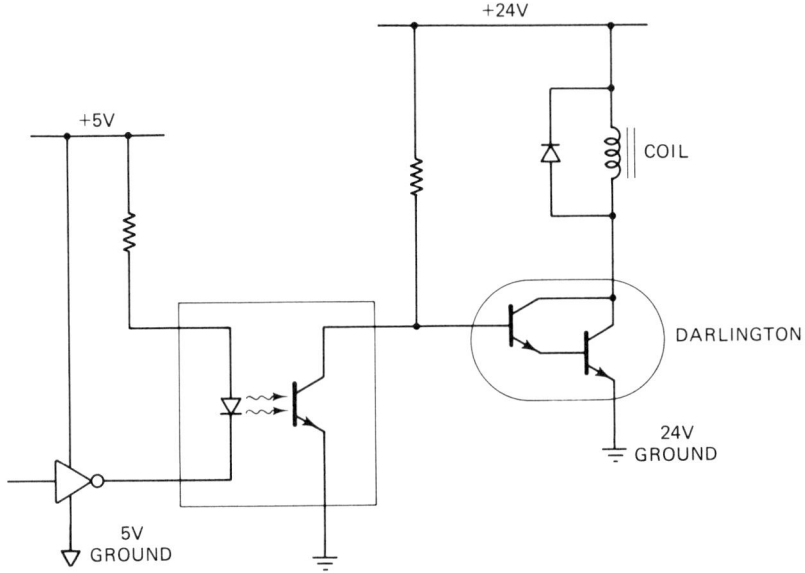

Figure 6.17 Solenoid driver for a dc coil.

6.4.2. AC Solenoids

Many industrial control solenoids and relays operate off the 120V ac mains, usually without transformer isolation. In such cases optical isolation is a necessity. Also, the driver device will be a triac instead of a transistor because a triac can conduct both ways, as required for AC current.

> **EXAMPLE 6.9 An AC Solenoid Driver**
>
> Figure 6.18 shows an ac solenoid interface. The resistor-capacitor circuit across the coil is a snubber. It does the same job as the diode across a dc coil, and is often required for larger ac solenoids. The optoisolator differs from what we saw earlier in that it uses a photosensitive triac in place of the phototransistor because the gate of the main triac requires ac drive. The R-C network on the gate is to prevent turn-on due to noise, or *false triggering*.

6.4.3 Relay Terminology

All that has been said about switch contacts, including bounce, also applies to relays. In addition, relay contacts are sometimes described in terms of their form: A N.O. contact pair is called form A; a N.C. pair is called form B; and a SPDT contact arrangement is called form C. The number of contact pairs is specified by a

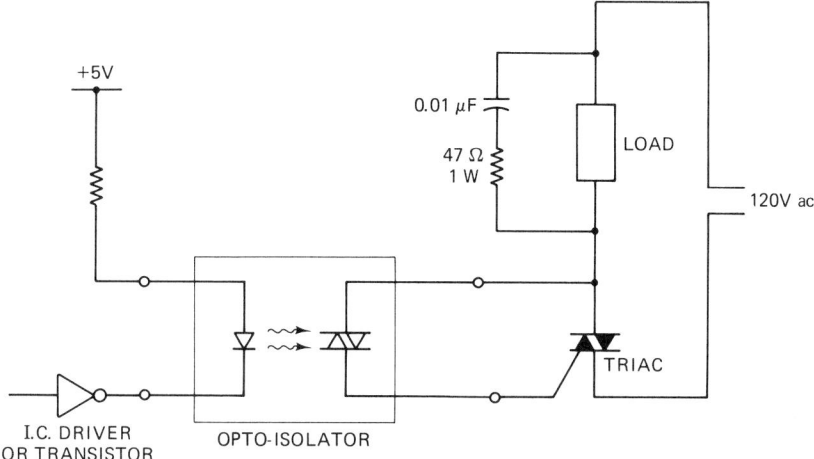

Figure 6.18 AC solenoid interface.

digit, so 1A2B on a relay means it contains a single N.O. pair and two N.C. pairs of contacts. Figure 6.19 shows the schematic symbols for relay contacts drawn in their deactivated (i.e., coil de-energized) state.

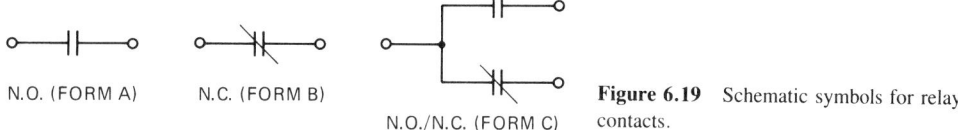

Figure 6.19 Schematic symbols for relay contacts.

Relays are divided into ac or dc according to their coil voltage and then further specified by voltage level. Voltages of 5V dc, 12V dc, 24V ac, and 120V ac are common. Note that not all coils of the same voltage draw the same current. Larger relays usually have lower resistance coils.

Relays have some built-in hysteresis. When the coil is energized, the steel pole moves to close the contacts but also shortens the magnetic path. So the pull-in voltage is higher than the drop-out voltage. Additional hysteresis may be needed to prevent *relay chatter*.

6.4.4 Solid State Relays

Solid state relays often combine the isolation, driving, and contact closure functions into a single package. Those meant to control ac loads typically use a triac in place of mechanical contacts. Hybrid designs combine solid state drive with metallic contacts. Solid state relays are fast, quiet, and last indefinitely (if not abused).

6.4.5 Software Toggles and Selectors

Many applications use software to make a momentary push-button switch act like a *toggle*. One push turns something on; the next push shuts it off.

EXAMPLE 6.10 A Software Toggle Switch

The program here will drive one bit of an output port alternately high and low each time a switch press is detected. The port can be assumed to drive a relay that controls, for example, a motor. DBNCE is a debounce routine, similar to the program in Example 6.3. Note that FLAG in the program does not refer to the 8085 flags but is used generically. When a program reads a value stored in a register or a memory location and then uses that value to alter the flow of execution, the value is called a flag.

```
               MVI   B,OFF      ; INITIALIZE FLAG
               MVI   A,00       ; AND TURN MOTOR
               OUT   RELAY      ; RELAY OFF

       LOOP:   IN    PB1        ; WAIT FOR
               CPI   OPEN       ; SWITCH
               JZ    LOOP       ; PRESS

               CALL  DBNCE      ; DEBOUNCE
               MOV   A,B        ; GET FLAG
               CPI   ON         ; WAS IT ON?
               JZ    TOFF       ; YES, SO JUMP

               MVI   B,ON       ; NO, SO CHANGE FLAG
               MVI   A,01       ; AND TURN
               OUT   RELAY      ; MOTOR ON
               JMP   LOOP       ; GO GET NEXT PRESS

       TOFF:   MVI   B,OFF      ; CHANGE FLAG AND
               MVI   A,00       ; TURN MOTOR
               OUT   RELAY      ; OFF
               JMP   LOOP       ; GO GET NEXT PRESS
```

Another common technique is to simulate a selector switch. Each press of a push button will energize a different "contact" in a fixed sequence.

EXAMPLE 6.11 A Software Selector Switch

This program has each press of a switch drive the bits of a port sequentially.

```
               MVI   B,01       ; INITIALIZE
               MOV   A,B        ; SELECTOR
               OUT   PORT       ; OUTPUT

       LOOP:   IN    SWITCH     ; WAIT
               CPI   OPEN       ; FOR
               JZ    LOOP       ; PRESS

               CALL  DBNCE      ; DEBOUNCE IT

               MOV   A,B        ; GET SELECTOR
               RLC              ; ROTATE IT
               MOV   B,A        ; SAVE IT
               OUT   PORT       ; NEXT SELECTION
               JMP   LOOP       ; GO WAIT
```

6.5 DISPLAYS AND PRINTERS

In this section we look at some common display and printing hardware and associated software.

6.5.1 LEDs

Light-emitting diodes (LEDs) have all but replaced incandescent lamps on display panels because of their power efficiency and long life. Because they can be turned on and off rapidly, high-power LEDs are sometimes used to drive digital data as pulses of light through fiber-optic cables.

> **EXAMPLE 6.12 LED Drive**
>
> Figure 6.20a shows a TTL circuit driving a low-power LED. If we assume a 1.6V drop across the LED, the 330-ohm resistor will allow approximately 10 mA of current, a typical level for good brightness. Higher power LEDs will require a transistor (or IC) driver, as shown in Fig. 6.20b.
>
>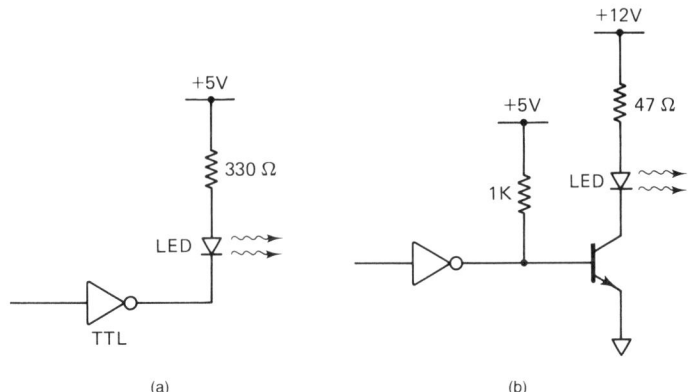
>
> **Figure 6.20** LED drive. (a) Low power. (b) High power.

6.5.2 Segment Displays

We briefly discussed seven-segment displays in Chapter 4. They have been implemented in several technologies, including liquid crystal (LCD), fluorescent, and plasma, as well as LED. LED seven-segment displays come in two configurations: *common anode* and *common cathode,* as shown in Fig. 6.21. Each LED corresponds to a segment.

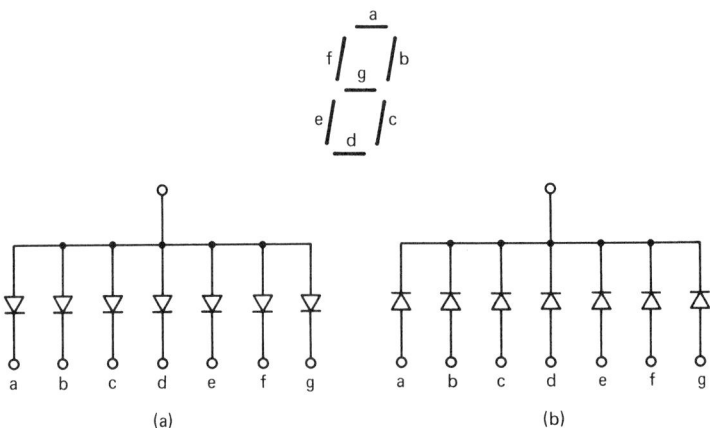

Figure 6.21 LED seven-segment displays. (a) Common anode. (b) Common cathode.

With only seven segments, a display is limited to showing only numeric digits and a few letters, enough for a hexadecimal number. To show a complete alphanumeric character set, a display needs more segments. Figure 6.22 shows a 16-segment display and its character set.

Segment displays can be driven by connecting each segment to a port bit (through transistor drivers), or they can be driven by *decoder/driver* ICs designed for the purpose. A decoder/driver chip will accept a parallel input (binary or ASCII) and drive the display to show the corresponding character.

Figure 6.22 Sixteen-segment display and its character set. (*Source:* Patrick O'Conner, *Digital and Microprocessor Technology,* © 1983, p. 407. Reprinted by permission of Prentice-Hall, Inc., Englewood Cliffs, N.J.)

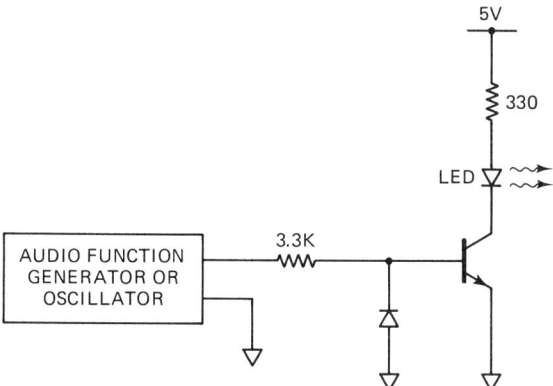

Figure 6.23 Circuit for a miltiplexed display.

6.5.3 Multiplexed Displays

Suppose a battery-powered instrument has a display of ten seven-segment characters. If each LED uses 10 mA and each segment is lit (all 8s), the total current demand on the battery would be 700 mA just to light the display. In order to conserve power most displays are *multiplexed*.

To multiplex such a display, the first character would be turned on for a brief period of time and then turned off. Then the second character would be flashed on and off; then the third. We would continue until the tenth character was shown and then start the cycle over. Only one seven-segment display would be lit at a time, so the maximum current would be only 70 mA. However, if the multiplexing is done fast enough, human vision integrates the light (smooths it out), so no flickering is seen. Television and motion pictures rely on the same effect. Most people perceive 20 flashes per second or faster as a steady light. To measure your own threshold, build the circuit in Fig. 6.23 and slowly increase the frequency until the flashing appears to give way to a constant light.

Figure 6.24 shows a block diagram of a multiplexed display. Note that a resistor is used for each segment instead of a single resistor for each display. The

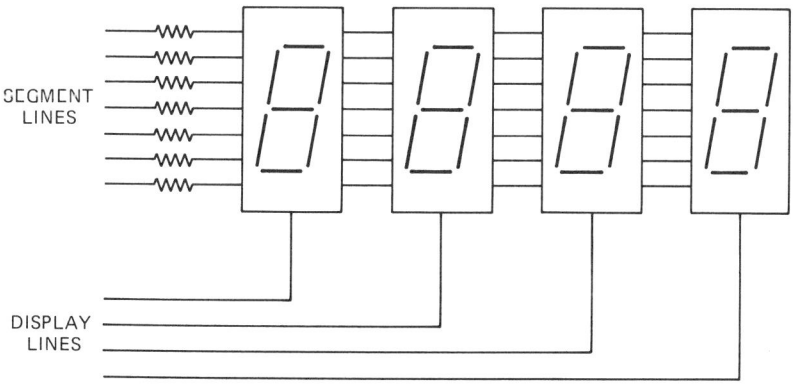

Figure 6.24 Block diagram of a multiplexed display.

voltage drop across each LED in a display is slightly different, and the lowest one would hog all the current from a single resistor.

EXAMPLE 6.13 Multiplexed Display Program

This program drives a four-digit multiplexed display. The port named DISP is assigned to the display drivers, 1 bit for each digit. Because only 4 digits are used, only the lower 4 bits of the port need be connected. The number held in register C will be used to drive DISP. It is initialized to 11 hex, or 00010001 binary, so every four rotations will cause the sequence to repeat. The numbers to be displayed are held in four consecutive memory locations starting at address NUMS. The subroutine CONVRT converts the binary number to the proper seven-segment equivalent using a look-up table (see Chap. 4). The port named SEGS drives the segments. Note that all the displays are off when the segments are changed to prevent cross-talk between the displays.

```
              MVI   C,11H      ; SET UP SEQUENCE
LOOP:   MVI   B,04       ; NUMBER OF DIGITS
        LXI   H,NUMS     ; ADDRESS OF DIGITS
NEXT:   SUB   A          ; CLEAR ACCUMULATOR
        OUT   DISP       ; TURN OFF DISPLAYS
        MOV   A,M        ; GET A DIGIT
        CALL  CONVRT     ; BINARY TO 7-SEG
        OUT   SEGS       ; OUTPUT DIGIT
        INX   H          ; ADVANCE DIGIT POINTER
        MOV   A,C        ; GET DISPLAY ENABLE
        OUT   DISP       ; TURN ON THE DISPLAY
        RLC              ; ADVANCE DISPLAY ENABLE
        MOV   C,A        ; SAVE IT
        CALL  DELAY      ; DIGIT ON-TIME
        DCR   B          ; DONE ALL DIGITS?
        JNZ   NEXT       ; NO, GET NEXT DIGIT
        JMP   LOOP       ; YES, REPEAT WHOLE CYCLE
```

6.5.4 Dot-Matrix Characters

As the name implies, a *dot-matrix* character is formed from a two-dimensional array of dots, as shown in Fig. 6.25a. Array sizes are given as width by height, such as 5×7 or 7×9. A higher number of dots can approximate fully formed or *near letter quality* (NLQ) characters. In addition to displays, dot-matrix technology is used in printers and other such hard-copy output devices. The dot patterns for the characters are typically stored in a ROM table. Changing character sets (fonts) can be as easy as changing the ROM chip.

EXAMPLE 6.14 5 × 7 Dot-Matrix Characters

As shown in Fig. 6.25, 5×7 characters can be stored as 7-bit patterns in 5 consecutive bytes of storage.

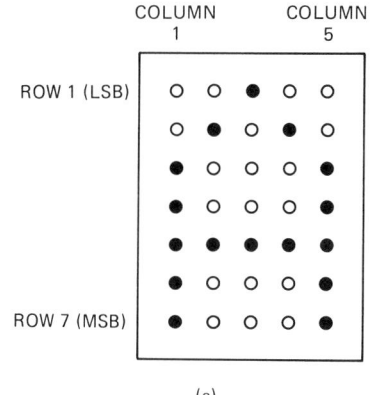

ADDRESS	CONTENT
1000	7C
1001	12
1002	11
1003	12
1004	7C

(b)

Figure 6.25 Dot-matrix printing. (a) 5 × 7 matrix displaying the letter A. (b) ROM table for storage of dot patterns.

Figure 6.26 shows a generalized dot-matrix printhead. It is a single vertical row because the motion of the head as it is pulled across the paper provides the horizontal dimension. An *impact printer* uses solenoids to press an inked ribbon onto the paper. A *drop-on-demand* type *ink-jet* printer uses piezoelectric crystals (or sometimes solenoids) to shoot drops of ink onto the paper. A *thermal* printer uses heat to "burn" each dot onto special paper. An *electrostatic* printer passes pulses of current through special aluminum-coated paper to burn dots.

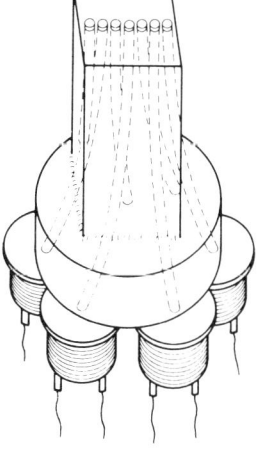

Figure 6.26 Dot-matrix printhead. (*Source:* Adapted from Patrick O'Connor, *Digital and Microprocessor Technology,* © 1983, p. 424. Reprinted by permission of Prentice-Hall, Inc., Englewood Cliffs, N.J.)

EXAMPLE 6.15 A Dot-Matrix Driver

The subroutine PRLINE in this program will drive a 5 × 7 printhead to print a single line of text terminated by a carriage return (CR). The line is held in a RAM buffer starting at address LBUFF. PRLINE calls CRLF (carriage-return line-feed) to get the printhead to a fresh line. Subroutine LOOKUP will take the ASCII character in the accumulator and return in DE the ROM address of the start of the dot character. Subroutine PULSE will print one column of dots, and STEP moves the printhead over to the next column.

```
PRLINE:   PUSH  PSW         ; SAVE
          PUSH  B           ; ALL
          PUSH  D           ; THE
          PUSH  H           ; REGISTERS

          CALL  CRLF        ; NEW LINE
          LXI   H,LBUFF     ; ADDRESS OF LINE BUFFER

LOOP1:    MOV   A,M         ; GET ASCII CHARACTER
          CPI   CR          ; END OF LINE?
          JZ    DONE        ; YES, GO HOME
          CALL  LOOKUP      ; NO, GET DOT CHARACTER
          MVI   B,05        ; SET UP COLUMN COUNT

LOOP2:    LDAX  D           ; GET A DOT COLUMN
          OUT   HEAD        ; SEND COL TO HEAD
          CALL  PULSE       ; PRINT A COLUMN
          CALL  STEP        ; NEXT COLUMN POSITION
          INX   D           ; NEXT COLUMN IN ROM
          DCR   B           ; ONE LESS COL TO PRINT
          JNZ   LOOP2       ; FINISHED THIS CHARACTER?

          CALL  STEP        ; YES, MAKE SPACE
          CALL  STEP        ; BETWEEN CHARACTERS

          JMP   LOOP1       ; GET NEXT CHAR FROM BUFF

DONE:     POP   H           ; RESTORE
          POP   D           ; ALL
          POP   B           ; THE
          POP   PSW         ; REGISTERS
          RET               ; OUT OF HERE
```

6.6 HANDSHAKING

Handshaking is the exchange of status bits between the processor and an I/O device. Status bits tell such things as whether the device is ready to receive data or if it has data it wishes to send. Often masking will be used to examine a specific bit in a status word and looping is used to wait for the bit to change. A printer, for example, typically has a buffer memory. When the buffer is full, it cannot accept any more characters until some are removed by printing.

Note that the essence of handshaking is an *exchange* of status information. A subroutine may ask a device, "are you ready?" When the device finally says "Yes," the subroutine responds with the (possibly formatted) data and says, "Here it is." The device takes it, and may then reply, "Thanks, I've got it" to complete the handshake. The signal to "do something" (e.g., print) is called a *strobe*. The signal "OK, it's done" is called an *acknowledgment* (ACK).

6.7 CENTRONICS PARALLEL INTERFACE

The parallel interface first used by Centronics Company on its line of inexpensive printers fast became a de facto industry standard.

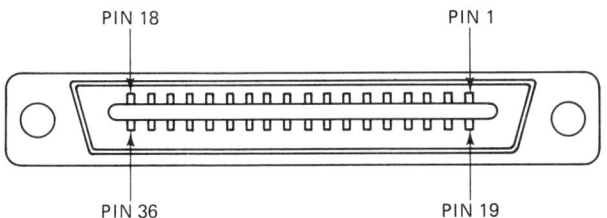

Figure 6.27 Thirty-six-pin Centronics printer interface connector.

TABLE 6.1 CENTRONICS PARALLEL INTERFACE SIGNAL DESCRIPTION

Pin	Name	Direction*	Description
1	$\overline{\text{STROBE}}$	to printer	indicates valid data on D1–D8
2	D1	to printer	data line 1 (least significant)
3	D2	,,	data line 2
4	D3	,,	data line 3
5	D4	,,	data line 4
6	D5	,,	data line 5
7	D6	,,	data line 6
8	D7	,,	data line 7
9	D8	,,	data line 8 (most significant)
10	$\overline{\text{ACK}}$	from printer	indicates data was accepted
11	BUSY	from printer	indicates printer is printing
12	PE	from printer	indicates "no paper" or "no ribbon"
13	SLCT	from printer	indicates printer is on-line
14	GND	none	signal ground
15			no connection
16	GND	none	signal ground
17	CHS	none	chassis ground (green wire ground)
18	VCC	from printer	positive 5 Volts, 20 mA maximum
19–30	GND	none	signal grounds
31	$\overline{\text{RESET}}$	to printer	puts printer into initial state
32	$\overline{\text{ERROR}}$	from printer	indicates printing failure or jam
33–36			no connection

*Note: the above interface is sometimes used bidirectionally

6.7.1 Brief Description

As shown in Fig. 6.27, the parallel interface uses a 36-pin connector (e.g., Amphenol part 57-30360) on a ribbon cable up to 15 feet long. It operates at TTL voltage levels. Table 6.1 gives the pin descriptions. Note that the parallel interface can be used for applications other than printers.

6.7.2 A Programming Example

The subroutine in Example 6.16 uses the Centronics interface to send a character to a printer each time it is called.

EXAMPLE 6.16 Centronics Interface Program

In the subroutine, port DATA is connected to the data pins (2–9). Port STATUS is connected to $\overline{\text{ERROR}}$, PE, SLCT, BUSY, and $\overline{\text{ACK}}$, with $\overline{\text{ERROR}}$ as the LSB (the upper 3 bits of STATUS are not used). If the status is not "normal," the subroutine returns with CY set. Bit 0 of port STRB is connected to $\overline{\text{STROBE}}$. The strobe pulse must be a minimum of 0.5 μsec long, and the data must remain stable for at least 0.5 μsec before and after the strobe.

```
PRINT:   PUSH  B          ; SAVE REGS

         MOV   B,A        ; SAVE THE CHARACTER
         IN    STATUS     ; READ STATUS
         ANI   07         ; MASK OFF BITS
         CPI   05         ; COMPARE TO NORMAL
         MOV   A,B        ; GET CHARACTER
         JZ    OK         ; WAS PRINTER OK?
         POP   B          ; NO, RESTORE REGS
         STC              ; SET ERROR FLAG
         RET              ; GO HOME

OK:      OUT   DATA       ; YES, PRINT CHAR
         NOP              ; ALLOW SET-UP TIME
         SUB   A          ; GET 00 IN ACC
         OUT   STRB       ; STROBE ACTIVE LOW
         NOP              ; STRETCH STROBE PULSE
         INR   A          ; GET 01 IN ACC
         OUT   STRB       ; END STROBE PULSE

ACKLP:   IN    STATUS     ; READ STATUS
         ANI   10H        ; JUST LOOK AT ACK\
         JNZ   ACKLP      ; IS IT DONE? JUMP IF NO

         SUB   A          ; DONE, SO CLEAR CY
         MOV   A,B        ; PUT CHAR BACK INTO ACC

         POP   B          ; RESTORE REGS
         RET              ; GO HOME
```

As written, PRINT will not return until the character is acknowledged. It keeps jumping back in a loop until $\overline{\text{ACK}}$ goes low. We should note that, in real life, the printer might fail and the program could wait forever. A better design would wait a finite amount of time and then handle the situation, perhaps with an error message sent to a CRT terminal.

6.8 IEEE-488 BUS (GPIB)

Hewlett-Packard Corporation (HP) developed a parallel bus to interconnect its line of programmable instruments. The bus, originally called the Hewlett-Packard Interface Bus (HPIB), became a de facto standard among instrument makers and became known as the General Purpose Instrumentation Bus (GPIB). In 1975, the Institute of Electrical and Electronic Engineers (IEEE) formalized GPIB into the published standard IEEE-488.

6.8.1 Brief Description

As shown in Fig. 6.28, the bus consists of 8 bidirectional data lines, 5 bus management lines, 3 handshake lines, and 8 grounds for a total of 24. As many as 15 devices may be connected to the bus. Devices can be separated by no more than 2 m, with a maximum cable length of 20 m. The maximum data transfer rate is 1 million bytes per second. Connections to the bus are by open collector or tristate logic. Because devices are connected to the bus in parallel, all devices must put a high on a line before the line actually goes high. Any device that puts a low on a line pulls that line down for all devices.

Four classes of devices can be hung on the bus:

1. A **Listener** is a device that, when addressed, can only receive data and commands over the bus. An example is a printer. Several listeners can be active simultaneously.
2. A **Talker** is a device that, when addressed, can send data and status over the bus. An example is a digital voltmeter. Only one talker at a time can be active.
3. A **Listener/Talker** is a device that can switch between being a listener and a talker.
4. A **Controller** is a device, typically microprocessor based, that coordinates the activities of the listeners and talkers. There can be more than one controller, but only one can be active at a time.

6.8.2 The Three-Wire Handshake

The three handshake signals are as follows:

DAV   **Data Available:** It is asserted high by a talker or controller to indicate that the data on the bus are valid.
NRFD   **Not Ready for Data:** A device pulls NRFD low to indicate that it is not ready to receive. A high means ready.

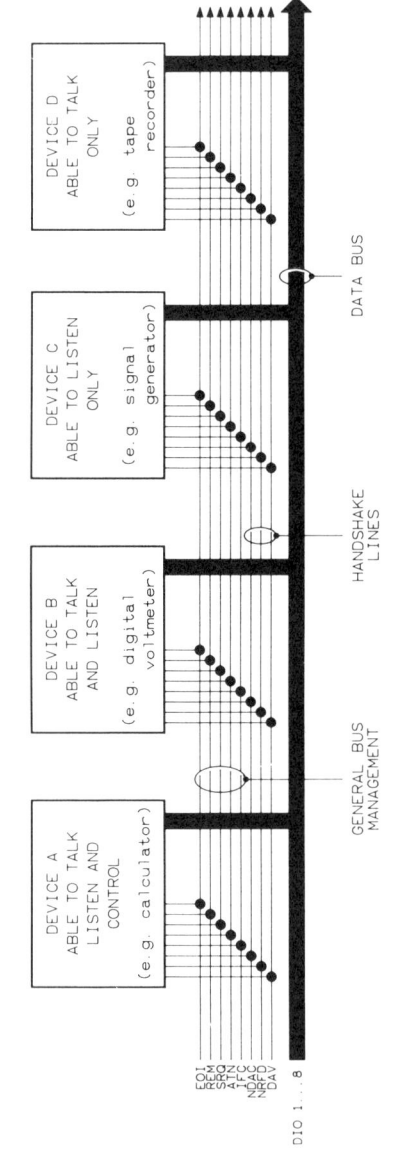

Figure 6.28 GPIB (IEEE-488) bus interface. (*Source:* Courtesy of Hewlett-Packard Co.)

NDAC   **Not Data Accepted:** A device pulls NDAC low while it is reading data off the bus. When finished, it lets NDAC go high.

> **EXAMPLE 6.17   A Handshake Sequence**
>
> Figure 6.29 shows a typical handshake sequence. A talker puts data on the bus and waits for NRFD to go high. For the NRFD line to go high, all devices must be ready. The talker then asserts DAV and waits for NDAC to go high. Again, all devices that are listening must accept the data before the NDAC line will go high. The talker can then drop DAV.

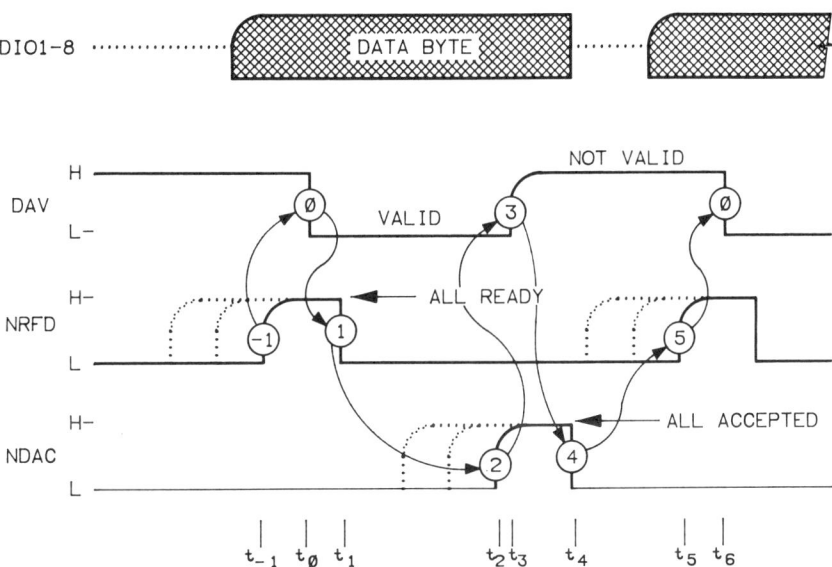

Figure 6.29   The IEEE-488 three-wire handshake. (*Source:* Courtesy of Hewlett-Packard Co.)

6.8.3 Bus Management

Bus management is done with the following signals:

IFC   **Interface Clear:** When asserted, it causes devices to cease the current bus activity.
ATN   **Attention:** It is asserted when a new talker or controller wishes to take over the bus.
SRQ   **Service Request:** A device asserts SRQ to interrupt the current bus activity so it can get service from the controller.
REN   **Remote Enable:** It is used to select remote or local control of a device.

EOI   **End or Identity:** It is used to identify a device when polled as well as to indicate the end of an operation.

6.9 RS-232C (EIA-232)   SERIAL INTERFACE

The venerable RS-232 standard (now known as EIA-232) published by the Electronic Industries Association (EIA) is old but still going strong. It is a common data communications physical level (meaning hardware) protocol.

6.9.1 Brief Description

The traditional implementation uses a 25-pin D-type connector (DB25). You will find other types, such as a 9-pin DIN connector, as rarely are all 25 pins used. Table 6.2 gives the descriptions of the commonly used pins. The nominal maximum cable length is 50 feet, although some are longer. Typical voltage levels are ±12V. For data, positive voltage represents binary 0 *(space)* and negative represents binary 1 *(mark)*. For the status pins, positive is true (on) and negative is false (off). When no data are being sent, the data line is held high (kept *marking*).

A complete description of RS-232C is not given here because it can be found in any data communications text. Briefly, data are sent, 1 bit at a time (serially), over an RS-232C link in the form of asynchronous frames. *Asynchronous* simply means that the timing between the frames can vary. As shown in Fig. 6.30, each frame consists of a start bit (always low), data bits, a parity bit, and a stop bit (always high). Data are sent LSB first. The rate at which the frame bits are sent is called the *baud rate* (or just baud) and is essentially the same as bits per second (bps). Note that while one stop bit is typical, one and a half or two stop bits are used in certain applications (e.g., low baud electromechanical equipment).

Common baud rates are 300, 600, 1200, 2400, 4800, and 9600. A frame may contain 5, 6, 7, or 8 data bits. The parity bit is optional, and may be odd or even.

TABLE 6.2 RS-232C PIN ASSIGNMENT

Pin number	Abbreviation	Description
1	GWG	Protective chassis ground
2	TD, SD	Transmit (send) data
3	RD	Receive data
4	RTS, RS	Request to send
5	CTS, CS	Clear to send
6	DSR	Data set ready
7	GND	Signal ground
8	CD, DCD	Carrier detect
20	DTR	Data terminal ready
22	RI	Ring indicator

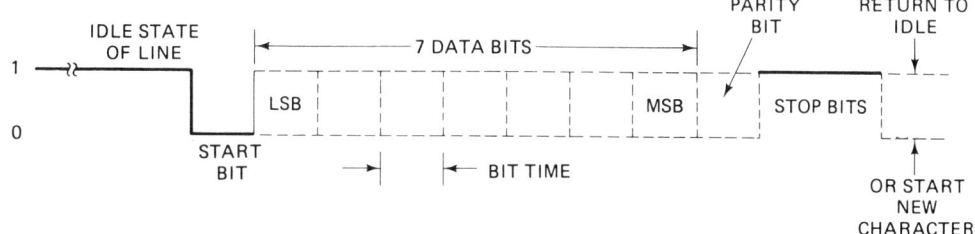

Figure 6.30 RS-232C (EIA-232) serial interface. (*Source:* Adapted from Kenneth Short, *Microprocessors and Programmed Logic*, © 1981, p. 282. Reprinted by permission of Prentice-Hall, Inc., Englewood Cliffs, N.J.)

Considering the many variations on RS-232, it may be wise to select a printer with a parallel interface. Modems especially require RS-232.

6.9.2 A Programming Example

Serial data are usually handled by a universal asynchronous receiver transmitter (UART) chip. The 8085, however, has the SID and SOD 1-bit ports, so a UART can be implemented in software.

EXAMPLE 6.18 Using SOD for Serial Data

This subroutine will send a serial frame when called. SOD would be connected to a line driver chip to convert the TTL voltage to RS-232C levels. The basic handshake is for the processor to *assert* (i.e., make true) RTS and wait for CTS as the go-ahead to send.

```
SEND:     PUSH  PSW         ; SAVE THE
          PUSH  B           ; WORKING REGISTERS

          MOV   B,A         ; SAVE THE DATA
          MVI   C,09        ; BIT COUNT: 8 DATA +START
          MVI   A,TRUE      ; ASSERT
          OUT   RTS         ; RTS

CTSLP:    IN    CTS         ; WAIT FOR
          CPI   TRUE        ; CTS
          JNZ   CTSLP       ; TO GO TRUE

          SUB   A           ; SET UP START BIT
LOOP:     ANI   80H         ; MASK OFF DATA BIT (MSB)
          ORI   40H         ; INSERT SOE BIT
          SIM               ; SEND IT
          CALL  DELAY       ; WAIT 1 BIT-TIME
          MOV   A,B         ; GET NEXT DATA
          RRC               ; BIT INTO MSB
          MOV   B,A         ; SAVE ROTATED DATA
          DCR   C           ; DEC LOOP COUNT
          JNZ   LOOP        ; FINISHED?
```

```
        MVI   A,0C0H    ; YES, SEND
        SIM             ; STOP BIT
        CALL  DELAY     ; WAIT LAST BIT TIME

        POP   B         ; RESTORE
        POP   PSW       ; REGISTERS
        RET             ; TO WHENCE YOU CAME
```

6.9.3 Checksums

When data are transmitted any distance, it is inevitable that errors will creep in. If you can't prevent it, you must detect and correct it. A full treatment of error detection and correction is beyond the scope of this text; however, we will look at the simple but very effective technique of *checksums*.

In comparison to simple parity, which is based on a single frame, checksums are based on a *block*. To implement checksums, the data are broken down into fixed-size blocks. For example, a 2K data file could be divided into eight blocks of 256 bytes each. All the bytes in a block are added up, even if they are ASCII characters, to get a 16-bit total. The addition is *modulo,* meaning you don't worry about overflow. The checksum is then formed by taking the two's complement of the total.

The checksum is sent as 2 bytes at the end of each block. As the receiver receives the data, it generates its own version of the checksum and compares it to the 2 bytes it received at the end of the block. If they agree, the block is assumed to be good. Otherwise, the block is bad and must be retransmitted. The receiver will send either a positive or negative acknowledgment (ACK or NAK) back to the transmitter after each block. (Actually, to verify the checksum the receiver just has to add up all the received bytes and then add the checksum. If the total is zero, the checksum is valid and the block is good.)

EXAMPLE 6.19   Checksum Calculation

To simplify the arithmetic, let's find an 8-bit checksum for four 4-bit words.

```
word 1 =     1001         one's complement of total is:   11010100
word 2 =     0110
word 3 =     1111         two's complement of total is the check-
word 4 =     1101         sum:   11010101
total  = 00101011
```

```
Verification:    1001
                 0110
                 1111           received data
                 1101
              00101011          sum of received data
           + 11010101           add the checksum
             00000000           total is zero; data are good
```

6.10 SOME 8155 APPLICATIONS

The 8155 is designed to give the 8085 a flexible I/O structure that includes a hardware handshake option. Also, the 8155 RAM is a good place to store I/O variables or implement a stack. In this section we look at some typical applications. Refer to section 2.6 as you read the following programs.

6.10.1 Stepper Motor Sequencer

Most motors spin continuously when voltage is applied. As the name implies, stepper motors move in discrete steps. A full treatment of stepper motors can be found in Gayakwad and Sokoloff. Briefly, the armature of a stepper is surrounded by a number of coils. As the coils are energized in a certain sequence, the armature will move in steps of a fixed angular size. The faster the sequence is repeated, the faster the motor turns. When the coils are held energized in a fixed state, the motor is held (locked) in position.

> **EXAMPLE 6.20 Stepper Motor Sequencer Program**
>
> Figure 6.31a shows the schematic of a four-phase (four-coil) motor and the associated coil drive sequence. If the sequence is executed from top to bottom, the motor turns clockwise (CW); bottom to top execution gives CCW rotation. Steppers are specified by steps per revolution (e.g., 200 steps/rev), as well as by speed and holding torque.

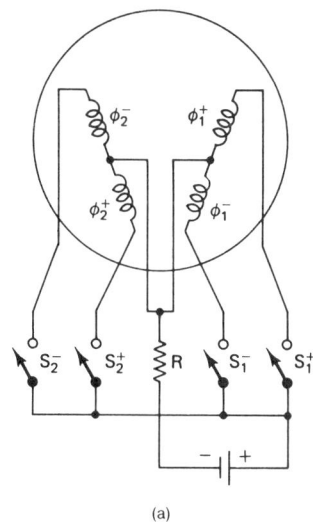

Step	S_1^+	S_1^-	S_2^+	S_2^-	HEX
1	X			X	9
2		X		X	5
3		X	X		6
4	X		X		A
1	X			X	9

(a)   (b)

Figure 6.31 Stepper motor sequencer. (a) Schematic of a four-phase (four-coil) motor. (b) Associated coil drive sequence. (*Source:* Adapted from Gayakwad/Sokoloff, *Analog and Digital Control Systems*, © 1988, p. 153. Reprinted by permission of Prentice-Hall, Inc., Englewood Cliffs, N.J.)

The program in this example will set up the 8155 command/status register (CSR), initialize the step pattern, read in from port A the number of steps to move, and call subroutine MOVE. MOVE will turn the stepper the number of steps given in the accumulator, save the step pattern, and return. The program assumes that an appropriate driver is connected to port B, such as the Sprague ULS-2068H quad Darlington switch.

```
MAIN:    MVI   A,02      ; INITIALIZE
         OUT   CSR       ; THE 8155
         MVI   A,09      ; INITIALIZE
         OUT   PORTB     ; STEP SEQUENCE
         MOV   D,A       ; AND SAVE IT
         CALL  DELAY     ; WAIT 1 STEP-TIME
MLOOP:   IN    PORTA     ; READ NUMBER OF STEPS
         CALL  MOVE      ; CALL STEPPER DRIVER
         JMP   MLOOP     ; DO IT AGAIN

                *
                *
                *

MOVE:    CPI   00        ; ZERO STEPS?
         RZ              ; YES, RETURN
         PUSH  B         ; NO, SAVE REGS
         MOV   B,A       ; SAVE STEP COUNT
SLOOP:   MOV   A,D       ; GET STEP PATTERN
         CPI   09        ; WAS IT 1001?
         JNZ   TRY5      ; NO, TRY NEXT ONE
         MVI   A,05      ; YES, MAKE IT 0101
         JMP   STEP      ; GO DO IT
TRY5:    CPI   05        ; WAS IT 0101?
         JNZ   TRY6      ; NO, TRY NEXT ONE
         MVI   A,06      ; YES, MAKE IT 0110
         JMP   STEP      ; GO DO IT
TRY6:    CPI   06        ; WAS IT 0110?
         JNZ   TRYA      ; NO, MUST BE LAST ONE
         MVI   A,0AH     ; YES, MAKE IT 1010
         JMP   STEP      ; GO DO IT
TRYA:    MVI   A,09      ; BACK TO 1001
STEP:    MOV   D,A       ; SAVE STEP PATTERN
         OUT   PORTB     ; ONE SMALL STEP FOR...
         CALL  DELAY     ; WAIT 1 STEP-TIME
         DCR   B         ; ONE LESS STEP
         JNZ   SLOOP     ; DONE? JUMP IF NO
         POP   B         ; RESTORE REGS
         RET             ; OUTA HERE
```

6.10.2 Strobed I/O: A Printer Example

The 8155 port C can be used for handshaking in ALT 3 and ALT 4. In the program in Example 6.21 data will be read from an ASCII keyboard and sent to a printer over a parallel interface, as shown in Fig. 6.32.

EXAMPLE 6.21 Strobed I/O

The $\overline{\text{DAV}}$ pulse from the keyboard will be used to drive the port B input strobe (B STB) on port C pin 5 (PC5). The port A buffer full signal (A BF) from PC1 will drive the Centronics $\overline{\text{STROBE}}$ pin; note the extra gates used to ensure the required 0.5-μsec delay. The one shot is positive edge-triggered and its output is a negative-going pulse. The $\overline{ACK}$ pulse will, in turn, be the acknowledgment back to the 8155 on PC2.

```
START:  MVI   A,09      ; SET UP
        OUT   CSR       ; THE 8155

LOOP1:  IN    CSR       ; READ STATUS
        ANI   10H       ; GET B BF
        JZ    LOOP1     ; WAIT FOR KEYPRESS

        IN    PORTB     ; GET CHARACTER
        OUT   PORTA     ; PRINT IT

LOOP2:  IN    CSR       ; READ STATUS
        ANI   02        ; GET A BF
        JNZ   LOOP2     ; WAIT FOR ACK\

        JMP   LOOP1     ; GET NEXT CHAR
```

Note that the interrupts were not used. The program polls the status register to check the handshake bits. Remember that, in this mode, writing to port A will automatically set A BF high, and reading from port B will clear B BF.

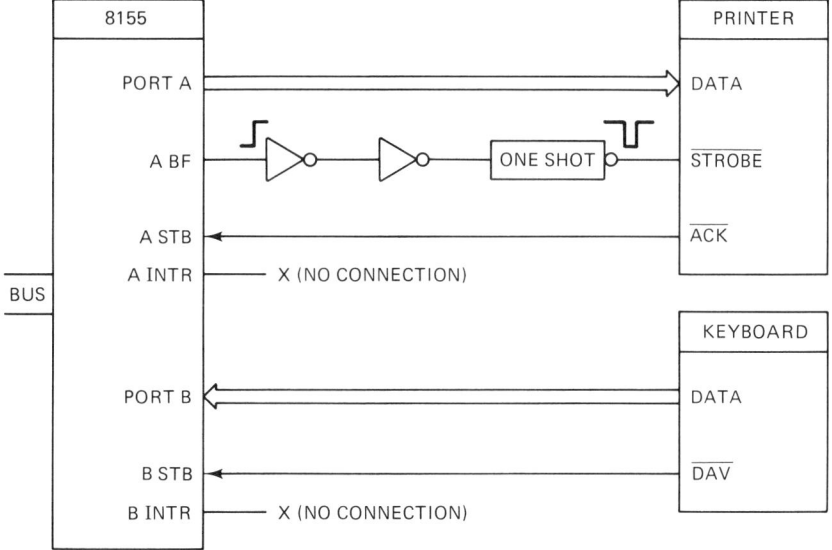

Figure 6.32 Strobed I/O.

6.11 SOME INTERRUPT-DRIVEN APPLICATIONS

In programs like that in Example 6.21, the computer spends all its time in a polling loop waiting for something to happen. Because I/O is often a rare event (in the time frame of a CPU), we could let the processor do something else until an I/O device demands service through an interrupt. However, interrupts must be used with care because they can cause intermittent bugs that are hard to track down.

6.11.1 Interrupt I/O: An 8155 Example

If Fig. 6.32 were modified so that B INTR was connected to one of the hardware restarts, RST 5.5, for example, then the programmed I/O of Example 6.21 could be changed into an *interrupt service routine*.

> **EXAMPLE 6.22   Interrupt I/O**
>
> Refer to the program below. Note that the CSR must be initialized with the interrupt function (INTE B) enabled. Also, the M5.5 mask must be enabled with a SIM instruction.
>
> ```
> MAIN:    ORG   002CH      ; RST 5.5 VECTOR ADDRESS
>          JMP   KBINT      ; JUMP TO SERVICE ROUTINE
>
>          ORG   START      ; BEGINNING OF MAIN PROG
>
>          MVI   A,29H      ; SET UP
>          OUT   CSR        ; THE 8155
>          MVI   A,1EH      ; ENABLE THE
>          SIM              ; M5.5 MASK
>          EI               ; ENABLE INTERRUPTS
>
>          < THE REST OF THE PROGRAM >
>                  *
>                  *
>                  *
> KBINT:   PUSH  PSW        ; SAVE ACC & FLAGS
>
>          IN    PORTB      ; GET KEYSTROKE CHAR
>          OUT   PORTA      ; SEND TO PRINTER
>
> LOOP:    IN    CSR        ; READ STATUS
>          ANI   02         ; GET A BF
>          JNZ   LOOP       ; WAIT FOR ACK\
>
>          POP   PSW        ; RESTORE ACC & FLAGS
>          EI               ; RE-ENABLE INTERRUPTS
>          RET              ; BACK TO BUSINESS
> ```
>
> The 8085 interrupts are enabled in the main program and reenabled at the end of the service routine. Remember, an interrupt automatically disables further interrupts until EI is executed again. Also, EI doesn't actually take effect until the instruction following EI has been executed, thus allowing a return from the service routine before another interrupt.

6.11.2 A Real-Time Clock (RTC)

Basically, an RTC keeps accurate track of time. Peripheral devices such as the National Semiconductor MM58274 (Fig. 6.33) are available that will give hours, minutes, seconds, and tenths of seconds, as well as month and day of the week.

National Semiconductor Corporation

May 1987

MM58274B Microprocessor Compatible Real Time Clock

General Description

The MM58274B is fabricated using low threshold metal gate CMOS technology and is designed to operate in bus oriented microprocessor systems where a real time clock and calendar function are required. The on-chip 32.768 kHz crystal controlled oscillator will maintain timekeeping down to 2.2V to allow low power standby battery operation. This device is pin compatible with the MM58174A but continues timekeeping up to tens of years. The MM58274B is a direct replacement for the MM58274 offering improved Bus access cycle times.

Applications

- Point of sale terminals
- Teller terminals
- Word processors
- Data logging
- Industrial process control

Features

- Same pin-out as MM58174A and MM58274
- Timekeeping from tenths of seconds to tens of years in independently accessible registers
- Leap year register
- Hours counter programmable for 12 or 24-hour operation
- Buffered crystal frequency output in test mode for easy oscillator setting
- Data-changed flag allows simple testing for time rollover
- Independent interrupting time with open drain output
- Fully TTL compatible
- Low power standby operation (10µA at 2.2V)
- Low cost 16-pin DIP and 20-pin PCC

Block Diagram

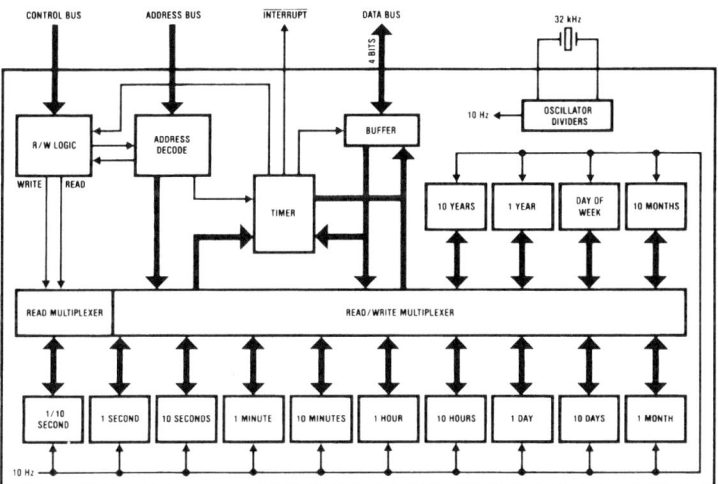

FIGURE 1

TRI-STATE® is a registered trademark of National Semiconductor Corp.
Microbus™ is a trademark of National Semiconductor Corp.

Figure 6.33 National Semiconductor MM58274.

Sec. 6.11   Some Interrupt-Driven Applications

Sometimes it is necessary to implement a simple RTC in software. For example, an industrial control program may need to monitor parameters such as temperature and pressure periodically. In such a case the "ticks of the clock" are usually interrupts generated by a *time base,* such as a crystal oscillator or even the 60-Hz (50-Hz in Europe) ac line (suitably isolated, of course).

Sometimes the RTC function is part of another interrupt routine. For example, a system may want to poll all its inputs once every 10 sec. An interrupt every second would invoke the service routine, which would increment the clock and do the poll every tenth interrupt. Also, multitasking systems use an interrupt RTC to determine when to activate (wake up) and deactivate programs (tasks).

EXAMPLE 6.23 Real-Time Clock

This program uses the 8155 timer to divide down a 60-Hz input to a 1-Hz square wave, which, in turn, is connected to the edge-triggered RST 7.5 interrupt pin. The interrupt service routine keeps track of seconds as two BCD numbers stored in memory.

```
                  ORG   003CH       ; RST7.5 ADDRESS

                  JMP   RTC         ; GO TO SERVICE ROUTINE

                  ORG   START       ; START ADDRESS

       MAIN:      SUB   A           ; PUT ZERO INTO
                  STAX  SEC01       ; UNITS OF SECONDS
                  STAX  SEC10       ; AND TENS OF SECONDS
                  MVI   A,1BH       ; ENABLE RST7.5
                  SIM               ; MASK
                  MVI   A,40H       ; CONT SQ WAVE
                  OUT   CLRH        ; CNT LEN REG HI
                  MVI   A,3CH       ; DIVIDE BY 60
                  OUT   CLRL        ; CNT LEN REG LO
                  MVI   A,0C0H      ; TIMER MODE 11
                  OUT   CSR         ; TURN IT ON
                  EI                ; ENABLE INTERRUPTS

                      <REST OF PROGRAM>

       RTC:       PUSH  PSW         ; SAVE ACC & FLAGS
                  LDAX  SEC01       ; GET UNITS
                  INR   A           ; INCREMENT
                  CPI   10          ; PAST 9?
                  JZ    TENS        ; JUMP IF YES
                  STAX  SEC01       ; NO, SAVE UNITS
                  JMP   DONE        ; GO HOME
       TENS:      SUB   A           ; PUT A ZERO
                  STAX  SEC01       ; IN UNITS
                  LDAX  SEC10       ; AND
                  INR   A           ; INCREMENT
                  STAX  SEC10       ; TENS
                  CPI   10          ; PAST 9?
                  JNZ   DONE        ; JUMP IF NO
                  SUB   A           ; YES, SO PUT A
                  STAX  SEC10       ; ZERO IN TENS
       DONE:      POP   PSW         ; RESTORE ACC & FLAGS
                  EI                ; RE ENABLE INTERRUPTS
                  RET               ; RETURN TO MAIN
```

> Note that when the main program wants to read the time it must first disable interrupts. Otherwise, an error could occur as follows: Suppose the time is 49 sec and the main program reads the 4. But an interrupt occurs before the 9 is read, so the second digit will be changed to 0 before the main routine gets a chance to read it. After the interrupt, the program reads the next digit and gets a time of 40 sec instead of the correct value.

A section of code that cannot be interrupted is often called a *critical region*, and is an example of the sort of synchronization required when programs are run *concurrently*. The RTC and the program that reads the time are concurrent; in effect, they are running at the same time even though they share a single processor. A problem with using critical regions with an RTC is that, unless an interrupt is latched or held pending while in the region, the clock may miss ticks and slowly fall behind the correct time. Remember that RST 7.5 is latched by the 8085.

6.12 ANALOG/DIGITAL INTERFACING

Microprocessors process digital numbers, but most of the things we want to measure and control, things out in the real world, are *analog*. Examples are pressure in a boiler, speed of a motor, and position of a robot arm. They are analog because they can take on any value within their range and can change smoothly and continuously from one value to another. Even though we use transducers to convert such things to an electrical signal, those signals vary in the same manner as (i.e., they are analogs of) the actual thing itself. On the other hand, digital numbers can have only discrete values in a range determined by the number of bits in the digital word. For example, an 8-bit binary number can go from 0 to 255 *full scale* and has a *resolution* of 1 LSB or approximately 0.4 percent of full scale (1/255).

What we need are analog to digital converters (A/D or ADC) and digital to analog converters (D/A or DAC). Such devices can be characterized in terms of the following: *speed* (how many times per second can it convert; also called sample rate), *resolution* (how many bits does it have), *accuracy* (how many bits are correct), *linearity* (how close does output track input), and *monotonicity* (does the output always go in the same direction as the input). The digital end of DACs and ADCs is usually pure binary, but may also be BCD or some other code.

ADCs and DACs can be connected to the CPU through I/O ports, or, if they have the appropriate interface, they can be connected to the CPU bus lines and treated as memory locations (i.e., they can be memory mapped). Microprocessor-compatible devices have the bus interface built in.

6.12.1 Digital to Analog Converters (DACs)

The output of a DAC can be current or voltage. It can be *unipolar* (e.g., 0 to +10V) or *bipolar* (e.g., −5 to +5V). Output voltages are derived from a *reference*, which can be either built-in or external. If the reference can be varied, it is a *multiplying DAC*, where the output is proportional to the binary input times the reference voltage. The speed of the DAC, often specified as a *settling time*, determines how often the program can send data to it. For example, a 10-μsec settling time means 100,000 conversions/sec (1 conversion/10 μsec).

Interfacing a DAC to a microprocessor is relatively straightforward. Basically, it has a number of input lines for the bits and an analog output line. There may be separate analog and digital ground lines. Refer to the simplified diagram in Fig. 6.34. If it is *microprocessor compatible,* it is simply connected to the bus lines and written to by moves to the appropriate "memory" addresses. If the DAC is connected to an I/O port, there are two things to consider:

> **First,** the binary input must be *latched* to hold it constant while the DAC converts it to analog. For example, the 8155 ports are latched. If the DAC contains its own latch, then the microprocessor can use a nonlatched output port. Data are written to the port and the latch-strobe line on the DAC is pulsed to latch it. The data must not change during the strobe pulse.
>
> **Second,** the DAC word size may exceed the CPU word size. For example, the ports may be 8 bits while the DAC is 12 bits. Because two successive OUT instructions will be needed to send data to the DAC, the DAC output will be at some arbitrary value (a glitch) in between the two OUTs. In such a case *double buffering* can be used. A shown in Fig. 6.35, double buffering allows the CPU to output the first part of the 12-bit word to an 8-bit "holding area." It then outputs the second part. After both parts are in place, it strobes the 12-bit latch so that the DAC sees the new word "all in one piece."

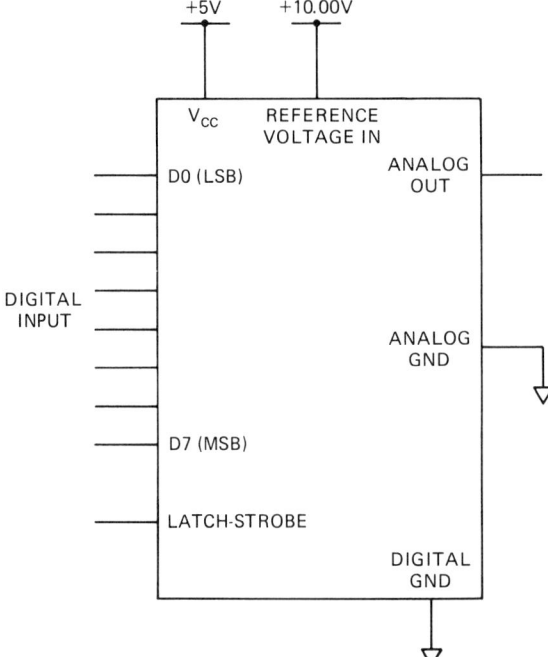

Figure 6.34 Eight-bit DAC with built-in latch.

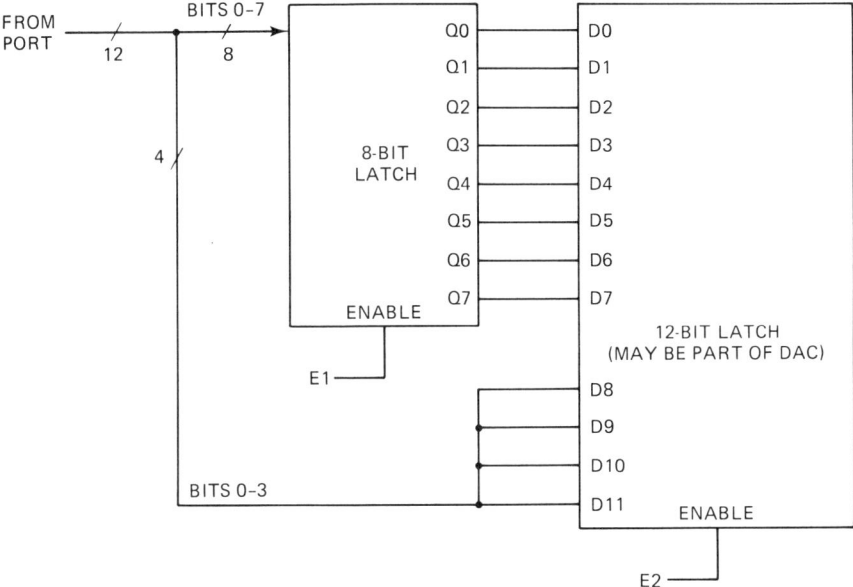

Figure 6.35 Double buffering.

6.12.2 Analog to Digital Converters (ADCs)

A full treatment of A/D design is beyond the scope of this book. In this section we look at the basics of interfacing to an ADC.

There are three main classes of ADCs:

1. *Integrating types* use a technique known as dual-slope conversion. They provide good accuracy at low cost but are slow. They are commonly used in such things as hand-held voltmeters.
2. *Flash converters,* as the name implies, are very fast. Also expensive, they have limited resolution.
3. *Successive-approximation* (SA) types are the garden-variety ADCs. They come in many combinations of speed, accuracy, and cost. The following discussion focuses on SA types.

An ADC consists of two main functional blocks: a *sample-and-hold* (S&H) and the actual A/D. A S&H is needed because an analog signal is typically a "moving target," that is, it is continuously changing while the ADC is trying to convert it to binary. The S&H, in effect, takes a "snapshot" of the analog input and holds it constant while it is converted into digital. The S&H may be built in or on a separate chip.

The minimum handshake between an ADC and a CPU requires two lines: *start-of-conversion* (SOC) and *end-of-conversion* (EOC). Typically, the program starts the process by pulsing the SOC line, which causes the ADC to take a sample and start the conversion. When the digital word is available, the EOC line is activated. EOC can be polled or used to generate an interrupt. The program responds to EOC by reading the digital word and, if necessary, pulsing SOC to start the process over. Figure 6.36 shows a block diagram and the timing. Note that SOC and EOC are active-low.

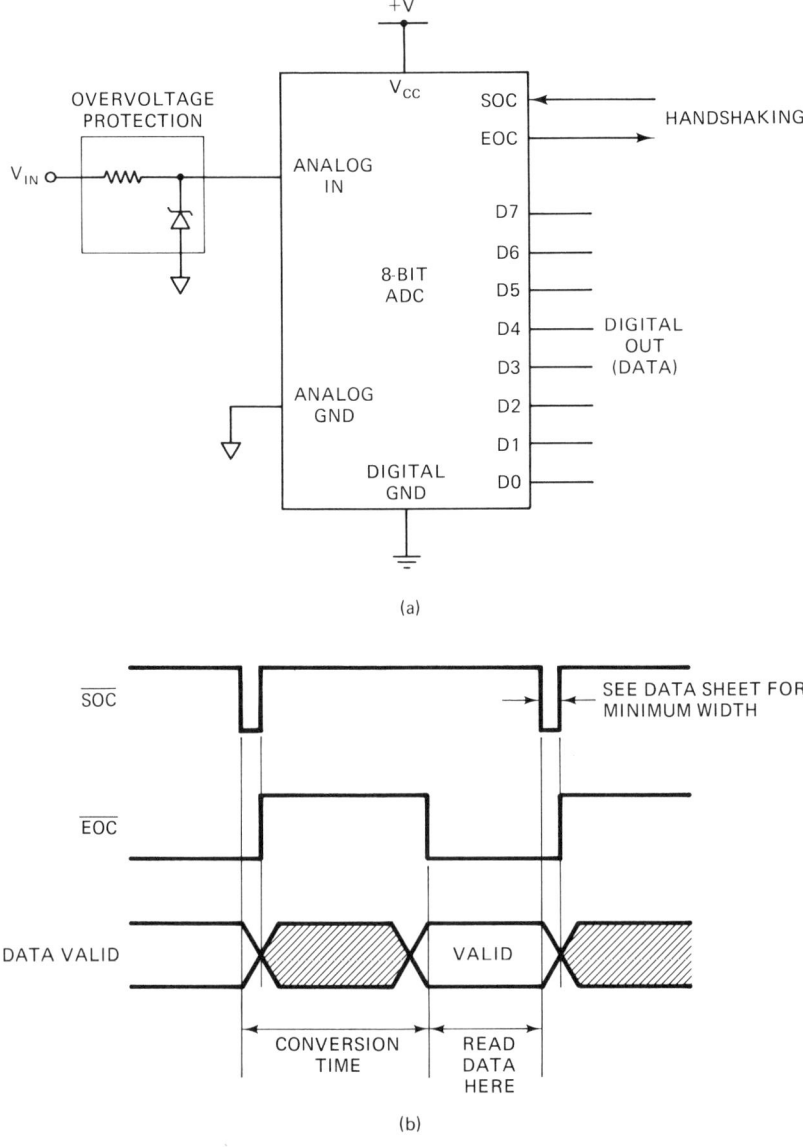

Figure 6.36 ADC converter.

EXAMPLE 6.24 Interfacing to an ADC

Assume we have an 8085 connected to the ADC in Fig. 6.36 through three ports: STATUS (input), DATA (input), and CONTROL (output). SOC is on bit 0 of CONTROL and EOC is on bit 0 of STATUS. Each time the following subroutine is called, it will get one sample from the ADC.

```
A_TO_D:    MVI   A,00      ; PULL SOC LOW
           OUT   CONTROL   ; TO ACTIVATE
           NOP             ; STRETCH OUT THE
           NOP             ; SOC PULSE
           MVI   A,01      ; PULL SOC
           OUT   CONTROL   ; BACK TO HI
LOOP:      IN    STATUS    ; READ EOC
           ANI   01        ; IS IT READY?
           JNZ   LOOP      ; JUMP IF NO
           IN    DATA      ; READY, READ DATA
           RET             ; RETURN WITH DATA
```

6.13 SUMMARY

In this chapter we discussed mechanical and solid state switches as input devices, including the need for debouncing. We looked at relays and solenoids, including drivers, as output devices. We noted the need for isolation and protection from inductive spikes. *Seven-segment* displays and *multiplexing* were discussed, as were such printing techniques as dot matrix. We defined *handshaking*, and the Centronics, IEEE-488, and RS-232C interfaces were examined. Interfacing applications were done using the 8155, including stepper motors, printing, and a real-time clock. We discussed the interface between the analog world and the digital microprocessor. D/A and A/D converters were described in terms of the interfacing requirements.

CHAPTER REVIEW

Questions

1. Explain contact bounce.
2. What is a limit switch?
3. What does break-before-make mean?
4. Why is hysteresis important?
5. Explain how a switch matrix is scanned.
6. How does two-key rollover differ from N-key rollover?
7. Why is isolation important?
8. Explain what a solenoid is and what it does in a relay.
9. Explain what an inductive spike is and how it is suppressed.

10. Draw a schematic for a 1A1C relay.
11. Compare and contrast a seven-segment and a dot-matrix display.
12. Describe a multiplexed display.
13. What is handshaking?
14. Compare and contrast handshaking on the Centronics and IEEE-488 interfaces.
15. Describe RS-232C.
16. What is a DAC?
17. What is an ADC?

Problems

1. Write a program using SID to receive serial data. Use a polling loop to detect the start bit.
2. Write a subroutine for the stepper motor of Fig. 6.31 that, when called, will rotate the motor one revolution CCW. Assume 64 steps/rev.
3. Write a calling routine that uses the RTC code of the program of Example 6.23 but that uses SIM to turn the interrupt mask on and off instead of DI and EI.
4. Write a program to generate a sawtooth wave by incrementing the accumulator and outputting it to a DAC in a continuous loop. The frequency of the sawtooth wave is determined by calling a time-delay subroutine (kills time) after each output. Assume a 1-MHz clock and get a frequency of 1000 Hz.
5. Rewrite the subroutine of Example 6.24 assuming that both SOC and EOC are active-high.
6. Rewrite the subroutine of Example 6.24 to use an 8155. Assume these hex addresses: CSR = 08, port A = 90, port B = 0A, port C = 0B. Data are to be read through Port A. Use Port B for SOC and port C for EOC.
7. Find the manufacturer's specs for a "bus-compatible" chip, such as an A/D converter, and write a program to use it via the 8155.

chapter 7

The Z80 Microprocessor

OBJECTIVES

After completing this chapter, you should be able to

1. Compare and contrast the Z80 to the 8085
2. Explain the three Z80 interrupt modes
3. Write short programs in Z80 assembly language
4. Explain context switching

7.1 INTRODUCTION

Zilog introduced the Z80 in 1976, and it soon became one of the most commonly used general-purpose 8-bit microprocessors. The Z80 was designed to be an enhanced version of the 8080. In fact, some of the people who worked on the 8080 at Intel designed the Z80 at Zilog. It executes a superset of the 8080 instructions, which means it will execute all the 8080 instructions—and all 8085 instructions except RIM and SIM—plus a set of additional instructions. If you liked the 8085, you will love the Z80.

The Z80 is second-sourced by Mostek and other semiconductor companies and is available in CMOS versions. Also, National Semiconductor makes the NSC800, a CMOS device combining hardware features of the 8085 with the instruction set of the Z80. The Zilog Z800 is a family of processors that are object-code compatible with the Z80 but include enhanced instruction sets, higher speed, and additional hardware features.

7.2 HARDWARE OVERVIEW

The Z80 is software compatible with the 8085 at the machine code level. Except for RIM and SIM, a ROM containing an 8085 program could be used in a Z80 system. However, the Z80 is not compatible at the hardware level. You cannot plug a Z80 into a socket meant for an 8080 or 8085 chip.

Figure 7.1 shows the Z80 pinout with the pins divided into functional groups. Each group is explained below. The Z80 requires a single +5V power supply and is available in an 8-MHz version.

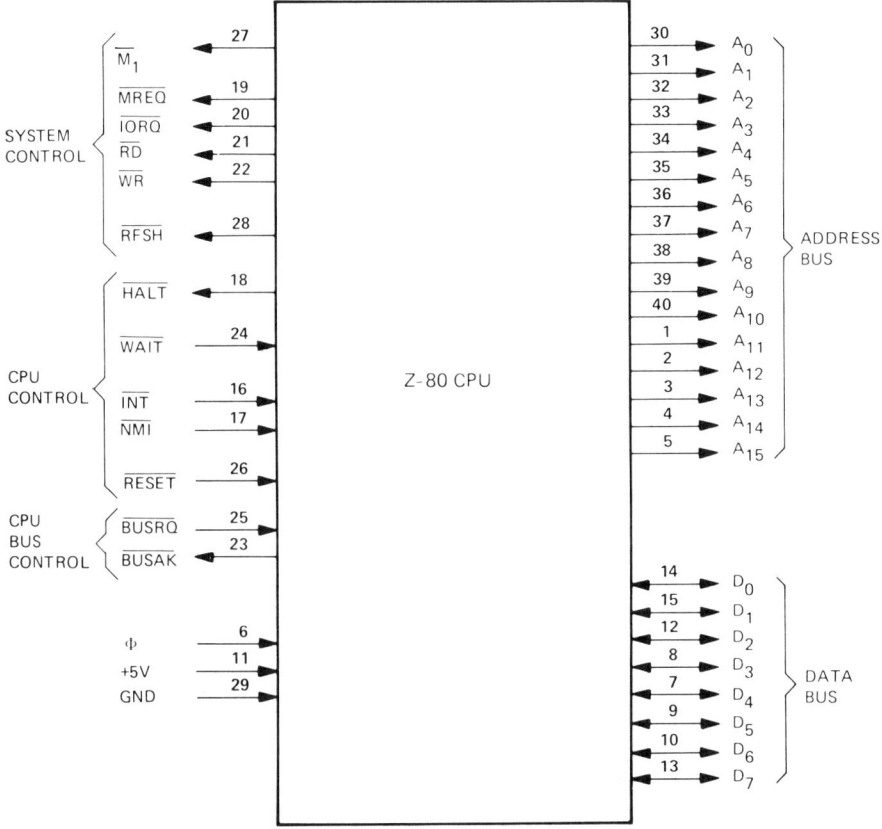

Figure 7.1 Z80 pin configuration. (*Source:* Reproduced by permission. © Copyright 1989 Zilog, Inc. This material shall not be reproduced without the written consent of Zilog, Inc.)

7.2.1 Clock

In contrast to the 8085, the Z80 must be driven by an external square-wave oscillator, typically crystal controlled. The clock pin on the standard Z80 has a capacitance to ground of 35 pF as compared to 5 pF for its other input pins. The result is that the circuit used to drive the clock pin must be able to supply high peak currents to charge the capacitance, especially at high speeds. For speeds below 4 MHz, the clock pin can be driven by a TTL gate with a 330-ohm pull-up resistor, as shown in Fig. 7.2a. For higher speeds, a driver circuit similar to the one in Fig. 7.2b is required. The Z80 uses static registers, so there is no minimum clock speed.

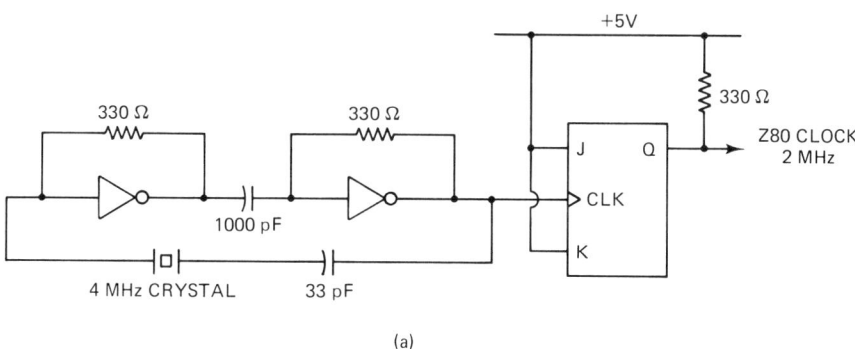

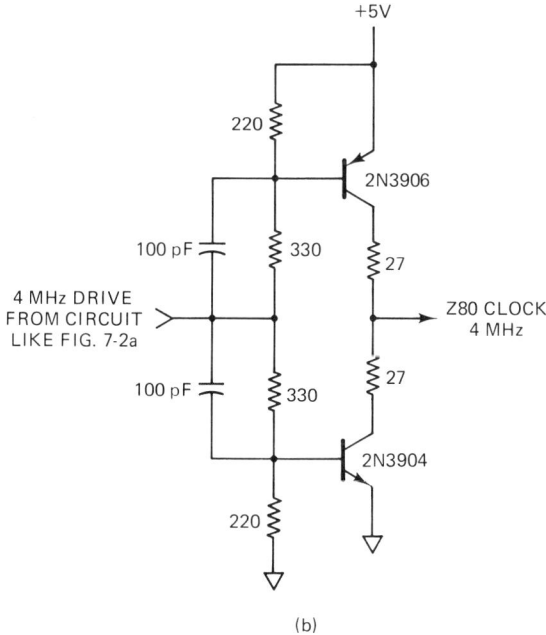

Figure 7.2 Clock pin circuits.

7.2.2 Address and Data Buses

Unlike the 8085, the Z80 does not use multiplexing. It has a separate 16-bit unidirectional address bus and an 8-bit bidirectional data bus. It can address 64K bytes of memory and 256 ports. During I/O, port addresses appear on the lower 8 address bits (A7–A0). The address bus is also used during a refresh cycle, as described in Sec. 7.2.7.

7.2.3 System Control

There are six pins in the system control group, all outputs:

$\overline{\text{M1}}$ **Machine Cycle 1:** Goes low only during an op-code fetch.

$\overline{\text{MREQ}}$ **Memory Request:** Goes low to indicate that the address bus holds a valid address for a memory read or write.

$\overline{\text{IORQ}}$ **I/O Request:** Goes low to indicate that the lower half of the address bus holds a valid port address for I/O read or write. Also, $\overline{\text{IORQ}}$ and $\overline{\text{M1}}$ will go low together as an interrupt acknowledge to indicate that an interrupt vector can be put on the data bus.

$\overline{\text{RD}}$ **Read:** Goes low during memory or I/O read operations. Used to strobe the data onto the data bus for the CPU to read.

$\overline{\text{WR}}$ **Write:** Goes low during memory or I/O write operations. Used to strobe the data off the data bus into the memory chip or I/O device.

$\overline{\text{RFSH}}$ **Refresh:** Goes low to indicate that the lower 7 bits of the address bus hold a valid refresh address. Special hardware will use this signal together with $\overline{\text{MREQ}}$ to refresh dynamic memory chips.

For systems requiring two pairs of read and write signals, one for memory and one for I/O, the system control signals can be combined, as shown in Fig. 7.3.

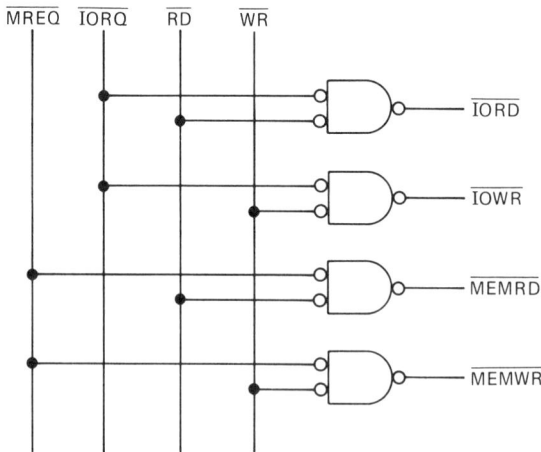

Figure 7.3 System control signals.

7.2.4 CPU Control

There are five pins in the CPU control group:

$\overline{\text{HALT}}$ **Halt:** (output) goes low to indicate that the CPU is in the halt state. While halted, the CPU executes NOPs so that memory refresh will continue.

$\overline{\text{WAIT}}$ **Wait:** (input) used by slow memory or I/O device to stretch out a data transfer cycle. CPU will continue wait states as long as $\overline{\text{WAIT}}$ is pulled low.

$\overline{\text{INT}}$ **Interrupt Request:** (input) pulled low by an external device to initiate an interrupt. $\overline{\text{INT}}$ interrupts must be enabled in software or they will not be recognized. Can be blocked by $\overline{\text{WAIT}}$ or $\overline{\text{BUSRQ}}$ because the current instruction must finish before an interrupt can be recognized.

$\overline{\text{NMI}}$ **Nonmaskable Interrupt:** (input) negative edge-triggered. When pulled low, the CPU will push the return address onto the stack and branch to 0066H. Cannot be disabled in software. Can be blocked by $\overline{\text{WAIT}}$ and overridden by $\overline{\text{BUSRQ}}$.

$\overline{\text{RESET}}$ **Reset:** (input) when pulled low the following happens:

1. Program counter is reset to 0000H.
2. Interrupt enable is reset (disabled).
3. Interrupts are set to mode 0.
4. The I register is reset to 00H.
5. The R register is reset to 00H.
6. While $\overline{\text{RESET}}$ is low, the address and data buses are in the high-impedance state. All control outputs go to the inactive state. Note that $\overline{\text{RESET}}$ must be applied *after* the clock has begun and must be held low for *at least three* clock periods. An improper reset can "hang up" the Z80. Subsequent resets will not get it out of hangup; you will have to remove power.

7.2.5 Bus Control

There are two pins in the bus control group:

$\overline{\text{BUSRQ}}$ **Bus Request:** (input) when pulled low the CPU will float its tristate bus lines at the end of the current instruction. $\overline{\text{BUSRQ}}$ is used by such devices as DMA controllers.

$\overline{\text{BUSAK}}$ **Bus Acknowledge:** (output) goes low in response to $\overline{\text{BUSRQ}}$ to indicate that the CPU has relinquished control of the bus.

7.2.6 Bus Timing

As shown in Fig. 7.4a, the basic Z80 CPU timing is an *instruction cycle* consisting of one or more *machine cycles*. Each machine cycle requires a number of clock periods called *T cycles*. An op-code fetch is shown in Fig. 7.4b.

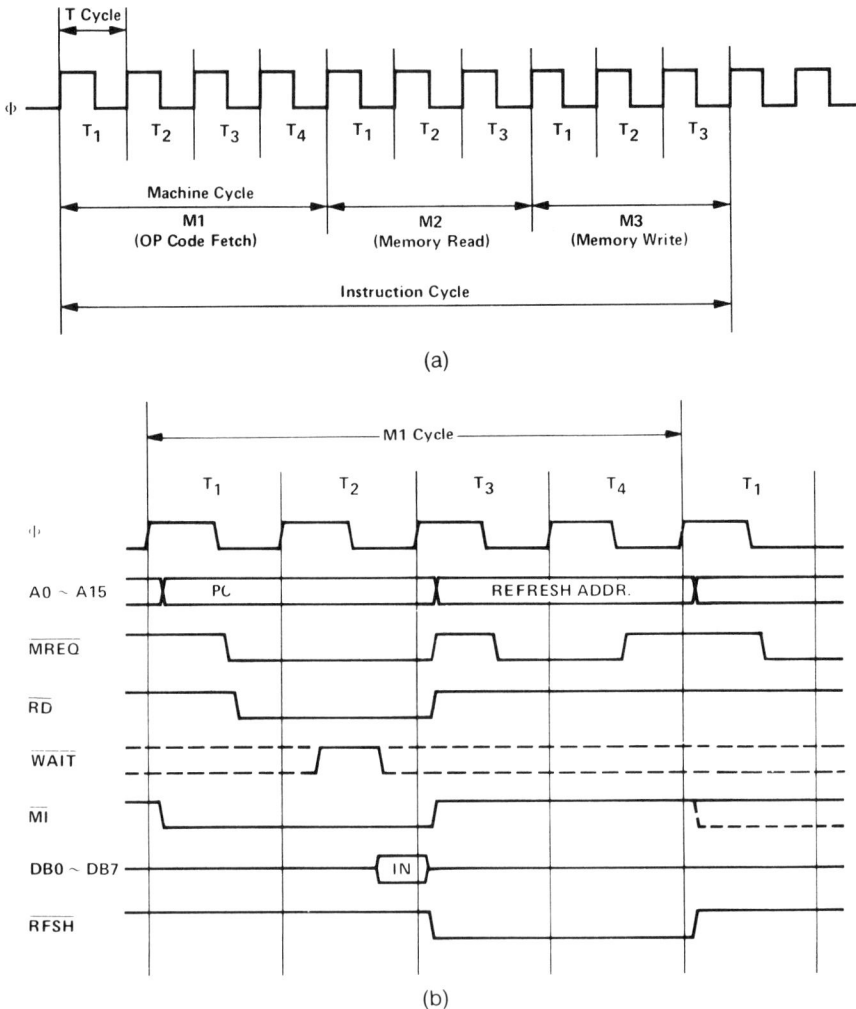

Figure 7.4 (a) Basic CPU timing example. (b) Instruction op-code fetch. (*Source:* Reproduced by permission. © Copyright 1989 Zilog, Inc. This material shall not be reproduced without the written consent of Zilog, Inc.)

The op-code is fetched during the first machine cycle (M1). Depending on the instruction, it will require three, four, five, or six T cycles. As the instruction is executed, it may require additional **machine** cycles to move data between the CPU and memory or I/O ports. Machine cycles after M1 may require three, four, or five

T cycles. Of course, the number of T cycles required in any machine cycle can be increased by using $\overline{\text{WAIT}}$.

Figure 7.5 shows a timing diagram for a memory read followed by a memory write. Note the relationships between the system control lines and the address and data buses. Figure 7.6 shows an I/O cycle (read or write). Note that a wait state is

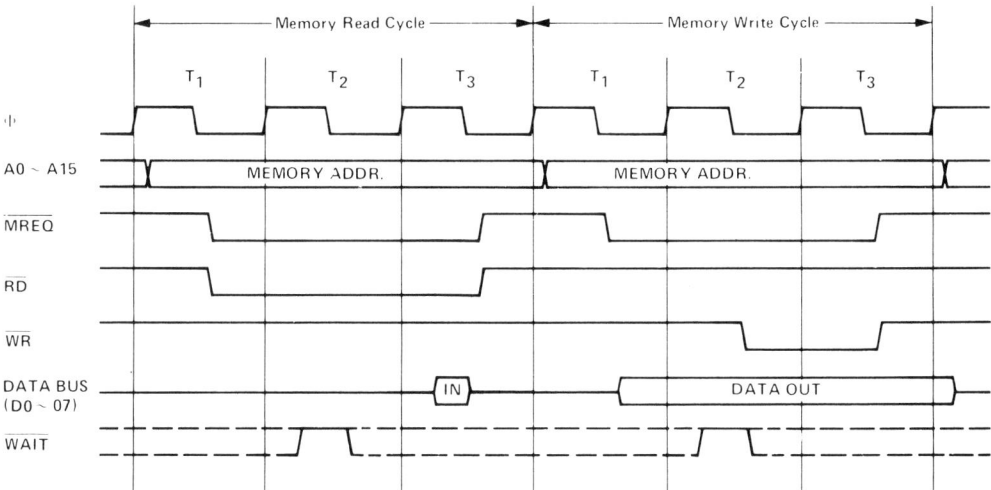

Figure 7.5 Memory read or write cycles. (*Source:* Reproduced by permission. © Copyright 1989 Zilog, Inc. This material shall not be reproduced without the written consent of Zilog, Inc.)

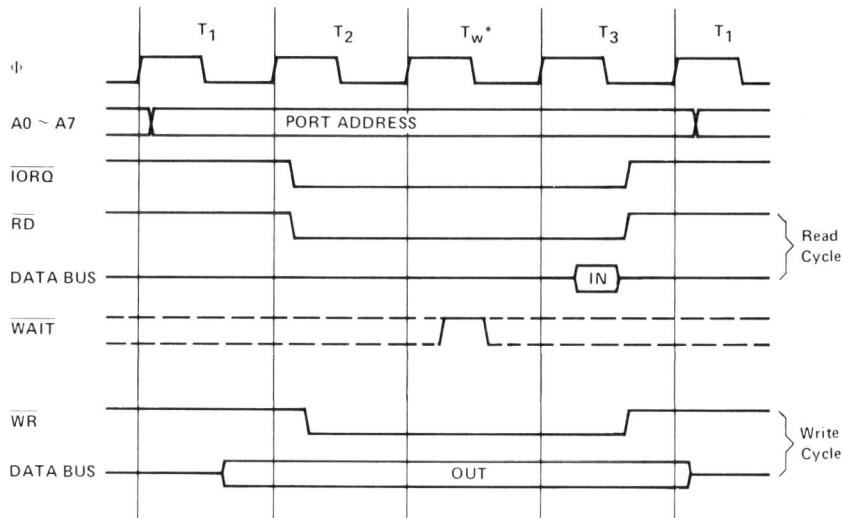

*T_W is an automatically inserted wait state.

Figure 7.6 Input or output cycles. (*Source:* Reproduced by permission. © Copyright 1989 Zilog, Inc. This material shall not be reproduced without the written consent of Zilog, Inc.)

Sec. 7.2   Hardware Overview

automatically inserted to compensate for the short time the Z80 has between when $\overline{\text{IORQ}}$ goes low and when $\overline{\text{WAIT}}$ must be asserted. The automatic wait state gives the I/O device time to request additional wait states if it wants them.

7.2.7 Dynamic Memory Refresh

In order to cut down on the number of pins, dynamic memory chips typically multiplex their address pins. For example, the 4116 memory chip shown in Fig. 7.7 holds 16K 1-bit words and would be arranged in groups of eight for byte-sized memory. However, the 4116 only has 7 address pins. The chip is organized internally into 128 rows, each with 128 columns.

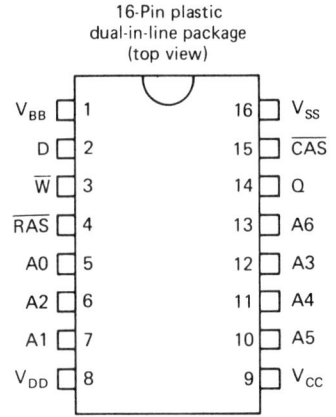

Figure 7.7 Pinout of the TMS4116 DRAM. (*Source:* Reprinted by permission of Texas Instruments.)

To address a bit, first give the 4116 the 7-bit row address and strobe the row-address-select ($\overline{\text{RAS}}$) pin. Next apply the column address and strobe the column-address-select ($\overline{\text{CAS}}$) pin. The full 14-bit address is now latched into the 4116 and data can be read or written using $\overline{\text{RD}}$ and $\overline{\text{WR}}$ combined with other control signals. See Fig. 7.8.

To refresh the 2118, it is only necessary to give it a row address and assert $\overline{\text{RAS}}$; $\overline{\text{CAS}}$, as well as $\overline{\text{RD}}$ and $\overline{\text{WR}}$, are not used. Referring again to Fig. 7.4b, note that during the machine cycle immediately following an op-code fetch the Z80 puts a refresh address on the lower 8 bits of the address line but pulses $\overline{\text{RFSH}}$ instead of $\overline{\text{RD}}$ or $\overline{\text{WR}}$. With suitable decoding, $\overline{\text{RFSH}}$ allows a simple refresh circuit to be implemented. The refresh address is obtained from the R register, as described in Sec. 7.3.2.

Read cycle timing

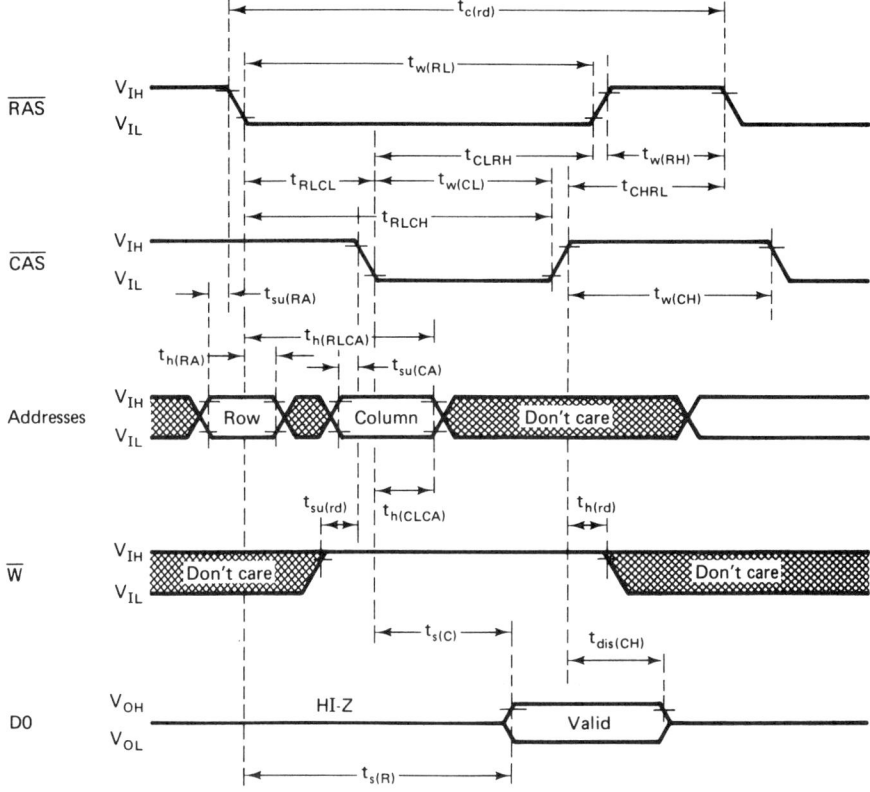

Figure 7.8 Read cycle timing for the 4116. (*Source:* Reprinted by permission of Texas Instruments.)

7.3 PROGRAMMING MODEL

The programming model of the Z80 is a superset of the 8085 model. The Z80 does not have the 8085 hardware restarts, but it does have more registers.

7.3.1 General-Purpose Registers

As shown in Fig. 7.9, the Z80 contains two register sets, each with its own accumulator and flags. Only one set is active at a time, and the programmer can switch between sets. Data in the inactive registers are not lost.

The general-purpose 8-bit registers have the same designations as in the 8085. Register pairs are specified as BC, DE, and HL. Note that the combination of accumulator and flags is not called PSW but, rather, AF. When describing Z80

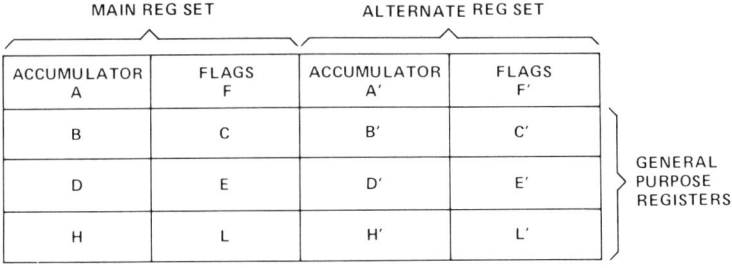

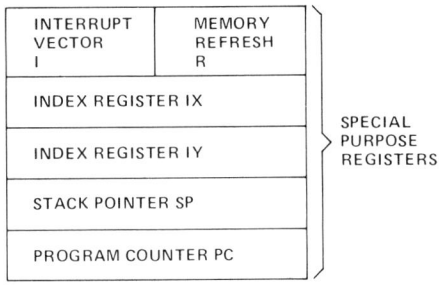

Figure 7.9 Z80 CPU register configuration.

instructions in this chapter we use the phrase "a register" or "any register." Such phrases should be understood to mean the registers A, B, C, D, E, H, or L.

7.3.2 Special-Purpose Registers

The special-purpose registers include the stack pointer and program counter, as in the 8085. However, they also include the 8-bit I and R registers and the 16-bit IX and IY index registers. The use of IX and IY is discussed in section 7.4.

The I (interrupt page) register is used to hold the upper 8 bits of a 16-bit address. Its use is discussed in Sec. 7.12. The R (refresh) register is used as counter. The most significant bit of R will stay at the level it was set to by the program. The lower 7 bits will be incremented after each instruction fetch. The content of R will be put on the address bus during dynamic memory refresh, as described in Section 7.2.7. If the system does not use dynamic memory, the value in R is a don't care.

7.3.3 The Flags

The flag register contains six flag bits, as shown in Fig. 7.10. The remaining two flag bits of the register are not used. The Z80 flags are almost the same as the 8085 flags. As usual, various conditional instructions will test the flag values to control execution.

7	6	5	4	3	2	1	0
S	Z	X	H	X	P/V	N	C

X = NOT USED

Figure 7.10 Flag register bit assignments.

The flags are as follows:

S   **Sign Flag:** After an arithmetic or logic operation, the MSB of the affected register (usually the accumulator) is copied to the sign flag. If the contents of the register are being used as a signed number, then a sign bit of 0 indicates a positive number and a 1 indicates a negative number.

Z   **Zero Flag:** Z is set to a 1 if an ALU operation on an 8-bit register results in the contents of the register going to zero. Note that moving zero into a register will not set Z because it doesn't involve the ALU.

H   **Half Carry Flag:** Similar to the AC flag in the 8085. The DAA instruction will test H in order to restore BCD numbers back to the correct format after arithmetic. Unlike the 8085, DAA will work for subtraction as well as addition.

P/V   **Parity/Overflow Flag:** A dual-purpose flag. Its parity function is the same as in the 8085. After an ALU operation, an 8-bit register may contain an odd or even number of 1s. If the number of 1s is even, the P flag is set to a 1. If the number of 1s is odd, P is reset to 0. When doing arithmetic with signed numbers, V will go high when an overflow occurs. Overflow occurs if adding two numbers with the same sign gives a result with the opposite sign. For example, adding 1 to +127 (01111111) will cause an overflow. This flag is also affected by block transfers, searches, and interrupts.

N   **Add/Subtract Flag:** Used by the ALU to distinguish the results of an addition from those of a subtraction. If the previous operation was a subtraction, N will be set to 1. N allows DAA to work for subtraction.

CY   **Carry Flag:** The carry flag is set or reset according to the result of ALU operations on 8-bit registers, including rotates, as well as addition with 16-bit registers. The carry can be considered as the ninth bit of the accumulator. For example, the addition of two 8-bit numbers may produce a result too big to fit into the accumulator. The resulting carry out of the accumulator MSB will set the carry flag. The carry will also be set during subtraction if a "borrow" occurs (i.e., a bigger number is subtracted from a smaller number). The Z80 has instructions both to set and complement the CY flag.

A flag is said to be *high, set,* or *true* if its value is 1; it is *reset, clear, low,* or *false* if its value is 0. The flags most often used in programming are CY and Z; the others are used only for certain specific functions.

7.4 INSTRUCTION SET OVERVIEW

The Z80 instruction set is summarized in Fig. 7.11. The instructions that affect the flags are given in Fig. 7.12. Many things, such as the way PUSH and POP work, are the same as in the 8085. Also, 2-byte numbers such as jump addresses are stored with the higher byte at the higher address, the same as in the 8085. Other things have been added.

The Z80 mnemonics are quite different from the 8085 mnemonics. One reason is that mnemonics are copyrighted. Another reason is that because of the sheer number of Z80 instructions, the mnemonics had to be simplified so that the programmer need remember only a few instruction formats.

> **EXAMPLE 7.1 The LD Mnemonic**
>
> To move data, the 8085 has MOV, MVI, LXI, LDA, STA, LDAX, and STAX. The Z80 has only LD.

In Z80 assembly language, things inside parentheses are addresses of operands.

> **EXAMPLE 7.2 Use of Parentheses**
>
> LD A,100H means load (move) the number 100H into the accumulator, but LD A,(100H) means load the number *stored in memory location* 100H into the accumulator.

7.4.1 Addressing Modes

The Z80 has 10 addressing modes. The first seven correspond to instructions common to both the Z80 and the 8085. The last three correspond to specific Z80 features not found in the 8085. The Z80 addressing modes described by Zilog are the following:

Register Addressing Where the mnemonic specifies that registers are involved.

> **EXAMPLE 7.3 Register Addressing**
>
> LD A,B will move a copy of the content of register B into the accumulator and is equivalent to the 8085 MOV A,B. LD stands for *load*.

Implied Addressing Instructions where an operand is not stated but is known implicitly.

> **EXAMPLE 7.4 Implied Addressing**
>
> SUB B will subtract the content of register B from the accumulator. SUB A,B is not used; the A is implied.

The following is a summary of the Z80, Z80A instruction set showing the assembly language mnemonic and the symbolic operation performed by the instruction. A more detailed listing appears in the Z80-CPU technical manual, and assembly language programming manual. The instructions are divided into the following categories:

- 8-bit loads
- 16-bit loads
- Exchanges
- Memory Block Moves
- Memory Block Searches
- 8-bit arithmetic and logic
- 16-bit arithmetic
- General purpose Accumulator & Flag Operations
- Miscellaneous Group
- Rotates and Shifts
- Bit Set, Reset and Test
- Input and Output
- Jumps
- Calls
- Restarts
- Returns

In the table the following terminology is used.

- b ≡ a bit number in any 8-bit register or memory location
- cc ≡ flag condition code
  - NZ ≡ non zero
  - Z ≡ zero
  - NC ≡ non carry
  - C ≡ carry
  - PO ≡ Parity odd or no over flow
  - PE ≡ Parity even or over flow
  - P ≡ Positive
  - M ≡ Negative (minus)
- d ≡ any 8-bit destination register or memory location
- dd ≡ any 16-bit destination register or memory location
- e ≡ 8-bit signed 2's complement displacement used in relative jumps and indexed addressing
- L ≡ 8 special call locations in page zero. In decimal notation these are 0, 8, 16, 24, 32, 40, 48 and 56
- n ≡ any 8-bit binary number
- nn ≡ any 16-bit binary number
- r ≡ any 8-bit general purpose register (A, B, C, D, E, H, or L)
- s ≡ any 8-bit source register or memory location
- s_b ≡ a bit in a specific 8-bit register or memory location
- ss ≡ any 16-bit source register or memory location
- subscript "L" ≡ the low order 8 bits of a 16-bit register
- subscript "H" ≡ the high order 8 bits of a 16-bit register
- ( ) ≡ the contents within the ( ) are to be used as a pointer to a memory location or I/O port number

8-bit registers are A, B, C, D, E, H, L, I and R
16-bit register pairs are AF, BC, DE and HL
16-bit registers are SP, PC, IX and IY

Addressing Modes implemented include combinations of the following:
- Immediate
- Immediate extended
- Modified Page Zero
- Relative
- Extended
- Indexed
- Register
- Implied
- Register Indirect
- Bit

	Mnemonic	Symbolic Operation	Comments
8-BIT LOADS	LD r, s	r ← s	s ≡ r, n, (HL), (IX+e), (IY+e)
	LD d, r	d ← r	d ≡ (HL), r, (IX+e), (IY+e)
	LD d, n	d ← n	d ≡ (HL), (IX+e), (IY+e)
	LD A, s	A ← s	s ≡ (BC), (DE), (nn), I, R
	LD d, A	d ← A	d ≡ (BC), (DE), (nn), I, R
16-BIT LOADS	LD dd, nn	dd ← nn	dd ≡ BC, DE, HL, SP, IX, IY
	LD dd, (nn)	dd ← (nn)	dd ≡ BC, DE, HL, SP, IX, IY
	LD (nn), ss	(nn) ← ss	ss ≡ BC, DE, HL, SP, IX, IY
	LD SP, ss	SP ← ss	ss ≡ HL, IX, IY
	PUSH ss	(SP-1) ← ss_H; (SP-2) ← ss_L	ss ≡ BC, DE, HL, AF, IX, IY
	POP dd	dd_L ← (SP); dd_H ← (SP+1)	dd ≡ BC, DE, HL, AF, IX, IY
EXCHANGES	EX DE, HL	DE ↔ HL	
	EX AF, AF'	AF ↔ AF'	
	EXX	$\begin{pmatrix} BC \\ DE \\ HL \end{pmatrix} \leftrightarrow \begin{pmatrix} BC' \\ DE' \\ HL' \end{pmatrix}$	
	EX (SP), ss	(SP) ↔ ss_L, (SP+1) ↔ ss_H	ss ≡ HL, IX, IY

	Mnemonic	Symbolic Operation	Comments
MEMORY BLOCK MOVES	LDI	(DE) ← (HL), DE ← DE+1 HL ← HL+1, BC ← BC-1	
	LDIR	(DE) ← (HL), DE ← DE+1 HL ← HL+1, BC ← BC-1 Repeat until BC = 0	
	LDD	(DE) ← (HL), DE ← DE-1 HL ← HL-1, BC ← BC-1	
	LDDR	(DE) ← (HL), DE ← DE-1 HL ← HL-1, BC ← BC-1 Repeat until BC = 0	
MEMORY BLOCK SEARCHES	CPI	A-(HL), HL ← HL+1 BC ← BC-1	A-(HL) sets the flags only. A is not affected
	CPIR	A-(HL), HL ← HL+1 BC ← BC-1, Repeat until BC = 0 or A = (HL)	
	CPD	A-(HL), HL ← HL-1 BC ← BC-1	
	CPDR	A-(HL), HL ← HL-1 BC ← BC-1, Repeat until BC = 0 or A = (HL)	
8-BIT ALU	ADD s	A ← A + s	CY is the carry flag s ≡ r, n, (HL), (IX+e), (IY+e)
	ADC s	A ← A + s + CY	
	SUB s	A ← A - s	
	SBC s	A ← A - s - CY	
	AND s	A ← A ∧ s	
	OR s	A ← A ∨ s	
	XOR s	A ← A ⊕ s	

Figure 7.11 Z80 instruction set (*Source:* Reproduced by permission. © Copyright 1989 Zilog, Inc. This material shall not be reproduced without the written consent of Zilog, Inc.)

	Mnemonic	Symbolic Operation	Comments
8-BIT ALU	CP s	A - s	s = r, n (HL) (IX+e), (IY+e)
	INC d	d ← d + 1	d = r, (HL) (IX+e), (IY+e)
	DEC d	d ← d - 1	
16-BIT ARITHMETIC	ADD HL, ss	HL ← HL + ss	ss ≡ BC, DE, HL, SP
	ADC HL, ss	HL ← HL + ss + CY	
	SBC HL, ss	HL ← HL - ss - CY	
	ADD IX, ss	IX ← IX + ss	ss ≡ BC, DE, IX, SP
	ADD IY, ss	IY ← IY + ss	ss ≡ BC, DE, IY, SP
	INC dd	dd ← dd + 1	dd ≡ BC, DE, HL, SP, IX, IY
	DEC dd	dd ← dd - 1	dd ≡ BC, DE, HL, SP, IX, IY
GP ACC. & FLAG	DAA	Converts A contents into packed BCD following add or subtract.	Operands must be in packed BCD format
	CPL	A ← $\overline{A}$	
	NEG	A ← 00 - A	
	CCF	CY ← $\overline{CY}$	
	SCF	CY ← 1	
MISCELLANEOUS	NOP	No operation	
	HALT	Halt CPU	
	DI	Disable Interrupts	
	EI	Enable Interrupts	
	IM 0	Set interrupt mode 0	8080A mode
	IM 1	Set interrupt mode 1	Call to 0038_H
	IM 2	Set interrupt mode 2	Indirect Call
ROTATES AND SHIFTS	RLC s		s ≡ r, (HL) (IX+e), (IY+e)
	RL s		
	RRC s		
	RR s		
	SLA s		
	SRA s		
	SRL s		
	RLD		
	RRD		

	Mnemonic	Symbolic Operation	Comments
BIT S. R. & T	BIT b, s	Z ← $\overline{s_b}$	Z is zero flag s ≡ r, (HL) (IX+e), (IY+e)
	SET b, s	s_b ← 1	
	RES b, s	s_b ← 0	
INPUT AND OUTPUT	IN A, (n)	A ← (n)	
	IN r, (C)	r ← (C)	Set flags
	INI	(HL) ← (C), HL ← HL + 1 B ← B - 1	
	INIR	(HL) ← (C), HL ← HL + 1 B ← B - 1 Repeat until B = 0	
	IND	(HL) ← (C), HL ← HL - 1 B ← B - 1	
	INDR	(HL) ← (C), HL ← HL - 1 B ← B - 1 Repeat until B = 0	
	OUT(n), A	(n) ← A	
	OUT(C), r	(C) ← r	
	OUTI	(C) ← (HL), HL ← HL + 1 B ← B - 1	
	OTIR	(C) ← (HL), HL ← HL + 1 B ← B - 1 Repeat until B = 0	
	OUTD	(C) ← (HL), HL ← HL - 1 B ← B - 1	
	OTDR	(C) ← (HL), HL ← HL - 1 B ← B - 1 Repeat until B = 0	
JUMPS	JP nn	PC ← nn	cc { NZ PO, Z PE, NC P, C M }
	JP cc, nn	If condition cc is true PC ← nn, else continue	
	JR e	PC ← PC + e	
	JR kk, e	If condition kk is true PC ← PC + e, else continue	kk { NZ NC, Z C }
	JP (ss)	PC ← ss	ss = HL, IX, IY
	DJNZ e	B ← B - 1, if B = 0 continue, else PC ← PC + e	
CALLS	CALL nn	(SP-1) ← PC_H (SP-2) ← PC_L, PC ← nn	cc { NZ PO, Z PE, NC P, C M }
	CALL cc, nn	If condition cc is false continue, else same as CALL nn	
RESTARTS	RST L	(SP-1) ← PC_H (SP-2) ← PC_L, PC_H ← 0 PC_L ← L	
RETURNS	RET	PC_L ← (SP), PC_H ← (SP+1)	
	RET cc	If condition cc is false continue, else same as RET	cc { NZ PO, Z PE, NC P, C M }
	RETI	Return from interrupt, same as RET	
	RETN	Return from non-maskable interrupt	

Figure 7.11 *(continued)*

Instruction	C	Z	P/V	S	N	H	Comments
ADD A, s; ADC A,s	↕	↕	V	↕	0	↕	8-bit add or add with carry
SUB s; SBC A, s, CP s, NEG	↕	↕	V	↕	1	↕	8-bit subtract, subtract with carry, compare and negate accumulator
AND s	0	↕	P	↕	0	1	Logical operations
OR s; XOR s	0	↕	P	↕	0	0	And set's different flags
INC s	•	↕	V	↕	0	↕	8-bit increment
DEC m	•	↕	V	↕	1	↕	8-bit decrement
ADD DD, ss	↕	•	•	•	0	X	16-bit add
ADC HL, ss	↕	↕	V	↕	0	X	16-bit add with carry
SBC HL, ss	↕	↕	V	↕	1	X	16-bit subtract with carry
RLA; RLCA, RRA, RRCA	↕	•	•	•	0	0	Rotate accumulator
RL m; RLC m: RR m; RRC m SLA m: SRA m: SRL m	↕	↕	P	↕	0	0	Rotate and shift location m
RLD, RRD	•	↕	P	↕	0	0	Rotate digit left and right
DAA	↕	↕	P	↕	•	↕	Decimal adjust accumulator
CPL	•	•	•	•	1	1	Complement accumulator
SCF	1	•	•	•	0	0	Set carry
CCF	↕	•	•	•	0	X	Complement carry
IN r, (C)	•	↕	P	↕	0	0	Input register indirect
INI; IND; OUTI; OUTD	•	↕	X	X	1	X	Block input and output
INIR; INDR; OTIR; OTDR	•	1	X	X	1	X	Z = 0 if B ≠ 0 otherwise Z = 1
LDI, LDD	•	X	↕	X	0	0	Block transfer instructions
LDIR, LDDR	•	X	0	X	0	0	P/V = 1 if BC ≠ 0, otherwise P/V = 0
CPI, CPIR, CPD, CPDR	•	↕	↕	↕	1	X	Block search instructions Z = 1 if A = (HL), otherwise Z = 0 P/V = 1 if BC ≠ 0, otherwise P/V = 0
LD A, I; LD A, R	•	↕	IFF	↕	0	0	The content of the interrupt enable flip-flop (IFF) is copied into the P/V flag
BIT b, s	•	↕	X	X	0	1	The state of bit b of location s is copied into the Z flag
NEG	↕	↕	V	↕	1	↕	Negate accumulator

The following notation is used in this table:

Symbol	Operation
C	Carry/link flag. C=1 if the operation produced a carry from the MSB of the operand or result.
Z	Zero flag. Z=1 if the result of the operation is zero.
S	Sign flag. S=1 if the MSB of the result is one.
P/V	Parity or overflow flag. Parity (P) and overflow (V) share the same flag. Logical operations affect this flag with the parity of the result while arithmetic operations affect this flag with the overflow of the result. If P/V holds parity, P/V=1 if the result of the operation is even, P/V=0 if result is odd. If P/V holds overflow, P/V=1 if the result of the operation produced an overflow.
H	Half-carry flag. H=1 if the add or subtract operation produced a carry into or borrow from into bit 4 of the accumulator.
N	Add/Subtract flag. N=1 if the previous operation was a subtract.
	H and N flags are used in conjunction with the decimal adjust instruction (DAA) to properly correct the result into packed BCD format following addition or subtraction using operands with packed BCD format.
↕	The flag is affected according to the result of the operation.
•	The flag is unchanged by the operation.
0	The flag is reset by the operation.
1	The flag is set by the operation.
X	The flag is a "don't care."
V	P/V flag affected according to the overflow result of the operation.
P	P/V flag affected according to the parity result of the operation.
r	Any one of the CPU registers A, B, C, D, E, H, L.
s	Any 8-bit location for all the addressing modes allowed for the particular instruction.
ss	Any 16-bit location for all the addressing modes allowed for that instruction.
ii	Any one of the two index registers IX or IY.
R	Refresh counter.
n	8-bit value in range <0, 255>
nn	16-bit value in range <0, 65535>
m	Any 8-bit location for all the addressing modes allowed for the particular instruction.

Figure 7.12 Summary of flag operation. (*Source:* Reproduced by permission. © Copyright 1989 Zilog, Inc. This material shall not be reproduced without the written consent of Zilog, Inc.)

Immediate Addressing   Instructions where the byte following the op-code is an operand value.

> **EXAMPLE 7.5   Immediate Addressing**
> LD A,5 will load the number 05 into the accumulator.

Suppose that the variable B1 has been set equal to 5 by an EQU statement. Then, in the instruction LD A,B1, a Z80 assembler will have to read all the characters up to and including the 1 before it can distinguish the instruction from LD A,B. In contrast, the 8085 assembly language uses different mnemonics: MVI A,B1 as compared to MOV A,B.

Immediate Extended   Instructions where the 2 bytes following the op-code form a 16-bit operand value.

> **EXAMPLE 7.6   Immediate Extended Addressing**
> LD HL,1234H puts 12h into register H and 34h into register L. The corresponding 8085 instruction is LXI H,1234H.

Modified Page Zero Addressing   These are the 1-byte RESTART calls RST 0 to RST 38. Page zero refers to the first 256 bytes of memory, where the RST target addresses are located.

> **EXAMPLE 7.7   A Restart**
> RST 38 will cause a call to address 0038h. The equivalent 8085 instruction is RST 7.

Extended Addressing   Instructions where the 2 bytes following the op-code form the 16-bit address of a memory location.

> **EXAMPLE 7.8   Extended Addressing**
> JP 1200H causes a jump to address 1200H, and LD A,(1000H) loads the accumulator with the byte stored in memory location 1000H. The equivalent 8085 instructions are JMP 1200H and LDA 1000H.

Register Indirect Addressing   These instructions specify a register pair that holds the address of an operand.

> **EXAMPLE 7.9 Register Indirect Addressing**
>
> LD A,(HL) copies a byte from memory into the accumulator. The address of the byte is held in the HL register pair. The equivalent 8085 instruction is MOV A,M.

Relative Addressing

No equivalent in the 8085. The Z80 has a group of 2-byte jump instructions where the destination address is relative to the address of the jump instruction itself. The second byte of a relative jump is a signed two's complement number in the range $+127$ to -128. That signed number is added to the address of the instruction *following* the relative jump, giving a range of 129 bytes forward and 126 bytes back from the relative jump itself.

> **EXAMPLE 7.10 Relative Jumps**
>
> JR 0 jumps to the very next location. JR 0FEH jumps to itself (jumps -2 bytes).

Indexed Addressing

No equivalent in the 8085. The Z80 contains two 16-bit index registers: IX and IY. Instructions using indexed addressing specify one of the index registers as well as an 8-bit displacement that is added to the value in the index register to form a 16-bit address of an operand. The content of the index register is not altered by the displacement; the addition is done "outside" it.

> **EXAMPLE 7.11 Indexed Addressing**
>
> LD A,(IX+04) will copy a byte from memory into the accumulator. The address of the byte is formed by adding 4 to the 16-bit number stored in IX.

Bit Addressing

No equivalent in the 8085. The Z80 has a group of instructions that can set or clear any bit in any register or memory location. It can also test any bit to see if the bit is 1 or 0.

> **EXAMPLE 7.12 Bit Addressing**
>
> SET 0,A will set bit 0 of the accumulator to 1. RES 3,B will reset bit 3 of register B to 0.

7.4.2 Instruction Length

Because the 8085 has fewer than 256 different instructions, all instructions have a 1-byte op-code and are 1, 2, or 3 bytes long. The Z80 has more than 256 different instructions, so some of the Z80 op-codes are 2 bytes long. Z80 instructions can be as long as 4 bytes.

To maintain compatibility, the Z80 uses some of the unused 8085 op-codes (CB, DD, ED, FD) to form a sort of prefix for "Z80 only" instructions.

> **EXAMPLE 7.13 Z80 Op-Code Prefix**
>
> 77 is the hex op-code for LD A,(HL) in the Z80 and the equivalent MOV A,M in the 8085, but DD 77 is the 2-byte Z80 op-code for LD A,(IX+d).

7.5 MOVING AND SEARCHING

The Z80 has extended the power of the 8085 move instructions by adding the use of index registers (IX and IY) and also by adding block move and search instructions. All moves use the mnemonic LD and have the form **LD dest,source** where dest is the destination of the move. Remember that flags are not affected by moves.

7.5.1 8-Bit Loads

A few examples will suffice to show the format of the 8-bit moves:

I and R Registers: LD I,A; LD R,A; LD A,I; LD A,R are the only instructions referencing the I and R registers.

Register to Register: LD B,C content of register C copied to register B.

Register Immediate: LD D,2 number 2 loaded into register D.

Extended: LD A,(1000) the byte stored at location 1000 is copied to the accumulator. The inverse operation is LD (1000),A. Note that the register must be the accumulator.

Register Indirect: LD A,(HL) the number in the HL register pair is used as the address of the byte that is copied to the accumulator. The inverse operation is LD (HL),A. If HL is used as the register pair, then the register can be A, B, C, D, E, H, or L. If the register pair is BC or DE, then the register must be A.

Immediate Indirect: LD (HL),2 the number 2 is loaded into a memory location. The address of the location is held in the HL register pair.

Register Indexed: LD B,(IX+10H) copies a byte from memory to register B. The address of the byte is formed by adding the displacement 10H to the 16-bit number stored in the IX index register. Remember that the addition of the displacement is done as part of the instruction execution; it does *not* change the number in the index register. The inverse instruction would be LD (IX+10H),B.

Immediate Indexed: LD (IY+0),12H loads the number 12H into the memory location whose address is held in IY. Note that the displacement can be zero, as in the example.

7.5.2 16-Bit Loads

The 16-bit loads have four formats, as shown in the following examples:

Register: LD SP,HL; LD SP,IX; LD SP,IY are three instructions used to load the stack pointer from the HL register pair, from IX, or from IY. Note that LD SP,HL is the same as the 8085 SPHL instruction.

Immediate: LD BC,1234H will put 12h into H and 34h into L.

Extended: LD DE,(1234H) will load E with a copy of the byte stored at 1234h and will load D with a copy of the byte stored at 1235h. The inverse instruction is LD (1234H),DE.

Stack: PUSH AF will push the accumulator and flags onto the stack the same as the accumulator and flags onto the stack the same as the 8085 PUSH PSW instruction. The inverse instruction is POP AF. AF, BC, DE, HL, IX, and IY can be PUSHed and POPed but *not* SP.

7.5.3 Exchanges

There are six exchange instructions:

EX AF,AF'	Will exchange the accumulator and flags of the currently active register set with the accumulator and flags of the alternate register set.
EXX	Will exchange the BC, DE, and HL register pairs of the currently active register set with the corresponding register pairs of the alternate register set.
EX DE,HL	Will exchange the 16-bit contents of the HL and DE register pairs. Same as the 8085 XCHG instruction.
EX (SP),HL	Will exchange the contents of the HL register pair with the 2 bytes on top of the stack. Same as the 8085 XTHL instruction.
EX (SP),IX	Similar to EX (SP),HL but with IX taking the place of HL.
EX (SP),IY	Same as EX (SP),IX except uses IY in place of IX.

7.5.4 Block Transfers

A common software task is to move a block of data from one part of memory to another. Consider the following 8085 subroutine, which moves 500 bytes from a block of memory starting at address 1000h and puts them into a block of memory starting at address 2000h. After each move, the pointers are incremented and the loop count is decremented. The loop continues until the count is zero. As shown in Example 7.14, the same job can be done with a shorter Z80 subroutine.

```
                LXI     B,500       ; LOOP COUNT
                LXI     H,1000H     ; FROM ADDRESS
                LXI     D,2000H     ; TO ADDRESS
        LOOP:   MOV     A,M         ; GET A BYTE
                STAX    D           ; MOVE IT
                INX     H           ; INCREMENT THE
                INX     D           ; POINTERS
                DCX     B           ; DECREMENT LOOP COUNT
                MVI     A,0         ; SET UP COMPARE
                CMP     B           ; IS REG B ZERO?
                JNZ     LOOP        ; JUMP IF NO

                CMP     C           ; IS REG C ZERO?
                JNZ     LOOP        ; JUMP IF NO

                RET                 ; ALL DONE
```

EXAMPLE 7.14 Block Transfer

```
                LD      BC,500      ; LOOP COUNT
                LD      HL,1000H    ; FROM ADDRESS
                LD      DE,2000H    ; TO ADDRESS
                LDIR                ; DO IT
                RET                 ; ALL DONE
```

The reason the Z80 routine is shorter is the Z80 LDIR instruction (load, increment, repeat), which does the following:

1. Moves a byte using HL as the *from* pointer and DE as the *to* pointer; shown symbolically as (DE) ← (HL).
2. Increments HL and DE.
3. Decrements BC.
4. Repeats the first three steps until BC contains zero.

The LDI instruction is the same as LDIR except it does not repeat. For cases where you want to *decrement* the pointers after each move, the Z80 has the LDDR (repeating) and LDD (nonrepeating) instructions.

7.5.5 Block Searches

The block searches are similar to the block transfer instructions in that a pointer is automatically updated and a counter is automatically decremented. The difference is that a comparison is made instead of a move. As above, we can look at an 8085 subroutine as a starting point.

Consider the 8085 code in the following subroutine, which searches through a block of text until either the target character is found or until the loop count is decremented down to zero. The same job can be done with a shorter Z80 subroutine, as in Example 7.15.

```
            LXI     B,500           ; LOOP COUNT
            LXI     H,1000H         ; START OF TEXT
LOOP:       MVI     A,'$'           ; TARGET CHARACTER
            MOV     D,M             ; GET A BYTE
            CMP     D               ; COMPARE TO TARGET
            JZ      FOUND           ; JUMP IF MATCH

            INX     H               ; INCREMENT THE POINTER
            DCX     B               ; DECREMENT LOOP COUNT
            MVI     A,0             ; SET UP COMPARE
            CMP     B               ; IS REG B ZERO?
            JNZ     LOOP            ; JUMP IF NO

            CMP     C               ; IS REG C ZERO?
            JNZ     LOOP            ; JUMP IF NO

FOUND:      RET                     ; ALL DONE
```

EXAMPLE 7.15   Block Search

```
            LD      A,'$'           ; TARGET CHARACTER
            LD      BC,500          ; LOOP COUNT
            LD      HL,1000H        ; START OF TEXT
            CPIR                    ; DO IT
            RET                     ; ALL DONE
```

The Z80 version is shorter because of the CPIR instruction (compare, increment, repeat), which does the following:

1. Compares the byte pointed to by HL to the byte in the accumulator. Neither byte is changed. The zero flag is affected as for a compare instruction.
2. Increments HL.
3. Decrements BC.
4. Repeats the first three steps until a match is found or until BC contains zero.

The CPI instruction is the same as CPIR, except it does not repeat. For cases where you want to *decrement* the HL pointer after each move, the Z80 has the CPDR (repeating) and CPD (nonrepeating) instructions.

Other block moves involving the I/O ports are described in Sec. 7.9.

7.6 ARITHMETIC AND LOGIC

Except for the mnemonics and the inclusion of the IX and IY registers, arithmetic and logic instructions on the Z80 are almost the same as on the 8085.

7.6.1 8-Bit Operations

As in the 8085, all arithmetic and logic operations use the accumulator. Where the 8085 mnemonics always leave the accumulator implied (as in ADD B or SUB B), the Z80 sometimes requires the accumulator to be specified (as in ADD A,B) and sometimes not (as in SUB B). When programming, it's a good idea to have a Z80 assembly language pocket reference card handy until you remember the mnemonics.

A nice feature of the instruction set is that the same mnemonic is used whether the operands are immediate, register, or indirect.

> **EXAMPLE 7.16   8-Bit ADC Instructions**
>
> ADC A,5; ADC A,B; ADC A,(HL) are all *add-with-carry* instructions.

A more important difference between the 8085 and the Z80 is that because of the half-carry flag (H), the DAA instruction will work after BCD subtraction as well as after BCD addition.

7.6.2 16-Bit Operations

As with the 8-bit operations, the Z80 16-bit operations are basically the same as the 8085 operations except for the mnemonics. However, a significant difference is the addition of two new 16-bit operations that affect the flags: ADC HL,rp and SBC HL,rp, where rp can be BC, DE, HL, or SP.

> **EXAMPLE 7.17   16-Bit ADC**
>
> ADC HL,BC will add the contents of the BC register pair as well as the value of the carry flag to the contents of the HL register pair. For the purpose of this addition, the carry flag can be thought of as a 16-bit number with only two possible values: 0000h or 0001h. The result of the addition is left in HL.
>
> The following flags are affected by the result: S, Z, V, N, and C.

7.6.3 Miscellaneous

Under the heading "General-purpose arithmetic and CPU control," we can list the following instructions:

DAA	**Decimal Adjust Accumulator:** Same as 8085, except also works after subtraction.
CPL	**Complement the Accumulator:** Same as 8085 CMA.
NEG	**Negate the Accumulator:** Replaces the content of the accumulator with its two's complement. No equivalent 8085 instruction.
CCF	**Complement Carry Flag:** Same as 8085 CMC.
SCF	**Set Carry Flag:** Same as 8085 STC.
NOP	**No Operation.**
HALT	Same as 8085 HLT.
DI:	**Disable Interrupts.**
EI	**Enable Interrupts.**
IM 0	**Set Interrupt Mode 0:** Z80 specific.

IM 1 **Set Interrupt Mode 1:** Z80 specific.
IM 2 **Set Interrupt Mode 2:** Z80 specific.

7.7 ROTATES AND SHIFTS

Rotating and shifting registers is a common task. The Z80 has greatly expanded the number of such instructions over the 8085.

7.7.1 Rotates

The Z80 has four single-byte instructions to rotate the accumulator: RLCA, RLA, RRCA, and RRA, which correspond to the 8085 instructions RLC, RAL, RRC, and RAR. In addition, the Z80 has four new instructions to rotate any register or memory location: RLC, RL, RRC, and RR. In operation, RLC is like RLCA, RL is like RLA, RRC is like RRCA, and RR is like RRCA. The new instructions take an operand that can be

  A register [example: RLC B]
  A location pointed to by HL [example: RL (HL)]
  A location pointed to by IX or IY [examples: RRC (IX+5); RR (IY+1)]

7.7.2 Shifts

The 8085 has only rotates. The Z80 has added four shift instructions. A *shift* is similar to a rotate except that the bit shifted out one end is not shifted back in the other end. The Z80 shift instructions take an operand that can be a register, HL as a pointer, or an index register as a pointer; any register or memory location can be shifted.
  In Chapter 4 we describe the difference between logic and arithmetic shifts. The Z80 has both.

> **EXAMPLE 7.18 Example Z80 Shifts**
>
> SLA B   **Shift Left Arithmetic** register B. Shifts the content of register B 1 bit to the left. The MSB (bit 7) is copied to the carry flag. A zero is shifted into bit 0.
> SRA (HL)   **Shift Right Arithmetic** location pointed to by HL. The content of the memory location is shifted right 1 bit. The MSB does not change. The LSB (bit 0) is copied to the carry flag.
> SRL (IX+0) **Shift Right Logical** location pointed to by IX plus the specified displacement. The content of the memory location is shifted right 1 bit. A zero is shifted into the MSB. The LSB is copied to the carry flag.

7.7.3 Swapping Nibbles

The Z80 has two instructions that are useful in BCD applications. They move 4-bit nibbles between the accumulator and the memory location pointed to by HL. In the following descriptions, (HL) refers to "the byte pointed to by HL," and A refers to the accumulator.

RLD   **Rotate Left Digit:** The lower nibble of (HL) is moved to the upper nibble of the same byte. The upper nibble of (HL) is moved to the lower nibble of A. The lower nibble of A is moved to the lower nibble of (HL).

> **EXAMPLE 7.19   RLD**
>
> Suppose A holds 12h and (HL) holds 34h. After RLD, A will hold 13h and (HL) will hold 42h.

RRD   **Rotate Right Digit:** Same as RRD, except rotates in the opposite direction.

> **EXAMPLE 7.20   RRD**
>
> Suppose A holds 12h and (HL) holds 34h. After RRD, A will hold 14h and (HL) will hold 23h.

7.8 JUMPS AND LOOPING

The Z80 has increased the power of the jump group over the 8085 by adding relative jumps as well as a looping instruction (DJNZ).

7.8.1 Direct and Indirect

The Z80 includes all the 8085 jump instructions using the mnemonic JP. One helpful by-product of the mnemonic structure is that an indirect jump is now recognized as such. For example, it may not be obvious what the 8085 instruction PCHL does, but the Z80 instruction JP (HL) obviously means "jump to the address held in the HL register pair." The Z80 also has the non-8085 instructions JP (IX) and JP (IY). Note that this is one of the few times that the index registers are used as operands without a displacement.

7.8.2 Relative

Compared to full address jump instructions, the relative jumps have two advantages:

   1. They are 2 bytes long instead of 3, so they save memory space.

2. A block of code containing only relative jumps can be executed from any part of memory without having to change jump addresses.

The disadvantage is that the relative jump range is limited to 256 bytes, as described in Sec. 7.4.1. Normally, you will write a relative jump such as JR LBL1 and the assembler will figure out where LBL1 is and calculate the appropriate numeric displacement. If LBL1 is out of range, the assembler will tell you.

7.8.3 DJNZ (Decrement and Jump-Not-Zero)

Consider the following typical 8085 loop:

```
            MVI    B, LPCNT
LOOP:       NOP
            < BODY OF THE LOOP >
            DCR    B
            JNZ    LOOP
```

The Z80 equivalent is given in Example 7.21.

EXAMPLE 7.21 Using DJNZ

```
            LD     B, LPCNT
LOOP:       NOP
            < BODY OF LOOP >
            DJNZ   LOOP
```

In operation, DJNZ will decrement register B. If B does not contain zero after the decrement, then DJNZ will do a relative jump back to the address specified in the operand (LOOP). If B does contain zero after the decrement, then the loop terminates and the instruction following DJNZ will be executed. The assembler will tell you if LOOP is out of range.

7.9 INPUT/OUTPUT

The 8085 has two I/O instructions, IN and OUT, both using the accumulator and affecting no flags. The 8085 requires port addresses to be fixed in code as immediate operands. In contrast, the Z80 has additional I/O instructions for indirect addressing and block transfer.

7.9.1 Immediate and Indirect

The Z80 includes the 8085 I/O instructions but with the format IN A,(n) and OUT (n),A, where n is the port address. Note that the port address is an immediate operand; it cannot be changed during program execution.

The Z80 adds new I/O instructions in the form IN r,(C) and OUT (C),r; where r is an 8-bit register and (C) means that the port address is held in register C. Because the port address is in a register, it can be changed during execution. Also, the new instructions will affect the S, Z, H, and P flags according to the byte moved.

EXAMPLE 7.22 I/O Using Register C

The following fragment of code will input a byte from port address 23h into register B and output it to port address 24h:

```
LD    C, 23H
IN    B, (C)
INC   C
OUT   (C), B
```

7.9.2 Block I/O

The Z80 extends the block move idea to I/O. The instruction INIR will do the following:

1. Using the content of C as the port address and the contents of HL as a memory pointer, a byte will be read from the port and stored in memory.
2. Register B, assumed to be a loop counter, is decremented.
3. The pointer in HL is incremented.
4. The first three steps are repeated until B equals zero.

The INI instruction is the same as INIR, except it does not repeat. For cases where you want to decrement the pointers after each move, the Z80 has the INDR (repeating) and IND (nonrepeating) instructions. The corresponding output instructions are OTIR (increment/repeating), OUTI (increment/nonrepeating). OTDR (decrement/repeating), and OUTD (decrement/nonrepeating). Note that INI, IND, OUTI, and OUTD affect the Z flag according to the result of decrementing B. INIR, INDR, OTIR, and OTDR leave Z set.

EXAMPLE 7.23 Block I/O

The following code fragment will get 5 bytes from port 17h and store them in five consecutive memory locations starting at 1000h:

```
LD    HL, 1000H
LD    B, 5
LD    C, 17H
INIR
```

7.10 CALLS AND RETURNS

Like the 8085, the Z80 contains conditional and unconditional subroutine calls and returns. It also contains 1-byte restart instructions that work the same as the 8085 RST 0–RST 7; except in Z80 mnemonics, the number after RST is 0, 8, 16, 24, 32, 40, 48, or 56.

Unlike the 8085, the Z80 has separate instructions for returning from certain interrupts. RETN is an unconditional return from nonmaskable interrupt, and RETI is an unconditional return from a maskable mode 2 interrupt. RET is a return from mode 0 and mode 1 maskable interrupts as well as from subroutine calls and restarts. We discuss Z80 interrupts further in Sec. 7.12.

7.11 BIT MANIPULATION

As mentioned earlier, the Z80 has instructions to set, reset, or test any bit in any register or memory location. When combined with I/O, bit instructions greatly simplify programming for control applications where individual status and control bits must be manipulated.

7.11.1 Testing

The BIT instruction copies the complement of the specified bit to the Z flag. The actual testing is done by a conditional instruction such as JP Z. The byte containing the bit can be

A register [example: Bit 1,B]
A location pointed to by HL [example: Bit 2,(HL)]
A location pointed to by an index register [example: Bit 3,(IX+5)]

Note that the number following the mnemonic BIT is the bit number within the byte with the LSB being 0 and the MSB being 7.

Remember that it is the *complement* of the specified bit that gets copied to the Z flag. For example, if register B contains 01, then BIT 7,B will cause Z to be set to 1 and BIT 0,B will reset Z to 0.

7.11.2 Setting and Resetting

Setting forces the specified bit to 1; resetting forces it to 0. The corresponding mnemonics are SET and RES, and the instructions follow the same format as BIT.

EXAMPLE 7.24 SET and RES

SET 0,B will force the LSB of register B high. RES 7,(HL) will force low the MSB of the location pointed to by HL.

7.12 INTERRUPTS

The Z80 has one nonmaskable interrupt (NMI) and three different modes of maskable interrupts. One of the maskable modes (mode 2) is vectored. A priority scheme is incorporated into the architecture of Z80 peripheral chips.

7.12.1 The Z80 Interrupt Process

Figure 7.13 shows a flow diagram summarizing the Z80 interrupt sequence. Note the priority of responses to external events. Bus requests are honored first, followed by nonmaskable interrupts, followed by maskable interrupts.

Also note that the process requires that four internal flip-flops (F/F) be used. The NMI F/F and the maskable INT F/F are flags that indicate an interrupt has been recognized. IFF1 is the mask bit; it must be set for a maskable interrupt to occur. IFF2 is a place to save a copy of IFF1 when a nonmaskable interrupt occurs.

7.12.2 Nonmaskable Interrupt (NMI)

Figure 7.14 shows the nonmaskable interrupt sequence. It happens when the $\overline{\text{NMI}}$ pin on the Z80 is pulled low, and the effect is similar to a call to memory address 0066h. Note that besides pushing the return address onto the stack, IFF1 was copied to IFF2. IFF2 will be copied back to IFF1 when RETN is executed, thus saving the NMI service routine the problem of having to figure out whether or not to reenable interrupts before returning. If you want to see what is in IFF2, it is copied into the P flag when either LD A,I or LD A,R is executed.

7.12.3 Maskable Interrupt Modes

The Z80 has three maskable interrupt modes to serve three levels of complexity (see Fig. 7.15). Each is described below. Before enabling interrupts, the program must select a mode by executing either IM 0, IM 1, or IM 2. The choice can be changed by disabling interrupts, executing IM n, and reenabling interrupts.

In any mode, a maskable interrupt will occur (assuming it is enabled) when the Z80 $\overline{\text{INT}}$ pin is pulled low. At the end of the service routine, EI must be executed before returning, because, as in the 8085, when an interrupt occurs, further interrupts are automatically disabled.

7.12.4 Mode 0

Figure 7.15a shows the mode 0 interrupt sequence. Mode 0 is simply the old 8080 interrupt scheme discussed in Chapter 5. In the Z80, the interrupting device must put an instruction onto the data bus when $\overline{\text{IORQ}}$ goes active during the M1 cycle acknowledging the interrupt. The instruction is usually a 1-byte RST.

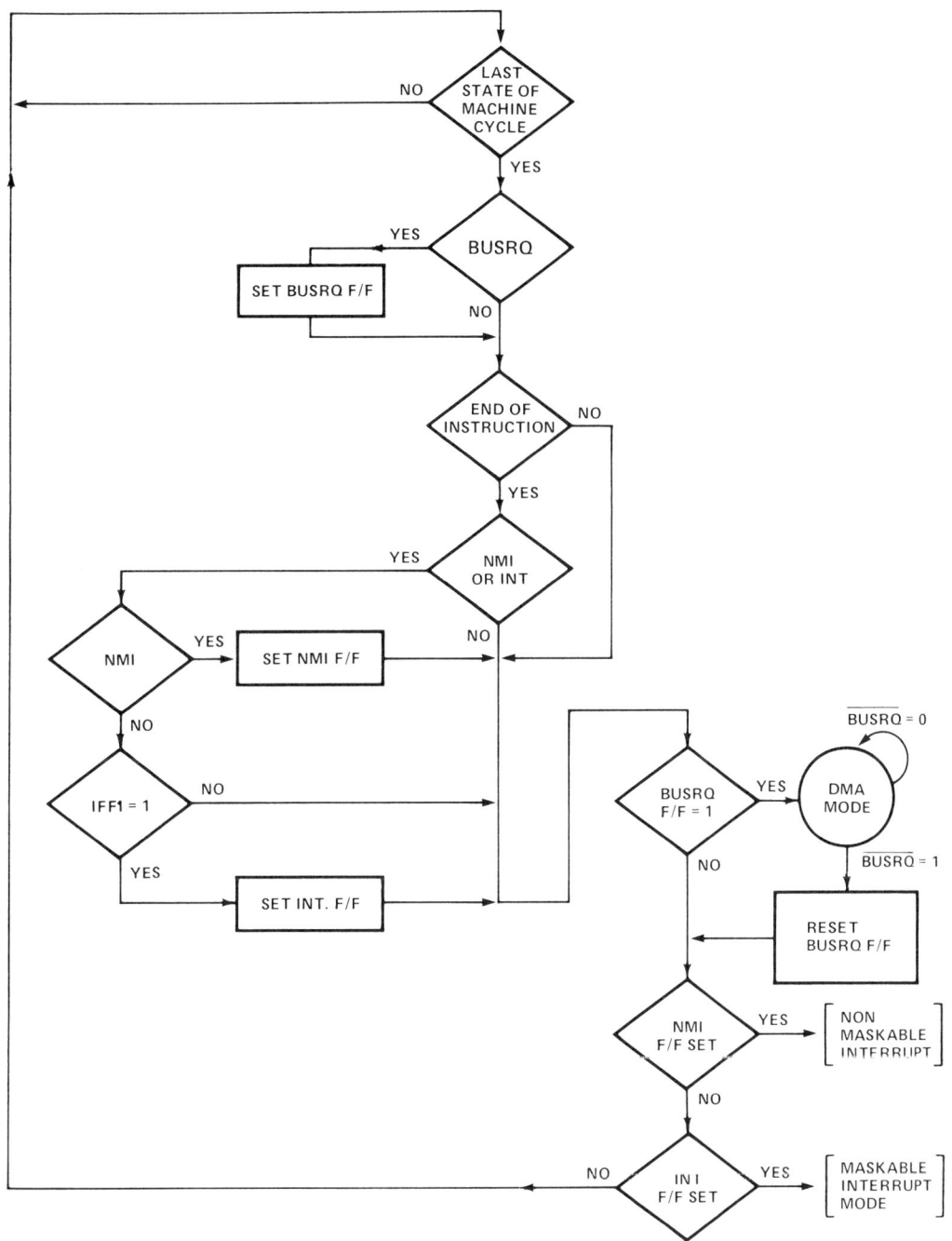

Figure 7.13 Z80 flow diagram: interrupt sequence. (*Source:* Reproduced by permission. © Copyright 1989 Zilog, Inc. This material shall not be reproduced without the written consent of Zilog, Inc.)

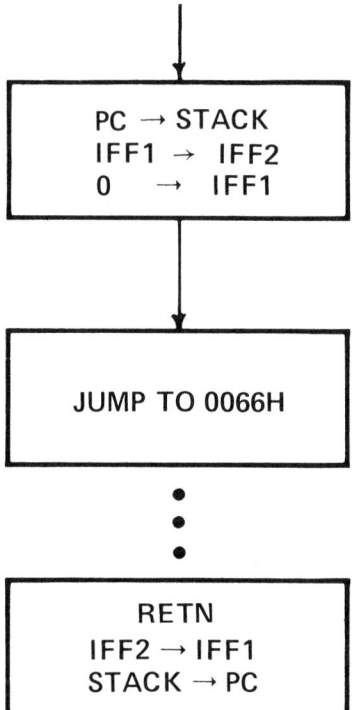

Figure 7.14 Nonmaskable interrupt sequence. (*Source:* Reproduced by permission. © Copyright 1989 Zilog, Inc. This material shall not be reproduced without the written consent of Zilog, Inc.)

7.12.5 Mode 1

Figure 7.15b shows the mode 1 interrupt sequence. In operation, it makes the Z80 INT pin act similar to one of the 8085 hardware restarts. A mode 1 interrupt will cause an automatic call to memory location 0038h. Mode 1 is useful for minimal complexity interrupt applications.

7.12.6 Mode 2

Figure 7.15c shows the mode 2 interrupt sequence. Mode 2 is vectored and is the most powerful of the three modes because it allows an indirect call to any location in memory.

Mode 2 makes use of a jump table, which can be located anywhere in memory. The jump table holds the 16-bit addresses of the various interrupt service routines, so each entry is 2 consecutive bytes in the table.

The 16-bit address of the jump table entry is formed from two 8-bit halves. The upper half of the table address is held in the I register (IREG), which the program loads with a LD I,A instruction. The lower half of the table address is supplied by the interrupting device, which puts it on the data bus during the interrupt-acknowledgment M1 cycle.

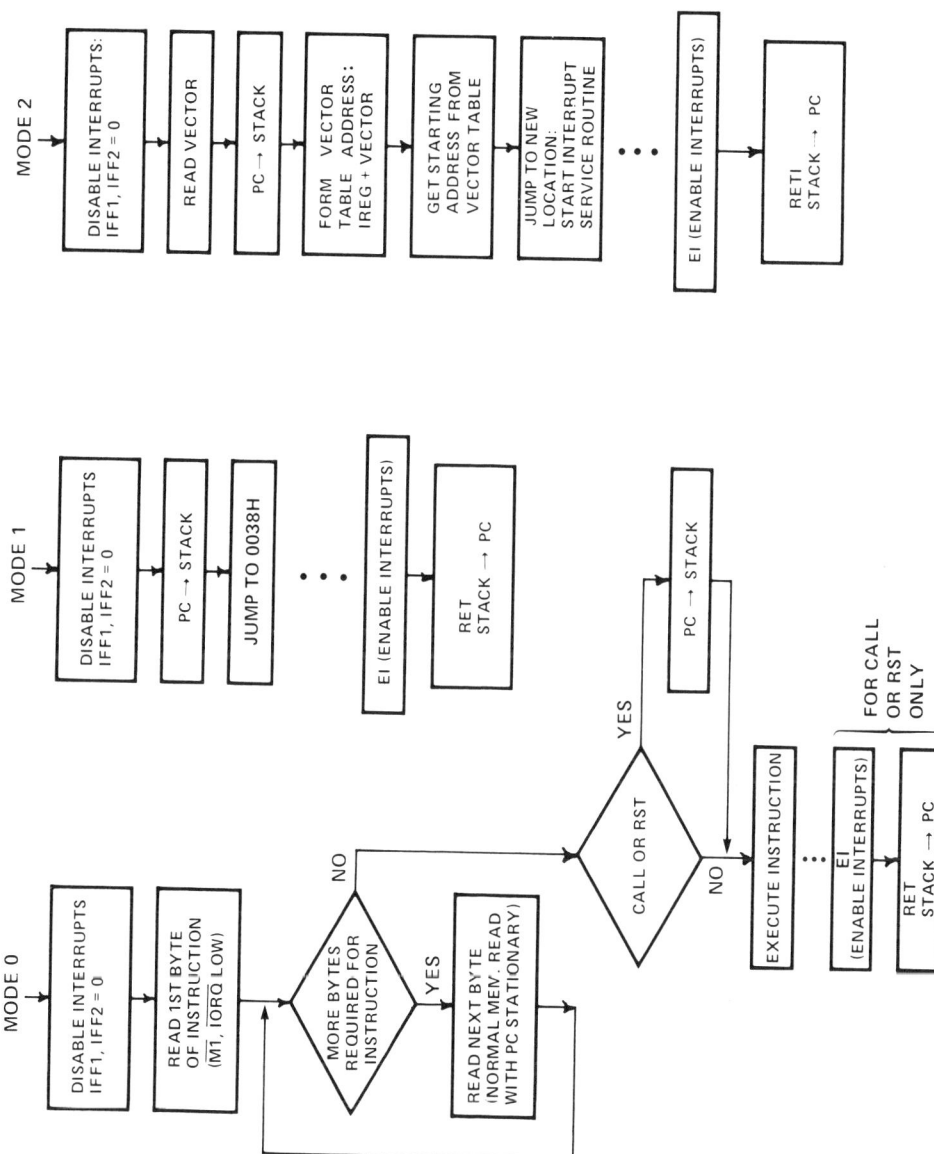

Figure 7.15 Maskable interrupt sequences. (a) Mode 0. (b) Mode 1. (c) Mode 2. (*Source*: Reproduced by permission. © Copyright 1989 Zilog, Inc. This material shall not be reproduced without the written consent of Zilog, Inc.)

229

Once the address of the table location is formed, the processor will get the 2 consecutive bytes stored there and use them as the 16-bit jump address. Note that because the table stores 2-byte addresses, the 8 bits supplied by the interrupting device must end in a 0. In other words, only the 7 most significant bits are used. The vector processing sequence is shown in Fig. 7.16.

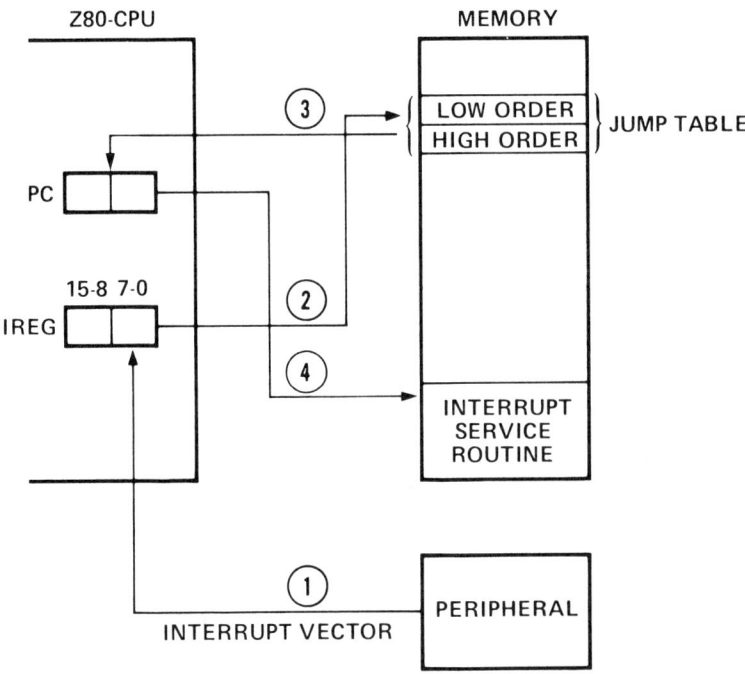

Figure 7.16 Vector processing sequence. (*Source:* Reproduced by permission. © Copyright 1989 Zilog, Inc. This material shall not be reproduced without the written consent of Zilog, Inc.)

EXAMPLE 7.25 Mode 2

The following piece of code will sit in a loop waiting for an interrupt from one of two devices (call them DEV1 and DEV2) operating in Z80 interrupt mode 2. The code initializes I to 35h. To form the 16-bit address into the jump table, DEV1 will supply 00h and DEV2 will supply 04h. Note the use of a NOP to force the second entry in the jump table to be at an even address (sometimes called a 16-bit boundary).

```
          ORG   200H        ; STARTING ADDRESS
          LD    A,35H       ; SET UP UPPER HALF
          LD    I,A         ; OF INTERRUPT VECTOR
LOOP:     JR    LOOP        ; WAIT HERE FOR INTERRUPT
```

```
          ORG   400H              ; ADDRESS OF SR_1
          <SERVICE ROUTINE SR_1>
          RETI                    ; RETURN BACK TO LOOP
          ORG   500H              ; ADDRESS OF SR_2
          <SERVICE ROUTINE SR_2>
          RETI                    ; RETURN BACK TO LOOP
          ORG   3500H             ; ADDRESS OF JUMP TABLE
          JP    400H              ; JUMP TO SR_1
          NOP                     ; MAKE NEXT ADDRESS EVEN
          JP    500H              ; JUMP TO SR_2
```

7.12.7 The Priority Daisy Chain

The Z80 resolves interrupt priority by daisy chaining peripherals that have been designed for the purpose. Such devices have pins labeled IEI (interrupt-enable-in) and IEO (interrupt-enable-out). The IEI pin must be high before the device can request an interrupt. When such a device does request an interrupt, it will also pull its own IEO pin low.

All the peripheral devices are tied to the common $\overline{INT}$ line. The priority chain is formed by connecting the IEI pin of the highest priority peripheral to +5V. The IEO pin of the highest priority device is connected to the IEI of the second priority device, the IEO of which is connected to the IEI pin of the third, and so on. The IEO of the lowest priority device is left unterminated. Thus, any device requesting an interrupt will inhibit all lower priority devices from requesting simultaneous interrupts. However, higher priority devices *can* interrupt lower priority devices *if* the lower priority device's interrupt service routine contains an EI as one of its early instructions.

EXAMPLE 7.26 A Daisy Chain

Figure 7.17 shows two devices, labeled CTC and PIO, in a daisy chain. The CTC (counter/timer chip) has higher priority, and the PIO (parallel I/O) has lower priority chip. If the CTC generates an interrupt, it will pull its IEO line low. The IEO line will not go high again until the CTC chip sees the 2 consecutive bytes ED 4D (the RETI instruction) on the data bus.

7.13 CONTEXT SWITCHING

The term *multitasking* is used to describe a computer system that can execute more than one program (task) at a time. For the traditional machine having one CPU, multitasking actually means that the CPU's time is divided among several different

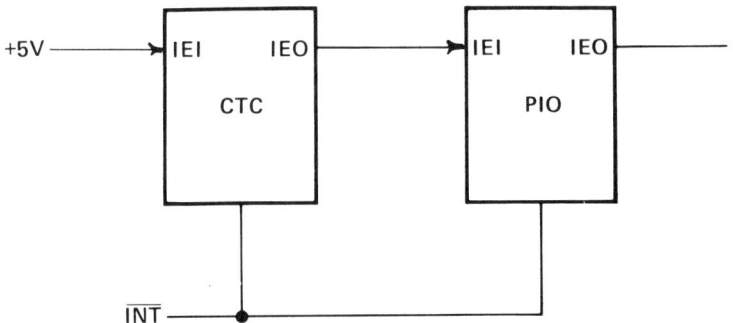

Figure 7.17 CTC/PIO priority chain. (*Source:* Reproduced by permission. © Copyright 1989 Zilog, Inc. This material shall not be reproduced without the written consent of Zilog, Inc.)

tasks residing in different parts of memory. It is done so fast that it appears to us that all the tasks are running simultaneously.

Because the Z80 has two accumulators, two flag registers, and two sets of general-purpose registers, it is relatively easy to implement a two-program multi-tasking system. In some applications, one task is said to be in the *foreground* and the other in the *background*. Alternating CPU time between the two tasks is called *context switching*.

EXAMPLE 7.27 Context Switching

The program in this example assumes an external oscillator is generating a mode 1 interrupt 100 times a second. The program will switch to the other task at each interrupt. Assuming a 4-MHz CPU clock, the Z80 can execute about 500 instructions between interrupts.

```
        ORG     0000            ; RESET HERE

        DI                      ; DISABLE INTERRUPTS
        IM      1               ; SELECT MODE 1
        LD      HL,STPTR2       ; SAVE THE
        LD      SP,HL           ;   STACK POINTER
        DEC     HL              ;   FOR
        DEC     HL              ;   TASK2
        LD      (STKPTR),HL     ; PUSH TASK2 ADDRESS
        LD      HL,TASK2        ;   ONTO TASK2 STACK
        PUSH    HL              ;   FOR CONTEXT SWITCH RET
        LD      SP,STPTR1       ; SET UP SP FOR TASK1
        EI                      ; ENABLE INTERRUPTS
        JP      TASK1           ; GO START TASK1


        ORG     0038H           ; INTERRUPT ADDRESS

        LD      (HLTMP),HL      ; FREE UP HL
        LD      (SPTMP),SP      ; FREE UP SP
        LD      SP,(STKPTR)     ; GET OTHER STACK POINTER
        LD      HL,(SPTMP)      ; SAVE THE PREVIOUS
```

```
        LD      (STKPTR),HL     ;  STACK POINTER
        LD      HL,(IYS)        ;  GET OTHER IY
        PUSH    HL              ;  PUT IT ON THE STACK
        LD      HL,(IXS)        ;  GET OTHER IX
        PUSH    HL              ;  PUT IT ON THE STACK
        LD      (IYS),IY        ;  SAVE CURRENT IY
        LD      (IXS),IX        ;  SAVE CURRENT IX
        POP     IX              ;  OTHER IX OFF STACK
        POP     IY              ;  OTHER IY OFF STACK
        LD      HL,(HLTMP)      ;  RESTORE HL
        EX      AF,AF'          ;  EXCHANGE ACC & FLAG REGS
        EXX                     ;  EXCHANGE OTHER REGS
        EI                      ;  ENABLE INTERRUPTS
        RET                     ;  BACK TO OTHER TASK

TASK1:  <PROGRAM 1>

TASK2:  <PROGRAM 2>
```

Note the initialization that is done starting at address 0000. Two stack areas are required, one for each task, as well as two stack pointers. SP holds the stack pointer for the active task, and the other pointer is saved in memory location STKPTR. TASK1 will start first, and the address of TASK2 is pushed onto the TASK2 stack.

When an interrupt occurs, the stack pointers are swapped, IX and IY are swapped with saved values, and the alternate register sets are swapped. After all the swaps, the RET instruction will pop off the stack the resume address for the task that has just "woken up." The other task is "put to sleep."

7.14 SUMMARY

In this chapter we have examined the Z80 processor and contrasted it to the 8085. We looked at the Z80 bus structure and instruction set and we pointed out the extensions of the Z80 over the 8080/8085 design. We examined the interrupt structure, consisting of a nonmaskable and three maskable modes. We looked at the daisy-chain priority scheme used by Z80 peripheral chips. Finally, we examined the possibility for context switching inherent in the Z80 architecture.

CHAPTER REVIEW

Questions

1. Compare and contrast the Z80 to the 8085 in terms of architecture.
2. Compare and contrast the Z80 to the 8085 in terms of programming model.
3. Explain the three Z80 interrupt modes.
4. Explain the significance of the dual register set, including context switching.
5. Describe the Z80 dynamic memory refresh system.

6. Describe the use of relative jumps.
7. Describe the use of block transfer instructions.
8. Describe the use of block search instructions.
9. Describe the use of block I/O instructions.
10. Describe the Z80 bit manipulation capability.

Problems

1. Using the instructions LD A,(IX+0), LD (IY+0),A and DJNZ, write a program to move 10 memory bytes. Move them from the block starting at 1000h to the destination block starting at 2000h.
2. Using SLA, write a program that inputs a byte from port 5, multiplies it by 16, and sends it out to port 6.
3. Modify the program of Example 7.15 so that the byte to be searched for is read in from I/O port 5. If the byte is found, the program should output the address to ports 6 (high half) and 7 (low half).
4. Write a program using BIT that will search through memory starting at location 1000h. It should continue until one of two things happens: a byte is found with its MSB = 0 or 128 bytes have been searched.
5. Select some 8085 programs from previous chapters and rewrite them in the Z80 instruction set. Try to use specific Z80 features, such as relative jumps and DJNZ.

chapter 8

The 8051 Single-Chip Microcontroller

OBJECTIVES

Upon completion of this chapter, you should be able to

1. Understand and use the special terminology of a microcontroller
2. Describe the function of every pin on the 8051
3. Describe the 8051 memory organization
4. Describe the uses of the various special function registers
5. Describe the Boolean processor
6. Describe the 8051 instruction groups

8.1 INTRODUCTION

Single-chip *microcontrollers* are devices designed for use in products that are not usually considered computers, per se, but that require the sophisticated and flexible control that a computer can provide. An example of such a product is an office copier. In contrast to standard microprocessors such as the 8085, microcontrollers typically integrate RAM, ROM, and I/O, as well as the CPU, onto the same chip. Also, since on-chip program storage (ROM space) is limited on a microcontroller, the instruction set is designed to consist mostly of short, preferably single-byte, instructions.

Many of the applications of microcontrollers fall into one of two categories: *open-loop* or *closed-loop* control systems. Open loop, often called *sequential* control, is used in applications where the process or device being controlled is characterized by a sequence of states, with the progression from state to state being triggered by discrete events. That is, the application is *event driven*. An example is a vending machine that accepts various value coins, recognizes product selection, vends the product, finds the price, and returns the correct change. If the coins were insufficient or the product out of stock, then appropriate messages would be displayed.

Closed-loop control is characterized by the use of *real-time* monitoring of a process to achieve effectively continuous control. The output of the process is monitored using various transducers and A/D converters and the process is continuously modified to achieve the desired result. Examples of closed-loop control can be found in automatic machine tools and robotics.

The use of microcontrollers is not limited to control systems. Other applications include those that require the manipulation of data structures, such as might be found in robot vision or data communications systems.

Microcontrollers are often called *embedded* controllers because they are used as a component of a larger system. The user of the system may not be aware that it contains a processor. On the other hand, users of a stand-alone system, such as a personal computer, are aware that they are running a program even when using the system in a control application. The use of microcontrollers can be very cost-effective, especially in such mass-produced items as microwave ovens, smart modems, and VCRs.

A good example of an advanced 8-bit microcontroller is the Intel MCS-51 family of devices. This family, typified by the 8051, has been designed mainly for sequential control applications. In this chapter we examine the hardware and software features of the 8051 and at points compare them to features in the 8085. However, for a complete and detailed description, the student should obtain and read the Intel literature listed in the references at the end of this chapter.

8.2 8051 HARDWARE OVERVIEW

There are three basic members of the MCS-51 family: the 8051, the 8031, and the 8751. The 8051 contains 4K bytes of ROM, 128 bytes of RAM, 32 I/O lines, two 16-bit counter/timers, five interrupt sources (two external), a duplex serial port, and a bit level Boolean processor. The 8031 has no on-board ROM and uses external memory for program storage. The 8751 is the same as the 8051 except that the ROM is replaced by UVEPROM. The 8751 is relatively expensive and is meant to be a program development tool, to be replaced in production by the 8051 containing factory-masked ROM. Three newer devices—the 8052, the 8032, and the 8752—are expanded versions with 8K of ROM, 256 bytes of RAM, and three timers. In addition, there are low-power CMOS versions designated 80C51, 80C31, and 87C51. A block diagram of the 8051/8052 is shown in Fig. 8.1. The 40-pin dual in-line package (DIP) pin connections are shown in Fig. 8.2.

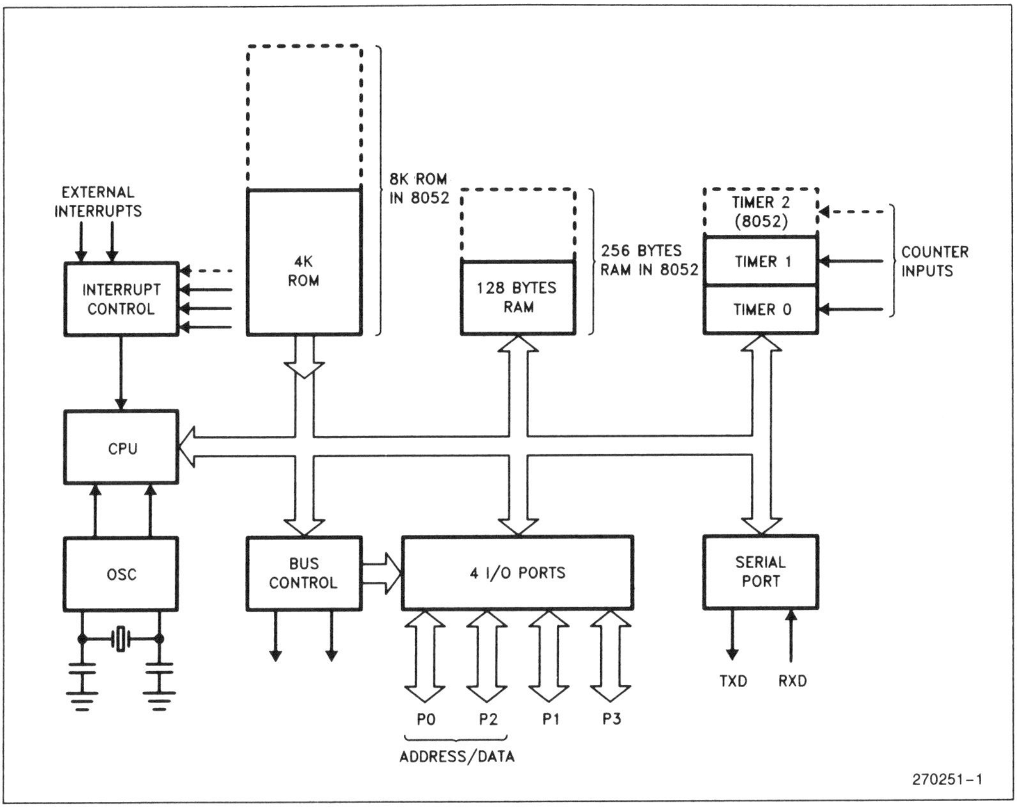

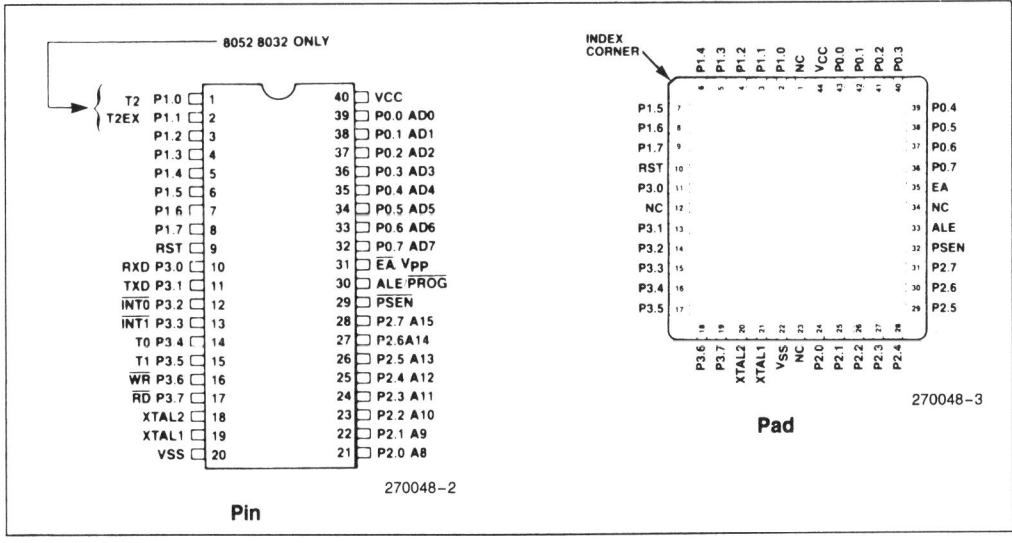

Figure 8.1 Block diagram of the 8051/8052AH. (*Source:* Reprinted by permission of Intel Corporation, Copyright © Intel Corporation 1987.)

Figure 8.2 Forty-pin dual in-line package. (*Source:* Reprinted by permission of Intel Corporation, Copyright © Intel Corporation 1987.)

8.3 CPU TIMING

8.3.1 Clock Frequency

The smallest unit of CPU timing is the oscillator period, also called the *clock*. The 8051 contains an on-chip oscillator that requires a crystal be connected between the pins designated XTAL1 and XTAL2. Alternatively, the 8051 can be driven by an external clock signal. For the standard (HMOS) device, the external clock is applied to XTAL2 and XTAL1 is connected to ground (V_{SS}). For the CMOS device, external clock is applied to XTAL1 and XTAL2 is left unconnected. The maximum clock frequency is currently 12 MHz.

8.3.2 Machine Cycles

A machine cycle consists of six states, designated S1 through S6. Each state is divided into two phases, P1 and P2, each phase lasting one clock period. Thus, a machine cycle is 12 clock periods long, and a 12-MHz clock would give a 1-µsec machine cycle lasting from S1P1 to S6P2. Many instructions require only one cycle for execution. Refer to Fig. 8.18.

8.3.3 Reset

To reset the 8051, a high level must be applied to the RST pin for *at least two* machine cycles. When designing a reset circuit to be activated by a momentary switch or some other short duration signal, the circuit must *stretch out* the signal to last at least 24 clock periods using either an RC time constant or a digital counting scheme. Often a *power-on reset* is implemented by connecting the RST pin to ground through a resistor and connecting a capacitor from RST to the V_{CC} power rail. Typical values are 8.2K and 10 MFD. Such a simple circuit only works under two conditions: V_{CC} comes on with a fast rise time and the clock oscillator starts within a few milliseconds of power on. Because many power supplies have a soft-start feature, the two conditions may not be met and a more complex circuit will be needed for a positive reset.

8.4 MEMORY ORGANIZATION

8.4.1 Memory Space Separation and Size

In contrast to processors such as the 8085, the 8051 has separate address spaces: one for program storage (usually ROM) and another for data storage (RAM). A given numeric address can refer to two logically and physically different memory locations, depending on the type of instruction using the address. The 8051 supports up to 64K bytes of program storage, the lowest 4K (8K for the 8052) being on chip, the rest external. In addition to on-chip RAM, the 8051 supports up to 64K of external data storage. Note that the 8051 instructions that reference program storage can only read. Even if the physical device used for external program storage is read/write, it is effectively read-only for the 8051. The storage (memory) structure is shown in Fig. 8.3.

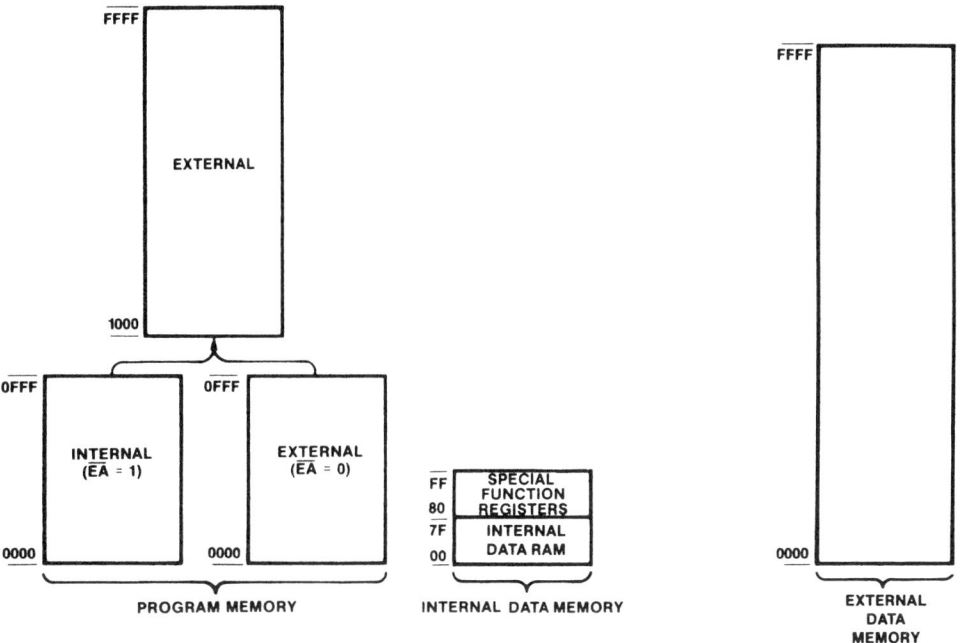

Figure 8.3 MCS®-51 memory map (excluding 8032/8052). (*Source:* Reprinted by permission of Intel Corporation, Copyright © Intel Corporation 1987.)

8.4.2 Program Storage

After reset, the CPU begins fetching instructions starting at address 0000H. The physical location of address 0000H is either on chip or external, depending on the 8051 pin designated EA (external address). If EA is *low*, address 0000H and all other program storage addresses will reference external memory. If EA is *high*, addresses 0000H to 0FFFH (to 1FFFH for the 8052) will reference on-chip ROM; higher address will automatically reference external memory. Note that the 8031 must operate with EA connected low because it does not contain any on-chip ROM. As is discussed later, some of the I/O pins are used for address and data when using external memory.

Also, each interrupt is associated with a fixed memory location, the first being address 0003H. An interrupt causes the CPU to jump to that location, which is assumed to be the start of the interrupt service routine. See Fig. 8.4.

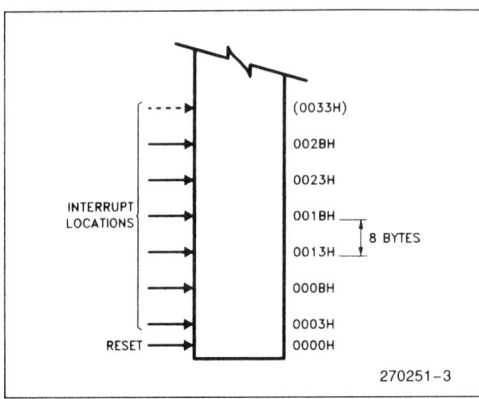

Figure 8.4 Interrupt vector addresses. (*Source:* Reprinted by permission of Intel Corporation, Copyright © Intel Corporation 1987.)

8.4.3 Data Storage

The internal data storage of the 8051 consists of the lower 128 bytes and the SFR (special function registers) space, also 128 bytes. The 8052 contains additional storage called the upper 128 bytes. The lowest 32 bytes of the lower 128 are grouped into four banks of eight registers. Only one bank at a time can be in active use, and it is selected by means of 2 bits in the PSW register that are under program control. The eight registers in the active bank are designated R0 through R7 and can be used by certain software instructions. After reset, the stack pointer (SP) is pointing to the top register of the lowest bank (address 07H). Usually the program loads a new value into SP.

The 16 bytes above the register banks form a block that can be addressed as either bytes or as 128 individual bits. The byte addresses are 20H to 2Fh. The bit addresses are from 00H to 7Fh. Even though the same numeric address (e.g., 20H) can refer to either a byte or a bit, there is no ambiguity. The instruction that uses the address determines if the reference is to be a byte or a bit.

8.4.4 On-Chip ROM

The contents of the on-chip ROM in the 8051 are *masked* at the factory. That means that the designer develops a program for the 8051 and sends it to the chip manufacturer. The manufacturer translates the program into a pattern on a photographic mask that is used to define a set of interconnections in the silicon during a final step in chip production. Once the chips are masked, the program cannot be altered.

Three major facts must be understood about masking. First, the system using a mask programmed part should be stable; that is, it should not require frequent modification of the program. Second, cost savings occur only when enough systems can be sold to pay for the costs associated with developing the mask and making a production run of devices (mass-produced consumer items such as VCRs often qualify). Third, the designer must be absolutely sure the program works and is bug-free before signing off on the mask. Ten thousand bad chips in a box on your desk could ruin your whole day.

The 8031 version of the microcontroller has no on-chip ROM and cannot be masked. Because it uses some of its port pins for the required external program memory, the 8031 does not have the I/O capability of the 8051 unless an external peripheral chip is used. However, for systems with short production runs or frequently updated code the trade-off may be well worth it. Also, the requirement often is to get to market first and lower the production costs later.

The 8751 is the equivalent of the 8051 except that the on-chip ROM is field programmable and erasable with ultraviolet light. The ALE pin on the 8751 also serves as the program pulse input pin during programming, and the EA pin is biased to V_{PP}, the 21V programming supply. Typically, a special piece of equipment (which may attach to a personal computer) is required to program an 8071. Where the cost of the processor is a small part of the total system cost, it is possible that the 8071 could be the production part.

8.5 SFR SPACE: SPECIAL FUNCTION REGISTERS

The registers associated with important functions of the 8051 are assigned memory locations in the on-chip data storage space, allowing them to be addressed by program instructions. Some of the SFR locations are *bit addressable* as well as byte addressable. This is a feature not found in processors such as the 8085. Referring to the SFR map in Fig. 8.5, we see that not all addresses are occupied. In general, unoccupied addresses are not implemented (or at least not documented) and the result of reading or writing to them is indeterminate. Unoccupied addresses in SFR space are reserved for use in future versions of the 8051 and should not be used in programs for the current version.

8 Bytes

F8									FF
F0	B								F7
E8									EF
E0	ACC								E7
D8									DF
D0	PSW								D7
C8	(T2CON)		(RCAP2L)	(RCAP2H)	(TL2)	(TH2)			CF
C0									C7
B8	IP								BF
B0	P3								B7
A8	IE								AF
A0	P2								A7
98	SCON	SBUF							9F
90	P1								97
88	TCON	TMOD	TL0	TL1	TH0	TH1			8F
80	P0	SP	DPL	DPH				PCON	87

Figure 8.5 SFR map. (*Source:* Reprinted by permission of Intel Corporation, Copyright © Intel Corporation 1987.)

Table 8.1 shows the contents of the SFR area after reset. Although RAM is not affected by a reset while the 8051 is running, the contents of RAM on power up are indeterminate.

TABLE 8.1 RESET VALUES OF THE SFRS

SFR name	Reset value
PC	0000H
ACC	00H
B	00H
PSW	00H
SP	07H
DPTR	0000H
P0–P3	FFH
IP (8051)	XXX00000B
IP (8052)	XX000000B
IE (8051)	0XX00000B
IE (8052)	0X000000B
TMOD	00H
TCON	00H
TH0	00H
TL0	00H
TH1	00H
TL1	00H
TH2 (8052)	00H
TL2 (8052)	00H
RCAP2H (8052)	00H
RCAP2L (8052)	00H
SCON	00H
SBUF	Indeterminate
PCON (HMOS)	0XXXXXXXB
PCON (CHMOS)	0XXX0000B

Source: Reprinted by permission of Intel Corporation, Copyright © Intel Corporation 1987.

8.5.1 Accumulator (ACC) and B Register

When referring to the accumulator as a location in the SFR, the mnemonic ACC is used. Accumulator-specific instructions designate the accumulator as A. The accumulator in the 8051 has the same functions as the accumulator in processors such as the 8085. It is also used in some instructions as an *index register*.

The B register has a specific function in multiply and divide operations. Otherwise, it can be used as a general-purpose scatchpad register.

8.5.2 Program Status Word (PSW)

The PSW contains flag bits, as shown in Fig. 8.6. Notice the notation used under the heading "Position" in the figure. A specific bit can be designated by the name of the register followed by a decimal point followed by the number of the bit position within the register. The MSB is position 7 and the LSB is position 0. Thus, the bit designated by the symbol AC can also be designated as PSW.6, as shown. This convention is also followed in the assembly language.

```
         (MSB)                                    (LSB)
         ┌────┬────┬────┬────┬────┬────┬────┬────┐
         │ CY │ AC │ F0 │RS1 │RS0 │ OV │ —  │ P  │
         └────┴────┴────┴────┴────┴────┴────┴────┘
```

Symbol	Position	Name and Significance	Symbol	Position	Name and Significance
CY	PSW.7	Carry flag.	OV	PSW.2	Overflow flag.
AC	PSW.6	Auxiliary Carry flag. (For BCD operations.)	—	PSW.1	User definable flag.
F0	PSW.5	Flag 0 (Available to the user for general purposes.)	P	PSW.0	Parity flag. Set/cleared by hardware each instruction cycle to indicate an odd/even number of "one" bits in the Accumulator, i.e., even parity.
RS1	PSW.4	Register bank select control bits 1 &			
RS0	PSW.3	0. Set/cleared by software to determine working register bank (see Note).			

NOTE:
The contents of (RS1, RS0) enable the working register banks as follows:

    (0.0)—Bank 0   (00H–07H)
    (0.1)—Bank 1   (08H–0FH)
    (1.0)—Bank 2   (10H–17H)
    (1.1)—Bank 3   (18H–1FH)

Figure 8.6 Progam status word register. (*Source:* Reprinted by permission of Intel Corporation, Copyright © Intel Corporation 1987.)

In addition to the usual flags, such as CY and AC, the 8051 has two general-purpose flags not associated with any specific CPU state or function: the bits PSW.5 (symbol F0) and PSW.1 (no symbol). The programmer may use F0 as a flag bit for a user-defined purpose. It may be set and reset by the program as a function of some special condition or be read in from a port pin. The Intel documentation indicates that PSW.1 is reserved for future use and should not be used in programs.

Note that although the PSW does not have a zero flag, this is not a problem because the 8051 has specific instructions to test the accumulator for zero. As mentioned earlier, the PSW also contains two programmable bits (RS0 and RS1) that select which register bank is active.

8.5.3 Stack Pointer (SP)

Because the stack pointer is 8 bits wide, it allows a maximum stack size of 256 bytes. In contrast to the 8085, the stack in the 8051 grows upward through memory; therefore, the SP is incremented before data are stored as a result of a PUSH or CALL instruction. The stack may reside anywhere in on-chip RAM by loading the appropriate address into the SP. After reset, the SP contains the address 07H, causing the stack to start at location 08H in a register bank. Because the program typically has other uses for the register banks, the stack is usually moved higher in RAM by loading a new address into SP before doing any PUSH or CALL instructions.

8.5.4 Data Pointer (DPTR)

The DPTR is a 16-bit quantity held in two 8-bit parts: the high byte in DPH and the low byte in DPL. The main purpose of the DPTR is to hold a 16-bit address for certain instructions. It can be used as a single 16-bit register or as two 8-bit registers.

8.5.5 Port Latches (P0, P1, P2, P3)

The 32 I/O pins are organized into four 8-bit ports designated P0–P3. Each port has an associated 8-bit latch, the outputs of which drive the matching I/O pins. The contents of the latches can be read from or written to in the SFR.

8.5.6 Serial Data Buffer (SBUF)

The SBUF is actually two separate registers sharing a common address: One is read-only and the other write-only. When data are written to SBUF, they go to a transmit buffer and are held there for serial transmission. When data are read from SBUF, they come from the serial data receive buffer.

8.5.7 Timer Registers

Registers TH0 and TL0 are the high and low bytes, respectively, of the 16-bit counting register for timer/counter 0. Likewise, TH1 and TL1 are for timer/counter 1. In the 8052, TH2 and TL2 are for timer/counter 2. Also, the 8052 contains two 8-bit capture registers (RCAP2H and RCAP2L) used to hold copies of the TH2 and TL2 register contents.

8.5.8 Control Registers

The SFR contains registers used for the control and status of the interrupt system, the timer/counters, and the serial port. They are IP (interrupt priority), IE (interrupt enable), TMOD (timer mode), TCON (timer control), T2CON (8052 timer 2 control), SCON (serial port control), and PCON (power control, used mainly in 80C51). Each is discussed in a later section.

8.6 I/O PORTS

One of the most useful features of the 8051 is the I/O, consisting of four bidirectional ports. Each port has an 8-bit latch in the SFR space, an output driver, and an input buffer. The ports can be used for general I/O, as address and data lines, and for certain special functions.

8.6.1 Input, Loading, and Output Drive

Ports 1, 2, and 3 have the equivalent of internal pull-up resistors. When used as inputs, the pins of P1, P2, and P3 will be high (logic 1) when open-circuited and will source current when pulled low by an external device. Port 0 does not have the same pull-up feature and is floating (high impedance) when used as an input. A clarification is needed for the phrase "read a port." Some instructions read the actual level on the I/O pin; others read the level in the latch. A condition can occur where the port is being used to output a high (logic level 1) but the external load attached to the port pin is of such low resistance that the voltage on the pin is at the same level as a low (logic level 0). Reading the latch would show a 1, but reading the pin would show a 0. Instructions that do a read-modify-write operation (e.g., INC) read the latch.

When used as outputs, ports 1, 2, and 3 each can drive the equivalent of four LS TTL inputs. Port 0 can drive eight such equivalent inputs. To speed up 0 to 1 output transitions (i.e., to overcome capacitance effects) on ports 1, 2, and 3, an additional internal pull-up is activated briefly during output.

8.6.2 Alternate Port Functions

All the pins of port 3 (and in the 8052, two P1 pins) have an *alternate function,* as listed in Fig. 8.7. To enable an alternate function, a 1 must be written to the corresponding bit in the port latch.

8.6.3 Accessing External Memory

Because the 8051 has separate program memory and data memory, it uses different hardware signals to access the corresponding external storage devices. The PSEN (program store enable) signal is used as the read strobe for program memory, and RD and WR are used as the read and write strobes to access data memory. Note that RD and WR are alternate functions of the P3.6 and P3.7 pins, as described above. Also, ports 0 and 2 are used to access external memory.

Accesses to external program store always use a 16-bit address. Accesses to external data store may use either an 8-bit or a 16-bit address, depending on the instruction being executed. In the case of a 16-bit address, the high-order 8 bits of the address are output on port 2, where they are held constant during the entire memory access cycle. The prior contents of the port 2 latches in the SFR are not lost but are restored after the memory access cycle. If an 8-bit address is being used, the contents of port 2 are unchanged, which allows some of the port 2 pins to be used to select 256-byte pages for the lower 8 bits of the address.

The low-order 8 bits of the address are multiplexed with the data byte on port 0. When used in this mode, the port 0 pins are connected to an internal active pull-

Port Pin	Alternative Function
P3.0	RXD (serial input port)
P3.1	TXD (serial output port)
P3.2	$\overline{\text{INT0}}$ (external interrupt 0)
P3.3	$\overline{\text{INT1}}$ (external interrupt 1)
P3.4	T0 (Timer 0 external input)
P3.5	T1 (Timer 1 external input)
P3.6	$\overline{\text{WR}}$ (external data memory write strobe)
P3.7	$\overline{\text{RD}}$ (external data memory read strobe)

(MSB)							(LSB)
RD	WR	T1	T0	INT1	INT0	TXD	RXD

Symbol	Position	Name and Significance
RD	P3.7	Read data control output. Active low pulse generated by hardware when external data memory is read.
WR	P3.6	Write data control output. Active low pulse generated by hardware when external data memory is written.
T1	P3.5	Timer/counter 1 external input or test pin.
T0	P3.4	Timer/counter 0 external input or test pin.
INT1	P3.3	Interrupt 1 input pin. Low-level or falling-edge triggered.
INT0	P3.2	Interrupt 0 input pin. Low-level or falling-edge triggered.
TXD	P3.1	Transmit Data pin for serial port in UART mode. Clock output in shift register mode.
RXD	P3.0	Receive Data pin for serial port in UART mode. Data I/O pin in shift register mode.

Figure 8.7 Alternate functions of port 3 pins. (*Source:* Reprinted by permission of Intel Corporation, Copyright © Intel Corporation 1987.)

up; they do not float. The prior contents of the port 0 latches are lost. The ALE (address latch enable) signal must be used to capture the low-order address bits in an external latch, much the same as is done with the 8085.

8.7 TIMER/COUNTERS

The 8051 has two 16-bit registers that can be used as either timers or counters. They are designated timer 0 and timer 1. The 8052 has an additional 16-bit register designated timer 2. These registers are in the SFR as pairs of 8-bit registers.

When used as a timer, the register is incremented once per machine cycle, which is equal to once per 12 clock periods. When used as a counter, the register is incremented on a 1–0 transition (a negative edge) applied to the appropriate input pin: T0 or T1 (or T2 in the 8052). Remember that T0, T1, and T2 are alternate functions of port pins (refer to Fig. 8.7). It takes two complete machine cycles for the 8051 to see the 1–0 transition; the input must be held high for at least one cycle and then low for at least one cycle.

8.7.1 Timer 0 and Timer 1

The way that timer 0 and timer 1 will operate is determined by the 8 bits written to the TMOD register, as detailed in Fig. 8.8a. The bits M0 and M1 (a pair for each timer) are used to select one of four operating modes: mode 0, mode 1, mode 2, or mode 3. Both counters work the same in modes 0, 1, and 2 but differently in mode 3.

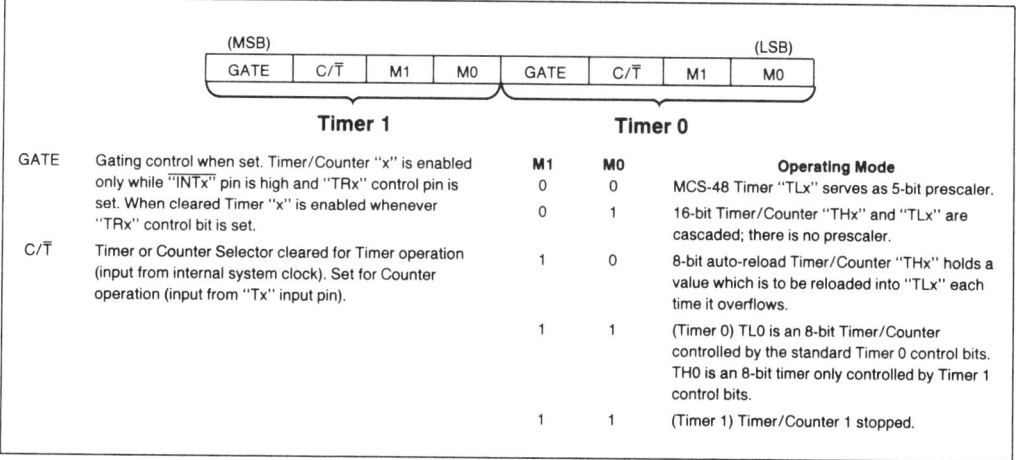

Figure 8.8a Timer/counter mode control register. (*Source:* Reprinted by permission of Intel Corporation, Copyright © Intel Corporation 1987.)

Figure 8.8b Timer/counter control register. (*Source:* Reprinted by permission of Intel Corporation, Copyright © Intel Corporation 1987.)

Sec. 8.7   Timer/Counters

8.7.2 Mode 0 and Mode 1

In mode 0 the timer is configured as a 13-bit counter that can be thought of as an 8-bit counter preceded by a 5-bit divide-by-32 prescaler. The 8-bit count is in the TH register (TH0 or TH1, depending on which counter is in use), and the 5-bit prescaler is the lower 5 bits of the TL register. The upper 3 bits of the TL register are random and should be ignored. As the 13-bit count in TL and TH goes from all 1s to all 0s, the timer interrupt flag (TF0 or TF1) is set. The timer interrupt is the connection between the counter hardware and the program software.

As in Fig. 8.9, the source of input to the counter is selected by the C/T bit in TMOD. The counting process can be turned on and off (enabled or disabled) independent of the input. In order for counting to proceed, the TR bit (TR0 or TR1) in the TCON register (Fig. 8.8b) must be a 1 at the same time that one of the following is true: Either the appropriate GATE bit in the TMOD register is a 0, or the appropriate INT pin (INT0 or INT1) is held low. The use of GATE or TR allows counting to be controlled by *software;* the use of INT allows counting to be controlled by external hardware. Remember that INT0 and INT1, as well as T0 and T1 inputs, are alternate functions of port 3 pins. Mode 1 is the same as mode 0, except that the timer register is 16 bits long, with all 8 bits of TL being used.

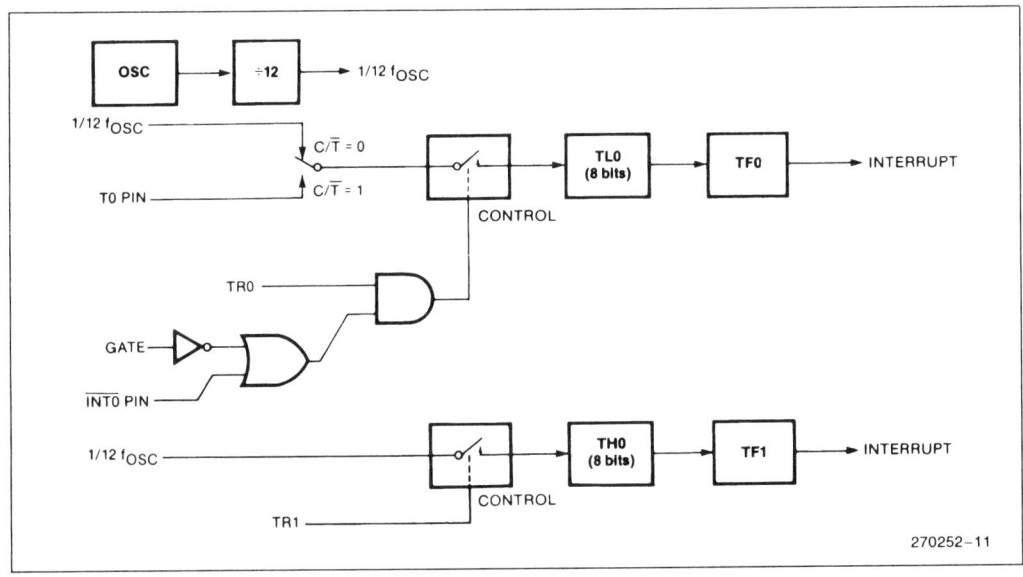

Figure 8.9 Timer/counter 0 mode 3: two 8-bit counters. (*Source:* Reprinted by permission of Intel Corporation, Copyright © Intel Corporation 1987.)

8.7.3 Mode 2

Mode 2 operation is much the same as mode 0, except that the TL register is used as an 8-bit counter and the TH register is used to hold a preset number. When the contents of TL go from all 1s to all 0s, the interrupt (TF) is set and the contents of TH are transferred to TL. The contents of TH remain unchanged. Because the contents of TH are under software control, the counter can be made to divide the count source by any number from 1 to 255 by means of the automatic reload of TH into TL.

8.7.4 Mode 3

In mode 3, timer 1 is disabled but holds its count; it is essentially frozen. Timer 0 in mode 3 is split into two separate counters (see Fig. 8.9). The first counter is the same as mode 0, except TL0 is used as an 8-bit counter and there is no prescaler. The second counter uses TH0 as an 8-bit counter. The count source is the oscillator divided by 12 and the enable control is the TR1 bit in the TCON register. Note that the first counter sets the TF0 interrupt flag and the second counter sets TF1.

8.7.5 Timer 2

Timer 2 is a 16-bit timer/counter in the 8052 group of devices; it does not appear in the 8051 group. Like the timers already described, the input source for timer 2 can be the clock (timer operation) or an external input (counter operation). Timer 2 has three operating modes: capture, auto-load, and baud rate generator. The input source and operating mode are selected by bits in the T2CON control register. A detailed description of timer 2 can be found in the Intel literature listed at the end of this chapter.

8.8 SERIAL PORT INTERFACE

The 8051 has a full duplex serial port that allows data to be transmitted and received simultaneously in hardware while the software is doing other things. A serial port interrupt is generated by the hardware to get the attention of the program in order to read or write serial port data. The receiver hardware is *double buffered*, meaning that a received frame of data can be held for reading while a second frame is being received. Double buffering allows the receiver interrupt service routine to be less time critical, but the stored frame must be read before reception of the second frame is complete or the stored frame will be overwritten and lost. To obtain the same level of performance with a processor such as the 8085, the use of a separate USART (universal synchronous/asynchronous receiver/transmitter) chip is required.

As mentioned, both the transmit and receive buffers are accessed at the same location in the SFR space: the SBUF register. Writing to SBUF loads the transmit buffer, and reading from SBUF obtains the contents of the receive buffer. Any instruction that writes to SBUF initiates serial transmission. The serial port has four modes of operation: mode 0, mode 1, mode 2, and mode 3. (Note that these modes are not to be confused with the timer/counter modes; a designation such as "mode 1" must be understood in the context of the hardware feature being discussed.)

8.8.1 Serial Port Control Register (SCON)

SCON is the serial port control and status register (see Fig. 8.10). Bits SM0 and SM1 are used to select the operating mode. The SM2 bit is used in a multiprocessor system where one 8051 acts as a master unit, sending commands to one or more slave units. Such systems are beyond the scope of this book, and the reader is referred to the Intel documentation for more information.

```
          (MSB)                                    (LSB)
         | SM0 | SM1 | SM2 | REN | TB8 | RB8 | TI | RI |
```

Where SM0, SM1 specify the serial port mode, as follows:

SM0	SM1	Mode	Description	Baud Rate
0	0	0	shift register	$f_{osc.}/12$
0	1	1	8-bit UART	variable
1	0	2	9-bit UART	$f_{osc.}/64$ or $f_{osc.}/32$
1	1	3	9-bit UART	variable

- SM2 enables the multiprocessor communication feature in Modes 2 and 3. In Mode 2 or 3, if SM2 is set to 1 then RI will not be activated if the received 9th data bit (RB8) is 0. In Mode 1, if SM2 = 1 then RI will not be activated if a valid stop bit was not received. In Mode 0, SM2 should be 0.
- REN enables serial reception. Set by software to enable reception. Clear by software to disable reception.
- TB8 is the 9th data bit that will be transmitted in Modes 2 and 3. Set or clear by software as desired.
- RB8 in Modes 2 and 3, is the 9th data bit that was received. In Mode 1, if SM2 = 0, RB8 is the stop bit that was received. In Mode 0, RB8 is not used.
- TI is transmit interrupt flag. Set by hardware at the end of the 8th bit time in Mode 0, or at the beginning of the stop bit in the other modes, in any serial transmission. Must be cleared by software.
- RI is receive interrupt flag. Set by hardware at the end of the 8th bit time in Mode 0, or halfway through the stop bit time in the other modes, in any serial reception (except see SM2). Must be cleared by software.

Figure 8.10 Serial port control and status register. (*Source:* Reprinted by permission of Intel Corporation, Copyright © Intel Corporation 1987.)

8.8.2 Serial Port Modes

Mode 0 is *half-duplex synchronous* operation. Data are sent and received (but not simultaneously) through the RXD pin in 8-bit frames, LSB first. The bit rate is fixed at one-twelfth the oscillator frequency. The shift clock, which is the same frequency as the bit rate, is sent out the TXD pin during both transmission and reception and is used to synchronize the receiver to the sender. A shift clock edge will occur during the valid state of each data bit. Note that TXD and RXD are alternate functions of port 3 pins. In mode 0, reception is initiated when bit REN is set to 1 and bit RI is cleared to 0 in the SCON register.

Mode 1 is *full duplex asynchronous* operation. Data are sent out TXD and received through RXD. A complete frame consists of a start bit (always a 0), followed by 8 data bits (LSB first), followed by a stop bit (always a 1). The start and stop bits are added by the hardware; the software writes the 8-bit data byte to, or reads it from, SBUF. The baud rate is variable and can be obtained by using timer 1 as a baud rate generator, as described in Sec. 8.8.3.

Mode 2 is similar to mode 1, with two exceptions. First, the frame is 11 bits long; a ninth data bit is inserted before the stop bit. When transmitting, the ninth bit is obtained from TB8 in SCON. It is assumed that TB8 was written into before initiating transmission. When receiving, the ninth bit can be read from RB8 in SCON. A common use for the ninth bit is as a parity bit for 8-bit data. The second difference is that the baud rate is either 1/32nd or 1/64th of the oscillator frequency, as selected by the SMOD bit (bit 7) in the PCON register. If SMOD is set to 1, the 1/32 number is used. If SMOD is cleared to 0, 1/64 is used.

Mode 3 is the same as mode 2, except that the baud rate is variable and can be obtained in the same way as in mode 1.

Reception for modes 1, 2, and 3 is enabled when the REN bit in SCON is set to 1. Actual reception is initiated when an incoming start bit causes a high to low transition on the RXD pin. As mentioned earlier, transmission is initiated by writing to SBUF in any serial mode.

8.8.3 Timer 1 as Baud Rate Generator

Although it is possible to use the timer/counter as a baud rate generator in any of its modes, its most common use is as a timer (i.e., clock-sourced) in auto-reload mode (timer mode 2). The baud rate is then given by the expression

$$\text{Baud rate} = \frac{\text{Oscillator frequency}}{N[256 - (TH1)]}$$

where N depends on the SMOD bit in the PCON register (bit PCON.7). If SMOD = 0, then N = 384. If SMOD = 1, then N = 192. The term (TH1) represents the contents of register TH1.

When selecting a crystal to set the oscillator frequency in a system that will use the serial port, consider the following. Because the value stored in TH1 must, by definition, be an integer number, the oscillator frequency must be an integer multiple of both the baud rate and N in order to obtain an exact baud rate using the above expression.

EXAMPLE 8.1 Crystal Selection

PROBLEM Pick a crystal frequency close to 12 MHz that will allow baud rates of 300, 600, and 1200 bits/sec.

SOLUTION Assume we set SMOD so that N = 384. Find a value for (TH1) in the range 0–255 for one baud rate and check it for the others:

$$1200 \times 384 \times [256 - (TH1)] = 12 \times 10^6 \quad \text{(approximately)}$$

$$(TH1) = 256 - (12 \times 10^6)/(384 \times 1200)$$

$$(TH1) = 256 - 26.04 = 230 \quad \text{(must be an integer)}$$

Next, use (TH1) = 230 to find the exact crystal frequency:

$$F = 1200 \times 384 \times 26 = 11.981 \text{ MHz} \quad \text{(to 3 decimal points)}$$

Next, verify other baud rates (note the baud rate ratios).

For 600 baud: 256 − (TH1) = 2 × 26 = 52, so (TH1) = 204

$$(11.981 \times 10^6)/(384 \times 52) = 600 \quad \textit{verified}$$

For 300 baud: 256 − (TH1) = 2 × 52 = 104, so (TH1) = 152

$$(11.981 \times 10^6)/(384 \times 104) = 300 \quad \textit{verified}$$

8.8.4 The PCON Register

Of the 8 bits in the PCON power control register, only bit 7, SMOD, is implemented in the standard 8051. As discussed, SMOD is used in setting the baud rate of the serial port. Bits 0, 1, 2, and 3 are implemented in the CMOS version. Bits 0 and 1 are used in power-saving modes and bits 2 and 3 are general-purpose flags. Details of the use of PCON in the CMOS devices can be found in the Intel literature.

8.9 INTERRUPTS

The 8051 has five sources of interrupts: two from external pins (INT0 and INT1), two from the timer/counters (TF0 and TF1), and one from the serial port (TI or SI). A useful feature of the 8051 is that the interrupt sources are associated with bit locations in registers. Those bits can be set or cleared by software, with the same results as when the bits are set or cleared by hardware.

As shown in Fig. 8.11, all interrupts or each individual interrupt can be enabled or disabled by setting or clearing the appropriate bit in the IE register. If enabled, an interrupt will cause a call to one of the predefined locations in RAM, as discussed in section 8.4.2 The return address is automatically pushed onto the stack before jumping and is popped back off when an RETI (return-from-interrupt) instruction is executed. If an interrupt occurs while it is disabled, or while a higher priority one is running, it becomes *pending*. As soon as a pending interrupt is enabled, it will cause a call, unless it was cancelled by software while it was still pending or a higher priority interrupt was simultaneously made active.

8.9.1 Priority Levels

The 8051 has a *two-tier* priority structure. The top tier has two priority levels: high and low. Each interrupt source can be assigned to either high-level or low-level status by setting the appropriate bits in the IP register, as shown in Fig. 8.12. When two interrupts of different levels are received simultaneously, the high-level interrupt is serviced first. The second tier of priority is used to resolve simultaneous

	(MSB)						(LSB)
	EA	—	ET2	ES	ET1	EX1	ET0	EX0

Symbol	Position	Function
EA	IE.7	disables all interrupts. If EA = 0, no interrupt will be acknowledged. If EA = 1, each interrupt source is individually enabled or disabled by setting or clearing its enable bit.
—	IE.6	reserved.
ET2	IE.5	enables or disables the Timer 2 Overflow or capture interrupt. If ET2 = 0, the Timer 2 interrupt is disabled.
ES	IE.4	enables or disables the Serial Port interrupt. If ES = 0, the Serial Port interrupt is disabled.
ET1	IE.3	enables or disables the Timer 1 Overflow interrupt. If ET1 = 0, the Timer 1 interrupt is disabled.
EX1	IE.2	enables or disables External Interrupt 1. If EX1 = 0, External Interrupt 1 is disabled.
ET0	IE.1	enables or disables the Timer 0 Overflow interrupt. If ET0 = 0, the Timer 0 interrupt is disabled.
EX0	IE.0	enables or disables External Interrupt 0. If EX0 = 0, External Interrupt 0 is disabled.

User software should never write 1s to unimplemented bits, since they may be used in future MCS-51 products.

Figure 8.11 Interrupt enable register. (*Source:* Reprinted by permission of Intel Corporation, Copyright © Intel Corporation 1987.)

	(MSB)						(LSB)
	—	—	PT2	PS	PT1	PX1	PT0	PX0

Symbol	Position	Function
—	IP.7	reserved
—	IP.6	reserved
PT2	IP.5	defines the Timer 2 interrupt priority level. PT2 = 1 programs it to the higher priority level.
PS	IP.4	defines the Serial Port interrupt priority level. PS = 1 programs it to the higher priority level.
PT1	IP.3	defines the Timer 1 interrupt priority level. PT1 = 1 programs it to the higher priority level.
PT0	IP.1	defines the Timer 0 interrupt priority level. PT0 = 1 programs it to the higher priority level.
PX0	IP.0	defines the External Interrupt 0 priority level. PX0 = 1 programs it to the higher priority level.

User software should never write 1s to unimplemented bits, since they may be used in future MCS-51 products.

Figure 8.12 Interrupt priority control register. (*Source:* Reprinted by permission of Intel Corporation, Copyright © Intel Corporation 1987.)

interrupts within the same level. The *priority-within-level* ordering from highest to lowest is fixed as follows: IE0, TF0, IE1, TF1, RI, or TI.

Note that bits 7, 6, and 5 in the IP register are unimplemented in the 8051 and should not be used by the software. Bit 5 does have a use in the 8052.

8.9.2 Interrupt Timing and Handling

As shown in Fig. 8.13, a "snap-shot" (sample) of the interrupt flags is taken by the 8051 hardware at the end of a typical machine cycle (C1). During the following machine cycle (C2), the sample from the previous cycle is examined. If one of the flags sampled during C1 is found to be set, then a call to the appropriate interrupt vector will be generated during cycles C3 and C4. Execution of the interrupt service routine will start with cycle C5 and continue for as long as is required by the routine.

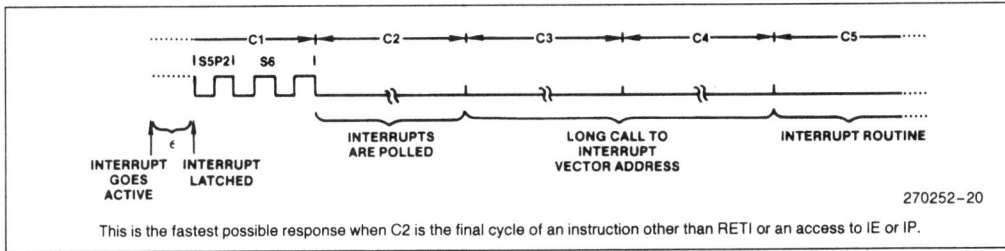

Figure 8.13 Interrupt response timing diagram. (*Source:* Reprinted by permission of Intel Corporation, Copyright © Intel Corporation 1987.)

The hardware will not generate the interrupt call if one of the following is true:

1. An interrupt of equal or higher priority is *already in progress*. A lower priority interrupt can itself be interrupted by a higher priority interrupt, assuming the higher one is enabled.
2. The current machine cycle is *not the final cycle* of the instruction being executed. The instruction in progress must be completed before jumping to the interrupt service instructions.
3. The instruction in progress is RETI or any instruction that writes to the IE or IP register. At least one *additional instruction* must be executed following those before jumping to the interrupt vector address. The reason for this condition is to prevent an interrupt from occurring in the middle of a routine that is in the process of reconfiguring the interrupts. Interrupt-driven applications are sufficiently complex without the added chaos of not being able to gain access to the interrupt control registers due to repeated interrupts.

The time between the activation of an interrupt and the start of execution of the service routine is the *response time*. In the 8051, the shortest response time is three machine cycles and the longest (worst case) is nine machine cycles. In time-critical applications, the worst case condition must be assumed to happen.

8.9.3 Activation Levels and Flag Clearing

In general, interrupts can be either *level-activated* or *transition-activated* (level-triggered or edge-triggered). Because a transition-activated event is, by definition, a transient, when the flag bit associated with the interrupt is cleared, the interrupt event itself is cleared. On the other hand, clearing the flag bit of a level-activated interrupt will have no effect if the external level causing the interrupt stays active.

In the 8051, the external interrupts INT0 and INT1 can be individually configured to be either transition activated or level activated, depending on the value of the bits IT0 and IT1 in the TCON register. The flag bit will be set when the interrupt occurs and cleared automatically when the call is made to the interrupt vector.

For the timers, the TF0 and TF1 flags are set when the count in the corresponding counter register rolls over from all 1s to all 0s; the counter interrupts are in effect transition activated. TF0 and TF1 are also cleared automatically during interrupt service.

The serial port interrupt is generated when either the RI bit or the TI bit is set to 1. However, RI and TI are not automatically cleared. The interrupt service routine will have to determine which bit caused the interrupt and then clear it as part of the routine.

8.10 INSTRUCTIONS AND ADDRESSING

The programming model for the 8085 is essentially the accumulator, the flags, a few registers, and a relatively simple vectored interrupt system. In contrast, the programming model for the 8051 has taken the first nine sections of this chapter to describe. Likewise, the assembly language of the 8051 contains features, such as Boolean operations, not seen in similar processors but that give the 8051 its flexibility and power as a control device. The language, however, is not complex.

The 8051 has five addressing modes and five groups of instructions. Each is described in the following sections. The complete instruction set is described in Appendix D.

8.10.1 Direct Addressing

Instructions using direct addressing are 2 bytes long: an 8-bit op-code followed by an 8-bit address. The address is a location in internal RAM or in the SFR area. Depending on the type of instruction, the address refers to either a byte location or a specific bit in a bit-addressable byte.

EXAMPLE 8.2 Some Direct Instructions

MOV A,07;   Move contents of RAM *byte* location 07 to the accumulator.
CLR 07;   Clear bit address 07, the MSB of byte address 20H.

Figure 8.14 shows the bit-addressable bytes in RAM together with the bit-addressable bytes in the SFR area. Assemblers for the 8051 usually have predefined mnemonic symbols corresponding to important bit and byte addresses. Table 8.2 shows the bit address names, and Table 8.3 shows the byte address names.

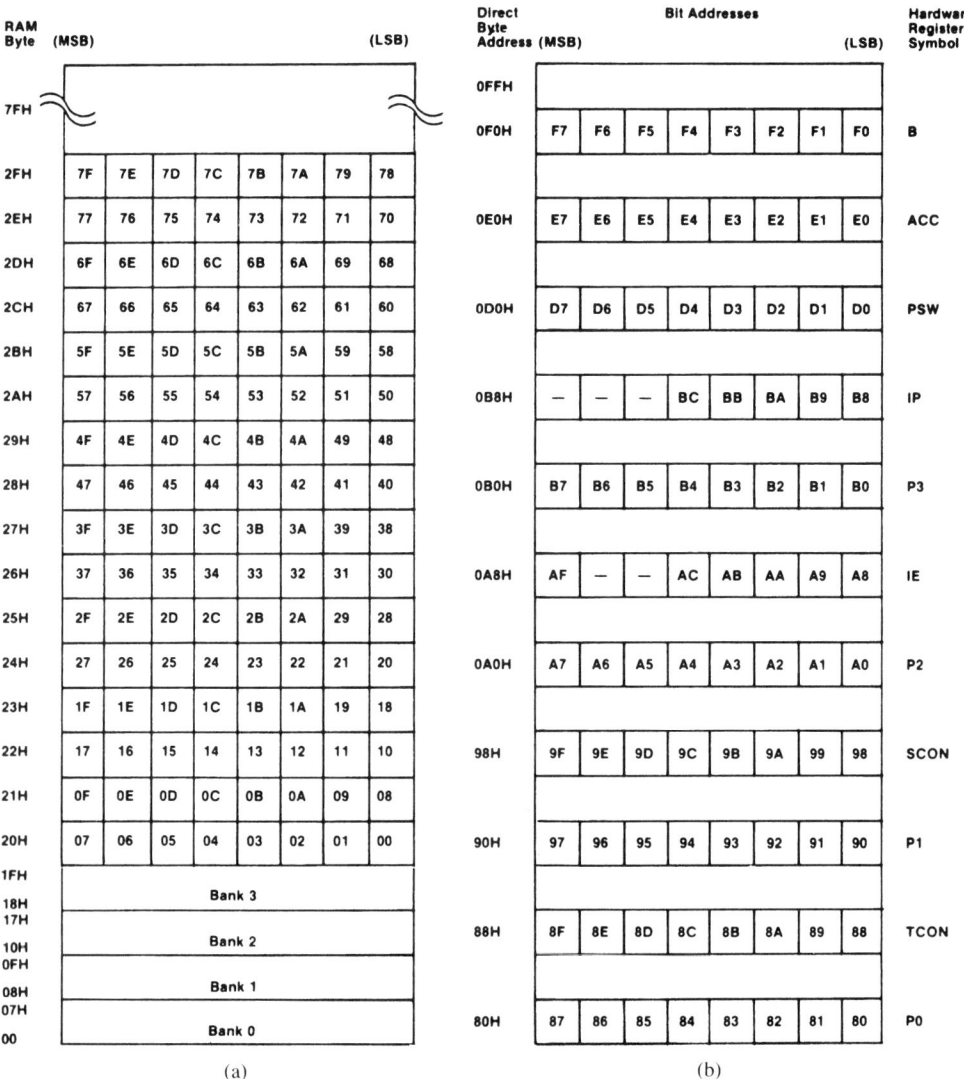

Figure 8.14 (a) RAM bit addresses. (b) Special function register bit addresses. (*Source:* Reprinted by permission of Intel Corporation, Copyright © Intel Corporation 1987.)

TABLE 8.2 PREDEFINED BIT ADDRESSES FOR 8051

Symbol	Bit position	Bit address	Meaning
CY	PSW.7	D7H	Carry Flag
AC	PSW.6	D6H	Auxiliary Carry Flag
F0	PSW.5	D5H	Flag 0
RS1	PSW.4	D4H	Register Bank Select Bit 1
RS0	PSW.3	D3H	Register Bank Select Bit 0
OV	PSW.2	D2H	Overflow Flag
P	PSW.0	D0H	Parity Flag
TF1	TCON.7	8FH	Timer 1 Overflow Flag
TR1	TCON.6	8EH	Timer 1 Run Control Bit
TF0	TCON.5	8DH	Timer 0 Overflow Flag
TR0	TCON.4	8CH	Timer 0 Run Control Bit
IE1	TCON.3	8BH	Interrupt 1 Edge Flag
IT1	TCON.2	8AH	Interrupt 1 Type Control Bit
IE0	TCON.1	89H	Interrupt 0 Edge Flag
IT0	TCON.0	88H	Interrupt 0 Type Control Bit
SM0	SCON.7	9FH	Serial Mode Control Bit 0
SM1	SCON.6	9EH	Serial Mode Control Bit 1
SM2	SCON.5	9DH	Serial Mode Control Bit 2
REN	SCON.4	9CH	Receiver Enable
TB8	SCON.3	9BH	Transmit Bit 8
RB8	SCON.2	9AH	Receive Bit 8
TI	SCON.1	99H	Transmit Interrupt Flag
RI	SCON.0	98H	Receive Interrupt Flag
EA	IE.7	AFH	Enable All Interrupts
ES	IE.4	ACH	Enable Serial Port Interrupt
ET1	IE.3	ABH	Enable Timer 1 Interrupt
EX1	IE.2	AAH	Enable External Interrupt 1
ET0	IE.1	A9H	Enable Timer 0 Interrupt
EX0	IE.0	A8H	Enable External Interrupt 0
RD	P3.7	B7H	Read Data for External Memory
WR	P3.6	B6H	Write Data for External Memory
T1	P3.5	B5H	Timer/Counter 1 External Flag
T0	P3.4	B4H	Timer/Counter 0 External Flag
INT1	P3.3	B3H	Interrupt 1 Input Pin
INT0	P3.2	B2H	Interrupt 0 Input Pin
TXD	P3.1	B1H	Serial Port Transmit Pin
RXD	P3.0	B0H	Serial Port Receive Pin
PS	IP.4	BCH	Priority of Serial Port Interrupt
PT1	IP.3	BBH	Priority of Timer 1 Interrupt
PX1	IP.2	BAH	Priority of External Interrupt 1
PT0	IP.1	B9H	Priority of Timer 0
PX0	IP.0	B8H	Priority of External Interrupt 0

Source: Reprinted by permission of Intel Corporation, Copyright © Intel Corporation 1987.

TABLE 8.3 PREDEFINED DATA ADDRESSES FOR 8051

Symbol	Hexadecimal address	Meaning
ACC	E0	Accumulator
B	F0	Multiplication Register
DPH	83	Data Pointer (high byte)
DPL	82	Data Pointer (low byte)
IE	A8	Interrupt Enable
IP	B8	Interrupt Priority
P0	80	Port 0
P1	90	Port 1
P2	A0	Port 2
P3	B0	Port 3
PSW	D0	Program Status Word
SBUF	99	Serial Port Buffer
SCON	98	Serial Port Controller
SP	81	Stack Pointer
TCON	88	Timer Control
TH0	8C	Timer 0 (high byte)
TH1	8D	Timer 1 (high byte)
TL0	8A	Timer 0 (low byte)
TL1	8B	Timer 1 (low byte)
TMOD	89	Timer Mode

Source: Reprinted by permission of Intel Corporation, Copyright © Intel Corporation 1987.

8.10.2 Indirect Addressing

An instruction using direct addressing specifies the fixed address of the operand, an instruction using indirect addressing specifies a register that contains the address of the operand. Because the contents of the register can be changed by the program, indirect addressing is a powerful technique. Also, most of the instructions that use indirect addressing are only 1 byte long, making them efficient in memory space and execution time.

Indirect addressing can access external RAM as well as internal, and addresses can be 8 bits or 16 bits. The 8-bit addresses use the registers designated R0–R7; the 16-bit addresses use the DPTR register. Remember that DPTR is actually the two 8-bit registers DPH and DPL treated as one 16-bit register. Also remember that different banks of registers can be selected for R0–R7, depending on bits in the PSW.

EXAMPLE 8.3 Some Indirect Instructions

MOV A,@R3;   Move to the accumulator the internal RAM byte pointed to by register R3.

MOVX A,@DPTR;   Move to the accumulator the external RAM byte pointed to by the DPTR register.

8.10.3 Register Instructions

Register instructions use the contents of one of the registers, typically R0–R7, as the operand. All register instructions have the efficiency of being 1 byte long. A few register instructions are register specific; they do not allow the programmer to specify the operand register.

> **EXAMPLE 8.4   Some Register Instructions**
>
> MOV A,R3;   Move contents of register R3 to the accumulator.
> MUL AB;   Multiply the contents of accumulator by the contents of the B register.

8.10.4 Immediate Operand Instructions

Instructions using an immediate operand have a numeric constant (or its symbolic name) following the op-code. The constant can be 8 or 16 bits long, depending on the instruction.

> **EXAMPLE 8.5   Some Immediate Instructions**
>
> MOV A,#NUM8;   Move the 8-bit number NUM8 to the accumulator.
> MOV DPTR,#NUM16;   Move the 16-bit number NUM16 to the data pointer.

8.10.5 Indexed Addressing

The 8051 has two uses for indexed addressing: reading data tables from program memory space and implementing jump tables. In either case, a 16-bit register holds a base address and the accumulator holds an 8-bit displacement or index. The address of the data byte (or the jump address, as the case may be) is the sum of the 16-bit base and the unsigned 8-bit displacement. Because the addition is unsigned, the result is always a forward reference from the base of 0 to 255 bytes. The base register is either DPTR or PC.

> **EXAMPLE 8.6   Some Indexed Instructions**
>
> MOVC A,@A+PC;   Move code byte relative to PC to the accumulator.
> JMP @A+DPTR;   Jump relative to DPTR.

8.10.6 Operand Modifiers: @ and

The 8051 assembly language uses two special symbols to distinguish operand types: the at symbol (@) and the number sign (#). The @ before an operand means that indirect addressing is being used; # before an operand means it is an immediate operand (a constant).

EXAMPLE 8.7 Use of Operand Modifiers

ADD A,R2;   Add to the accumulator the contents of register 2 of the selected bank.
ADD A,@R2;   Add to the accumulator the contents of the RAM location whose address is in register 2 of the selected bank.
ADD A, 05;   Add to the accumulator the contents of RAM address 05.
ADD A,#05;   Add to the accumulator the number 05.

8.11 INSTRUCTION GROUPS

The 8051 has 111 instruction types: 49 one-byte, 45 two-byte, and 17 three-byte. Counting the variations within each type, there are 255 separate instructions; every hex code from 00 to FF corresponds to a valid instruction except A5, which is reserved for future use. The instructions fall into five groups: arithmetic, logic, data transfer, Boolean, and branching. A brief description of each group is given below. Refer to Appendix D for a complete description.

8.11.1 Arithmetic Operations

The 8051 has the usual operations of an 8-bit processor: add (ADD), add-with-carry (ADDC), subtract-with-borrow (SUBB), increment (INC), decrement (DEC), and decimal-adjust-accumulator (DA). It also has two operations not typical of 8-bit micros: multiply (MUL AB) and divide (DIV AB).

MUL AB multiplies the contents of the accumultor by the contents of the B register as unsigned 8-bit integers to give a 16-bit result. The low-order 8 bits of the result will be in the accumulator and the high-order 8 bits will be in B. DIV AB causes the contents of the accumultor to be divided by the contents of B as unsigned integer numbers. The integer part of the result will be in the accumultor, and the remainder is left in B.

The addressing modes used by arithmetic instructions are direct, indirect, register, and immediate.

8.11.2 Logic Operations

The logic operations include *and* (ANL), *or* (ORL), *exclusive-or* (XRL), *clear* and *complement* (CLR and CPL), and *rotates* (RL, RLC, RR, RRC). Also included is the SWAP A instruction. SWAP A swaps nibbles within the accumulator. That is, it exchanges the lower 4 bits in the accumulator with the upper 4 bits. SWAP is useful for working with 4-bit quantities such as BCD numbers, which can be packed two to the byte.

Note that neither the arithmetic nor the logic group contains a compare instruction. The function of a compare instruction has been absorbed into a special branching instruction, as discussed in Sec. 8.11.5.

8.11.3 Data Transfers

The basic data transfer instruction is *move,* which has three forms: MOV, MOVC, and MOVX. Also included in this group are PUSH, POP, and XCH (exchange). All addressing modes are used in this group.

MOV instructions are used to reference internal RAM and SFR space. The two MOVC instructions are used to move bytes from program memory into the accumulator, as from a data table. MOVX instructions are used to reference external RAM.

8.11.4 Boolean Operations

This group of instructions is associated with the single-bit Boolean processor hardware of the 8051. The group includes *set* and *clear,* as well as *and, or,* and *complement* instructions. Also included are bit level move instructions and conditional *jumps,* which test bit values. In effect, this group makes up a miniature assembly language for the Boolean processor.

8.11.5 Branching Instructions

Included in this group are the subroutine calls and returns, as well as various conditional and unconditional jumps. The conditional jumps are relative to the first byte of the next instruction. Because the jump is given as a signed two's complement 8-bit number, the range is -128 to $+127$ bytes, thereby allowing forward and backward branching.

The jump instruction has three basic versions: the short jump (SJMP), the long jump (LJMP), and the absolute jump (AJMP). The *short jump* uses a relative offset as described above. The *long jump* (as well as the long call) uses a 16-bit address as part of the instruction, which makes the instruction 3 bytes long but enables it to reference any location in the 64K program memory space. The *absolute jump* (and the absolute call) uses an 11-bit address, which is split into 8 lower bits and 3 upper bits. The 3 upper bits are combined with a 5-bit operation specifier to make an 8-bit op-code. Thus, the entire instruction is only 2 bytes long. During execution, the 11 bits of the address are substituted for the lower 11 bits in the program counter (PC), which means that the location referenced must be within 2K bytes of the instruction following the AJMP (the upper 5 bits in PC remain the same).

An important instruction in this group is CJNE, which combines the functions of separate compare and jump instructions.

> **EXAMPLE 8.8 Using CJNE**
>
> CJNE A,07,03 will compare the contents of the accumulator with the contents of direct RAM address 07. If they are not equal, a jump is made to the instruction 3 bytes past the beginning of the next instruction. If they are equal, the next instruction, which could be an unconditional jump, is executed.

Also included in this group, by default, is NOP: a 1-byte instruction that does nothing, and takes one machine cycle to do it. One use for the NOP is in padding out delay loops to get exact times. Often a device attached to an output port pin will require a pulse of some minimum duration. NOPs can be used to determine the pulse width.

8.12 SINGLE-BIT BOOLEAN PROCESSOR

The Boolean processor can be thought of as a built-in bit-level coprocessor complete with its own set of instructions: the Boolean group. (It is not a true coprocessor; it doesn't run separately.) All the port lines, as well as 128 bits in RAM and many bits in the SFR registers, have bit addresses. Such a hardware and software combination makes the 8051 well suited for control applications that have many on/off kinds of inputs and outputs, such as switches, lamps, relays, stepper motor drives, and the like.

8.12.1 Carry: The Boolean Accumulator

The carry bit (bit 7 of the PSW) is the equivalent of an accumulator for the Boolean processor. The symbolic name CY is used to designate the carry bit when referring to it as a bit address; the symbol C is used in register-specific instructions that reference the carry bit. For example, CLR C is a 1-byte register-specific instruction that clears the carry bit to 0; CLR CY is a 2-byte instruction that clears the carry bit by referencing its address in the SFR space. The assembler will translate the symbol CY to the number D7H, the address of the carry bit. The instruction CLR PSW.7 is equivalent to CLR CY; it will generate the same code. CLR C generates different code but has the same effect.

Bits from the SFR registers, from internal RAM, and from I/O ports can be read into CY. Operations such as AND and OR can be performed on CY and the result written back to a bit address. Program branching can be conditional on the state of CY or any other addressable bit. Extensive bit manipulation can be done without having to use extraneous code to mask off bits to extract them from bytes, as is done in processors such as the 8085. Also, operations and testing can be done directly on bits without first moving them to CY.

8.12.2 An Application Example

The following example, taken from Intel application note AP-70, illustrates the advantage of a Boolean processor.

EXAMPLE 8.9 A Boolean Application

Figure 8.15 shows a logic circuit implemented with both gates and relays. The Boolean equation for the circuit is

$$Q = (U \cdot (V + W)) + (X \cdot Y) + Z$$

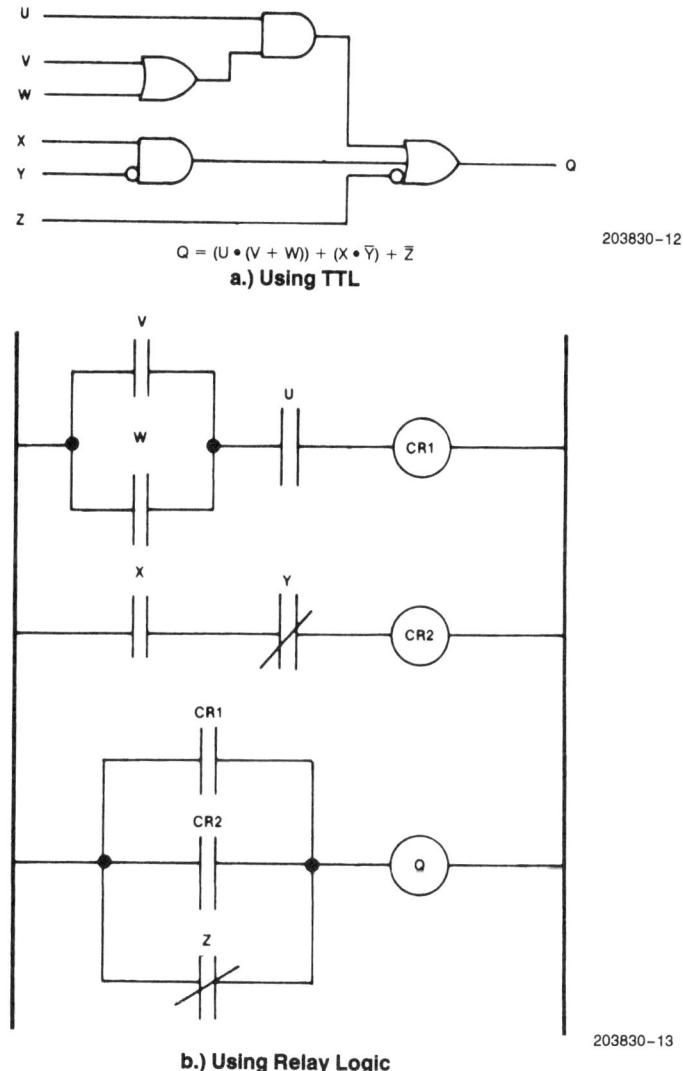

Figure 8.15 Hardware implementations of Boolean functions. (*Source:* Reprinted by permission of Intel Corporation, Copyright © Intel Corporation 1987.)

The 8051 program segment to implement the equation follows. Note the elegance of the straight-line code made possible by the use of Boolean operations. It is left as an exercise for the student to implement the same equation in 8085 code; the comparison should be enlightening.

```
          *
          *
          *
    MOV   C,V      ;GET V INPUT
    ORL   C,W      ;OUTPUT OF OR GATE
    ANL   C,U      ;OUTPUT OF TOP AND GATE
    MOV   F0,C     ;SAVE INTERMEDIATE STATE
    MOV   C,X      ;GET X INPUT
    ANL   C,Y      ;OUTPUT OF BOTTOM AND GATE
    ORL   C,F0     ;INCLUDE SAVED STATE
    ORL   C,Z      ;INCLUDE Z INPUT
    MOV   Q,C      ;OUTPUT COMPUTED RESULT
          *
          *
          *
```

8.13 SYSTEM EXAMPLES: EXTERNAL ROM, RAM, I/O

Because so much is included on the chip, microcontrollers typically do not require much in the way of peripheral chip support. More often, a device such as the 8051 is interfaced directly to the input and output devices it is controlling. However, in order to illustrate the use of the 8051 two simple examples are included here.

EXAMPLE 8.10 External Program Memory

Figure 8.16 shows the 8051 interfaced to a 2732 EPROM. Note the use of the ALE and PSEN pins, as well as the use of port 0 pins as data lines. Also note the use of port 2 pins as high-order address lines.

EXAMPLE 8.11 External RAM and I/O Expansion

Figure 8.17 shows the 8051 interfaced to an 8155 peripheral device. Note the use of $\overline{\text{RD}}$ and $\overline{\text{WR}}$ as strobes to the RAM data store. Also note the use of P2.0 to control the IO/$\overline{\text{M}}$ pin on the 8155.

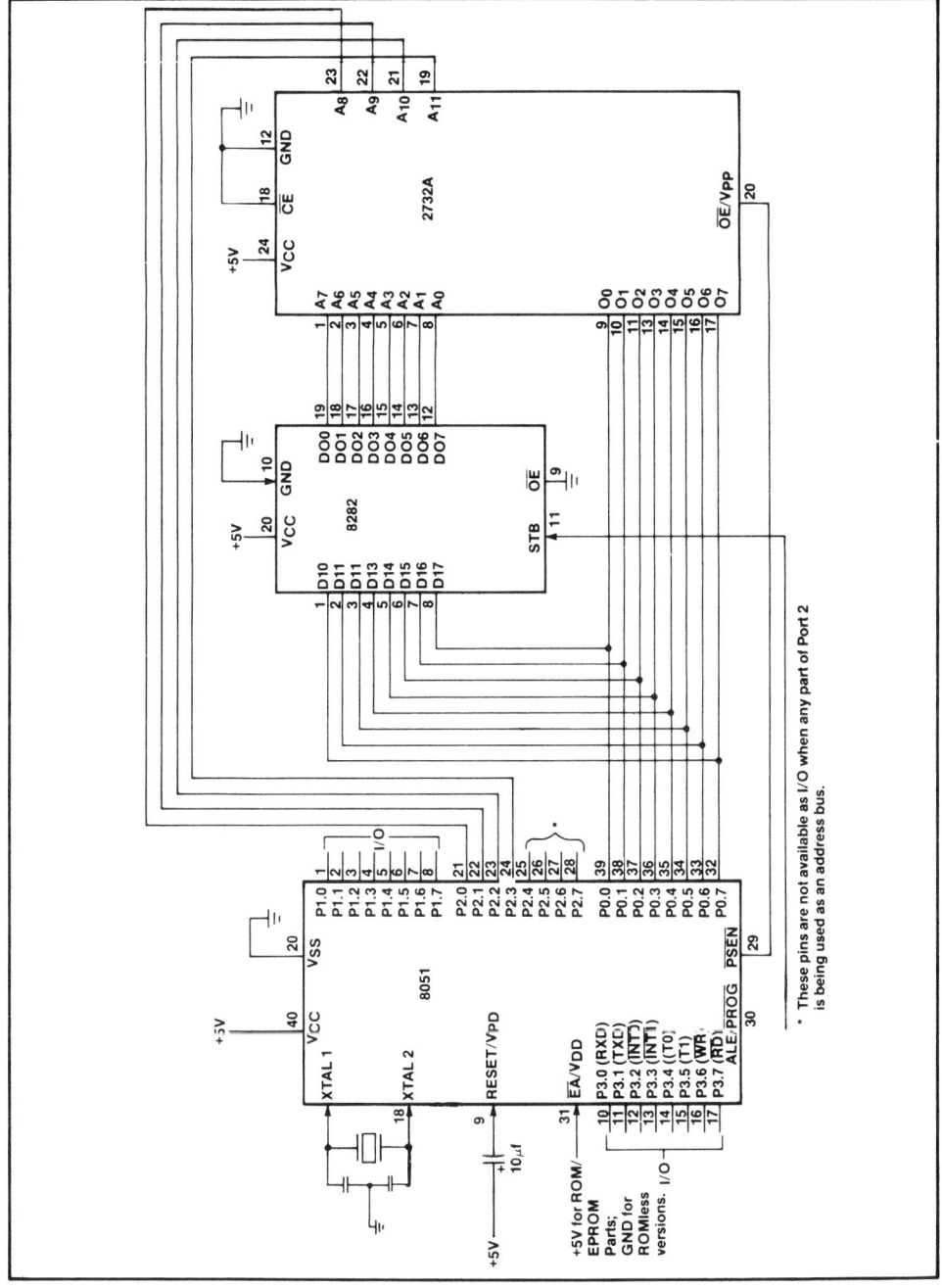

Figure 8.16 External program memory using a 2732. (*Source*: Reprinted by permission of Intel Corporation, Copyright © Intel Corporation 1987.)

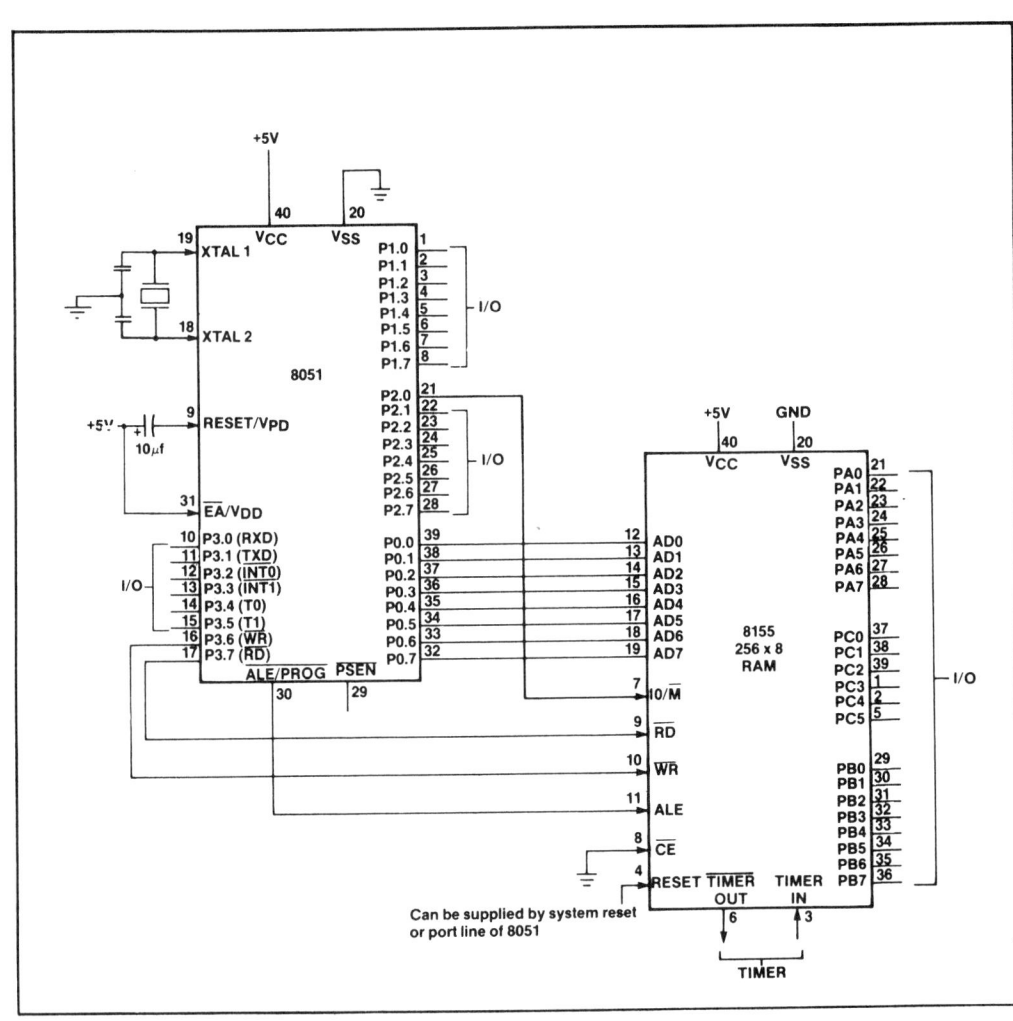

Figure 8.17 Adding a data memory and I/O expander. (*Source:* Reprinted by permission of Intel Corporation, Copyright © Intel Corporation 1987.)

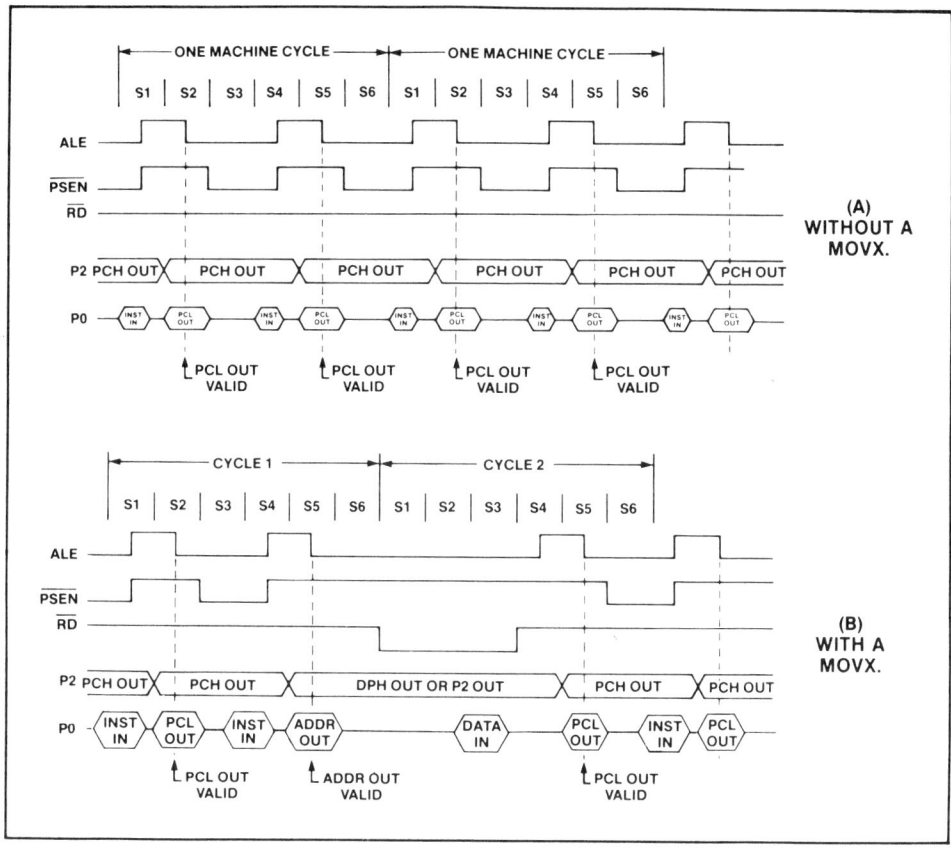

Figure 8.18 Bus cycles in MCS©-51 devices executing from external program memory. (*Source:* Reprinted by permission of Intel Corporation, Copyright © Intel Corporation 1987.)

8.14 SUMMARY

Microcontrollers are devices that combine memory, I/O, and other functions with a CPU to form a sophisticated component level device for use in embedded control applications. The 8051, as an example of a microcontroller, has been examined in terms of its hardware and software. Key features include

- On-board RAM and ROM
- 32 I/O lines
- Hardware timer/counters
- On-board USART
- Sophisticated vectored interrupt system
- Boolean processor
- RAM resident control registers

REFERENCES

Intel Embedded Controller Handbook (1987), Intel order number 210918-005.

Intel Microcontroller Handbook (1983), Intel order number 210918-001.

Intel MCS-51 Macro Assembler User's Guide, Intel order number 9800937-03.

Intel MCS-51 Macro Assembler User's Guide for DOS Systems, Intel order number 122753-001.

The 8051: Programming, Interfacing, Applications (Howard Boyet and Ron Katz, MTI Publications, Inc., 14 E. 8 St., New York, NY 10003).

CHAPTER REVIEW

Questions

1. Explain the term *embedded*.
2. How do open-loop and closed-loop applications differ?
3. How does the 8031 differ from the 8051?
4. How many clocks are in an 8051 machine cycle?
5. How many phases are in an 8051 machine cycle?
6. Explain how program memory and data memory are treated by the 8051.
7. What is the function of the EA pin?
8. What is in the SFR area?
9. What bits are in the PSW?
10. Can jump-on-zero be done without a zero flag bit? How?
11. What is in SP at power up?
12. What control register is associated with SBUF?
13. What control registers are associated with the timers?
14. Which port can drive the heaviest load?
15. Which port is used for address and data with external memory?
16. Which port has alternate functions for its pins?
17. How does the use of PSEN differ from the use of $\overline{RD}$ and $\overline{WR}$?
18. When can the contents of port 0 latches be lost?
19. When is a counter advanced from an external source?
20. Explain how mode 2 differs from mode 0 in a counter.
21. Explain a possible use for counter mode 3.
22. Explain double buffering.
23. Which serial port modes allow full duplex asynchronous operation with variable baud rate?
24. In what register is the SMOD bit found?
25. What does it mean to say an interrupt is pending?
26. Name the interrupt sources in the 8051.
27. Explain the two-tier interrupt priority system.

28. Assuming both interrupts are high level and occur simultaneously, which gets done first, RI or TF0?
29. Does the ordering of the within-level priorities make sense to you? Explain your answer.
30. Explain the special timing involved when an interrupt occurs during the execution of a RETI instruction. What might happen if the timing were otherwise?
31. What controls the state of the flag for an external level-activated interrupt?
32. Name an interrupt flag that is not automatically cleared when the hardware generates the call to the service routine.
33. How long must a reset level be applied to the 8051?
34. How does the 8051 distinguish between a byte address and a bit address?
35. Explain indexed addressing in the 8051.
36. What holds the index number?
37. How many instruction types does the 8051 have? How many do you think you would actually use?
38. Explain what a Boolean processor does. How does it differ from what a byte processor does?
39. Write a program that reads a byte from port 1 and uses it as an index into a jump table starting at address 02B0H.
40. Write a program that will read a byte from port 0 and, depending on which bit in the byte is a 1, jump to one of eight different locations. Use Boolean instructions.

Problems

1. Select a crystal frequency to get a baud rate of 9600, assuming SMOD = 0 and TH1 contains 254. Will the 8051 run that fast?
2. Will a crystal frequency of 11.059 MHz allow the following baud rates: 600, 1200, 2400, 4800? What value or values are required to be in TH1?
3. Write the program suggested in Example 8.9.

chapter 9

Programming and the 8051

OBJECTIVES

Upon completion of this chapter, you should be able to

1. Explain what a state machine is and why it is useful
2. Read and make transition diagrams and state tables
3. Read and explain algorithms coded in 8051 assembly language
4. Write short programs in 8051 assembly language

9.1 INTRODUCTION

As we pointed out in Chapter 8, when a CPU is combined with ROM, RAM, I/O ports, and other hardware features all on a single chip, the result is a single-chip microcomputer. The most common uses for such devices are as embedded controllers (or bit bangers), which effectively substitute software for hardware. For example, a single 8051 can replace an entire board of TTL chips (including a UART). If we consider that additional chips cost money but additional copies of a program don't, the desirability of replacing hardware with software is obvious. The reduction in hardware made possible by microcontrollers can be seen in Example 9.1.

EXAMPLE 9.1 An Embedded Controller

Figure 9.1 shows a smart modem built with an 80C51, a single-chip modem, and a handful of parts.

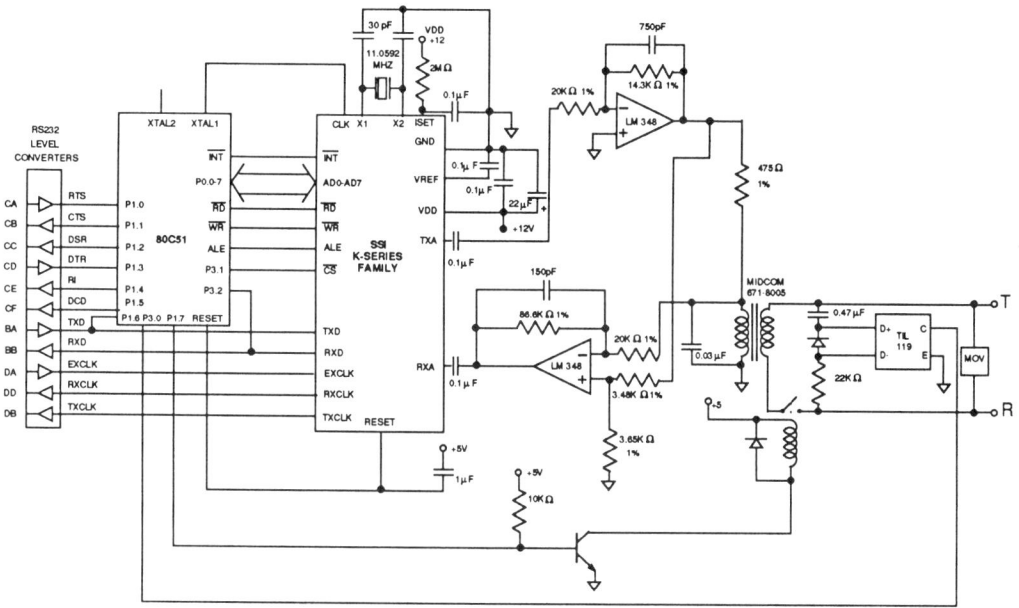

Figure 9.1 Basic box modem (12V version). (*Source:* Courtesy of Silicon Systems Inc.)

Because of the increasing use of microcontrollers, today's designer of electronic equipment (or electronically controlled equipment) must be as adept at software as at hardware.

9.2 FINITE STATE MACHINES

A *finite state machine* (FSM), or just *state machine,* is an abstraction. It can be built with hardware or it can be implemented in code. In software, its purpose is to allow a routine or algorithm to decide what to do next based on both the present set of inputs and the current machine state. State machines are powerful tools for bringing order to complex programming tasks.

At any given time, a program is in one of a finite number of valid *states.* When input arrives (perhaps through an interrupt), the program will make a *transition* to another state. Different inputs will cause different transitions. At each state, some particular action may take place. Before writing the code to implement them, designers put state machines on paper using diagrams, as described below.

9.2.1 State Transition Diagrams

An FSM can best be explained by a small example. We will build a *recognizer* for the two words AND and ADD. Assume the words are entered one letter at a time via a keypad. Each time a key is pressed, an interrupt is generated, a letter is read, and the program must decide which of three conditions is true:

1. The word is complete and the appropriate action should be done.
2. More letters are needed to complete the word.
3. An error has been made entering the word.

Note that the full job of the program extends over more than one interrupt from the keypad.

EXAMPLE 9.2 State Transition Diagram

Figure 9.2 shows the state transition diagram for the recognizer routine. We start in state 0 waiting for a key press. Note that in any state, only specific inputs are accepted as valid. Nonvalid intputs will cause an error routine to be executed and the FSM will return to state 0 to start over.

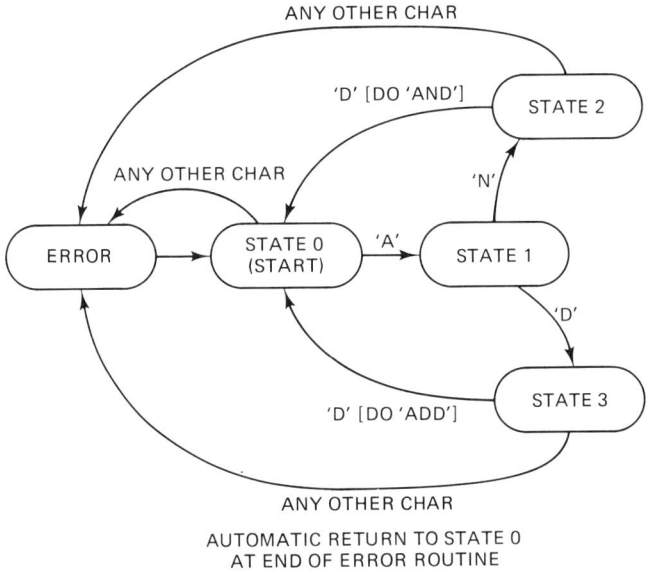

Figure 9.2 State transition diagram for recognizer routine.

As an example of a nontrivial problem, Fig. 9.3 shows the state diagram for the K224DEMO software package written by Silicon Systems to test its model K224 single-chip modem. The software is written in 8051 assembly language.

272 Programming and the 8051 Chap. 9

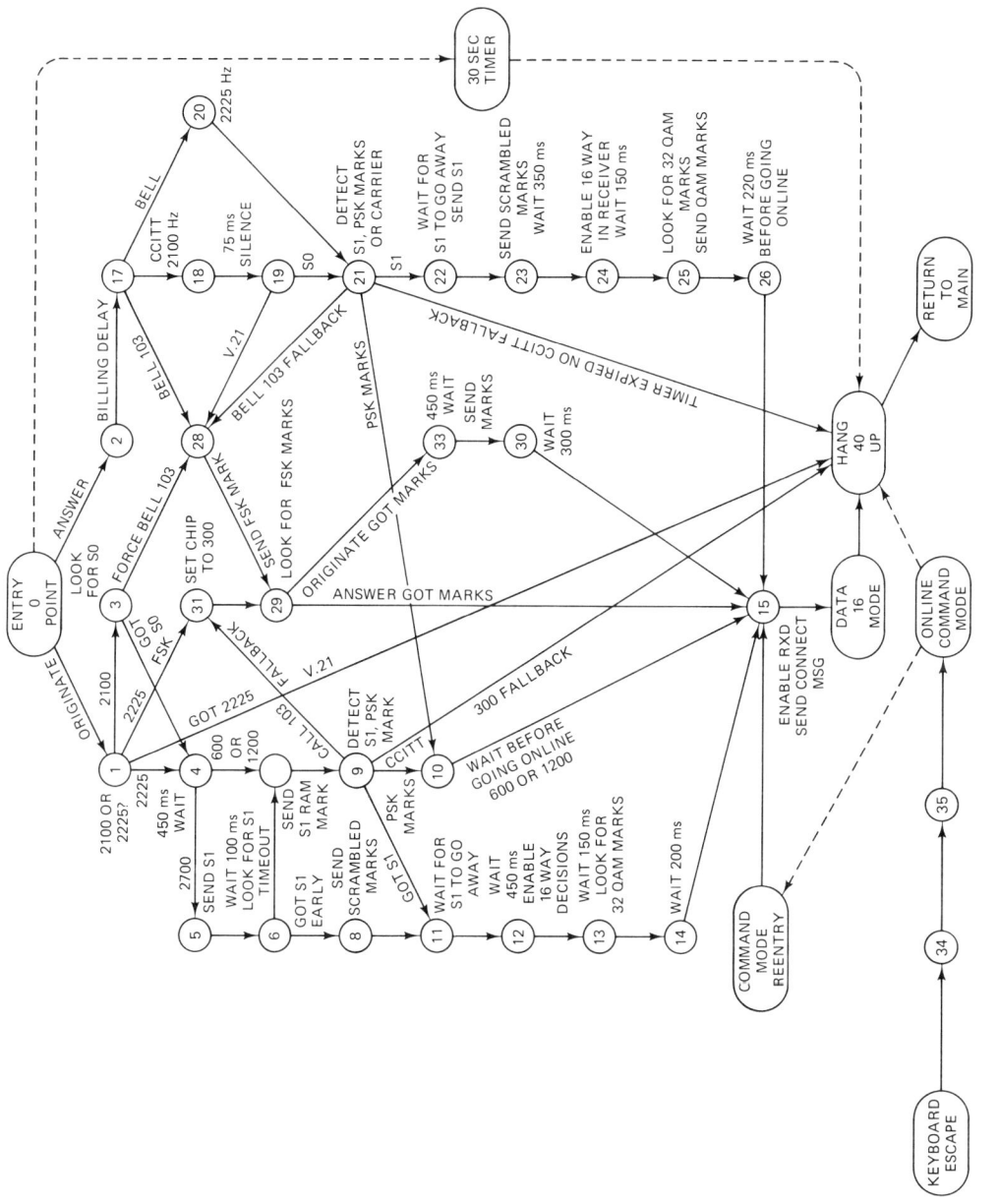

Figure 9.3 Flowchart for K224DEMO state machine. (*Source*: Courtesy of Silicon Systems Inc.)

9.2.2 State Tables

An FSM routine sometimes will keep track of which state it is in by means of a number stored in a RAM location. Other times the state is implicit. When input is received, the routine may decide which transition to make by looking at the state number together with the input. Or, as in Example 9.3, the input will cause different transitions, depending on what state the program is in when the input is received.

An action may be associated with a state. The action taken may be no more than just changing the state number, or it may include some task. An FSM can be summarized in a table. Routines which include the table as a data structure are referred to as *table driven*.

EXAMPLE 9.3 A State Table

Figure 9.4 shows the state table for the recognizer.

		STATES			
		0	1	2	3
I N P U T S	'A'	GO TO STATE_1	DO ERROR ACTION GO TO STATE_0	DO ERROR ACTION GO TO STATE_0	DO ERROR ACTION GO TO STATE_0
	'N'	DO ERROR ACTION GO TO STATE_0	GO TO STATE_2	DO ERROR ACTION GO TO STATE_0	DO ERROR ACTION GO TO STATE_0
	'D'	DO ERROR ACTION GO TO STATE_0	GO TO STATE_3	DO 'AND' ACTION GO TO STATE_0	DO 'ADD' ACTION GO TO STATE_0
	ANY OTHER LETTER	DO ERROR ACTION GO TO STATE_0	DO ERROR ACTION GO TO STATE_0	DO ERROR ACTION GO TO STATE_0	DO ERROR ACTION GO TO STATE_0

Figure 9.4 State table for the recognizer.

Note that table driven routines can be divided into two sections: the table itself, and the code which uses the table (called the *engine*). Such a division makes it possible to generate a general purpose state machine. All that needs to be changed is a data table. Even if you do not include a table into the program, it is still a good idea to make a table for reference while writing the code.

9.2.3 An 8051 Implementation

In this section we develop an 8051 code fragment for the recognizer. The code description is given in Example 9.4.

EXAMPLE 9.4 Recognizer Code

The code is given in the accompanying program. Note that we use busy loops to wait in states 0, 1, and 2. We don't have to wait in state 3 because there is no state 4; we just return to state 0. GOTKEY is a bit location and KEY is a byte location, both in RAM. Assume that an interrupt service routine gets a character from a keyboard and puts it into KEY; it then sets GOTKEY high as a flag to indicate a key was pressed.

```
ST_0:   JBC     GOTKEY,TRYA     ; JUMP ON KEY PRESS
        SJMP    ST_0            ; OTHERWISE, WAIT
TRYA:   MOV     A,KEY           ; GET CHARACTER
        CJNE    A,#'A',ERROR    ; IS IT 'A'? GOTO ERROR IF NO

ST_1:   JBC     GOTKEY,TRYN     ; JUMP ON KEY PRESS
        SJMP    ST_1            ; OTHERWISE, WAIT
TRYN:   MOV     A,KEY           ; GET CHARACTER
        CJNE    A,#'N',TRYD1    ; IS IT 'N'?  TRY 'D' IF NO

ST_2:   JBC     GOTKEY,TRYD2    ; WAIT FOR
        SJMP    ST_2            ; NEXT KEY PRESS
        MOV     A,KEY           ; GET CHARACTER
        CJNE    A,#'D',ERROR    ; IS IT 'D'? GOTO ERROR IF NO
        LCALL   DO_AND          ; YES, DO 'AND' ACTION
        SJMP    ST_0            ; BACK TO STATE_0

TRYD1:  CJNE    A,#'D',ERROR    ; IS IT 'D'? GOTO ERROR IF NO

ST_3:   JBC     GOTKEY,TRYD3    ; WAIT FOR
        SJMP    ST_3            ; NEXT CHARACTER
        CJNE    A,#'D',ERROR    ; IS IT 'D'? GOTO ERROR IF NO
        LCALL   DO_ADD          ; YES, DO 'ADD' ACTION
        SJMP    ST_0            ; BACK TO STATE_0

ERROR:  LCALL   DO_ERR          ; DO ERROR ACTION
        SJMP    ST_0            ; BACK TO STATE_0
```

In state 0, the only valid input is 'A'. Receiving 'A' causes a transition to state 1; any other input is an error. When in state 1, the routine will accept as valid input either 'N' or 'D'. The letter 'N' will cause a transition to state 2, and 'D' will cause a transition to state 3. In both state 2 and state 3, the only valid input is a 'D'. The difference is that in state 2 'D' will cause the 'AND' action to be done, whereas in state 3 the same input will cause the 'ADD' action to be done. After either action is complete, the routine returns to state 0.

Note the use of the JBC instruction for testing bits. If the bit is low, JBC will fall through to the next instruction. If the bit is high, JBC will not only jump but will also reset the tested bit back low. Also note that we did not use an explicit state number. The states are implicit in the flow of control.

You could probably come up with an equivalent program without the aid of a state diagram and transition table for the simple case we just examined. But imagine a recognizer for, say, an assembly language. Another example is the K224DEMO software. State machines can keep us from getting totally lost in complicated situations. They can also be automated with the help of special software tools like *scanner generators,* which can create recognizers from a high-level description.

9.2.4 FSM Limitations

While state machines are useful tools, they are not the 'universal solvent'. There are many tasks which can not be done by an FSM. A classic example is the job of reading a line of text to determine if it contains an equal number of left and right parentheses. The problem is that an FSM doesn't know what took place in previous states. The test is: if you can't draw a state transition diagram of finite size, you can't make an FSM for the task.

9.3 EXAMPLE PROGRAMS

Space does not allow for an exhaustive examination of every 8051 instruction. In this section we look at a few short applications to get a feel for 8051 programming. As you read the code, it will be useful to refer to the appropriate sections in Chap. 6.

Note the use of predefined bit and byte names, such as TCON, in the example programs. They are a common feature of 8051 assemblers, and are discussed in Chap. 8 and Sec. 9.2.4. Such names, along with the op-codes and directives, are called *reserved symbols* and should not be used except for their intended purposes.

9.3.1 An Easy Move

Some of the things to notice in the program of Example 9.5 are the selection of the register bank, the initialization of the stack pointer, and the use of indexed addressing with the DPTR register.

EXAMPLE 9.5 Data Moves

This small procedure is programmed in 8051 code that reads 10 bytes from a data table in program memory and stores each byte in a RAM location. After each byte is read, a subroutine is called, which, presumably, uses the data byte.

```
                              *
                              *
                              *
;               SELECT REGISTER BANK 1

        SETB    C               ; SET CARRY TO 1 FOR
        MOV     RS1,C           ; LSB OF BANK SELECT
        CLR     C               ; CLEAR CARRY TO 0 FOR
        MOV     RS0,C           ; MSB OF BANK SELECT

;               MOVE STACK POINTER

        MOV     SP,#2FH         ; START STACK AT 30H

;               INITIALIZE LOOP

        MOV     R0,00           ; INITIAL VALUE OF INDEX
        MOV     R2,0AH          ; LOOP COUNT = 10
        MOV     R1,20H          ; INITIAL RAM ADDR FOR SAVING
        MOV     DPTR,#0200H     ; BASE ADDRESS OF TABLE IN ROM

;               EXECUTE LOOP

LOOP:   MOV     A,R0            ; MOVE INDEX VAL TO ACCUMULATOR
        MOVC    A,@A+DPTR       ; GET BYTE FROM TABLE
        MOV     @R1,A           ; STORE BYTE IN RAM
        ACALL   SUB             ; CALL ROUTINE THAT USES BYTE
        INC     R0              ; INCREMENT THE INDEX
        INC     R1              ; INCREMENT RAM ADDRESS
        DJNZ    R2,LOOP         ; DEC COUNT, JUMP IF NOT 0

                <REST OF PROGRAM>
                              *
                              *
                              *
```

9.3.2 Jump Table

In Chapter 4 we examined jump tables in 8085 code. Example 9.6 shows a similar routine in 8051 code. Note the use of base-displacement addressing.

EXAMPLE 9.6 Jump Table

The DPTR register is initialized to the beginning address of the table. The variable NUMBER is used to form the displacement. NUMBER is the sequential integer number of the program to which we will jump; it can have the value 1, 2, 3, or 4. Note that no check is made for values outside that range. The displacement, held in A, must be adjusted prior to the JMP @A+DPTR instruction. Because LJMP is 3 bytes long, NUMBER must be converted to a multiple of 3 (0, 3, 6, 9) before it is added to DPTR.

```
JTABLE: MOV     DPTR,#TABLE     ; GET TABLE ADDRESS AS BASE
        MOV     A,NUMBER        ; GET PROGRAM NUMBER
        RL      A               ; MULTIPLY NUMBER BY 2
        ADD     A,NUMBER        ; GET 3 TIMES NUMBER
        JMP     @A+DPTR         ; HOP TO IT
```

```
        TABLE:    LJMP    PROG1         ; NOTE THAT
                  LJMP    PROG2         ; LONG JUMPS
                  LJMP    PROG3         ; ARE 3 BYTES
                  LJMP    PROG4         ; IN LENGTH
```

9.3.3 ASCII to Hex Conversion

This is another example that we saw earlier in 8085 code. The routines shown in Example 9.7 were adapted from Silicon System's K224DEMO package, and are good examples of typical 8051 code.

EXAMPLE 9.7 ASCII to HEX

The code is given in the following program. Some features to note are

```
        ; ROUTINE TO CONVERT 2 ASCII CHARACTERS TO HEX
        ;   R1 POINTS TO FIRST ASCII CHARACTER
        ;   HEX NUMBER RETURNED IN ACCUMULATOR
        ;   ERROR CAUSES RETURN WITH CARRY SET

        A2HEX:
                MOV     R7,#2           ; INITIALIZE LOOP COUNT
        CNV_1:
                MOV     A,@R1           ; GET ASCII CHARACTER
                LCALL   VAL_HEX         ; IS IT 0-9 OR A-F ?
                JC      INVHEX          ; IF NOT, JUMP TO RETURN
                CJNE    R7,#2,CNV_2     ; 2ND CHAR? JUMP IF YES
                SWAP    A               ; SWAP NIBBLES IN ACC
                MOV     R6,A            ; SAVE MSD
                INC     R1              ; POINT TO NEXT CHAR
                DJNZ    R7,CNV_1        ; FINISHED? JUMP IF NO
        CNV_2:
                ORL     A,R6            ; COMBINE HALVES
                CLR     C               ; NO ERROR, CLEAR CARRY
        INVHEX:
                RET                     ; GO HOME


        ; SUBROUTINE TO CHECK FOR VALID ASCII HEX DIGIT
        ;    RETURNS LOWER 4 BITS OF VALID DIGIT
        ;    SETS CARRY HIGH IF INVALID

        VAL_HEX:
                CLR     C               ; CLEAR CARRY INITIALLY
                SUBB    A,#30H          ; REDUCES TO HEX IF 0-9
                JC      BADHEX          ; JUMP IF IT'S BELOW '0'
                SUBB    A,#0AH          ; BIGGER THAN '9' ?
                JC      VH_2            ; JUMP IF NO
                SUBB    A,#27H          ; BETWEEN '9' AND 'A' ?
                JC      BADHEX          ; JUMP TO ERROR IF YES
                SUBB    A,#06H          ; TEST FOR A-F
                JC      VH_1            ; JUMP IF IN RANGE
                SETB    C               ; SET ERROR FLAG
                SJMP    BADHEX          ; JUMP TO RETURN
        VH_1:
                ADD     A,#06H          ; RENORMALIZE HEX
        VH_2:
                ADD     A,#0AH          ; FIX UP 0-9
                CLR     C               ; SET NO-ERROR FLAG
        BADHEX:
                RET                     ; GO BACK
```

1. The use of registers to hold the working variables and the loop counter. Register instructions are short and quick.
2. The use of carry (C) as an error flag.
3. The use of SWAP to get at the lower 4 bits of a character.
4. The use of CJNE to combine compare and conditional jump.
5. The use of DJNZ to implement a loop.
6. Because subtract-with-borrow (SUBB) is the only subtraction the 8051 has, the carry bit must be cleared to effect a simple subtraction.
7. The use of @ and # operand modifiers.

Every programmer tends to develop a personal style. However, that style is affected by the processor's instruction set. The reader should compare the 8051 code to the 8085 version to see both the similarities and differences.

9.3.4 A/D Converter Interface

Figure 9.5 shows the ADC0801 analog to digital converter (ADC) interfaced to the 8051. Port 1 is used to read the 8-bit result from the ADC. The handshake timing is shown in Fig. 9.6. Note that the ADC0801 start-of-conversion (SOC) signal is

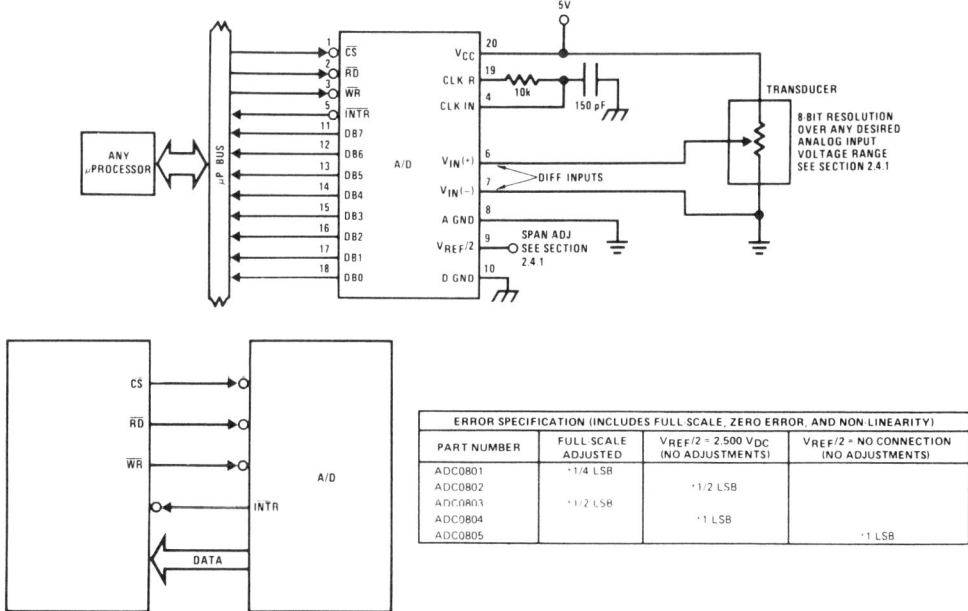

Figure 9.5 ADC0801 analog to digital converter interfaced to the 8051. (*Source:* Reprinted with permission of National Semiconductor Corporation.)

Sec. 9.3   Example Programs

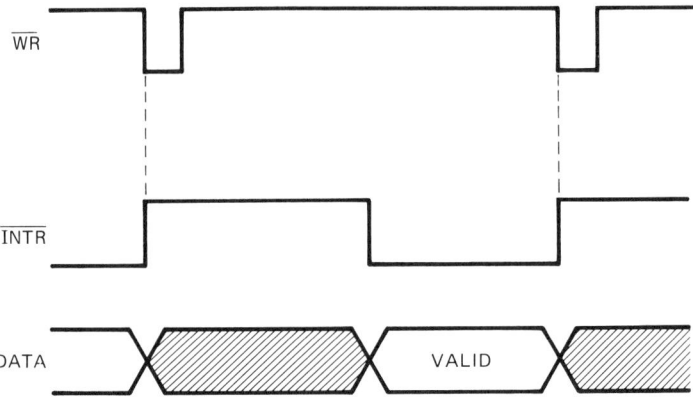

Figure 9.6 Timing diagram.

labeled $\overline{WR}$ and the end-of-conversion (EOC) signal is called $\overline{INTR}$. We will use port 2 bit 0 (P2.0) to activate the SOC. The EOC will be connected to external interrupt pin INT0.

EXAMPLE 9.8 A/D Interface

In the program here, note that the variable DATA was declared in the data segment (DSEG) because it must be a RAM location. Remember that the 8051 uses different address spaces for code and data. Also note that at the interrupt vector address (0003H) we jumped to location 0050H to start the service routine. We did that to leave room for the next interrupt service routine, which starts at address 000BH. There is no interrupt enable instruction at the end of the service routine; that function is done by RETI.

```
              ORG   0003H          ; INTERRUPT VECTOR ADDRESS

              SJMP  GETNUM         ; LEAVE ROOM FOR OTHERS

              ORG   0050H          ; START SERVICE ROUTINE HERE

   GETNUM:    PUSH  ACC            ; SAVE ACCUMULATOR
              PUSH  PSW            ; SAVE FLAGS
              MOV   A,P1           ; INPUT FROM PORT_1
              MOV   DATA,A         ; SAVE THE DATA
              CLR   P2.0           ; PULL SOC LOW & HIGH TO
              SETB  P2.0           ; START NEXT CONVERSION
              POP   PSW            ; RESTORE FLAGS
              POP   ACC            ; RESTORE ACCUMULATOR
              RETI                 ; RETURN FROM INTERRUPT

              ORG   0100H          ; START OF MAIN PROGRAM
   MAIN:      MOV   IP,01          ; SET INT0 TO HIGH PRIORITY
              MOV   TCON,01        ; MAKE INT0 EDGE TRIGGERED
              MOV   IE,81H         ; ENABLE EXTERNAL INT0
              MOV   P1,#0FFH       ; FORCE PORT_1 PINS HIGH
              SETB  P2.0           ; GENERATE A
              CLR   P2.0           ; START-OF-CONVERSION
              SETB  P2.0           ; PULSE ON SOC
```

```
                    <REST OF PROGRAM>

            DSEG                ; DATA SEGMENT IN RAM
    DATA    DS      1           ; 1-BYTE TEMPORARY STORAGE
```

The port 1 pins are driven high prior to using them for input. That creates the equivalent of a pull-up resistor on the inputs and allows the external device to pull them low.

9.3.5 Pulse Width Modulator (PWM) D/A

Many IC devices, such as the DAC0808 shown in Fig. 9.7, are available for digital to analog conversion. We can also implement a cheap, simple, slow-speed DAC by

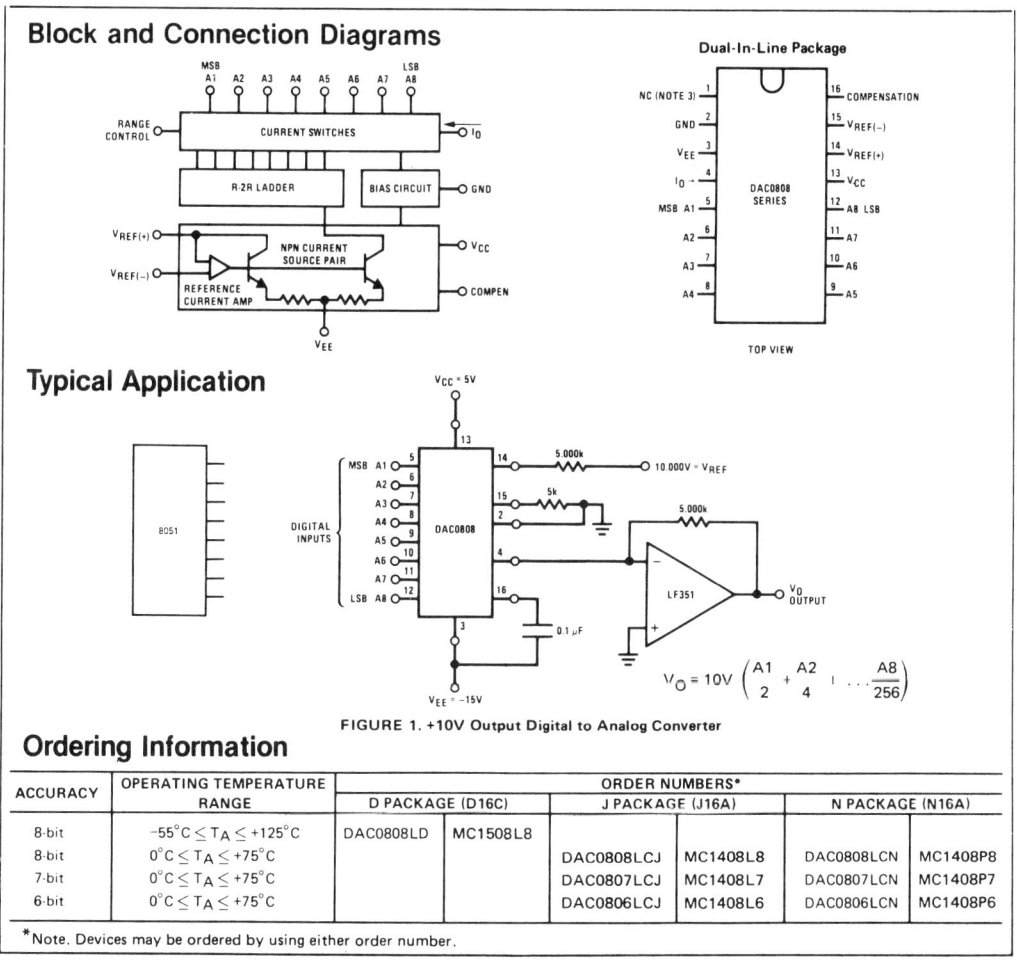

Figure 9.7 DAC0808 IC device. (*Source:* Reprinted with permission of National Semiconductor Corporation.)

using a single I/O bit to output a constant frequency pulse train and integrating it with a low-pass filter, as shown in Fig. 9.8. By digitally varying the duty cycle (on/off ratio) of the pulse, the analog dc voltage out of the filter will be proportional to the digital input.

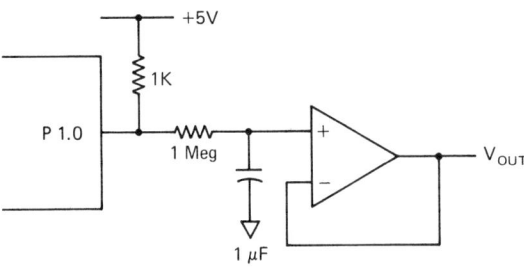

Figure 9.8 Simple, slow-speed DAC.

We will use two 8-bit numbers in this routine: the binary number to be converted and the duration count (initialized to 255). We will initialize the I/O bit high and set up the timer to generate an interrupt every 100 μsec (assuming a 12-MHz clock). Remember that in timer mode, the clock is automatically divided by 12 before it is used.

The interrupt service routine will decrement both the binary number and the duration count. When the binary number is decremented to zero, the I/O bit is forced low. The duration count continues to be decremented until it reaches zero, at which point the I/O bit is forced high, the duration count is reset to 255, and the binary number is restored. The result is a pulse train with a constant period of 25.5 msec and a duty cycle that varies with the binary number.

EXAMPLE 9.9 Pulse Width Modulator

In the code here, note that timer 0 is being used in mode 2. Also note the push instruction is PUSH ACC instead of PUSH A. The push and pop instructions refer to 8-bit addresses because the 8051 uses on-board RAM for the special function register (SFR) locations.

```
JTABLE:   MOV    DPTR,#TABLE    ; GET TABLE ADDRESS AS BASE
          MOV    A,NUMBER       ; GET PROGRAM NUMBER
          DEC    A              ; ADJUST OFFSET
          MOV    B,#3           ; SET UP FOR MULTIPLY
          MUL    AB             ; MULTIPLY NUMBER BY 3
          JMP    @A+DPTR        ; HOP TO IT

TABLE:    LJMP   PROG1          ; NOTE THAT
          LJMP   PROG2          ; LONG JUMPS
          LJMP   PROG3          ; ARE 3 BYTES
          LJMP   PROG4          ; IN LENGTH
```

Pay careful attention to the initialization of the IE, TMOD, TCON, TH0, and TL0 registers. Convert the hex values to binary and go back to Chapter 8 for descriptions of what each bit does. For example, the 82H put into IE is

10000010B and activates $\overline{EA}$ and ET0. ET0 high enables the timer 0 interrupt; the other low bits disable the other interrupts.

9.3.6 Serial I/O

As described in Chap. 8, the 8051 has the equivalent of an on-board USART. The program of Example 9.10 uses the 8051 in serial mode 1 to send and receive simultaneously asynchronous data at a baud rate of 1200 bits per second (bps). We will use timer 1 in auto-reload mode (timer mode 2) to generate the bit clock. We will use a CPU clock frequency of 11.059 MHz because that is a multiple of the baud rate.

EXAMPLE 9.10 Serial I/O

The serial port generates an interrupt when either a frame is received or when a frame being sent gets to the last (stop) bit. The interrupt service routine must determine which event occurred by testing both the TI and RI flag bits. TI and RI are set by the hardware when the corresponding interrupt occurs but must be reset in software as part of the service routine.

```
      PCON    EQU    87H          ; NOT PREDEFINED IN MY ASSEMBLER
      COUNT   EQU    0E8H         ; TIMER RELOAD VALUE
      SFLG    BIT    20H.0        ; SEND FLAG

              ORG    0023H        ; SERIAL INTERRUPT VECTOR

              PUSH   PSW          ; SAVE FLAGS
              JNB    TI,NXT       ; JUST SENT FRAME? JUMP IF NO
              CLR    TI           ; YES, CLEAR XMIT INTERRUPT FLAG
              CLR    SFLG         ; AND TELL THE SUBROUTINE
      NXT:    JNB    RI,BYE       ; JUMP IF NO FRAME RECEIVED
              MOV    A,SBUF       ; GET THE 8-BIT DATA WORD
              MOV    DATA,A       ; AND SAVE IT FOR MAIN
              CLR    RI           ; CLEAR RCVE INTERRUPT FLAG
      BYE:    POP    PSW          ; RESTORE FLAGS
              RETI                ; RETURN FROM INTERRUPT

      MAIN:   MOV    SP,30H       ; MOVE SP TO HIGH RAM
              MOV    TH1,COUNT    ; INIT COUNT
              MOV    TL1,COUNT    ; FOR BAUD RATE
              MOV    TMOD,#20H    ; INIT TIMER 1 MODE 2
              MOV    TCON,#40H    ; INIT TIMER CONTROL
              MOV    IE,#90H      ; ENABLE SERIAL INTERRUPTS
              MOV    SCON,#70H    ; SERIAL MODE 1 (10 BIT FRAME)
              MOV    PCON,#00H    ; SET SMOD TO 0

              MOV    A,'G'        ; GET FIRST ASCII CHAR
              LCALL  SEND         ; AND SEND IT
              MOV    A,'O'        ; GET SECOND ASCII CHAR
              LCALL  SEND         ; AND SEND IT

                   <REST OF PROGRAM>

                          *
                          *
```

```
        SEND:   PUSH    ACC             ; SAVE ACCUMULATOR
                MOV     SBUF,A          ; LOAD OUTPUT BUFFER
                SETB    SFLG            ; SET FLAG TO BUSY STATUS
        SLP:    JB      SFLG,SLP        ; WAIT FOR INTERRUPT TO
                CJNE    A,#DONE,SLP     ; CHANGE FLAG TO DONE
                POP     ACC             ; RESTORE ACCUMULATOR
                RET                     ; RETURN FROM SUBROUTINE


                DSEG                    ; DATA SEGMENT IN RAM

        DATA    DS      1               ; RECEIVED DATA STORAGE
```

Note that the subroutine can be anywhere in the program address space because we called it with the 3-byte LCALL instruction. If the subroutine is within a 2K range, we can use the 2-byte ACALL. Many assemblers have a generic CALL instruction that automatically gets replaced with either ACALL or LCALL, as is appropriate; the assembler computes the address range. Also note that subroutine returns use RET, whereas interrupt returns use RETI.

Note the use of the JB and JNB instructions to test the value of individual bits. The 8051 RAM locations with byte address 20H to 2FH are bit addressable with bit addresses 00H to 7FH (20H.0 = 00). Using the BIT directive, we can assign names to the bit addresses and use them as flags, as is done in the program with SFLG. Actually, SFLG is redundant because we could have just looked at T1 directly.

As before, the student should do a bit-by-bit analysis of the initialization of the various control registers to be sure that the value of each bit is understood in terms of its function.

9.4 SUMMARY

The purpose of this chapter was threefold: (1) to introduce the idea of a state machine as an aid to program design; (2) to illustrate the use of the 8051 instruction set; and (3) to give the flavor of 8051 programming.

CHAPTER REVIEW

Questions

1. Compare and contrast the 8051 to the 8085 in terms of architecture.
2. Compare and contrast the 8051 to the 8085 in terms of programming model.

Problems

1. Draw a state transition diagram for a recognizer that can distinguish between the words 'CAT', 'CAN' and 'BAT'.
2. Design the state table for problem 1.
3. Write an 8051 assembly language program to implement the recognizer of problem 1.
4. A certain machine control has three push-button switches: forward, stop, and reverse. If the machine is running forward, it must be stopped before it can be run in reverse. Likewise, if it is running in reverse, it must be stopped before running forward. Draw the state transition diagram, draw a state table, and write the 8051 code to implement such a controller.
5. Pick some of the 8085 code examples given in previous chapters and rewrite them in 8051 code.
6. Rewrite the program of Example 9.4 so that it is table driven.

chapter 10

Peripheral Devices

OBJECTIVES

Upon completion of this chapter, you should be able to

1. Write routines to use the 8255 chip
2. Write routines to use the 8279 chip
3. Write routines to use the LTC1091 chip
4. Write routines to use the 8251

10.1 INTRODUCTION

Peripheral chips are integrated circuits that either share the bus with a microprocessor or "talk" to one over port lines. They do jobs such as input/output, DMA, and A/D. Some peripherals are designed for specific microprocessors, such as the 8155 for the 8085; others are generic and will work with many processors.

We have already discussed two peripherals, the 8155 and the 8257. In this chapter we examine four typical devices: a relatively "plain vanilla" I/O chip, a specialized keyboard/display I/O chip, an analog data acquisition chip, and a serial I/O chip.

10.2 THE 8255 PROGRAMMABLE PERIPHERAL INTERFACE

The 8255 block diagram and pin configuration are shown in Fig. 10.1. It is a general-purpose I/O device with 24 lines divided into three 8-bit ports designated A, B, and C. When used for output, the pins of port B or C will source as much as 1 mA at 1.5V for driving Darlington transistor inputs.

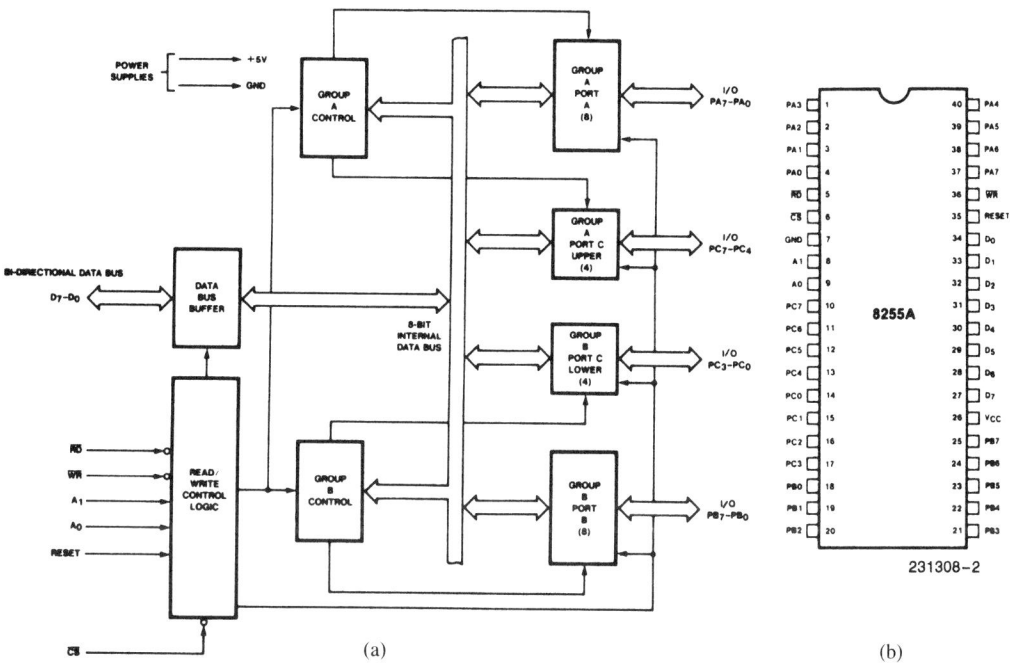

Figure 10.1 8255 interface. (a) 8255A block diagram. (b) Pin configuration. (*Source:* Reprinted by permission of Intel Corporation, Copyright © Intel Corporation 1987.)

As shown in Fig. 10.2, the 8255 has three modes of operation to configure the I/O pins in a variety of ways, as described below.

10.2.1 8255 Bus Connections

The 8255 connects to the system bus through the following pins:

D0–D7   **Data:** Connect to the system data bus. The CPU communicates to the 8255 through these bidirectional pins.

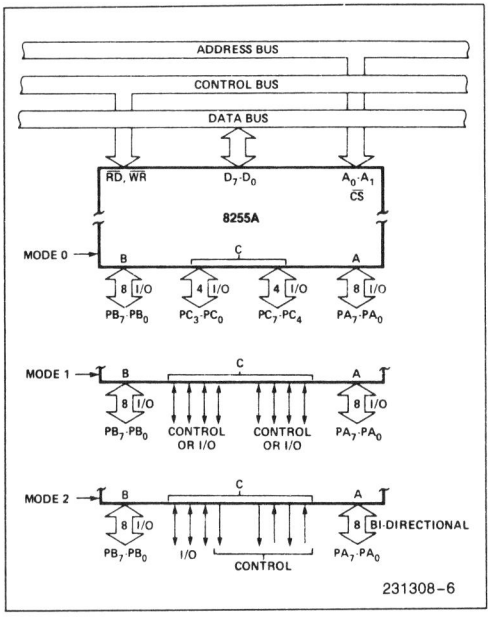

Figure 10.2 Basic mode definitions and bus interface. (*Source:* Reprinted by permission of Intel Corporation, Copyright © Intel Corporation 1987.)

$\overline{\text{CS}}$ **Chip Select:** Obtained by decoding the appropriate address lines above A1.

$\overline{\text{RD}}$ **Read:** Pulled low by the CPU IOREAD signal to read data from the 8255. IOREAD may have to be derived using a signal such as IO/$\overline{\text{M}}$.

$\overline{\text{WR}}$ **Write:** Pulled low by the CPU IOWRITE signal to write data or control words to the 8255. IOWRITE may have to be derived using a signal such as IO/$\overline{\text{M}}$.

A0/A1   **Address:** Lowest 2 bits of the address bus. Used with $\overline{\text{RD}}$ and $\overline{\text{WR}}$ to select one of the 8255 ports.

RESET   A high on reset clears the control register and sets the ports to input mode.

The functions of the 8255 bus connections are summarized in Fig. 10.3. Note how A1 and A0 are used to select either port A, port B, port C, or the control word.

10.2.2 The 8255 Control Word

The mode of operation and the direction of the port lines (in or out) are selected by writing the appropriate byte to the control register. Note that the control register is write-only; you can't read it. The mode definition format is shown in Fig. 10.4.

A_1	A_0	$\overline{RD}$	$\overline{WR}$	$\overline{CS}$	Input Operation (READ)
0	0	0	1	0	Port A → Data Bus
0	1	0	1	0	Port B → Data Bus
1	0	0	1	0	Port C → Data Bus
					Output Operation (WRITE)
0	0	1	0	0	Data Bus → Port A
0	1	1	0	0	Data Bus → Port B
1	0	1	0	0	Data Bus → Port C
1	1	1	0	0	Data Bus → Control
					Disable Function
X	X	X	X	1	Data Bus → 3-State
1	1	0	1	0	Illegal Condition
X	X	1	1	0	Data Bus → 3-State

Figure 10.3 8255A basic operation. (*Source:* Reprinted by permission of Intel Corporation, Copyright © Intel Corporation 1987.)

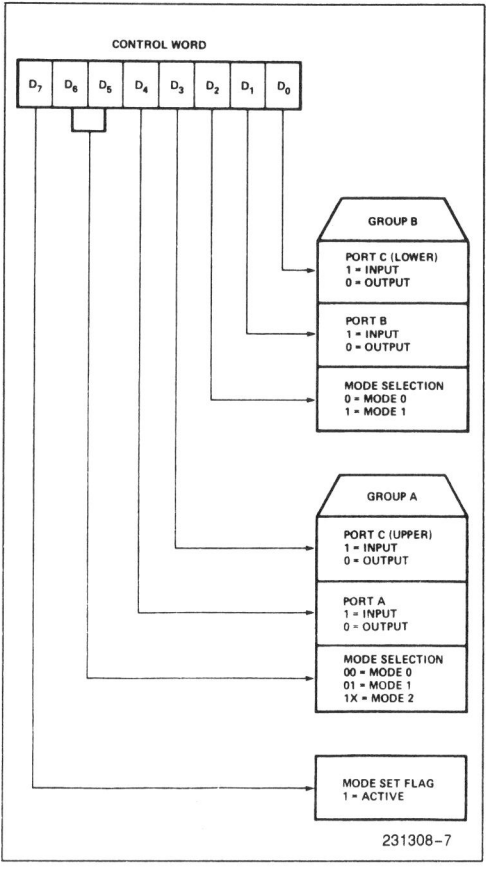

Figure 10.4 Mode definition format. (*Source:* Reprinted by permission of Intel Corporation, Copyright © Intel Corporation 1987.)

The MSB (D7) of the byte written to the control word must be a 1 when setting the mode. If the MSB is a 0, the control word becomes the bit set/reset feature.

10.2.3 Single-Bit Set/Reset Feature

In control applications it is often required to control individual I/O bits. The 8255 uses the control word to set or reset any of the port C bits individually, as shown in Fig. 10.5. Note that the particular pin on port C is selected by D1–D3, and the value to be written to the pin is held in D0.

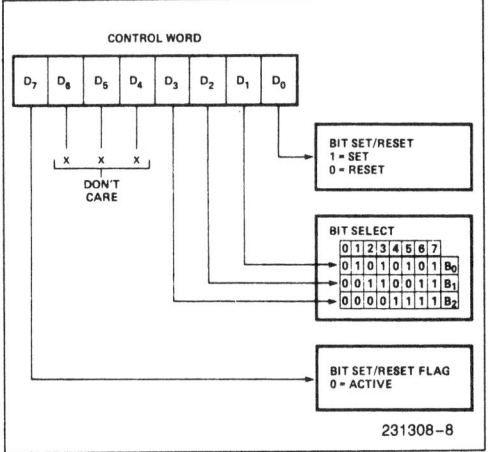

Figure 10.5 Bit set/reset format. (*Source:* Reprinted by permission of Intel Corporation, Copyright © Intel Corporation 1987.)

EXAMPLE 10.1   8255 Port C Bit Set/Reset

PROBLEM   Reset bit 6 of port C (i.e., PC6) to a 0.

SOLUTION   Using Fig. 10.5, we must get the correct byte in the accumulator and output it to the control word. For a reset, the LSB (D0) should be a 0. The 3-bit binary number for 6 is 110, so the next 3 bits above the LSB (D3, D2, D1) should be 110. The next 3 bits (D4, D5, D6) are don't cares, so we can make them 000. The MSB (D7) is the bit set/reset flag and must be 0 to activate this mode. Putting it all together, the byte we want is 00001100, or 0Ch. The 8085 instructions to reset the bit would be

```
MVI  A,0CH   ; LOAD THE COMMAND BYTE
OUT  CWPORT  ; WRITE TO CONTROL WORD
```

The single-bit set/reset feature is useful for controlling the port C bits used for INTE, as described in Sec. 10.2.5.

10.2.4 Mode 0

Mode 0 is simple input/output with no handshaking. The basic configuration is two 8-bit ports (A and B) and two 4-bit ports (upper half of C and lower half of C). Any port can be input or output. Outputs are latched, inputs are not. The 16 possible configurations are summarized in Fig. 10.6.

A		B		Group A		#	Group B	
D_4	D_3	D_1	D_0	Port A	Port C (Upper)		Port B	Port C (Lower)
0	0	0	0	OUTPUT	OUTPUT	0	OUTPUT	OUTPUT
0	0	0	1	OUTPUT	OUTPUT	1	OUTPUT	INPUT
0	0	1	0	OUTPUT	OUTPUT	2	INPUT	OUTPUT
0	0	1	1	OUTPUT	OUTPUT	3	INPUT	INPUT
0	1	0	0	OUTPUT	INPUT	4	OUTPUT	OUTPUT
0	1	0	1	OUTPUT	INPUT	5	OUTPUT	INPUT
0	1	1	0	OUTPUT	INPUT	6	INPUT	OUTPUT
0	1	1	1	OUTPUT	INPUT	7	INPUT	INPUT
1	0	0	0	INPUT	OUTPUT	8	OUTPUT	OUTPUT
1	0	0	1	INPUT	OUTPUT	9	OUTPUT	INPUT
1	0	1	0	INPUT	OUTPUT	10	INPUT	OUTPUT
1	0	1	1	INPUT	OUTPUT	11	INPUT	INPUT
1	1	0	0	INPUT	INPUT	12	OUTPUT	OUTPUT
1	1	0	1	INPUT	INPUT	13	OUTPUT	INPUT
1	1	1	0	INPUT	INPUT	14	INPUT	OUTPUT
1	1	1	1	INPUT	INPUT	15	INPUT	INPUT

Figure 10.6 Mode 0 port definition. (*Source:* Reprinted by permission of Intel Corporation, Copyright © Intel Corporation 1987.)

EXAMPLE 10.2 8255 Mode 0 Configuration

PROBLEM In mode 0, configure the 8255 ports as follows:

```
                A : Input
                B : Output
    Upper Half  C : Output
    Lower Half  C : Output
```

SOLUTION We must get the correct byte in the accumulator and output it to the control word. Looking at Fig. 10.6, we find that the configuration we want is 8. For 8, Fig. 10.6 tells us that D0 = 0, D1 = 0, D3 = 0, and D4 = 1. For all the entries in Fig. 10.5, D7 = 1 and the other bits (D6, D5, D2) = 0. Putting it all together, the byte we want is 10010000, or 90h. The 8085 instructions to implement this configuration are:

```
MVI  A,90H   ; LOAD THE COMMAND BYTE
OUT  CWPORT  ; WRITE TO CONTROL WORD
```

10.2.5 Mode 1

Mode 1 is strobed I/O; that is, it uses handshaking. The basic configuration is two groups (A and B) where each group contains an 8-bit data port and a 4-bit control/status port.

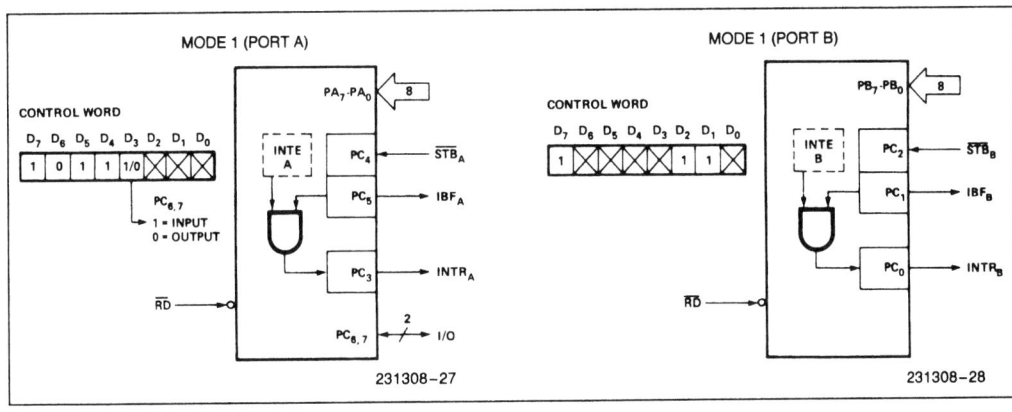

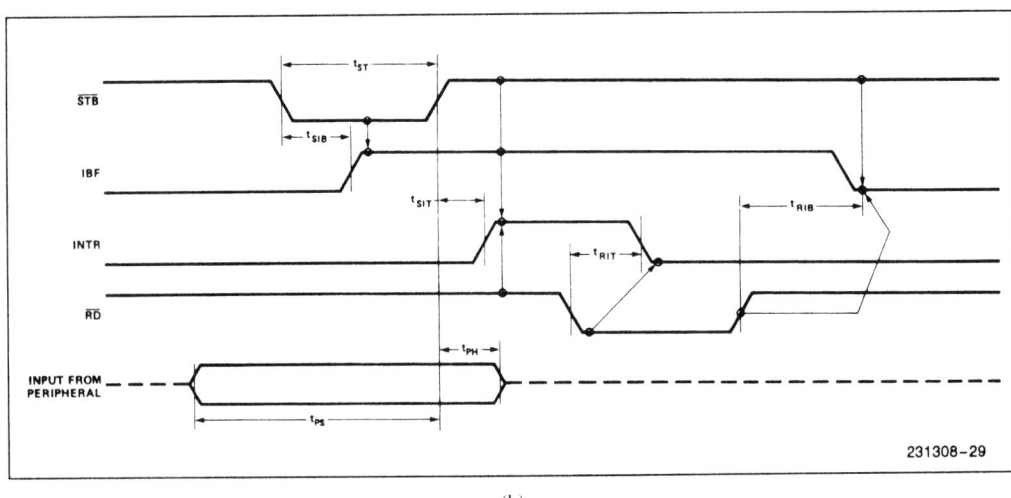

Figure 10.7 (a) Mode 1 input. (b) Mode 1 (strobed input). (*Source:* Reprinted by permission of Intel Corporation, Copyright © Intel Corporation 1987.)

Mode 1 input. Figure 10.7 shows ports A and B in mode 1 input. Note the use of port C pins for handshaking, as follows:

STB **Input Strobe:** A low pulse on this pin loads the data into the input latch, where the data are held.

IBF **Input Buffer Full:** Acknowledgment of $\overline{\text{STB}}$. Goes high when $\overline{\text{STB}}$ is pulsed and goes back low when the CPU activates $\overline{\text{RD}}$. IBF is used to tell an external device when it is free to strobe another byte into the port.

INTR **Interrupt Request:** This output can be connected to the CPU to generate an interrupt. INTR goes high when IBF is high and INTE is a 1. INTE is actually PC4 for port A and PC2 for port B and can be set/reset with the control register, as described in Example 10.1.

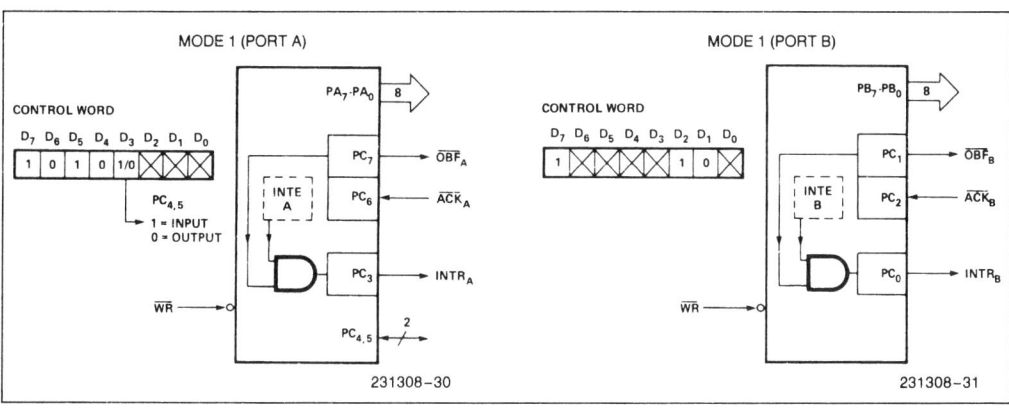

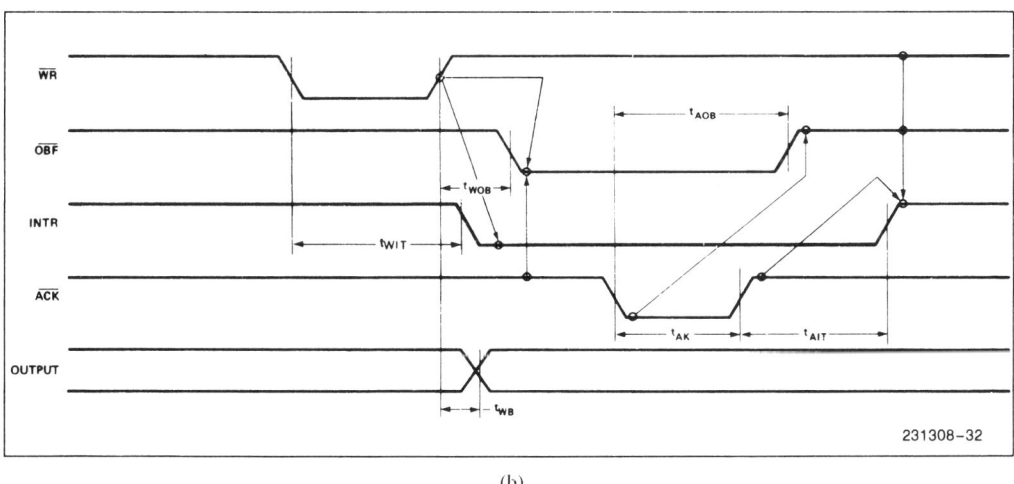

Figure 10.8 (a) Mode 1 output. (b) Mode 1 (strobed output). (*Source:* Reprinted by permission of Intel Corporation, Copyright © Intel Corporation 1987.)

Mode 1 output. Figure 10.8 shows ports A and B in mode 1 output. Note the use of port C pins for handshaking, as follows:

$\overline{\text{OBF}}$ **Output Buffer Full:** Goes low when the CPU writes data to the port. Goes high when $\overline{\text{ACK}}$ is pulsed low.

$\overline{\text{ACK}}$ **Acknowledge Input:** Pulsed low by the external device to indicate that the last data output has been read.

INTR **Interrupt Request:** Can be connected to the CPU to generate an interrupt. INTR goes high when $\overline{\text{OBF}}$ is high, $\overline{\text{ACK}}$ is high, and INTE is a 1. INTR is reset by the $\overline{\text{WR}}$ pulse from the CPU. As with input, INTE is PC6 for port A and PC2 for port B and can be set/reset with the control register (see Example 10.1).

Because mode 1 uses port C for status and control, the program can read port C to test the status. For example, in input configuration, the status of IBF can be read to see if data have been strobed into the 8255 and are waiting to be read by the CPU.

EXAMPLE 10.3   8255 Mode 1 Configuration

PROBLEM   In mode 1, configure the 8255 ports as follows:

```
A : Input
B : Output
C : bits 6 & 7 input
Interrupts INTE A and INTE B Enabled
```

SOLUTION   We must get the correct byte in the accumulator and output it to the control word. Mode 1 input is found in Fig. 10.7, where we find that for A to be input the 4 bits D7, D6, D5, and D4 = 1011. For port C bits 6 and 7 (PC6, 7) to be input, D3 = 1. Mode 1 output is found in Fig. 10.8, where we find that for B to be output the 2 bits D2 and D1 = 10. D0 is a don't care, so D0 = 0. Putting it all together, the byte we want is 10111100, or BCh. To set the interrupt flags, we must use the bit set command, as described in Example 10.1. The 8085 instructions to implement this configuration are

```
MVI   A,0BCH  ; LOAD THE COMMAND BYTE
OUT   CWPORT  ; WRITE TO CONTROL WORD
MVI   A,09    ; SETUP PC4 TO BE A 1
OUT   CWPORT  ; MAKE INTE_A A 1
MVI   A,05    ; SETUP PC2 TO BE A 1
OUT   CWPORT  ; MAKE INTE_B A 1
```

10.2.6 Mode 2

Mode 2 is strobed bidirectional bus I/O. It allows both input and output through the same 8-bit port and uses port C pins as handshake signals to support direction and flow control. The basic configuration is port A as the bidirectional 8-bit port and five of the port C bits used for handshaking. The remaining three port C bits can be used for I/O. As shown in Fig. 10.9b and 10.9c, mode 2 combines the handshake signals of mode 1 input and mode 1 output.

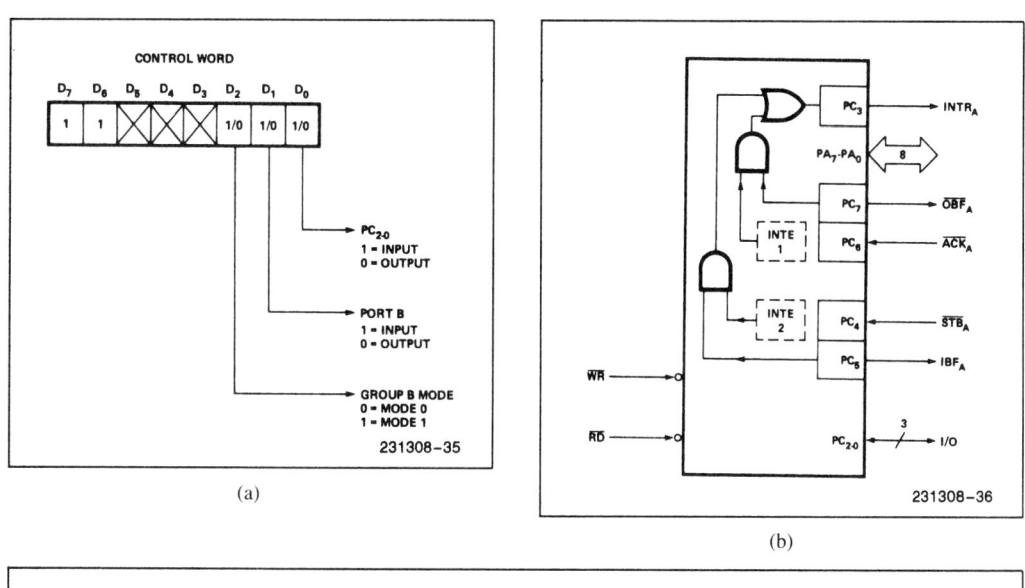

Figure 10.9 (a) Mode control word. (b) Mode 2. (c) Mode 2 (bidirectional). (*Source:* Reprinted by permission of Intel Corporation, Copyright © Intel Corporation 1987.)

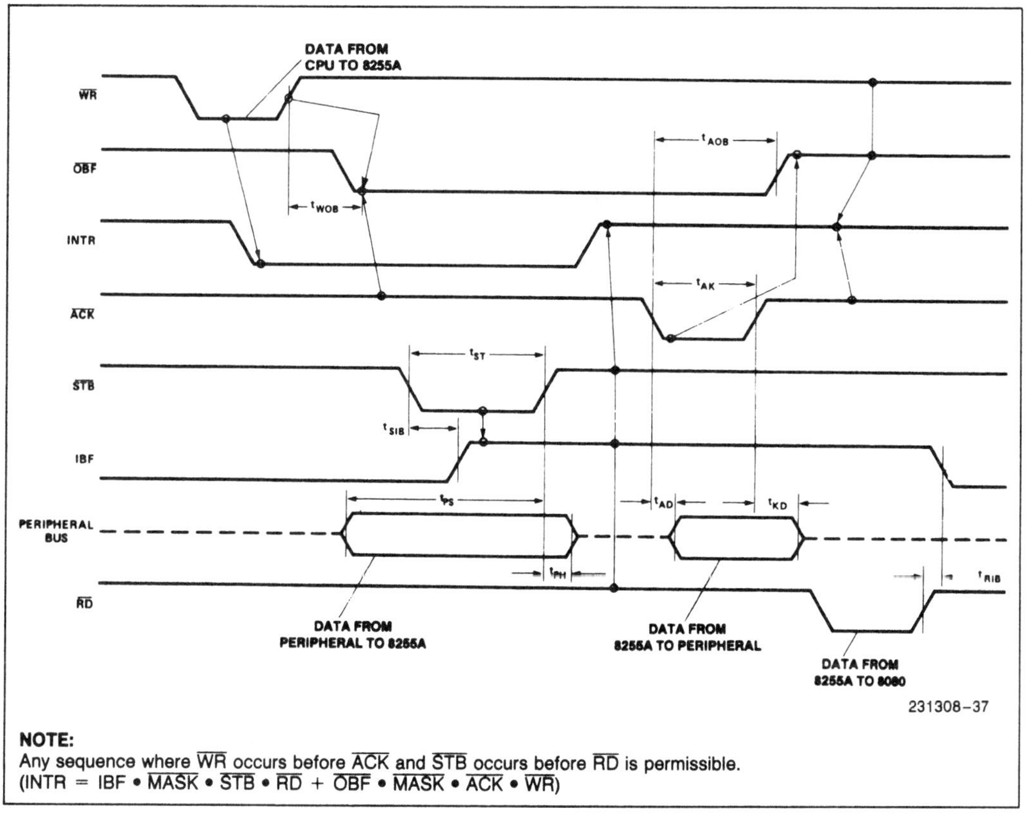

Note the two interrupt enables: INTE 1 associated with $\overline{OBF}$ (output buffer full) and INTE 2 associated with IBF (input buffer full). INTE 1 can be enabled/disabled (set/reset) by using a bit set command to PC6. Likewise, INTE 2 can be enabled/disabled by a bit set command to PC4.

Mode 2 affects port A only. Figure 10.9a shows that the mode 2 control word allows port B to be configured into either mode 0 or mode 1 independent of port A. Note that if mode 0 is selected for port B, then port C bits 0, 1, and 2 can be

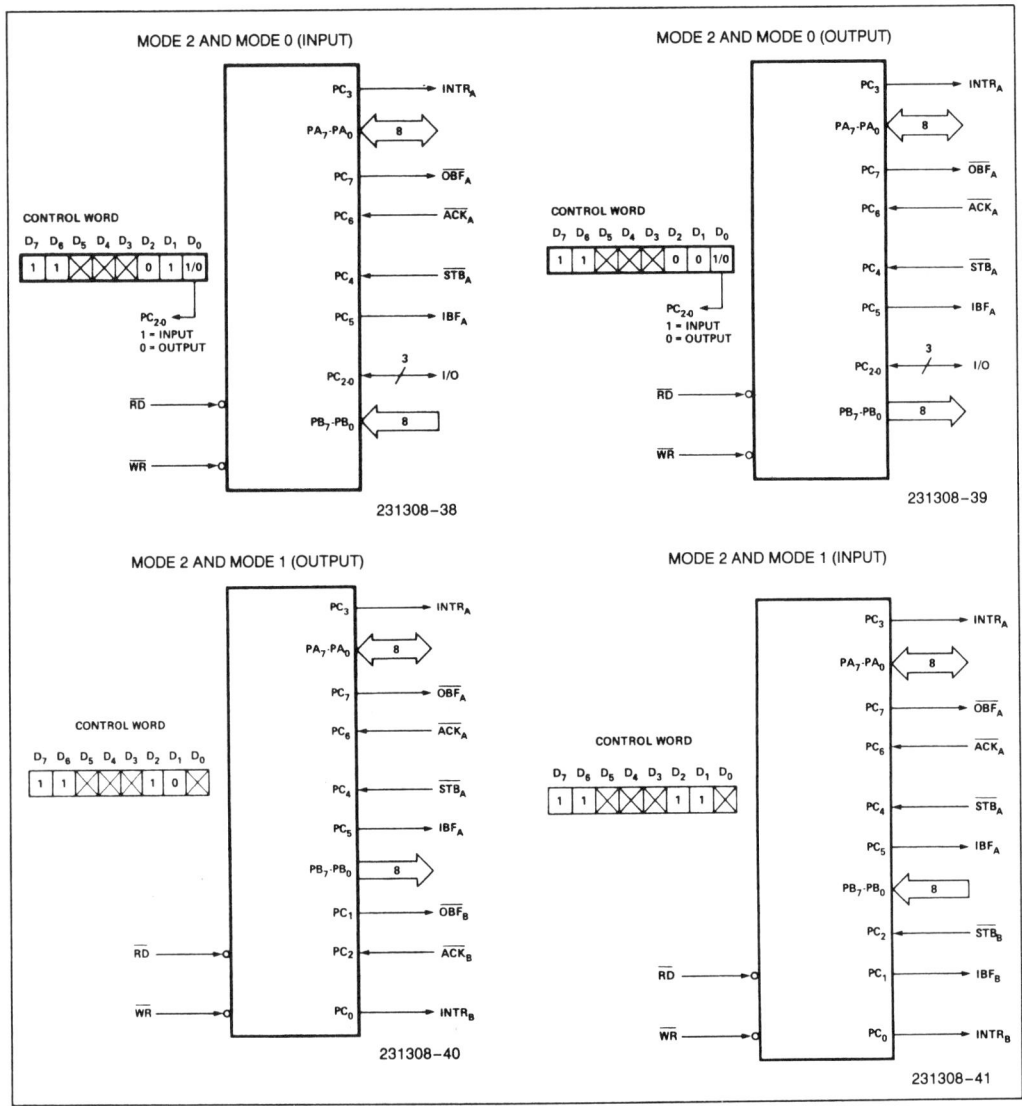

Figure 10.10 Mode 1/4 combinations. (*Source:* Reprinted by permission of Intel Corporation, Copyright © Intel Corporation 1987.)

used for I/O. The direction is selected by D0 of the control word. If mode 1 is selected for port B, then PC0, PC1, and PC2 are used for handshaking and D0 of the control word becomes a don't care. Figure 10.10 shows various modes of port B when port A is in mode 2. Note the control words used for configuration.

> **EXAMPLE 10.4 8255 Mode 2 Configuration**
>
> **PROBLEM** In mode 2, configure the 8255 ports as follows:
>
> ```
> A : Input
> B : Mode 0 Output
> C : bits 0, 1, 2 Input
> Interrupts INTE 1 and INTE 2 Enabled
> ```
>
> **SOLUTION** We must get the correct byte in the accumulator and output it to the control word. Mode 2 is found in Fig. 10.9a, where we find that the bits D7 and D6 = 11. The next 3 bits are don't cares, so D5, D4, and D3 = 000. Port B mode 0 is selected by D2 = 0. Port B is made an output by D1 = 0. The unused port C bits (PC2, PC1, PC0) are made inputs by D0 = 1. Putting it all together, the byte we want is 11000001, or C1h. To set the interrupt flags, we must use the bit set command, as described in Example 10.1. The 8085 instructions to implement this configuration are
>
> ```
> MVI   A, 0C1H  ; LOAD THE COMMAND BYTE
> OUT   CWPORT   ; WRITE TO CONTROL WORD
> MVI   A, 0DH   ; SETUP PC6 TO BE A 1
> OUT   CWPORT   ; MAKE INTE_1 = 1
> MVI   A, 09    ; SETUP PC4 TO BE A 1
> OUT   CWPORT   ; MAKE INTE_2 = 1
> ```

10.3 THE 8279 KEYBOARD/DISPLAY INTERFACE

The 8279 is a device for interfacing a CPU to both a keyboard of up to 64 keys and a display of up to 16 characters. The 8279 can also be used with sensor switch input. Like many peripheral devices, the 8279 achieves flexibility by being programmable. Figure 10.11 shows the logic symbol and pin configuration, and Fig. 10.12 is a block diagram of the internal structure.

10.3.1 8279 Bus Connections

The 8279 connects to the system bus through the following pins:

DB0–DB7 Connect to the system data bus. The CPU communicates data and commands to the 8279 through these bidirectional pins.

$\overline{\text{CS}}$ **Chip Select:** Obtained by decoding the appropriate address lines above A0.

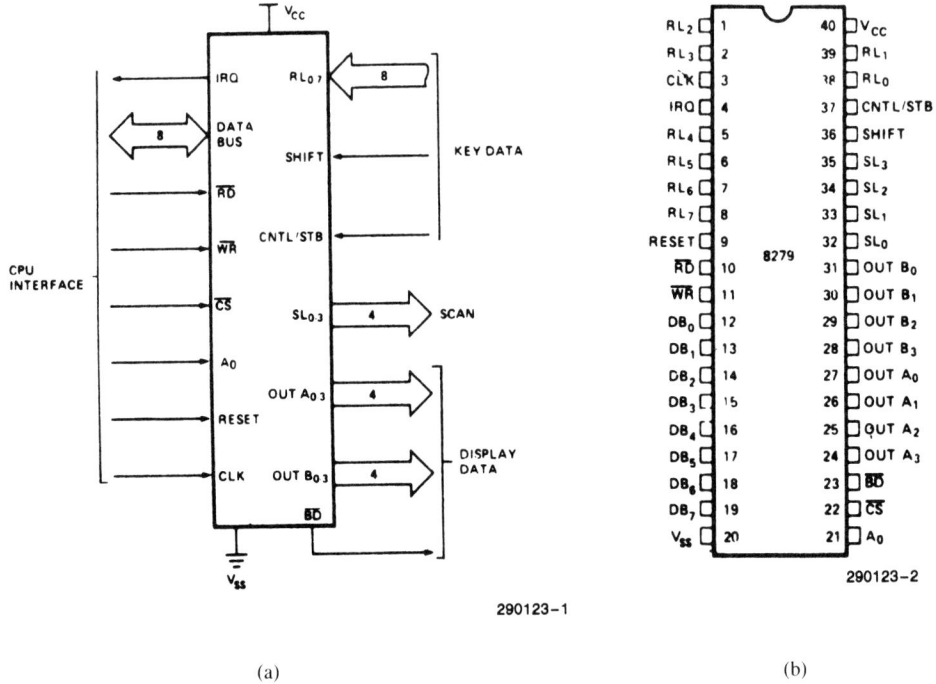

Figure 10.11 8279 interface. (a) Logic symbol. (b) Pin configuration. (*Source:* Reprinted by permission of Intel Corporation, Copyright © Intel Corporation 1987.)

$\overline{RD}$	**Read:** Pulled low by the CPU IOREAD signal to read data from the 8279. IOREAD may have to be derived using a signal such as $IO/\overline{M}$.
$\overline{WR}$	**Write:** Pulled low by the CPU IOWRITE signal to write data or control words to the 8279. IOWRITE may have to be derived using a signal such as $IO/\overline{M}$.
A0	Lowest bit of the address bus. Used to distinguish data words from command words. Bytes written to the 8279 with A0 high are interpreted as commands; bytes read or written with A0 low are data (except when reading status word; see Sec. 10.3.3).
RESET	Sets the 8279 to 16-character left-entry display and encoded scan input with 2-key lockout. Clock prescaler set to 31.
CLOCK	System clock used for internal timing.
IRQ	**Interrupt Request:** Goes high when there are data in the FIFO from a key press. Can be connected to the CPU interrupt line to invoke a service routine.

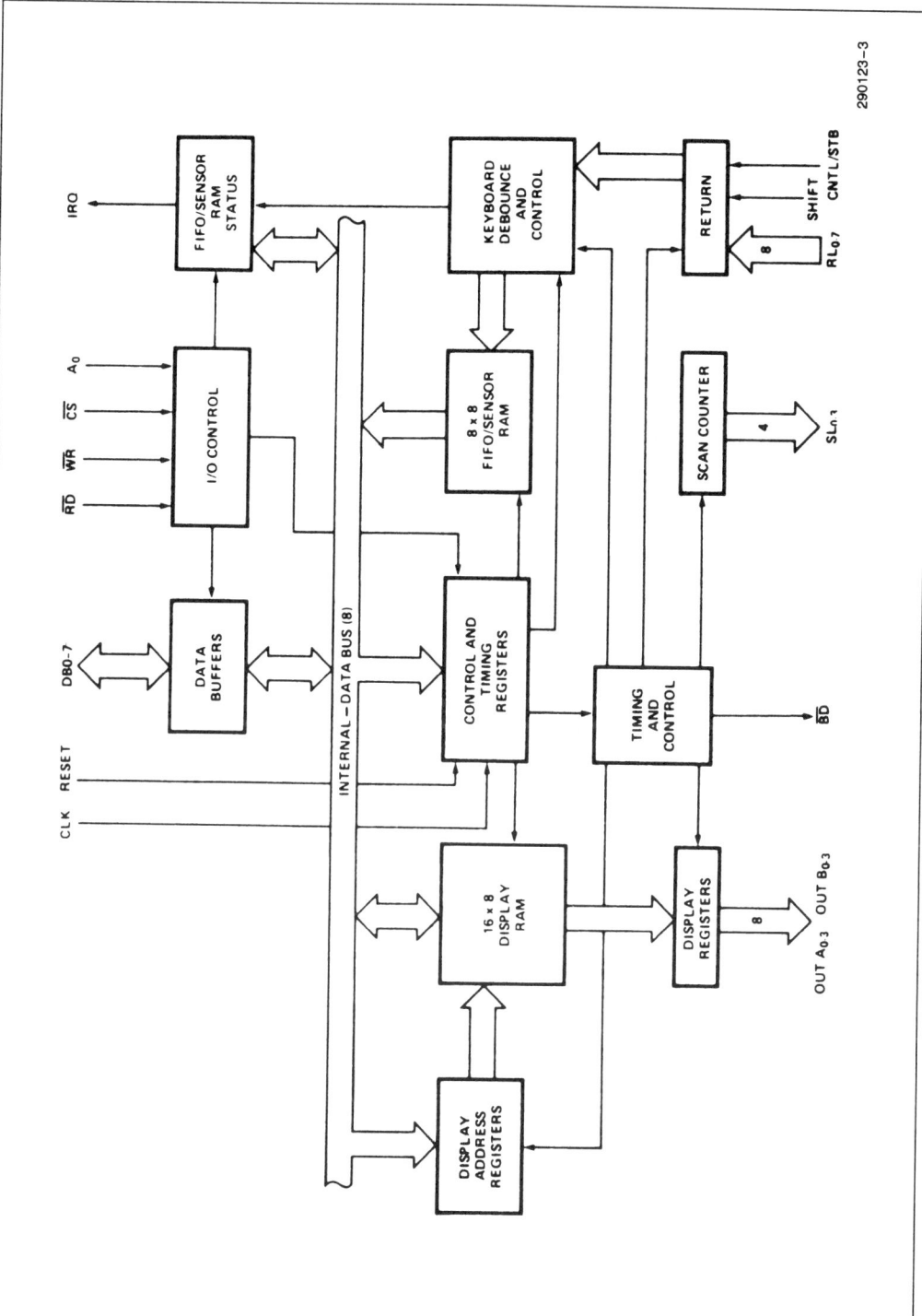

Figure 10.12 Block diagram of internal structure. (*Source*: Reprinted by permission of Intel Corporation, Copyright © Intel Corporation 1987.)

10.3.2 Brief Description of Operation

Figure 10.13 shows a typical 8279 system using a scanned keyboard matrix of 64 keys (8 rows by 8 columns) and a 16-character display. Note that two additional input keys (shift and control) are not scanned but are connected to the 8279 individually.

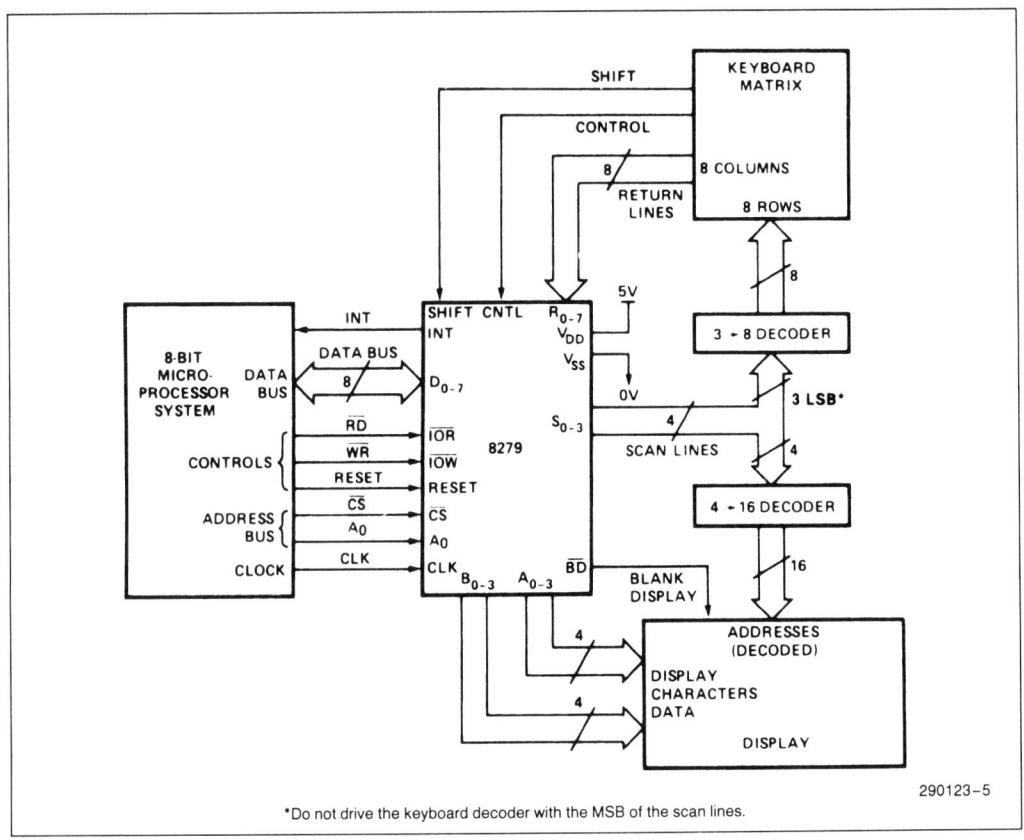

Figure 10.13 System block diagram. (*Source:* Reprinted by permission of Intel Corporation, Copyright © Intel Corporation 1987.)

When one of the keys is pressed, a unique 8-bit number is entered into the 8279's FIFO input buffer and IRQ goes high. Key presses are debounced and accepted by the 8279 with either 2-key *lockout* or N-key *rollover*. If several keys are pressed simultaneously, only the first key pressed is accepted with lockout. With rollover, the key presses are accepted in the order they are scanned. The FIFO can hold up to eight entries, corresponding to eight key presses, before overflow.

In an interrupt-driven system, the CPU will respond to IRQ with a service routine to read the FIFO and send the appropriate character to the 8279 display buffer. In a noninterrupt system, the CPU can periodically check the FIFO status to look for key presses. The 8279 will drive multiplexed seven-segment displays from the contents of the output buffer automatically.

10.3.3 The 8279 Commands and Status

Commands are written to the 8279 with A0 high. The upper 3 bits of the command byte determine the type of command, and the lower 5 bits determine what the command does.

The status byte is read from the 8279 with A0 high; all other data are read with A0 low. The status byte, shown in Fig. 10.14, tells how many characters are in the input FIFO, if the FIFO has overflowed (overrun error), or if an empty FIFO has been read (underrun error). The display unavailable bit indicates that you cannot write to the display buffer because a clear operation is in progress.

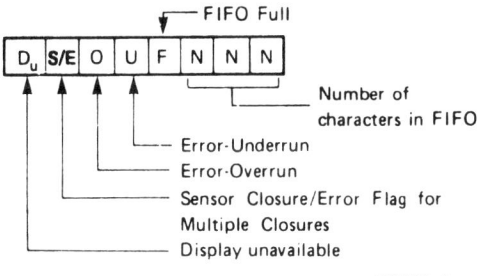

Figure 10.14 FIFO status word. (*Source:* Reprinted by permission of Intel Corporation, Copyright © Intel Corporation 1987.)

EXAMPLE 10.5 8279 Status

PROBLEM
a. How is the status byte read?
b. If the status byte = 85h, what does it mean?

SOLUTION
a. The status byte is read from the command port (let's call it CMNDP), as, for example, with the 8085 instruction IN CMNDP.
b. 85h = 10000101. Referring to Fig. 10.14 and reading the byte left to right, we see that the display is unavailable right now (so don't write to it), there are no multiple closure errors (nobody pressed two keys at once), the FIFO has not overrun or underrun (we've been processing the key presses more or less as they've arrived), the FIFO is not full, and in fact there are five entries in the FIFO.

10.3.4 Keyboard and Display Mode Set

The mode of operation of both the keyboard input and display output must be specified by writing a command in the following format:

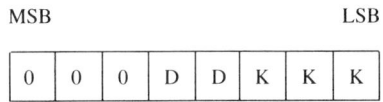

The 2 bits DD select the display mode as follows:

D D DESCRIPTION

0 0 Eight 8-bit characters with left entry
0 1 Sixteen 8-bit characters with left entry (default mode)
1 0 Eight 8-bit characters with right entry
1 1 Sixteen 8-bit characters with right entry

An 8-bit character can correspond to a seven-segment display with a decimal point, although the display device used is up to the user. The terms left entry and right entry correspond to the order in which successive characters appear on the display: from the left side or from the right. An example of right entry is seen on an ordinary hand-held calculator.

The 3 bits KKK select the keyboard mode as follows:

K K K DESCRIPTION

0 0 0 Encoded Scan with 2-Key Lockout   * (reset default mode)
0 0 1 Decoded Scan with 2-Key Lockout   *
0 1 0 Encoded Scan with N-Key Rollover   *
0 1 1 Decoded Scan with N-Key Rollover   *
1 0 0 Encoded Scan Sensor Matrix
1 0 1 Decoded Scan Sensor Matrix
1 1 0 Strobed Input with Encoded Display Scan
1 1 1 Strobed Input with Decoded Display Scan

Note: The first four table entries are scanned keyboard modes. We will not discuss sensor matrix mode; refer to Intel documentation.

EXAMPLE 10.6 8279 Mode Set

PROBLEM Set up the 8279 as follows:

- Displays : eight 8-bit characters, right entry
- Keyboard: N-key rollover
- Scan   : encoded

SOLUTION We must get the correct byte in the accumulator and output it to the command port. Using the information given in Sec. 10.3.4, we see that the lower 3 bits (KKK) determine both keyboard entry format (lockout vs. rollover) and scan mode (encoded/decoded). The value of KKK for this problem is found to be 010. The next 2 bits (DD) determine the display mode. For this problem the value is found to be 10. The upper 3 bits for mode set are always 000. Putting it all together, we see that the command byte is 00010010, or 12h. The 8085 instructions to set this mode are

```
MVI  A, 12H  ; LOAD THE COMMAND BYTE
OUT  CMNDP   ; SEND IT TO THE COMMAND PORT
```

10.3.5 The Clock Prescaler

The multiplex timing of the 8279 is derived from the clock on pin 3 (often the system clock) by means of an internal prescaler. The program sets the prescale value with the following command:

MSB   LSB

| 0 | 0 | 1 | P | P | P | P | P |

The bits PPPPP specify a divisor in the range of 1 to 31. The value used should produce a result close to 100 kHz when divided into the clock frequency.

EXAMPLE 10.7 Setting the 8279 Clock Prescaler

PROBLEM Pin 3 of the 8279 is being clocked at 2 MHz. Set up the prescaler.

SOLUTION Use the equation $N = F/(100,000)$, where F is the 8279 clock frequency and N is rounded off to an integer in the range 1–31. Convert N to a 5-bit binary number PPPPP and embed it in the command byte as 001PPPPP. In this problem, $N = (2 \times 10^6)/(1 \times 10^5) = 20$. Then 20 converts to binary 10100, so the command byte is 00110100, or 34h. The 8085 instructions to set the prescaler are

```
MVI  A, 34H  ; LOAD THE COMMAND BYTE
OUT  CMNDP   ; SEND IT TO THE COMMAND PORT
```

10.3.6 Reading the FIFO

Because all reads are done through a common port address, the 8279 must first be told what is being read by writing a command. Before the FIFO can be read, the following command must be written:

MSB							LSB
0	1	0	AI	X	A	A	A

X = Don't Care

In the scan keyboard mode, only the first 3 bits count; the rest are don't cares. After this command, all reads will be from the FIFO until a different "read-from" command is written.

EXAMPLE 10.8 Reading the 8279 FIFO

PROBLEM   Get the first 2 bytes out of the FIFO and save them in 8085 registers B and C. The 8279 is in a scan keyboard mode.

SOLUTION   First we write a "read-FIFO" command to the 8279. Then we do two successive data reads. The command byte is 010XXXXX, where the Xs are don't cares, so we will use 01000000, or 40h. The 8085 instructions are

```
MVI   A,40H    ; LOAD THE COMMAND BYTE
OUT   CMNDP    ; SEND IT TO THE COMMAND PORT
IN    DATAP    ; READ 1ST FIFO BYTE FROM DATA PORT
MOV   B,A      ; SAVE IT IN REG_B
IN    DATAP    ; READ 2ND FIFO BYTE FROM DATA PORT
MOV   C,A      ; SAVE IT IN REG_C
```

10.3.7 Reading the Display RAM

Before the display RAM can be read, the following command must be written:

MSB							LSB
0	1	1	AI	A	A	A	A

The address bits AAAA select one of the 16 rows of the display RAM. AI is the auto-increment flag. When AI is set to 1, the row address will be incremented after each read or write. If AI is reset to 0, each read will be from the same address until a command changes AAAA.

EXAMPLE 10.9 Reading the 8279 Display RAM

PROBLEM Get the 2 bytes out of rows 7 and 8 of the display RAM and save them in 8085 registers B and C.

SOLUTION First we write a "read-display-RAM" command to the 8279. We will use auto-increment mode and do two successive data reads. The upper 3 bits of the command byte are 011, followed by the AI bit set to 1 for auto-increment. The last 4 bits are the starting address and for row 7 should be 0111. Putting it all together, the command byte is 01110111, or 77h. The 8085 instructions are

```
MVI  A,77H   ; LOAD THE COMMAND BYTE
OUT  CMNDP   ; SEND IT TO THE COMMAND PORT
IN   DATAP   ; READ 1ST RAM BYTE FROM DATA PORT
MOV  B,A     ; SAVE IT IN REG_B
IN   DATAP   ; READ 2ND RAM BYTE FROM DATA PORT
MOV  C,A     ; SAVE IT IN REG_C
```

10.3.8 Writing the Display RAM

Before writing data to the display RAM, the following command must be written:

MSB							LSB
1	0	0	AI	A	A	A	A

The functions of AI and AAAA are the same as for reading the display RAM.

EXAMPLE 10.10 Writing the 8279 Display RAM

PROBLEM Using HL as a pointer, get 16 bytes from 8085 memory starting at location 1000h and write them to the 8279 display RAM.

SOLUTION First we write a "write-display-RAM" command to the 8279. We will use auto-increment mode and do 16 successive data writes. The upper 3 bits of the command byte are 100, followed by the AI bit set to 1 for auto-increment. The last 4 bits are the starting address. We will start at row 0, so AAAA will be 0000. Putting it all together, the command byte is 10010000, or 90h. The 8085 instructions are

```
        MVI  A,90H    ; LOAD THE COMMAND BYTE
        OUT  CMNDP    ; SEND IT TO THE COMMAND PORT
        LXI  H,1000H  ; SET UP POINTER
        MVI  B,16     ; SET UP LOOP COUNTER
LOOP:   MOV  A,M      ; GET A CHARACTER
        OUT  DATAP    ; WRITE CHAR TO DATA PORT
        INX  H        ; INCREMENT POINTER
        DCR  B        ; DECREMENT LOOP COUNTER
        JNZ  LOOP     ; REPEAT 16 TIMES
```

10.3.9 Display Write Inhibit/Blanking

```
MSB              A    B    A    B
| 1 | 0 | 1 | X | IW | IW | BL | BL |
```

The 8-bit display output is divided into two 4-bit ports: A and B. It is possible to connect both of the 4-bit ports to BCD decoders, in which case it is often desirable to be able to write a byte to the display RAM and change only one BCD display. By setting the appropriate IW bit to 1, the corresponding port output is frozen, and subsequent writes to the display RAM will not affect it.

Normally, anything written to the display RAM will be displayed. If the user wants a certain bit combination to be interpreted as a blank (i.e., not displayed), then the BL flag must be set to 1. For 8-bit displays, both BL flags must be set. The bit combination used for the blank character is selected with the clear command.

Note that pin 23 of the 8279 is the $\overline{BD}$ (blank display) output. It is used to disable the display driver during blanking. $\overline{BD}$ also blanks the display during digit switching irrespective of BL.

10.3.10 The Clear Command

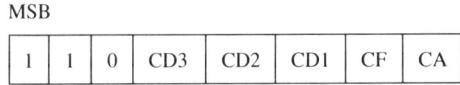

The bit combination used to represent the blank character is selected by CD2 and CD1 as follows:

CD2	CD1	Blanking Code	Display Size
0	X	All zeros (X = don't care)	4-bit or 8-bit
1	0	ASCII blank (20h = 00100000)	8-bit only
1	1	All ones	4-bit or 8-bit

On power up or after a system reset, the default blanking code is all zeros. When the command is written with CD3 set, all rows in the display RAM will be cleared to the blanking code selected. However, the display will not be blanked unless the BL flags were set, as discussed previously.

When the command is written with CF set to 1, the FIFO status is cleared, meaning that whatever was in the FIFO is lost. Writing the command with CA set is equivalent to having both CD3 and CF set.

> **EXAMPLE 10.11 Selecting an 8279 Blank Character**
>
> **PROBLEM** Set up the 8279 so that ASCII blank (20h) will appear as a blank on the display. Also, initialize the display to all blanks but save the FIFO contents.
>
> **SOLUTION** We must use both the display write blanking command and the clear command. First, we will build the blanking command. The upper 3 bits are 101 followed by a don't care, so we have 1010 so far. Because ASCII characters are 7 bits, we can assume that the displays are being driven by both of the 8279 4-bit display ports and the IW bits should be 00. Likewise, to allow blanking, the BL bits are 11. Putting it together, we have 10100011, or A3h, for the first command. For the clear command, the upper 3 bits are 110. CD3 controls the display RAM, and is 1 to blank the display. CD2 and CD1 select the blank char, and are 10 for ASCII blank. To save the FIFO, CF is 0 and CA is 0. Putting it together, we have 11011000, or D8h, as the second command. The 8085 instructions are
>
> ```
>         MVI   A,0A3H  ; BLANKING ENABLED
>         OUT   CMNDP   ; SEND TO COMMAND PORT
>         MVI   A,0D8H  ; SELECT BLANKING
>         OUT   CMNDP   ; SEND TO COMMAND PORT
> ```

10.3.11 The Scan Lines

The 8279 uses the four scan lines SL0–SL3 both to scan the keyboard and multiplex the displays. The scan lines operate in one of two modes as selected by the mode set command: encoded or decoded.

In encoded mode, the scan lines are active high and provide a binary count that must be decoded externally, as shown in Fig. 10.13. In decoded mode, the scan lines are active-low and provide a 1-out-of-4 scan. Note that in decoded mode only the first four entries in the display RAM can be displayed.

10.3.12 Keyboard Data Format

In scanned keyboard mode, each key press enters a byte into the FIFO with the following format:

MSB							
CNTL	SHIFT	SB2	SB1	SB0	RB2	RB1	RB0

The first 2 bits are the status of the CNTL (control) and SHIFT lines. The next 3 bits (SB2–SB0) are the scan line count and indicate which row the key was in. The last 3 bits (RB2–RB0) tell the number of the active return line and indicate which column the key was in.

Every character on the keyboard has a unique combination of row number and column number. Which character corresponds to what combination is determined by the system hardware designer.

In strobed input mode, an 8-bit number is entered into the FIFO from the return lines by a rising edge on the STB line (CNTL does double duty as STB). The format is

Strobed input mode is useful for interfacing to encoded keyboards, switch matrices, or even something like an A/D converter.

EXAMPLE 10.12 8279 Scanned Keyboard Data

PROBLEM A certain keyboard has the letter C in row 4, column 3. What will the FIFO entries be for the following:

- Lowercase C
- Uppercase C
- Control C

SOLUTION The lower 3 bits of a FIFO entry represent the column the key was in, and in this case they are 011. The next 3 bits represent the row of the key and in this case they are 100. So all three answers will be in the form CS100011, where C = 1 if the control key is pressed and S = 1 if the shift key is pressed. Thus, we get

- Lowercase C has FIFO entry 00100011 (23h).
- Uppercase C has FIFO entry 01100011 (63h).
- Control C has FIFO entry 10100011 (A3h).

10.3.13 Display Entry

Initially, display RAM address 0 corresponds to the leftmost display position, and address 15 (address 7 in an 8-character display) is the rightmost display position.

In left-entry mode, the correspondence between address and position is maintained. Writing data to the display RAM with auto-increment causes no surprises, as is shown in Fig. 10.15a. In right-entry mode, the relationship between address and position rotates, as shown in Fig. 10.15b. Right-entry mode with auto-increment should always be sequential from address 0 to avoid confusion.

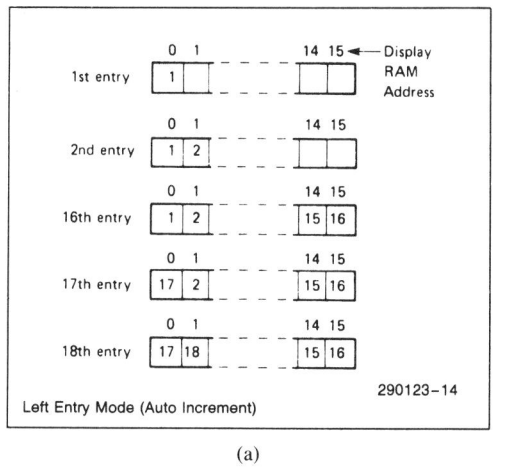
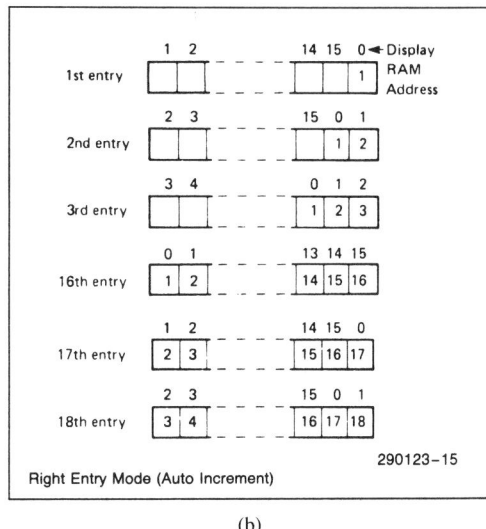

Figure 10.15 (a) Right-entry mode (auto-increment). (b) Left-entry mode (auto-increment). (*Source:* Reprinted by permission of Intel Corporation, Copyright © Intel Corporation 1987.)

10.4 THE LTC1091 DATA ACQUISITION CHIP

The Linear Technology Corporation LTC109X family of data acquisition chips is a good example of a modern high-performance programmable device designed for use with a variety of microprocessors. The family includes 1, 2, 6, and 8-channel, 10-bit A/D converters with on-chip sample and holds (S&H). Inputs can be unipolar (0 to +V) or bipolar (−V to +V), single-ended (input to ground) or differential (+ input to − input). Conversion time is typically 20 μsec with an error of ±1/2 LSB. Data and commands are exchanged with the microprocessor over a synchronous, half-duplex, serial interface.

The device we will examine is the 2-channel, unipolar LTC1091. Its pin configuration is shown in Fig. 10.16 and its pin functions are shown in Fig. 10.17.

10.4.1 The Serial Interface

To interface to the LTC1091 the MPU must have some I/O lines available. Devices such as the 8051 have built-in lines, whereas devices such as the Z80 require additional hardware, such as an 8255. Four LTC1091 pins are used to talk to the MPU: $\overline{CS}$ (chip select), CLK (shift clock), Dout (data out), and Din (data in).

Commands from the MPU are shifted into the LTC1091 over Din, and data from the LTC1091 are shifted back to the MPU over Dout. Because operation is half duplex, Din and Dout can be tied together, assuming that the MPU can use the

ABSOLUTE MAXIMUM RATINGS

(Notes 1 and 2)

Supply Voltage (V_{CC}) to GND or V^- 12V
Negative Supply Voltage (V^-) .... –6V to GND
Voltage
  Analog Reference and LTC1091/2 $\overline{CS}$
  Inputs .... (V^-) – 0.3V to V_{CC} + 0.3V
  Digital Inputs (except LTC1091/2 $\overline{CS}$) ..... –0.3V to 12V
  Digital Outputs .... –0.3V to V_{CC} + 0.3V

Power Dissipation 500mW
Operating Temperature Range
  LTC1091-4AC, LTC1091-4C .... –40°C to 85°C
  LTC1091-4AM, LTC1091-4M .... –55°C to 125°C
Storage Temperature Range .... –65°C to 150°C
Lead Temperature (Soldering, 10 sec.) .... 300°C

PACKAGE/ORDER INFORMATION

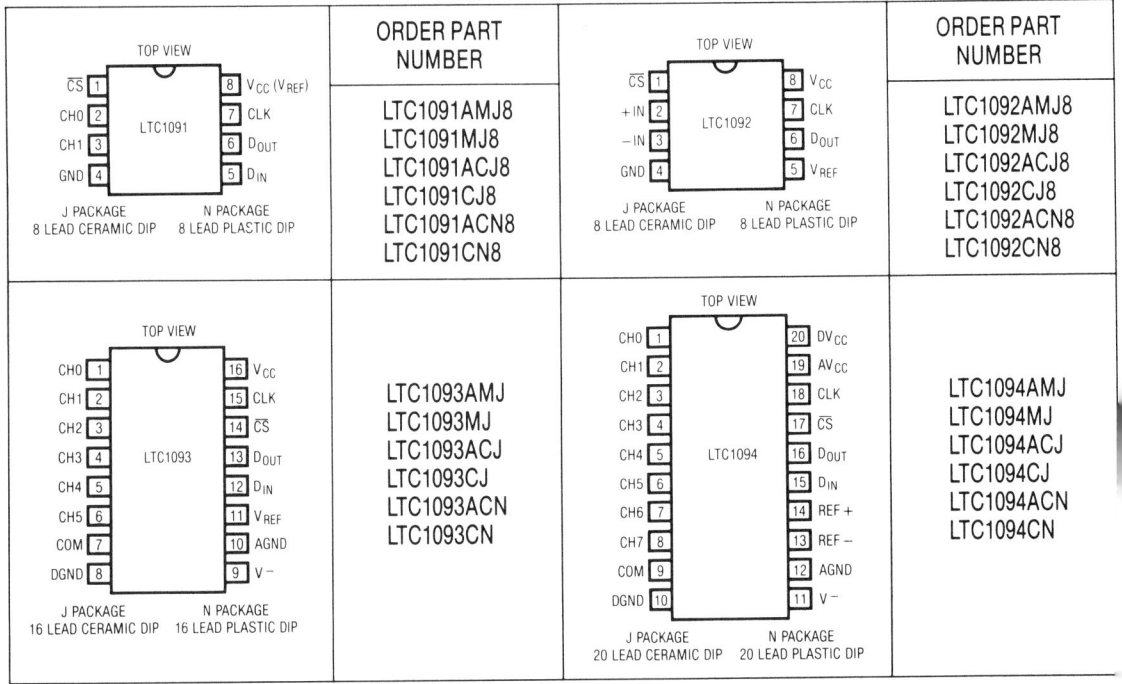

PRODUCT GUIDE

PART NUMBER	# CHANNELS	CONVERSION MODES		REDUCED SPAN CAPABILITY (SEPARATE V_{REF})	±5V CAPABILITY	
		UNIPOLAR	BIPOLAR			
LTC1091	2	●				Pin for pin 10-bit upgrade of ADC083
LTC1092	1	●		●		Pin for pin 10-bit upgrade of ADC083
LTC1093	6	●	●	●	●	
LTC1094	8	●	●	●	●	

Figure 10.16 Pin configuration of the 2-channel, unipolar LTC1091. (*Source:* Courtesy of Linear Technology Corp. Milpitas, CA.)

PIN FUNCTIONS LTC1091/2

LTC1091 #	LTC1092 #	PIN	FUNCTION	DESCRIPTION
1	1	$\overline{CS}$	Chip Select Input	A logic low on this input enables the LTC1091/2.
2, 3		CH0, CH1	Analog Inputs	These inputs must be free of noise with respect to GND.
	2, 3	IN+, IN−	Analog Inputs	These inputs must be free of noise with respect to GND.
4	4	GND	Analog Ground	GND should be tied directly to an analog ground plane.
5		D_{IN}	Digital Data Input	The multiplexer address is shifted into this input.
	5	V_{REF}	Reference Input	The reference input defines the span of the A/D converter and must be kept free of noise with respect to AGND.
6	6	D_{OUT}	Digital Data Output	The A/D conversion result is shifted out of this output.
7	7	CLK	Shift Clock	This clock synchronizes the serial data transfer.
8		V_{CC} (V_{REF})	Positive Supply and Reference Voltage	This pin provides power and defines the span of the A/D converter. It must be kept free of noise and ripple by bypassing directly to the analog ground plane.
	8	V_{CC}	Positive Supply Voltage	This pin provides power to the A/D converter. It must be kept free of noise and ripple by bypassing directly to the analog ground plane.

Figure 10.17 Pin functions of the 2-channel, unipolar LTC1091. (*Source:* Courtesy of Linear Technology Corp. Milpitas, CA.)

same line for both input and output. Bits are sent on the falling edge of CLK and received on the rising edge of CLK.

10.4.2 The Command/Data Exchange

Serial transfer is initiated when $\overline{CS}$ goes low, after which the LTC1091 looks for a start bit on Din. The start bit is active-high, and all leading zeros are ignored. After the start bit, a 3-bit command is sent to configure the LTC1091 and start the conversion.

After one null bit (one pulse on CLK with no serial transfer) the result of the conversion is shifted out Dout. At the end of the data, $\overline{CS}$ should be brought high to reset the LTC1091 for the next conversion.

Note that each conversion is a command/data exchange, as shown in Fig. 10.18.

10.4.3 Command Word

The 3-bit command word sent to the LTC1091 has the following format:

SGL/DIFF	ODD/SIGN	MSBF

SGL/DIFF When this bit is a 1, single-ended operation is selected and the selected input is with respect to ground. When this bit is a 0, differential operation is selected and the selected input is with respect to the other input.

ODD/SIGN When this bit is a 0, CH0 is the selected input. When this bit is a 1, CH1 is the selected input.

MSBF When this bit is a 1, data appear on Dout MSB first. After the LSB appears, zeros will be sent until $\overline{CS}$ goes high. When this bit is a 0, data will appear on Dout MSB first, but after the LSB, the data will be repeated LSB first followed by zeros until $\overline{CS}$ goes high. Refer to Fig. 10.18.

10.4.4 An 8051 Interface Example

Figure 10.19, taken from the Linear Technology Corporation applications manual, shows the connections and software to interface the LTC1091 to the Intel 8051.

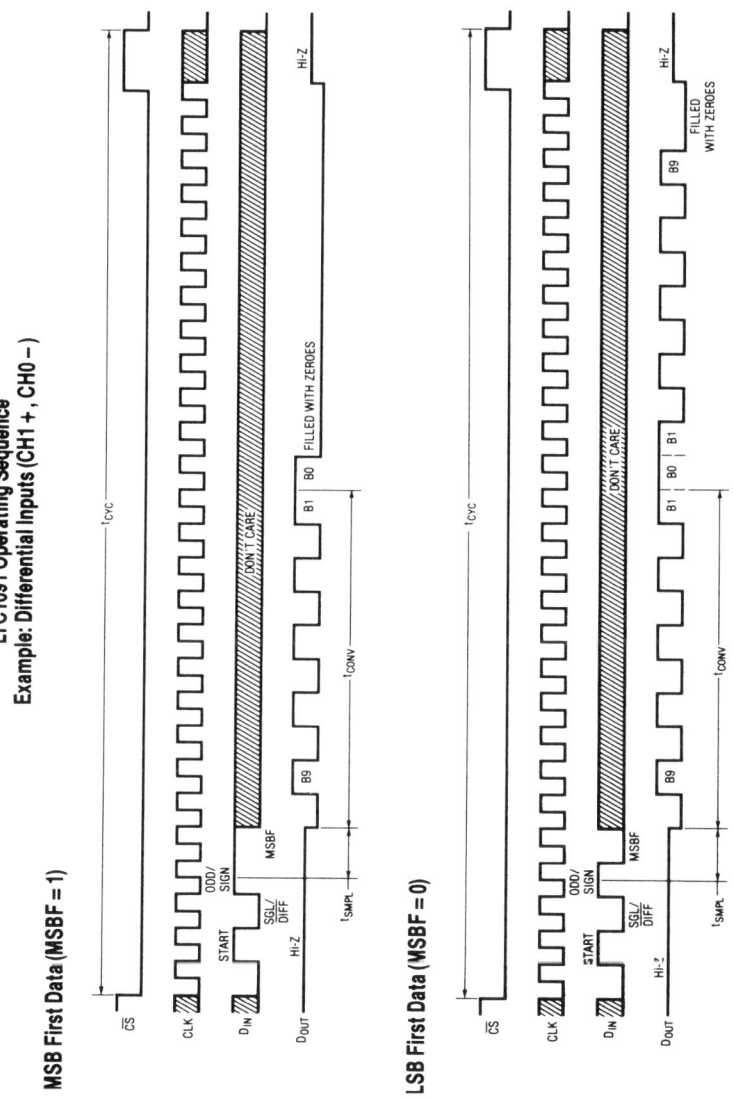

Figure 10.18 Command/data exchange. (*Source*: Courtesy of Liner Technology Corp. Milpitas, CA.)

LTC1091/LTC1092
LTC1093/LTC1094

APPLICATIONS INFORMATION

Interfacing to the Parallel Port of the Intel 8051 Family

The Intel 8051 has been chosen to demonstrate the interface between the LTC1091 and parallel port microprocessors. Normally the $\overline{CS}$, SCLK and D_{IN} signals would be generated on 3 port lines and the D_{OUT} signal read on a 4th port line. This works very well. However, we will demonstrate here an interface with the D_{IN} and D_{OUT} of the LTC1091 tied together as described in section 4. This saves one wire.

The 8051 first sends the start bit and MUX address to the LTC1091 over the data line connected to P1.2. Then P1.2 is reconfigured as an input (by writing to it a one) and the 8051 reads back the 10-bit A/D result over the same data line.

LABEL	MNEMONIC	OPERAND	COMMENTS
	MOV	A, #FFH	D_{IN} word for LTC1091
	SETB	P1.4	Make sure $\overline{CS}$ is high
	CLR	P1.4	$\overline{CS}$ goes low
	MOV	R4, #04	Load counter
LOOP 1	RLC	A	Rotate D_{IN} bit into Carry
	CLR	P1.3	SCLK goes low
	MOV	P1.2, C	Output D_{IN} bit to LTC1091
	SETB	P1.3	SCLK goes high
	DJNZ	R4, LOOP 1	Next bit
	MOV	P1, #04	Bit 2 becomes an input
	CLR	P1.3	SCLK goes low
	MOV	R4, #09	Load counter
LOOP	MOV	C, P1.2	Read data bit into Carry
	RLC	A	Rotate data bit into Acc.
	SETB	P1.3	SCLK goes high
	CLR	P1.3	SCLK goes low
	DJNZ	R4, LOOP	Next bit
	MOV	R2, A	Store MSBs in R2
	MOV	C, P1.2	Read data bit into Carry
	SETB	P1.3	SCLK goes high
	CLR	P1.3	SCLK goes low
	CLR	A	Clear Acc.
	RLC	A	Rotate data bit from Carry to Acc.
	MOV	C, P1.2	Read data bit into Carry
	RRC	A	Rotate right into Acc.
	RRC	A	Rotate right into Acc.
	MOV	R3, A	Store LSBs in R3
	SETB	P1.4	$\overline{CS}$ goes high

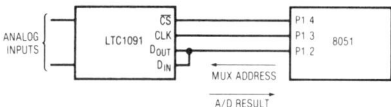

D_{OUT} from LTC1091 stored in 8051 RAM

	MSB							
R2	B9	B8	B7	B6	B5	B4	B3	B2
	LSB							
R3	B1	B0	0	0	0	0	0	0

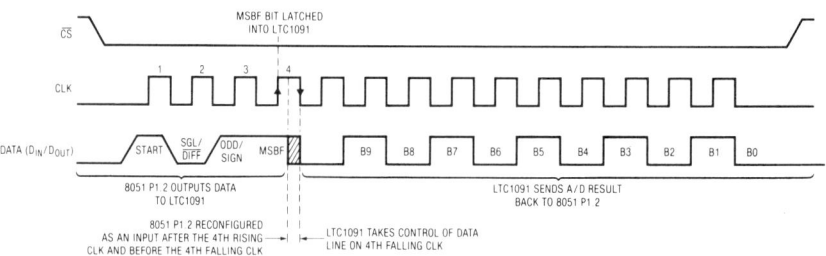

Figure 10.19 Interfacing of the LTC1091 to the Intel 8051. (*Source:* Courtesy of Linear Technology Corp. Milpitas, CA.)

10.5 THE 8251A PROGRAMMABLE USART

The 8251, which Intel calls a programmable communication interface, is a *universal synchronous/asynchronous receiver/transmitter* (USART). The pin configuration and block diagram are shown in Fig. 10.20.

10.5.1 8251A Bus Connections

The 8251 connects to the system bus through the following pins:

D0–D7 **Data:** Connect to the system data bus. The CPU communicates to the 8251 through these bidirectional pins.

$\overline{\text{CS}}$ **Chip Select:** Obtained by decoding the appropriate address lines other than the one used for C/D (see below).

$\overline{\text{RD}}$ **Read:** Pulled low by the CPU IOREAD signal to read data from the 8251. IOREAD may have to be derived using a signal such as IO/$\overline{\text{M}}$.

$\overline{\text{WR}}$ **Write:** Pulled low by the CPU IOWRITE signal to write data or control words to the 8251. IOWRITE may have to be derived using a signal such as IO/$\overline{\text{M}}$.

C/D **Control/Data:** Connect to an address line. C/D = 1 when reading status or writing commands to the 8251. C/D = 0 when reading or writing data.

RE-SET A high on RESET puts the 8251 into *idle* mode. The clock (CLK) must be running, and RESET must be high for six clock periods to effect a reset.

CLK **Clock:** Used for internal timing. Must be a TTL level signal in the frequency range 750 kHz to 3.1 MHz. Can be connected to the CLK output of 8085 or another source.

Note that the 8251 CLK frequency must be higher than the data clock frequencies (T×C and R×C) by a multiplier that depends on the *baud rate factor* selected by the mode command (described in Sec. 10.5.8). If the baud rate factor is 1×, then the multiplier must be at least 30. If the baud rate factor is 16× or 64×, the multiplier must be at least 5. For example, if T×C and R×C are both 4800 Hz and 16× mode is selected, then CLK should be at least 24,000 Hz. If 1× mode was selected, CLK would have to be at least 144,000 Hz. If the baud rate factor can change, use the higher CLK frequency. Note that synchronous mode is a 1× mode.

10.5.2 What Is a USART

Basically, a USART is a device that accepts parallel data from the CPU and converts the data to a serial data stream. It will also accept serial data as input and convert the data to parallel data to be read by the CPU. Because it can both send and receive data, a USART is said to operate in a *duplex* mode. Sending and re-

8251A
PROGRAMMABLE COMMUNICATION INTERFACE

- Synchronous and Asynchronous Operation
- Synchronous 5–8 Bit Characters; Internal or External Character Synchronization; Automatic Sync Insertion
- Asynchronous 5–8 Bit Characters; Clock Rate—1, 16 or 64 Times Baud Rate; Break Character Generation; 1, 1½, or 2 Stop Bits; False Start Bit Detection; Automatic Break Detect and Handling
- Synchronous Baud Rate—DC to 64K Baud
- Asynchronous Baud Rate—DC to 19.2K Baud
- Full-Duplex, Double-Buffered Transmitter and Receiver
- Error Detection—Parity, Overrun and Framing
- Compatible with an Extended Range of Intel Microprocessors
- 28-Pin DIP Package
- All Inputs and Outputs are TTL Compatible
- Available in EXPRESS
  —Standard Temperature Range
  —Extended Temperature Range

The Intel® 8251A is the enhanced version of the industry standard, Intel 8251 Universal Synchronous/Asynchronous Receiver/Transmitter (USART), designed for data communications with Intel's microprocessor families such as MCS-48, 80, 85, and iAPX-86, 88. The 8251A is used as a peripheral device and is programmed by the CPU to operate using virtually any serial data transmission technique presently in use (including IBM "bi-sync"). The USART accepts data characters from the CPU in parallel format and then converts them into a continuous serial data stream for transmission. Simultaneously, it can receive serial data streams and convert them into parallel data characters for the CPU. The USART will signal the CPU whenever it can accept a new character for transmission or whenever it has received a character for the CPU. The CPU can read the complete status of the USART at any time. These include data transmission errors and control signals such as SYNDET, TxEMPTY. The chip is fabricated using N-channel silicon gate technology.

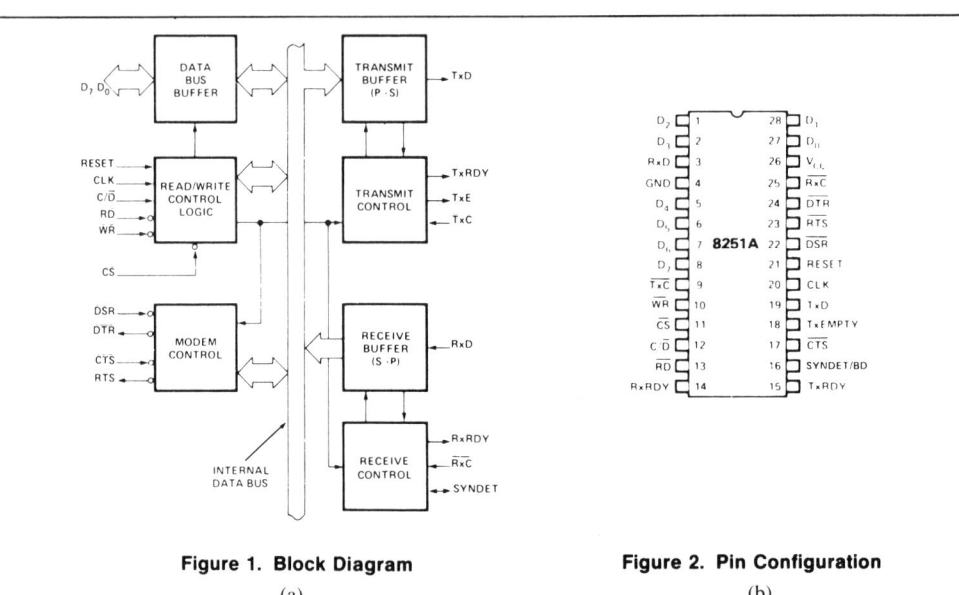

Figure 1. Block Diagram
(a)

Figure 2. Pin Configuration
(b)

Figure 10.20 USART. (a) Block diagram. (b) Pin configuration. (*Source:* Reprinted by permission of Intel Corporation, Copyright © Intel Corporation 1987.)

ceiving simultaneously is called *full duplex* (FDX). Alternating between sending and receiving is called *half duplex* (HDX).

Although the data being sent and received could be just arbitrary binary numbers, they are more likely to be code characters. The two most common codes are ASCII (American Standard Code for Information Interchange) and IBM's EBCDIC (Extended Binary Coded Decimal Interchange Code). As shown in appendix F, ASCII is a 7-bit code of 128 characters; EBCDIC is an 8-bit code of 256 characters.

10.5.3 Asynchronous Data

Asynchronous data communications equipment goes back to the teletypewriter machines developed at the end of the nineteenth century. In such machines, characters were represented by fixed length *frames,* where each frame held one character as a sequence of *marks* and *spaces* (i.e., 1s and 0s: the serial bits). The frames were generated as someone typed at a keyboard. The term *asynchronous* refers to the fact that while the bits per second (bps) of a frame was fixed, the time between frames could vary. A *start bit* (always a 0) is used to identify the beginning of an asynch frame and a *stop bit* (always a 1) is used at the end. The start and stop bits are called *framing bits* and are added by the USART during transmission and are removed by the USART at reception.

When configuring a USART for asynchronous operation, you must tell it how many data bits you want after the start bit (choices are 5, 6, 7, or 8), whether or not you want to use parity, whether parity is odd or even, and how many stop bits you want (1, 1.5, or 2). The sequence of bits as they are sent out the USART is start bit, data bits (LSB first), parity bit (if used), and stop bit (or bits). See Fig. 10.21.

In turn, the USART will tell you (through status bits) if a receiving error has occurred due to parity (didn't agree with data), framing (didn't get the right *number* of bits), or overrun (a second frame arrived before the first frame was read by the CPU). The 8251A asynchronous baud rate is from 0 to 19,200 bps.

10.5.4 Synchronous Data

Synchronous data communication does not use individual frames. Blocks of characters are sent and received as one long continuous bit stream. Because synchronous transmission does not use start and stop bits, it is more efficient, as virtually all the bits sent are data. However, the receiver has the problem of determining which is the first bit of the first data character. After that, it just counts bits. For example, it would count off 8 bits per EBCDIC character.

In order to achieve initial synchronization, the transmitter sends a series of SYN characters (16h in ASCII, 32h in EBCDIC) prior to sending data. In *hunt* mode, the receiver shifts the data in and looks for SYN. If it doesn't find it, it shifts in another bit and looks again. The effect is like a ''moving window'' sliding across the bit stream until a SYN is found. If it receives a SYN, it knows it is synchronized to the transmitter and reports it to the CPU on an output pin (SYNDET

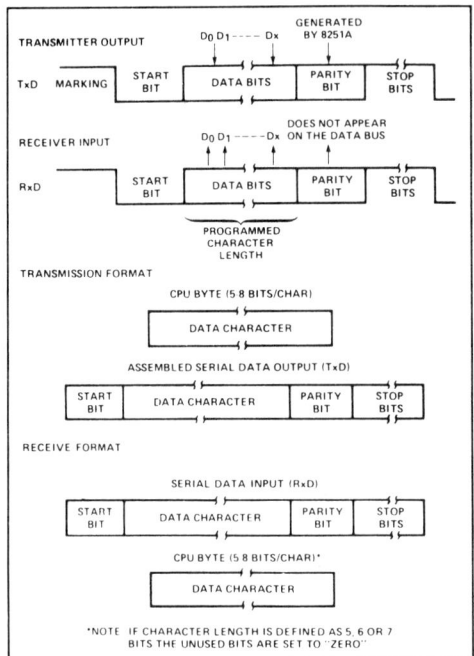

Figure 10.21 Asynchronous mode. (*Source:* Reprinted by permission of Intel Corporation, Copyright © Intel Corporation 1987.)

in the 8251A). Often it wants to see two consecutive SYNs before reporting synchronization. After that, the first character it sees that is not a SYN is the start of the data. During transmission, if the CPU does not supply a character, the USART will automatically send a SYN. The 8251A synchronous baud rate is from 0 to 64,000 bps.

10.5.5 T×D, R×D, and MODEM Control Lines

USARTs usually interface to the outside world through an RS-232 connection, and the outside world is often a modem. The 8251 has the following connections to facilitate an RS-232 interface:

T×D   **Transmit Data:** The serial data out of the USART, normally connected to the Rs-232 line through an inverting line driver (which converts TTL levels to RS-232 levels). T×D stays high (said to be "marking") when there are no data to send or when in an idle state after reset. Can be forced low by a break command.

R×D   **Receive Data:** The serial data into the USART, normally connected to the RS-232 line through an inverting line receiver (which converts RS-232 levels to TTL levels).

$\overline{\text{DSR}}$ **Data Set Ready:** An inverting 1-bit input port (a 0 on the pin is read in as a 1). Normally used to read DSR from a modem through an inverting line receiver.

$\overline{\text{DTR}}$ **Data Terminal Ready:** An inverting 1-bit output port. Normally used to send DTR to a modem through an inverting line driver

$\overline{\text{RTS}}$ **Request to Send:** An inverting 1-bit output port. Normally used to send RTS to a modem through an inverting line driver.

$\overline{\text{CTS}}$ **Clear to Send:** An inverting input. Normally accepts the modem CTS through an inverting line receiver.

> *Note:* $\overline{\text{CTS}}$ must be *low* to enable transmission.

If $\overline{\text{CTS}}$ is high, the 8251 cannot transmit. If $\overline{\text{CTS}}$ goes high while data are being sent, the USART will finish sending what it contains and then stop.

10.5.6 Transmitter Control

The 8251 has 3 pins to allow control of serial data transmission:

T×RDY **Transmitter Ready:** Goes high when the USART transmitter is ready to accept a character. Can be used to generate an interrupt by connecting it to the appropriate CPU pin (e.g., one of the 8085 hardware restart pins). The CPU can mask off T×RDY with the T×EN command bit (see Sec. 10.5.9). For polled operation, the CPU can check T×RDY by reading the 8251 status register (see below). Note that masking off T×RDY does not affect its value in the status register: it can always be polled.

T×E **Transmitter Empty:** Goes high when the USART has no characters in its buffer to send. Note that T×RDY can be high while T×E is low because the 8251 is *double buffered*. While it is sending one character it can accept a second character and hold it until the first is gone. The second character then takes the place of the first and the USART can accept another character (T×RDY goes high). If the first is sent and there is no second character waiting, then T×E goes high.

$\overline{\text{T×C}}$ **Transmitter Clock:** Controls the bits-per-second rate (baud rate) at which data are sent out T×D. In synchronous mode, $\overline{\text{T×C}}$ is 1× the baud rate (i.e., equal to the baud rate). In asynchronous mode, $\overline{\text{T×C}}$ can be 1×, 16×, or 64× the baud rate. For example, assume the baud rate is 300 bps. Then, in 1× mode, $\overline{\text{T×C}}$ must be 300 Hz; in 16× mode, $\overline{\text{T×C}}$ must be 4800 Hz; and in 64× mode, $\overline{\text{T×C}}$ must be 19,200 Hz. $\overline{\text{T×C}}$ must be supplied by an external clock source. Often it is divided down from the system clock, or a special baud rate generator circuit is used with its own crystal-controlled oscillator. Normally, $\overline{\text{T×C}}$ is the same frequency as $\overline{\text{R×C}}$.

10.5.7 Receiver Control

The 8251 has three pins to allow control of serial data reception. The first two are used in both synchronous and asynchronous modes:

R×RDY **Receiver Ready:** Goes high when the USART receiver contains a character. As with T×RDY, R×RDY can be used to generate an interrupt. The CPU can mask off T×RDY with the R×E command bit (see below). For polled operation, the CPU can check R×RDY by reading the 8251 status register (see below). Note that masking off R×RDY with R×E keeps the R×RDY status bit low.

$\overline{R \times C}$ **Receiver Clock:** Controls the bits-per-second rate (baud rate) at which data are read from R×D. In synchronous mode, $\overline{R \times C}$ is 1× the baud rate (i.e., equal to the baud rate). In asynchronous mode, $\overline{R \times C}$ can be 1×, 16×, or 64× the baud rate. (See the discussion of $\overline{T \times C}$.) Normally, $\overline{R \times C}$ is the same frequency as $\overline{T \times C}$, and the two pins can be tied together.

The third pin does double duty. In synchronous mode it is called SYNDET; in asynchronous mode it is called BRKDET.

SYNDET **Sync Detect:** Can be programmed as either an input or an output. As an *output*, it goes high to indicate that the USART has received a SYN character (or two successive SYN characters in bisync mode). Useful for initial data stream synchronization. Also, during data transmission, the sender may insert SYNs into the data stream as a way of "stalling for time." SYNDET allows the receiver software to detect these extra SYNs and disregard them. As an *input*, it is used to tell the USART that it is OK to start accepting data. Configuring SYNDET as an input disables the internal SYN detection.

BRKDET **Break Detect:** If R×D stays low for a time equal to two frames, BRKDET goes high to indicate there is a break in the data link. BRKDET goes low on reset or when T×D returns high.

10.5.8 Mode Selection

After a reset, prior to sending or receiving data, the 8251 must be configured by writing a pair of commands to the control/status port address (C/$\overline{D}$ is a 1). The first command must select either synchronous or asynchronous mode:

Asynchronous Mode is selected when the mode command is as shown in Fig. 10.22. Note that bits in the command word select the baud rate factor, the character length, parity enable, odd/even parity (a don't care if parity is not selected), and the number of stop bits.

Synchronous Mode is selected when the mode command is as shown in Fig. 10.23. Note that the last two bits (D0, D1) must be zeros. Character length and

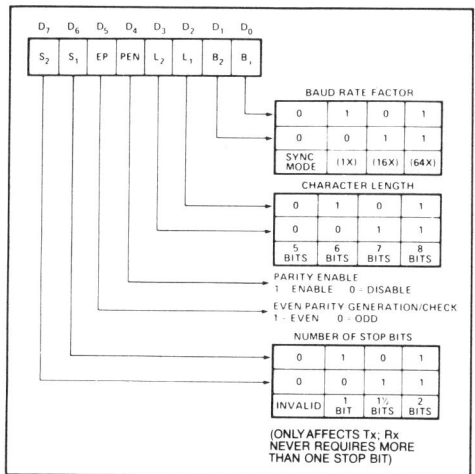

Figure 10.22 Mode instruction format, asynchronous mode. (*Source:* Reprinted by permission of Intel Corporation, Copyright © Intel Corporation 1987.)

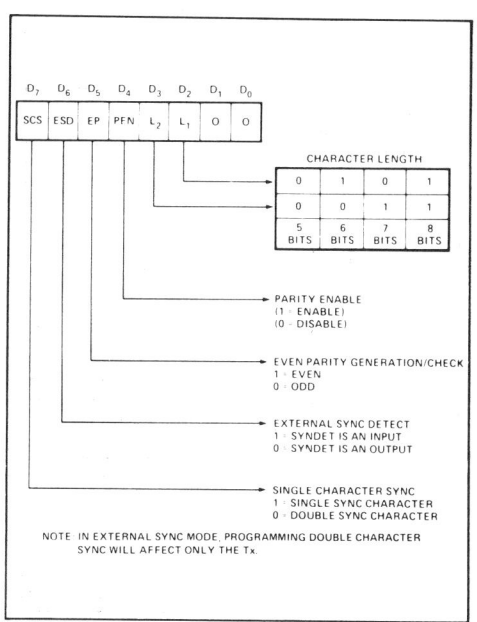

Figure 10.23 Mode instruction format, synchronous mode. (*Source:* Reprinted by permission of Intel Corporation, Copyright © Intel Corporation 1987.)

parity are selected as described above. In addition, the direction of SYNDET must be selected. When SYNDET is an output, the USART will look for SYN characters in the data stream. The number of SYN characters to check (1 or 2) before SYNDET (as an output) can go high is also selected.

10.5.9 The Command Instruction

Once the mode has been selected (as described above), the second thing that must be written to the 8251A is the *command instruction*. Remember that control writes (mode select and command instructions) are to the port address with C/$\overline{\text{D}}$ = 1. Data writes are to the 8251A port address with C/$\overline{\text{D}}$ = 0. Note that setting the DTR bit (D1) to 1 makes the $\overline{\text{DTR}}$ pin go low and likewise for the RTS bit and the $\overline{\text{RTS}}$ pin.

Figure 10.24 shows the command instruction format and explains the function of each bit in the command. Especially note these two:

T×EN bit (D0): Must be set to a 1 to enable data transmission.

Internal Reset (D6): 8251A can be reset by setting the IR bit to 1. An internal reset allows the mode selection to be changed.

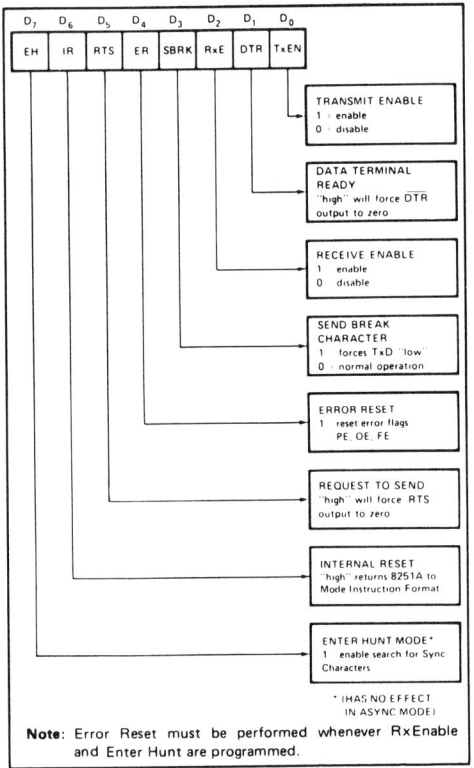

Figure 10.24 Command instruction format. (*Source:* Reprinted by permission of Intel Corporation, Copyright © Intel Corporation 1987.)

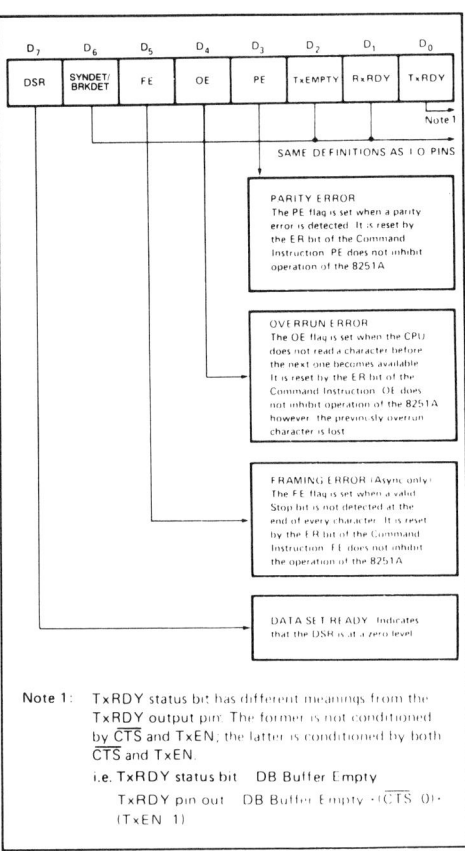

Figure 10.25 Status read format. (*Source:* Reprinted by permission of Intel Corporation, Copyright © Intel Corporation 1987.)

10.5.10 Reading Status

Figure 10.25 shows the format of the status byte. Like a control write, a status read is done from the 8251A port with C/D = 1. Note that the DSR status bit (D7) goes high when the $\overline{\text{DSR}}$ pin is low. Also note that the important external signals (T×RDY, R×RDY, T×E, SYNDET/BRKDET) have corresponding bits in the status byte. That allows the software to operate in a polling mode, or the pins can be used to generate interrupts.

Note: The T×RDY status bit does not depend on T×EN or $\overline{\text{CTS}}$; it goes high when the data buffer can accept data. The T×RDY pin goes high when the buffer can accept *and* $\overline{\text{CTS}}$ is low *and* T×EN is set to 1.

322   Peripheral Devices   Chap. 10

10.5.11 Programming Examples

EXAMPLE 10.13 Asynchronous Operation

Assume that the 8251A is at I/O port address 1000000X, where X is the C/$\overline{\text{D}}$ pin. Then data will be through port 80h and command/status will be through port 81h. We will initialize the USART, go into a loop to send data, and use an interrupt service routine to receive data. Interrupts will be generated by the R×RDY pin.

We will use 8 data bits per frame and 1 stop bit. We will not use parity. It is usually more efficient to find errors elsewhere in the communications software by the use of checksums or CRC numbers. We will assume that both T×C and R×C are 16× the baud rate, the most common choice. Thus, the mode byte is 01001110, or 4Eh. The command instruction byte is 00110111, or 37h. The 8085 code is

```
        DATA     EQU    80H
        CONTROL  EQU    DATA+1
        STATUS   EQU    CONTROL
        MODE     EQU    4EH
        CINSTR   EQU    37H

                 MVI    A,MODE      ; ASYNC MODE SELECTION
                 OUT    CONTROL     ; MAKE IT SO
                 MVI    A,CINSTR    ; COMMAND INSTRUCTION
                 OUT    CONTROL     ; MAKE IT SO
                 LXI    H,RECBUF    ; DATA BUFFER FOR RX
                 SHLD   HLTMP       ; SAVE FOR SERVICE ROUTINE
                 LXI    H,SENDBUF   ; DATA BUFFER FOR TX
                 EI                 ; ENABLE INTERRUPTS

        TLOOP:   IN     STATUS      ; READ STATUS
                 RLC                ; GET DSR IN CY
                 JNC    TLOOP       ; DATA GET READY? JUMP IF NO
                 RRC                ; RESTORE STATUS
                 RRC                ; GET TXRDY IN CY
                 JNC    TLOOP       ; JUMP IF TX NOT READY
                 MOV    A,M         ; GET A CHARACTER
                 OUT    DATA        ; SEND IT
                 INX    H           ; MOVE POINTER
                 JMP    TLOOP       ; DO IT AGAIN

                 ORG    INTADR      ; INTERRUPT ADDRESS
                 PUSH   PSW         ; SAVE ACC & FLAGS
                 PUSH   H           ; SAVE H & L REGS
                 LHLD   HLTMP       ; GET POINTER TO REC BUFF
                 IN     DATA        ; READ DATA CHARACTER
                 MOV    M,A         ; SAVE IT IN BUFFER
                 INX    H           ; INC POINTER
```

```
              SHLD     HLTMP      ; SAVE POINTER
              POP      H          ; RESTORE H & L
              POP      PSW        ; RESTORE ACC & FLAGS
              RET                 ; GO BACK TO SENDING
```

EXAMPLE 10.14 Synchronous Operation

Assume that the 8251A is at I/O port address 1000000X, where X is the $C/\overline{D}$ pin. Then data will be through port 80h and command/status will be through port 81h. We will initialize the USART, go into a loop to send data, and use an interrupt service routine to receive data. Interrupts will be generated by the R×RDY pin.

We will use 8 data bits per frame. As in Example 10.13, we will not use parity; synchronous data usually include CRC numbers at the end. We will use internal sync detect (SYNDET is output) and require one SYN character. Thus, the mode byte is 00001100, or 0Ch. We will have to achieve initial synchronization, so we will first have to enter hunt mode. Then the command instruction byte is 10110111, or B7h. The 8085 code is

```
        DATA     EQU     80H
        CONTROL  EQU     DATA+1
        STATUS   EQU     CONTROL
        MODE     EQU     0CH
        HUNT     EQU     0B7H        ; COMMAND WITH HUNT
        NORM     EQU     37H         ; COMMAND NORMAL

                 MVI     A, MODE     ; SYNC MODE SELECTION
                 OUT     CONTROL     ; MAKE IT SO
                 MVI     A, HUNT     ; COMMAND INSTRUCTION
                 OUT     CONTROL     ; MAKE IT SO

        SLOOP:   IN      STATUS      ; GET STATUS BYTE
                 RLC                 ; ROTATE TWICE TO
                 RLC                 ; GET SYNDET IN CY
                 JNC     SLOOP       ; SYN? JUMP IF NO
                 MVI     A, NORM     ; TURN OFF HUNT MODE
                 OUT     CONTROL     ; WE ARE SYNCHED

                 LXI     H, RECBUF   ; DATA BUFFER FOR RX
                 SHLD    HLTMP       ; SAVE FOR SERVICE ROUTINE
                 LXI     H, SENDBUF  ; DATA BUFFER FOR TX
                 EI                  ; ENABLE INTERRUPTS

        TLOOP:   IN      STATUS      ; READ STATUS
                 RLC                 ; GET DSR IN CY
                 JNC     TLOOP       ; DATA SET READY? JUMP IF NO
                 RRC                 ; RESTORE STATUS
                 RRC                 ; GET TXRDY IN CY
```

```
              JNC    TLOOP      ; JUMP IF TX NOT READY
              MOV    A,M        ; GET A CHARACTER
              OUT    DATA       ; SEND IT
              INX    H          ; MOVE POINTER
              JMP    TLOOP      ; DO IT AGAIN

              ORG    INTADR     ; INTERRUPT ADDRESS
              PUSH   PSW        ; SAVE ACC & FLAGS
              PUSH   H          ; SAVE H & L REGS
              LHLD   HLTMP      ; GET POINTER TO REC BUFF
              IN     STATUS     ; READ STATUS BYTE
              RLC               ; GET SYNDET
              RLC               ; INTO CY
              IN     DATA       ; READ DATA CHARACTER
              JC     BYE        ; SYN CHAR? JUMP IF YES
              MOV    M,A        ; SAVE IT IN BUFFER
              INX    H          ; INC POINTER
              SHLD   HLTMP      ; SAVE POINTER
      BYE:    POP    H          ; RESTORE H & L
              POP    PSW        ; RESTORE ACC & FLAGS
              RET               ; GO BACK TO SENDING
```

Note that the subroutine disregards SYN characters. However, all characters must be read to avoid overrun errors. The receiver is double buffered, so the amount of time to read a character must be less than the time to receive the next frame.

Examples 10.13 and 10.14 do not check for errors or breaks. It is left as an exercise for the reader to modify the code to include such features.

10.6 SUMMARY

In this chapter we have examined four peripheral chips, each typical of a class of devices. The 8255 is a general-purpose I/O chip that provides a microprocessor with parallel ports, the configurations of which are programmable and flexible. The 8279 is specialized to take on the tasks of keyboard scanning and display multiplexing, thus allowing the MPU time to do other things. The LTC1091 is an analog subsection on a chip with a serial interface to an MPU. The 8251 is a USART. It unburdens the CPU of the timing, framing, and handshaking involved in serial data communications.

CHAPTER REVIEW

Questions

1. Compare and contrast the 8155 and the 8255.
2. Explain what asynchronous data are.

3. Explain what synchronous data are.
4. Explain what a USART does.
5. Explain keyboard scanning.
6. Explain display multiplexing.
7. Explain the advantage of doing an I/O chore (e.g., keyboard scanning) in hardware as compared to doing it in software. What is the disadvantage?

Problems

For the following problems, assign your own port addresses.

1. Write an 8085 program to use the 8255 in mode 0 as follows: Read a byte in from port A and send it out port B in an infinite loop.
2. Repeat Prob. 1 except with the 8255 in mode 1. Use loops to monitor the handshake lines.
3. Repeat Prob. 2 using the 8085 hardware interrupts.
4. Write an 8085 program to use the 8255 in mode 2 as follows: Read a byte in and send back its two's complement.
5. Draw a schematic showing the 8279 scanning a 4 × 4 hex keypad and driving eight seven-segment displays.
6. For the circuit of Prob. 5, write an 8085 program that waits for a key press and then displays the appropriate hex digit on the next sequential display using left entry. Assume a 2.5-MHz clock.
7. Assume you have an 8155 connected to an 8085. Write a program to use the LTC1091 to get a reading from both channels once every 2 sec. Assume a 1-MHz clock.
8. Modify the initialization equates of Example 10.13 to use odd parity.
9. Modify Example 10.13 to check for breaks and errors. If found, call an ERROR or BREAK subroutine (you don't have to write the subroutines, just assume they handle the errors).
10. Modify the initialization equates of Example 10.14 to use two SYN characters.

chapter 11

The 8086 Processor

OBJECTIVES

After finishing this chapter, you should be able to

1. Explain the key hardware features of the 8086
2. Explain the key assembly language features of the 8086
3. Compare and contrast the 8086 to the 8085, Z80, and 8051.

11.1 INTRODUCTION

The purpose of this chapter is to introduce the reader to 16-bit microprocessors by examining a popular 16-bit device: the 8086. However, a complete treatment of the 8086 is a book in itself. So our goal here is to get enough of a feel for the 8086 to be able to compare and contrast it to the 8-bit devices we have studied. For more information, the reader is referred to the many books available, such as *The 8086 Microprocessor* by Triebel and Singh (Prentice Hall) and *The 8086 Book* by Rector and Alexy (McGraw-Hill).

Introduced by Intel in 1978, the 8086 is a true 16-bit machine, meaning that it has 16-bit internal and external data paths and 16-bit registers and performs operations on 16-bit words. The 8088 is similar to the 8086 but uses an 8-bit external data bus; it is software compatible with the 8086. From the 8086, Intel has introduced a succession of devices, including the 80186, 80286, and 80386 processors, as well as the 8087, 80287, and 80387 math coprocessors. The many popular MS-DOS–based personal computers use the 8088, 80286, or 80386.

11.2 THE 8086 ARCHITECTURE

The 8086 differs from the 8-bit devices we have discussed in more than just its word length. Three of its key features are its modes, its use of pipelining, and its segmented addressing. Also, even though it is a 16-bit machine, the 8086 can reference memory a byte at a time.

11.2.1 Modes and Pin Functions

The 8086 pin layout is shown in Fig. 11.1. The processor is designed to operate in one of two modes, *minimum* or *maximum,* as selected by the MN/MX pin. MN/MX is "tied high" (connected to V_{CC}) for minimum mode and "tied low" (connected to GND) for maximum mode. The main difference between the modes is that maximum mode allows a system to have multiple processors sharing the bus, whereas minimum mode has a single CPU. Use of the 8086 in maximum mode requires external support chips such as the 8288 bus controller and the 8289 bus arbiter.

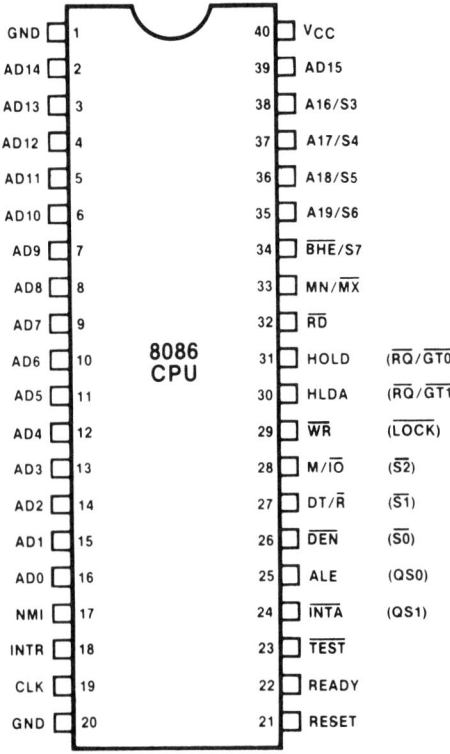

Figure 11.1 Pin layout of the 8086 microprocessor. (*Source:* Reprinted by permission of Intel Corporation, Copyright © Intel Corporation 1987.)

Figure 11.1 shows that some of the pins have multiple names, indicating that they have multiple functions. For one thing, the data lines are multiplexed with the lower 16 address lines, similar to the 8085. Note that, like the 8085, the 8086 has an ALE pin. Also, some 8086 pin functions depend on the mode. The table in Fig. 11.2 shows which functions are common to both modes, which are for minimum mode, and which are for maximum mode. Figure 11.3 shows typical address/data demultiplexing logic for both the 8086 and the 8088.

Common Signals		
Name	Function	Type
AD15-AD0	Address/Data Bus	Bidirectional, 3-State
A19/S6-A16/S3	Address/Status	Output, 3-State
$\overline{BHE}$/S7	Bus High Enable/Status	Output, 3-State
MN/$\overline{MX}$	Minimum/Maximum Mode Control	Input
$\overline{RD}$	Read Control	Output, 3-State
$\overline{TEST}$	Wait On Test Control	Input
READY	Wait State Control	Input
RESET	System Reset	Input
NMI	Non-Maskable Interrupt Request	Input
INTR	Interrupt Request	Input
CLK	System Clock	Input
V_{CC}	+5V	Input
GND	Ground	

(a)

Minimum Mode Signals (MN/$\overline{MX}$ = V_{CC})		
Name	Function	Type
HOLD	Hold Request	Input
HLDA	Hold Acknowledge	Output
$\overline{WR}$	Write Control	Output, 3-State
M/$\overline{IO}$	Memory/IO Control	Output, 3-State
DT/$\overline{R}$	Data Transmit/Receive	Output, 3-State
$\overline{DEN}$	Data Enable	Output, 3-State
ALE	Address Latch Enable	Output
$\overline{INTA}$	Interrupt Acknowledge	Output

(b)

Figure 11.2 (a) Signals common to both minimum and maximum modes. (b) Unique minimum mode signals. (c) Unique maximum mode signals. (*Source:* Reprinted by permission of Intel Corporation, Copyright © Intel Corporation 1987.)

Maximum Mode Signals (MN/$\overline{\text{MX}}$ = GND)		
Name	Function	Type
$\overline{\text{RQ}}/\overline{\text{GT}}$1, 0	Request/Grant Bus Access Control	Bidirectional
$\overline{\text{LOCK}}$	Bus Priority Lock Control	Output, 3-State
$\overline{\text{S2}}$-$\overline{\text{S0}}$	Bus Cycle Status	Output, 3-State
QS1, QS0	Instruction Queue Status	Output

(c)

Figure 11.2 (*continued*)

11.2.2 The BIU, EU, and Instruction Queue

Figure 11.4 shows a block diagram of the 8086 internal architecture. Note the division into *bus interface unit* (BIU) and *execution unit* (EU). The BIU is responsible for managing the address and data buses, including such tasks as fetching instructions and operands, writing to memory, and doing I/O to ports. The EU is responsible for executing instruction.

An important feature of the 8086 is its *pipeline architecture*. The BIU and the EU operate asynchronously, meaning that new operations can be prefetched while previous operations are being executed. The BIU holds the prefetched instructions in a 6-byte FIFO *instruction queue*. The BIU fills the queue from sequential memory locations, and the EU pulls instructions from it as needed. If the needed instruction is not in the queue, due perhaps to a JUMP, the pipeline will be "flushed" and the needed instruction fetched from memory. Figure 11.5 shows EU, BIU, and bus activity as a block diagram.

11.2.3 Segments and Addressing

All the 8086 registers are 16 bits, including the instruction pointer (IP) and the stack pointer (SP). With 16 bits you can directly address up to 64K bytes. However, the 8086 has a 20-bit address bus and can address up to a megabyte (1 M = 2^{20} = 1,048,576) of memory. The 8086 gets around the problem by segmenting memory into multiple 64K blocks.

The 8086 contains four 16-bit segment registers: CS (code segment), DS (data segment), SS (stack segment), and ES (extra segment). A 20-bit *physical address* is formed by adding a 16-bit *offset* to the content of the appropriate segment register. The number in the segment register is the starting address of a 64K block. For instruction fetches, IP is added to CS; for stack reference, SP is added to SS. DS and ES are used for moving data bytes around in memory.

Figure 11.6 shows that logic addresses are not added to segment registers directly. The contents of the segment register are first shifted left by 4 bits. Then the offset is added. For example, suppose the instruction pointer contains 1004h and

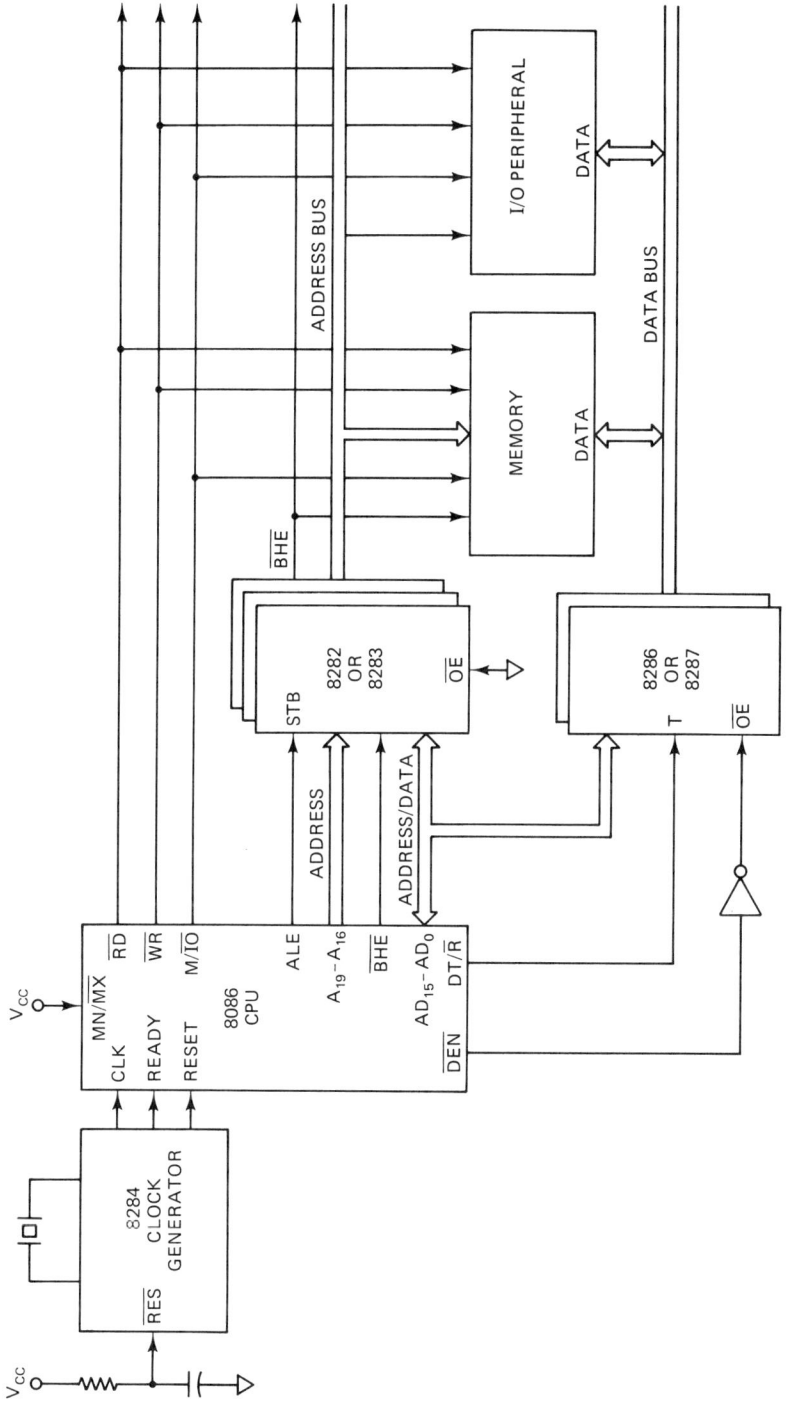

Figure 11.3 Bus demultiplexers and buffers for the Intel microprocessors. (a) Demultiplexing and buffering the 8086 address and data bases. (b) Demultiplexing the 8088 address/data bus. (Source: Reprinted by permission of Intel Corporation, Copyright © Intel Corporation 1981.)

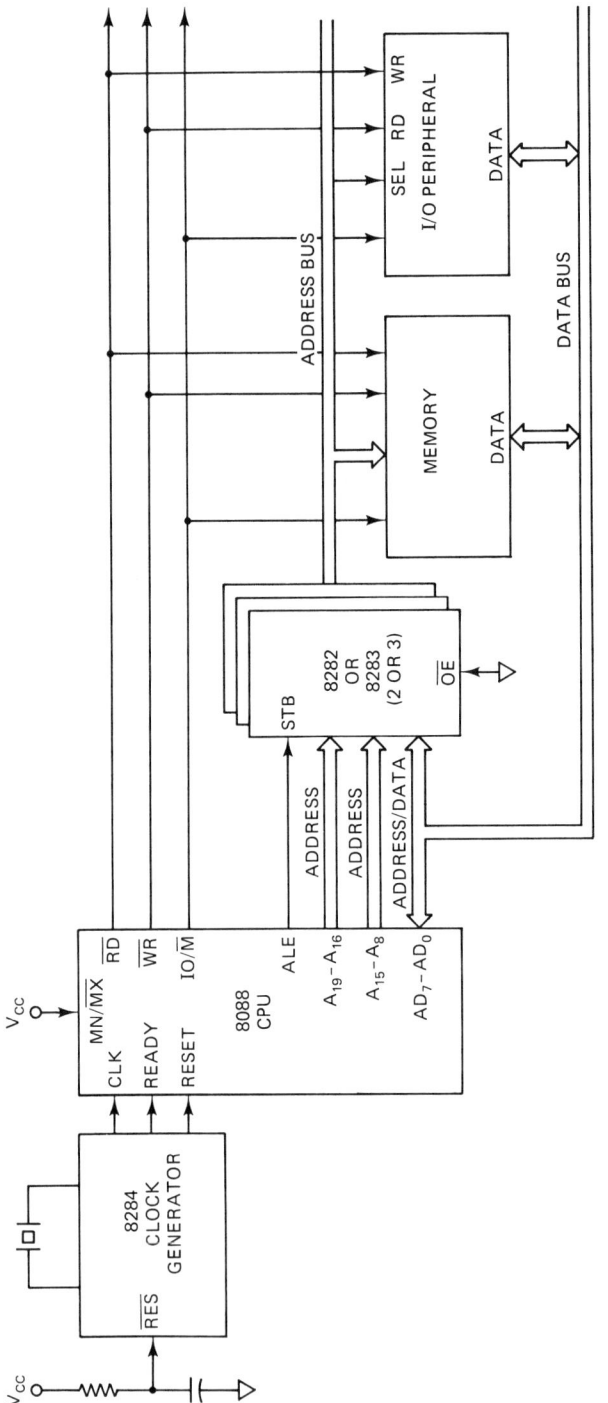

Figure 11.3 (*continued*)

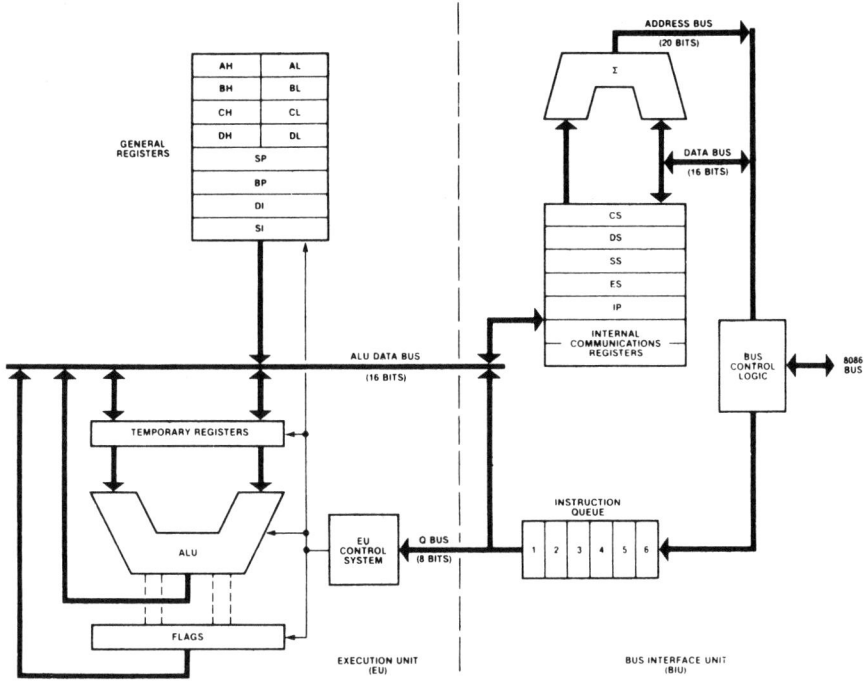

Figure 11.4 Internal architecture of the 8086 microprocessor. (*Source:* Reprinted by permission of Intel Corporation, Copyright © Intel Corporation 1987.)

the CS register contains 8050h. The physical address of the next instruction is 81504h.

The addition is done automatically by the 8086 and does not change the register contents. The segment registers must be loaded initially with the correct values. In ROM-based systems, the segment registers may have to be initialized to absolute values by the programmer's linker. In disk-based systems the linker will produce relocatable code and the operating system will determine the run-time values in the segment registers.

Note that the segments may overlap. In fact, if everything will fit into 64K, then all the segment registers can contain the same value.

11.2.4 Clock Generation and Reset

Note that Fig. 11.3 shows an 8284 clock generator, which also provides the reset function. The frequency of the crystal connected to the 8284 is divided by 3 to drive the 8086. For example, a 15-MHz crystal will generate a 5-MHz clock. The 8284 also supplies a secondary clock of half the CPU clock frequency for use by peripherals.

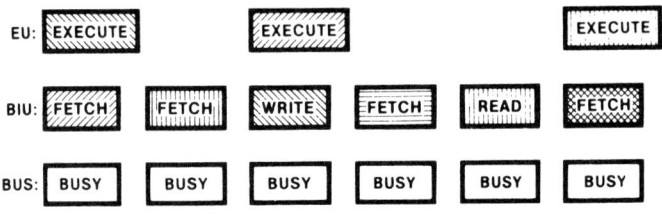

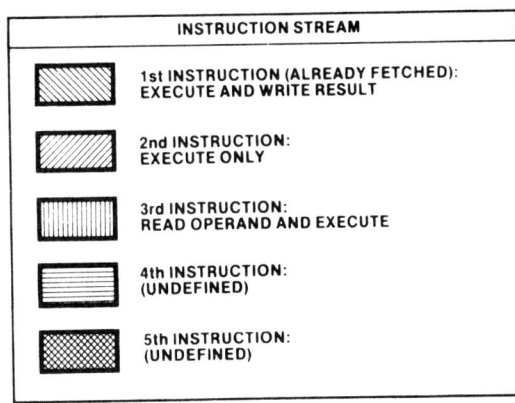

Figure 11.5 Overlapping instruction fetch and execution. (*Source:* Reprinted by permission of Intel Corporation, Copyright © Intel Corporation 1987.)

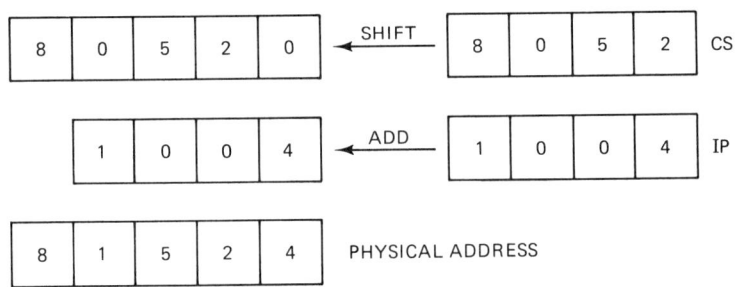

Figure 11.6 20 Bit address formation.

On power up, pin 21 of the 8086 must be held high for at least 50 μsec to generate a reset. If the 8086 is running, the minimum reset pulse must be four clock cycles long. Figure 11.7 shows a typical 8284 circuit.

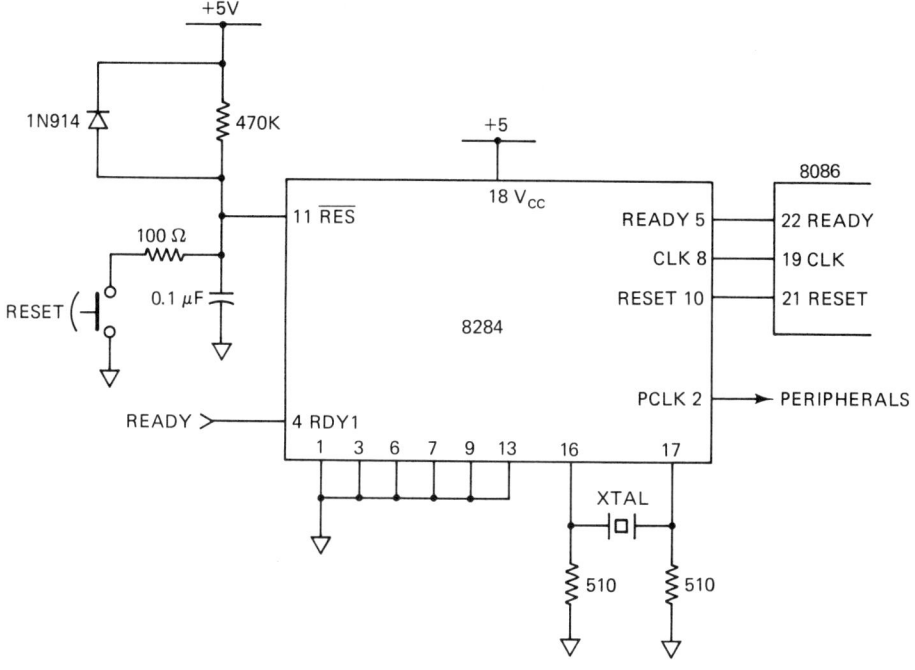

Figure 11.7 Typical 8284 circuit.

The results of a reset are summarized in Table 11.1. Note that the CS register is initialized to FFFFh and the IP is reset to 0000h. The result is that after reset the first instruction fetched will be from address FFFF0h, not 00000h. Location FFFF0h, often implemented as ROM, will typically contain a jump to the actual start of the program.

TABLE 11.1
RESULTS OF A
RESET

CPU section	Content
Flags	Clear
IP reg	0000h
CS reg	FFFFh
DS reg	0000h
SS reg	0000h
ES reg	0000h
Queue	Empty

Sec. 11.2 The 8086 Architecture

11.3 THE MINIMUM MODE INTERFACE

Figure 11.8 shows the block diagram of a minimum mode system. In minimum mode, the 8086 provides all the control signals it needs. They can be divided into several groups: address/data bus, status signals, control signals, and interrupt/DMA signals.

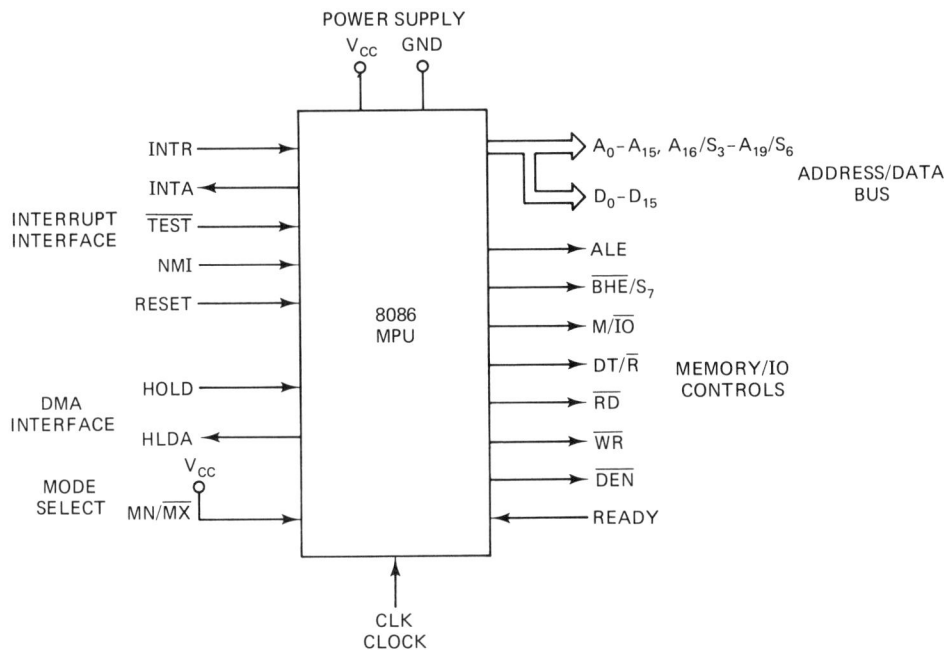

Figure 11.8 Block diagram of the minimum mode 8086 MPU. (*Source:* Triebel/Singh, *The 8086 Microprocessor: Architecture, Software, and Interfacing Techniques,* © 1985, p. 18. Reprinted by permission of Prentice-Hall, Inc., Englewood Cliffs, N.J.)

11.3.1 Address/Data Bus

AD0–AD15   Lower address bits multiplexed with the data bits. Must be demultiplexed, as shown in Fig. 11.3.

A16–A19/S3–S6   Upper address bits multiplexed with status bits S3, S4, S5, and S6. The status bits are described in the next section.

11.3.2 Status Signals

QS0, QS1   Not used in minimum mode. In maximum mode they indicate the status of the queue.

S0–S2   Not used in minimum mode. In maximum mode they indicate which CPU cycle is on the bus.

S3–S6   S6 is always a 0. S5 tells the state of the 8086 interrupt enable flag. S4 and S3 form a 2-bit code that identifies which of the segment registers was used to generate the address. The code is 00 = ES, 01 = SS, 10 = CS, 11 = DS. S3–S6 can be demultiplexed along with the data.

S7   Multiplexed with $\overline{BHE}$. S7 is active-low and is used to indicate the beginning of an interrupt acknowledge cycle.

11.3.3 Control Signals

The control signals are used to interface the 8086 to memory and I/O devices as follows:

READY Used to force the CPU to insert wait states in current bus cycle. Can be synchronized through the 8284 chip.

ALE **Address Latch Enable:** The falling edge of ALE is used to latch A0–A15 into an external circuit such as the 8282.

$\overline{BHE}$ **Bank High Enable:** Enables the upper byte of a 16-bit memory word during read or write. Used in conjunction with address bit A0, as shown in Fig. 11.9. To access the entire word, both A0 and $\overline{BHE}$ will go low. To access the upper byte, $\overline{BHE}$ will go low while A0 stays high. To access the lower byte, A0 will go low while $\overline{BHE}$ stays high.

$M/\overline{IO}$ **Memory/IO:** This line is high to indicate a memory access and low to indicate I/O transfer.

DT/R **Data Transmit/Receive:** Indicates direction of data bus. When DT/$\overline{R}$ is 1, data are either being written to memory or output to a port. When DT/R is a 0, data are either being read from memory or input from a port. Can be used to control the direction of bidirectional buffers.

$\overline{WR}$ **Write:** Goes low to indicate the CPU is writing data onto the data bus.

$\overline{RD}$ **Read:** Goes low to indicate the CPU is reading data off the data bus.

$\overline{DEN}$ **Data Enable:** During read operations, $\overline{DEN}$ is used to tell external devices (such as RAM chips) when to put data onto the data bus.

11.3.4 Interrupt and DMA Signals

INTR **Interrupt Request:** Level-triggered. INTR is pulled high by an external device to request an interrupt. The current instruction finishes execution before INTR is recognized. INTR interrupts must be enabled in software (see IF flag, described in Sec. 11.6.3).

$\overline{INTA}$ **Interrupt Acknowledge:** $\overline{INTA}$ is pulsed low twice in response to INTR. The first pulse tells the interrupting device that INTR has been

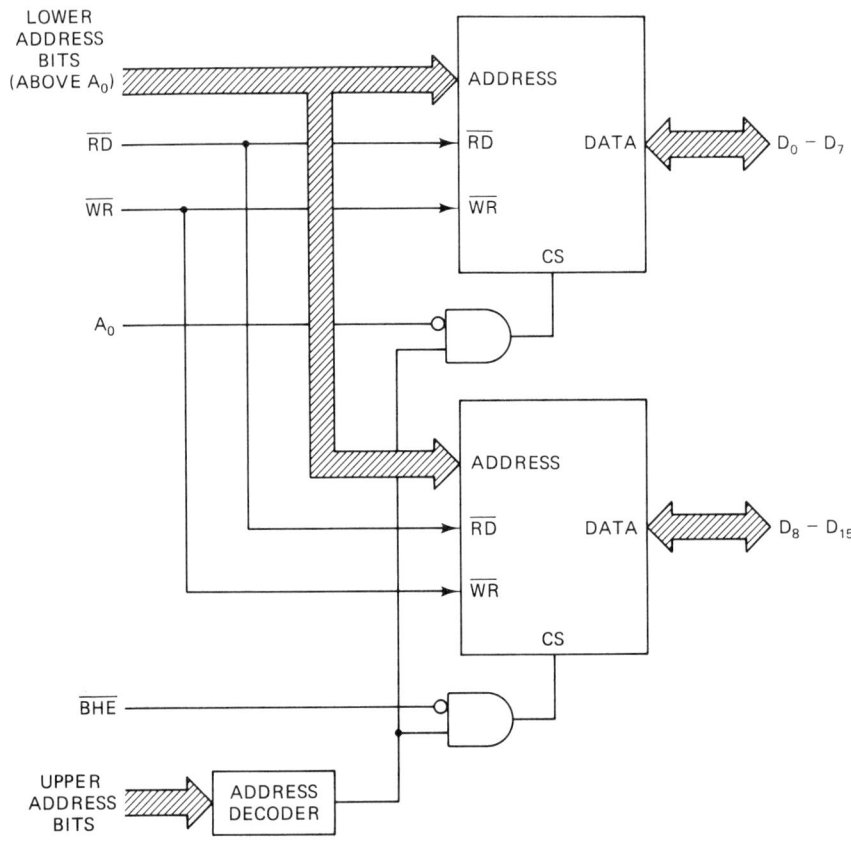

Figure 11.9 Use of A_0 and $\overline{BHE}$.

	recognized. The second pulse tells the interrupting device to put an 8-bit interrupt code on D0–D7.
NMI	**Nonmaskable Interrupt:** Positive edge-triggered. Causes a type 2 interrupt, as described in Sec. 11.4.
$\overline{\text{TEST}}$	Interrupts the CPU, but causes no jump to a service routine. $\overline{\text{TEST}}$ is sampled when a WAIT instruction (not to be confused with a wait state) is executed. If $\overline{\text{TEST}}$ is a 0, it is ignored and the next instruction is executed. If $\overline{\text{TEST}}$ is a 1, further execution is suspended until $\overline{\text{TEST}}$ goes low. $\overline{\text{TEST}}$ can be used to "put the 8086 to sleep" in order to synchronize its timing to some external device or event.
HOLD	Pulled high by external device to initiate DMA. Causes 8086 to float its buses to allow external device to control them.
HOLDA	Goes high to indicate the external device that 8086 is in HOLD state. Acknowledgment to hold.

11.4 INTERRUPT VECTORING

The 8086 uses the first 1K of memory (00000h to 003FFh) to hold an interrupt vector table, as shown in Fig. 11.10. Each entry is 4 bytes long. The lower 2 bytes hold an offset to be loaded into the IP register and the upper 2 bytes hold a value for the CS register. The table must be initialized in software before any interrupts occur.

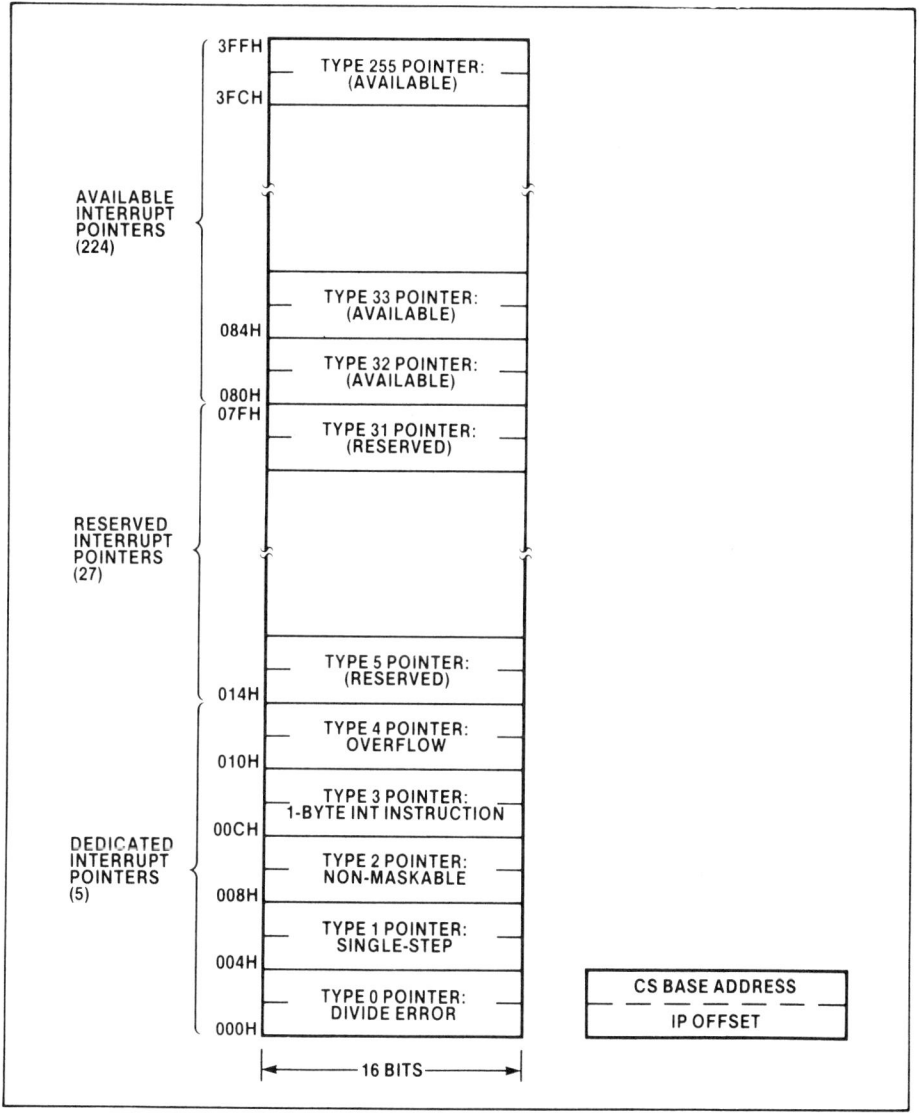

Figure 11.10 8086/8088 interrupt vector table. (*Source:* Reprinted by permission of Intel Corporation, Copyright © Intel Corporation 1981.)

When an interrupt occurs, the current contents of CS and IP are pushed onto the stack. The appropriate values from the interrupt table are then loaded into CS and IP, effectively causing a jump to the service routine. At the end of the service routine, a return instruction will pop the old values of CS and IP off the stack and the program resumes from where it was interrupted.

Note that each table entry has a type number in the range 0 to 255 in decimal, 00–FF in hex. When an INTR type interrupt occurs, the external device must put the type number onto the data bus on the second $\overline{\text{INTA}}$ pulse. NMI automatically causes a type 2 interrupt. An error in executing the divide instruction (e.g., divide by 0) causes a type 0 interrupt.

11.5 MINIMUM MODE TIMING

The timing relationships of the address, data, and control signals for a minimum mode system are detailed in this section.

11.5.1 Basic Timing

Figure 11.11 shows the basic system timing. Note that a basic cycle is four clock cycles long (T1–T4) plus any wait states caused by the READY line. Also note the points from which memory access time is measured.

11.5.2 Read Cycle

Figure 11.12 shows a minimum mode read cycle. Note the relationships between ALE, M/$\overline{\text{IO}}$, and the address lines. Also note the relationships between DT/$\overline{\text{R}}$, $\overline{\text{RD}}$, $\overline{\text{DEN}}$, and valid data.

11.5.3 Write Cycle

Figure 11.13 shows a minimum mode write cycle. Compare the timing relationships to those in Fig. 11.12. Also note that the bottom of Fig. 11.13 shows an $\overline{\text{INTA}}$ cycle. It is actually the second of the two $\overline{\text{INTA}}$ cycles used to acknowledge an interrupt. Note the relationships between DT/$\overline{\text{R}}$, $\overline{\text{INTA}}$, $\overline{\text{DEN}}$, and the pointer (interrupt type number) placed on the data lines.

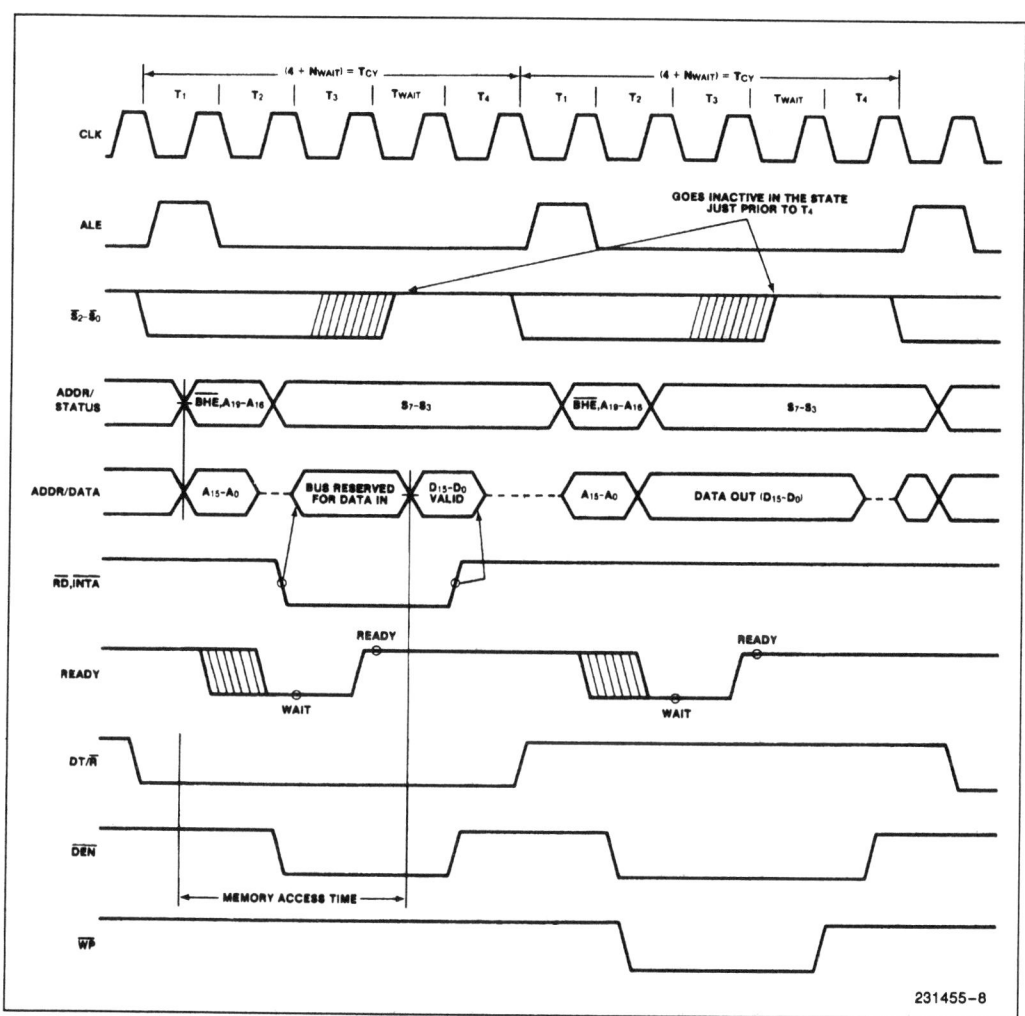

Figure 11.11 Basic system timing. (*Source:* Reprinted by permission of Intel Corporation, Copyright © Intel Corporation 1987.)

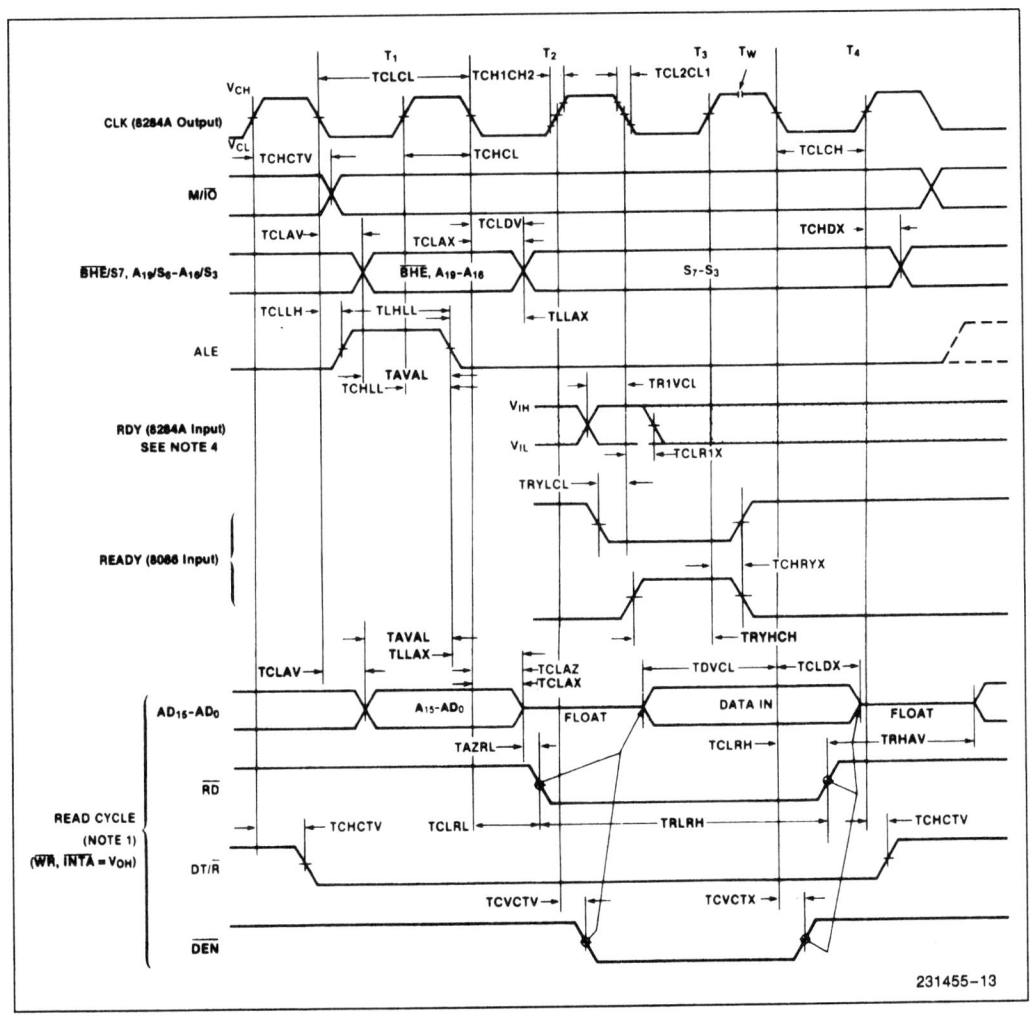

Figure 11.12 Minimum mode read cycle. (*Source:* Reprinted by permission of Intel Corporation, Copyright © Intel Corporation 1987.)

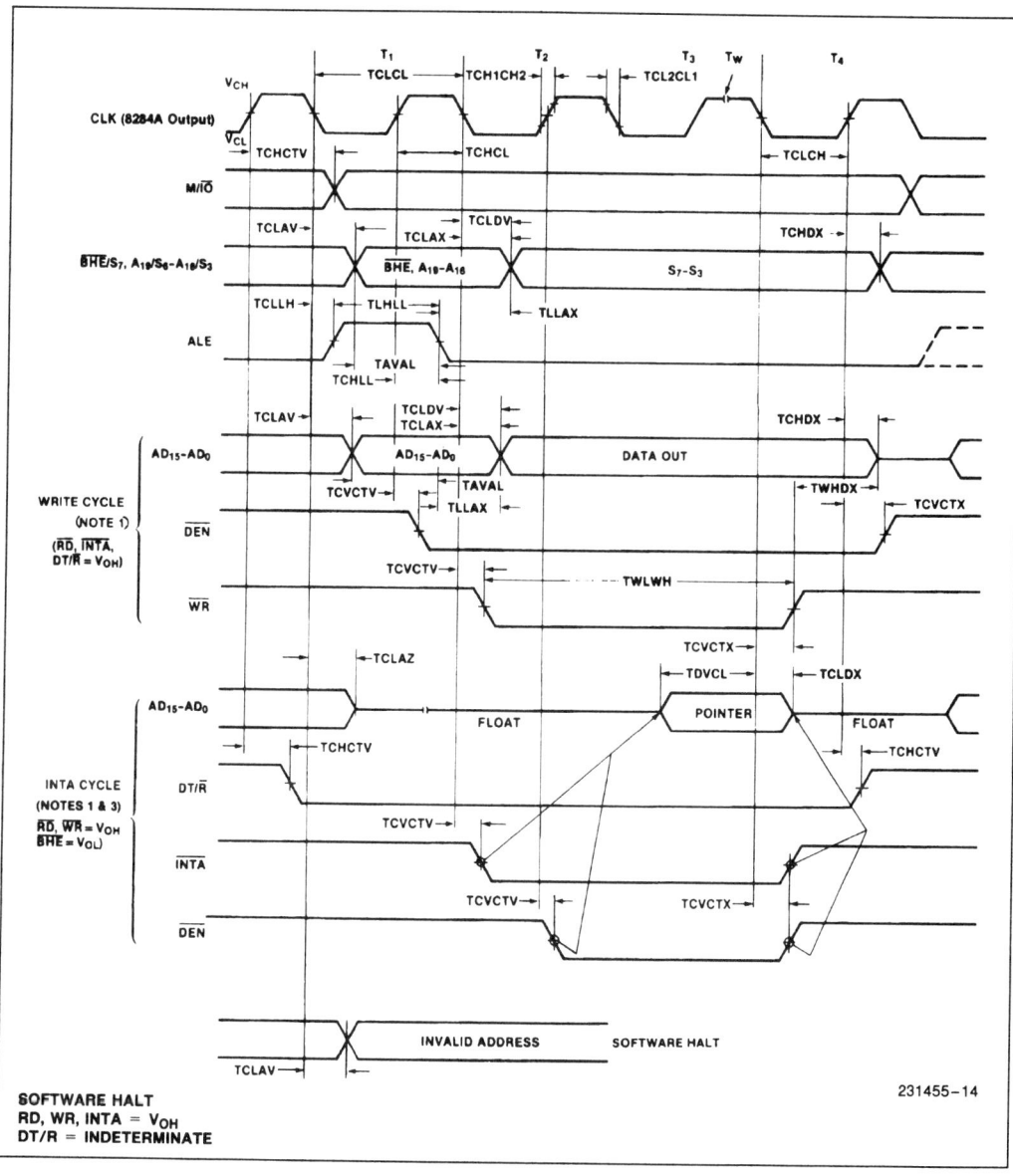

Figure 11.13 Minimum mode write cycle. (*Source:* Reprinted by permission of Intel Corporation, Copyright © Intel Corporation 1987.)

11.6 THE PROGRAMMING MODEL

Figure 11.14 shows a block diagram of the registers making up the 8086 programming model (software model).

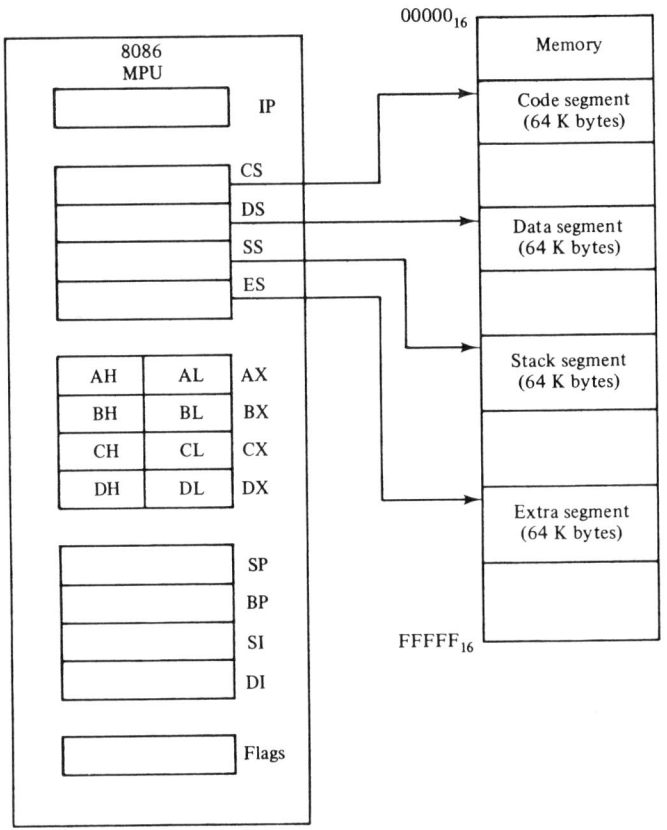

Figure 11.14 Software model of the 8086 microprocessor. (*Source:* Triebel/Singh, *The 8086 Microprocessor: Architecture, Software, and Interfacing Techniques,* © 1985, p. 41. Reprinted by permission of Prentice-Hall, Inc., Englewood Cliffs, N.J.)

11.6.1 General-Purpose Registers

The 8086 has four general-purpose 16-bit registers: AX, BX, CX, and DX. Each 16-bit register can also be addressed as two 8-bit registers, in which case the X suffix is changed to either H (high byte) or L (low byte). For example, the 2 bytes of AX can be addressed as AH and AL.

As shown in Fig. 11.15, the registers are associated with certain functions of the instruction set. AX is the accumulator. BX can be used as a base register for

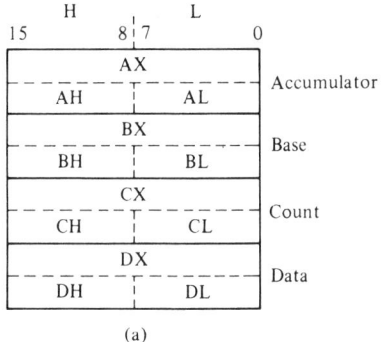

Figure 11.15 (a) General-purpose registers. (b) Dedicated register functions. (*Source:* Reprinted by permission of Intel Corporation, Copyright © Intel Corporation 1987.)

base-displacement addressing. CX is used by certain instructions to hold a count. DX is a data register in some applications; it is also used in indirect I/O to hold a port address.

11.6.2 Pointer and Index Registers

This group consists of four 16-bit registers:

SP   **Stack Pointer:** Used to hold the offset from SS during push, pop, call, and other stack operations.

BP   **Base Pointer:** BP is also used to hold an offset from SS. Parameters are often passed to a subroutine on the stack. The subroutine can use BP to read them off the stack without disturbing the stack pointer.

SI   **Source Index:** Used to hold an offset from DS for addressing data in the data segment.

DI   **Destination Index:** Used to hold an offset from ES for addressing data in the extra segment.

Although each pointer and index register is associated with a certain segment register, the association can be overridden. The above are the default associations.

11.6.3 The Flags

Figure 11.16 shows the 16-bit flag register. Note that there are 9 bits: six status flags and three control flags. The *status flags* depend on the results of ALU operations, as follows:

C   **Carry Flag (CF):** Set to 1 if a carry out or borrow in occurs in the MSB; otherwise, reset to 0. Can also be set and reset directly in software.

P   **Parity Flag (PF):** Set to 1 if a result contains an even number of 1s; otherwise, reset to 0.

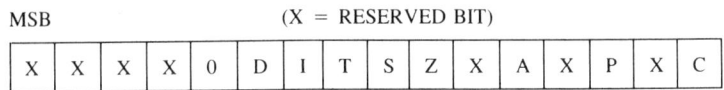

Figure 11.16 Sixteen-bit flag register.

A   **Auxiliary Carry Flag (AF):** For BCD operations on lower byte of a 16-bit word. Set to 1 on carry out or borrow in between lower 4 bits and upper 4 bits.
Z   **Zero Flag (ZF):** Set to 1 if the result is zero; otherwise, reset to 0.
S   **Sign Flag (SF):** The MSB of the result is copied to SF. SF = 1 indicates a negative result; SF = 0 indicates a positive result.
O   **Overflow Flag (OF):** Set to 1 if an operation on a signed number gives an out-of-range result; otherwise, reset to 0.

The *control flags* are set or reset by software and are used to make the 8086 operate in specific ways, as follows:

T   **Trap Flag (TF):** If TF is set to 1 the 8086 operates in single-step mode. After each instruction is executed, the 8086 will automatically initiate a type 1 interrupt. The service routine would then determine when to return to the next instruction, perhaps through use of the $\overline{\text{TEST}}$ input. Single stepping is useful in debugging.
I   **Interrupt Flag (IF):** Must be set to 1 to enable maskable interrupts to be recognized. Has no effect on NMI.
D   **Direction Flag (DF):** The 8086 has string move instructions that automatically increment or decrement the address for each move. If DF is set to 1, addresses are incremented. If DF is reset to 0, addresses are decremented.

11.7 8086 ASSEMBLY LANGUAGE

The 8086 instruction set is summarized in Appendix E. We will not be able to cover fully 8086 assembly language programming in this chapter. As in the case of hardware, we will just try to get enough of a feel for the 8086 language features to be able to compare and contrast them to the 8-bit processors.

With simple 8-bit processors like the 8085, it is possible (although tedious) to assemble code by hand. The 8086 is too complex for that, and an assembler is required. Intel supplies assemblers for its development systems. Third-party software companies, such as Microsoft and Borland International, sell assemblers for use on MS-DOS–based personal computers.

11.7.1 Instruction Types

The 8086 has all the usual types of instructions of a stack-oriented, multiple register machine. Like the Z80 LD, almost all data moves use the single mnemonic MOV. The arithmetic instructions include multiply and divide. The 8086 also has a set of string move instructions that can combine looping and address incrementing. Another interesting 8086 feature is that interrupts can be initiated from software as well as from hardware.

11.7.2 Addressing and Effective Address

As was discussed, memory addressing always involves the segment registers. Particular instructions will imply the use of particular segment registers by default. In most cases, however, the implied register can be overridden by an explicitly specified register. Table 11.2 shows the default segment register associated with types of memory reference together with alternatives.

TABLE 11.2 USE OF SEGMENT REGISTERS

Type of memory reference	Default segment register	Alternate segment register	Offset
Instruction fetch	CS	None	IP
Stack operation	SS	None	SP
Data variable	DS	CS, ES, SS	Effective address
String source	DS	CS, ES, SS	SI
String destination	ES	None	DI
BP used as base register	SS	CS, DS, ES	Effective address
BX used as base register	DS	CS, ES, SS	Effective address

The EU calculates the address of an operand as a 16-bit offset from the start of the segment in which the operand resides. That 16-bit offset is called the effective address.

11.7.3 Instruction Format

Figure 11.17 shows a generalized format of an 8086 assembly language instruction after it has been assembled into hex code. There are four possible bytes:

SEGMENT OVERRIDE Can be considered as a modifier to the op-code. It overrides the default segment register, as described above.

OP-CODE The operation code. Specifies the instruction.

ADDRESS MODE Distinguishes between memory and register ad-

BYTE 0	BYTE 1	BYTE 2	BYTE 3	BYTE 4
SEG OVERRIDE	OP CODE	ADDRESS MOD	DISP 1	DISP 2

Figure 11.17 Format of an 8086 assembly language instruction.

dressing, specifies what register (if any), specifies the addressing mode.

DISPLACEMENT BYTES A 16-bit displacement given low byte first.

11.7.4 Addressing Modes

The 8086 instructions use about 24 different addressing modes to arrive at the effective address. However, they are combinations of a few basic modes, as described below.

Register operands. These are instructions that only refer to registers, for example, MOV AX,BX.

Immediate operands. These instructions contain an operand as part of the instruction, for example, MOV AL,43.

Direct addressing. These instructions include the effective address as part of the instruction, for example, MOV AL,NUM1, where NUM1 is the label on a byte in the data segment. NUM1 is not a variable; the assembler will replace it with its numeric value. Note that DS is assumed. If NUM1 were actually in the extra segment, we could override the default segment as follows: MOV AL,ES:NUM1. Note that the desired segment register is prefixed to the address with a colon.

Register indirect addressing. The effective address of an operand can be held in one of the following registers: BP, BX, SI, or DI, for example, MOV AL,[SI]. Note the use of brackets to indicate "address of." Remember that the number in SI is the 16-bit offset of a variable in the data segment. The segment override could be used as in MOV AL,ES:[SI].

If the operand we want were stored at NUM1, SI could have been loaded with the instruction LEA SI,NUM1 (LEA stands for load effective address). Another way is with the OFFSET directive provided by some assemblers: MOV SI,OFFSET NUM1.

Base addressing. Base addressing is similar to register indirect addressing with two changes. First, only BP or BX can be used as the register. Second, a constant displacement is added to the content of the register to form the effective address. The register content is not changed by the addition. For example, assume that BX holds 1000h. Then MOV AL,[BX+5] will give an effective address of 1005h. The instruction could also be written as MOV AL,[BX][5].

Indexed addressing. Indexed addressing is similar to arrays in a high-level language. A register takes the place of the subscript. For example, assume that ARRAY is the label of the first byte in an array of bytes. Also assume that SI contains 3. Then the instruction MOV AL,ARRAY[SI] will move the byte from ARRAY + 3 into AL. The power of the instruction is that SI can be changed during execution. A constant displacement can be included, such as in MOV AL,ARRAY[SI+4]. The allowable registers are SI, DI, BP, and BX. As always, they have implied segment registers.

Based Indexed addressing. As the name implies, based indexed addressing is a combination of based addressing and indexed addressing. The base register is selected from either BX or BP. The index register is selected from either SI or DI. An example instruction is MOV AL,[BX][SI]. A constant displacement can be added, as in MOV AL,[BX][SI+4].

String addressing. A typical string operation is to move a block of consecutive bytes from one part of memory to another. In such operations, SI is assumed to point to the source and DI is assumed to point to the destination.

Port addressing. Port addresses are specified in one of two ways. The first is to specify the port address in the instruction such as IN AL,45H. The other is to have the port address in the DX register such as IN AL,DX.

11.7.5 Software Interrupts

As mentioned, an interrupt can be initiated from software. The instruction is INT nn, where nn is the type number in the range 00h to FFh. Also, the INTO instruction can be used following an arithmetic instruction to generate a type 4 interrupt on overflow. Typically, INT instructions are used to allow programs to request services from the operating system. For example, MS-DOS uses INT 21h to allow programs access to the disk, screen, keyboard, and other system resources.

11.8 SUMMARY

In this chapter we have sketched the features of the 8086 processor. We looked at the pipeline architecture, which allows overlapping of instruction fetches and instruction execution to increase throughput. We looked at the control signals and timing for a minimum mode system. The use of segmented addressing was examined, as was the powerful vectored interrupt scheme. The programming model was discussed, together with the use of registers particular to the 8086. The basic 8086 addressing modes were defined.

CHAPTER REVIEW

Questions

1. Explain "pipelining."
2. What does the BIU do?
3. What does the EU do?
4. What are the two 8086 operating modes, and how do they differ?
5. Explain the use of the segment registers.
6. If CS contains F430h and IP contains 1010h, what is the physical address they form?
7. What does an 8284 do?
8. Name the 8086 control signals used in minimum mode and explain what they do.
9. Explain the 8086 interrupt vectoring scheme.
10. Explain the relationship between DT/$\overline{\text{R}}$, $\overline{\text{RD}}$\, and $\overline{\text{DEN}}$\.
11. Name the 8086 general-purpose registers.
12. Name the 8086 flags and tell what they mean.
13. What is an "effective address"?
14. Explain segment override.
15. Explain register indirect addressing.
16. Explain base addressing.
17. Explain indexed addressing.
18. Explain based indexed addressing.
19. Compare and contrast the 8086 to the 8085.
20. Compare and contrast the 8086 to the Z80.

chapter 12

System Design Techniques

OBJECTIVES

Upon completion of this chapter you should be able to:

1. Describe the steps in the system design cycle.
2. Given a description of a simple electronic design project, write:
   A. System Requirements
   B. System Specifications
   C. Software Modularization
   D. Pseudocode
   E. Assembly Language

12.1 INTRODUCTION: THE SYSTEM DESIGN CYCLE

When microprocessors were first used as the basis for electronic systems, a large system might have only a thousand lines of code, but in the past few years microcomputer-based systems have become much more complex. Large systems now might require hundreds of times as much code and contain several microprocessors. The use of *bottom-up* design techniques, where the parts of the system are designed as the need for them becomes apparent, is no longer sufficient. Rather, systematic techniques are called for. This section describes the basic steps used in *top-down* design.

12.1.1 System Requirements

The first step in the design cycle is to generate the *system requirements*. This is a document that describes exactly the capabilities desired of the finished system. It must contain a list of all the tasks that the system is to support for the end user. The system requirements are best done in consultation between the design team and the customer or end user of the system.

12.1.2 System Specifications

From the system requirements, the *system specifications* are produced. The design team must decide how the system is to interact with the user and specify the inputs and outputs of the device. This second step in the cycle also includes a list of functions that the system must perform in order to implement the user-defined tasks. Whereas the system requirements show what the device must do, the system specifications detail how the system must operate in order to perform the tasks.

12.1.3 Partitioning

The third step is to determine how the functions should be *partitioned* between hardware and software. In many cases, it is obvious whether a particular function should be implemented in hardware or software. If there is a possibility of doing it either way, considerations such as cost or development time should point to the more practical method. The general problem of which way to do it is called the *hardware-software trade-off*.

12.1.4 Modularization

At this point in the design cycle, the project is split between a hardware design team and a software design team. Each team performs the fourth step, the *modularization*. The hardware team resolves the hardware design into a number of modules, each of which implements one or more of the hardware functions. The software is also partitioned into a hierarchy of modules, each of which performs one or more of the tasks to be implemented in software. The modules might be further divided into procedures, which are routines to perform particular functions. The final software modules consist of groups of procedures that are closely related to each other.

12.1.5 Software Design

In this discussion, concentrate on the software side of the cycle. The fifth step is to produce a *pseudo-code* image of the software. Each procedure is written in a syntax-free high-level language. This language has typical high-level program constructs, such as DO WHILE or IF THEN ELSE, and is used to establish the outline of the program, much as a flowchart would be used. Pseudo-code also introduces documentation constructs, to improve the readability and maintainability of the software.

The sixth step in the software design cycle is to verify that the pseudo-code is correct before the software is coded in the actual microprocessor language. A member of the software team other than the writer of the procedure executes the procedure "in his head" to make sure that the procedure actually does the function. This step is called the pseudo-code *walk-through*.

The procedure is then coded in some high-level language such as PASCAL or PL/M or in the assembly language for the processor. Each procedure is translated to machine code and tested. This seventh step in the software design cycle results in a set of machine language procedures that have been tested so far as can be in a stand-alone, one-at-a-time mode.

12.1.6 Integration and Evaluation

The eighth step involves integrating the software procedures. That is, the procedures are combined and tested for their interaction with each other. This usually involves more than just linking the programs and executing the resulting program. Instead, the highest level procedures (in terms of subroutine calling) are first tested with simplified versions (commonly called *stubs*) of the lower level procedures. As the program flow is verified, more and more complete procedures are substituted until the entire program is tested. If lower level procedures are finished first, they can be tested with short *driver* programs that call them as a higher level procedure would. Tools such as *simulators* and *in-circuit emulators* are available to aid in this task.

The ninth step is to integrate the hardware and software. It might be possible to do this by installing a prom with the completed system software into the hardware and exercising the resultant system. If extensive debugging is required, tools like the microcomputer *analyzer* and in-circuit emulator may be required.

The tenth step is to evaluate the entire system for satisfaction of the original requirements. The customer or end user of the system is the one who ultimately will decide on the suitability of the final product. After all, the customer is the one who must be happy with the performance of the system.

The entire design process is iterative; detection of errors at any point means looping back to an earlier point in the cycle. Figure 12.1 shows a diagram of the software system design cycle.

12.1.7 Documentation and Maintenance

In the previous steps, the designers have generated records of all the tasks they have performed during the design cycle. The complete collection of these records, organized in a logical manner, is the *system documentation*. If the records are incomplete or unclear, particularly in a large or complex system, it will be difficult to maintain the software. After the delivery of the system to the customer, it often needs to be modified, either because of undetected errors that only surface in the field or because the system is updated to perform additional functions. This *software maintenance* can be very costly, often accounting for up to 80 percent of the total software costs. Good design techniques and good documentation lead to easier and less costly system maintenance.

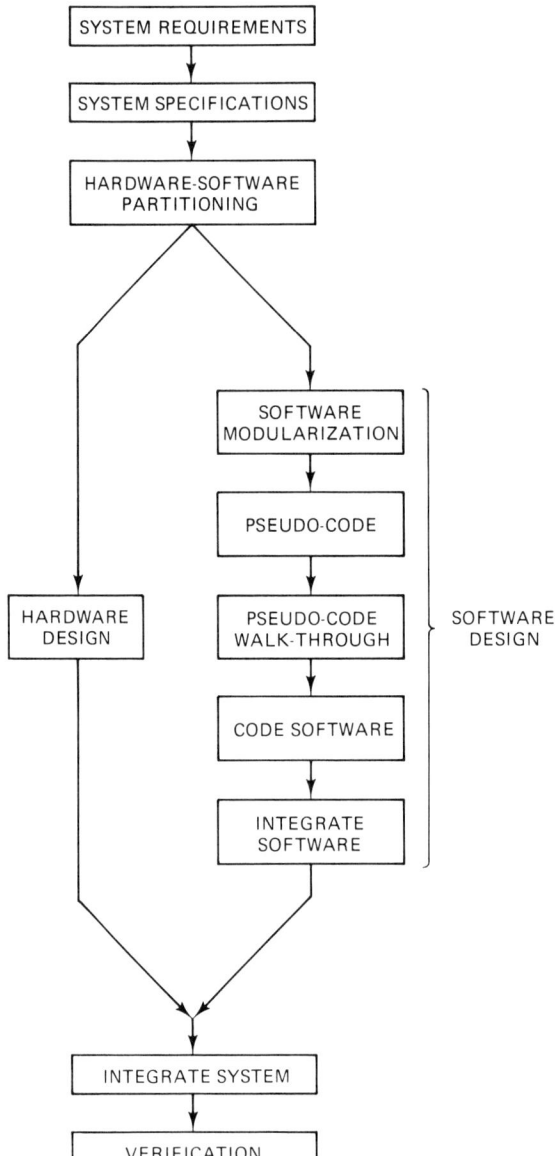

Figure 12.1 Software design cycle.

12.1.8 A Design Example

Let's illustrate the design process by an example: the design of a trainer microcomputer. This is the sort of basic computer that would be used by a student who is learning the assembly language for some processor. The trial programs would be hand-coded into machine language, entered, and executed. By this process, the student gets practical experience in writing and debugging software. Because the student is also learning about peripheral devices, the computer would be more useful if it had user I/O ports so that it could interact with and control external hardware. The design example will result in a real product that can be constructed as a project. Appendix A includes a complete description of the hardware and of the subsystem that controls the displays and keyboard.

12.2 TOP-DOWN VS. BOTTOM-UP DESIGN

When a system is designed, it is often immediately apparent that some subsystems are necessary. These subsystems are usually low-level parts of the project that implement very specific tasks. For example, many systems need a keyboard and displays for entry and display of data. If we start by designing these subsystems first, we are embarking on a *bottom-up* design cycle. This might be a reasonable thing to do for a small system that has a small number of subsystems and minimal interaction between them. The bottom-up method allows the designers and programmers to concentrate on the subsystems without having to get bogged down in the planning of the overall system. The problem often comes near the end of the project, when it is discovered that the subsystems do not mesh well, and extensive modification of the subsystems is required. It also might lead to more complicated higher level functions, as the high-level modules bind the subsystems together.

Top-down structured design is meant to remedy some of the drawbacks of the bottom-up design. First, the complete system function is specified, and the design is partitioned into a series of subfunctions, each of which might also have subfunctions. In this manner, the complex design is resolved into a series of more easily implemented functions. As each subfunction is specified, it limits and defines the properties of its subfunctions. In this way, the properties of the low-level functions can be expected to combine properly at system integration time.

The design proceeds from consideration of higher to lower modules, from more general to more specific considerations. The highest level is the *system design specification*. For the hardware, the highest level would be a *block diagram;* for the software, it would be the *software modularization*. The lower level functions, such as keyboards and displays, would only be specified later, when it is clear how they will fit in with the higher level modules. Implementation of the low-level functions would not be attempted until the partitioning process was completed.

12.3 SYSTEM REQUIREMENTS FOR THE PROJECT

As an example, let us consider the design of a trainer microcomputer. The question is, what should the computer be able to do for the student? A complete and correct answer to this question will lead to the system requirements. There is always the temptation to add too many bells and whistles, but the requirements should include only items actually needed by the user. We will attempt to answer the question in a simple and straightforward way.

12.3.1 The Trainer

The unit, like any system, must "come to life" when powered up so that the user knows it is ready to be used. The system has to be ready to accept a user program. Because it is extremely easy to make a mistake when entering a machine language program, it must be feasible to check the program before it is executed. There has to be some way to run the program, and there should be some indication to the user that the execution is proceeding. In case the program does not execute properly, it is important to provide at least some minimal debugging capability. There should be provision for display of an error message if the user makes an operational mistake such as an illegal series of keystrokes. The computer must be able to recover from such an error.

Because the student will be learning about interfacing to peripherals, the unit should have some way to exchange electrical signals with other devices. Finally, because handling devices in real time is an important application to learn about, we will provide the system with the ability to support interrupts.

12.3.2 System Requirements

From this discussion we will prepare the *system requirements*. The computer must provide

1. Visual feedback to the user
   a. Show prompt sign on power up
   b. Show error message on illegal operation
   c. Show run indication while executing user programs
2. Ability to enter, examine, and execute a user program. In order to do this, the computer must be able to
   a. Accept any address
   b. Examine the contents of any address
   c. Modify the contents of some addresses
   d. Execute a program from any starting address
3. Program debugging tools
   a. Breakpoint
   b. Display of the CPU register contents
4. Serial and parallel I/O ports
5. Support for interrupts (including vectored interrupts)

Many other requirements might be included, such as performance of a self-test upon power up, or having the device prompt the user by issuing instructions about how to operate the system. We also could have included a single-step mode of operation, or specified more complicated I/O, like an interface to a tape drive. We will assume, however, that the list details all the properties of the trainer.

12.4 SYSTEM SPECIFICATIONS FOR THE PROJECT

From the list of system requirements, we prepare a detailed description of how the device should interact with its environment and what processes it must perform to satisfy the list. Notice that the requirements describe what tasks the scale should perform. Now we are going to detail how the computer must perform to do the tasks. We will prepare a list of inputs, outputs, and processes to complete the *system specifications*.

12.4.1 Inputs

1. Sixteen data keys; a hexadecimal keypad
2. A "high address" key (H)
3. A "low address" key (L)
4. A "store or see" key (S)
5. An "execute" key (G), for "Go"
6. A "reset" key (R)
7. Hardware inputs

12.4.2 Outputs

1. Six, seven-segment displays
2. Hardware outputs

The keyboard and display for the computer is shown in Fig. 12.2. The keys labeled U1, U2, and U3 are *user* keys, recognized only by user programs.

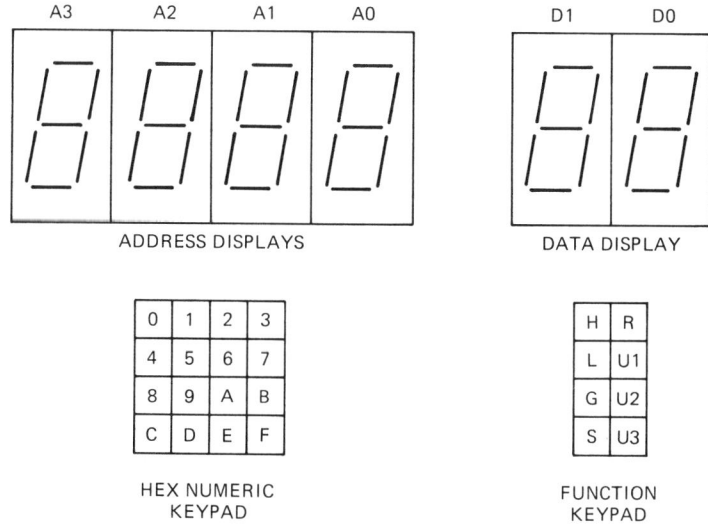

Figure 12.2 Keyboard/display.

12.4.3 Processes

1. Upon power up, the five leftmost displays will show the power-on prompt message "ready". The user must then strike any key except the reset key. See Fig. 12.3.

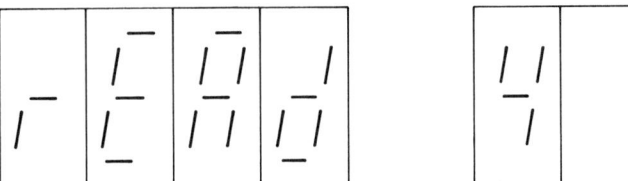

Figure 12.3 Prompt display.

2. Upon the first keystroke, the four leftmost displays will show the starting address 1400H, and the other two will show the hexadecimal value of the contents of that address (the data). The computer will wait for the user to strike a key. See Fig. 12.4.

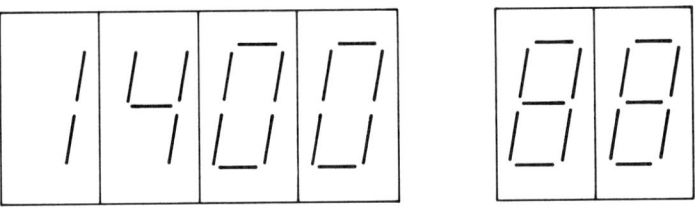

Figure 12.4 Starting address display.

3. Striking the R key will cause the same action as power up, independent of the present mode of operation.
4. The H key will be used to modify the address. Depression of H causes the values on the data displays to appear in the two leftmost displays. As the new address appears, the data displays are updated to the contents of that new address.
5. The L key causes the same action as the H key, but it operates on the low byte of the address.
6. Data key depression will cause the data displays to be changed, in a right-entry mode of operation. The rightmost display will accept the key value, and its value will be shifted left to the other data display.
7. The S key allows the user to examine or change the contents of memory. Hitting the S key causes the data shown on the displays to be stored in the memory location pointed to by the current address. The address is then automatically incremented, and the new data are displayed.
8. The G key causes execution of the program stored at the current address. While the program is running, the displays will show "run". See Fig. 12.5.

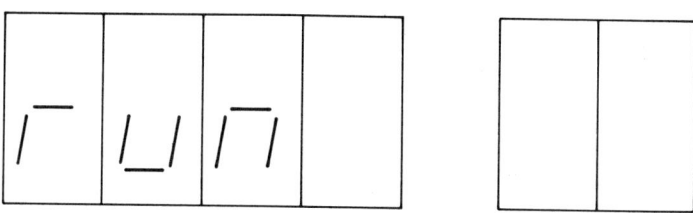

Figure 12.5 Run prompt display.

9. The debugging mode is entered through software. The user must enter a RST 6 code into the program at the point she or he wants the program to break. (The user must replace the proper code later.) When the processor executes the RST 6, the register display mode is entered. The two rightmost displays now identify the register pair, and the contents of that register pair appear in the four leftmost displays. Any keystroke (except the R key) now changes the register pair displayed, in the order AF (the 8085 accumulator and flags), BC, DE, HL, and SP. One more keystroke causes the address of the breakpoint and the RST 6 code to show. At this time any key could be used. The contents of the internal registers are not modified by this routine. See Fig. 12.6.

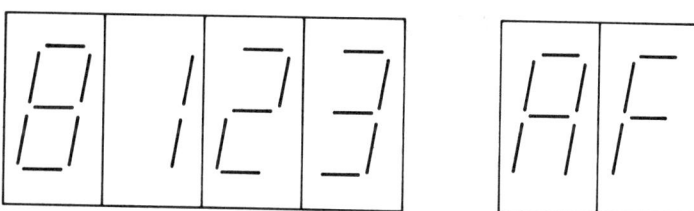

Figure 12.6 Register display.

10. "Error" will be displayed if two or more keys are touched at once. See Fig. 12.7. To recover, the operator presses the R key.

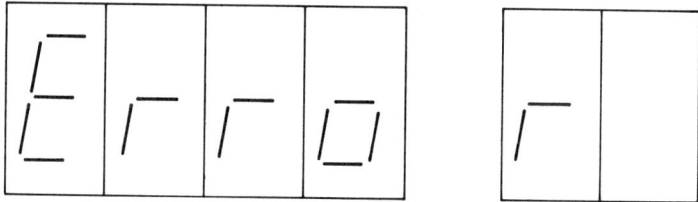

Figure 12.7 Error display.

11. Serial user I/O is provided by use of the 8085 pins SID and SOD. Parallel hardware I/O will be done through an 8155 programmable I/O chip.

12.4.4 Comparison

If we compare the specifications with the requirements, it can be seen that the specifications follow from the requirements but are much more detailed. They describe every action that the computer must take in order to perform the user-required tasks. Notice that the specifications are still mostly in terms of English descriptions, with few references to programs or specific hardware. Although specifications 9 and 11 could have been made in more general terms, it has already been decided to use the Intel 8085A microprocessor, and the specifications mirror this decision.

12.5 HARDWARE DESIGN

At this point in the design cycle, a decision must be made about whether to implement the various functions in hardware or software. The system needs a microprocessor, ROM and RAM to store the operating software, RAM to store user programs, and interfaces to the keyboard and displays. Figure 12.8 is an example of how the system might be configured.

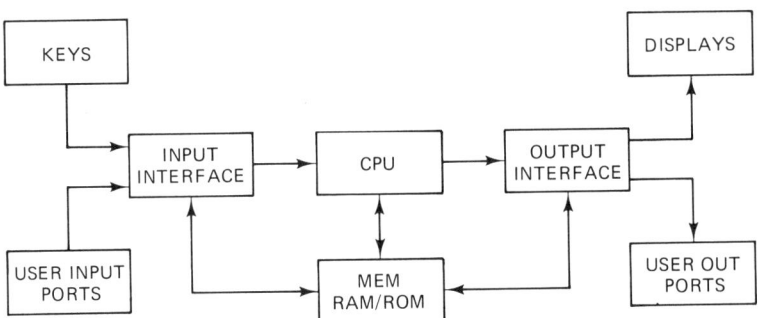

Figure 12.8 Hardware modular block diagram.

The only blocks in the diagram that might be implemented in software are the blocks for the input and output interfaces. In fact, they are good examples of how the design of a module might be shifted between hardware and software implementation. The keyboard might just be a set of momentary contact keys wired in a row-column matrix. This would be minimal hardware, but the software would be relatively complex. It must scan the matrix, check for key bounces, make sure the same keystroke is not detected more than once, decode keys for their numeric value, and a host of other considerations. On the other hand, the hardware could detect, debounce, decode, and latch the keycodes and provide a key-detected status bit. Then the software would be simple; it would only have to poll the status and input the keycode when it is ready. Similar considerations apply to the output interface, where the displays could be multiplexed in software or hardware.

The Intel 8279 programmable keyboard/display controller, which is described elsewhere in this book, would be one approach to solving both interface problems.

This would be a highly hardware-oriented solution. We will use an 8155 and an interrupt-driven software package to realize this part of the system.

12.5.1 Keyboard/Display Subsystem

Because this chapter is mainly concerned with the software design cycle, the hardware design considerations and descriptions are given in Appendix A. The I/O interface design will be done as a subsystem, and is also presented in the same appendix as another design example. We must, however, specify how the I/O driver will interact with the operating software we are designing.

The interaction is through eight reserved memory locations. Two of these are dedicated to the keyboard. The location KEY_STB is set to one when a legal keystroke is detected, and the location KEYCODE is loaded with the keycode. All that the software we are considering needs to do is poll KEY_STB until it is set, clear KEY_STB, and read KEYCODE. The keycodes are the actual numeric values for the hex keys, and the keycodes for H, L, S, and G are 10H through 13H, respectively. The R key is hardwired to the 8085 reset terminal.

The other reserved locations are six contiguous bytes called DIS_BUF, DIS_BUF+1, . . ., DIS_BUF+5. Our operating system must place the seven-segment codes for whatever we want to display in these locations. The I/O driver multiplexes these codes out to the displays. The code in DIS_BUF is sent to the rightmost display, DIS_BUF+1 to the second rightmost, and so on. All the software has to do to update the displays is write into this display buffer. The seven-segment codes are the same as described elsewhere in this book.

12.6 SOFTWARE DESIGN

Many people first learn about programming with a highly interactive language such as BASIC. The tendency is to sit at the terminal and bang out code without sufficient planning. The resulting programs are usually inefficient, hard to document and test, and extremely difficult to maintain. Just as top-down techniques are desirable for system design, so are they desirable for software design. The software design should be *modular,* that is, divided into small, manageable units. *Structured programming techniques,* where all the control and branching operations are done in a standard way, should be used. A plan for the overall program flow must be developed, often with the use of state transition diagrams. The software must be modularized, and pseudo-code written and tested, before the final code for each module can be produced.

12.6.1 Top-Down Software Design

Let us consider what a typical top-down structured program looks like. There is a *hierarchical* arrangement of all the routines that make up the package. At the top level is a main driver routine, often called the *executive program.* The function of the executive is to control the overall flow of the program. The actual tasks that must be executed to make the system work are written as a series of subroutines or procedures. The executive contains a section that initializes the system. Then it enters an endless loop that examines the inputs or controls of the system (often through one of the subroutines). The values gathered are tested and the executive conditionally calls the appropriate routines to do the current task. In a more complicated system, the executive might call one of several subexecutive programs, and many of the working procedures might have subroutines of their own. In any case, program control flows from the executive to the other procedures and *always* returns back to the executive.

12.6.2 State Transition Diagrams

We must now examine the system specifications to determine what software we need to write. Notice that although there are 21 different input keys, there are only 5 different types of keys. The system behaves in the same way if any of the hexadecimal keys are depressed. We will call them data keys. Striking any of these keys causes the data display to change but does not modify the memory. Both the H and L keys cause the address to change and the data displays to show the new data. H and L will be called address keys. Similarly, G, S, and R have well-defined effects on the state of the system. (The R key is actually implemented in hardware; it is the 8085 reset.)

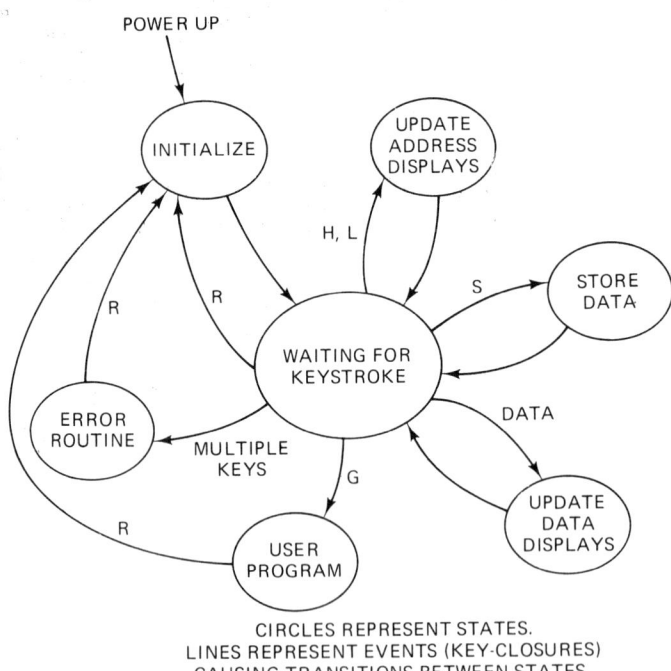

Figure 12.9 State transition diagram.

If we examine the outputs of the system, we can readily group them into address displays and data displays. Perhaps not so obvious is that the state of the system not only is determined by the status of the displays but also by the memory. The H, L, R, and S keys all have the effect of causing the data displays to assume the value of the contents of the current address. Data keys alter this correspondence, and the S key forces the data display value into the memory. The G key passes control away from the program. Thus there are many identifiable output states, depending on the address displays, the data displays, the memory, and whether we are in a user program. A complete state transition diagram is beyond the scope of this text, but see Fig. 12.9 for a simplified version.

12.7 SOFTWARE MODULARIZATION FOR THE PROJECT

Once the different procedures or subroutines needed are identified, it is usual to collect them into related groups called modules. There are many reasons for this. For example, all the programs in a particular module might do similar tasks so that they are functionally related. The programs might have to be executed in a narrow time interval, like the procedures invoked by a particular interrupt device. They might be a routine and all its subroutines, or they might just be the programs that didn't seem to fit into any of the other modules.

When we examine the system specifications or the transition diagrams, we see that several programs are going to be needed. In any case, we will need an executive program to control the overall program flow. We will call the executive program MONITOR and define an EXECUTIVE module to hold this. The software to interact with the inputs (through KEY_STB and KEYCODE) will be named GET-KEY and will be placed in the INPUT module. Software must be provided to send output codes to the memory locations DIS_BUF, . . ., DIS_BUF+5. These are routines to update the address and data displays. The routines DIS_HI and DIS_LO will be used to modify the contents of the high and low bytes of the address displays. The routine DIS_DAT will change the data displays. Also needed is a routine to cause messages such as "run" and "error" to appear on the displays. Because these routines will copy set tables of seven-segment codes into the display buffer, we will conceive a program BLK_MOV to do this task. DIS_HI, DIS_LO, DIS_DAT, and BLK_MOV make up the OUTPUT module.

Now we examine the processes section of the specifications. From process A, it can be seen that we need to initialize the address displays and data displays. The hardware for the system (programming the 8155, which is controlling the keyboard and displays) will be initialized in that subsystem software. Most systems would have an INIT module, containing programs like INITSW and INITHW to initialize the software and hardware. In our design, we place the procedure INITSW into the EXECUTIVE module. Process B, as mentioned before, is implemented in hardware. Both processes C and D have to do with modifying the address. Module ADDRESS will contain the programs HI and LO, which will be invoked upon detection of an H or L key. Processes E and F will define another module DATA, containing a program DATA to handle data keystrokes and a program STORE. Following specification G, a module RUN will be set up. RUN contains the routine GO, which enters the user program, and the program DIS_RUN. The next two processes suggest a module DEBUG, which contains the programs REGISTERS and DIS_REG and the module ERROR containing ERROR and DIS_ERR. Upon consideration of how the routines might work, we can determine what other routines are needed.

Notice that the routines HI and LO are very similar in function. Each must read the current data display, place the data in the high or low byte of the address displays, and display the new data at that address. Implicit in this process is that the system have a digital image of the current address and data (the image in the display buffer is in terms of seven-segment codes). Assume that the current address is stored in two contiguous memory locations, ADD_BUF and ADD_BUF+1, and the data are stored in location DAT_BUF. The algorithm for implementing HI would be to read DAT_BUF and write those data into ADD_BUF+1 to get the new address. Then that memory location would be read and the result written into DAT_BUF.

All that remains to be done is to update the displays to reflect the new status. The routines DIS_HI and DIS_DAT could be called to do this. But because these

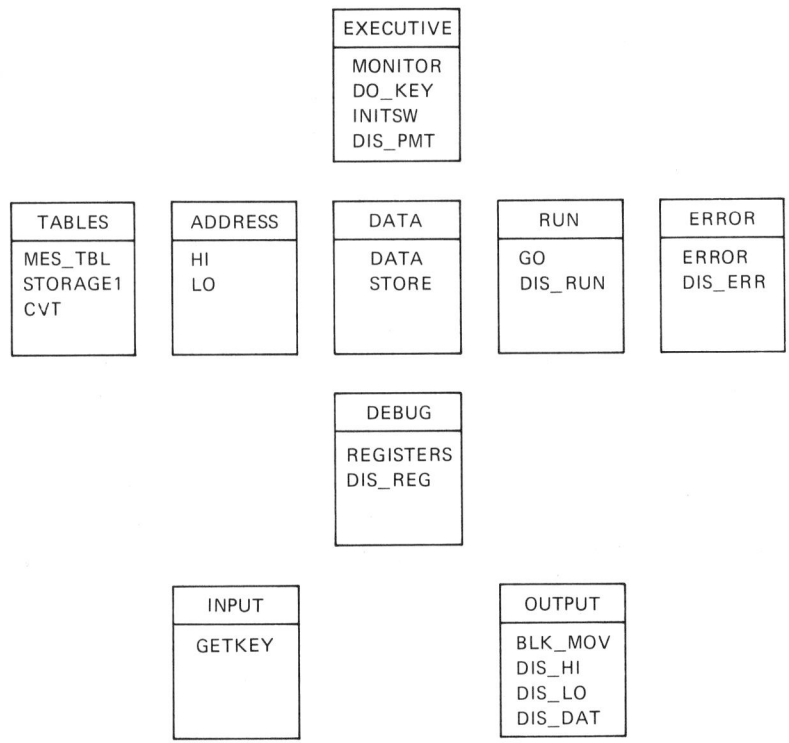

Figure 12.10 Software modularization for the trainer microcomputer.

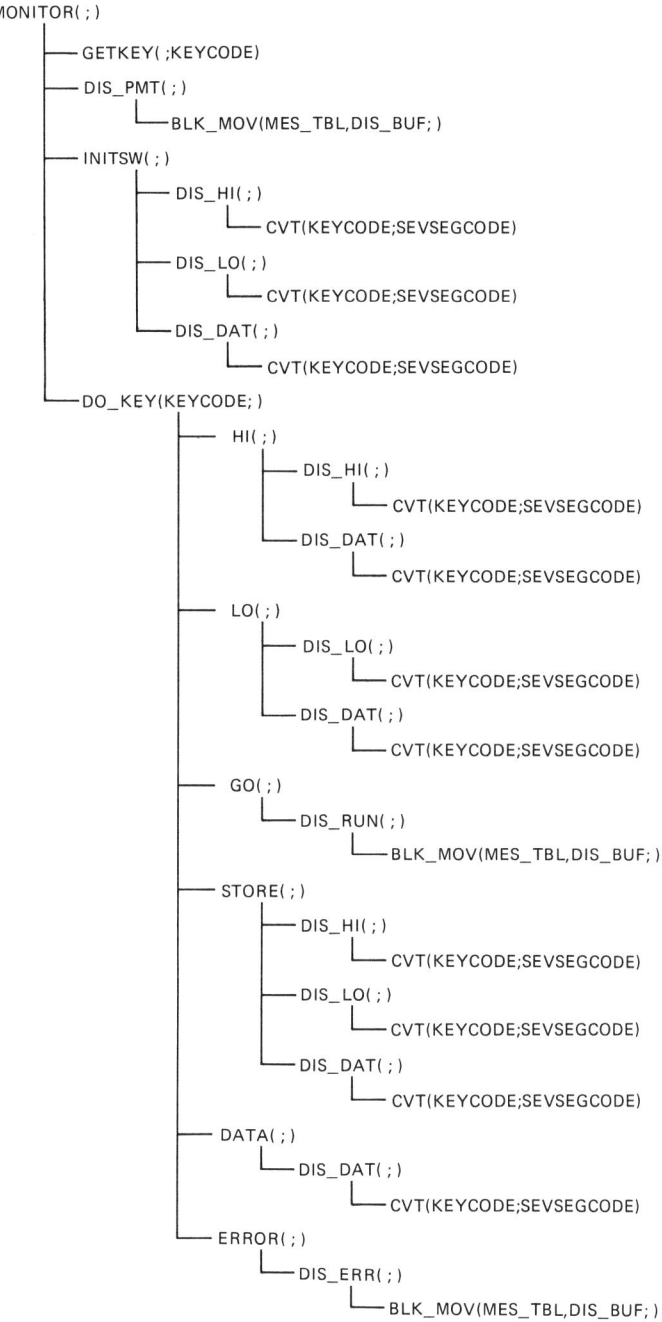

Figure 12.11 Procedure calling tree for the trainer.

programs read a digital image from the data and address buffers, and must place a seven-segment code image in the display buffer, they might each call a routine called CVT. CVT would be a look-up routine that is entered with a hexadecimal digit and returns the seven-segment code. The CVT routine accesses a table of seven-segment codes that is stored in the system ROM.

In addition to CVT, this discussion introduces two other programs. We define the procedure STORAGE1, which sets up reserved memory locations for the address and data buffers and any others we might need. The procedure MES_TBL will define the seven-segment code table and any other tables we must implement.

Consideration of how STORE and DATA work does not lead to any more new procedures. The programs DIS_ERR and DIS_RUN need seven-segment code tables for their messages, but these can be defined in procedure MES_TBL. The DISREG routine needs reserved memory to save the registers; this can be done in STORAGE1.

This completes the software modularization. There are, of course, a great variety of ways the procedures and modules can be chosen. For example, DIS_RUN, DIS_PMT, and DIS_ERR cause a message to show on the display; they could have been grouped together in a module called MESSAGE. A diagrammatic representation of the software modules is shown in Fig. 12.10.

At this point it is usual to introduce another diagram, the procedure calling tree, shown in Fig. 12.11. This diagram organizes the procedures in a way that highlights the relationship between called and calling procedures. The diagram includes a notation to specify parameters passed between the procedures.

12.8 PSEUDO-CODE FOR THE PROJECT

Nearly everyone who learns how to program is introduced to the technique of using flowcharts to aid in the program development. Flowcharts, which are graphical devices to depict the algorithm for the software being constructed, have the advantage of familiarity. However, they have several disadvantages. Unlike pseudo-code, the flowchart does not force the programmer to follow tenets of modular, structured programming. There is seldom room on the flowchart to describe program steps fully. Furthermore, it is difficult to keep the documentation current; any change involves a complete redrawing of the chart.

Pseudo-code, on the other hand, contains documentation and program structures and is easily updated with a word processor. Pseudo-code, or programming design language (PDL), is the technique we will describe and employ.

What are the properties that a pseudo-code should possess? The code should, like such languages as PASCAL or PL/M, support the constructs necessary to impose proper structure to the software. Such languages, however, are meant to be read by computers and are very inflexible with respect to syntax. The pseudo-code should not need exact punctuation or have a special set of reserved words. Rather, the ideas that express the algorithm for the software should be coded in plain English statements. For example, if we wanted to set a counter to zero, the PASCAL statement would be "COUNT := 0;". In pseudo-code, it could be "SET COUNT TO ZERO," or "RESET COUNT," or any other statement that is easily understood by the reader.

Documentation constructs that encourage the programmer to use modular design and to provide a complete description of the software are an important part of the design language. This includes items such as packages to outline modules and procedures and headers, or prologues, to document properly the contents of the package. Each module could be declared a MODULE...END MODULE construct. The module prologue might contain such items as authorship, date, a list of the procedures contained, and a list of data accessed or modified. The procedure declaration might be similar, such as PROCEDURE...(header)...BEGIN PROCEDURE...(code)...END PROCEDURE.

Program constructs must be included to ensure proper structured design. Each construct defines a program segment that has single entry and exit points and implements a certain, well-defined function. It is possible to define a set of program constructs such that proper program flow control is easily attained. The structures could be classified as

1. Sequence of statements
2. Conditional structures
3. Loop constructs

The sequence construct would be "DO (series of statements) END". It is possible to invoke an entire procedure (which could be thought of as a sequence) with the "CALL...RETURN" construct. The conditional structures would be "IF(condition)THEN(series of statements)" and "IF(condition)THEN(series of statements)ELSE(series of statements)." The loop constructs would include the endless loop "DO ALWAYS...END" and conditional loops "DO WHILE (condition)...END" and "DO UNTIL(condition)...END." Other constructs also follow the rules for good structure, but we will use only those mentioned here. The "GOTO..." structure will be avoided.

An important aspect of modular design is how to keep track of parameters. As each procedure is invoked, the calling procedure might be required to send some information to its subroutine. This routine might also want to pass data back to the calling routine. Each procedure name will be appended with an input and output parameter list to keep track of the information flow. The format will be

NAME(parm1;parm2)

where parm1 is an input parameter and parm2 is an output parameter. Multiple parameters will be separated with commas. An example would be an addition routine; the calling procedure would pass in the two addends and receive back the sum. The complete name of such a routine might be ADDER(addend1,addend2;sum).

We will illustrate the use of design language by continuing the design of the trainer microcomputer.

12.8.1 Pseudo-Code for the Module Executive

A review of the design specifications, the state transition diagram, the software modularization, and what we have said about how the software driver must work enables us to develop an algorithm for the MONITOR procedure. Evidently, it must invoke DIS_PMT to set up the initial display status. Then it would call GETKEY to wait for the first keystroke. Upon the first keystroke, and after return to MONITOR, INITSW must be called to initialize the buffers and displays to show the starting address. The program would then go into an endless loop, at the head of which is an invocation of the procedure GETKEY to detect key closures by the operator. The procedure DO_KEY would be called in order to test the keycode and selectively invoke the appropriate routine, one for each type of key. Notice that the control always returns to MONITOR, and thus to GETKEY, where the computer is waiting for the next keystroke.

The DO_KEY routine may call six other routines: HI, LO, DATA, GO, STORE, and ERROR. The author of the DO_KEY software does not need to know the details of how each of these routines is constructed. All that is required is the assurance that a routine to implement the task described in the specifications exists or will exist, and what parameters must be passed. We will note that GETKEY gathers the keycode and returns it to MONITOR. Thus, GETKEY has an output parameter KEYCODE. The procedure DO_KEY needs to know which key was pressed; this information is passed into DO_KEY as the input parameter KEYCODE. No other routines directly pass information, but all of the other routines access or modify the memory locations ADD_BUF and DAT_BUF. These locations will be defined as program variables.

12.8.2 Pseudo-Code for the Procedure MONITOR

A first pass at writing the pseudo-code for MONITOR is shown in the following segment.

```
PROCEDURE MONITOR

    (PROCEDURE HEADING TO BE ADDED LATER)

    BEGIN PROCEDURE MONITOR

        CALL DIS_PMT
        CALL GETKEY
        CALL INITSW
        DO FOREVER
            CALL GETKEY
            CALL DO_KEY
        END

    END PROCEDURE MONITOR
```

Examine the code first for the documentation constructs. The prologue is always placed between the procedure declaration and "BEGIN PROCEDURE," and the body, or executable code, follows. Indentions and blank lines set off the different parts of the program to facilitate easy reading. The body of the program is a series of statements; look for some of the program constructs we have defined. Indention is also employed to set off the various program constructs. We have yet to complete the procedure heading and to show the relationship for the parameters.

Now we verify that the code actually implements the task that has been set. Does this code cause the ready prompt to appear upon power up? Does it then wait for the user to touch a key? Is there provision for setting up the proper starting address? Does it finally go into an endless loop that monitors the keypad and invokes the routine that implements the command issued from the keypad? This process of verification by a thought process is the design walk-through and must be done for each procedure before conversion to the final programming language.

12.8.3 Pseudo-Code for the Procedure INITSW(;)

The procedure INITSW should initialize the memory locations ADD_BUF and DAT_BUF. After the address and data displays are updated to reflect this new information, the task of INITSW is over. Let us write the pseudo-code for INITSW, but this time attempt to include a proper procedure heading and keep track of any parameters or variables. The code is shown in the following procedure.

```
PROCEDURE INITSW( ; )

    WRITTEN BY: G. THOMAS HUETTER   DATE: 2/21/88

    CALLED BY:
        DIS_HI( ; ), DIS_LO( ; ), DIS_DAT( ; )

    DATA STRUCTURE:
        INPUT PARAMETERS:    NONE
        OUTPUT PARAMETERS:   NONE
        PROGRAM VARIABLES:   ADDRESS BUFFER, DATA BUFFER

    BEGIN PROCEDURE INITSW( ; )

        SAVE ENVIRONMENT
        SET ADDRESS BUFFER TO 1400H
        CALL DIS_HI( ; )
        CALL DIS_LO( ; )
        READ CONTENTS OF 1400H
        STORE IT IN DATA BUFFER
        CALL DIS_DAT( ; )
        RESTORE ENVIRONMENT
        RETURN

    END PROCEDURE INITSW( ; )
```

INITSW does not accept any parameters from MONITOR, nor does it pass any back. Although there are no parameters in this routine, there must be a standard notation to identify the parameters of a procedure. The notation for this procedure name will be INITSW(;). The field inside the parentheses is meant to contain the parameter list, with input parameters preceding the semicolon and output parameters following. Each procedure should have information in the procedure header. This should include authorship, purpose of the program, how the procedure is invoked, and the programs it invokes and should show how the program handles data. The subheading data structure is used to describe any parameters and to show variables or memory locations that are modified by the procedure.

As for the body of procedure INITSW(;), we should perform a walk-through to verify correct operation. Does it properly initialize the address buffer and data buffer? Does it cause the proper response on the displays? When answering these questions, we assume that properly functioning subroutines such as DIS_HI(;), DIS_LO(;), and DIS_DAT(;) exist.

12.8.4 Pseudo-Code for the Procedure DO_KEY(KEYCODE;)

The code for this procedure must identify which key was struck and invoke the appropriate procedure to implement the function desired for that keystroke. For example, when any data key is touched, the routine DATA should run to cause the value of the data key to appear in the data displays. This routine must know the value of the keycode, but returns no data back to DO_KEY(KEYCODE;); thus it will be called DATA(KEYCODE;). Similarly, strokes of the H, L, G, and S keys must, respectively, call the routines HI(;), LO(;), GO(;), and STORE(;). Any other key should lead to execution of the routine ERROR(;). Walk through the pseudo-code shown here to verify proper operation. Notice that the procedure prologue shows authorship, has a thumbnail description of the purpose of the software, and identifies KEYCODE as the only datum involved.

```
PROCEDURE DO_KEY(KEYCODE; )

    WRITTEN BY:  G. THOMAS HUETTER   DATE: 2/21/88

    CALLED BY:
        MONITOR( ; )

    PROCEDURES CALLED:
        HI( ; ), LO( ; ), DATA(KEYCODE; ), STORE( ; )
        GO( ; ), ERROR( ; )

    DATA STRUCTURE:
        INPUT PARAMETERS:  KEYCODE
        OUTPUT PARAMETERS: NONE

    BEGIN PROCEDURE DO_KEY(KEYCODE; )

        IF KEYCODE IS FOR "H" KEY
            THEN CALL HI( ; )
        IF KEYCODE IS FOR A DATA KEY
            THEN CALL DATA(KEYCODE; )
        IF KEYCODE IS FOR "L" KEY
            THEN CALL LO( ; )
        IF KEYCODE IS FOR "G" KEY
            THEN CALL GO( ; )
        IF KEYCODE IS FOR "S" KEY
            THEN CALL STORE( ; )
        IF KEYCODE IS AN ILLEGAL KEY
            THEN CALL ERROR( ; )
        RETURN

    END PROCEDURE DO_KEY(KEYCODE; )
```

12.8.5 Pseudo-Code for the Procedure DIS_PMT(;)

Upon power up, the computer is supposed to show the prompt "ready" in the displays. In order to do this, a table of seven-segment codes stored in the ROM must be copied to the display buffer. Because there are other messages to be sent out at other times, we have a program BLKMOV that can copy the required 6 bytes from one set of memory locations to another. What DIS_PMT(;) must do is to set up pointers to the message table and to the display buffer. The parameters MES_TBL and DIS_BUF are the respective pointers. MES_TBL can have different values, depending on the message to be sent—in this case, PMT_TBL. The copy subroutine will be called BLKMOV(MES_TBL,DIS_BUF;) and in this instance MES_TBL will be PMT_TBL.

The pseudo-code for DIS_PMT(;) is shown below. Verify proper operation and documentation for the procedure. The procedures DIS_RUN(;) and DIS_ERR (;) would be identical except for the value of MES_TBL.

```
PROCEDURE DIS_PMT( ; )

    WRITTEN BY:   G. THOMAS HUETTER   DATE: 2/20/88

    CALLED BY:
        MONITOR( ; )

    PROCEDURES CALLED:
        BLK_MOV(MES_TBL,DIS_BUF; )

    DATA STRUCTURE:
        INPUT PARAMETERS:  NONE
        OUTPUT PARAMETERS: NONE

    BEGIN PROCEDURE DIS_PMT( ; )

        POINT TO DISPLAY BUFFER
        POINT TO PROMPT MESSAGE TABLE
        CALL BLK_MOV(MES_TBL,DIS_BUF; )
        RETURN

    END PROCEDURE DIS_PMT( ; )
```

12.8.6 Complete Pseudo-Code for the Module EXECUTIVE

Following is the complete pseudo-code for the module EXECUTIVE.

```
MODULE EXECUTIVE

    WRITTEN BY:  G. THOMAS HUETTER
    DATE:        3/2/88

    PROCEDURES: MONITOR( ; ), INITSW( ; ), DO_KEY(KEYCODE; ),
                DIS_PMT( ; )

    EXTERNAL PROCEDURES: GETKEY( ; ), DIS_HI( ; ), DIS_LO( ; ),
                         DIS_DAT( ; ), HI( ; ), LO( ; ), GO( ; ),
                         DATA(KEYCODE; ), STORE( ; ), ERROR( ; )
```

```
PROCEDURE MONITOR( ; )

    WRITTEN BY:  G. THOMAS HUETTER   DATE: 2/19/88

    CALLED BY:
        THIS PROCEDURE IS INVOKED UPON POWER-UP
        OR UPON A COLD OR WARM RESTART.

    PROCEDURES CALLED:
        DIS_PMT( ; ), GETKEY( ;KEYCODE),
        INITSW( ; ), DO_KEY(KEYCODE; )

    DATA STRUCTURE:
        INPUT PARAMETERS:  NONE
        OUTPUT PARAMETERS: NONE

    BEGIN PROCEDURE MONITOR( ; )

        CALL DIS_PMT( ; )
        CALL GETKEY( ;KEYCODE)
        CALL INITSW( ; )
        DO FOREVER
            CALL GETKEY( ;KEYCODE)
            CALL DO_KEY(KEYCODE; )
        END

    END PROCEDURE MONITOR( ; )

PROCEDURE INITSW( ; )

    WRITTEN BY:  G. THOMAS HUETTER   DATE: 2/21/88

    CALLED BY:
        MONITOR( ; )

    PROCEDURES CALLED:
        DIS_HI( ; ), DIS_LO( ; ), DIS_DAT( ; )

    DATA STRUCTURE:
        INPUT PARAMETERS:  NONE
        OUTPUT PARAMETERS: NONE
        PROGRAM VARIABLES: ADDRESS BUFFER, DATA BUFFER

    BEGIN PROCEDURE INITSW( ; )

        SAVE ENVIRONMENT
        SET ADDRESS BUFFER TO 1000H
        CALL DIS_HI( ; )
        CALL DIS_LO( ; )
        READ CONTENTS OF 1000H
        STORE IT IN DATA BUFFER
        CALL DIS_DAT( ; )
        RESTORE ENVIRONMENT
        RETURN

    END PROCEDURE INITSW( ; )

PROCEDURE DO_KEY(KEYCODE; )

    WRITTEN BY:  G. THOMAS HUETTER   DATE: 2/21/88

    CALLED BY:
        MONITOR( ; )
```

```
        PROCEDURES CALLED:
            HI( ; ), LO( ; ), DATA(KEYCODE; )
            STORE( ; ), GO( ; ), ERROR( ; )

        DATA STRUCTURE:
            INPUT PARAMETERS:  KEYCODE
            OUTPUT PARAMETERS: NONE

        BEGIN PROCEDURE DO_KEY(KEYCODE; )

            IF KEYCODE IS FOR "H" KEY
                THEN CALL HI( ; )
            IF KEYCODE IS FOR A DATA KEY
                THEN CALL DATA(KEYCODE; )
            IF KEYCODE IS FOR "L" KEY
                THEN CALL LO( ; )
            IF KEYCODE IS FOR "G" KEY
                THEN CALL GO( ; )
            IF KEYCODE IS FOR "S" KEY
                THEN CALL STORE( ; )
            IF KEYCODE IS AN ILLEGAL KEY
                THEN CALL ERROR( ; )
            RETURN

        END PROCEDURE DO_KEY(KEYCODE; )

    PROCEDURE DIS_PMT( ; )

        WRITTEN BY:  G. THOMAS HUETTER    DATE: 2/21/88

        CALLED BY:
            MONITOR( ; )

        PROCEDURES CALLED:
            BLK_MOV(MES_TBL,DIS_BUF; )

        DATA STRUCTURE:
            INPUT PARAMETERS:  NONE
            OUTPUT PARAMETERS: NONE

        BEGIN PROCEDURE DIS_PMT( ; )

            POINT TO DISPLAY BUFFER
            POINT TO PROMPT MESSAGE TABLE
            CALL BLK_MOV(MES_TBL,DIS_BUF; )
            RETURN

        END PROCEDURE DIS_PMT( ; )

END MODULE EXECUTIVE
```

This document collects together all the procedures for the module EXECUTIVE. The module header shows authorship, a list of the procedures included, and a list of external (i.e., in a different module) procedures called. Walk through each procedure in the module to verify correct operation.

A similar process must be performed for each module in the system. When this is done, a complete pseudo-code implementation of the system software will be available. The completion of the pseudo-code for the microprocessor trainer is left as an exercise.

12.9 ASSEMBLY LANGUAGE FOR THE PROJECT

The software must now be translated into machine code for the microprocessor being used—in this case, 8085 machine code. However, the pseudo-code is never translated directly into machine code but rather is encoded into some high-level language such as PASCAL, PL/M, or C. A compiler would then generate the machine language for each procedure from the high-level language implementation. Critical sections of the software, for example, procedures that must execute at maximum speed, would be written in the assembly language for the processor. Although in modern practice high-level language implementation is common, because the languages described in this text are assembly languages, we will encode all the procedures into 8085 assembly language.

The task of generating the machine level code has several levels. Each pseudo-code procedure must be converted to 8085 assembly language. Each must then be assembled, with a program such as CASM85. The output of the assembler would include an object-code program, which would be machine language, but probably not in executable form. These individual machine code programs must then be combined or linked into a complete executable program. The software must be tested for proper operation, and if there are errors they must be located and corrected. Testing should not wait for completion of the linking procedure; there are techniques for testing individual machine code programs. In the rest of this section conversion to assembly language and linking is discussed. Testing is deferred until Sec. 12.10, on software integration.

In order to illustrate the process of conversion to assembly language, we assume that we are working on a project that needs several software delay programs. Three delays are needed: a 10-msec, a 20-msec, and a 50-msec delay. Each will be implemented by calling a 1-msec delay the proper number of times. Thus, the procedure DEL_10_MSEC will call the procedure DEL_1_MSEC 10 times. Note that both of these programs are subroutines that will be called by other programs. The pseudo-code for the procedure DEL_10_MSEC might look like this:

```
PROCEDURE DEL_10_MSEC
    Save environment
    Set COUNT to 10
    Do Until COUNT = 0
        Call DEL_1_MSEC
        Decrement COUNT
    End
    Restore environment
END PROCEDURE
```

The variable COUNT must be kept track of by the computer. It might be stored in a reserved memory location or in one of the CPU registers. We will assign the 8085 register C for this task. The DO UNTIL. . .END loop could be implemented by calling DEL_1_MSEC, decrementing the C register, and looping back to the call until the C register is empty, after moving 10 into the C register. This routine would only use the C register and the PSW, so the Saves and Restores would only involve the BC and PSW register pairs.

The assembly language version might thus look like this:

```
DEL_10_MSEC:    PUSH    PSW
                PUSH    B
                MVI     C,COUNT
LOOP1:          CALL    DEL_1_MSEC
                DCR     C
                JNZ     LOOP1
                POP     B
                POP     PSW
                RET
```

However, this program would not assemble correctly. The assembler would not be able to evaluate the symbols COUNT and DEL_1_MSEC, and would report so in error messages. The problem with COUNT could be taken care of by the use of the EQU assembler directive, but there is no way to evaluate the label DEL_1_MSEC because we do not know where that program will be stored in memory. In fact, that program might not even have been written yet. The solution is to declare such symbols as "external" variables. This causes the assembler to go ahead and assemble the program even though it can't evaluate the symbol. The symbol can be evaluated later, at link time, when all the procedures are presented in concert.

If these details were taken care of, the program would assemble on many assemblers, although some may require additional structure such as an END statement. There would still be a problem, however. The variables LOOP1 and DEL_10_MSEC would be treated as "local" variables; that is, they would be known only inside this program. This would be an advantage for LOOP1, because then some other program could also use the same label. But consider DEL_10_MSEC. This label must have been declared external in the program that called this program. If DEL_10_MSEC is a local variable, it will not be able to be passed to the calling routine at link time. The solution to this dilemma is to declare such labels "global," that is, known to all the programs that are being linked together. Notice that because DEL_1_MSEC is external in this program, it must be declared global in that subroutine.

With these changes, the assembly routine might look like this:

```
                GLB     DEL_10_MSEC     ;Global declaration
                EXT     DEL_1_MSEC      ;External declaration
                CODE                    ;Code segment declaration

COUNT           EQU     10              ;Count is defined

DEL_10M_SEC:    PUSH    PSW             ;
                PUSH    B               ;Save environment
                MVI     C,COUNT         ;Initialize Count
LOOP1:          CALL    DEL_1_MSEC      ;
                DCR     C               ;
                JNZ     LOOP1           ;Do ten calls
                POP     B               ;
                POP     PSW             ;Restore environment
                RET
```

The use of the assembler directive CODE is for the linker and is discussed below. Several more examples are shown in Sec. 12.9.1, on assembly language for the module EXECUTIVE.

The linking procedure usually involves presenting a list of the programs to be linked to the linker software. It is at this time that the external variable will be evaluated, and the output of the linker is an executable program. Another task of the linker is to place the software in the proper area of memory. For example, the bulk of the procedures in this project are executable procedures that must be placed in the system ROM. The tables, such as the prompt and look-up tables for the seven-segment codes for the numeric characters are also stored in the ROM. The procedures that set up reserved memory locations, such as the programs STORAGE1 (described above) and the program STORE (see Appendix A), must refer to the RAM locations. The stack also must be located in the RAM. In this project, for example, the code must be placed in system ROM, which lies in the address range 0 through 7FFH, and the reserved memory locations must lie in the range 3000H through 30FFH. The linker (or, in some systems, a locator program) must then be able to look through the input list of procedures and decide which area to place them. This is accomplished by use of different segments. Any procedure to be placed in ROM might be declared to be in the code segment, while the reserved memory locations might be declared as being in the data segment. This is the reason for the CODE declaration in the preceding program. In the linker used to prepare the software for this project, CODE is the default declaration, and may be suppressed in any program meant to be stored in ROM.

The linker must also provide some error diagnostic capacity. The most prevalent problem is that of unresolved externals. This means that the linker could not evaluate some label that had been declared external. Typical causes for this error are forgetting to include some procedure in the link list, forgetting to declare some symbol to be global, or misspelling of the symbol in one or the other file.

At the end of this process of translation to assembly language, assembly of each procedure, and linking of the object-code programs, a complete *absolute*, or executable, program would exist. The final version of the software must then be tested for any remaining bugs.

12.9.1 Assembly Language for the Module EXECUTIVE

It is now time to encode the pseudo-code procedures into assembly language. As examples of this process, we will generate assembly code for the four programs in the module EXECUTIVE. Refer to the pseudo-code for the module.

Assembly language for the procedure MONITOR(;). The MONITOR procedure is entered by the command JMP MONITOR in the program INIT, which is part of the I/O subsystem described in Appendix A. Therefore, the program must have an entry label MONITOR, which must be declared global. The (;) notation must be suppressed in the assembly language, as the assembler will only accept alphanumeric characters (and the character _) as components of a symbol.

Because MONITOR calls four other routines—GET_KEY, DIS_PMT, DO_KEY, and INITSW—these symbols must be declared external. There are no parameters to be assigned. The body of the procedure involves the first three calls and then an endless loop of alternate calls of GET_KEY and DO_KEY.

Each assembly routine should also have a header. This should include similar information to the pseudo-code header, such as authorship, calling routine(s), called routine(s), and parameters, and it should keep track of any registers or memory locations affected. Another necessary item for the HP64000 assembler is the notation "8085," which tells the system the type of microprocessor for which the assembly code is written. Examine the following segment and notice the relationship between the pseudo-code and assembly code.

```
        "8085"

;THIS IS THE MONITOR PROGRAM
;WRITTEN BY: G. THOMAS HUETTER
; CALLED BY: INVOKED AT POWER-UP, OR UPON EXECUTION OF "RST 7"
; SUBROUTINES CALLED: DIS_PMT, GETKEY, INITSW, DO_KEY
; PARAMETERS:    INPUT: NONE        OUTPUT: NONE
; REGISTERS AFFECTED: PSW
; MEMORY LOCATIONS AFFECTED: ADD_BUF, ADD_BUF+1, DAT_BUF
;                            DIS_BUF THROUGH DIS_BUF+5
;
         GLB    MONITOR
         EXT    GETKEY, DIS_PMT, DO_KEY, INITSW

         CODE

MONITOR: CALL   DIS_PMT     ;DISPLAY THE POWER-ON PROMPT
         CALL   GETKEY      ;WAIT FOR FIRST KEYSTROKE
         CALL   INITSW      ;DISPLAY STARTING ADDRESS
L1:      CALL   GETKEY      ;GET THE NEXT KEYCODE
         CALL   DO_KEY
         JMP    L1
```

Assembly language for the procedure INITSW(;). The conversion for the procedure INITSW is similar. INITSW should be the entry label and be a global quantity, and the subroutine entry labels should be declared external. The major difference is the existence of the variables ADDRESS BUFFER and DATA BUFFER. Because 8085 data are 1 byte long, a single memory location, which will be called DAT_BUF, will be sufficient. 8085 addresses require 2 bytes, so two consecutive memory locations will be reserved, with ADD_BUF being the pointer to them. The method for setting up these reserved locations is discussed at the end of this section, where they are defined and made global. We may then assume that they exist and make them external in this procedure.

How should we set ADD_BUF to 1400H? Familiarity with the way the 8085 works might suggest putting 1400H in a register pair and transferring their contents into memory. Because we also have to use this same address as a pointer to memory, the logical choice is to use register pair HL. We can then, later in the program, bring the contents of memory location 1400H into the accumulator and send that accumulator's contents out to location DAT_BUF. Accordingly, a possible version of the routine could be that shown here:

```
     "8085"

;THIS PROCEDURE INITIALIZES ADD_BUF TO STARTING ADDRESS 1400H,
;AND DISPLAYS ADDRESS AND THE PROPER DATA.
;WRITTEN BY: G. THOMAS HUETTER   3/22/88
; CALLED BY: MONITOR
; PARAMETERS:  INPUT: NONE      OUTPUT: NONE
; REGISTERS AFFECTED: NONE
; MEMORY LOCATIONS AFFECTED: ADD_BUF, ADD_BUF+1, DAT_BUF
;                            DIS_BUF  THROUGH  DIS_BUF+5

        GLB  INITSW
        EXT  ADD_BUF, DAT_BUF, DIS_HI, DIS_LO, DIS_DAT

        CODE
INITSW: PUSH H            ;
        PUSH PSW          ;SAVE ENVIRONMENT
        LXI  H,1400H      ;
        SHLD ADD_BUF      ;INIT ADDRESS BUFFER TO 1400H
        CALL DIS_HI       ;
        CALL DIS_LO       ;DISPLAY STARTING ADDRESS
        MOV  A,M          ;GET CONTENTS OF ADDRESS 1400H
        STA  DAT_BUF      ;STORE CURRENT DATA IN DATA BUFFER
        CALL DIS_DAT      ;DISPLAY DATA
        POP  PSW          ;
        POP  H            ;RESTORE ENVIRONMENT
        RET
```

Assembly language for the procedure DO_KEY(;). This procedure is implemented with a series of IF...THEN statements. In assembly code this must correspond to a series of arithmetic tests followed by conditional execution of each task. The conditional execution could be done by a conditional jump that either falls through and executes the task or jumps and skips over the task. But, because each of the tasks is in a separate subroutine of this software driver program, it would make sense to use conditional calls of each subroutine. Remembering that the keycode is in the accumulator (it is an input parameter of this program), the test part of the IF...THEN should correspond to a comparison of the accumulator contents to the known keycode for each function. With the keycode assignments shown in the hardware description, the following program will successfully separate data keys from function keys and invoke the proper functions. It will also invoke the ERROR routine if an undefined key is struck.

```
     "8085"

;THIS PROCEDURE DETERMINES WHICH KEY WAS STRUCK, AND INVOKES THE
;APPROPRIATE PROCEDURE TO IMPLEMENT THE KEYSTROKE FUNCTION.
;WRITTEN BY: G. THOMAS HUETTER   3/15/88
; CALLED BY: MONITOR
; SUBROUTINES CALLED: HI, LO, GO, STORE, DATA, ERROR
; PARAMETERS:  INPUT: NONE      OUTPUT: NONE
; REGISTERS AFFECTED: FLAGS
; MEMORY LOCATIONS AFFECTED: ADDBUF, ADDBUF+1, DAT_BUF,
;                            DIS_BUF  THROUGH  DIS_BUF+5

        GLB  DO_KEY
        EXT  HI, LO, GO, STORE, DATA, ERROR
```

```
DO_KEY:  CPI   10H          ;IS IT THE "H" KEY?
         CZ    HI           ;IF YES, CALL HI
         CC    DATA         ;IF KEYCODE IS BELOW 10H IT IS DATA KEY
         CPI   11H          ;IS IT THE "L" KEY?
         CZ    LO           ;IF YES, CALL LO
         CPI   12H          ;IS IT THE "G" KEY?
         CZ    GO           ;IF YES, CALL GO
         CPI   13H          ;IS IT THE "S" KEY?
         CZ    STORE        ;IF YES, CALL STORE
         CPI   14H          ;IS IT AN ILLEGAL KEY?
         CNC   ERROR        ;IF YES, CALL ERROR
         RET
```

Assembly language for the procedure DIS_PMT(;). As described earlier, the function of this program is to set up a copy of data from a table of seven-segment codes to the display buffer in order to show the ready prompt. The pointer to the display buffer is DIS_BUF, and the HL register pair will be used to hold it. Register pair DE will be used to hold the pointer to the seven-segment codes, PMT_TBL. With these definitions, the assembly language follows.

```
"8085"

;THIS PROGRAM CAUSES "READY" TO APPEAR ON THE DISPLAYS.
;WRITTEN BY: G. THOMAS HUETTER    3/16/88
; CALLED BY: MONITOR
; SUBROUTINES CALLED: BLK_MOV
; PARAMETERS:   INPUT: NONE           OUTPUT: NONE
; REGISTERS AFFECTED: NONE
; MEMORY LOCATIONS AFFECTED: DIS_BUF  THROUGH  DIS_BUF+5

         GLB   DIS_PMT

         EXT   DIS_BUF, PMT_TBL, BLK_MOV

DIS_PMT: PUSH  H            ;
         PUSH  D            ;SAVE ENVIRONMENT
         LXI   H,DIS_BUF    ;POINTER TO THE DISPLAY BUFFER
         LXI   D,PMT_TBL    ;POINTER TO DATA FOR "READY"
         CALL  BLK_MOV      ;COPY DATA FOR "READY" TO DISPLAY BUFFER
         POP   D            ;
         POP   H            ;RESTORE ENVIRONMENT
         RET
```

This completes the conversion of the pseudo-code for the module EXECUTIVE to assembly code. There are two other procedures from other modules that are instructive to consider now.

Assembly language for procedures MES_TBL(;) & STORAGE1 (;). In the software for the programs in the module EXECUTIVE, there were references to reserved memory locations, such as DIS_BUF, ADD_BUF, and DAT_BUF. The location DIS_BUF is defined as part of the I/O driver submodule in the program STORAGE and is described in the appendix. ADD_BUF and DAT_BUF must be defined, and the program STORAGE1 will do this. These memory locations must, however, be in the system RAM, rather than in the ROM. In order to do this, the procedure will be declared to be in the DATA segment. At link time, the locations defined will be concatenated with the locations already defined in the I/O driver. Definition of the locations is accomplished by use of the DS assembler directive, whose argument is the number of bytes to be reserved for each location. The following shows procedure STORAGE1.

```
"8085"

;SETS UP RESERVED MEMORY LOCATIONS.
;THIS IS NOT AN EXECUTABLE ROUTINE.

        DATA

        GLB   ADD_BUF, DAT_BUF, HL_BUF, DE_BUF, BC_BUF, PSW_BUF

ADD_BUF: DS   2        ;RESERVE 16 BIT BUFFER FOR CURRENT ADDRESS
DAT_BUF: DS   1        ;RESERVE  8 BIT BUFFER FOR CURRENT DATA
HL_BUF:  DS   2        ;RESERVE 16 BIT BUFFER TO SAVE RECORD OF (HL)
DE_BUF:  DS   2        ;RESERVE 16 BIT BUFFER TO SAVE RECORD OF (DE)
BC_BUF:  DS   2        ;RESERVE 16 BIT BUFFER TO SAVE RECORD OF (BC)
PSW_BUF: DS   2        ;RESERVE 16 BIT BUFFER TO SAVE RECORD OF (PSW)
```

According to the software modularization, there are other messages to be sent to the displays besides the ready prompt. The seven-segment codes for the numeric characters must also be defined and stored in the ROM. The procedure MES_TBL uses the assembler directive DB to accomplish this task. Here is the assembly version of the procedure.

```
"8085"

;SETS UP MESSAGE TABLES.
;THIS IS NOT AN EXECUTABLE ROUTINE.

        GLB   RUN_TBL, PMT_TBL, ERR_TBL, CVT_TBL

        CODE

RUN_TBL: DB   0,0,0,54H,1CH,50H       ;DATA TO DISPLAY "run"
PMT_TBL: DB   0,66H,5EH,77H,79H,50H   ;DATA TO DISPLAY "rEAdY"
ERR_TBL: DB   0,50H,5CH,50H,50H,79H   ;DATA TO DISPLAY "Error"
CVT_TBL: DB   3FH,06H,5BH,4FH         ;7-SEGMENT CODES FOR 0,1,2,3
         DB   66H,6DH,7DH,07H         ;7-SEGMENT CODES FOR 4,5,6,7
         DB   7FH,69H,77H,73H         ;7-SEGMENT CODES FOR 8,9,A,b
         DB   39H,57H,79H,71H         ;7-SEGMENT CODES FOR C,d,E,F
```

12.9.2 Software Integration

We now test and combine the individual procedures into a complete functioning program. Each assembly language procedure must be assembled, a process that generates an 8085 machine code image of the procedure. However, these routines are usually not executable routines, because of undefined quantities, the variables that have been declared external. The external variables are evaluated by the linker, as soon as the program that has defined the external has been linked to it. It might thus appear that all the procedures must be completed and linked together before any testing may be done. It is better to write simplified versions (called *stubs*) of the lower level procedures, which contain just enough information to define the externals and parameters required for that procedure. Then the link process can proceed properly, and the resulting code can be tested at least to the extent that the completed procedures (which would be the higher level procedures) successfully invoke the yet unwritten lower level programs. A repetitive process of executing the software on a simulator, software emulator, or other debugging tool, fixing any problems that might crop up and adding in completed lower level procedures, will result in a complete machine language of the software. This software will have been tested so far as possible without interaction with the actual system hardware.

As an example, suppose that the software already described in the assembly language section had been written, but not the rest. If these procedures were submitted to the linker, many unresolved external errors would be reported, and the resulting machine code could not execute properly. In the procedure DO_KEY alone, for example, there are six undefined variables—HI, LO, GO, STORE, DATA, and ERROR. Each of these is a subroutine name, and each would be defined temporarily by a stub. Each stub could be as simple as the one shown for HI:

```
        ''8085''

        ; STUB FOR HI

                GLB     HI

        HI:     RET
```

For routines with input or output parameters, the stub would be somewhat more complicated because it would have to simulate proper operation of the parameters.

Once the software to be tested and its stubs have been linked, the resulting program could be tested. We might single step through the program. We could begin execution from the label MONITOR and verify that all of the routines are invoked at the proper time. Notice that when we call GET_KEY from the label L1 the program is to return with some keycode in the accumulator. This could be done by a simulation in GET_KEY or by using the register modification function of the simulator. Subsequent execution of DO_KEY could then be checked for invocation of the proper routine (HI, LO, etc.). As each routine is completed, it could be added and tested, until the software is complete.

12.10 SYSTEM INTEGRATION AND EVALUATION

At this point, the hardware and software must be combined. A possible way to accomplish the task is to burn the software into an EPROM and install the EPROM into the system hardware. The system is then fired up and exercised in order to evaluate the operation. It is easily possible that the software does not operate properly in the real system hardware, even if it seemed to work correctly in the simulations of the software integration phase. This could be caused by either software or hardware problems, and such bugs must be traced and corrected, using tools such as logic analyzers and microcomputer analyzers. Each time a mistake is found in the software, the EPROM must be erased and reburned. In large systems, or in systems where there is a lot of interaction between the hardware and the software, this method is likely to be quite difficult and time-consuming.

12.10.1 The In-Circuit Emulator

A tool that can greatly enhance the integration phase is the in-circuit emulator (ICE). This consists of an emulation pod and emulation software. The emulation pod contains a microprocessor that is connected both to the development system and to a ribbon cable with a socket plug. The plug is inserted into the microprocessor socket of the system hardware, so that the processor in the pod becomes the system (called the "target" system) processor. Now, when the target system is exercised, the development system, under the influence of the emulation software, can monitor and control execution of the software under test. A full range of debugging tools is usually available, including memory and register examination and modification, breakpoints, single stepping, program tracing, and control of the I/O ports.

An important feature of the ICE is the existence of emulation memory. This is memory in the development system that can be used to overlay memory in the target system. When the target system is exercised, the overlay memory appears to be part of the target system. This can be very advantageous during integration; for example, the system can be tested before the entire system memory has been constructed. In fact, the entire target system memory map could be overlayed in emulation memory, and the software integration could be performed by use of the ICE. Another important use of the overlay memory is to overlay the system ROM. Then the system software can be loaded by the emulator, eliminating the necessity to burn an EPROM. Each cycle of discovering and eliminating a software bug then means a new load of the program rather than reburning an EPROM.

Because the emulator can control the memory and I/O of the target system, it can also be used for testing the system hardware. Even in the absence of any system software, the target hardware can be exercised through the memory and I/O commands of the ICE and tested with short test programs that simulate some of the functions of the target system. The hardware can also be tested in a modular manner because some parts of the system memory can be provided temporarily by emulation memory. Use of the ICE can yield considerable economy of time and effort in hardware integration and testing.

If the software integration phase has been completed, and the hardware has been tested in a stand-alone mode, then system integration can proceed, except that the need for reburning EPROMS is eliminated and the sophisticated debugging features of the ICE are available.

12.10.2 Integration in Concert

Rather than individual integration of the software, hardware, and system, it is often advantageous to proceed with integration of all phases in concert. In order to do this, a hardware prototype must be available early in the software development process. Then the early software integration can be done with the use of an ICE along with the actual system hardware. This allows a modularized, top-down approach to the integration and testing, where the hardware and software are done together.

A typical scheme for in-concert integration would involve preparation of the highest level software module (the EXECUTIVE) and the lowest level ones (the INPUT and OUTPUT). The software in these modules is then linked with any stubs required to resolve the external variables and satisfy the requirements for parameters. Similarly, the hardware should have the highest (CPU) and lowest (I/O) level modules completed. Now the ICE is used to provide emulation memory and the system can be tested for proper operation of the I/O (keyboard and display, for example) and for overall program flow. Problems that crop up can much more easily be found and repaired than if we waited until the entire system was constructed (as at system integration time in the scheme above).

As software and hardware modules are completed, they are integrated into the system. At each step, as the functionality of the system is increased, testing and debugging continue. When all the modules are in place, the system is ready for the final evaluation to make sure that it satisfies all the original requirements and specifications.

12.11 SUMMARY

In this chapter we have discussed some techniques for design of microprocessor-based electronic systems. We have described the software system design cycle and have shown the importance of proper top-down design. As an example of these techniques, we have embarked upon the design of a simple single-board computer, such as might be used as an aid in learning assembly language.

The design of this trainer computer was initiated with the generation of the system requirements. From them, the system specifications were written, and a software modularization was constructed. A particular module was then selected (the EXECUTIVE module), and pseudo code and assembly language were written to implement the module.

Finally, we discussed software integration, system integration, and evaluation of the system.

12.12 REFERENCES

FREEDMAN AND EVANS, *Designing Systems with Microcomputers* (Englewood Cliffs: Prentice Hall, 1983).

YOURDAN, *Structured Walkthroughs* (Englewood Cliffs: Prentice Hall, 1980).

CHAPTER REVIEW

Problems

1. Generate the system requirements for an automated scale, such as might be used in a delicatessen or butcher shop. Consider the following questions (and others that you can think of) as an aid:
   - How would the unit determine the weight of the product?
   - How would the user enter the unit cost (price/lb) of the product?
   - How would the scale display the weight, unit cost, and total cost to the user and to the customer?
   - How would the scale compensate for the tare of a container holding the product to be sold?
2. Write system requirements for a point-of-sale (POS) terminal, as would be used in a fast-food restaurant. First list an appropriate set of questions similar to those in Prob. 2.
3. Write system specifications for the automated scale of Prob. 1.
4. Write the specifications for the computer-controlled POS terminal of Prob. 2.
5. Assume that the scale of Prob. 1 uses a load cell and an A/D converter to weigh the item, so that a digital image of the weight is available, and that an I/O driver subsystem similar to the one used for the trainer's keypad and displays exists. Generate a software modularization for the system, including a state transition diagram, a thumbnail description of each procedure, a module diagram, and a procedure calling tree.
6. Write the modularization for the POS terminal.
7. Write pseudo-code for the programs in the module OUTPUT of the trainer. Review the material in the specifications and software modularization sections to see how the procedures work. Include proper documentation, and keep track of any parameters used.
8. Write pseudo-code for the procedures in the modules ADDRESS and STORE.
9. Complete the pseudo-code for the trainer.
10. Write assembly language for the procedures in the module OUTPUT. Write the code in a fashion that a typical assembler would accept (proper syntax). Don't forget global and external declarations and include headers and comments.
11. Write the assembly for the procedures in the modules ADDRESS and DATA.
12. Complete the assembly language for the trainer.

appendices

A Project Design

B 8085 Instruction Set Summary

C Z80 Instruction Set Summary

D 8051 Instruction Set Summary

E 8086 Instruction Set Summary

F ASCII and EBCDIC Tables

Appendix A: Project Design

A.1 HARDWARE DESCRIPTION OF THE PROJECT

Upon review of the system requirements and specifications of the project as developed in Chap. 12, it can be seen that the following hardware modules are needed:

1. CPU
2. System ROM to hold system software
3. System RAM for stack and system reserved memory
4. System I/O to interface to keypad and displays
5. User RAM to store user programs
6. User I/O for interface to user-supplied devices
7. "Glue chips" to integrate the main chips into a system.

A.1.1 The Chip Set for the Project

An Intel 8085 will be used for the CPU. An inexpensive and easily available chip, the 2716 2K EPROM is a likely choice for the system ROM. The 6116 2K Static RAM is pin compatible with the 2716, and will be selected as user RAM. An 8155 RAM-I/O IC provides user I/O and storage for system reserved memory locations.

A second 8155 is used for interface to the keypad/displays. This 8155 stores the system stack and user-defined interrupt vectors.

The CPU requires an address latch to demultiplex the low half of the address from the data. An Intel 8282 is used for this task. A 74LS138 gated octal decoder is used for chip select logic. Differentiation between memory and I/O operations is supplied by a 74LS32 quad 2-input or gate.

A.1.2 Chip Select Decoding and the Memory Map

The five most significant bits of the address bus are decoded by the 74LS138. This causes each output of the decoder to correspond to a 2K-wide address range, with a maximum available memory space of 16K. Memory space can be expanded by addition of more decoders. Each 74LS138 output also corresponds to an eightfold range of I/O addresses and must be qualified with the 8085 control signal IO/M. For the 2716 and the 6116, this is accomplished by gating the proper outputs of the decoder with IO/M by use of the or gate. The 8155 has its own IO/M input, so the decoding is done internally for the 8155s.

Because the 8085 fetches from address zero after a reset, the system software must start at address zero. Thus, the system ROM will be selected by the least significant output (output 0) of the decoder. Output 1 will be reserved for an additional 2K of EPROM. Output 2 will select the user RAM, and outputs 3 through 5 are reserved for expansion RAM or user I/O. Output 6 selects the 8155 for user I/O, and the memory in this 8155 holds system reserve memory. Finally, the last output selects the 8155 that controls the keypad and displays and that holds the system stack. The memory space of each 8155 is only 256 bytes, so each memory location has eight addresses, or seven "mirror" addresses.

On the basis of the discussion above, the memory and I/O map of the project follows:

MEMORY MAP

ADDRESS RANGE (HEX)	FUNCTION
0000-07FF	2K EPROM-System ROM
0800-0FFF	2K Hole-Expansion ROM
1000-17FF	2K SRAM-User RAM
1800-2FFF	6K Hole-Expansion RAM or I/O
3000-30FF	256 SRAM-System reserve memory
3100-37FF	Mirror addresses
3800-38FF	256 SRAM-System stack
3900-3FFF	Mirror addresses
4000-FFFF	Expansion (Needs more decoders)

I/O MAP

8155 REGISTER	C/S	PA	PB	PC	TL	TH
USER 8155	30H	31H	32H	33H	34H	35H
SYSTEM 8155	38H	39H	3AH	3BH	3CH	3DH

A.1.3 SCHEMATIC FOR THE PROJECT

The schematic for the microcomputer trainer project is shown in Fig. A.1. The connections between the 8155 and the keypad/display are shown on the keypad/display subsystem design, Fig. A.2. The reader should verify that the schematics are consistent with the memory and I/O maps shown below.

A.2 THE I/O DRIVER SUBSYSTEM

This section shows the documentation for the design of the keypad/display driver subsystem. The properties of this subsystem are outlined in Sec. 12.5.1. Table A.1 shows a summary of the reserved memory locations used by the I/O subsystem. Table A.2 shows, for each key, the binary number output on Port C (SEL_PORT), the corresponding number input on Port B (KEY_PORT), and the final keycode that is placed in the location KEYCODE.

TABLE A.1

RESERVED MEMORY LOCATIONS

Location	Contents
DIS_BUF	"D0"
DIS_BUF+1	"D1"
DIS_BUF+2	"A0"
. +3	"A1"
. +4	"A2"
DIS_BUF+5	"A3"
KEYCODE	0 → 16H
KEY_STB	0 OR 1
SEL_CODE	1011 1111B 1111 1110B
INT_CNT	6 → 0
ARM_KYBRD	0 or 1
DEBOUNCE_CNT	3 → 0

TABLE A.2

Key	Port C	Port B	Code
0	1101 1111	1110 0000	00H
1	1110 1111	1110 0000	01H
2	1111 0111	1110 0000	02H
3	1111 1011	1110 0000	03H
4	1101 1111	1101 0000	04H
5	1110 1111	1101 0000	05H
6	1111 0111	1101 0000	06H
7	1111 1011	1101 0000	07H
8	1101 1111	1011 0000	08H
9	1110 1111	1011 0000	09H
A	1111 0111	1011 0000	0AH
B	1111 1011	1011 0000	0BH
C	1101 1111	0111 0000	0CH
D	1110 1111	0111 0000	0DH
E	1111 0111	0111 0000	0EH
F	1111 1011	0111 0000	0FH
F0	1111 1101	1110 0000	10H
F1	1111 1101	1101 0000	11H
F2	1111 1101	1011 0000	12H
F3	1111 1101	0111 0000	13H
F4	1111 1110	1101 0000	14H
F5	1111 1110	1011 0000	15H
F6	1111 1110	0111 0000	16H

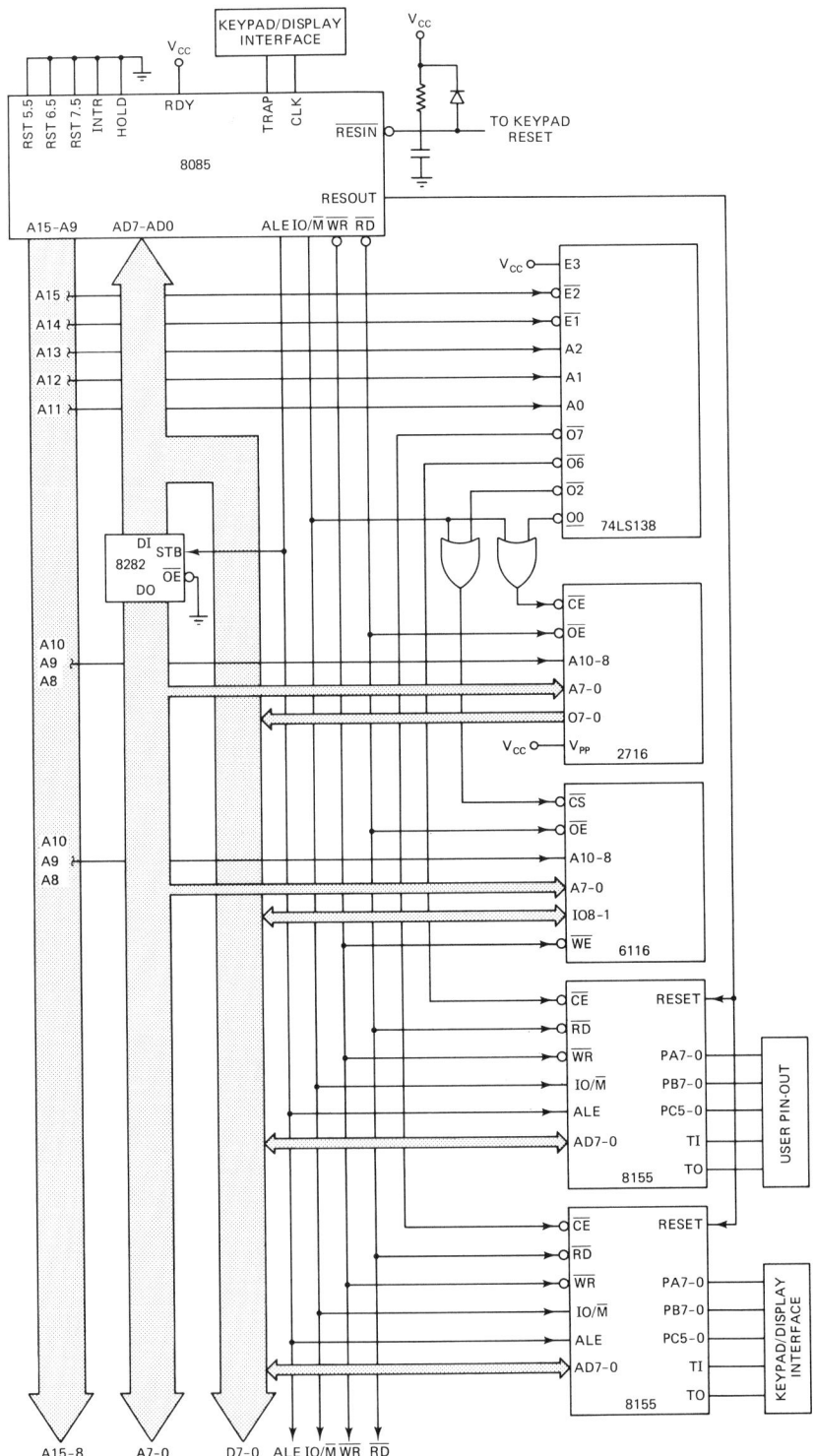

Figure A.1

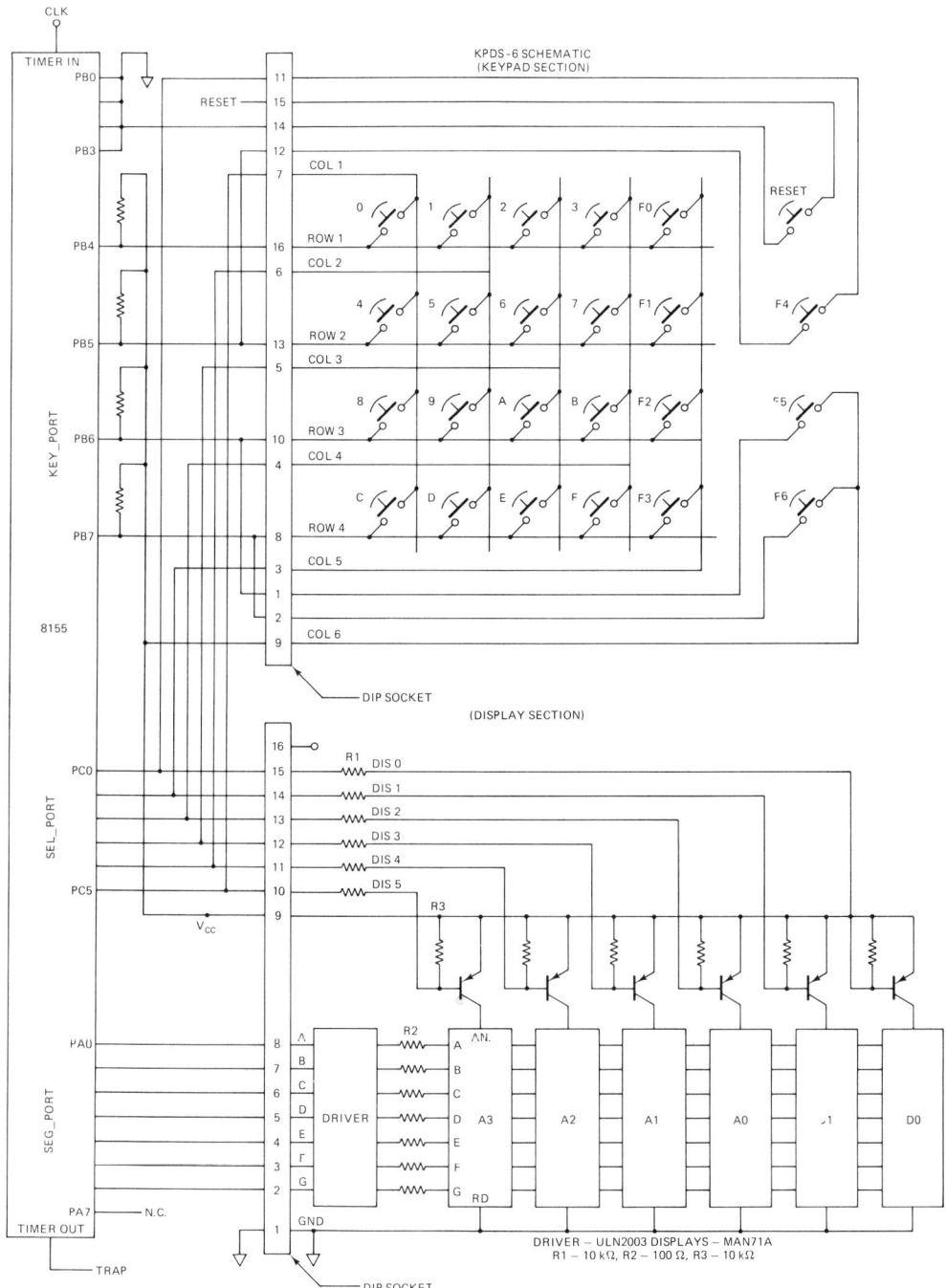

Figure A.2

A.2.1 SYSTEM REQUIREMENTS

A. Accept seven-segment codes from the monitor program and pass them to the seven-segment displays.
B. Scan, debounce, and decode the keypad and pass keycodes and a keystrobe to the monitor program.
C. Ensure that a single keystroke causes a single action (so that the monitor does not accept an "old" keystroke).
D. The displays and keypad must be accessible at all times, including when a user program is running.
E. The formalism used for this design must illustrate the software design cycle and provide a model for the student's design of the monitor program.

A.2.2 SYSTEM SPECIFICATIONS

I. Input/Output
   A. Six reserved memory locations will accept seven-segment codes from the monitor program. This program will time division multiplex the six codes across the six seven-segment displays of the devry KPDS-6. Each of the displays should be on for about two milliseconds.
   B. The program will check for any key closure once for each complete multiplexing of the displays (once every twelve milliseconds). If any key is closed for three consecutive scans, that keystroke is considered to be debounced, and the keypad is scanned to detect which key is depressed. The keypad is then disarmed until that key opens, so that the same keystroke is not captured twice. The program then decodes the keystroke and passes the keycode and a keystrobe to the monitor program. (The monitor program must reset the keystrobe upon acceptance of the keycode.)
   C. Refer to existing hardware design for I/O port specifications.
II. Functions
   A. This software will be interrupt driven through the trap interrupt request input to ensure continuous accessibility.
   B. The displays will be selected one at a time by the contents of the 8155 output port C. The corresponding seven-segment code will be passed through port A. Each subsequent run of the program will multiplex to the next display. Reserved memory locations will keep track of the current display selected and when to re-initialize back to first display.
   C. Once each complete multiplexing of the display status of the keypad is checked. This is accomplished by driving all columns of the keypad low through port C, and checking the condition of the rows on port B.
   D. The keypad will be armed upon detection of all keys open. It will be disarmed upon successful debouncing of a keystroke. The status of keypad arming will be in a reserved memory location.
   E. If any key is detected closed for three consecutive multiplexing cycles, with the keypad armed, then the keystroke is considered to be debounced. A

debounce counter keeps track of number of cycles (debounce time is 24 mSEC).

F. For a debounced keystroke, the keyboard is disarmed, and the keypad is scanned. The debounce count is reinitiated (re-inited).

G. The information about a captured keystroke is decoded to an absolute (hexadecimal) keycode. The keycode is passed to the monitor program in a reserved memory location. A keystrobe is passed to the monitor program in another reserved memory location. After the monitor gathers the keycode it must reset the keystrobe.

The hardware design has been completed and is shown, together with information about keycodes and reserved memory locations, in Section A.1.

A list of reserved memory location follows.

```
DIS_BUF    THROUGH   DIS_BUF+5
     SIX BYTES FOR PASSING DISPLAY CODES

KEYCODE
     PASSES KEYCODE TO MONITOR

KEY_STB
     PASSES KEYSTROBE TO MONITOR

SEL_CODE
     POINTS TO CURRENT DISPLAY (THROUGH PORT C)

INT_CNT
     COUNTS DISPLAYS FOR STARTING NEW CYCLE

ARM_KYBRD
     GIVES STATUS OF KEYPAD ARMING

DEBOUNCE_CNT
     COUNTS KEY CLOSURE DETECTIONS FOR DEBOUNCE
```

A.2.3 SOFTWARE MODULARIZATION

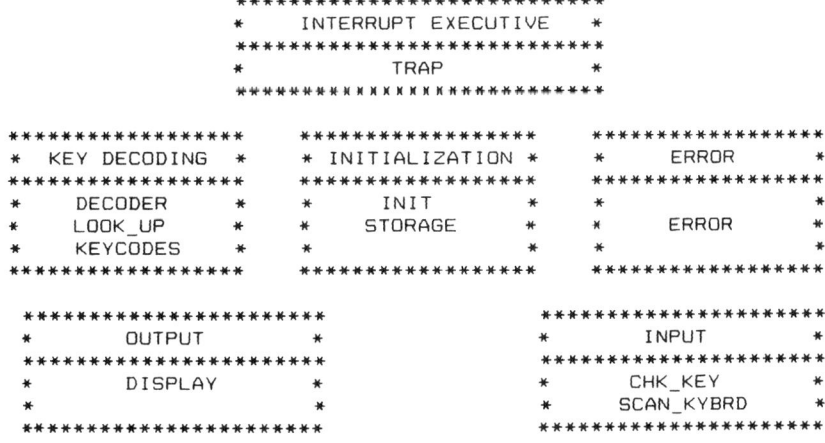

A.2.4 PSEUDO-CODE

All the following modules, procedures and routines were written by G. Thomas Huetter.

```
MODULE INTERRUPT EXECUTIVE

    PROCEDURES:
        TRAP( ; )
    EXTERNAL PROCEDURES CALLED:
        CHK_KEY( ; ROW_STATUS)
        SCAN_KYBRD( ; ROW_STATUS,COL_STATUS)
        DECODER(ROW_STATUS,COL_STATUS ; KEYCODE)
        DISPLAY( ; )

PROCEDURE TRAP( ; )

    CALLED BY:
        THIS PROCEDURE IS ACCESSED BY EXTERNAL HARDWARE THROUGH THE TRAP
        INPUT.  THE PROCEDURE IS INVOKED EVERY TWO MILLISECONDS

    PROCEDURES CALLED:
        CHK_KEY( ; ROW_STATUS)
        SCAN_KBRD( ; ROW_STATUS,COL_STATUS)
        DECODER(ROW_STATUS,COL_STATUS ; KEYCODE)
        DISPLAY( ; )
    DATA STRUCTURE:
        INPUT PARAMETERS:
            NONE
        OUTPUT PARAMETERS:
            NONE
        PROGRAM VARIABLES
            INT_CNT             (1 BYTE)
            ARM_KYBRD           (1 BYTE)
            DEBOUNCE_CNT        (1 BYTE)

BEGIN PROCEDURE

    SAVE ENVIRONMENT
    IF THIS IS FIRST DISPLAY
        THEN CALL CHK_KEY( ; ROW_STATUS)
        ELSE DO
                CALL DISPLAY( ; )
                RESTORE OLD INTERRUPT STATUS
                RESTORE ENVIRONMENT
                RETURN
             END
    IF NO KEY IS DEPRESSED
        THEN DO
                ARM KEYBOARD
                CALL DISPLAY( ; )
                RESTORE OLD INTERRUPT STATUS
                RESTORE ENVIRONMENT
                RETURN
             END
        ELSE IF KEYBOARD IS ARMED
                THEN DECREMENT DEBOUNCE COUNTER
                ELSE DO
                        CALL DISPLAY( ; )
                        RESTORE OLD INTERRUPT STATUS
                        RESTORE ENVIRONMENT
                        RETURN
                     END
```

```
            IF DEBOUNCE COUNTER IS NOT ZERO
                THEN DO
                        CALL DISPLAY( ; )
                        RESTORE OLD INTERRUPT STATUS
                        RESTORE ENVIRONMENT
                        RETURN
                    END
            SET DEBOUNCE COUNTER
            CALL SCAN_KYBRD( ; ROW_STATUS,COL_STATUS)
            CALL DECODER(ROW_STATUS,COL_STATUS ; KEYCODE)
            PASS CODE AND KEYSTROBE
            DISARM KEYBOARD
            CALL DISPLAY( ; )
            RESTORE OLD INTERRUPT STATUS
            RESTORE ENVIRONMENT
            RETURN

    END PROCEDURE TRAP

    END MODULE INTERRUPT EXECUTIVE



    MODULE OUTPUT

        PROCEDURES:
            DISPLAY( ; )

    PROCEDURE DISPLAY( ; )

        THIS PROCEDURE TRANSFERS A BYTE FROM THE DISPLAY BUFFER TO THE
        DISPLAY SEGMENT PORT AND MUXES OVER TO THE NEXT DISPLAY.  THIS
        ALSO SELECTS THE NEXT COLUMN OF THE KEYPAD.

        CALLED BY:
            TRAP( ; )
        PROCEDURES CALLED:
            NONE
        DATA STRUCTURE:
            INPUT PARAMETERS:
                NONE
            OUTPUT PARAMETERS:
                NONE
            PROGRAM VARIABLES
                DIS_BUF             ( 6 BYTES )
                INT_CNT             ( 1 BYTE )
                SEL_CODE            ( 1 BYTE )

    BEGIN PROCEDURE

        UPDATE INTERRUPT COUNTER
        POINT TO CURRENT DISPLAY DATA
        OUTPUT SEVEN SEGMENT CODE
        UPDATE SELECT CODE
        SELECT CURRENT DISPLAY
        IF THIS IS NOT LAST DISPLAY
            THEN RETURN
        REINITIALIZE INTERRUPT COUNTER AND SELECT CODE
        RETURN

    END PROCEDURE DISPLAY

    END MODULE OUTPUT
```

```
MODULE INPUT

    PROCEDURES:
        CHK_KEY( ; ROW_STATUS)
        SCAN_KYBRD( ; ROW_STATUS,COL_STATUS)

PROCEDURE CHK_KEY( ; ROW_STATUS)

    THIS PROCEDURE CHECKS FOR ANY KEY CLOSURE. IF KEY IS CLOSED,
    ROW STATUS  (ROW_CODE) WILL CONTAIN THAT INFORMATION.

    CALLED BY:
        TRAP( ; )
    DATA STRUCTURE
        OUTPUT PARAMETERS:
            ROW_STATUS              ( 1 BYTE )

BEGIN PROCEDURE

    DRIVE ALL COLUMNS LOW
    READ ROW STATUS
    RETURN

END PROCEDURE  CHK_KEY


PROCEDURE SCAN_KYBRD( ; ROW_STATUS,COL_STATUS)

    THIS PROCEDURE RETURNS THE "RAW" KEYCODE, WHICH IS ENCODED
    IN TERMS OF WHICH ROW AND COLUMN CONTAINS THE DEPRESSED KEY.
    CALLED BY:
        TRAP( ; )
    DATA STRUCTURE:
        OUTPUT PARAMETERS:
            ROW_STATUS              ( 1 BYTE )
            COL_STATUS              ( 1 BYTE )

BEGIN PROCEDURE
    INITIALIZE COLUMN STATUS
    DO FOREVER
        POINT TO NEXT COLUMN
        DRIVE A COLUMN LOW
        IF THIS COLUMN IS PAST LAST COLUMN
            THEN DO
                FIX STACK POINTER
                DISARM KEYBOARD
                GO TO ERROR
        SAVE COLUMN STATUS
        READ STATUS OF ROWS
        IF A KEY IS DEPRESSED
            THEN RETURN
            ELSE RESTORE COLUMN STATUS
    END

END PROCEDURE SCAN_KYBRD

END MODULE INPUT


MODULE  KEY DECODING

    PROCEDURES:
        DECODER(ROW_STATUS,COL_STATUS ; KEYCODE)
        LOOK_UP(RAWCODE ; KEYCODE)
        KEYCODES( ; )
```

```
PROCEDURE DECODER(ROW_STATUS,COL_STATUS ; KEYCODE)

    THIS PROCEDURE ACCEPTS THE "RAW" KEYCODE IN TERMS OF TWO BYTES
    THAT DEFINE THE ROW AND COLUMN OF THE KEY AND COMPRESSES THAT
    INFORMATION INTO A SINGLE BYTE INTERMEDIATE (HALF_COOKED) KEYCODE,
    CALLED THE RAWCODE.  THE RAWCODE IS PASSED TO PROCEDURE LOOK_UP.

    CALLED BY:
        TRAP( ; )
    DATA STRUCTURE:
        INPUT PARAMETERS:
            ROW_STATUS                ( 1 BYTE )
            COL_STATUS                ( 1 BYTE )
        OUTPUT PARAMETERS:
            KEYCODE                   ( 1 BYTE )

BEGIN PROCEDURE
    SAVE ROW STATUS
    IF KEY IS DATA KEY
        THEN DO
                    MASK COL STATUS FOR D2 THRU D5
                    SHIFT RIGHT TWICE
                    OR WITH ROW STATUS TO GENERATE HALF-COOKED KEYCODE
                    POINT TO DATA TABLE
                    INIT COUNT TO 10H
             END
        ELSE DO
                    MASK COL STATUS FOR D0 THRU D3
                    OR WITH ROW STATUS (HALF-COOKED KEYCODE)
                    POINT TO FUNCTION TABLE
                    INIT COUNT TO 07H
             END
    CALL LOOK_UP(RAWCODE ; KEYCODE)
    RETURN
END PROCEDURE


PROCEDURE LOOK_UP(RAWCODE ; KEYCODE)

    THIS PROCEDURE ACCEPTS INTERMEDIATE KEYCODE (RAWCODE), AND
    GENERATES THE FINAL KEYCODE BY COMPARISON TO KEYCODE TABLE.

    CALLED BY:
        DECODER(ROW_STATUS,COL_STATUS ; KEYCODE)
    DATA STRUCTURE:
        INPUT PARAMETERS
            RAWCODE
        OUTPUT PARAMETERS:
            KEYCODE

BEGIN PROCEDURE

    SAVE COUNT
    DO FOREVER
        COMPARE TABLE ENTRY TO HALF-COOKED KEYCODE
        IF KEYCODE AGREES
            THEN DO
                        TEST FOR FUNCTION OR DATA KEY
                        MOVE KEYCODE TO ACCUMULATOR
                        RETURN
                 END
        POINT TO NEXT TABLE ENTRY
        IF PAST END OF TABLE (NO VALID KEYCODE FOUND)
            THEN DO
                        FIX STACK POINTER
```

```
                    DISARM KEYBOARD
                    GO TO ERROR
        END

END PROCEDURE

PROCEDURE KEYCODES

        THE PURPOSE OF THIS PROCEDURE IS TO PROVIDE A LOOK-UP TABLE
        FOR THE PROGRAM LOOK_UP.  THE ENTRIES ARE THE HALF_COOKED
        CODES GENERATED BY PROGRAM SCAN_KYBR.

        THE CODES ARE ENTERED BY USE OF THE "HEX" ASSEMBLER DIRECTIVE.

END PROCEDURE

END MODULE KEY DECODING


MODULE INITIALIZATION

        PROCEDURES:
            INIT( ; )
            STORAGE( ; )

PROCEDURE INIT( ; )

        THIS PROCEDURE IS INVOKED UPON COLD RESTART (POWER-UP OR
        RESET BUTTON).  IT SETS UP 8155 FOR CONTROL OF KEYPAD/DISPLAY,
        INTIALIZES RESERVED MEMORY LOCATIONS, AND CLEARS 8085 REGISTERS.

        CALLED BY:
              THIS PROGRAM IS INVOKED BY POWER-UP OR RESET BUTTON

BEGIN PROCEDURE

        INITIALIZE 8155 PORTS AND TIMER
        INITIALIZE  RESERVED MEMORY LOCATIONS
        CLEAR 8085 INTERNAL REGISTERS
        GO TO STUDENT'S MONITOR PROGRAM

END PROCEDURE

PROCEDURE STORAGE

        THIS PROCEDURE RESERVES MEMORY LOCATIONS FOR:
            A.  DISPLAY BUFFER (SIX LOCATIONS)
            B.  KEYCODE AND KEY_STB
            C.  PROGRAM VARIABLES FOR KEYPAD/DISPLAY DRIVER
                (SEE LIST ON PAGE SIX.)

        THE LOCATIONS ARE RESERVED BY USE OF THE "DS" ASSEMBLER
        DIRECTIVE.  IF THE STUDENT WISHES TO RESERVE MORE LOCATIONS,
        THIS PROCEDURE COULD BE MODIFIED (BY ADDING MORE LOCATIONS).
END PROCEDURE

END MODULE INITIALIZATION


MODULE ERROR

        PROCEDURES:  ERROR( ; )

PROCEDURE ERROR( ; )
```

```
            THIS PROCEDURE IS A TEMPORARY ERROR PROGRAM TO ALLOW THE
            LINK OF THE TEST MONITOR TO PROCEED.  IT WILL CAUSE ALL
            DISPLAYS TO SHOW "8'S" IF ILLEGAL KEYCODES ARE ENCOUNTERED.

            CALLED BY:
                LOOK_UP(RAWCODE ; KEYCODE)
BEGIN PROCEDURE

     DO FOREVER
          DISPLAY ALL "8'S"
     END

END PROCEDURE

END MODULE ERROR
```

A.2.5 DESIGN WALKTHROUGH

Each design language procedure would be checked for logical errors by "walking through" the steps, that is executing the procedure in a thought experiment. The design walkthrough would precede the assembly language implementation.

The complete design language could be implemented prior to writing any of the assembly language procedures, or alternatively, assembly language procedures could be done as soon as the corresponding design language procedure is written and walked through.

A.2.6 PROCEDURE CALLING TREE

In this diagram the parameters are denoted as input parameters above the lines and output parameters below the lines.

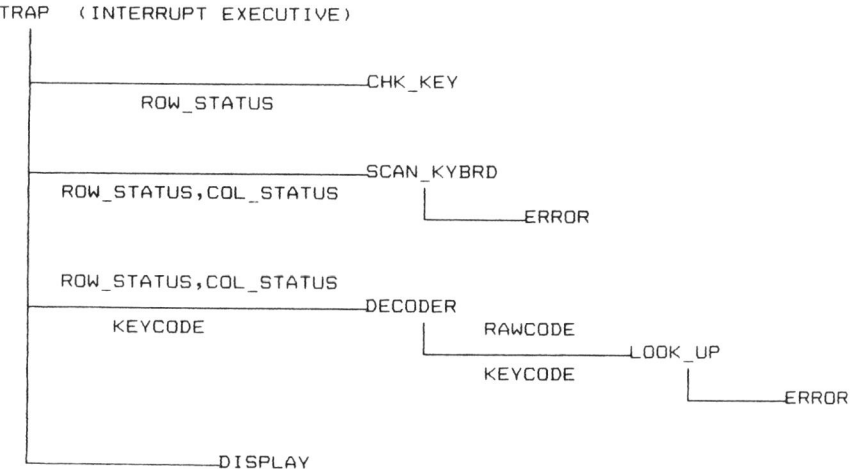

The procedure INIT is invoked upon power-up or cold restart (reset). The "procedures" STORAGE and KEYCODES are not executable code, rather they are data set-up procedures.

A.2.7 ASSEMBLY LANGUAGE

An assembly language implementation follows. The order of the assembly language procedures is the same as the order of the design language procedures. The procedures can be linked in any order, so long as the procedure trap is first in the link list and is located at address zero.

```
                        PROCEDURE TRAP

"8085"
;THIS PROGRAM WAS WRITTEN BY G. THOMAS HUETTER.
;IT WILL CONTROL THE KEYPAD AND THE LED READ-OUTS, IF THE HARDWARE
;IS AS DESCRIBED IN CLASS.

                GLB             TRAP
                GLB             SEG_PORT,KEY_PORT,SEL_PORT
;RESERVED MEMORY LOCATIONS, DEFINED IN PROGRAM "STORAGE"
                EXT
INT_CNT,ARM_KYBRD,DEBOUNCE_CNT
                EXT             KEYCODE,KEY_STB,SEL_CODE
;ENTRY LABELS FOR SUBROUTINES OF "TRAP"
                EXT             CHK_KEY,SCAN_KYBRD,DISPLAY
                EXT             DECODER,INIT,W_STRT,REGISTERS
;THESE EQUATES DEFINE THE PORT ASSIGNMENTS FOR YOUR SYSTEM.
SEG_PORT        EQU             39H             ;CONTROLS SEGMENTS
KEY_PORT        EQU             3AH             ;ACCEPTS RAW KEYCODES
SEL_PORT        EQU             3BH             ;SELECTS DISPLAY & KEY

START           JMP             INIT            ;RST 0  INT. VECTOR
                HEX             0,0,0,0,0       ;PAD TO NEXT INT. VECTOR
                JMP             3808H           ;RST 1
                HEX             0,0,0,0,0
                JMP             3810H           ;RST 2
                HEX             0,0,0,0,0
                JMP             3818H           ;RST 3
                HEX             0,0,0,0,0
                JMP             3820H           ;RST 4
                HEX             0
                JMP             TRAP            ;TRAP VECTOR
                HEX             0
                JMP             3828H           ;RST 5
                HEX             0
                JMP             382CH           ;RST 5.5
                HEX             0
                JMP             REGISTERS       ;RST 6
                HEX             0
                JMP             3834H           ;RST 6.5
                HEX             0
                JMP             W_STRT          ;RST 7
                HEX             0
                JMP             383CH           ;RST 7.5
```

```
TRAP            PUSH        PSW                     ;SAVE ENVIRONMENT
                PUSH        B
                PUSH        D
                PUSH        H
                LDA         INT_CNT                 ;FIND IF FIRST DISPLAY
                CPI         06H
                JNZ         EXIT                    ;IF NOT, DON'T DO KEYS
                CALL        CHK_KEY                 ;IF SO, LOOK FOR KEY
                CPI         0F0H                    ;ROW_STATUS FOR NO KEY
                JZ          ARM                     ;NO KEY GO ARM KEYBRD
                LDA         ARM_KYBRD               ;IS KEYBRD ARMED?
                CPI         01H                     ;CODE FOR ARMED KEYBRD
                JNZ         EXIT                    ;IF NOT ARMED, DON'T
                                                    ;BEBOUNCE
                LDA         DEBOUNCE_CNT            ;IF ARMED BEBOUNCE
                DCR         A                       ;IF DEBOUNCED, Z FLAG IS
                                                    ;SET
                STA         DEBOUNCE_CNT
                JNZ         EXIT
                MVI         A,02H
                STA         DEBOUNCE_CNT            ;REINIT.  DEBOUNCE ;COUNTER
                CALL        SCAN_KYBRD              ;FIND WHICH KEY (RAW
                                                    ;KEYCODE)
                CALL        DECODER                 ;GET COOKED KEYCODE
                STA         KEYCODE                 ;PASS KEYCODE
                MVI         A,01H
                STA         KEY_STB                 ;PASS KEY STROBE
                XRA         A                       ;DISARM KEYBRD
                JMP         DO_IT
ARM             MVI         A,01H                   ;ARM KEYBRD
DO_IT           STA         ARM_KYBRD
EXIT            CALL        DISPLAY                 ;SERVICE DISPLAY MUXING
                RIM                                 ;READ INT.  MASK
                ANI         08H                     ;CHECK IE BEFORE TRAP
                JZ          LEAVE                   ;INT. WAS DISABLE BEFORE
                                                    ;TRAP
                EI                                  ;RE-ENABLE INTERRUPTS
LEAVE           POP         H                       ;RESTORE ENVIRONMENT
                POP         D
                POP         B
                POP         PSW
                RET                                 ;GO BACK



                PROCEDURE DISPLAY

"8085"
;THIS PROGRAM WAS WRITTEN BY G. THOMAS HUETTER.
;IT WILL MULTIPLEX THE DISPLAYS TO THE NEXT ONE
;EVERY TIME THE TRAP SUBROUTINE RUNS.
                EXT         INT_CNT
                EXT         SEG_PORT
                EXT         SEL_PORT
                EXT         SEL_CODE,DIS_BUFH
                GLB         DISPLAY
DISPLAY         LXI         H,DIS_BUF               ;POINT TO DISPLAY BUFFER
                LDA         INT_CNT                 ;
                DCR         A                       ;UPDATE INTERRUPT COUNT
                STA         INT_CNT                 ;
                MOV         L,A                     ;POINT TO CURRENT DISPLAY
                MOV         A,M                     ;GET SEVEN SEG CODE
                OUT         SEG_PORT                ;OUTPUT DISPLAY CODE
```

```
                    LDA         SEL_CODE        ;
                    RRC                         ;UPDATE SELECT CODE
                    STA         SEL_CODE        ;
                    OUT         SEL_PORT        ;TURN ON CURRENT DISPLAY
                    RNZ                         ;GO BACK IF NOT LAST
                                                ;DISPLAY
RE_INIT             MVI         A,06H           ;
                    STA         INT_CNT         ;
                    MVI         A,0BFH          ;ELSE REINIT.  COUNTERS
                    STA         SEL_CODE        ;
                    RET                         ;GO BACK


                    PROCEDURE CHK_KEY

"8085"
;THIS PROGRAM WAS WRITTEN BY G. THOMAS HUETTER.
;IT WILL CHECK IF ANY KEY IS CLOSED.
                    EXT         SEL_PORT
                    EXT         KEY_PORT
                    GLB         CHK_KEY
CHK_KEY             XRA         A
                    OUT         SEL_PORT        ;DRIVE ALL COLS LOW
                    IN          KEY_PORT        ;CHECK ROW STATUS
                    RET                         ;ROW_STATUS IS IN ACC.


                    PROCEDURE SCAN_KYBRD

"8085"
;THIS PROGRAM WAS WRITTEN BY G. THOMAS HUETTER.
;IT WILL SCAN THE KEYBOARD AND WILL RETURN WITH
;A RAW KEY CODE (COLUMN IN B REG. AND ROW IN ACC.).
                    EXT         ERROR
                    EXT         SEL_PORT
                    EXT         KEY_PORT
                    GLB         SCAN_KYBRD
SCAN_KYBRD          MVI         A,0BFH          ;INIT COL_STATUS
NEXT_COL            RRC                         ;UPDATE COL_STATUS
                    JNC         ERR             ;NO KEY FOUND
                    OUT         SEL_PORT        ;DRIVE A COL LOW
                    MOV         B,A             ;SAVE COL_STATUS
                    IN          KEY_PORT        ;CHECK ROW_STATUS
                    CPI         0F0H            ;IS KEY DOWN THIS COL?
                    RNZ                         ;IF DOWN, GO BACK
                    MOV         A,B             ;ELSE RESTORE COL_STATUS
                    JMP         NEXT_COL
ERR                 MVI         A,00H           ;
                    STA         ARM_KYBRD       ;DISARM KEYBOARD
                    LXI         H,000EH         ;
                    DAD         SP              ;
                    SPHL                        ;ADJUST STACK POINTER
                    JMP         ERROR


                    PROCEDURE DECODER

"8085"
;THIS PROGRAM WAS WRITTEN G. THOMAS HUETTER.  IT WILL COMBINE CON-
;TENTS OF REG A AND REG B TO FORM A ONE BYTE CODE TO BE PASSED TO
;THE LOOK_UP PROGRAM.
                    EXT         LOOKUP,KEY_TBL
                    GLB         DECODER
DECODER             MOV         C,A             ;SAVE ROW STATUS
                    MOV         A,B             ;GET COLUMN STATUS
```

```
                    ANI     03H                 ;MASK FOR FUNCTION COLS.
                    CPI     03H                 ;IS IT COL 5 OR 6?
                    JNZ     FUNC                ;IF SO GO TO FUNC
DATA                MOV     A,B                 ;RESTORE COLUMN DATA
                    ANI     3CH                 ;KEEP STATUS OF COLS 1,2,3,&4
                    RRC                         ;MOVE COL STATUS TO LOW NIBBLE
                    RRC
                    ORA     C                   ;COMBINE ROW STATUS WITH COL STATUS
                    LXI     H,KEY_TBL           ;POINT TO DATA LOOK-UP TABLE
                    MVI     B,10H
                    CALL    LOOKUP
                    RET
FUNC                MOV     A,B                 ;RESTORE COLUMN STATUS
                    ANI     0FH                 ;KEEP LOW NIBBLE
                    ORA     C                   ;COMBINE ROW STATUS WITH ROW STATUS
                    LXI     H,KEY_TBL+16        ;POINT TO FUNCTION LOOK-UP TABLE
                    MVI     B,07H
                    CALL    LOOKUP
                    RET
```

PROCEDURE LOOK_UP

```
"8085"
;THIS PROGRAM WAS WRITTEN BY G. THOMAS HUETTER
;IT WILL STROBE THROUGH A TABLE OF RAW KEYCODES
;AND RETURN THE FINAL KEYCODE IN ACC.
                    EXT     ERROR
                    GLB     LOOKUP
LOOKUP              MOV     C,B
LOOP                CMP     M
                    JZ      EXIT_LOOK
                    INX     H
                    DCR     B
                    JNZ     LOOP
                    JMP     ERR
EXIT_LOOK           MOV     A,C
                    CPI     07H
                    JZ      EXIT_FUNC
EXIT_DATA           DCR     B
                    MOV     A,B
                    CMA
                    ANI     0FH
                    RET
EXIT_FUNC           MOV     A,B
                    ORI     08H
                    CMA
                    ANI     1FH
                    RET
ERR                 MVI     A,00H               ;
                    STA     ARM_KYBRD           ;DISARM KEYBOARD
                    LXI     H,000EH             ;
                    DAD     SP                  ;
                    SPHL                        ;ADJUST STACK POINTER
                    JMP     ERROR
```

PROCEDURE KEYCODES (LOOK-UP TABLE)

```
"8085"
;WRITTEN BY G. THOMAS HUETTER.
;THIS IS A LOOK-UP TABLE WHICH IS ACCESSED BY LOOK_UP.
                    GLB     KEY_TBL
KEY_TBL             HEX     E7,EB,ED,EE         ;
                    HEX     D7,DB,DD,DE         ;
```

```
              HEX         B7,BB,BD,BE      ;
              HEX         77,7B,7D,7E      ;DATA LOOK-UP TABLE
              HEX         ED,DD,BD,7D      ;
              HEX         DE,BE,7E         ;FUNCTION LOOK-UP TABLE
```

                    PROCEDURE INIT

```
"8085"
;THIS PROGRAM WAS WRITTEN BY G. THOMAS HUETTER.
;THIS PROGRAM IS TO INITIALIZE SYSTEM FOR TEST OF
;THE TRAP ROUTINE.
              EXT   SEL_CODE
              EXT   INT_CNT
              EXT   ARM_KYBRD
              EXT   DEBOUNCE_CNT
              EXT   KEY_STB
              EXT   MONITOR
              GLB   INIT,W_STRT
INIT          LXI   SP,38FEH
;THIS SECTION OF THE PGM INITIALIZES THE 8155 FOR KEYBRD/DISPLAY.
              MVI   A,0CDH             ;8155 MODE SET
              OUT   38H
              MVI   A,57H              ;
              OUT   3CH                ;SET TIMER MODE AND
              MVI   A,66H              ;COUNT LENGTH
              OUT   3DH                ;
;THIS SECTION INITIALIZES RESERVED MEMORY LOCATIONS.
              MVI   A,0BFH             ;INITIALIZE DISPLAY SELECT
              STA   SEL_CODE
              MVI   A,06H              ;INITIALIZE INTERRUPT COUNTER
              STA   INT_CNT
              XRA   A
              STA   KEY_STB            ;NO KEY IS READY
              INR   A
              STA   ARM_KYBRD          ;ARM THE KEYBOARD
              MVI   A,03H              ;SET UP THE DEBOUNCE COUNTER
              STA   DEBOUNCE_CNT
;THIS SECTION CLEARS THE 8085 REGISTERS.
              XRA   A
              LXI   H,0
              LXI   D,0
              LXI   B,0
W_STRT        JMP   MONITOR            ;GO TO TEST MINIMONITOR
```

                    PROCEDURE STORAGE

```
"8085"
;THIS PROGRAM WAS WRITTEN BY G. THOMAS HUETTER.
;     THIS PROGRAM DEFINES AND RESERVES MEMORY LOCATIONS
;FOR THE MAILBOXES BETWEEN THE MONITOR AND THE KEYPAD/DISPLAY
;DRIVER SOFTWARE.  IT ALSO SETS UP RESERVED MEMORY LOCATIONS
;FOR THE VARIABLES USED BY THE KEYPAD/DISPLAY SOFTWARE.

              GLB
DIS_BUF,SEL_CODE,KEYCODE,KEY_STB
              GLB
INT_CNT,ARM_KYBRD,DEBOUNCE_CNT
```

```
                ORG         3000H
DIS_BUF         DS          6           ;SIX LOCATIONS FOR DISPLAY CODES
KEYCODE         DS          1           ;DECODED KEY CODE
KEY_STB         DS          1           ;HIGH MEANS KEY WAS STRUCK
SEL_CODE        DS          1           ;THIS MASK POINTS TO CURRENT
                                        ;COLUMN
INT_CNT         DS          1           ;TELLS WHICH DISPLAY
ARM_KYBRD       DS          1           ;ENABLES KEYBOARD
DEBOUNCE_CNT    DS          1           ;COUNTS DEBOUNCE CYCLES



                PROCEDURE ERROR

"8085"
;THIS PROGRAM WAS WRITTEN BY G. THOMAS HUETTER.
;THIS PROGRAM IS A TEMPORARY VERSION OF ERROR TO
;ALLOW THE LINK TO PROCEED.
                GLB         ERROR
ERROR           MVI         A,0FFH      ;IF ILLEGAL KEYCODE,
                STA         3000H       ;DISPLAY ALL "8's"
                STA         3001H       ;AND STOP.
                STA         3002H
                STA         3003H
                STA         3004H
                STA         3005H
LOOP            HLT
                JMP         LOOP
```

A.2.8 VERIFICATION

The assembly language procedures can be executed on a simulator or an emulator and checked for proper operation.

Appendix B 8085 Instruction Set Summary

Mnemonic	Description	D_7	D_6	D_5	D_4	D_3	D_2	D_1	D_0	Clock[2] Cycles
MOVE, LOAD, AND STORE										
MOV r1, r2	Move register to register	0	1	D	D	D	S	S	S	4
MOV M, r	Move register to memory	0	1	1	1	0	S	S	S	7
MOV r, M	Move memory to register	0	1	D	D	D	1	1	0	7
MVI r	Move immediate register	0	0	D	D	D	1	1	0	7
MVI M	Move immediate memory	0	0	1	1	0	1	1	0	10
LXI B	Load immediate register Pair B & C	0	0	0	0	0	0	0	1	10
LXI D	Load immediate register Pair D & E	0	0	0	1	0	0	0	1	10
LXI H	Load immediate register Pair H & L	0	0	1	0	0	0	0	1	10
LXI SP	Load immediate stack pointer	0	0	1	1	0	0	0	1	10
STAX B	Store A indirect	0	0	0	0	0	0	1	0	7
STAX D	Store A indirect	0	0	0	1	0	0	1	0	7
LDAX B	Load A indirect	0	0	0	0	1	0	1	0	7
LDAX D	Load A indirect	0	0	0	1	1	0	1	0	7
STA	Store A direct	0	0	1	1	0	0	1	0	13
LDA	Load A direct	0	0	1	1	1	0	1	0	13
SHLD	Store H & L direct	0	0	1	0	0	0	1	0	16
LHLD	Load H & L direct	0	0	1	0	1	0	1	0	16
XCHG	Exchange D & E, H & L Registers	1	1	1	0	1	0	1	1	4
STACK OPS										
PUSH B	Push register Pair B & C on stack	1	1	0	0	0	1	0	1	12
PUSH D	Push register Pair D & E on stack	1	1	0	1	0	1	0	1	12
PUSH H	Push register Pair H & L on stack	1	1	1	0	0	1	0	1	12
PUSH PSW	Push A and Flags on stack	1	1	1	1	0	1	0	1	12
POP B	Pop register Pair B & C off stack	1	1	0	0	0	0	0	1	10
POP D	Pop register Pair D & E off stack	1	1	0	1	0	0	0	1	10
POP H	Pop register Pair H & L off stack	1	1	1	0	0	0	0	1	10
POP PSW	Pop A and Flags off stack	1	1	1	1	0	0	0	1	10
XTHL	Exchange top of stack, H & L	1	1	1	0	0	0	1	1	16
SPHL	H & L to stack pointer	1	1	1	1	1	0	0	1	6
JUMP										
JMP	Jump unconditional	1	1	0	0	0	0	1	1	10
JC	Jump on carry	1	1	0	1	1	0	1	0	7/10
JNC	Jump on no carry	1	1	0	1	0	0	1	0	7/10
JZ	Jump on zero	1	1	0	0	1	0	1	0	7/10
JNZ	Jump on no zero	1	1	0	0	0	0	1	0	7/10
JP	Jump on positive	1	1	1	1	0	0	1	0	7/10
JM	Jump on minus	1	1	1	1	1	0	1	0	7/10
JPE	Jump on parity even	1	1	1	0	1	0	1	0	7/10
JPO	Jump on parity odd	1	1	1	0	0	0	1	0	7/10
PCHL	H & L to program counter	1	1	1	0	1	0	0	1	6
CALL										
CALL	Call unconditional	1	1	0	0	1	1	0	1	18
CC	Call on carry	1	1	0	1	1	1	0	0	9/18
CNC	Call on no carry	1	1	0	1	0	1	0	0	9/18
CZ	Call on zero	1	1	0	0	1	1	0	0	9/18
CNZ	Call on no zero	1	1	0	0	0	1	0	0	9/18
CP	Call on positive	1	1	1	1	0	1	0	0	9/18
CM	Call on minus	1	1	1	1	1	1	0	0	9/18
CPE	Call on parity even	1	1	1	0	1	1	0	0	9/18
CPO	Call on parity odd	1	1	1	0	0	1	0	0	9/18
RETURN										
RET	Return	1	1	0	0	1	0	0	1	10
RC	Return on carry	1	1	0	1	1	0	0	0	6/12
RNC	Return on no carry	1	1	0	1	0	0	0	0	6/12
RZ	Return on zero	1	1	0	0	1	0	0	0	6/12
RNZ	Return on no zero	1	1	0	0	0	0	0	0	6/12
RP	Return on positive	1	1	1	1	0	0	0	0	6/12
RM	Return on minus	1	1	1	1	1	0	0	0	6/12
RPE	Return on parity even	1	1	1	0	1	0	0	0	6/12
RPO	Return on parity odd	1	1	1	0	0	0	0	0	6/12
RESTART										
RST	Restart	1	1	A	A	A	1	1	1	12
INPUT/OUTPUT										
IN	Input	1	1	0	1	1	0	1	1	10
OUT	Output	1	1	0	1	0	0	1	1	10
INCREMENT AND DECREMENT										
INR r	Increment register	0	0	D	D	D	1	0	0	4
DCR r	Decrement register	0	0	D	D	D	1	0	1	4
INR M	Increment memory	0	0	1	1	0	1	0	0	10
DCR M	Decrement memory	0	0	1	1	0	1	0	1	10
INX B	Increment B & C registers	0	0	0	0	0	0	1	1	6
INX D	Increment D & E registers	0	0	0	1	0	0	1	1	6
INX H	Increment H & L registers	0	0	1	0	0	0	1	1	6
INX SP	Increment stack pointer	0	0	1	1	0	0	1	1	6
DCX B	Decrement B & C	0	0	0	0	1	0	1	1	6
DCX D	Decrement D & E	0	0	0	1	1	0	1	1	6
DCX H	Decrement H & L	0	0	1	0	1	0	1	1	6
DCX SP	Decrement stack pointer	0	0	1	1	1	0	1	1	6
ADD										
ADD r	Add register to A	1	0	0	0	0	S	S	S	4
ADC r	Add register to A with carry	1	0	0	0	1	S	S	S	4
ADD M	Add memory to A	1	0	0	0	0	1	1	0	7
ADC M	Add memory to A with carry	1	0	0	0	1	1	1	0	7
ADI	Add immediate to A	1	1	0	0	0	1	1	0	7
ACI	Add immediate to A with carry	1	1	0	0	1	1	1	0	7
DAD B	Add B & C to H & L	0	0	0	0	1	0	0	1	10
DAD D	Add D & E to H & L	0	0	0	1	1	0	0	1	10
DAD H	Add H & L to H & L	0	0	1	0	1	0	0	1	10
DAD SP	Add stack pointer to H & L	0	0	1	1	1	0	0	1	10
SUBTRACT										
SUB r	Subtract register from A	1	0	0	1	0	S	S	S	4
SBB r	Subtract register from A with borrow	1	0	0	1	1	S	S	S	4
SUB M	Subtract memory from A	1	0	0	1	0	1	1	0	7
SBB M	Subtract memory from A with borrow	1	0	0	1	1	1	1	0	7

Mnemonic	Description	D_7	D_6	D_5	D_4	D_3	D_2	D_1	D_0	Clock[2] Cycles
SUI	Subtract immediate from A	1	1	0	1	0	1	1	0	7
SBI	Subtract immediate from A with borrow	1	1	0	1	1	1	1	0	7
LOGICAL										
ANA r	And register with A	1	0	1	0	0	S	S	S	4
XRA r	Exclusive Or register with A	1	0	1	0	1	S	S	S	4
ORA r	Or register with A	1	0	1	1	0	S	S	S	4
CMP r	Compare register with A	1	0	1	1	1	S	S	S	4
ANA M	And memory with A	1	0	1	0	0	1	1	0	7
XRA M	Exclusive Or memory with A	1	0	1	0	1	1	1	0	7
ORA M	Or memory with A	1	0	1	1	0	1	1	0	7
CMP M	Compare memory with A	1	0	1	1	1	1	1	0	7
ANI	And immediate with A	1	1	1	0	0	1	1	0	7
XRI	Exclusive Or immediate with A	1	1	1	0	1	1	1	0	7
ORI	Or immediate with A	1	1	1	1	0	1	1	0	7
CPI	Compare immediate with A	1	1	1	1	1	1	1	0	7
ROTATE										
RLC	Rotate A left	0	0	0	0	0	1	1	1	4
RRC	Rotate A right	0	0	0	0	1	1	1	1	4
RAL	Rotate A left through carry	0	0	0	1	0	1	1	1	4
RAR	Rotate A right through carry	0	0	0	1	1	1	1	1	4
SPECIALS										
CMA	Complement A	0	0	1	0	1	1	1	1	4
STC	Set carry	0	0	1	1	0	1	1	1	4
CMC	Complement carry	0	0	1	1	1	1	1	1	4
DAA	Decimal adjust A	0	0	1	0	0	1	1	1	4
CONTROL										
EI	Enable Interrupts	1	1	1	1	1	0	1	1	4
DI	Disable Interrupt	1	1	1	1	0	0	1	1	4
NOP	No-operation	0	0	0	0	0	0	0	0	4
HLT	Halt	0	1	1	1	0	1	1	0	5
NEW 8085A INSTRUCTIONS										
RIM	Read Interrupt Mask	0	0	1	0	0	0	0	0	4
SIM	Set Interrupt Mask	0	0	1	1	0	0	0	0	4

NOTES: 1. DDD or SSS: B 000, C 001, D 010, E 011, H 100, L 101, Memory 110, A 111
2. Two possible cycle times, (6/12) indicate instruction cycles dependent on condition flags

*All mnemonics copyright ©Intel Corporation 1977

Source: Reprinted by permission of Intel Corporation, copyright © Intel Corporation.

Appendix C Z80 Instruction Set Summary

The following is a summary of the Z80, Z80A instruction set showing the assembly language mnemonic and the symbolic operation performed by the instruction. A more detailed listing appears in the Z80-CPU technical manual, and assembly language programming manual. The instructions are divided into the following categories:

8-bit loads	Miscellaneous Group
16-bit loads	Rotates and Shifts
Exchanges	Bit Set, Reset and Test
Memory Block Moves	Input and Output
Memory Block Searches	Jumps
8-bit arithmetic and logic	Calls
16-bit arithmetic	Restarts
General purpose Accumulator & Flag Operations	Returns

In the table the following terminology is used.

b ≡ a bit number in any 8-bit register or memory location
cc ≡ flag condition code
    NZ ≡ non zero
    Z ≡ zero
    NC ≡ non carry
    C ≡ carry
    PO ≡ Parity odd or no over flow
    PE ≡ Parity even or over flow
    P ≡ Positive
    M ≡ Negative (minus)

d ≡ any 8-bit destination register or memory location
dd ≡ any 16-bit destination register or memory location
e ≡ 8-bit signed 2's complement displacement used in relative jumps and indexed addressing
L ≡ 8 special call locations in page zero. In decimal notation these are 0, 8, 16, 24, 32, 40, 48 and 56
n ≡ any 8-bit binary number
nn ≡ any 16-bit binary number
r ≡ any 8-bit general purpose register (A, B, C, D, E, H, or L)
s ≡ any 8-bit source register or memory location
s_b ≡ a bit in a specific 8-bit register or memory location
ss ≡ any 16-bit source register or memory location
subscript "L" ≡ the low order 8 bits of a 16-bit register
subscript "H" ≡ the high order 8 bits of a 16-bit register
( ) ≡ the contents within the ( ) are to be used as a pointer to a memory location or I/O port number

8-bit registers are A, B, C, D, E, H, L, I and R
16-bit register pairs are AF, BC, DE and HL
16-bit registers are SP, PC, IX and IY

Addressing Modes implemented include combinations of the following:

Immediate	Indexed
Immediate extended	Register
Modified Page Zero	Implied
Relative	Register Indirect
Extended	Bit

	Mnemonic	Symbolic Operation	Comments
8-BIT LOADS	LD r, s	r ← s	s ≡ r, n, (HL), (IX+e), (IY+e)
	LD d, r	d ← r	d ≡ (HL), r (IX+e), (IY+e)
	LD d, n	d ← n	d ≡ (HL), (IX+e), (IY+e)
	LD A, s	A ← s	s ≡ (BC), (DE), (nn), I, R
	LD d, A	d ← A	d ≡ (BC), (DE), (nn), I, R
16-BIT LOADS	LD dd, nn	dd ← nn	dd ≡ BC, DE, HL, SP, IX, IY
	LD dd, (nn)	dd ← (nn)	dd ≡ BC, DE, HL, SP, IX, IY
	LD (nn), ss	(nn) ← ss	ss ≡ BC, DE, HL, SP, IX, IY
	LD SP, ss	SP ← ss	ss ≡ HL, IX, IY
	PUSH ss	(SP-1) ← ss_H; (SP-2) ← ss_L	ss ≡ BC, DE, HL, AF, IX, IY
	POP dd	dd_L ← (SP); dd_H ← (SP+1)	dd ≡ BC, DE, HL, AF, IX, IY
EXCHANGES	EX DE, HL	DE ↔ HL	
	EX AF, AF'	AF ↔ AF'	
	EXX	$\begin{pmatrix} BC \\ DE \\ HL \end{pmatrix} \leftrightarrow \begin{pmatrix} BC' \\ DE' \\ HL' \end{pmatrix}$	
	EX (SP), ss	(SP) ↔ ss_L, (SP+1) ↔ ss_H	ss ≡ HL, IX, IY

	Mnemonic	Symbolic Operation	Comments
MEMORY BLOCK MOVES	LDI	(DE) ← (HL), DE ← DE+1 HL ← HL+1, BC ← BC-1	
	LDIR	(DE) ← (HL), DE ← DE+1 HL ← HL+1, BC ← BC-1 Repeat until BC = 0	
	LDD	(DE) ← (HL), DE ← DE-1 HL ← HL-1, BC ← BC-1	
	LDDR	(DE) ← (HL), DE ← DE-1 HL ← HL-1, BC ← BC-1 Repeat until BC = 0	
MEMORY BLOCK SEARCHES	CPI	A-(HL), HL ← HL+1 BC ← BC-1	A-(HL) sets the flags only. A is not affected
	CPIR	A-(HL), HL ← HL+1 BC ← BC-1, Repeat until BC = 0 or A = (HL)	
	CPD	A-(HL), HL ← HL-1 BC ← BC-1	
	CPDR	A-(HL), HL ← HL-1 BC ← BC-1, Repeat until BC = 0 or A = (HL)	
8-BIT ALU	ADD s	A ← A + s	CY is the carry flag s ≡ r, n, (HL), (IX+e), (IY+e)
	ADC s	A ← A + s + CY	
	SUB s	A ← A - s	
	SBC s	A ← A - s - CY	
	AND s	A ← A ∧ s	
	OR s	A ← A ∨ s	
	XOR s	A ← A ⊕ s	

Category	Mnemonic	Symbolic Operation	Comments
8-BIT ALU	CP s	A - s	s = r, n (HL) (IX+e), (IY+e)
	INC d	d ← d + 1	d = r, (HL) (IX+e), (IY+e)
	DEC d	d ← d - 1	
16-BIT ARITHMETIC	ADD HL, ss	HL ← HL + ss	ss ≡ BC, DE, HL, SP
	ADC HL, ss	HL ← HL + ss + CY	
	SBC HL, ss	HL ← HL - ss - CY	
	ADD IX, ss	IX ← IX + ss	ss ≡ BC, DE, IX, SP
	ADD IY, ss	IY ← IY + ss	ss ≡ BC, DE, IY, SP
	INC dd	dd ← dd + 1	dd ≡ BC, DE, HL, SP, IX, IY
	DEC dd	dd ← dd - 1	dd ≡ BC, DE, HL, SP, IX, IY
GP ACC. & FLAG	DAA	Converts A contents into packed BCD following add or subtract.	Operands must be in packed BCD format
	CPL	A ← $\overline{A}$	
	NEG	A ← 00 - A	
	CCF	CY ← $\overline{CY}$	
	SCF	CY ← 1	
MISCELLANEOUS	NOP	No operation	
	HALT	Halt CPU	
	DI	Disable Interrupts	
	EI	Enable Interrupts	
	IM 0	Set interrupt mode 0	8080A mode
	IM 1	Set interrupt mode 1	Call to 0038$_H$
	IM 2	Set interrupt mode 2	Indirect Call
ROTATES AND SHIFTS	RLC s		s = r, (HL) (IX+e), (IY+e)
	RL s		
	RRC s		
	RR s		
	SLA s		
	SRA s		
	SRL s		
	RLD		
	RRD		

Category	Mnemonic	Symbolic Operation	Comments
BIT S, R, & T	BIT b, s	Z ← $\overline{s_b}$	Z is zero flag s ≡ r, (HL) (IX+e), (IY+e)
	SET b, s	s_b ← 1	
	RES b, s	s_b ← 0	
INPUT AND OUTPUT	IN A, (n)	A ← (n)	
	IN r, (C)	r ← (C)	Set flags
	INI	(HL) ← (C), HL ← HL + 1 B ← B - 1	
	INIR	(HL) ← (C), HL ← HL + 1 B ← B - 1 Repeat until B = 0	
	IND	(HL) ← (C), HL ← HL - 1 B ← B - 1	
	INDR	(HL) ← (C), HL ← HL - 1 B ← B - 1 Repeat until B = 0	
	OUT(n), A	(n) ← A	
	OUT(C), r	(C) ← r	
	OUTI	(C) ← (HL), HL ← HL + 1 B ← B - 1	
	OTIR	(C) ← (HL), HL ← HL + 1 B ← B - 1 Repeat until B = 0	
	OUTD	(C) ← (HL), HL ← HL - 1 B ← B - 1	
	OTDR	(C) ← (HL), HL ← HL - 1 B ← B - 1 Repeat until B = 0	
JUMPS	JP nn	PC ← nn	cc { NZ PO, Z PE, NC P, C M }
	JP cc, nn	If condition cc is true PC ← nn, else continue	
	JR e	PC ← PC + e	
	JR kk, e	If condition kk is true PC ← PC + e, else continue	kk { NZ NC, Z C }
	JP (ss)	PC ← ss	ss = HL, IX, IY
	DJNZ e	B ← B - 1, if B = 0 continue, else PC ← PC + e	
CALLS	CALL nn	(SP-1) ← PC_H (SP-2) ← PC_L, PC ← nn	cc { NZ PO, Z PE, NC P, C M }
	CALL cc, nn	If condition cc is false continue, else same as CALL nn	
RESTARTS	RST L	(SP-1) ← PC_H (SP-2) ← PC_L, PC_H ← 0 PC_L ← L	
RETURNS	RET	PC_L ← (SP), PC_H ← (SP+1)	
	RET cc	If condition cc is false continue, else same as RET	cc { NZ PO, Z PE, NC P, C M }
	RETI	Return from interrupt, same as RET	
	RETN	Return from non-maskable interrupt	

Source: Reproduced by permission. © Copyright 1989 Zilog, Inc. This material shall not be reproduced without the written consent of Zilog, Inc.

Appendix C   Z80 Instruction Set Summary

Appendix D 8051 Instruction Set Summary

Interrupt Response Time: Refer to Hardware Description Chapter.

Instructions that Affect Flag Settings[1]

Instruction	Flag			Instruction	Flag		
	C	OV	AC		C	OV	AC
ADD	X	X	X	CLR C	0		
ADDC	X	X	X	CPL C	X		
SUBB	X	X	X	ANL C,bit	X		
MUL	0	X		ANL C,/bit	X		
DIV	0	X		ORL C,bit	X		
DA	X			ORL C,/bit	X		
RRC	X			MOV C,bit	X		
RLC	X			CJNE	X		
SETB C	1						

[1] Note that operations on SFR byte address 208 or bit addresses 209-215 (i.e., the PSW or bits in the PSW) will also affect flag settings.

Note on instruction set and addressing modes:

Rn — Register R7–R0 of the currently selected Register Bank.

direct — 8-bit internal data location's address. This could be an Internal Data RAM location (0–127) or a SFR [i.e., I/O port, control register, status register, etc. (128–255)].

@Ri — 8-bit internal data RAM location (0–255) addressed indirectly through register R1 or R0.

#data — 8-bit constant included in instruction.

#data 16 — 16-bit constant included in instruction.

addr 16 — 16-bit destination address. Used by LCALL & LJMP. A branch can be anywhere within the 64K-byte Program Memory address space.

addr 11 — 11-bit destination address. Used by ACALL & AJMP. The branch will be within the same 2K-byte page of program memory as the first byte of the following instruction.

rel — Signed (two's complement) 8-bit offset byte. Used by SJMP and all conditional jumps. Range is −128 to +127 bytes relative to first byte of the following instruction.

bit — Direct Addressed bit in Internal Data RAM or Special Function Register.

* — New operation not provided by 8048AH/8049AH.

Mnemonic		Description	Byte	Oscillator Period
ARITHMETIC OPERATIONS				
ADD	A,Rn	Add register to Accumulator	1	12
ADD	A,direct	Add direct byte to Accumulator	2	12
ADD	A,@Ri	Add indirect RAM to Accumulator	1	12
ADD	A,#data	Add immediate data to Accumulator	2	12
ADDC	A,Rn	Add register to Accumulator with Carry	1	12
ADDC	A,direct	Add direct byte to Accumulator with Carry	2	12
ADDC	A,@Ri	Add indirect RAM to Accumulator with Carry	1	12
ADDC	A,#data	Add immediate data to Acc with Carry	2	12
SUBB	A,Rn	Subtract Register from Acc with borrow	1	12
SUBB	A,direct	Subtract direct byte from Acc with borrow	2	12
SUBB	A,@Ri	Subtract indirect RAM from ACC with borrow	1	12
SUBB	A,#data	Subtract immediate data from Acc with borrow	2	12
INC	A	Increment Accumulator	1	12
INC	Rn	Increment register	1	12
INC	direct	Increment direct byte	2	12
INC	@Ri	Increment direct RAM	1	12
DEC	A	Decrement Accumulator	1	12
DEC	Rn	Decrement Register	1	12
DEC	direct	Decrement direct byte	2	12
DEC	@Ri	Decrement indirect RAM	1	12

All mnemonics copyrighted © Intel Corporation 1980

Mnemonic		Description	Byte	Oscillator Period
ARITHMETIC OPERATIONS (Continued)				
INC	DPTR	Increment Data Pointer	1	24
MUL	AB	Multiply A & B	1	48
DIV	AB	Divide A by B	1	48
DA	A	Decimal Adjust Accumulator	1	12
LOGICAL OPERATIONS				
ANL	A,Rn	AND Register to Accumulator	1	12
ANL	A,direct	AND direct byte to Accumulator	2	12
ANL	A,@Ri	AND indirect RAM to Accumulator	1	12
ANL	A,#data	AND immediate data to Accumulator	2	12
ANL	direct,A	AND Accumulator to direct byte	2	12
ANL	direct,#data	AND immediate data to direct byte	3	24
ORL	A,Rn	OR register to Accumulator	1	12
ORL	A,direct	OR direct byte to Accumulator	2	12
ORL	A,@Ri	OR indirect RAM to Accumulator	1	12
ORL	A,#data	OR immediate data to Accumulator	2	12
ORL	direct,A	OR Accumulator to direct byte	2	12
ORL	direct,#data	OR immediate data to direct byte	3	24
XRL	A,Rn	Exclusive-OR register to Accumulator	1	12
XRL	A,direct	Exclusive-OR direct byte to Accumulator	2	12
XRL	A,@Ri	Exclusive-OR indirect RAM to Accumulator	1	12
XRL	A,#data	Exclusive-OR immediate data to Accumulator	2	12
XRL	direct,A	Exclusive-OR Accumulator to direct byte	2	12
XRL	direct,#data	Exclusive-OR immediate data to direct byte	3	24
CLR	A	Clear Accumulator	1	12
CPL	A	Complement Accumulator	1	12

Mnemonic		Description	Byte	Oscillator Period
LOGICAL OPERATIONS (Continued)				
RL	A	Rotate Accumulator Left	1	12
RLC	A	Rotate Accumulator Left through the Carry	1	12
RR	A	Rotate Accumulator Right	1	12
RRC	A	Rotate Accumulator Right through the Carry	1	12
SWAP	A	Swap nibbles within the Accumulator	1	12
DATA TRANSFER				
MOV	A,Rn	Move register to Accumulator	1	12
MOV	A,direct	Move direct byte to Accumulator	2	12
MOV	A,@Ri	Move indirect RAM to Accumulator	1	12
MOV	A,#data	Move immediate data to Accumulator	2	12
MOV	Rn,A	Move Accumulator to register	1	12
MOV	Rn,direct	Move direct byte to register	2	24
MOV	Rn,#data	Move immediate data to register	2	12
MOV	direct,A	Move Accumulator to direct byte	2	12
MOV	direct,Rn	Move register to direct byte	2	24
MOV	direct,direct	Move direct byte to direct	3	24
MOV	direct,@Ri	Move indirect RAM to direct byte	2	24
MOV	direct,#data	Move immediate data to direct byte	3	24
MOV	@Ri,A	Move Accumulator to indirect RAM	1	12

All mnemonics copyrighted ©Intel Corporation 1980

Mnemonic		Description	Byte	Oscillator Period
DATA TRANSFER (Continued)				
MOV	@Ri,direct	Move direct byte to indirect RAM	2	24
MOV	@Ri,#data	Move immediate data to indirect RAM	2	12
MOV	DPTR,#data16	Load Data Pointer with a 16-bit constant	3	24
MOVC	A,@A+DPTR	Move Code byte relative to DPTR to Acc	1	24
MOVC	A,@A+PC	Move Code byte relative to PC to Acc	1	24
MOVX	A,@Ri	Move External RAM (8-bit addr) to Acc	1	24
MOVX	A,@DPTR	Move External RAM (16-bit addr) to Acc	1	24
MOVX	@Ri,A	Move Acc to External RAM (8-bit addr)	1	24
MOVX	@DPTR,A	Move Acc to External RAM (16-bit addr)	1	24
PUSH	direct	Push direct byte onto stack	2	24
POP	direct	Pop direct byte from stack	2	24
XCH	A,Rn	Exchange register with Accumulator	1	12
XCH	A,direct	Exchange direct byte with Accumulator	2	12
XCH	A,@Ri	Exchange indirect RAM with Accumulator	1	12
XCHD	A,@Ri	Exchange low-order Digit indirect RAM with Acc	1	12

Mnemonic		Description	Byte	Oscillator Period
BOOLEAN VARIABLE MANIPULATION				
CLR	C	Clear Carry	1	12
CLR	bit	Clear direct bit	2	12
SETB	C	Set Carry	1	12
SETB	bit	Set direct bit	2	12
CPL	C	Complement Carry	1	12
CPL	bit	Complement direct bit	2	12
ANL	C,bit	AND direct bit to CARRY	2	24
ANL	C,/bit	AND complement of direct bit to Carry	2	24
ORL	C,bit	OR direct bit to Carry	2	24
ORL	C,/bit	OR complement of direct bit to Carry	2	24
MOV	C,bit	Move direct bit to Carry	2	12
MOV	bit,C	Move Carry to direct bit	2	24
JC	rel	Jump if Carry is set	2	24
JNC	rel	Jump if Carry not set	2	24
JB	bit,rel	Jump if direct Bit is set	3	24
JNB	bit,rel	Jump if direct Bit is Not set	3	24
JBC	bit,rel	Jump if direct Bit is set & clear bit	3	24
PROGRAM BRANCHING				
ACALL	addr11	Absolute Subroutine Call	2	24
LCALL	addr16	Long Subroutine Call	3	24
RET		Return from Subroutine	1	24
RETI		Return from interrupt	1	24
AJMP	addr11	Absolute Jump	2	24
LJMP	addr16	Long Jump	3	24
SJMP	rel	Short Jump (relative addr)	2	24

All mnemonics copyrighted ©Intel Corporation 1980

Mnemonic		Description	Byte	Oscillator Period
PROGRAM BRANCHING (Continued)				
JMP	@A+DPTR	Jump indirect relative to the DPTR	1	24
JZ	rel	Jump if Accumulator is Zero	2	24
JNZ	rel	Jump if Accumulator is Not Zero	2	24
CJNE	A,direct,rel	Compare direct byte to Acc and Jump if Not Equal	3	24
CJNE	A,#data,rel	Compare immediate to Acc and Jump if Not Equal	3	24

Mnemonic		Description	Byte	Oscillator Period
PROGRAM BRANCHING (Continued)				
CJNE	Rn,#data,rel	Compare immediate to register and Jump if Not Equal	3	24
CJNE	@Ri,#data,rel	Compare immediate to indirect and Jump if Not Equal	3	24
DJNZ	Rn,rel	Decrement register and Jump if Not Zero	2	24
DJNZ	direct,rel	Decrement direct byte and Jump if Not Zero	3	24
NOP		No Operation	1	12

All mnemonics copyrighted © Intel Corporation 1980

Source: Reprinted by permission of Intel Corporation, copyright © Intel Corporation.

Appendix E 8086 Instruction Set Summary

Mnemonic and Description	Instruction Code			
	7 6 5 4 3 2 1 0	7 6 5 4 3 2 1 0	7 6 5 4 3 2 1 0	7 6 5 4 3 2 1 0
DATA TRANSFER				
MOV = Move:				
Register/Memory to/from Register	1 0 0 0 1 0 d w	mod reg r/m		
Immediate to Register/Memory	1 1 0 0 0 1 1 w	mod 0 0 0 r/m	data	data if w = 1
Immediate to Register	1 0 1 1 w reg	data	data if w = 1	
Memory to Accumulator	1 0 1 0 0 0 0 w	addr-low	addr-high	
Accumulator to Memory	1 0 1 0 0 0 1 w	addr-low	addr-high	
Register/Memory to Segment Register	1 0 0 0 1 1 1 0	mod 0 reg r/m		
Segment Register to Register/Memory	1 0 0 0 1 1 0 0	mod 0 reg r/m		
PUSH = Push:				
Register/Memory	1 1 1 1 1 1 1 1	mod 1 1 0 r/m		
Register	0 1 0 1 0 reg			
Segment Register	0 0 0 reg 1 1 0			
POP = Pop:				
Register/Memory	1 0 0 0 1 1 1 1	mod 0 0 0 r/m		
Register	0 1 0 1 1 reg			
Segment Register	0 0 0 reg 1 1 1			
XCHG = Exchange:				
Register/Memory with Register	1 0 0 0 0 1 1 w	mod reg r/m		
Register with Accumulator	1 0 0 1 0 reg			
IN = Input from:				
Fixed Port	1 1 1 0 0 1 0 w	port		
Variable Port	1 1 1 0 1 1 0 w			
OUT = Output to:				
Fixed Port	1 1 1 0 0 1 1 w	port		
Variable Port	1 1 1 0 1 1 1 w			
XLAT = Translate Byte to AL	1 1 0 1 0 1 1 1			
LEA = Load EA to Register	1 0 0 0 1 1 0 1	mod reg r/m		
LDS = Load Pointer to DS	1 1 0 0 0 1 0 1	mod reg r/m		
LES = Load Pointer to ES	1 1 0 0 0 1 0 0	mod reg r/m		
LAHF = Load AH with Flags	1 0 0 1 1 1 1 1			
SAHF = Store AH into Flags	1 0 0 1 1 1 1 0			
PUSHF = Push Flags	1 0 0 1 1 1 0 0			
POPF = Pop Flags	1 0 0 1 1 1 0 1			

Mnemonics © Intel, 1978

Mnemonic and Description	Instruction Code			
	7 6 5 4 3 2 1 0	7 6 5 4 3 2 1 0	7 6 5 4 3 2 1 0	7 6 5 4 3 2 1 0
ARITHMETIC				
ADD = Add:				
Reg./Memory with Register to Either	0 0 0 0 0 0 d w	mod reg r/m		
Immediate to Register/Memory	1 0 0 0 0 0 s w	mod 0 0 0 r/m	data	data if s: w = 01
Immediate to Accumulator	0 0 0 0 0 1 0 w	data	data if w = 1	
ADC = Add with Carry:				
Reg./Memory with Register to Either	0 0 0 1 0 0 d w	mod reg r/m		
Immediate to Register/Memory	1 0 0 0 0 0 s w	mod 0 1 0 r/m	data	data if s: w = 01
Immediate to Accumulator	0 0 0 1 0 1 0 w	data	data if w = 1	
INC = Increment:				
Register/Memory	1 1 1 1 1 1 1 w	mod 0 0 0 r/m		
Register	0 1 0 0 0 reg			
AAA = ASCII Adjust for Add	0 0 1 1 0 1 1 1			
BAA = Decimal Adjust for Add	0 0 1 0 0 1 1 1			
SUB = Subtract:				
Reg./Memory and Register to Either	0 0 1 0 1 0 d w	mod reg r/m		
Immediate from Register/Memory	1 0 0 0 0 0 s w	mod 1 0 1 r/m	data	data if s w = 01
Immediate from Accumulator	0 0 1 0 1 1 0 w	data	data if w = 1	
SSB = Subtract with Borrow				
Reg./Memory and Register to Either	0 0 0 1 1 0 d w	mod reg r/m		
Immediate from Register/Memory	1 0 0 0 0 0 s w	mod 0 1 1 r/m	data	data if s w = 01
Immediate from Accumulator	0 0 0 1 1 1 w	data	data if w = 1	
DEC = Decrement:				
Register/memory	1 1 1 1 1 1 1 w	mod 0 0 1 r/m		
Register	0 1 0 0 1 reg			
NEG = Change sign	1 1 1 1 0 1 1 w	mod 0 1 1 r/m		
CMP = Compare:				
Register/Memory and Register	0 0 1 1 1 0 d w	mod reg r/m		
Immediate with Register/Memory	1 0 0 0 0 0 s w	mod 1 1 1 r/m	data	data if s w = 01
Immediate with Accumulator	0 0 1 1 1 1 0 w	data	data if w = 1	
AAS = ASCII Adjust for Subtract	0 0 1 1 1 1 1 1			
DAS = Decimal Adjust for Subtract	0 0 1 0 1 1 1 1			
MUL = Multiply (Unsigned)	1 1 1 1 0 1 1 w	mod 1 0 0 r/m		
IMUL = Integer Multiply (Signed)	1 1 1 1 0 1 1 w	mod 1 0 1 r/m		
AAM = ASCII Adjust for Multiply	1 1 0 1 0 1 0 0	0 0 0 0 1 0 1 0		
DIV = Divide (Unsigned)	1 1 1 1 0 1 1 w	mod 1 1 0 r/m		
IDIV = Integer Divide (Signed)	1 1 1 1 0 1 1 w	mod 1 1 1 r/m		
AAD = ASCII Adjust for Divide	1 1 0 1 0 1 0 1	0 0 0 0 1 0 1 0		
CBW = Convert Byte to Word	1 0 0 1 1 0 0 0			
CWD = Convert Word to Double Word	1 0 0 1 1 0 0 1			

Mnemonics © Intel, 1978

Mnemonic and Description	Instruction Code			
	7 6 5 4 3 2 1 0	7 6 5 4 3 2 1 0	7 6 5 4 3 2 1 0	7 6 5 4 3 2 1 0
LOGIC				
NOT = Invert	1 1 1 1 0 1 1 w	mod 0 1 0 r/m		
SHL/SAL = Shift Logical/Arithmetic Left	1 1 0 1 0 0 v w	mod 1 0 0 r/m		
SHR = Shift Logical Right	1 1 0 1 0 0 v w	mod 1 0 1 r/m		
SAR = Shift Arithmetic Right	1 1 0 1 0 0 v w	mod 1 1 1 r/m		
ROL = Rotate Left	1 1 0 1 0 0 v w	mod 0 0 0 r/m		
ROR = Rotate Right	1 1 0 1 0 0 v w	mod 0 0 1 r/m		
RCL = Rotate Through Carry Flag Left	1 1 0 1 0 0 v w	mod 0 1 0 r/m		
RCR = Rotate Through Carry Right	1 1 0 1 0 0 v w	mod 0 1 1 r/m		
AND = And:				
Reg./Memory and Register to Either	0 0 1 0 0 0 d w	mod reg r/m		
Immediate to Register/Memory	1 0 0 0 0 0 0 w	mod 1 0 0 r/m	data	data if w = 1
Immediate to Accumulator	0 0 1 0 0 1 0 w	data	data if w = 1	
TEST = And Function to Flags, No Result:				
Register/Memory and Register	1 0 0 0 0 1 0 w	mod reg r/m		
Immediate Data and Register/Memory	1 1 1 1 0 1 1 w	mod 0 0 0 r/m	data	data if w = 1
Immediate Data and Accumulator	1 0 1 0 1 0 0 w	data	data if w = 1	
OR = Or:				
Reg./Memory and Register to Either	0 0 0 0 1 0 d w	mod reg r/m		
Immediate to Register/Memory	1 0 0 0 0 0 0 w	mod 0 0 1 r/m	data	data if w = 1
Immediate to Accumulator	0 0 0 0 1 1 0 w	data	data if w = 1	
XOR = Exclusive or:				
Reg./Memory and Register to Either	0 0 1 1 0 0 d w	mod reg r/m		
Immediate to Register/Memory	1 0 0 0 0 0 0 w	mod 1 1 0 r/m	data	data if w = 1
Immediate to Accumulator	0 0 1 1 0 1 0 w	data	data if w = 1	
STRING MANIPULATION				
REP = Repeat	1 1 1 1 0 0 1 z			
MOVS = Move Byte/Word	1 0 1 0 0 1 0 w			
CMPS = Compare Byte/Word	1 0 1 0 0 1 1 w			
SCAS = Scan Byte/Word	1 0 1 0 1 1 1 w			
LODS = Load Byte/Wd to AL/AX	1 0 1 0 1 1 0 w			
STOS = Stor Byte/Wd from AL/A	1 0 1 0 1 0 1 w			
CONTROL TRANSFER				
CALL = Call:				
Direct within Segment	1 1 1 0 1 0 0 0	disp-low	disp-high	
Indirect within Segment	1 1 1 1 1 1 1 1	mod 0 1 0 r/m		
Direct Intersegment	1 0 0 1 1 0 1 0	offset-low	offset-high	
		seg-low	seg-high	
Indirect Intersegment	1 1 1 1 1 1 1 1	mod 0 1 1 r/m		

Mnemonics © Intel, 1978

Mnemonic and Description	Instruction Code		
	7 6 5 4 3 2 1 0	7 6 5 4 3 2 1 0	7 6 5 4 3 2 1 0
JMP = Unconditional Jump:			
Direct within Segment	1 1 1 0 1 0 0 1	disp-low	disp-high
Direct within Segment-Short	1 1 1 0 1 0 1 1	disp	
Indirect within Segment	1 1 1 1 1 1 1 1	mod 1 0 0 r/m	
Direct Intersegment	1 1 1 0 1 0 1 0	offset-low	offset-high
		seg-low	seg-high
Indirect Intersegment	1 1 1 1 1 1 1 1	mod 1 0 1 r/m	
RET = Return from CALL:			
Within Segment	1 1 0 0 0 0 1 1		
Within Seg Adding Immed to SP	1 1 0 0 0 0 1 0	data-low	data-high
Intersegment	1 1 0 0 1 0 1 1		
Intersegment Adding Immediate to SP	1 1 0 0 1 0 1 0	data-low	data-high
JE/JZ = Jump on Equal/Zero	0 1 1 1 0 1 0 0	disp	
JL/JNGE = Jump on Less/Not Greater or Equal	0 1 1 1 1 1 0 0	disp	
JLE/JNG = Jump on Less or Equal/ Not Greater	0 1 1 1 1 1 1 0	disp	
JB/JNAE = Jump on Below/Not Above or Equal	0 1 1 1 0 0 1 0	disp	
JBE/JNA = Jump on Below or Equal/ Not Above	0 1 1 1 0 1 1 0	disp	
JP/JPE = Jump on Parity/Parity Even	0 1 1 1 1 0 1 0	disp	
JO = Jump on Overflow	0 1 1 1 0 0 0 0	disp	
JS = Jump on Sign	0 1 1 1 1 0 0 0	disp	
JNE/JNZ = Jump on Not Equal/Not Zero	0 1 1 1 0 1 0 1	disp	
JNL/JGE = Jump on Not Less/Greater or Equal	0 1 1 1 1 1 0 1	disp	
JNLE/JG = Jump on Not Less or Equal/ Greater	0 1 1 1 1 1 1 1	disp	
JNB/JAE = Jump on Not Below/Above or Equal	0 1 1 1 0 0 1 1	disp	
JNBE/JA = Jump on Not Below or Equal/Above	0 1 1 1 0 1 1 1	disp	
JNP/JPO = Jump on Not Par/Par Odd	0 1 1 1 1 0 1 1	disp	
JNO = Jump on Not Overflow	0 1 1 1 0 0 0 1	disp	
JNS = Jump on Not Sign	0 1 1 1 1 0 0 1	disp	
LOOP = Loop CX Times	1 1 1 0 0 0 1 0	disp	
LOOPZ/LOOPE = Loop While Zero/Equal	1 1 1 0 0 0 0 1	disp	
LOOPNZ/LOOPNE = Loop While Not Zero/Equal	1 1 1 0 0 0 0 0	disp	
JCXZ = Jump on CX Zero	1 1 1 0 0 0 1 1	disp	
INT = Interrupt			
Type Specified	1 1 0 0 1 1 0 1	type	
Type 3	1 1 0 0 1 1 0 0		
INTO = Interrupt on Overflow	1 1 0 0 1 1 1 0		
IRET = Interrupt Return	1 1 0 0 1 1 1 1		

Mnemonic and Description	Instruction Code	
	7 6 5 4 3 2 1 0	7 6 5 4 3 2 1 0
PROCESSOR CONTROL		
CLC = Clear Carry	1 1 1 1 1 0 0 0	
CMC = Complement Carry	1 1 1 1 0 1 0 1	
STC = Set Carry	1 1 1 1 1 0 0 1	
CLD = Clear Direction	1 1 1 1 1 1 0 0	
STD = Set Direction	1 1 1 1 1 1 0 1	
CLI = Clear Interrupt	1 1 1 1 1 0 1 0	
STI = Set Interrupt	1 1 1 1 1 0 1 1	
HLT = Halt	1 1 1 1 0 1 0 0	
WAIT = Wait	1 0 0 1 1 0 1 1	
ESC = Escape (to External Device)	1 1 0 1 1 x x x	mod x x x r/m
LOCK = Bus Lock Prefix	1 1 1 1 0 0 0 0	

NOTES:
AL = 8-bit accumulator
AX = 16-bit accumulator
CX = Count register
DS = Data segment
ES = Extra segment
Above/below refers to unsigned value
Greater = more positive;
Less = less positive (more negative) signed values
if d = 1 then "to" reg; if d = 0 then "from" reg
if w = 1 then word instruction; if w = 0 then byte instruction
if mod = 11 then r/m is treated as a REG field
if mod = 00 then DISP = 0*, disp-low and disp-high are absent
if mod = 01 then DISP = disp-low sign-extended to 16 bits, disp-high is absent
if mod = 10 then DISP = disp-high; disp-low
if r/m = 000 then EA = (BX) + (SI) + DISP
if r/m = 001 then EA = (BX) + (DI) + DISP
if r/m = 010 then EA = (BP) + (SI) + DISP
if r/m = 011 then EA = (BP) + (DI) + DISP
if r/m = 100 then EA = (SI) + DISP
if r/m = 101 then EA = (DI) + DISP
if r/m = 110 then EA = (BP) + DISP*
if r/m = 111 then EA = (BX) + DISP
DISP follows 2nd byte of instruction (before data if required)
*except if mod = 00 and r/m = 110 then EA = disp-high; disp-low.

Mnemonics © Intel, 1978

if s w = 01 then 16 bits of immediate data form the operand
if s w = 11 then an immediate data byte is sign extended to form the 16-bit operand
if v = 0 then "count" = 1; if v = 1 then "count" in (CL)
x = don't care
z is used for string primitives for comparison with ZF FLAG

SEGMENT OVERRIDE PREFIX

0 0 1 reg 1 1 0

REG is assigned according to the following table:

16-Bit (w = 1)	8-Bit (w = 0)	Segment
000 AX	000 AL	00 ES
001 CX	001 CL	01 CS
010 DX	010 DL	10 SS
011 BX	011 BL	11 DS
100 SP	100 AH	
101 BP	101 CH	
110 SI	110 DH	
111 DI	111 BH	

Instructions which reference the flag register file as a 16-bit object use the symbol FLAGS to represent the file:
FLAGS = X:X:X:X:(OF):(DF):(IF):(TF):(SF):(ZF):X:(AF):X:(PF):X:(CF)

Source: Reprinted by permission of Intel Corporation, copyright © Intel Corporation.

Appendix F ASCII and EBCDIC Tables

ASCII-77 CODE—ODD PARITY

	Binary Code								Hex		Binary Code								Hex
Bit:	7	6	5	4	3	2	1	0		Bit:	7	6	5	4	3	2	1	0	
NUL	1	0	0	0	0	0	0	0	00	@	0	1	0	0	0	0	0	0	40
SOH	0	0	0	0	0	0	0	1	01	A	1	1	0	0	0	0	0	1	41
STX	0	0	0	0	0	0	1	0	02	B	1	1	0	0	0	0	1	0	42
ETX	1	0	0	0	0	0	1	1	03	C	0	1	0	0	0	0	1	1	43
EOT	0	0	0	0	0	1	0	0	04	D	1	1	0	0	0	1	0	0	44
ENQ	1	0	0	0	0	1	0	1	05	E	0	1	0	0	0	1	0	1	45
ACK	1	0	0	0	0	1	1	0	06	F	0	1	0	0	0	1	1	0	46
BEL	0	0	0	0	0	1	1	1	07	G	1	1	0	0	0	1	1	1	47
BS	0	0	0	0	1	0	0	0	08	H	1	1	0	0	1	0	0	0	48
HT	1	0	0	0	1	0	0	1	09	I	0	1	0	0	1	0	0	1	49
NL	1	0	0	0	1	0	1	0	0A	J	0	1	0	0	1	0	1	0	4A
VT	0	0	0	0	1	0	1	1	0B	K	1	1	0	0	1	0	1	1	4B
FF	1	0	0	0	1	1	0	0	0C	L	0	1	0	0	1	1	0	0	4C
CR	0	0	0	0	1	1	0	1	0D	M	1	1	0	0	1	1	0	1	4D
SO	0	0	0	0	1	1	1	0	0E	N	1	1	0	0	1	1	1	0	4E
SI	1	0	0	0	1	1	1	1	0F	O	0	1	0	0	1	1	1	1	4F
DLE	0	0	0	1	0	0	0	0	10	P	1	1	0	1	0	0	0	0	50
DC1	0	0	0	1	0	0	0	1	11	Q	0	1	0	1	0	0	0	1	51
DC2	1	0	0	1	0	0	1	0	12	R	0	1	0	1	0	0	1	0	52
DC3	0	0	0	1	0	0	1	1	13	S	1	1	0	1	0	0	1	1	53
DC4	1	0	0	1	0	1	0	0	14	T	0	1	0	1	0	1	0	0	54
NAK	0	0	0	1	0	1	0	1	15	U	1	1	0	1	0	1	0	1	55
SYN	0	0	0	1	0	1	1	0	16	V	1	1	0	1	0	1	1	0	56
ETB	1	0	0	1	0	1	1	1	17	W	0	1	0	1	0	1	1	1	57
CAN	1	0	0	1	1	0	0	0	18	X	0	1	0	1	1	0	0	0	58
EM	0	0	0	1	1	0	0	1	19	Y	1	1	0	1	1	0	0	1	59
SUB	0	0	0	1	1	0	1	0	1A	Z	1	1	0	1	1	0	1	0	5A
ESC	1	0	0	1	1	0	1	1	1B	[	0	1	0	1	1	0	1	1	5B
FS	0	0	0	1	1	1	0	0	1C	\	1	1	0	1	1	1	0	0	5C
GS	1	0	0	1	1	1	0	1	1D	]	0	1	0	1	1	1	0	1	5D
RS	1	0	0	1	1	1	1	0	1E	∧	0	1	0	1	1	1	1	0	5E
US	0	0	0	1	1	1	1	1	1F	—	1	1	0	1	1	1	1	1	5F
SP	0	0	1	0	0	0	0	0	20	`	1	1	1	0	0	0	0	0	60
!	1	0	1	0	0	0	0	1	21	a	0	1	1	0	0	0	0	1	61
"	1	0	1	0	0	0	1	0	22	b	0	1	1	0	0	0	1	0	62
#	0	0	1	0	0	0	1	1	23	c	1	1	1	0	0	0	1	1	63
$	1	0	1	0	0	1	0	0	24	d	0	1	1	0	0	1	0	0	64
%	0	0	1	0	0	1	0	1	25	e	1	1	1	0	0	1	0	1	65
&	0	0	1	0	0	1	1	0	26	f	1	1	1	0	0	1	1	0	66
'	1	0	1	0	0	1	1	1	27	g	0	1	1	0	0	1	1	1	67
(	1	0	1	0	1	0	0	0	28	h	0	1	1	0	1	0	0	0	68
)	0	0	1	0	1	0	0	1	29	i	1	1	1	0	1	0	0	1	69
*	0	0	1	0	1	0	1	0	2A	j	1	1	1	0	1	0	1	0	6A
+	1	0	1	0	1	0	1	1	2B	k	0	1	1	0	1	0	1	1	6B
,	0	0	1	0	1	1	0	0	2C	l	1	1	1	0	1	1	0	0	6C
-	1	0	1	0	1	1	0	1	2D	m	0	1	1	0	1	1	0	1	6D

	Binary Code								Hex		Binary Code								Hex
Bit:	7	6	5	4	3	2	1	0		Bit:	7	6	5	4	3	2	1	0	
.	1	0	1	0	1	1	1	0	2E	n	0	1	1	0	1	1	1	0	6E
/	0	0	1	0	1	1	1	1	2F	o	1	1	1	0	1	1	1	1	6F
0	1	0	1	1	0	0	0	0	30	p	0	1	1	1	0	0	0	0	70
1	0	0	1	1	0	0	0	1	31	q	1	1	1	1	0	0	0	1	71
2	0	0	1	1	0	0	1	0	32	r	1	1	1	1	0	0	1	0	72
3	1	0	1	1	0	0	1	1	33	s	0	1	1	1	0	0	1	1	73
4	0	0	1	1	0	1	0	0	34	t	1	1	1	1	0	1	0	0	74
5	1	0	1	1	0	1	0	1	35	u	0	1	1	1	0	1	0	1	75
6	1	0	1	1	0	1	1	0	36	v	0	1	1	1	0	1	1	0	76
7	0	0	1	1	0	1	1	1	37	w	1	1	1	1	0	1	1	1	77
8	0	0	1	1	1	0	0	0	38	x	1	1	1	1	1	0	0	0	78
9	1	0	1	1	1	0	0	1	39	y	0	1	1	1	1	0	0	1	79
:	1	0	1	1	1	0	1	0	3A	z	0	1	1	1	1	0	1	0	7A
;	0	0	1	1	1	0	1	1	3B	{	1	1	1	1	1	0	1	1	7B
<	1	0	1	1	1	1	0	0	3C	¦	0	1	1	1	1	1	0	0	7C
=	0	0	1	1	1	1	0	1	3D	}	1	1	1	1	1	1	0	1	7D
>	0	0	1	1	1	1	1	0	3E	~	1	1	1	1	1	1	1	0	7E
?	1	0	1	1	1	1	1	1	3F	DEL	0	1	1	1	1	1	1	1	7F

NUL = null
SOH = start of heading
STX = start of text
ETX = end of text
EOT = end of transmission
ENQ = enquiry
ACK = acknowledge
BEL = bell
BS = back space
HT = horizontal tab
NL = new line
VT = vertical tab
FF = form feed
CR = carriage return
SO = shift-out
SI = shift-in
DLE = data link escape

DC1 = device control 1
DC2 = device control 2
DC3 = device control 3
DC4 = device control 4
NAK = negative acknowledge
SYN = synchronous
ETB = end of transmission block
CAN = cancel
SUB = substitute
ESC = escape
FS = field separator
GS = group separator
RS = record separator
US = unit separator
SP = space
DEL = delete

Note: Standard ASCII is a 7-bit code. The parity bit (bit 7) is often not used. The Hex numbers given correspond to standard ASCII.

EBCDIC CODE

	Binary Code								Hex		Binary Code								Hex
Bit:	0	1	2	3	4	5	6	7		Bit:	0	1	2	3	4	5	6	7	
NUL	0	0	0	0	0	0	0	0	00		1	0	0	0	0	0	0	0	80
SOH	0	0	0	0	0	0	0	1	01	a	1	0	0	0	0	0	0	1	81
STX	0	0	0	0	0	0	1	0	02	b	1	0	0	0	0	0	1	0	82
ETX	0	0	0	0	0	0	1	1	03	c	1	0	0	0	0	0	1	1	83
	0	0	0	0	0	1	0	0	04	d	1	0	0	0	0	1	0	0	84
PT	0	0	0	0	0	1	0	1	05	e	1	0	0	0	0	1	0	1	85
	0	0	0	0	0	1	1	0	06	f	1	0	0	0	0	1	1	0	86
	0	0	0	0	0	1	1	1	07	g	1	0	0	0	0	1	1	1	87
	0	0	0	0	1	0	0	0	08	h	1	0	0	0	1	0	0	0	88
	0	0	0	0	1	0	0	1	09	i	1	0	0	0	1	0	0	1	89
	0	0	0	0	1	0	1	0	0A		1	0	0	0	1	0	1	0	8A
	0	0	0	0	1	0	1	1	0B		1	0	0	0	1	0	1	1	8B
FF	0	0	0	0	1	1	0	0	0C		1	0	0	0	1	1	0	0	8C
	0	0	0	0	1	1	0	1	0D		1	0	0	0	1	1	0	1	8D
	0	0	0	0	1	1	1	0	0E		1	0	0	0	1	1	1	0	8E
	0	0	0	0	1	1	1	1	0F		1	0	0	0	1	1	1	1	8F
DLE	0	0	0	1	0	0	0	0	10		1	0	0	1	0	0	0	0	90
SBA	0	0	0	1	0	0	0	1	11	j	1	0	0	1	0	0	0	1	91
EUA	0	0	0	1	0	0	1	0	12	k	1	0	0	1	0	0	1	0	92
IC	0	0	0	1	0	0	1	1	13	l	1	0	0	1	0	0	1	1	93
	0	0	0	1	0	1	0	0	14	m	1	0	0	1	0	1	0	0	94
NL	0	0	0	1	0	1	0	1	15	n	1	0	0	1	0	1	0	1	95
	0	0	0	1	0	1	1	0	16	o	1	0	0	1	0	1	1	0	96
	0	0	0	1	0	1	1	1	17	p	1	0	0	1	0	1	1	1	97
	0	0	0	1	1	0	0	0	18	q	1	0	0	1	1	0	0	0	98
EM	0	0	0	1	1	0	0	1	19	r	1	0	0	1	1	0	0	1	99
	0	0	0	1	1	0	1	0	1A		1	0	0	1	1	0	1	0	9A
	0	0	0	1	1	0	1	1	1B		1	0	0	1	1	0	1	1	9B
DUP	0	0	0	1	1	1	0	0	1C		1	0	0	1	1	1	0	0	9C
SF	0	0	0	1	1	1	0	1	1D		1	0	0	1	1	1	0	1	9D
FM	0	0	0	1	1	1	1	0	1E		1	0	0	1	1	1	1	0	9E
ITB	0	0	0	1	1	1	1	1	1F		1	0	0	1	1	1	1	1	9F
	0	0	1	0	0	0	0	0	20		1	0	1	0	0	0	0	0	A0
	0	0	1	0	0	0	0	1	21	~	1	0	1	0	0	0	0	1	A1
	0	0	1	0	0	0	1	0	22	s	1	0	1	0	0	0	1	0	A2
	0	0	1	0	0	0	1	1	23	t	1	0	1	0	0	0	1	1	A3
	0	0	1	0	0	1	0	0	24	u	1	0	1	0	0	1	0	0	A4
	0	0	1	0	0	1	0	1	25	v	1	0	1	0	0	1	0	1	A5
ETB	0	0	1	0	0	1	1	0	26	w	1	0	1	0	0	1	1	0	A6
ESC	0	0	1	0	0	1	1	1	27	x	1	0	1	0	0	1	1	1	A7
	0	0	1	0	1	0	0	0	28	y	1	0	1	0	1	0	0	0	A8
	0	0	1	0	1	0	0	1	29	z	1	0	1	0	1	0	0	1	A9
	0	0	1	0	1	0	1	0	2A		1	0	1	0	1	0	1	0	AA
	0	0	1	0	1	0	1	1	2B		1	0	1	0	1	0	1	1	AB
	0	0	1	0	1	1	0	0	2C		1	0	1	0	1	1	0	0	AC
ENQ	0	0	1	0	1	1	0	1	2D		1	0	1	0	1	1	0	1	AD
	0	0	1	0	1	1	1	0	2E		1	0	1	0	1	1	1	0	AE
	0	0	1	0	1	1	1	1	2F		1	0	1	0	1	1	1	1	AF
	0	0	1	1	0	0	0	0	30		1	0	1	1	0	0	0	0	B0
	0	0	1	1	0	0	0	1	31		1	0	1	1	0	0	0	1	B1

EBCDIC CODE

	Binary Code								Hex		Binary Code								Hex
Bit:	0	1	2	3	4	5	6	7		Bit:	0	1	2	3	4	5	6	7	
SYN	0	0	1	1	0	0	1	0	32		1	0	1	1	0	0	1	0	B2
	0	0	1	1	0	0	1	1	33		1	0	1	1	0	0	1	1	B3
	0	0	1	1	0	1	0	0	34		1	0	1	1	0	1	0	0	B4
	0	0	1	1	0	1	0	1	35		1	0	1	1	0	1	0	1	B5
	0	0	1	1	0	1	1	0	36		1	0	1	1	0	1	1	0	B6
EOT	0	0	1	1	0	1	1	1	37		1	0	1	1	0	1	1	1	B7
	0	0	1	1	1	0	0	0	38		1	0	1	1	1	0	0	0	B8
	0	0	1	1	1	0	0	1	39		1	0	1	1	1	0	0	1	B9
	0	0	1	1	1	0	1	0	3A		1	0	1	1	1	0	1	0	BA
	0	0	1	1	1	0	1	1	3B		1	0	1	1	1	0	1	1	BB
RA	0	0	1	1	1	1	0	0	3C		1	0	1	1	1	1	0	0	BC
NAK	0	0	1	1	1	1	0	1	3D		1	0	1	1	1	1	0	1	BD
	0	0	1	1	1	1	1	0	3E		1	0	1	1	1	1	1	0	BE
SUB	0	0	1	1	1	1	1	1	3F		1	0	1	1	1	1	1	1	BF
SP	0	1	0	0	0	0	0	0	40	{	1	1	0	0	0	0	0	0	C0
	0	1	0	0	0	0	0	1	41	A	1	1	0	0	0	0	0	1	C1
	0	1	0	0	0	0	1	0	42	B	1	1	0	0	0	0	1	0	C2
	0	1	0	0	0	0	1	1	43	C	1	1	0	0	0	0	1	1	C3
	0	1	0	0	0	1	0	0	44	D	1	1	0	0	0	1	0	0	C4
	0	1	0	0	0	1	0	1	45	E	1	1	0	0	0	1	0	1	C5
	0	1	0	0	0	1	1	0	46	F	1	1	0	0	0	1	1	0	C6
	0	1	0	0	0	1	1	1	47	G	1	1	0	0	0	1	1	1	C7
	0	1	0	0	1	0	0	0	48	H	1	1	0	0	1	0	0	0	C8
	0	1	0	0	1	0	0	1	49	I	1	1	0	0	1	0	0	1	C9
¢	0	1	0	0	1	0	1	0	4A		1	1	0	0	1	0	1	0	CA
.	0	1	0	0	1	0	1	1	4B		1	1	0	0	1	0	1	1	CB
<	0	1	0	0	1	1	0	0	4C		1	1	0	0	1	1	0	0	CC
(	0	1	0	0	1	1	0	1	4D		1	1	0	0	1	1	0	1	CD
+	0	1	0	0	1	1	1	0	4E		1	1	0	0	1	1	1	0	CE
¦	0	1	0	0	1	1	1	1	4F		1	1	0	0	1	1	1	1	CF
&	0	1	0	1	0	0	0	0	50	}	1	1	0	1	0	0	0	0	D0
	0	1	0	1	0	0	0	1	51	J	1	1	0	1	0	0	0	1	D1
	0	1	0	1	0	0	1	0	52	K	1	1	0	1	0	0	1	0	D2
	0	1	0	1	0	0	1	1	53	L	1	1	0	1	0	0	1	1	D3
	0	1	0	1	0	1	0	0	54	M	1	1	0	1	0	1	0	0	D4
	0	1	0	1	0	1	0	1	55	N	1	1	0	1	0	1	0	1	D5
	0	1	0	1	0	1	1	0	56	O	1	1	0	1	0	1	1	0	D6
	0	1	0	1	0	1	1	1	57	P	1	1	0	1	0	1	1	1	D7
	0	1	0	1	1	0	0	0	58	Q	1	1	0	1	1	0	0	0	D8
	0	1	0	1	1	0	0	1	59	R	1	1	0	1	1	0	0	1	D9
!	0	1	0	1	1	0	1	0	5A		1	1	0	1	1	0	1	0	DA
$	0	1	0	1	1	0	1	1	5B		1	1	0	1	1	0	1	1	DB
*	0	1	0	1	1	1	0	0	5C		1	1	0	1	1	1	0	0	DC
)	0	1	0	1	1	1	0	1	5D		1	1	0	1	1	1	0	1	DD
;	0	1	0	1	1	1	1	0	5E		1	1	0	1	1	1	1	0	DE
¬	0	1	0	1	1	1	1	1	5F		1	1	0	1	1	1	1	1	DF
-	0	1	1	0	0	0	0	0	60	\	1	1	1	0	0	0	0	0	E0
/	0	1	1	0	0	0	0	1	61		1	1	1	0	0	0	0	1	E1
	0	1	1	0	0	0	1	0	62	S	1	1	1	0	0	0	1	0	E2
	0	1	1	0	0	0	1	1	63	T	1	1	1	0	0	0	1	1	E3

	|	Binary Code							Hex		|	Binary Code							Hex
Bit:	0	1	2	3	4	5	6	7		Bit:	0	1	2	3	4	5	6	7	
	0	1	1	0	0	1	0	0	64	U	1	1	1	0	0	1	0	0	E4
	0	1	1	0	0	1	0	1	65	V	1	1	1	0	0	1	0	1	E5
	0	1	1	0	0	1	1	0	66	W	1	1	1	0	0	1	1	0	E6
	0	1	1	0	0	1	1	1	67	X	1	1	1	0	0	1	1	1	E7
	0	1	1	0	1	0	0	0	68	Y	1	1	1	0	1	0	0	0	E8
	0	1	1	0	1	0	0	1	69	Z	1	1	1	0	1	0	0	1	E9
	0	1	1	0	1	0	1	0	6A		1	1	1	0	1	0	1	0	EA
,	0	1	1	0	1	0	1	1	6B		1	1	1	0	1	0	1	1	EB
%	0	1	1	0	1	1	0	0	6C		1	1	1	0	1	1	0	0	EC
	0	1	1	0	1	1	0	1	6D		1	1	1	0	1	1	0	1	ED
>	0	1	1	0	1	1	1	0	6E		1	1	1	0	1	1	1	0	EE
?	0	1	1	0	1	1	1	1	6F		1	1	1	0	1	1	1	1	EF
	0	1	1	1	0	0	0	0	70	0	1	1	1	1	0	0	0	0	F0
	0	1	1	1	0	0	0	1	71	1	1	1	1	1	0	0	0	1	F1
	0	1	1	1	0	0	1	0	72	2	1	1	1	1	0	0	1	0	F2
	0	1	1	1	0	0	1	1	73	3	1	1	1	1	0	0	1	1	F3
	0	1	1	1	0	1	0	0	74	4	1	1	1	1	0	1	0	0	F4
	0	1	1	1	0	1	0	1	75	5	1	1	1	1	0	1	0	1	F5
	0	1	1	1	0	1	1	0	76	6	1	1	1	1	0	1	1	0	F6
	0	1	1	1	0	1	1	1	77	7	1	1	1	1	0	1	1	1	F7
	0	1	1	1	1	0	0	0	78	8	1	1	1	1	1	0	0	0	F8
▲	0	1	1	1	1	0	0	1	79	9	1	1	1	1	1	0	0	1	F9
:	0	1	1	1	1	0	1	0	7A		1	1	1	1	1	0	1	0	FA
#	0	1	1	1	1	0	1	1	7B		1	1	1	1	1	0	1	1	FB
@	0	1	1	1	1	1	0	0	7C		1	1	1	1	1	1	0	0	FC
▲	0	1	1	1	1	1	0	1	7D		1	1	1	1	1	1	0	1	FD
=	0	1	1	1	1	1	1	0	7E		1	1	1	1	1	1	1	0	FE
"	0	1	1	1	1	1	1	1	7F		1	1	1	1	1	1	1	1	FF

DLE = data link escape
DUP = duplicate
EM = end of medium
ENQ = enquiry
EOT = end of transmission
ESC = escape
ETB = end of transmission block
ETX = end of text
EUA = erase unprotected to address
FF = form feed
FM = field mark
IC = insert cursor

ITB = end of intermediate transmission block
NUL = null
PT = program tab
RA = repeat to address
SBA = set buffer address
SF = start field
SOH = start of heading
SP = space
STX = start of text
SUB = substitute
SYN = synchronous
NAK = negative acknowledge

Appendix F

Answers to Selected Questions and Problems

CHAPTER 1

Questions

1. Ada, Countess of Lovelace
5. CPU, memory, I/O, bus structure
24. The basic difference is that dynamic RAM loses data unless it is refreshed while static RAM does not. Dynamic RAM is usually cheaper and holds more data per chip.
41. A benchmark program contains a mix of instructions which is supposed to match the mix found in a certain class of programs. Thus, the results obtained (speed, accuracy, etc.) when a specific computer runs the benchmark is supposed to reflect how well that computer will handle a typical program represented by the benchmark.

Problems

1. $2^{24} = 16,777,216$ locations.

CHAPTER 2

Questions

2. An embedded controller is a microprocessor used as a component of a system where the main function of the system is not that of 'general purpose computer'. An example of such a system is an automobile ignition.

7. The largest memory is $2^{16} = 65{,}536$ bytes, or 64K bytes.
14. The clock is 4 MHz divided by 2, or 2 MHz.
23. The M in 8085 instructions means that the contents of the HL register pair is being used as a 16-bit pointer into memory. One of the operands is that memory location, as in MOV A,M.
29. LDAX B loads the accumulator from the memory location whose address is held in the BC register pair. MOV A,M loads the accumulator from the memory location whose address is held in the HL register pair. The MOV instruction can be used to load any register (such as MOV B,M) while LDAX can only load the accumulator.

Problems

3.
```
        LXI    H, 1230H
        MOV    D, M
        INX    H
        MOV    E, M
```

4. The binary number for the CSR command is 01010000, or 50H.

```
        MVI    A, 50H
        OUT    10H
```

CHAPTER 3

Questions

2. It converts an assembly language source file into a binary object file plus a listing file.
3. An assembly language has a one-to-one correspondence to the hardware features of the processor for which it was written. A high level language defines a virtual machine that is independent (more or less) of the processor, so programs are compact and portable.

Problems

1.
```
        ORG    0FE00H
        ADD    B
        END
```

CHAPTER 4

Questions

2. Write down a clear description of the problem to be solved or the task to be done.
4. Documentation is important because it makes explicit the methods and algorithms used in the design and implementation of the software. Documentation is vital for maintenance (modification and debugging).

14. Masking is the use of ANDing and ORing to select certain bits from a word while ignoring (masking off) others.
22. After adding two BCD numbers, DAA is used to restore the sum to a BCD format. On some processors, DAA also works after subtraction.

Problems

2.
```
        IN    PORT1;  GET ANY LETTER
        ANI   ODFH ;  MAKE BIT5 A 0
        OUT   PORT2;  SEND UPPER CASE LETTER
```

9. 2.574 milliseconds

CHAPTER 5

Questions

2. In general, an interrupt is a hardware means for forcing a processor to stop what it is doing and handle an event in the outside world as it occurs (i.e., in real time). Afterwards, the processor will resume from where it left off.
11. DMA is a way of moving data into and out of memory without going through the CPU. It requires special hardware which temporarily takes bus control away from the processor.

Problems

2. 5×20 mS = 100 mS
   (100 mS / 1000 mS) $\times$ 100% = 10%

CHAPTER 6

Questions

1. Contact bounce occurs in metallic contacts on relays and switches. When the contacts initially come together under the force of the mechanism, they will bounce off each other several times before coming to rest closed. Sometimes, a similar effect will occur when closed contacts first open.
4. Hysteresis is important because it prevents oscillation during switching in solid state devices. Such oscillation is equivalent to contact bounce.
9. Inductive spikes are short duration, high voltage transients that occur when current is switched in an inductive load. Such spikes can destroy solid state devices, and must be suppressed with diodes (DC loads) or snubber circuits (AC loads).

Problems

5.
```
A_TO_D:   MVI   A,01       ; PULL SOC HI
          OUT   CONTROL    ; TO ACTIVATE
          NOP              ; STRETCH OUT THE
          NOP              ; SOC PULSE
          MVI   A,00       ; PULL SOC
          OUT   CONTROL    ; BACK TO LO
LOOP:     IN    STATUS     ; READ EOC
          CMP   A          ; IS IT READY? (LO)
          JNZ   LOOP       ; JUMP IF NO
          IN    DATA       ; READY, READ DATA
          RET              ; RETURN WITH DATA
```

CHAPTER 7

Questions

4. The dual register set of the Z80 has two main advantages. First, it gives the programmer access to additional registers. Operations on data in registers is quicker than similar operations on data in memory, plus more pointers can be kept in register pairs. The second advantage is that subroutines and interrupts can be written so that pushes and pops are replaced by a fast context switch (i.e., switch to the other register set).

Problems

1.
```
          LD    IX,1000H
          LD    IY,2000H
          LD    B,10
LOOP:     LD    A,(IX+0)
          LD    (IY+0),A
          INC   IX
          INC   IY
          DJNZ  LOOP
          HALT
```

CHAPTER 8

Questions

3. The 8031 has no onboard ROM.
7. The EA pin allows external program memory to be used.
14. Port 0 can drive eight TTL loads.
24. SMOD is bit 7 of the PCON register.
32. RI and TI are not automatically cleared.

Problems

1. Let (TH1) = 253 and get f = 11.0592 MHz.

CHAPTER 9

Questions

1. Your answer should include the separation of program and data storage in the 8051 as well as the use of the SFR region.

Problems

1. Refer to the example in the chapter.

CHAPTER 10

Questions

2. The basic idea in asynchronous data is the frame. The time between frames can vary but the timing within a frame is fixed. The start and stop bits of the frame allow the receiver to sync on each frame.

Problems

1. Refer to example 10-2, as well as examples of looping in chap 4.

CHAPTER 11

Questions

1. The pipeline is basically the 6 byte instruction queue. The BIU puts instructions from memory into one end of the pipeline while the EU pulls instructions out of the other end.
6. F5310h

Index

A *reg*
  8085, 41
  Z80, 207
A/D. *See* ADC.
AC flag (8085)
  def, 42
  use, 120
ACALL *instr* (8051), 284
Access time, 11
ACI *instr* (8085), 46
ACK, 186
Acknowledgment, 186
Accumulator, 7
  8085, 30
  after RIM, 144
  before SIM, 143
Ada, 2
ADC chip, 193, 195
  conversion time, 196
  handshake, 196
ADC *instr*
  8085, 45
  Z80, 220
ADC0801 chip, 279

ADD *instr*
  8085, 45
  8051, 260
  Z80, 220
ADDC *instr* (8051), 260
ADI *instr* (8085), 46
Address, 3
  decoding, 21
  full, 22
  linear, 22
AF *reg* pair (Z80), 207
Aiken, Howard, 2
AJMP *instr* (8051), 261
al-Khwarizmi, 87
ALE
  8051, 246
  8085, 32
  8086, 337
  8155, 52
Algorithm, 48, 87
Alphanumeric display, 174
ALT1-ALT4 (8155), 54
ALU, 7
ANA *instr* (8085), 47

ANI *instr* (8085), 47
ANL *instr* (8085), 260
Apostrophes, 71
Apple, 2
Applications, 7
Architecture, 1
  Harvard, 6
Archive, 65
Arithmetic and logic unit.
  See ALU.
ASIC, 25
Assembler, 63, 374
  cross-, 65
  -passes, 66
  -directives, 69, 74
  macro-, 79
Assembly language, 63, 353, 374
Asynchronous
  data, 317
  frame, 184
Atanasoff, John, 2
AX *reg* (8086), 344, 345
AY-5-2376 encoder chip, 163

reg = register   *def* = definition   *instr* = instruction

B *reg*
  8051, 242
  8085, 41
  Z80, 242
Babbage, Charles, 2
Background, 232
Backplane, 19
Bandwidth, 25
Battery backup, 9
Baud, 184, 251
BCD, 117
Benchmark, 26
BF (8155), 55
BHE pin (8086), 337, 338
Binary numbers, 70
BIT *instr* (Z80), 225
Bits, 3
  flag, 7
Boolean processor (8051), 262
Boolean value, 113
Booth's algorithm, 125
Borrow, 98
Bottom-up design, 351, 355
BP *reg* (8086), 345
BRKDET, 320
Buffer, 19
Bug, 88
Bus, 3, 17
  8085, 31
  multiplexed, 17, 31
  STD, 20
Bus interface unit (8086), 330
BUSAK pin (Z80), 203
BUSRQ pin (Z80), 203
Busy loop, 95
BX *reg* (8086), 344, 345
Byte, 3

C *reg*
  8085, 41
  Z80, 207
Cache, 6
CALL *instr* (8085), 49
Call, subroutine, 11
Calling tree, 366
Card cage, 19
Carry. *See* CY.
CAS pin (DRAM), 206
Cell, 26
CC *instr* (8085), 49
CCF *instr* (Z80), 220
Central processing unit. *See* CPU.
Centronics, 179
Characters, 71
CISC, 25

CJNE *instr* (8051), 261
Clarity, 89
Clock, 4
CLK (8085), 33
CLR *instr* (8051), 260
CM *instr* (8085), 49
CMA *instr* (8085), 48
CMC *instr* (8085), 48
CMP *instr* (8085), 47
CNC *instr* (8085), 49
CNZ *instr* (8085), 49
Collision, 17
Comments, 67, 90
Common anode, 173
Common cathode, 173
Common mode voltage, 166
Compatibility, code, 29
Compiler, 64
Concurrent programs, 193
Configuration control, 65
Constructs, 352, 367
Contact bounce, 158
Contention, 17
Control flags (8086), 346
Control memory, 6
Control unit, 6
Coprocessor, 25, 328
CP *instr* (8085), 49
CPD, CPDR *instr*
  (Z80), 219
CPE *instr* (8085), 49
CPI *instr*
  8085, 48
  Z80, 219
CPIR *instr* (Z80), 219
CPL *instr*
  8051, 260
  Z80, 220
CPO *instr* (8085), 49
CPU, 4
  control unit, 6
  8085, 30
  modes, 6
Critical region, 134, 193
CR-LF sequence, 111
Cross license, 19
Cross talk, 21
Crystal selection (8051), 251
CSEG, 77
CSR (8155), 53
  command format, 54
  status format, 55
CTS, 185, 319
CX *reg* (8086), 344, 345
CY flag

8051 use, 262
8085, 42
  as error flag, 94
  passing, 94
  use in math, 98
  use with compare, 102
  use with signed numbers, 101
  use with rotate, 115
  use in DAA, 120
Z80, 209
cycle, machine, 4
cycle, fetch-execute, 5
CZ *instr* (8085), 49

D, DF flag (8086), 346
D/A. *See* DAC.
D *reg*
  8085, 41
  Z80, 207
DA, DAA *instr*
  8051, 260
  8085, 48, 117, 120
  Z80, 260
DAC, 193
  buffering, 194
  multiplying, 194
DAC0808 chip, 281
DAD *instr* (8085), 46, 100
Daisy chain, 133, 231
Datapoint, 2
Daughterboard, 19
DB, 76
DB25, 184
DCR *instr* (8085), 46
DCX *instr* (8085), 46, 100
Debug, 88
  tools, 353, 356, 359, 382
Debugger, 66
DEC *instr* (8051), 260
Decoding, address, 21
Decrement, 3
Demultiplexing, bus (8085), 40
DEN pin (8086), 337
Design
  cycle, 351, 353
  language, 88
Development system, 65
Dhrystone, 26
DI *instr*
  8085, 50, 137
  Z80, 220
DI *reg* (8086), 345, 349
Direct memory access. *See* DMA.
DIV AB *instr* (8051), 260
Displacement, 215

DJNZ *instr* (Z80), 223
DMA, 25, 130, 145
DPH, DPL *regs* (8051), 258
Documentation, 90, 353, 367, 368
Dot matrix printer, 177
Downloading, 65
DPTR *reg* (8051), 258, 276, 277
DS statement, 76
DSEG, 77
DSR, 318
DTR, 319
DT/R pin (8086), 337
Dummy parameter, 94
Dummy subtraction, 102
DSP, 25
DW, 76
DX reg (8086), 344, 345
Dynamic memory, 4, 9

E *reg*
  8085, 41
  Z80, 207
EAROM, 8
Editor, 64
EI *instr*
  8085, 50, 137, 140
  Z80, 220
EIA, 184
Embedded controller, 30, 133, 236
Emulation, 66
Emulator, 353, 382
END statement, 75
ENDIF directive, 82
Environment, 90
EOC, 196
EOF, 109
EOL, 109
EPROM, 8
EQ, 83
EQU, 69, 75
Equal flag, 102
Error detection/correction, 186
EX, EXX *instr* (Z80), 217
Execution unit (8086), 330
Executive, 361, 368, 371
EXTERNAL, 78, 375, 376

Faggin, Federico, 2
Fetch-executive cycle, 5
Files
  absolute-, 65
  binary-, 65
  hex-, 66
  list-, 65
  object-, 64

relocatable-, 65
source-, 64
FIFO, 301
Finite state machine. *See* FSM.
Firmware, 8
Flags, 7, 8
  passing, 94
  use in math, 97
Flowcharts, 87, 366
Foreground, 232
Formal parameters, 80
FSM, 271
  diagram, 272, 273, 362
  example, 275
  table, 274
Full-scale, 193

GATE bit (8051), 248
GLOBAL, 78, 375
GOTO, 88
GPIB, 181
GT, 83

H flag (Z80), 209
H *reg* (8085), 41
HALT (Z80)
  instr, 220
  pin, 203
Handshaking, 178
  8155, 55
  8255, 292, 293, 294
  interrupt, 131
  LTC1091, 312
  RTS/CTS, 319
Hardware design, 355, 360
Hardware/software tradeoff, 86, 352, 360
Harvard architecture, 6
Hash table, 122
Header, 367, 377
Hexadecimal numbers, 70, 174
Hewlett-Packard, 181
Hitachi, 14
Hoff, Ted, 2
HL *reg* pair (8085), 41
HLDA (8085), 33, 34
HLT *instr* (8085), 50, 133
HOLD pin
  8085, 33, 34
  8086, 338
HOLDA pin (8086), 338
HP, 181
HPIB, 181
HVAC, 107

I flag (8086), 346
I reg (Z80), 208, 228
ICE. *See* In-circuit emulation.
IE flag
  8051, 244
  8085, 143
  Z80. *See* IFF1, IFF2.
IF
  directive, 82
  flag (8086), 346
IEEE-488, 181, 182, 183
IEI (Z80), 231
IEO (Z80), 231
IFF1, IFF2 (Z80), 226
IM0, IM1, IM2 *instr* (Z80), 220, 221, 226, 228
IN *instr* (8085), 50
INC *instr*
  8051, 260
  Z80, 212
In-circuit emulation, 66
Increment, 3
IND, INDR *instr* (Z80), 224
Index register, 7. *See also* IX, IY.
INI, INIR *instr* (Z80), 224
Input/output, 15
Instruction, 5, 6
  -register, 6
INT pin
  8051, 248
  Z80, 203, 228
INT 21H, 349
INTA,
  8085 pin, 32, 137
  8085 control signal, 38
  8086 pin, 337
Integration, 353, 355, 380, 381, 383
Intel, 2
Interface, 155
Interrupt, 16, 130
  applications, 189
  8051, 254
INTR
  8085 pin, 33, 137
  8086 pin, 337
  8155, 55
INR *instr* (8085), 46, 52
Inverting, 106
INX *instr* (8085), 46, 100
I/O, 15
  subsystem, 355, 361, 376, 379
IO/M pin
  8085 pin, 32
  8085 control signal, 38
  8155 pin, 52

IORQ pin (Z80), 202
IP (8051), 244
IR *reg*, 6
Isolation, 165
IT0, IT1 (8051), 255
iteration, 108
IX, IY *reg* (Z80), 208, 216, 217

JC *instr* (8085), 49
JM *instr* (8085), 49
JMP *instr*
  8051, 259
  8085, 49, 52
  Z80. *See* JP.
JNC *instr* (8085), 49
JNZ *instr* (8085), 49
JP *instr*
  8085, 49
  Z80, 222
JPE *instr* (8085), 49
JPO *instr* (8085), 49
JZ *instr* (8085), 49

Key words, 69
Khwarizmi, al-, 87

L *reg* (8085), 41
Label, 67
Language
  assembly, 63, 353, 374
  BASIC, 85
  C, 86
  high-level, 63
  low-level, 62
  machine, 62
  PASCAL, 86
Latches, 16
LED, 173
LCALL *instr* (8051), 284
LCD, 173
LD *instr* (Z80), 210
LDD, LDDR *instr* (Z80), 218
LDI, LDIR *instr* (Z80), 218
LDA *instr* (8085), 44, 51
LDAX *instr* (8085), 45
LHLD *instr* (8085), 44
Libraries, 65
LIFO, 10
Linear Technology Corp., 309
Linker, 65, 353, 376, 380
LJMP *instr* (8051), 261
LOC, 75
Logical address (8086), 330
Loader, 65
Loading problem, 19

Logic analyzer, 39
Looping, 108
Lovelace, Countess of, 2
LT, 83
LTC1091, 309
LXI *instr* (8085), 44, 51

M *reg* (8085), 41
M0, M1 (8051), 247
M1 cycle (8085), 36
M1 pin (Z80), 202
Machine cycle, 4
Machine language, 62
Macro, 79, 80, 81
Maintenance, 67, 352, 353, 361
MAR *reg*, 6
Mark, 184
Mask byte, 104
Maskable interrupt, 131
Maximum mode (8086), 328
Mazor, Stan, 2
Minimum mode (8086), 328
MCS-51, 236
Memory, 3, 4, 6, 8, 9, 11
  8051, 238
  8085, 31
  8155, 52
Micro-Link, 20
Microcomputer, 3
Microcode, 6
Microcontroller, 133, 235
Minicomputer, 2
M/IO pin (8086), 337
MITS, 2
Mnemonic, 63, 67
Mode (CPU), 6
Modem, 185
Modules, modularization, 89, 352,
  355, 361, 363
Modulo addition, 186
Monotonicity, 193
MOS Technologies, 2
Mostek, 199
Motherboard, 19
Motorola, 2
Motors, 187
MOV *instr*
  8051, 258, 261
  8085, 44, 51, 94
MOVC *instr* (8051), 259, 261
MOVX *instr* (8051), 258, 261
MREQ pin (Z80), 202
MS-DOS, 328, 349
MSB, 7
MSE bit (8085), 141

MUL AB *instr* (8051), 259, 260
Multitasking, 89, 231
Murphy's Law, 140, 165
MVI *instr* (8085), 44, 51

N flag (Z80), 206
N-key rollover, 161
NAK, 186
Name, 69
National Semiconductor, 199
NEG *instr* (Z80), 220
Nibble, 3, 117, 222
Nine's complement, 121
NMI pin
  8086, 338
  Z80, 203, 226
Non-maskable interrupt, 131
Nonvolatility, 8, 140
NOP *instr*
  8051, 262
  8085, 50
  Z80, 220
NOT
  condition, 83
  operation, 107

O, OF flag (8086), 346
octal numbers, 70
offset, 74
  8086, 330
  Z80, *See* Displacement.
Op-code, 6, 63
  Z80 prefix, 216
Operand, 6, 67
Operating system, 7
Optocoupler, 166
Optoisolator, 165
ORA *instr* (8085), 47
ORG, 75
ORI *instr* (8085), 47
ORL *instr* (8051), 260
OTDR *instr* (Z80), 224
OTIR *instr* (Z80), 224
OUT *instr* (8085), 50, 52
OUTD *instr* (Z80), 224
OUTI *instr* (Z80), 224
Overflow, 8
  device, 130
  8086 flag, 346
Overlap, 6

P flag (8085), 42
P/V flag (Z80), 209
Pages, 8, 73, 245

Parameters, 367, 381
  passing, 92
Parentheses, 71
  Z80 use, 210
Partitioning, 352, 355
PASCAL, 88, 113
PC (8051), 259. *See also* Program.
PCHL *instr* (8085), 49, 124
PCON (8051), 244
Pending (interrupt), 131
Physical address (8086), 330
Pipeline, 6, 330
Pointer, 7, 95
  passing, 92
  stack, 10
  table, 92
Polling, 131
POP *instr*, 10
  8051, 261
  8085, 50
  Z80, 211
Predecrementing, 43
Prefetch, 6
Priority (interrupt)
  8051, 252
  8085, 140
  Z80, 231
Printers, 177
Processor status word. *See* PSW.
Procedure, 352, 353, 368, 374
Program, 8, 62, 87
  counter (PC), 6, 43
  design, 86, 87
  status word, 7. *See also* PSW.
  storage, 8
Pseudo language, pseudo code, 113, 352, 366, 371
Pseudo operations, 69, 74
PSW, 7
  8051, 243, 262
  8085, 41
  Z80. *See* AF.
PUBLIC, 78
PULL, 10
Pull-up resistor, 158
Pulse width modulation. *See* PWM.
PUSH *instr*, 10
  8051, 261
  8085, 50
  Z80, 211
PWM, 281, 282

QS0, QS1 pins (8086), 336
Queue, 6, 330

R *reg* (Z80), 208
Radix, 70
RAL *instr* (8085), 47, 115
RAM, 8, 9, 15
  8155, 58
RAR *instr* (8085), 47, 115
RAS pin (DRAM), 206
RB8 (8051), 251
RC *instr* (8085), 50
RD pin
  8051, 245
  8085, 33, 36, 38
  8086, 337
  Z80, 202
Read, 22
READY pin
  8085, 33
  8086, 337
Real time, 133, 236
  -clock, 190, 191
Register, 3, 6, 7
  page, 73
Relative jump, 74
Relay
  electromagnetic, 168, 169, 170, 171
  solid state, 171
REN bit (8051), 250
Requirements, 352, 356, 360
RES *instr* (Z80), 225
Reset, 4, 34
  Z80 pin (RESET), 203
RESET IN pin (8085), 32
RESET OUT pin (8085), 33
Resolution, 193
RET *instr*
  8051, 284
  8085, 49, 90, 139
  Z80, 225
RETI *instr*
  8051, 284
  Z80, 225
RETN *instr* (Z80), 225
Return, 11
RFSH pin (Z80), 202, 206
RI bit (8051), 250, 255
RIM *instr* (8085), 50, 143, 199
Ringing, 21
RISC, 25
RL *instr*
  8051, 260
  Z80, 221
RLA, RLCA *instr* (Z80), 221
RLC *instr*
  8051, 260

8085, 46, 115
Z80, 221
RLD *instr* (Z80), 222
RM *instr* (8085), 50
RNC *instr* (8085), 50
RNZ *instr* (8085), 49
Rollover, 161
ROM, 8
ROMable code, 78
RP *instr* (8085), 50
RPE *instr* (8085), 50
RPO *instr* (8085), 50
RR *instr*
  8051, 260
  Z80, 221
RRA, RRCA *instr* (Z80), 221
RRC *instr*
  8051, 260
  8085, 47, 115
  Z80, 221
RRD *instr* (Z80), 222
RS-232, 184, 318
RST nn *instr*
  8085, 49, 137, 138
  Z80, 225
RST 5.5, 6.5, 7.5 (8085), 32, 139
RTC, 190
RTS, 185, 319
RxC, 320
RXD, 250, 318
RxRDY, 320
RZ *instr* (8085), 50

S flag
  8085, 42, 101
  Z80, 209
S0, S1 (8085), 32, 38
S0-S7 pins (8086), 336, 337
Sample and hold (S&H), 195
SBB *instr* (8085), 46
SBC *instr* (Z80), 220
SBI *instr* (8085), 46
SBUF (8051), 249
SCADA, 107
Scanning, 161
SCF *instr* (Z80), 220
Schmitt trigger, 165, 166
SCON (8051), 244
Scratchpad, 7
Second-source, 19
Segments, memory, 8, 77, 78, 328, 330, 344, 347
Semantic errors, 66
Service routine, 132, 136

SET
  instr (Z80), 225
  statement, 75
Seven-segment display, 173
Shaft encoder, 166, 167, 168
Shifts, 115
SHLD *instr* (8085), 44
SI *reg* (8086), 345, 349
SID pin (8085), 33, 143, 185
Side effects, 88, 140
Sign bit, 101
SIM *instr* (8085), 50, 141, 199
Simulator, 66
Single quotes, use, 71
Sixteen-segment display, 174
SJMP *instr* (8051), 261
SLA *instr* (Z80), 221
SOC, 196
SOD pin (8085), 33, 141, 185
Soft-start, 34
Solenoid, 16, 169, 170
Sole-source, 19
SP *reg*, 10
  8051, 243
  8085, 41, 91
  8086, 345
  Z80, 208
Space, 184
Spaghetti code, 88
Speed, 25, 34
Specifications, 352, 355, 357, 360
SPHL *instr* (8085), 50, 127
SRA *instr* (Z80), 221
SRL *instr* (Z80), 221
STA *instr* (8085), 44, 51
Stack, 10, 43, 90, 93, 131
Stack pointer. *See* SP.
Start bit (RS232), 184
State machine. *See* FSM.
Stage diagram, 272, 273, 362
State table. *See* FSM.
Statement, 67
Static RAM, 4, 9
Status
  8085 signals, 38
  8086 flags, 345
STAX *instr* (8085), 45
STC *instr* (8085), 48
STB (8155), 55
STD bus, 20
Stepper motor, 187

Stop bit (RS232), 184
String, 71, 349
Structured programs, 361
Stubs, 353, 381
SUB *instr*
  8085, 46, 51
  Z80, 220
SUBB *instr* (8051), 260
Subroutine, 11, 8, 89
SUI *instr* (8085), 46, 51
SWAP A *instr* (8051), 260
Switch, 156, 157, 158, 159, 161, 164
Symbol table, 69
SYN character, 317
Synchronous data, 317
SYNDET, 317, 320
Syntax error, 66

T0, T1, T2 (8051), 246
T2CON (8052), 244
T, TF flag (8086), 346
T state (8085), 15
Target system, 65
TB8 (8051), 251
TCON (8051), 244
Ten's complement, 121
TEST pin (8086), 338
TF0, TF1 (8051), 248
TH, TL *regs* (8051), 244
3-state, three-state, tri-state, 11
Throughput, 25
TI bit (8051), 255
Time delay, 112
TMOD (8051), 244
Toggle, 156, 171
Top-down design, 351, 355, 361
TR bit (8051), 248
Transients, 21
Trap, 7
TRAP pin (8085), 32, 139, 140
Triac, 170
Turing, Alan, 2
TxC, 319
TXD, 250, 318
TxE, 319
TxEN, 321
TxRDY, 319, 322

UART, 185. *See also* USART.
Ultraviolet light, 8

USART, 249, 283, 315. *See also* UART.
User mode, 6
UVEPROM, 8

Vector table, 132
Virtual machine, 64
VM85, 66
Volatility, 8
Von Neumann, John, 2, 145

WAIT
  instr (8086), 338
  pin (Z80), 203
  states, 18, 36, 338
Watchdog timer, 4
Whetstone, 26
Wire-OR, 132
Word, 3
Work station, 65
WR pin
  8051, 245
  8085, 33, 38
  8086, 337
  Z80, 202
Write, 22

XCH *instr* (8051), 261
XCHG *instr* (8085), 45
XRA *instr* (8085), 47
XRI *instr* (8085), 47
XRL *instr* (8051), 260
XTHL *instr* (8085), 50

Z flag, 8
  8085, 42, 102
  Z80, 209
Z80, 199
  clock driver, 201
  CPU timing, 204
  DRAM refresh, 206
  flags, 209
  instruction set, 211
  interrupt sequence, 227, 228, 229
  memory timing, 205
  pin configuration, 200
  registers, 208
  vector processing modes, 230
Zero flag. *See* Z flag.
Zilog, 2, 199

Numbered Devices

2764 ROM chip, 12, 13
4116 RAM chip, 206
555 timer chip, 5
58274 real time clock chip, 191
74C923 keyboard scanner chip, 162
6264 RAM chip, 14
8051 Embedded Controller, 235
  block diagram, 237
  crystal selection, 251
  external ROM, 265
  interface to 8155, 266
  interface to modem chip, 271
  interrupt enable register, 253
  interrupt priority control *reg*, 253
  interrupt vectors, 240
  memory map, 239
  pin configuration, 237
  port-3 alternate functions, 246
  predefined bit addresses, 257
  predefined byte address, 258
  PSW, 243
  PWM output, 282
  RAM and SFR bit addresses, 241
  serial port control/status *reg*, 250
  serial port modes, 249
  SFR map, 241
  SFR reset values, 242
  timer modes, 247
  timer/counter mode control, 247
  timer/counter mode-3 diagram, 248
8085 CPU, 29
  block diagram, 30
  flags, 42
  instruction cycle, 36
  instruction set, 43
  machine cycle chart, 38
  M1 cycle, 36
  pins configuration, 31
  pin functions, 32
  registers, 41
  reset action, 35
  support chips, 39, 52
8086/8088 CPU chip, 327
  A0 and BHE, 338
  assembly language format, 348
  block diagram, 333
  bus circuits, 331, 332
  flag *reg,* 346
  fetch/execute overlap, 334
  interrupt vector table, 339
  minimum mode block diagram, 336
  pin configuration, 328
  pin functions, 329, 330
  segment registers, 347
  registers, 344, 345
  reset, 335
  timing
    read, 342
    system, 341
    write, 343
8155/8156 RAM/IO chip, 52
  applications, 187
  block diagram, 53
  command register bits, 54
  counter/timer, 57
  CSR, 53
  set up, 58
  pin configuration, 52
  port directions, 55
  registers, 53
  status register bits, 55
  strobed input/output, 56
  system example, 39
  timer register, 58
  use with 8051, 266
  waveshapes, 57
8251 USART chip, 315
  asynchronous mode, 318
  baud rate, 315
  block diagram, 316
  command instruction format, 322
  mode instruction format, 321
  pin configuration, 316
  status read format, 322
  SYNDET, 317
  TxRDY bit, pin, 322
8255 PPI chip, 287
  basic operation, 289
  bit set/reset format, 289
  block diagram, 287
  mode combinations, 296
  mode definition, 288, 289
  mode 0 port definition, 291
  mode 1 timing, 292, 293
  mode 2 summary, 295
  pin configuration, 287
8257 DMA chip, 147
  DRQ/DACK, 148
  DMA action codes, 149
  example use, 151, 152
  master/slave modes, 148
  register addresses, 150
8279 Keyboard/Display Interface chip, 297
  blank character selection, 307
  block diagram, 299
  display entry, right/left, 308, 309
  pin configuration, 298
  status word, 301
  system use, 300
8284 clock generator chip, 333
  diagram, 335